Kawasaki ZX600 & ZX750 Owners Workshop Manual

by Bob Henderson and John H Haynes
Member of the Guild of Motoring Writers

Models covered:

ZX600 A1 through A3 (Ninja 600R). 592cc. US 1985 through 1987
ZX600 A1 through A5 (GPZ600R). 592cc. UK 1985 through 1990
ZX600 B1aluminum frame model (Ninja 600RX). 592cc. US 1987
ZX600 C1 through C7 (Ninja 600R). 592cc. US 1988 through 1994
ZX600 C1 through C7 (GPX600R). 592cc. UK 1988 through 1994
ZX750 F1 through F4 (Ninja 750R). 748cc. US 1987 through 1990
ZX750 F1 through F3 (GPX750R). 748cc. UK 1987 through 1991
Note: Does not cover the 599cc ZX-6 (US) or ZZ-R600 (UK), the 748cc GPZ750R (UK), and the 748/749cc ZX-7 (US) or the ZXR750 (UK)

(6W1 - 1780)

ABCDE
FGHIJ
KLMNO
PQ

Haynes Publishing
Sparkford Nr Yeovil
Somerset BA22 7JJ England

Haynes North America, Inc
861 Lawrence Drive
Newbury Park
California 91320 USA

Acknowledgements

Our thanks to Kawasaki Motors (UK), Ltd. for permission to repro-
duce certain illustrations used in this manual. We would also like
to thank NGK Spark Plugs (UK) Ltd for supplying the color spark
plug condition photos.

A book in the **Haynes Owners Workshop Manual Series**

Printed in the USA

ISBN 1 56392 102 2

Library of Congress Catalog Card Number 94-77758

British Library Cataloguing in Publication Data
A catalogue record for this book is available from the British Library

94–272

Contents

1985 ZX600 – A1 (UK GPZ model shown, US Ninja model similar)

1988 ZX600 – C1 (UK GPX model shown, US Ninja model similar)

About this manual

Its purpose

The purpose of this manual is to help you maintain and repair your vehicle. It can do so in several ways. It can help you decide what work must be done, even if you choose to have it done by a dealer service department or a repair shop, it provides information and procedures for routine maintenance and it offers diagnostic and repair procedures to follow when trouble occurs.

It is hoped that you will use the manual to tackle the work yourself. For many simple jobs, doing it yourself may be quicker than arranging an appointment to get the machine into a shop and making the trips to leave it and pick it up. More importantly, a lot of money can be saved by avoiding the expense the shop must pass on to you to cover its labor and overhead costs. An added benefit is the sense of satisfaction and accomplishment that you feel after having done the job yourself.

Using the manual

The manual is divided into Chapters. Each Chapter is divided into numbered Sections which are headed in bold type between horizontal lines. Each Section consists of consecutively numbered paragraphs.

At the beginning of each numbered section you will be referred to any illustrations which apply to the procedures in that section. The reference numbers used in illustration captions pinpoint the pertinent Step within that section. That is, illustration 3.2 means the illustration refers to Section 3 and Step (or paragraph) 2 within that Section.

Procedures, once described in the text, are not normally repeated. When it is necessary to refer to another Chapter, the reference will be given as Chapter and Section number. Cross references given without use of the word "Chapter" apply to Sections and/or paragraphs in the same Chapter. For example, "see Section 8" means in the same Chapter.

Reference to the left or right side of the motorcycle is based on the assumption that one is sitting on the seat, facing forward.

Even though extreme care has been taken during the preparation of this manual, neither the publisher nor the author can accept responsibility for any errors in, or omissions from, the information given.

NOTE

A **Note** provides information necessary to properly complete a procedure or information which will make the procedure easier to understand.

CAUTION

A **Caution** provides a special procedure or special steps which must be taken while completing the procedure where the **Caution** is found. Not heeding a **Caution** can result in damage to the assembly being worked on.

WARNING

A **Warning** provides a special procedure or special steps which must be taken while completing the procedure where the **Warning** is found. Not heeding a **Warning** can result in personal injury.

Introduction to the Kawasaki ZX600 Ninja

Refer to Chapter 10 for information on the ZX750F model

The Kawasaki ZX600R is one of the most competent high-performance motorcycles in its class. Light weight, high output, outstanding brakes and excellent handling characteristics are what have made this machine one of the more popular mid-size bikes.

The engine is an inline four-cylinder, liquid-cooled, double overhead camshaft unit with four valves per cylinder. Fuel is delivered through four 32 mm Keihin carburetors.

The front suspension features an anti-dive system, designed to firm-up the suspension during hard braking to lessen the tendency of fork compression, which reduces suspension travel. On A and B models this is accomplished through the Automatic Variable Damping System (AVDS), which changes the fork valving as the front brake lever is squeezed. On C models, this action is performed by the Electric Suspension Control System (ESCS). Both of these variable damping systems are adjustable by turning a knob on each unit to one of three positions. The front suspension can be also be fine-tuned by adjusting the air pressure in the forks.

The rear end uses Kawasaki's proven Uni-trak suspension, which employs a shock absorber/spring unit mounted ahead of the swingarm, close to the center of gravity of the machine. The damping characteristics of the rear shock are adjustable (four possible settings) and air can also be added to suit various riding conditions and loads.

Identification numbers

Refer to Chapter 10 for information on the ZX750F model

The frame serial number is stamped into the right side of the steering head and the engine serial number is stamped into the right engine case. Both of these numbers should be recorded and kept in a safe place so they can be furnished to law enforcement officials in the event of theft.

The frame serial number, engine serial number and carburetor identification number should also be kept in a handy place (such as with your driver's license) so they are always available when purchasing or ordering parts for your machine.

The models covered by this manual are as follows:

ZX600-A1, A2, A3, A4, A5
ZX600-B1 – Aluminum frame model
ZX600-C1, C2, C3, C4, C5, C6, C7

The following table is a breakdown of the engine and frame numbers for the UK only by model and year of production:

Year	Model Code	Initial frame number (UK models only)	Initial engine number (UK models only)
A and B models (GPZ600R)			
1985	ZX600-A1	ZX600A-000001 on	ZX600AE000001 on
1986	ZX600-A2	ZX600A-025001 on	ZX600AE025001 on
1987	ZX600-A3	ZX600A-046001 on	ZX600AE052040 on
1988	ZX600-A4/A4A	ZX600A-054001 on	ZX600ZE052040 on
1989	ZX600-A5/A5A	ZX600A-055801 on	ZX600AE069501 on
C models (GPX600R)			
1988	ZX600-C1	ZX600C-000001 on	ZX600AE052040 on
1989	ZX600-C2	ZX600C-011501 on	ZX600AE069501 on
1990	ZX600-C3	ZX600C-019001 on	ZX600AE069501 on
1993	ZX600-C6	ZX600C-600001 on	ZX600AE069501 on
1994	ZX600-C7	ZX600C-601551 on	ZX600AE069501 on

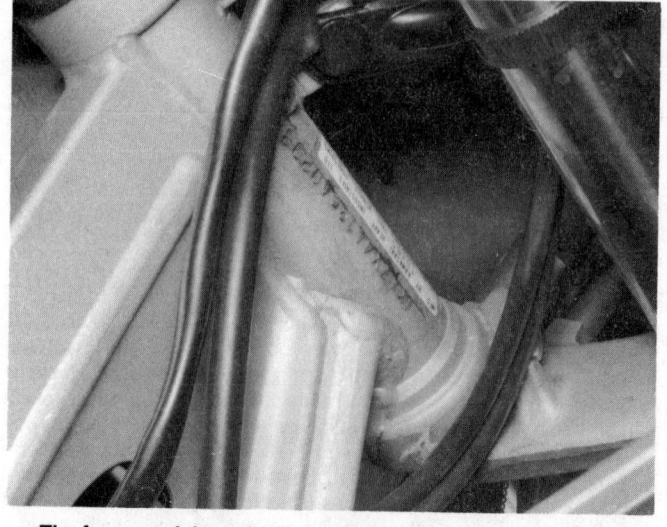

The frame serial number is stamped on the right side of the steering head

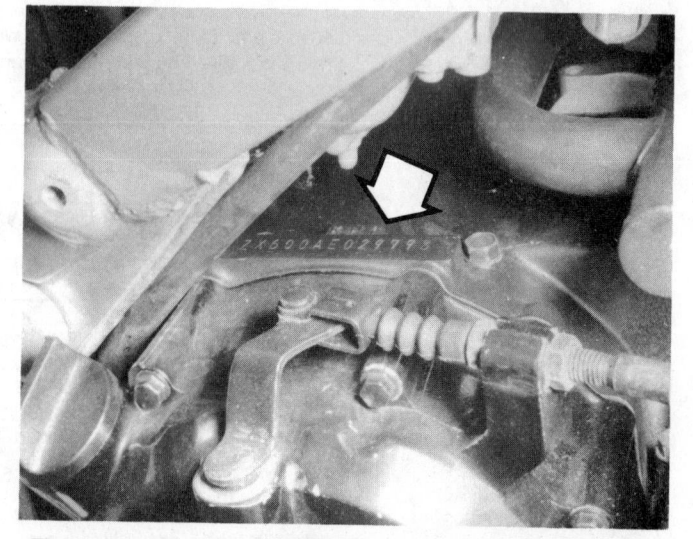

The engine serial number (arrow) is located on the right side of the engine case, just inboard of the clutch housing

Buying parts

Once you have found all the identification numbers, record them for reference when buying parts. Since the manufacturers change specifications, parts and vendors (companies that manufacture various components on the machine), providing the ID numbers is the only way to be reasonably sure that you are buying the correct parts.

Whenever possible, take the worn part to the dealer so direct comparison with the new component can be made. Along the trail from the manufacturer to the parts shelf, there are numerous places that the part can end up with the wrong number or be listed incorrectly.

The two places to purchase new parts for your motorcycle – the accessory store and the franchised dealer – differ in the type of parts they carry.

While dealers can obtain virtually every part for your cycle, the accessory dealer is usually limited to normal high wear items such as shock absorbers, tune-up parts, various engine gaskets, cables, chains, brake parts, etc. Rarely will an accessory outlet have major suspension components, cylinders, transmission gears, or cases.

Used parts can be obtained for roughly half the price of new ones, but you can't always be sure of what you're getting. Once again, take your worn part to the wrecking yard for direct comparison.

Whether buying new, used or rebuilt parts, the best course is to deal directly with someone who specializes in parts for your particular make.

General specifications

Refer to Chapter 10 for information on the ZX750F model

Frame and suspension

Wheelbase	
A and B models	56.3 in (1430 mm)
C models	56.1 in (1425 mm)
Overall length	
A and B models	84.3 in (2140 mm)
C models	82.5 in (2095 mm)
Overall width	
A and B models	26.3 in (670 mm)
C models	27.1 in (690 mm)
Overall height	
A and B models	46.6 in (1185 mm)
C models	45.3 in (1150 mm)
Seat height	
A and B models	30.3 in (770 mm)
C models	29.7 in (755 mm)
Dry weight	
A models	430 lbs (195 kg)
B model	420 lbs (190.6 kg)
C models	397 lbs (180 kg)
Front suspension	Telescopic fork
Rear suspension	Uni-trak
Front brake	Dual hydraulic discs
Rear brake	Single hydraulic disc
Fuel capacity	4.7 US gal (18 liters)

Engine

Type	Liquid cooled, 4-stroke, DOHC inline four-cylinder
Displacement	592 cc
Ignition system	Transistorized
Carburetor type	Four 32 mm Keihin carburetors
Clutch	Wet, multi-plate
Transmission	6-speed, constant mesh

Maintenance techniques, tools and working facilities

Basic maintenance techniques

There are a number of techniques involved in maintenance and repair that will be referred to throughout this manual. Application of these techniques will enable the amateur mechanic to be more efficient, better organized and capable of performing the various tasks properly, which will ensure that the repair job is thorough and complete.

Fastening systems

Fasteners, basically, are nuts, bolts and screws used to hold two or more parts together. There are a few things to keep in mind when working with fasteners. Almost all of them use a locking device of some type (either a lock washer, locknut, locking tab or thread adhesive). All threaded fasteners should be clean, straight, have undamaged threads and undamaged corners on the hex head where the wrench fits. Develop the habit of replacing all damaged nuts and bolts with new ones.

Rusted nuts and bolts should be treated with a penetrating oil to ease removal and prevent breakage. Some mechanics use turpentine in a spout type oil can, which works quite well. After applying the rust penetrant, let it "work" for a few minutes before trying to loosen the nut or bolt. Badly rusted fasteners may have to be chiseled off or removed with a special nut breaker, available at tool stores.

If a bolt or stud breaks off in an assembly, it can be drilled out and removed with a special tool called an E-Z out (or screw extractor). Most dealer service departments and motorcycle repair shops can perform this task, as well as others (such as the repair of threaded holes that have been stripped out).

Flat washers and lock washers, when removed from an assembly, should always be replaced exactly as removed. Replace any damaged washers with new ones. Always use a flat washer between a lock washer and any soft metal surface (such as aluminum), thin sheet metal or plastic. Special locknuts can only be used once or twice before they lose their locking ability and must be replaced.

Tightening sequences and procedures

When threaded fasteners are tightened, they are often tightened to a specific torque value (torque is basically a twisting force). Over-tightening the fastener can weaken it and cause it to break, while under-tightening can cause it to eventually come loose. Each bolt, depending on the material it's made of, the diameter of its shank and the material it is threaded into, has a specific torque value, which is noted in the Specifications. Be sure to follow the torque recommendations closely.

Fasteners laid out in a pattern (i.e. cylinder head bolts, engine case bolts, etc.) must be loosened or tightened in a sequence to avoid warping the component. Initially, the bolts/nuts should go on finger tight only. Next, they should be tightened one full turn each, in a criss-cross or diagonal pattern. After each one has been tightened one full turn, return to the first one tightened and tighten them all one half turn, following the same pattern. Finally, tighten each of them one quarter turn at a time until each fastener has been tightened to the proper torque. To loosen and remove the fasteners the procedure would be reversed.

Disassembly sequence

Component disassembly should be done with care and purpose to help ensure that the parts go back together properly during reassembly. Always keep track of the sequence in which parts are removed. Take note of special characteristics or marks on parts that can be installed more than one way (such as a grooved thrust washer on a shaft). It's a good idea to lay the disassembled parts out on a clean surface in the order that they were removed. It may also be helpful to make sketches or take instant photos of components before removal.

When removing fasteners from a component, keep track of their locations. Sometimes threading a bolt back in a part, or putting the washers and nut back on a stud, can prevent mixups later. If nuts and bolts can't be returned to their original locations, they should be kept in a compartmented box or a series of small boxes. A cupcake or muffin tin is ideal for this purpose, since each cavity can hold the bolts and nuts from a particular area (i.e. engine case bolts, valve cover bolts, engine mount bolts, etc.). A pan of this type is especially helpful when working on assemblies with very small parts (such as the carburetors and the valve train). The cavities can be marked with paint or tape to identify the contents.

Whenever wiring looms, harnesses or connectors are separated, it's a good idea to identify the two halves with numbered pieces of masking tape so they can be easily reconnected.

Gasket sealing surfaces

Throughout any motorcycle, gaskets are used to seal the mating surfaces between components and keep lubricants, fluids, vacuum or pressure contained in an assembly.

Many times these gaskets are coated with a liquid or paste type gasket sealing compound before assembly. Age, heat and pressure can sometimes cause the two parts to stick together so tightly that they are very difficult to separate. In most cases, the part can be loosened by striking it with a soft-faced hammer near the mating surfaces. A regular hammer can be used if a block of wood is placed between the hammer and the part. Do not hammer on cast parts or parts that could be easily damaged. With any particularly stubborn part, always recheck to make sure that every fastener has been removed.

Avoid using a screwdriver or bar to pry apart components, as they can easily mar the gasket sealing surfaces of the parts (which must remain smooth). If prying is absolutely necessary, use a piece of wood, but keep in mind that extra clean-up will be necessary if the wood splinters.

After the parts are separated, the old gasket must be carefully scraped off and the gasket surfaces cleaned. Stubborn gasket material can be soaked with a gasket remover (available in aerosol cans) to soften it so it can be easily scraped off. A scraper can be fashioned from a piece of copper tubing by flattening and sharpening one end. Copper is recommended because it is usually softer than the surfaces to be scraped, which reduces the chance of gouging the part. Some gaskets can be removed with a wire brush, but regardless of the method used, the mating surfaces must be left clean and smooth. If for some reason the gasket surface is gouged, then a gasket sealer thick enough to fill scratches will have to be used during reassembly of the components. For most applications, a non-drying (or semi-drying) gasket sealer is best.

Hose removal tips

Hose removal precautions closely parallel gasket removal precautions. Avoid scratching or gouging the surface that the hose mates against or the connection may leak. Because of various chemical reactions, the rubber in hoses can bond itself to the metal spigot that the hose fits over. To remove a hose, first loosen the hose clamps that secure it to the spigot. Then, with slip joint pliers, grab the hose at the clamp and rotate it around the spigot. Work it back and forth until it is completely free, then pull it off (silicone or other lubricants will ease removal if they can be applied between the hose and the outside of the spigot). Apply the same lubricant to the inside of the hose and the outside of the spigot to simplify installation.

If a hose clamp is broken or damaged, do not reuse it. Also, do not reuse hoses that are cracked, split or torn.

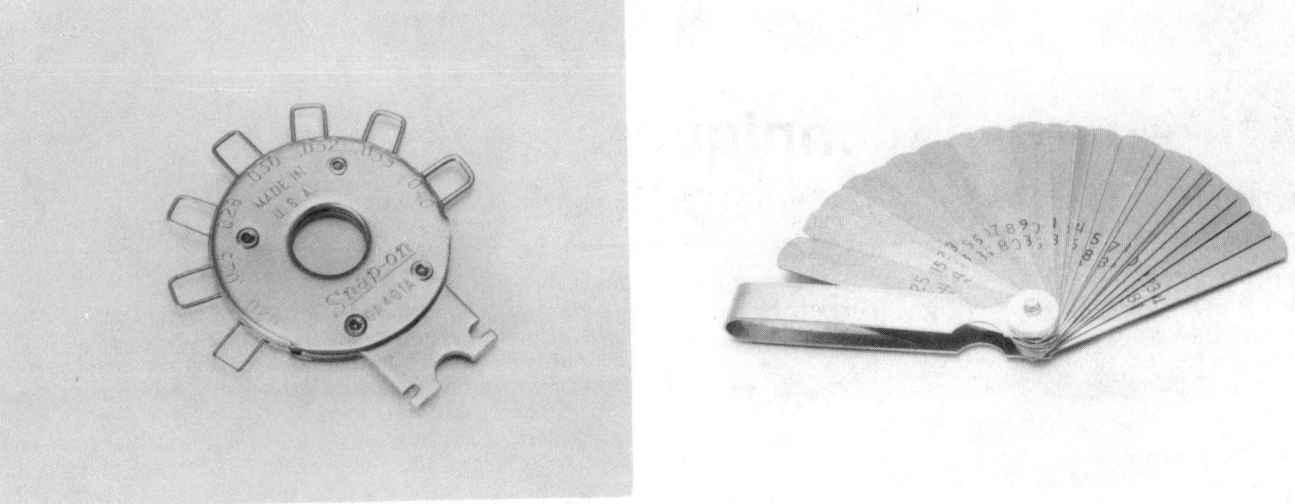

Spark plug gap adjusting tool

Feeler gauge set

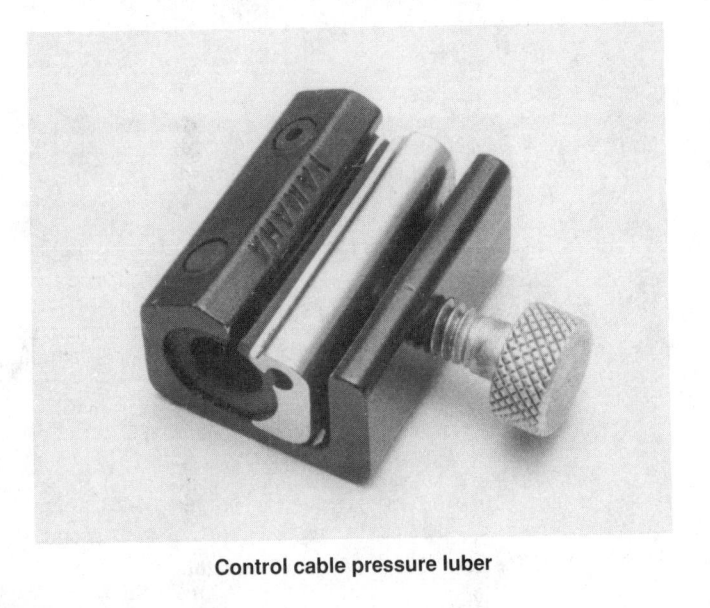

Control cable pressure luber

Hand impact screwdriver and bits

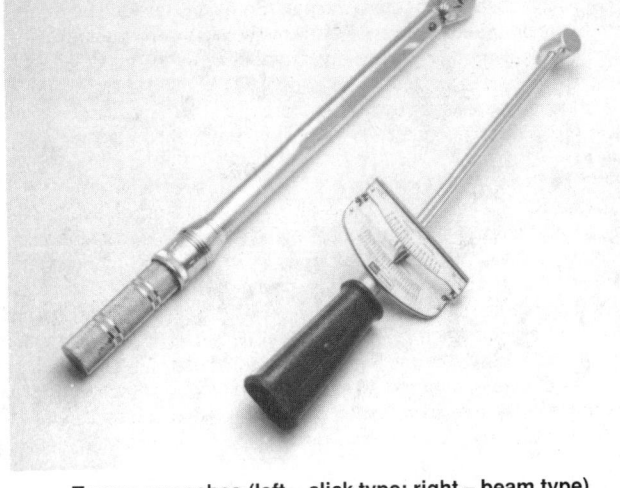

Torque wrenches (left – click type; right – beam type)

Tools

A selection of good tools is a basic requirement for anyone who plans to maintain and repair a motorcycle. For the owner who has few tools, if any, the initial investment might seem high, but when compared to the spiraling costs of routine maintenance and repair, it is a wise one.

To help the owner decide which tools are needed to perform the tasks detailed in this manual, the following tool lists are offered: Maintenance and minor repair, Repair and overhaul and Special. The newcomer to practical mechanics should start off with the Maintenance and minor repair tool kit, which is adequate for the simpler jobs. Then, as confidence and experience grow, the owner can tackle more difficult tasks, buying additional tools as they are needed. Eventually the basic kit will be built into the Repair and overhaul tool set. Over a period of time, the experienced do-it-yourselfer will assemble a tool set complete enough for most repair and overhaul procedures and will add tools from the Special category when it is felt that the expense is justified by the frequency of use.

Maintenance and minor repair tool kit

The tools in this list should be considered the minimum required for performance of routine maintenance, servicing and minor repair work. We recommend the purchase of combination wrenches (box end and open

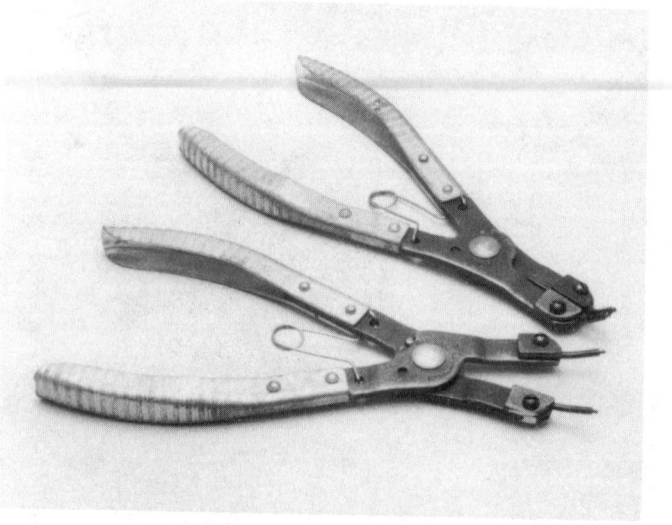

Snap-ring pliers (top – external; bottom – internal)

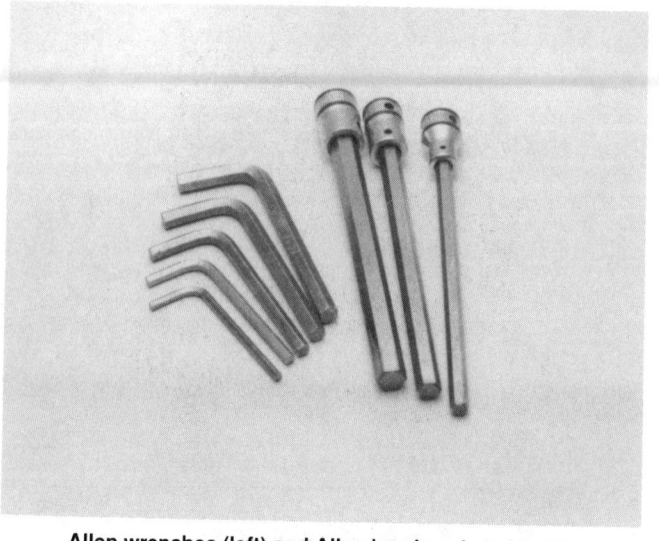

Allen wrenches (left) and Allen head sockets (right)

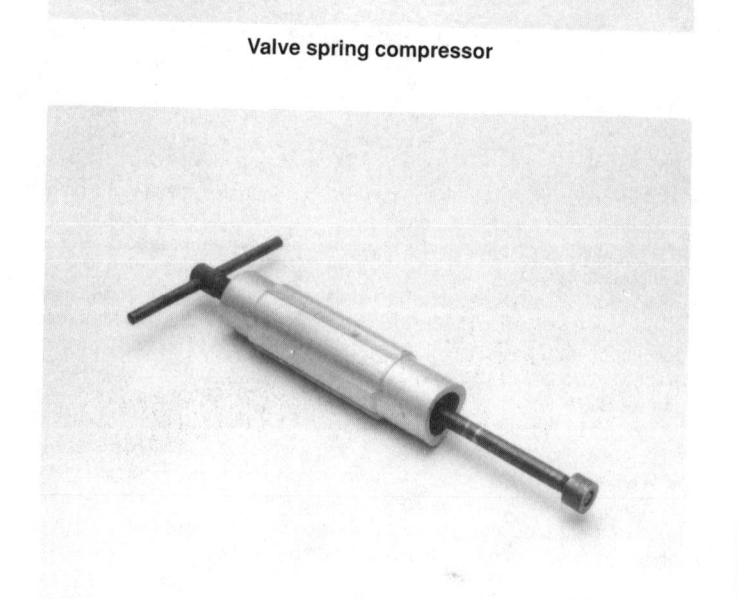

Valve spring compressor

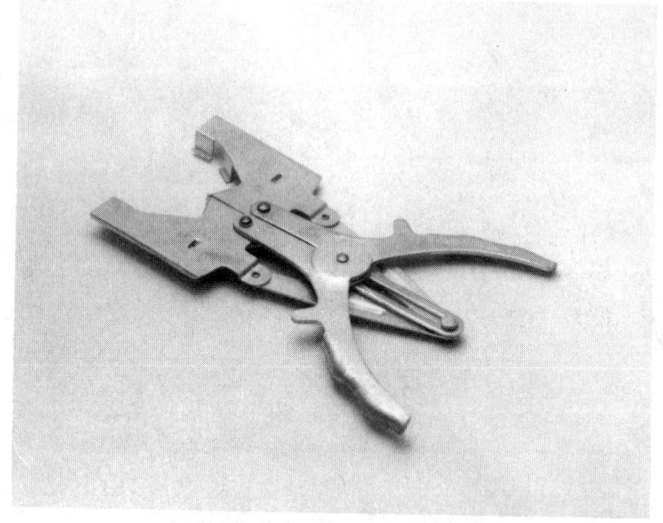

Piston ring removal/installation tool

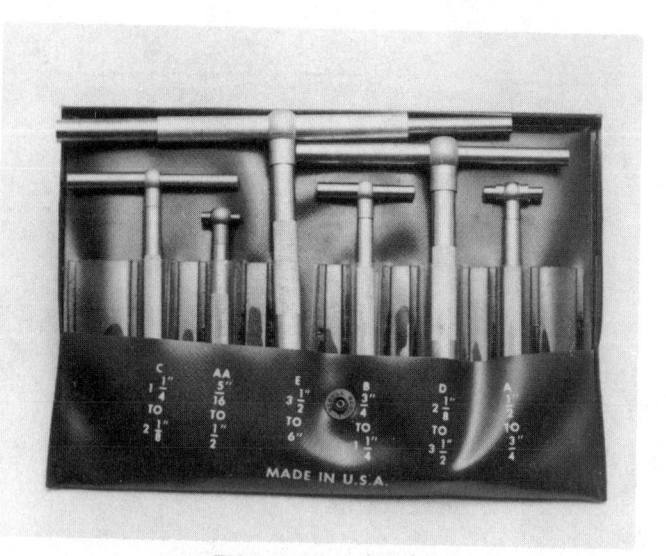

Piston pin puller

Telescoping gauges

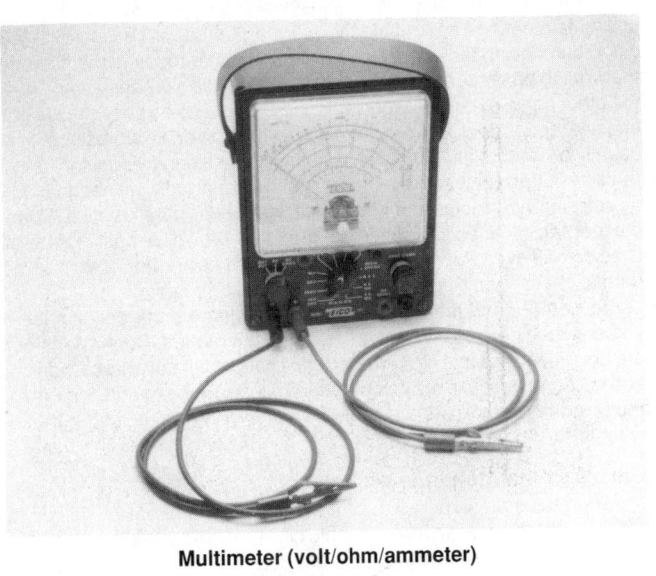

0-to-1 inch micrometer

Cylinder surfacing hone

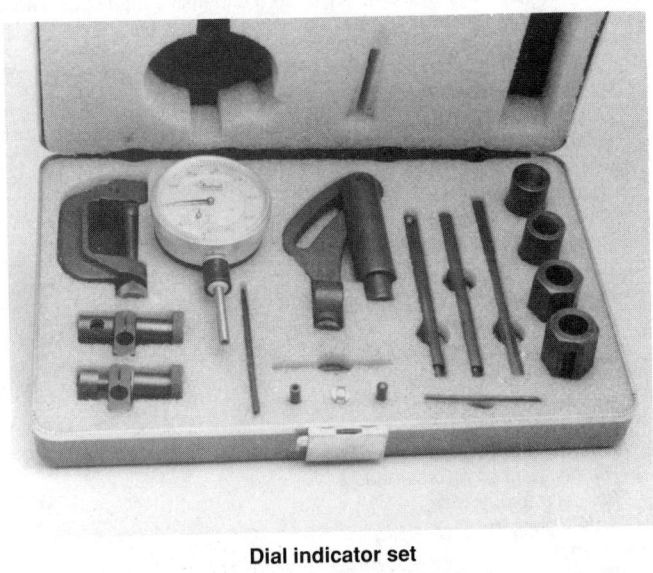

Cylinder compression gauge

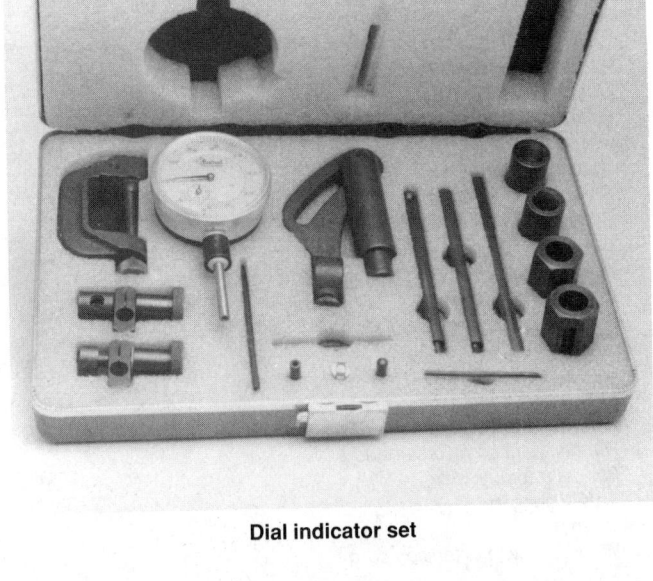

Dial indicator set

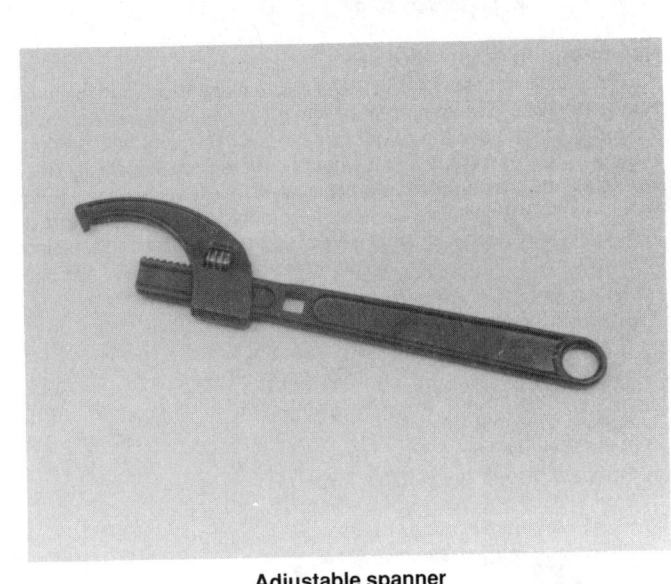

Multimeter (volt/ohm/ammeter)

Adjustable spanner

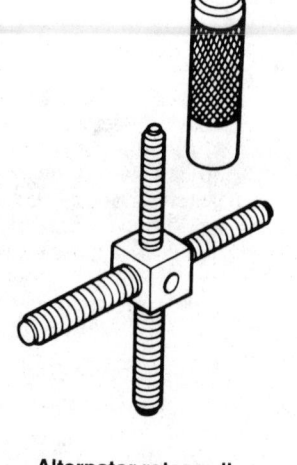

Alternator rotor puller

end combined in one wrench); while more expensive than open-ended ones, they offer the advantages of both types of wrench.

Combination wrench set (6 mm to 22 mm)
Adjustable wrench – 8 in
Spark plug socket (with rubber insert)
Spark plug gap adjusting tool
Feeler gauge set
Standard screwdriver (5/16 in x 6 in)
Phillips screwdriver (No. 2 x 6 in)
Allen (hex) wrench set (4 mm to 12 mm)
Combination (slip-joint) pliers – 6 in
Hacksaw and assortment of blades
Tire pressure gauge
Control cable pressure luber
Grease gun
Oil can
Fine emery cloth
Wire brush
Hand impact screwdriver and bits
Funnel (medium size)
Safety goggles
Drain pan
Work light with extension cord

Repair and overhaul tool set

These tools are essential for anyone who plans to perform major repairs and are intended to supplement those in the Maintenance and minor repair tool kit. Included is a comprehensive set of sockets which, though expensive, are invaluable because of their versatility (especially when various extensions and drives are available). We recommend the 3/8 inch drive over the 1/2 inch drive for general motorcycle maintenance and repair (ideally, the mechanic would have a 3/8 inch drive set and a 1/2 inch drive set).

Socket set(s)
Reversible ratchet
Extension – 6 in
Universal joint
Torque wrench (same size drive as sockets)
Ball pein hammer – 8 oz
Soft-faced hammer (plastic/rubber)
Standard screwdriver (1/4 in x 6 in)
Standard screwdriver (stubby – 5/16 in)
Phillips screwdriver (No. 3 x 8 in)
Phillips screwdriver (stubby – No. 2)
Pliers – locking
Pliers – lineman's

Pliers – needle nose
Pliers – snap-ring (internal and external)
Cold chisel – 1/2 in
Scriber
Scraper (made from flattened copper tubing)
Center punch
Pin punches (1/16, 1/8, 3/16 in)
Steel rule/straightedge – 12 in
Pin-type spanner wrench
A selection of files
Wire brush (large)

Note: Another tool which is often useful is an electric drill with a chuck capacity of 3/8 inch (and a set of good quality drill bits).

Special tools

The tools in this list include those which are not used regularly, are expensive to buy, or which need to be used in accordance with their manufacturer's instructions. Unless these tools will be used frequently, it is not very economical to purchase many of them. A consideration would be to split the cost and use between yourself and a friend or friends (i.e. members of a motorcycle club).

This list primarily contains tools and instruments widely available to the public, as well as some special tools produced by the vehicle manufacturer for distribution to dealer service departments. As a result, references to the manufacturer's special tools are occasionally included in the text of this manual. Generally, an alternative method of doing the job without the special tool is offered. However, sometimes there is no alternative to their use. Where this is the case, and the tool can't be purchased or borrowed, the work should be turned over to the dealer service department or a motorcycle repair shop.

Valve spring compressor
Piston ring removal and installation tool
Piston pin puller
Telescoping gauges
Micrometer(s) and/or dial/Vernier calipers
Cylinder surfacing hone
Cylinder compression gauge
Dial indicator set
Multimeter
Adjustable spanner
Alternator rotor holder
Alterantor rotor puller
Manometer or vacuum gauge set
Small air compressor with blow gun and tire chuck

Buying tools

For the do-it-yourselfer who is just starting to get involved in motorcycle maintenance and repair, there are a number of options available when purchasing tools. If maintenance and minor repair is the extent of the work to be done, the purchase of individual tools is satisfactory. If, on the other hand, extensive work is planned, it would be a good idea to purchase a modest tool set from one of the large retail chain stores. A set can usually be bought at a substantial savings over the individual tool prices (and they often come with a tool box). As additional tools are needed, add-on sets, individual tools and a larger tool box can be purchased to expand the tool selection. Building a tool set gradually allows the cost of the tools to be spread over a longer period of time and gives the mechanic the freedom to choose only those tools that will actually be used.

Tool stores and motorcycle dealers will often be the only source of some of the special tools that are needed, but regardless of where tools are bought, try to avoid cheap ones (especially when buying screwdrivers and sockets) because they won't last very long. The expense involved in replacing cheap tools will eventually be greater than the initial cost of quality tools.

Care and maintenance of tools

Good tools are expensive, so it makes sense to treat them with respect. Keep them clean and in usable condition and store them properly when not in use. Always wipe off any dirt, grease or metal chips before putting them away. Never leave tools lying around in the work area.

Some tools, such as screwdrivers, pliers, wrenches and sockets, can be hung on a panel mounted on the garage or workshop wall, while others should be kept in a tool box or tray. Measuring instruments, gauges, meters, etc. must be carefully stored where they can't be damaged by weather or impact from other tools.

When tools are used with care and stored properly, they will last a very long time. Even with the best of care, tools will wear out if used frequently. When a tool is damaged or worn out, replace it; subsequent jobs will be safer and more enjoyable if you do.

Working facilities

Not to be overlooked when discussing tools is the workshop. If anything more than routine maintenance is to be carried out, some sort of suitable work area is essential.

It is understood, and appreciated, that many home mechanics do not have a good workshop or garage available and end up removing an engine or doing major repairs outside (it is recommended, however, that the overhaul or repair be completed under the cover of a roof).

A clean, flat workbench or table of comfortable working height is an absolute necessity. The workbench should be equipped with a vise that has a jaw opening of at least four inches.

As mentioned previously, some clean, dry storage space is also required for tools, as well as the lubricants, fluids, cleaning solvents, etc. which soon become necessary.

Sometimes waste oil and fluids, drained from the engine or cooling system during normal maintenance or repairs, present a disposal problem. To avoid pouring them on the ground or into a sewage system, simply pour the used fluids into large containers, seal them with caps and take them to an authorized disposal site or service station. Plastic jugs (such as old antifreeze containers) are ideal for this purpose.

Always keep a supply of old newspapers and clean rags available. Old towels are excellent for mopping up spills. Many mechanics use rolls of paper towels for most work because they are readily available and disposable. To help keep the area under the motorcycle clean, a large cardboard box can be cut open and flattened to protect the garage or shop floor.

Whenever working over a painted surface (such as the fuel tank) cover it with an old blanket or bedspread to protect the finish.

Safety first!

Professional mechanics are trained in safe working procedures. However enthusiastic you may be about getting on with the job at hand, take the time to ensure that your safety is not jeopardized. A moment's lack of attention can result in an accident, as can failure to recognize certain simple safety precautions. The possibility of an accident will always exist, and the following points do not pretend to be a comprehensive list of all dangers; they are intended, rather, to make you aware of the risks and to encourage a safety-conscious approach to all work you carry out on your machine.

Essential DOs and DON'Ts

DON'T start the engine without first checking to see if the transmission is in Neutral.

DON'T use gasoline for cleaning parts.

DON'T attempt to drain the oil until you are sure it has cooled to the point that it will not burn you.

DON'T touch any part of the engine or exhaust system until it has cooled down sufficiently to avoid burns.

DON'T siphon toxic liquids such as gasoline, antifreeze and brake fluid by mouth, or allow them to remain on your skin.

DON'T inhale brake lining dust – it is potentially hazardous.

DON'T allow spilled oil or grease to remain on the floor – wipe it up before someone slips on it.

DON'T use loose fitting wrenches or other tools which may slip and cause injury.

DON'T push on wrenches when loosening or tightening nuts or bolts. Always try to pull the wrench towards you. If the situation calls for pushing the wrench away, push with an open hand to avoid scraped knuckles if the wrench should slip.

DON'T attempt to lift a heavy component which may be beyond your capability – get someone to help you.

DON'T rush or take unsafe shortcuts to finish a job.

DON'T allow children on or around the motorcycle while you are working on it.

DO wear eye protection when using power tools such as a drill, bench grinder, etc.

DO keep loose clothing and long hair well out of the way of moving parts.

DO make sure that any hoist used has a safe working load rating adequate for the job.

DO make sure that the machine is securely supported, especially when removing wheels.

DO get someone to check on you periodically when working alone.

DO carry out work in a logical sequence and make sure that everything is correctly assembled and tightened.

DO keep chemicals and fluids tightly capped and out of the reach of children and pets.

DO remember that your motorcycle's safety affects that of yourself and others. If in doubt on any point, get professional advice.

Asbestos

Certain friction, insulating, sealing, and other products – such as brake linings, clutch linings, high-temperature gaskets, etc. – may contain asbestos. Extreme care must be taken to avoid inhalation of dust from such products since it is hazardous to your health. If in doubt, assume that they do contain asbestos.

Fire

Remember at all times that gasoline is highly flammable. Never smoke or have any kind of open flame around when working on your machine. But, the risk does not end there; a spark caused by an electrical short-circuit, by two metal surfaces contacting each other, or even static electricity built up in your body under certain conditions, can ignite gasoline vapors, which in a confined space are highly explosive. Do not, under any circumstances, use gasoline for cleaning parts; use an approved safety solvent.

Always disconnect the battery ground cable before working on any part of the fuel system and never risk spilling fuel on a hot engine or exhaust.

It is highly recommended that a fire extinguisher suitable for use on fuel and electrical fires be kept handy in the garage or workshop at all times. Never try to extinguish a fuel or electrical fire with water.

Fumes

Certain fumes are highly toxic and can quickly cause unconsciousness and even death if inhaled to any extent. Gasoline vapor falls into this category, as do the vapors from some cleaning solvents. Any draining or pouring of such volatile fluids should be done in a well ventilated area.

When using cleaning fluids and solvents, read the instructions on the container carefully. Never use materials from unmarked containers.

Never run the engine in an enclosed space such as a garage; exhaust fumes contain carbon monoxide which is extremely poisonous. If you need to run the engine, always do so in the open air or at least have the rear of the machine outside the work area.

The battery

Never create a spark or allow a bare light bulb near the battery vent hose. It will normally be giving off a certain amount of hydrogen gas, which is highly explosive.

Always disconnect the battery ground cable before working on the fuel or electrical systems.

If possible, loosen the filler caps when charging the battery from an external source. Do not charge at an excessive rate or the battery may burst.

Take care when adding water and when carrying a battery. The electrolyte, even when diluted, is very corrosive and should not be allowed to contact clothing or skin.

Always wear eye protection when cleaning the battery to prevent the caustic deposits from entering your eyes.

Household current

When using an electric power tool, inspection light, etc., which operates on household current, always make sure that the tool is correctly connected to its plug and that, where necessary, it is properly grounded. Do not use such items in damp conditions and, again, do not create a spark or apply excessive heat in the vicinity of fuel or fuel vapor.

Secondary ignition system voltage

A severe electric shock can result from touching certain parts of the ignition system (such as the spark plug wires) when the engine is running or being cranked, particularly if components are damp or the insulation is defective. Where an electronic ignition system is installed, the secondary system voltage is much higher and could prove fatal.

Motorcycle chemicals and lubricants

A number of chemicals and lubricants are available for use in motorcycle maintenance and repair. They include a wide variety of products ranging from cleaning solvents and degreasers to lubricants and protective sprays for rubber, plastic and vinyl.

Contact point/spark plug cleaner is a solvent used to clean oily film and dirt from points, grime from electrical connectors and oil deposits from spark plugs. It is oil free and leaves no residue. It can also be used to remove gum and varnish from carburetor jets and other orifices.

Carburetor cleaner is similar to contact point/spark plug cleaner but it usually has a stronger solvent and may leave a slight oily reside. It is not recommended for cleaning electrical components or connections.

Brake system cleaner is used to remove grease or brake fluid from brake system components (where clean surfaces are absolutely necessary and petroleum-based solvents cannot be used); it also leaves no residue.

Silicone-based lubricants are used to protect rubber parts such as hoses and grommets, and are used as lubricants for hinges and locks.

Multi-purpose grease is an all purpose lubricant used wherever grease is more practical than a liquid lubricant such as oil. Some multi-purpose grease is colored white and specially formulated to be more resistant to water than ordinary grease.

Gear oil (sometimes called gear lube) is a specially designed oil used in transmissions and final drive units, as well as other areas where high friction, high temperature lubrication is required. It is available in a number of viscosities (weights) for various applications.

Motor oil, of course, is the lubricant specially formulated for use in the engine. It normally contains a wide variety of additives to prevent corrosion and reduce foaming and wear. Motor oil comes in various weights (viscosity ratings) of from 5 to 80. The recommended weight of the oil depends on the seasonal temperature and the demands on the engine. Light oil is used in cold climates and under light load conditions; heavy oil is used in hot climates and where high loads are encountered. Multi-viscosity oils are designed to have characteristics of both light and heavy oils and are available in a number of weights from 5W-20 to 20W-50.

Gas additives perform several functions, depending on their chemical makeup. They usually contain solvents that help dissolve gum and varnish that build up on carburetor and intake parts. They also serve to break down carbon deposits that form on the inside surfaces of the combustion chambers. Some additives contain upper cylinder lubricants for valves and piston rings.

Brake fluid is a specially formulated hydraulic fluid that can withstand the heat and pressure encountered in brake systems. Care must be taken that this fluid does not come in contact with painted surfaces or plastics. An opened container should always be resealed to prevent contamination by water or dirt.

Chain lubricants are formulated especially for use on motorcycle final drive chains. A good chain lube should adhere well and have good penetrating qualities to be effective as a lubricant inside the chain and on the side plates, pins and rollers. Most chain lubes are either the foaming type or quick drying type and are usually marketed as sprays.

Degreasers are heavy duty solvents used to remove grease and grime that may accumulate on engine and frame components. They can be sprayed or brushed on and, depending on the type, are rinsed with either water or solvent.

Solvents are used alone or in combination with degreasers to clean parts and assemblies during repair and overhaul. The home mechanic should use only solvents that are non-flammable and that do not produce irritating fumes.

Gasket sealing compounds may be used in conjunction with gaskets, to improve their sealing capabilities, or alone, to seal metal-to-metal joints. Many gasket sealers can withstand extreme heat, some are impervious to gasoline and lubricants, while others are capable of filling and sealing large cavities. Depending on the intended use, gasket sealers either dry hard or stay relatively soft and pliable. They are usually applied by hand, with a brush, or are sprayed on the gasket sealing surfaces.

Thread cement is an adhesive locking compound that prevents threaded fasteners from loosening because of vibration. It is available in a variety of types for different applications.

Moisture dispersants are usually sprays that can be used to dry out electrical components such as the fuse block and wiring connectors. Some types can also be used as treatment for rubber and as a lubricant for hinges, cables and locks.

Waxes and polishes are used to help protect painted and plated surfaces from the weather. Different types of paint may require the use of different types of wax polish. Some polishes utilize a chemical or abrasive cleaner to help remove the top layer of oxidized (dull) paint on older vehicles. In recent years, many non-wax polishes (that contain a wide variety of chemicals such as polymers and silicones) have been introduced. These non-wax polishes are usually easier to apply and last longer than conventional waxes and polishes.

Troubleshooting

Contents

Engine doesn't start or is difficult to start

1   Starter motor does not rotate

1   Engine stop switch Off.
2   Fuse blown. Check fuse block under the seat (Chapter 9).
3   Battery voltage low. Check and recharge battery (Chapter 9).
4   Starter motor defective. Make sure the wiring to the starter is secure. Make sure the starter solenoid (relay) clicks when the start button is pushed. If the solenoid clicks, then the fault is in the wiring or motor.
5   Starter solenoid (relay) faulty. It is located behind the left side cover. Check it according to the procedure in Chapter 9.
6   Starter button not contacting. The contacts could be wet, corroded or dirty. Disassemble and clean the switch (Chapter 9).
7   Wiring open or shorted. Check all wiring connections and harnesses to make sure that they are dry, tight and not corroded. Also check for broken or frayed wires that can cause a short to ground (see wiring diagram, Chapter 9).
8   Ignition switch defective. Check the switch according to the procedure in Chapter 9. Replace the switch with a new one if it is defective.
9   Engine stop switch defective. Check for wet, dirty or corroded contacts. Clean or replace the switch as necessary (Chapter 9).
10   Faulty starter lockout switch. Check the wiring to the switch and the switch itself according to the procedures in Chapter 9.

2   Starter motor rotates but engine does not turn over

1   Starter motor clutch defective. Inspect and repair or replace (Chapter 2).
2   Damaged idler or starter gears. Inspect and replace the damaged parts (Chapter 2).

3   Starter works but engine won't turn over (seized)

Seized engine caused by one or more internally damaged components. Failure due to wear, abuse or lack of lubrication. Damage can include seized valves, camshaft, pistons, crankshaft, connecting rod bearings, or transmission gears or bearings. Refer to Chapter 2 for engine disassembly.

4   No fuel flow

1   No fuel in tank.
2   Fuel tap vacuum hose broken or disconnected.
3   Tank cap air vent obstructed. Usually caused by dirt or water. Remove it and clean the cap vent hole.
4   Fuel tap clogged. Remove the tap and clean it and the filter (Chapter 4).
5   Fuel line clogged. Pull the fuel line loose and carefully blow through it.
6   Inlet needle valves clogged. For all of the valves to be clogged, either a very bad batch of fuel with an unusual additive has been used, or some other foreign object has entered the tank. Many times after a machine has been stored for many months without running, the fuel turns to a varnish-like liquid and forms deposits on the inlet needle valves and jets. The carburetors should be removed and overhauled if draining the float bowls does not alleviate the problem.

5   Engine flooded

1   Float level too high. Check and adjust as described in Chapter 4.

2   Inlet needle valve worn or stuck open. A piece of dirt, rust or other debris can cause the inlet needle to seat improperly, causing excess fuel to be admitted to the float bowl. In this case, the float chamber should be cleaned and the needle and seat inspected. If the needle and seat are worn, then the leaking will persist and the parts should be replaced with new ones (Chapter 4).
3   Starting technique incorrect. Under normal circumstances (i.e., if all the carburetor functions are sound) the machine should start with little or no throttle. When the engine is cold, the choke should be operated and the engine started without opening the throttle. When the engine is at operating temperature, only a very slight amount of throttle should be necessary. If the engine is flooded, turn the fuel tap off and hold the throttle open while cranking the engine. This will allow additional air to reach the cylinders. Remember to turn the gas back on after the engine starts.

6   No spark or weak spark

1   Ignition switch Off.
2   Engine stop switch turned to the Off position.
3   Battery voltage low. Check and recharge battery as necessary (Chapter 9).
4   Spark plug dirty, defective or worn out. Locate reason for fouled plug(s) using spark plug condition chart and follow the plug maintenance procedures in Chapter 1.
5   Spark plug cap or high-tension wiring faulty. Check condition. Replace either or both components if cracks or deterioration are evident (Chapter 5).
6   Spark plug cap not making good contact. Make sure the plug cap fits snugly over the plug end.
7   IC igniter defective. Check the unit, referring to Chapter 5 for details.
8   Pickup coil defective. Check the unit, referring to Chapter 5 for details.
9   Ignition coil(s) defective. Check the coils, referring to Chapter 5.
10   Ignition or stop switch shorted. This is usually caused by water, corrosion, damage or excessive wear. The switches can be disassembled and cleaned with electrical contact cleaner. If cleaning does not help, replace the switches (Chapter 9).
11   Wiring shorted or broken between:
   a) Ignition switch and engine stop switch
   b) IC igniter and engine stop switch
   c) IC igniter and ignition coil
   d) Ignition coil and plug
   e) IC igniter and pickup coils
12   Make sure that all wiring connections are clean, dry and tight. Look for chafed and broken wires (Chapters 5 and 9).

7   Compression low

1   Spark plug loose. Remove the plug and inspect the threads. Reinstall and tighten to the specified torque (Chapter 1).
2   Cylinder head not sufficiently tightened down. If the cylinder head is suspected of being loose, then there's a chance that the gasket or head is damaged if the problem has persisted for any length of time. The head bolts should be tightened to the proper torque in the correct sequence (Chapter 2).
3   Improper valve clearance. This means that the valve is not closing completely and compression pressure is leaking past the valve. Check and adjust the valve clearances (Chapter 1).
4   Cylinder and/or piston worn. Excessive wear will cause compression pressure to leak past the rings. This is usually accompanied by worn rings as well. A top end overhaul is necessary (Chapter 2).
5   Piston rings worn, weak, broken, or sticking. Broken or sticking piston rings usually indicate a lubrication or carburetion problem that causes excess carbon deposits or seizures to form on the pistons and rings. Top end overhaul is necessary (Chapter 2).

6   Piston ring-to-groove clearance excessive. This is caused by excessive wear of the piston ring lands. Piston replacement is necessary (Chapter 2).

7   Cylinder head gasket damaged. If the head is e allowed to become loose, or if excessive carbon build-up on the piston crown and combustion chamber causes extremely high compression, the head gasket may leak. Retorquing the head is not always sufficient to restore the seal, so gasket replacement is necessary (Chapter 2).

8   Cylinder head warped. This is caused by overheating or improperly tightened head bolts. Machine shop resurfacing or head replacement is necessary (Chapter 2).

9   Valve spring broken or weak. Caused by component failure or wear; the spring(s) must be replaced (Chapter 2).

10   Valve not seating properly. This is caused by a bent valve (from over-revving or improper valve adjustment), burned valve or seat (improper carburetion) or an accumulation of carbon deposits on the seat (from carburetion, lubrication problems). The valves must be cleaned and/or replaced and the seats serviced if possible (Chapter 2).

8   Stalls after starting

1   Improper choke action. Make sure the choke rod is getting a full stroke and staying in the "out" position. Adjustment of the cable slack is covered in Chapter 1.

2   Ignition malfunction. See Chapter 5.

3   Carburetor malfunction. See Chapter 4.

4   Fuel contaminated. The fuel can be contaminated with either dirt or water, or can change chemically if the machine is allowed to sit for several months or more. Drain the tank and float bowls (Chapter 4).

5   Intake air leak. Check for loose carburetor-to-intake manifold connections, loose or missing vacuum gauge access port cap or hose, or loose carburetor top (Chapter 4).

6   Idle speed incorrect. Turn idle speed adjuster screw until the engine idles at the specified rpm (Chapters 1 and 4).

9   Rough idle

1   Ignition malfunction. See Chapter 5.

2   Idle speed incorrect. See Chapter 1.

3   Carburetors not synchronized. Adjust carburetors with vacuum gauge set or manometer as outlined in Chapter 1.

4   Carburetor malfunction. See Chapter 4.

5   Fuel contaminated. The fuel can be contaminated with either dirt or water, or can change chemically if the machine is allowed to sit for several months or more. Drain the tank and float bowls. If the problem is severe, a carburetor overhaul may be necessary (Chapters 1 and 4).

6   Intake air leak (Chapter 4).

7   Air cleaner clogged. Service or replace air filter element (Chapter 1).

Poor running at low speed

10   Spark weak

1   Battery voltage low. Check and recharge battery (Chapter 9).

2   Spark plug fouled, defective or worn out. Refer to Chapter 1 for spark plug maintenance.

3   Spark plug cap or high tension wiring defective. Refer to Chapters 1 and 5 for details on the ignition system.

4   Spark plug cap not making contact.

5   Incorrect spark plug. Wrong type, heat range or cap configuration. Check and install correct plugs listed in Chapter 1. A cold plug or one with a recessed firing electrode will not operate at low speeds without fouling.

6   IC igniter defective. See Chapter 5.

7   Pickup coil defective. See Chapter 5.

8   Ignition coil(s) defective. See Chapter 5.

11   Fuel/air mixture incorrect

1   Pilot screw(s) out of adjustment (Chapters 1 and 4).

2   Pilot jet or air passage clogged. Remove and overhaul the carburetors (Chapter 4).

3   Air bleed holes clogged. Remove carburetor and blow out all passages (Chapter 4).

4   Air cleaner clogged, poorly sealed or missing.

5   Air cleaner-to-carburetor boot poorly sealed. Look for cracks, holes or loose clamps and replace or repair defective parts.

6   Fuel level too high or too low. Adjust the floats (Chapter 4).

7   Fuel tank air vent obstructed. Make sure that the air vent passage in the filler cap is open.

8   Carburetor intake manifolds loose. Check for cracks, breaks, tears or loose clamps or bolts. Repair or replace the rubber boots.

12   Compression low

1   Spark plug loose. Remove the plug and inspect the threads. Reinstall and tighten to the specified torque (Chapter 1).

2   Cylinder head not sufficiently tightened down. If the cylinder head is suspected of being loose, then there's a chance that the gasket and head are damaged if the problem has persisted for any length of time. The head bolts should be tightened to the proper torque in the correct sequence (Chapter 2).

3   Improper valve clearance. This means that the valve is not closing completely and compression pressure is leaking past the valve. Check and adjust the valve clearances (Chapter 1).

4   Cylinder and/or piston worn. Excessive wear will cause compression pressure to leak past the rings. This is usually accompanied by worn rings as well. A top end overhaul is necessary (Chapter 2).

5   Piston rings worn, weak, broken, or sticking. Broken or sticking piston rings usually indicate a lubrication or carburetion problem that causes excess carbon deposits or seizures to form on the pistons and rings. Top end overhaul is necessary (Chapter 2).

6   Piston ring-to-groove clearance excessive. This is caused by excessive wear of the piston ring lands. Piston replacement is necessary (Chapter 2).

7   Cylinder head gasket damaged. If the head is allowed to become loose, or if excessive carbon build-up on the piston crown and combution chamber causes extremely high compression, the head gasket may leak. Retorquing the head is not always sufficient to restore the seal, so gasket replacement is necessary (Chapter 2).

8   Cylinder head warped. This is caused by overheating or improperly tightened head bolts. Machine shop resurfacing or head replacement is necessary (Chapter 2).

9   Valve spring broken or weak. Caused by component failure or wear; the spring(s) must be replaced (Chapter 2).

10   Valve not seating properly. This is caused by a bent valve (from over-revving or improper valve adjustment), burned valve or seat (improper carburetion) or an accumulation of carbon deposits on the seat (from carburetion, lubrication problems). The valves must be cleaned and/or replaced and the seats serviced if possible (Chapter 2).

13   Poor acceleration

1   Carburetors leaking or dirty. Overhaul the carburetors (Chapter 4).

2   Timing not advancing. The pickup coil unit or the IC igniter may be defective. If so, they must be replaced with new ones, as they cannot be repaired.

3   Carburetors not synchronized. Adjust them with a vacuum gauge set or manometer (Chapter 1).
4   Engine oil viscosity too high. Using a heavier oil than that recommended in Chapter 1 can damage the oil pump or lubrication system and cause drag on the engine.
5   Brakes dragging. Usually caused by debris which has entered the brake piston sealing boot, or from a warped disc or bent axle. Repair as necessary (Chapter 7).

Poor running or no power at high speed

14   Firing incorrect

1   Air filter restricted. Clean or replace filter (Chapter 1).
2   Spark plug fouled, defective or worn out. See Chapter 1 for spark plug maintenance.
3   Spark plug cap or high tension wiring defective. See Chapters 1 and 5 for details on the ignition system.
4   Spark plug cap not in good contact. See Chapter 5.
5   Incorrect spark plug. Wrong type, heat range or cap configuration. Check and install correct plugs listed in Chapter 1. A cold plug or one with a recessed firing electrode will not operate at low speeds without fouling.
6   IC igniter defective. See Chapter 5.
7   Ignition coil(s) defective. See Chapter 5.

15   Fuel/air mixture incorrect

1   Main jet clogged. Dirt, water and other contaminants can clog the main jets. Clean the fuel tap filter, the float bowl area, and the jets and carburetor orifices (Chapter 4).
2   Main jet wrong size. The standard jetting is for sea level atmospheric pressure and oxygen content.
3   Throttle shaft-to-carburetor body clearance excessive. Refer to Chapter 4 for inspection and part replacement procedures.
4   Air bleed holes clogged. Remove and overhaul carburetors (Chapter 4).
5   Air cleaner clogged, poorly sealed or missing.
6   Air cleaner-to-carburetor boot poorly sealed. Look for cracks, holes or loose clamps, and replace or repair defective parts.
7   Fuel level too high or too low. Adjust the float(s) (Chapter 4).
8   Fuel tank air vent obstructed. Make sure the air vent passage in the filler cap is open.
9   Carburetor intake manifolds loose. Check for cracks, breaks, tears or loose clamps or bolts. Repair or replace the rubber boots (Chapter 2).
10   Fuel tap clogged. Remove the tap and clean it and the filter (Chapter 1).
11   Fuel line clogged. Pull the fuel line loose and carefully blow through it.

16   Compression low

1   Spark plug loose. Remove the plug and inspect the threads. Reinstall and tighten to the specified torque (Chapter 1).
2   Cylinder head not sufficiently tightened down. If the cylinder head is suspected of being loose, then there's a chance that the gasket and head are damaged if the problem has persisted for any length of time. The head bolts should be tightened to the proper torque in the correct sequence (Chapter 2).
3   Improper valve clearance. This means that the valve is not closing completely and compression pressure is leaking past the valve. Check and adjust the valve clearances (Chapter 1).
4   Cylinder and/or piston worn. Excessive wear will cause compression pressure to leak past the rings. This is usually accompanied by worn rings as well. A top end overhaul is necessary (Chapter 2).

5   Piston rings worn, weak, broken, or sticking. Broken or sticking piston rings usually indicate a lubrication or carburetion problem that causes excess carbon deposits or seizures to form on the pistons and rings. Top end overhaul is necessary (Chapter 2).
6   Piston ring-to-groove clearance excessive. This is caused by excessive wear of the piston ring lands. Piston replacement is necessary (Chapter 2).
7   Cylinder head gasket damaged. If the head is allowed to become loose, or if excessive carbon build-up on the piston crown and combustion chamber causes extremely high compression, the head gasket may leak. Retorquing the head is not always sufficient to restore the seal, so gasket replacement is necessary (Chapter 2).
8   Cylinder head warped. This is caused by overheating or improperly tightened head bolts. Machine shop resurfacing or head replacement is necessary (Chapter 2).
9   Valve spring broken or weak. Caused by component failure or wear; the spring(s) must be replaced (Chapter 2).
10   Valve not seating properly. This is caused by a bent valve (from over-revving or improper valve adjustment), burned valve or seat (improper carburetion) or an accumulation of carbon deposits on the seat (from carburetion, lubrication problems). The valves must be cleaned and/or replaced and the seats serviced if possible (Chapter 2).

17   Knocking or pinging

1   Carbon build-up in combustion chamber. Use of a fuel additive that will dissolve the adhesive bonding the carbon particles to the crown and chamber is the easiest way to remove the build-up. Otherwise, the cylinder head will have to be removed and decarbonized (Chapter 2).
2   Incorrect or poor quality fuel. Old or improper grades of gasoline can cause detonation. This causes the piston to rattle, thus the knocking or pinging sound. Drain old gas and always use the recommended fuel grade.
3   Spark plug heat range incorrect. Uncontrolled detonation indicates the plug heat range is too hot. The plug in effect becomes a glow plug, raising cylinder temperatures. Install the proper heat range plug (Chapter 1).
4   Improper air/fuel mixture. This will cause the cylinder to run hot, which leads to detonation. Clogged jets or an air leak can cause this imbalance. See Chapter 4.

18   Miscellaneous causes

1   Throttle valve doesn't open fully. Adjust the cable slack (Chapter 1).
2   Clutch slipping. Caused by a cable that is improperly adjusted or snagging or damaged, loose or worn clutch components. Refer to Chapters 1 and 2 for adjustment and overhaul procedures.
3   Timing not advancing.
4   Engine oil viscosity too high. Using a heavier oil than the one recommended in Chapter 1 can damage the oil pump or lubrication system and cause drag on the engine.
5   Brakes dragging. Usually caused by debris which has entered the brake piston sealing boot, or from a warped disc or bent axle. Repair as necessary.

Overheating

19   Cooling system not operating properly

1   Coolant level low. Check coolant level as described in Chapter 1. If coolant level is low, the engine will overheat.
2   Leak in cooling system. Check cooling system hoses and radiator for leaks and other damage. Repair or replace parts as necessary (Chapter 3).

3 Thermostat sticking open or closed. Check and replace as described in Chapter 3.
4 Faulty radiator cap. Remove the cap and have it pressure checked at a service station.
5 Coolant passages clogged. Have the entire system drained and flushed, then refill with new coolant.
6 Water pump defective. Remove the pump and check the components.
7 Clogged radiator fins. Clean them by blowing compressed air through the fins from the back side.

20 Firing incorrect

1 Spark plug fouled, defective or worn out. See Chapter 1 for spark plug maintenance.
2 Incorrect spark plug.
3 Faulty ignition coils (Chapter 5).

21 Fuel/air mixture incorrect

1 Main jet clogged. Dirt, water and other contaminants can clog the main jets. Clean the fuel tap filter, the float bowl area and the jets and carburetor orifices (Chapter 4).
2 Main jet wrong size. The standard jetting is for sea level atmospheric pressure and oxygen content.
3 Air cleaner poorly sealed or missing.
4 Air cleaner-to-carburetor boot poorly sealed. Look for cracks, holes or loose clamps and replace or repair.
5 Fuel level too low. Adjust the float(s) (Chapter 4).
6 Fuel tank air vent obstructed. Make sure the air vent passage in the filler cap is open.
7 Carburetor intake manifolds loose. Check for cracks, breaks, tears or loose clamps or bolts. Repair or replace the rubber boots (Chapter 2).

22 Compression too high

1 Carbon build-up in combustion chamber. Use of a fuel additive that will dissolve the adhesive bonding the carbon particles to the piston crown and chamber is the easiest way to remove the build-up. Otherwise, the cylinder head will have to be removed and decarbonized (Chapter 2).
2 Improperly machined head surface or installation of incorrect gasket during engine assembly. Check Specifications (Chapter 2).

23 Engine load excessive

1 Clutch slipping. Caused by an out of adjustment or snagging cable or damaged, loose or worn clutch components. Refer to Chapters 1 and 2 for adjustment and overhaul procedures.
2 Engine oil level too high. The addition of too much oil will cause pressurization of the crankcase and inefficient engine operation. Check Specifications and drain to proper level (Chapter 1).
3 Engine oil viscosity too high. Using a heavier oil than the one recommended in Chapter 1 can damage the oil pump or lubrication system as well as cause drag on the engine.
4 Brakes dragging. Usually caused by debris which has entered the brake piston sealing boot, or from a warped disc or bent axle. Repair as necessary.

24 Lubrication inadequate

1 Engine oil level too low. Friction caused by intermittent lack of lubrication or from oil that is "overworked" can cause overheating. The oil pro-

vides a definite cooling function in the engine. Check the oil level (Chapter 1).
2 Poor quality engine oil or incorrect viscosity or type. Oil is rated not only according to viscosity but also according to type. Some oils are not rated high enough for use in this engine. Check the Specifications section and change to the correct oil (Chapter 1).

25 Miscellaneous causes

Modification to exhaust system. Most aftermarket exhaust systems cause the engine to run leaner, which makes them run hotter. When installing an accessory exhaust system, always rejet the carburetors.

Clutch problems

26 Clutch slipping

1 No clutch lever play. Adjust clutch lever free play according to the procedure in Chapter 1.
2 Friction plates worn or warped. Overhaul the clutch assembly (Chapter 2).
3 Steel plates worn or warped (Chapter 2).
4 Clutch springs broken or weak. Old or heat-damaged (from slipping clutch) springs should be replaced with new ones (Chapter 2).
5 Clutch release not adjusted properly. See Chapter 1.
6 Clutch inner cable hanging up. Caused by a rusty or frayed cable or kinked outer cable. Replace the cable. Repair of a frayed cable is not advised.
7 Clutch release mechanism defective. Check the shaft, cam, actuating arm and pivot. Replace any defective parts (Chapter 2).
8 Clutch hub or housing unevenly worn. This causes improper engagement of the discs. Replace the damaged or worn parts (Chapter 2).

27 Clutch not disengaging completely

1 Clutch lever play excessive. adjust at bars or at engine (Chapter 1).
2 Clutch plates warped or damaged. this will cause clutch drag, which in turn causes the machine to creep. Overhaul the clutch assembly (Chapter 2).
3 Clutch spring tension uneven. Usually caused by a sagged or broken spring. Check and replace the springs (Chapter 2).
4 Engine oil deteriorated. Old, thin, worn out oil will not provide proper lubrication for the discs, causing the clutch to drag. Replace the oil and filter (Chapter 1).
5 Engine oil viscosity too high. Using a heavier oil than recommended in Chapter 1 can cause the plates to stick together, putting a drag on the engine. Change to the correct weight oil (Chapter 1).
6 Clutch housing seized on shaft. Lack of lubrication, severe wear or damage can cause the housing to seize on the shaft. Overhaul of the clutch, and perhaps transmission, may be necessary to repair damage (Chapter 2).
7 Clutch release mechanism defective. Worn or damaged release mechanism parts can stick and fail to apply force to the pressure plate. Overhaul the clutch cover components (Chapter 2).
8 Loose clutch hub nut. Causes housing and hub misalignment putting a drag on the engine. Engagement adjustment continually varies. Overhaul the clutch assembly (Chapter 2).

Gear shifting problems

28 Doesn't go into gear or lever doesn't return

1 Clutch not disengaging. See Section 27.
2 Shift fork(s) bent or seized. Often caused by dropping the machine or from lack of lubrication. Overhaul the transmission (Chapter 2).
3 Gear(s) stuck on shaft. Most often caused by a lack of lubrication or excessive wear in transmission bearings and bushings. Overhaul the transmission (Chapter 2).
4 Shift drum binding. Caused by lubrication failure or excessive wear. Replace the drum and bearings (Chapter 2).
5 Shift lever return spring weak or broken (Chapter 2).
6 Shift lever broken. Splines stripped out of lever or shaft, caused by allowing the lever to get loose or from dropping the machine. Replace necessary parts (Chapter 2).
7 Shift mechanism pawl broken or worn. Full engagement and rotary movement of shift drum results. Replace shaft assembly (Chapter 2).
8 Pawl spring broken. Allows pawl to "float", causing sporadic shift operation. Replace spring (Chapter 2).

29 Jumps out of gear

1 Shift fork(s) worn. Overhaul the transmission (Chapter 2).
2 Gear groove(s) worn. Overhaul the transmission (Chapter 2).
3 Gear dogs or dog slots worn or damaged. The gears should be inspected and replaced. No attempt should be made to service the worn parts.

30 Overshifts

1 Pawl spring weak or broken (Chapter 2).
2 Shift drum stopper lever not functioning (Chapter 2).
3 Overshift limiter broken or distorted (Chapter 2).

Abnormal engine noise

31 Knocking or pinging

1 Carbon build-up in combustion chamber. Use of a fuel additive that will dissolve the adhesive bonding the carbon particles to the piston crown and chamber is the easiest way to remove the build-up. Otherwise, the cylinder head will have to be removed and decarbonized (Chapter 2).
2 Incorrect or poor quality fuel. Old or improper fuel can cause detonation. This causes the piston to rattle, thus the knocking or pinging sound. Drain the old gas and always use the recommended grade fuel (Chapter 4).
3 Spark plug heat range incorrect. Uncontrolled detonation indicates that the plug heat range is too hot. The plug in effect becomes a glow plug, raising cylinder temperatures. Install the proper heat range plug (Chapter 1).
4 Improper air/fuel mixture. This will cause the cylinder to run hot and lead to detonation. Clogged jets or an air leak can cause this imbalance. See Chapter 4.

32 Piston slap or rattling

1 Cylinder-to-piston clearance excessive. Caused by improper assembly. Inspect and overhaul top end parts (Chapter 2).

2 Connecting rod bent. Caused by over-revving, trying to start a badly flooded engine or from ingesting a foreign object into the combustion chamber. Replace the damaged parts (Chapter 2).
3 Piston pin or piston pin bore worn or seized from wear or lack of lubrication. Replace damaged parts (Chapter 2).
4 Piston ring(s) worn, broken or sticking. Overhaul the top end (Chapter 2).
5 Piston seizure damage. Usually from lack of lubrication or overheating. Replace the pistons and bore the cylinders, as necessary (Chapter 2).
6 Connecting rod bearing and/or piston pin-end clearance excessive. Caused by excessive wear or lack of lubrication. Replace worn parts.

33 Valve noise

1 Incorrect valve clearances. Adjust the clearances by referring to Chapter 1.
2 Valve spring broken or weak. Check and replace weak valve springs (Chapter 2).
3 Camshaft or cylinder head worn or damaged. Lack of lubrication at high rpm is usually the cause of damage. Insufficient oil or failure to change the oil at the recommended intervals are the chief causes. Since there are no replaceable bearings in the head, the head itself will have to be replaced if there is excessive wear or damage (Chapter 2).

34 Other noise

1 Cylinder head gasket leaking. This will cause compression leakage into the cooling system (which may show up as air bubbles in the coolant in the radiator). Also, coolant may get into the oil (which will turn the oil gray). In either case, have the cooling system checked by a dealer service department.
2 Exhaust pipe leaking at cylinder head connection. Caused by improper fit of pipe(s) or loose exhaust flange. All exhaust fasteners should be tightened evenly and carefully. Failure to do this will lead to a leak.
3 Crankshaft runout excessive. Caused by a bent crankshaft (from over-revving) or damage from an upper cylinder component failure. Can also be attributed to dropping the machine on either of the crankshaft ends.
4 Engine mounting bolts loose. Tighten all engine mount bolts to the specified torque (Chapter 2).
5 Crankshaft bearings worn (Chapter 2).
6 Camshaft chain tensioner defective. Replace according to the procedure in Chapter 2.
7 Camshaft chain, sprockets or guides worn (Chapter 2).
8 Loose alternator rotor. Tighten the mounting bolt to the specified torque (Chapter 2).

Abnormal driveline noise

35 Clutch noise

1 Clutch housing/friction plate clearance excessive (Chapter 2).
2 Loose or damaged clutch pressure plate and/or bolts (Chapter 2).

36 Transmission noise

1 Bearings worn. Also includes the possibility that the shafts are worn. Overhaul the transmission (Chapter 2).
2 Gears worn or chipped (Chapter 2).
3 Metal chips jammed in gear teeth. Probably pieces from a broken clutch, gear or shift mechanism that were picked up by the gears. This will cause early bearing failure (Chapter 2).

4   Engine oil level too low. Causes a howl from transmission. Also affects engine power and clutch operation (Chapter 1).

37   Chain or final drive noise

1   Chain not adjusted properly (Chapter 1).
2   Sprocket (primary sprcket or rear sprocket) loose. Tighten fasteners (Chapter 6).
3   Sprocket(s) worn. Replace sprocket(s) (Chapter 6).
4   Rear sprocket warped. Replace (Chapter 6).
5   Wheel coupling worn. Replace coupling (Chapter 6).

Abnormal frame and suspension noise

38   Front end noise

1   Low fluid level or improper viscosity oil in forks. This can sound like "spurting" and is usually accompanied by irregular fork action (Chapter 6).
2   Spring weak or broken. Makes a clicking or scraping sound. Fork oil, when drained, will have a lot of metal particles in it (Chapter 6).
3   Steering head bearings loose or damaged. Clicks when braking. Check and adjust or replace as necessary (Chapter 6).
4   Fork clamps loose. Make sure all fork clamp pinch bolts are tight (Chapter 6).
5   Fork tube bent. Good possibility if machine has been dropped. Replace tube with a new one (Chapter 6).
6   Front axle or axle clamp bolt loose. Tighten them to the specified torque (Chapter 7).

39   Shock absorber noise

1   Fluid level incorrect. Indicates a leak caused by defective seal. Shock will be covered with oil. Replace shock (Chapter 6).
2   Defective shock absorber with internal damage. This is in the body of the shock and cannot be remedied. The shock must be replaced with a new one (Chapter 6).
3   Bent or damaged shock body. Replace the shock with a new one (Chapter 6).

40   Disc brake noise

1   Squeal caused by shim not installed or positioned correctly (Chapter 7).
2   Squeal caused by dust on brake pads. Usually found in combination with glazed pads. Clean using brake cleaning solvent (Chapter 7).
3   Contamination of brake pads. Oil, brake fluid or dirt causing brake to chatter or squeal. Clean or replace pads (Chapter 7).
4   Pads glazed. Caused by excessive heat from prolonged use or from contamination. Do not use sandpaper, emery cloth, carborundum cloth or any other abrasive to roughen the pad surfaces as abrasives will stay in the pad material and damage the disc. A very fine flat file can be used, but pad replacement is suggested as a cure (Chapter 7).
5   Disc warped. Can cause a chattering, clicking or intermittent squeal. Usually accompanied by a pulsating lever and uneven braking. Replace the disc (Chapter 7).

Oil pressure indicator light comes on

41   Engine lubrication system

1   Engine oil pump defective (Chapter 2).

2   Engine oil level low. Inspect for leak or other problem causing low oil level and add recommmended lubricant (Chapters 1 and 2).
3   Engine oil viscosity too low. Very old, thin oil or an improper weight of oil used in engine. Change to correct lubricant (Chapter 1).
4   Camshaft or journals worn. Excessive wear causing drop in oil pressure. Replace cam and/or head. Abnormal wear could be caused by oil starvation at high rpm from low oil level or improper oil weight or type (Chapter 1).
5   Crankshaft and/or bearings worn. Same problems as paragraph 4. Check and replace crankshaft and/or bearings (Chapter 2).

42   Electrical system

1   Oil pressure switch defective. Check the switch according to the procedure in Chapter 9. Replace it if it is defective.
2   Oil pressure indicator light circuit defective. Check for pinched, shorted, disconnected or damaged wiring (Chapter 9).

Excessive exhaust smoke

43   White smoke

1   Piston oil ring worn. The ring may be broken or damaged, causing oil from the crankcase to be pulled past the piston into the combustion chamber. Replace the rings with new ones (Chapter 2).
2   Cylinders worn, cracked, or scored. Caused by overheating or oil starvation. The cylinders will have to be rebored and new pistons installed.
3   Valve oil seal damaged or worn. Replace oil seals with new ones (Chapter 2).
4   Valve guide worn. Perform a complete valve job (Chapter 2).
5   Engine oil level too high, which causes oil to be forced past the rings. Drain oil to the proper level (Chapter 1).
6   Head gasket broken between oil return and cylinder. Causes oil to be pulled into combustion chamber. Replace the head gasket and check the head for warpage (Chapter 2).
7   Abnormal crankcase pressurization, which forces oil past the rings. Clogged breather or hoses usually the cause (Chapter 4).

44   Black smoke

1   Air cleaner clogged. Clean or replace the element (Chapter 1).
2   Main jet too large or loose. Compare the jet size to the Specifications (Chapter 4).
3   Choke stuck, causing fuel to be pulled through choke circuit (Chapter 4).
4   Fuel level too high. Check and adjust the float level as necessary (Chapter 4).
5   Inlet needle held off needle seat. Clean float bowl and fuel line and replace needle and seat if necessary (Chapter 4).

45   Brown smoke

1   Main jet too small or clogged. Lean condition caused by wrong size main jet or by a restricted orifice. Clean float bowl and jets and compare jet size to Specifications (Chapter 4).
2   Fuel flow insufficient. Fuel inlet needle valve stuck closed due to chemical reaction with old gas. Float level incorrect. Restricted fuel line. Clean line and float bowl and adjust floats if necessary (Chapter 4).

3   Carburetor intake manifolds loose (Chapter 4).
4   Air cleaner poorly sealed or not installed (Chapter 1).

Poor handling or stability

46   Handlebar hard to turn

1   Steering stem locknut too tight (Chapter 6).
2   Bearings damaged. Roughness can be felt as the bars are turned from side-to-side. Replace bearings and races (Chapter 6).
3   Races dented or worn. Denting results from wear in only one position (i.e., straight ahead) from impacting an immovable object or hole or from dropping the machine. Replace races and bearings (Chapter 6).
4   Steering stem lubrication inadequate. Causes are grease getting hard from age or being washed out by high pressure car washes. Disassemble steering head and repack bearings (Chapter 6).
5   Steering stem bent. Caused by hitting a curb or hole or from dropping the machine. Replace damaged part. Do not try to straighten stem (Chapter 6).
6   Front tire air pressure too low (Chapter 1).

47   Handlebar shakes or vibrates excessively

1   Tires worn or out of balance (Chapter 7).
2   Swingarm bearings worn. Replace worn bearings by referring to Chapter 6.
3   Rim(s) warped or damaged. Inspect wheels for runout (Chapter 7).
4   Wheel bearings worn. Worn front or rear wheel bearings can cause poor tracking. Worn front bearings will cause wobble (Chapter 7).
5   Handlebar clamp bolts loose (Chapter 6).
6   Steering stem or fork clamps loose. Tighten them to the specified torque (Chapter 6).
7   Motor mount bolts loose. Will cause excessive vibration with increased engine rpm (Chapter 2).

48   Handlebar pulls to one side

1   Frame bent. Definitely suspect this if the machine has been dropped. May or may not be accompanied by cracking near the bend. Replace the frame (Chapter 6).
2   Wheel out of alignment. Caused by improper location of axle spacers or from bent steering stem or frame (Chapter 6).
3   Swingarm bent or twisted. Caused by age (metal fatigue) or impact damage. Replace the arm (Chapter 6).
4   Steering stem bent. Caused by impact damage or from dropping the motorcycle. Replace the steering stem (Chapter 6).
5   Fork leg bent. Disassemble the forks and replace the damaged parts (Chapter 6).
6   Fork oil level uneven.

49   Poor shock absorbing qualities

1   Too hard:
   a) Fork oil level excessive (Chapter 6).
   b) Fork oil viscosity too high. Use a lighter oil, (see the Specifications in Chapter 6).
   c) Fork tube bent. Causes a harsh, sticking feeling (Chapter 6).
   d) Shock shaft or body bent or damaged (Chapter 6).
   e) Fork internal damage (Chapter 6).
   f) Shock internal damage.
   g) Tire pressure too high (Chapters 1 and 7).

2   Too soft:
   a) Fork or shock oil insufficient and/or leaking (Chapter 6).
   b) Fork oil level too low (Chapter 6).
   c) Fork oil viscosity too light (Chapter 6).
   d) Fork springs weak or broken (Chapter 6).

Braking problems

50   Brakes are spongy, don't hold

1   Air in brake line. Caused by inattention to master cylinder fluid level or by leakage. Locate problem and bleed brakes (Chapter 7).
2   Pad or disc worn (Chapters 1 and 7).
3   Brake fluid leak. See paragraph 1.
4   Contaminated pads. Caused by contamination with oil, grease, brake fluid, etc. Clean or replace pads. Clean disc thoroughly with brake cleaner (Chapter 7).
5   Brake fluid deteriorated. Fluid is old or contaminated. Drain system, replenish with new fluid and bleed the system (Chapter 7).
6   Master cylinder internal parts worn or damaged causing fluid to bypass (Chapter 7).
7   Master cylinder bore scratched. From ingestion of foreign material or broken spring. Repair or replace master cylinder (Chapter 7).
8   Disc warped. Replace disc (Chapter 7).

51   Brake lever pulsates

1   Disc warped. Replace disc (Chapter 7).
2   Axle bent. Replace axle (Chapter 6).
3   Brake caliper bolts loose (Chapter 7).
4   Brake caliper shafts damaged or sticking, causing caliper to bind. Lube the shafts and/or replace them if they are corroded or bent (Chapter 7).
5   Wheel warped or otherwise damaged (Chapter 7).
6   Wheel bearings damaged or worn (Chapter 7).

52   Brakes drag

1   Master cylinder piston seized. Caused by wear or damage to piston or cylinder bore (Chapter 7).
2   Lever balky or stuck. Check pivot and lubricate (Chapter 7).
3   Brake caliper binds. Caused by inadequate lubrication or damage to caliper shafts (Chapter 7).
4   Brake caliper piston seized in bore. Caused by wear or ingestion of dirt past deteriorated seal (Chapter 7).
5   Brake pad damaged. Pad material separating from backing plate. Usually caused by faulty manufacturing process or from contact with chemicals. Replace pads (Chapter 7).
6   Pads improperly installed (Chapter 7).
7   Rear brake pedal free play insufficient.

Electrical problems

53   Battery dead or weak

1   Battery faulty. Caused by sulphated plates which are shorted through the sedimentation or low electrolyte level. Also, broken battery terminal making only occasional contact (Chapter 9).
2   Battery cables making poor contact (Chapter 9).

3   Load excessive. Caused by addition of high wattage lights or other electrical accessories.

4   Ignition switch defective. Switch either grounds internally or fails to shut off system. Replace the switch (Chapter 9).

5   Regulator/rectifier defective (Chapter 9).

6   Stator coil open or shorted (Chapter 9).

7   Wiring faulty. Wiring grounded or connections loose in ignition, charging or lighting circuits (Chapter 9).

54   Battery overcharged

1   Regulator/rectifier defective. Overcharging is noticed when battery gets excessively warm or "boils" over (Chapter 9).

2   Battery defective. Replace battery with a new one (Chapter 9).

3   Battery amperage too low, wrong type or size. Install manufacturer's specified amp-hour battery to handle charging load (Chapter 9).

Chapter 1   Tune-up and routine maintenance

Refer to Chapter 10 for information on the ZX750F model

Contents

1

Specifications

Engine

Spark plugs
  Type
    US models .... NGK D9EA or ND X27ES-U
    UK and Canadian models .... NGK DR8ES or ND X27ESR-U
  Gap .... 0.024 to 0.028 in (0.6 to 0.7 mm)
Engine idle speed
  All except California models .... 1050 ± 50 rpm
  California models .... 1300 ± 50 rpm
Valve clearances (COLD engine)
  Intake .... 0.005 to 0.007 in (0.13 to 0.18 mm)
  Exhaust .... 0.007 to 0.009 in (0.18 to 0.23 mm)
Cylinder compression pressure
  Acceptable range .... 109 to 171 psi
  Maximum difference between cylinders .... 14 psi
Carburetor synchronization (vacuum difference
  between cylinders) .... Less than 0.391 in (2 cm) Hg
Cylinder numbering (from left side to right side of bike) 1-2-3-4
Firing order 1-2-4-3

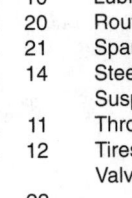

Cylinder locations

Miscellaneous

Brake pad minimum thickness .... 0.040 in (1.0 mm)
Freeplay adjustments
  Throttle grip .... 0.08 to 0.12 in (2 to 3 mm)
    Clutch lever (gap between lever and lever bracket
      when freeplay is taken up) .... 0.08 to 0.12 in (2 to 3 mm)

Drive chain
  Slack . . . . 1.38 to 1.57 in (35 to 40 mm)
  20-link length . . . . 12.73 in (323 mm) maximum
Battery electrolyte specific gravity . . . . 1.260 minimum
Minimum tire tread depth . . . . 0.040 in (1.0 mm)
Tire pressures (cold)
  Front . . . . 32 psi
  Rear . . . . 36 psi
Suspension air pressures
  Forks
    A and B models . . . . 7 to 10 psi
    C models . . . . 0 psi (atmospheric pressure)
  Rear shock absorber
    A and B models . . . . 0 to 50 psi
    C models . . . . 0 to 28 psi

Torque specifications

Ft-lb (unless otherwise indicated)

Oil drain plug 14.5
Oil filter mounting bolt 14.5
Coolant drain bolt . . . . 69 in-lbs
Spark plugs . . . . 120 in-lbs
Valve cover bolts . . . . 87 in-lbs

Recommended lubricants and fluids

Engine/transmission oil
  Type . . . . API grade SG multigrade and fuel efficient oil
  Viscosity
    In cold climates . . . . SAE 10W40 or 10W50
    In warm climates . . . . SAE 20W40 or 20W50
  Capacity
    With filter change . . . . 3.2 US qt (3.0 liters)
    Oil change only . . . . 2.7 US qt (2.6 liters)
Coolant
  Type . . . . 50/50 mixture of ethylene glycol based antifreeze and soft water
  Capacity
    A and B models . . . . 2.1 US qt (2.0 liters)
    C models . . . . 2.4 US qt (2.3 liters)
Brake fluid . . . . DOT 3
Fork oil
  Type . . . . SAE 10W20 – fork oil
  Amount
    A and B models
      Dry fill . . . . 321 ± 4 mL
      At oil change . . . . Approximately 273 mL
    C models
      Dry fill
        Left fork tube . . . . 311 ± 4 mL
        Right fork tube . . . . 356 ± 4 mL
      At oil change
        Left fork tube . . . . Approximately 265 mL
        Right fork tube . . . . Approximately 305 mL
  Oil level
    A and B models (forks fully extended – no spring) . . . . 13.16 ± 0.008 in (334 ± 2 mm)
    C models (forks fully compressed – no spring)
      Left fork tube . . . . 7.2 ± 0.008 in (182 ± 2 mm)
      Right fork tube . . . . 6.07 ± 0.008 in (154 ± 2 mm)
Miscellaneous
  Wheel bearings . . . . Medium weight, lithium-based multi-purpose grease
  Swingarm pivot bearings . . . . Medium weight, lithium-based multi-purpose grease
  Cables and lever pivots . . . . Chain and cable lubricant or 10W30 motor oil
  Sidestand/centerstand pivots . . . . Chain and cable lubricant or 10W30 motor oil
  Brake pedal/shift lever pivots . . . . Chain and cable lubricant or 10W30 motor oil
  Throttle grip . . . . Multi-purpose grease or dry film lubricant

1 Kawasaki ZX600 Ninja
Routine maintenance intervals

Routine maintenance intervals

Note: The pre-ride inspection outlined in the owner's manual covers checks and maintenance that should be carried out on a daily basis. It's condensed and included here to remind you of its importance. Always perform the pre-ride inspection at every maintenance interval (in addition to the procedures listed). The intervals listed below are the shortest intervals recommended by the manufacturer for each particular operation during the model years covered in this manual. Your owner's manual may have different intervals for your model.

Daily or before riding

Check the engine oil level
Check the fuel level and inspect for leaks
Check the engine coolant level and look for leaks
Check the operation of both brakes – also check the fluid level and look for leakage
Check the tires for damage, the presence of foreign objects and correct air pressure
Check the throttle for smooth operation and correct freeplay
Check the operation of the clutch – make sure the freeplay is correct
Make sure the steering operates smoothly
Check for proper operation of the headlight, taillight, brake light, turn signals, indicator lights and horn
Make sure the sidestand and centerstand return to their fully up positions and stay there under spring pressure
Make sure the engine STOP switch works properly

Every 200 miles

Lubricate the drive chain

After the initial 500 miles

Perform all of the daily checks plus:
Check and adjust the valve clearances
Clean the air filter element
Check/adjust the idle speed
Check/adjust the carburetor synchronization
Check/adjust the drive chain slack
Change the engine oil and oil filter
Check the evaporative emission control system (California models)
Check the cooling system hoses
Check the battery electrolyte level
Check the tightness of all fasteners

Every 500 miles

Check/adjust the drive chain slack

Every 3000 miles

Clean and gap the spark plugs
Check the operation of the air suction valve (if equipped)
Check/adjust the idle speed
Check/adjust the carburetor synchronization
Check the evaporative emission control system (California models)
Adjust the clutch freeplay

2   Introduction to tune-up and routine maintenance

This Chapter covers in detail the checks and procedures necessary for the tune-up and routine maintenance of your motorcycle. Section 1 includes the routine maintenance schedule, which is designed to keep the machine in proper running condition and prevent possible problems. The remaining Sections contain detailed procedures for carrying out the items listed on the maintenance schedule, as well as additional maintenance information designed to increase reliability.

Since routine maintenance plays such an important role in the safe and

Check the drive chain and sprockets for wear
Check the brake fluid level
Check the brake discs and pads
Check/adjust the brake pedal position
Check the operation of the brake light
Lubricate all cables
Lubricate the clutch and brake lever pivots
Lubricate the shift/brake lever pivots and the sidestand/centerstand pivots
Change the engine oil and oil filter
Clean the air filter element
Check the steering
Check the tires and wheels
Check the battery electrolyte level
Check the exhaust system for leaks and check the tightness of the fasteners

Every 6000 miles

All of the items above plus:
Check the cleanliness of the fuel system and the condition of the fuel and vacuum hoses
Lubricate the swingarm needle bearings and Uni-trak linkage
Replace the spark plugs

Every 18,000 miles

Check the cooling system and replace the coolant
Change the fork oil

Once a year

Clean the coolant filter (UK models only)

Every two years

Change the brake fluid (Chapter 7)
Replace the anti-dive brake plunger parts (A and B models – Chapter 7)
Rebuild the brake calipers and master cylinders (Chapter 7)
Lubricate the steering head bearings (Chapter 6)
Check and lubricate the wheel bearings (Chapter 7)
Lubricate the speedometer gear

Every four years

Replace the fuel hoses (Chapter 4)
Replace the brake hoses (Chapter 7)

efficient operation of your motorcycle, it is presented here as a comprehensive check list. For the rider who does all his own maintenance, these lists outline the procedures and checks that should be done on a routine basis.

Deciding where to start or plug into the routine maintenance schedule depends on several factors. If you have a motorcycle whose warranty has recently expired, and if it has been maintained according to the warranty standards, you may want to pick up routine maintenance as it coincides with the next mileage or calendar interval. If you have owned the machine for some time but have never performed any maintenance on it, then you may want to start at the nearest interval and include some additional pro-

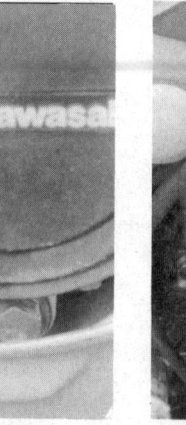

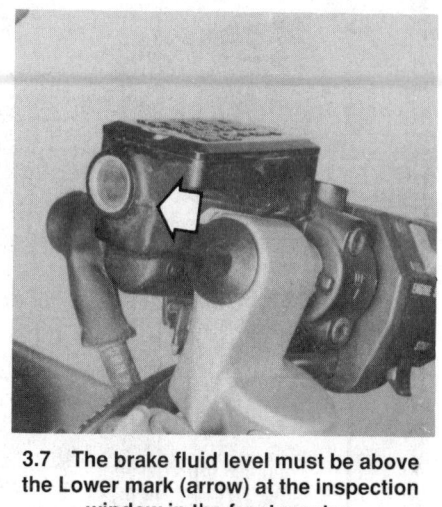

3.3 The engine oil level must be between the Minimum and Maximum marks (arrows) at the window

3.4 The engine oil filler cap is located on the right crankcase cover (arrow)

3.7 The brake fluid level must be above the Lower mark (arrow) at the inspection window in the front master cylinder reservoir

cedures to ensure that nothing important is overlooked. If you have just had a major engine overhaul, then you may want to start the maintenance routine from the beginning. If you have a used machine and have no knowledge of its history or maintenance record, you may desire to combine all the checks into one large service initially and then settle into the maintenance schedule prescribed.

The Sections which actually outline the inspection and maintenance procedures are written as step-by-step comprehensive guides to the actual performance of the work. They explain in detail each of the routine inspections and maintenance procedures on the check list. References to additional information in applicable Chapters is also included and should not be overlooked.

Before beginning any actual maintenance or repair, the machine should be cleaned thoroughly, especially around the oil filter housing, spark plugs, cylinder head covers, side covers, carburetors, etc. Cleaning will help ensure that dirt does not contaminate the engine and will allow you to detect wear and damage that could otherwise easily go unnoticed.

---

3 Fluid levels – check

Engine oil

Refer to illustrations 3.3 and 3.4

1   Place the motorcycle on the centerstand, then start the engine and allow it to reach normal operating temperature. **Caution:** *Do not run the engine in an enclosed space such as a garage or shop.*

2   Stop the engine and allow the machine to sit undisturbed on the centerstand for about five minutes.

3   With the engine off, check the oil level in the window located at the lower part of the right crankcase cover. The oil level should be between the Maximum and Minimum level marks on the window **(see illustration)**.

4   If the level is below the Minimum mark, remove the oil filler cap from the right crankcase cover **(see illustration)** and add enough oil of the recommended grade and type to bring the level up to the Maximum mark. Do not overfill.

Brake fluid

Refer to illustrations 3.7 and 3.13

5   In order to ensure proper operation of the hydraulic disc brakes, the fluid level in the master cylinder reservoirs must be properly maintained.

6   With the motorcycle on the centerstand, turn the handlebars until the top of the master cylinder is as level as possible. If necessary, loosen the brake lever clamp bolts and rotate the master cylinder assembly slightly to make it level.

7   Look closely at the inspection window in the master cylinder reservoir. Make sure that the fluid level is above the Lower mark on the reservoir **(see illustration)**.

8   If the level is low, the fluid must be replenished. Before removing the master cylinder cap, cover the gas tank to protect it from brake fluid spills (which will damage the paint) and remove all dust and dirt from the area around the cap.

9   Remove the screws and lift off the cap and rubber diaphragm. **Note:** *Do not operate the brake lever with the cap removed.*

10   Add new, clean brake fluid of the recommended type until the level is above the inspection window. Do not mix different brands of brake fluid in the reservoir, as they may not be compatible.

11   Replace the rubber diaphragm and the cover. Tighten the screws evenly, but do not overtighten them.

12   Wipe any spilled fluid off the reservoir body and reposition and tighten the brake lever and master cylinder assembly if it was moved.

13   To check the fluid level in the rear master cylinder reservoir, remove the right side cover. Wipe off the cap and the side of the reservoir – the fluid level should be between the Upper and Lower marks **(see illustration)**. If not, unscrew the cap and add brake fluid of the recommended type until the level is at the Upper mark.

14   If the brake fluid level was low in either check, inspect the front or rear brake system for leaks.

Coolant

Refer to illustrations 3.15a and 3.15b

15   The engine must be cold for the results to be accurate, so always perform this check before starting the engine for the first time each day. On A and B models, the reservoir is visible through the slot in the front of the lower fairing **(see illustration)**. On C models, The reservoir is located in the left side of the upper fairing **(see illustration)**.

3.13 The brake fluid level in the rear master cylinder reservoir must be between the Upper and Lower marks

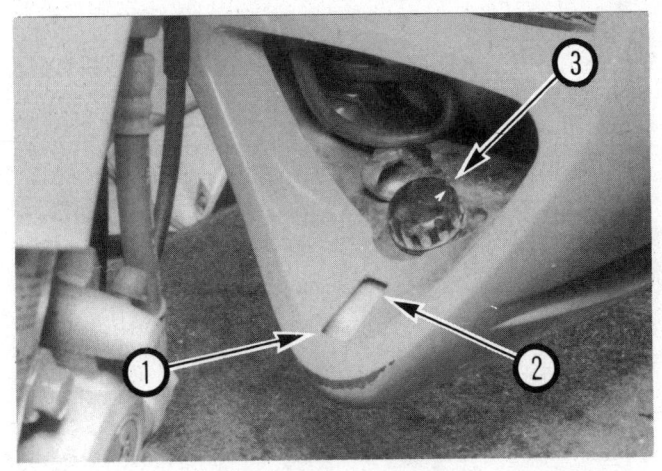

3.15a   On A and B models, check the coolant level through the slot in the lower fairing

1 Low mark	2 Full mark	3 Cap

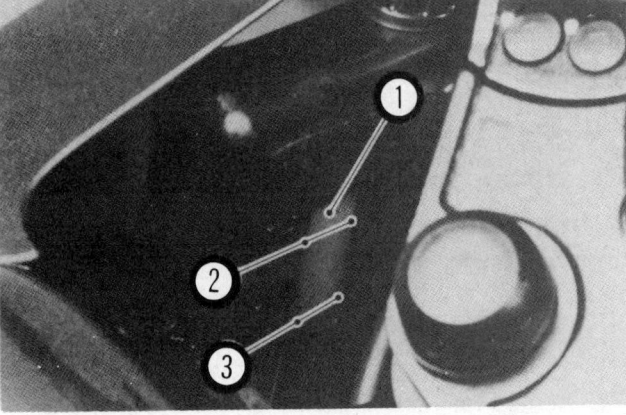

3.15b   On C models, turn the handlebars to the right and look into the left side of the upper fairing to check the coolant level

1 Reservoir tank	2 Full mark	3 Low mark

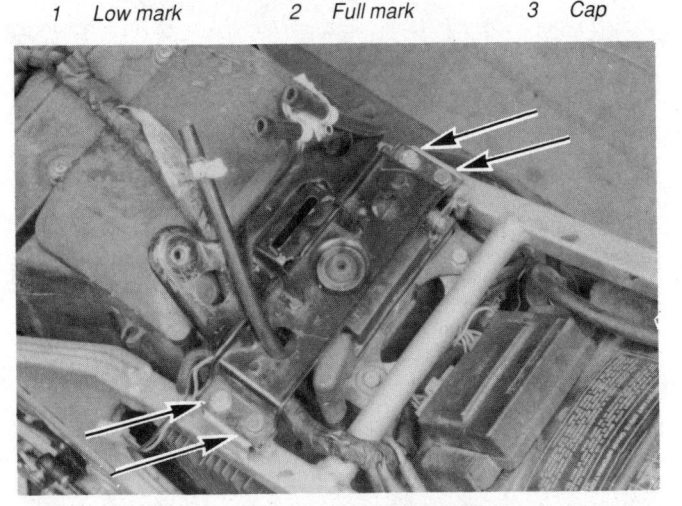

4.1   To gain access to the battery, unbolt the fuel tank from the rear mount, then remove the bolts (arrows) securing the mount to the frame (fuel tank removed for clarity)

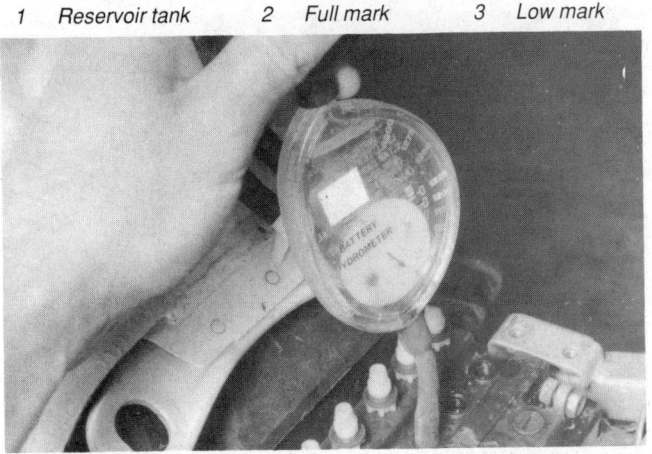

4.5   Check the specific gravity with a hydrometer

below the Low mark, add the recommended coolant mixture (see this Chapter's Specifications) until the Full level is reached. If the coolant level seems to be consistently low, check the entire cooling system for leaks.

4   Battery electrolyte level/specific gravity – check

Refer to illustrations 4.1, 4.2 and 4.5

Caution: *Be extremely careful when handling or working around the battery. The electrolyte is very caustic and an explosive gas (hydrogen) is given off when the battery is charging.*

1   To check and replenish the battery electrolyte, it will be necessary to remove the seat and the fuel tank bracket **(see illustration)**.

2   Remove the bolts securing the battery cables to the battery terminals (remove the negative cable first, positive cable last) **(see illustration)**. Pull the battery straight up to remove it. The electrolyte level will now be visible through the opaque battery case – it should be between the Upper and Lower level marks.

3   If it is low, remove the cell caps and fill each cell to the upper level mark with distilled water. Do not use tap water (except in an emergency), and do not overfill. The cell holes are quite small, so it may help to use a plastic squeeze bottle with a small spout to add the water. If the level is within the marks on the case, additional water is not necessary.

4   Next, check the specific gravity of the electrolyte in each cell with a small hydrometer made especially for motorcycle batteries (if the electrolyte level is known to be sufficient it won't be necessary to remove the battery. These are available from most dealer parts departments or motorcycle accessory stores.

5   Remove the caps, draw some electrolyte from the first cell into the hydrometer **(see illustration)** and note the specific gravity. Compare the

4.2   To remove the battery, unscrew the bolts securing the battery cables to the terminals (negative first, positive last), then pull the battery straight up

1 Negative cable	2 Positive cable and boot

16   The coolant level is satisfactory if it is between the Low and Full marks on the reservoir **(see illustrations 3.15a and 3.15b).** If the level is at or

1

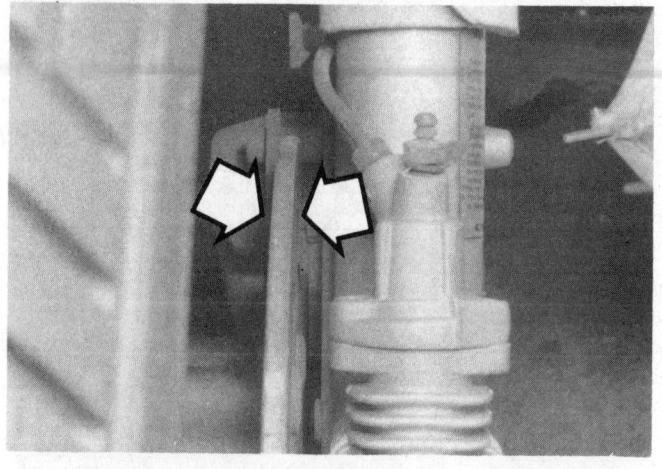

5.2   The front brake pads (arrows) are visible from the front of the bike – these pads look like they're ready for replacement

5.3   Check the rear pads (arrows) by looking between the caliper and disc

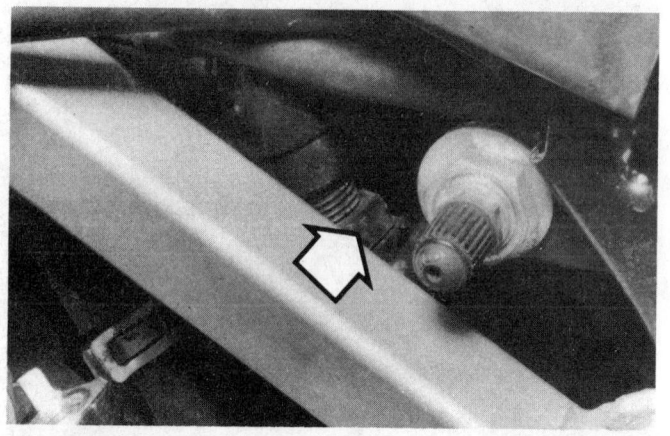

6.6   To adjust the rear brake light switch, turn the adjusting nut to move the switch in or out to activate the brake light when the pedal is depressed about 11 mm (7/16 inch)

7.1   The top of the brake pedal should be about 40 mm (1–9/16 inches) below the top of the footpeg

reading to the Specifications listed in this Chapter. **Note:** *Add 0.004 points to the reading for every 10-degrees F above 68-degrees F – subtract 0.004 points from the reading for every 10-degrees below 68-degrees F.* Return the electrolyte to the appropriate cell and repeat the check for the remaining cells. When the check is complete, rinse the hydrometer thoroughly with clean water.

6   If the specific gravity of the electrolyte in each cell is as specified, the battery is in good condition and is apparently being charged by the machine's charging system.

7   If the specific gravity is low, the battery is not fully charged. This may

be due to corroded battery terminals, a dirty battery case, a malfunctioning charging system, or loose or corroded wiring connections. On the other hand, it may be that the battery is worn out, especially if the machine is old, or that infrequent use of the motorcycle prevents normal charging from taking place.

8   Be sure to correct any problems and charge the battery if necessary. Refer to Chapter 9 for additional battery maintenance and charging procedures.

9   Install the battery cell caps, tightening them securely. Reconnect the cables to the battery, attaching the positive cable first and the negative cable last. Make sure to install the insulating boot over the positive terminal. Install the fuel tank mount and the seat. Be very careful not to pinch or otherwise restrict the battery vent tube (if equipped), as the battery may build up enough internal pressure during normal charging system operation to explode.

5   Brake pads – wear check

Refer to illustrations 5.2 and 5.3

1   The brake pads should be checked at the recommended intervals and replaced with new ones when worn beyond the limit listed in this Chapter's Specifications.

2   To check the front brake pads, position the front wheel so you can see clearly into the front of the brake caliper. The brake pads are visible from this angle and should have at least the specified minimum amount of lining material remaining on the metal backing plate **(see illustration)**. Be sure to check the pads in both calipers.

3   Check the rear brake pads by looking into the caliper from the rear of the machine **(see illustration)**.

4   If the pads are worn excessively, they must be replaced with new ones (see Chapter 7).

6   Brake system – general check

Refer to illustration 6.6

1   A routine general check of the brakes will ensure that any problems are discovered and remedied before the rider's safety is jeopardized.

2   Check the brake lever and pedal for loose connections, excessive play, bends, and other damage. Replace any damaged parts with new ones (see Chapter 7).

3   Make sure all brake fasteners are tight. Check the brake pads for wear (see Section 5) and make sure the fluid level in the reservoir is correct (see Section 3). Look for leaks at the hose connections and check for cracks in the hoses. If the lever is spongy, bleed the brakes as described in Chapter 7.

4   Make sure the brake light operates when the brake lever is depressed.

8.4   Use an accurate gauge to check the air pressure in the tires

5   Make sure the brake light is activated when the rear brake pedal is depressed approximately 11 mm (7/16 in).

6   If adjustment is necessary, hold the switch and turn the adjusting nut on the switch body **(see illustration)** until the brake light is activated when required. Turning the switch out will cause the brake light to come on sooner, while turning it in will cause it to come on later. If the switch doesn't operate the brake lights, check it as described in Chapter 9.

7   The front brake light switch is not adjustable. If it fails to operate properly, replace it with a new one (see Chapter 9).

7   Brake pedal position – check and adjustment

Refer to illustration 7.1

1   Rear brake pedal position is largely a matter of personal preference. Locate the pedal so that the rear brake can be engaged quickly and easily without excessive foot movement. The recommended factory setting is approximately 40 mm below the top of the footpeg **(see illustration)**.

2   To adjust the position of the pedal, loosen the locknut on the master cylinder clevis, then remove the master cylinder (see Chapter 7). To lower the brake pedal, turn the clevis clockwise. To raise the position of the brake pedal, turn the clevis counterclockwise.

3   Install the master cylinder, fill the rear brake master cylinder with the recommended brake fluid, then bleed the air from the system (see Chapter 7). If necessary, adjust the brake light switch (see Section 6).

8   Tires/wheels – general check

Refer to illustration 8.4

1   Routine tire and wheel checks should be made with the realization that your safety depends to a great extent on their condition.

2   Check the tires carefully for cuts, tears, embedded nails or other sharp objects and excessive wear. Operation of the motorcycle with excessively worn tires is extremely hazardous, as traction and handling are directly affected. Measure the tread depth at the center of the tire and replace worn tires with new ones when the tread depth is less than specified.

3   Repair or replace punctured tires as soon as damage is noted. Do not try to patch a torn tire, as wheel balance and tire reliability may be impaired.

4   Check the tire pressures when the tires are cold and keep them properly inflated **(see illustration)**. Proper air pressure will increase tire life and provide maximum stability and ride comfort. Keep in mind that low tire pressures may cause the tire to slip on the rim or come off, while high tire pressures will cause abnormal tread wear and unsafe handling.

5   The cast wheels used on this machine are virtually maintenance free, but they should be kept clean and checked periodically for cracks and other damage. Never attempt to repair damaged cast wheels; they must be replaced with new ones.

6   Check the valve stem locknuts to make sure they are tight. Also, make sure the valve stem cap is in place and tight. If it is missing, install a new one made of metal or hard plastic.

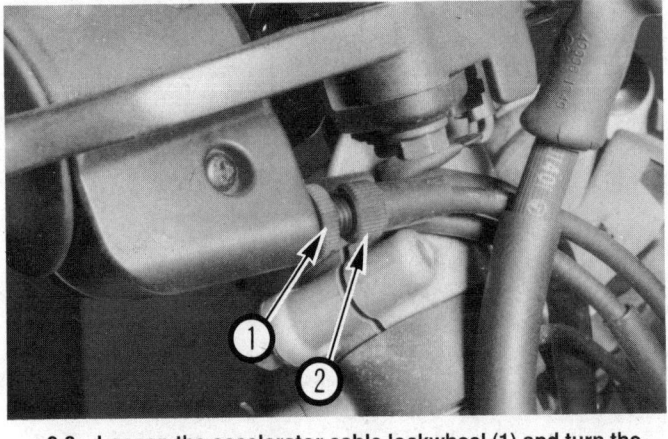

9.3   Loosen the accelerator cable lockwheel (1) and turn the adjuster (2) in or out to obtain the correct throttle freeplay

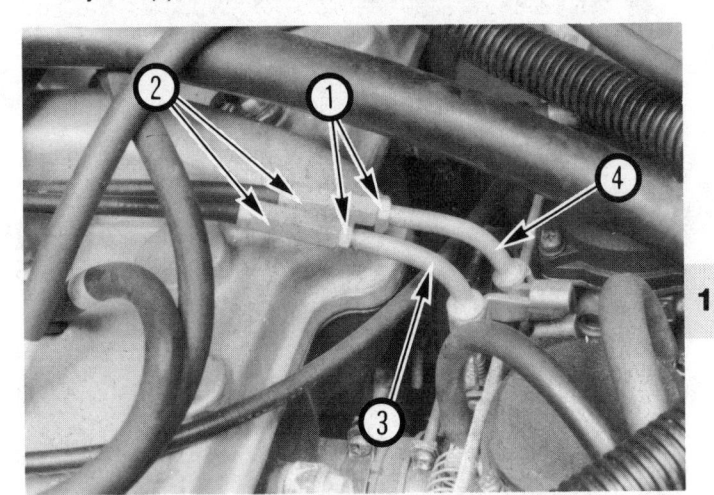

9.5   Throttle cable details (A and B models)

1	Locknuts	3	Decelerator cable
2	Adjusting nuts	4	Accelerator cable

9   Throttle operation/grip freeplay – check and adjustment

Check

1   Make sure the throttle grip rotates easily from fully closed to fully open with the front wheel turned at various angles. The grip should return automatically from fully open to fully closed when released. If the throttle sticks, check the throttle cables for cracks or kinks in the housings. Also, make sure the inner cables are clean and well-lubricated.

2   Check for a small amount of freeplay at the grip and compare the freeplay to the value listed in this Chapter's Specifications.

Adjustment

Refer to illustration 9.3

Note: *These motorcycles use two throttle cables – an accelerator cable and a decelerator cable.*

3   Freeplay adjustments can be made at the throttle end of the cable. Loosen the lockwheel on the cable **(see illustration)** and turn the adjuster until the desired freeplay is obtained, then retighten the lockwheel.

4   If the cables can't be adjusted at the grip end, adjust them at the lower ends. To do this, first remove the fuel tank (see Chapter 4).

A and B models

Refer to illustrations 9.5 and 9.7

5   Loosen the locknuts on both throttle cables **(see illustration)**, then turn both adjusting nuts in completely.

9.7   The throttle linkage lever must contact the idle adjusting screw (arrow) when the throttle is closed

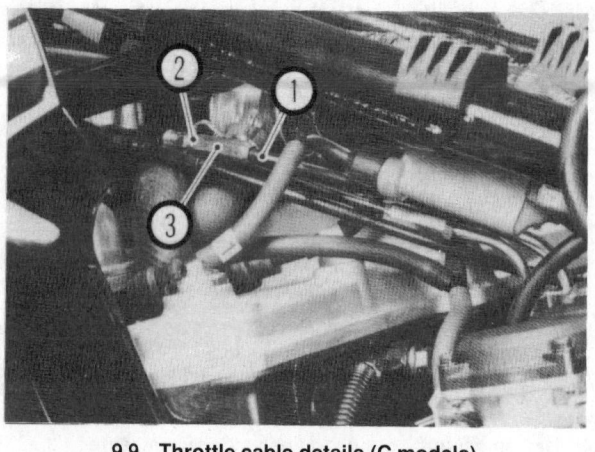

9.9   Throttle cable details (C models)

1   Accelerator cable   2   Locknut   3   Adjusting nut

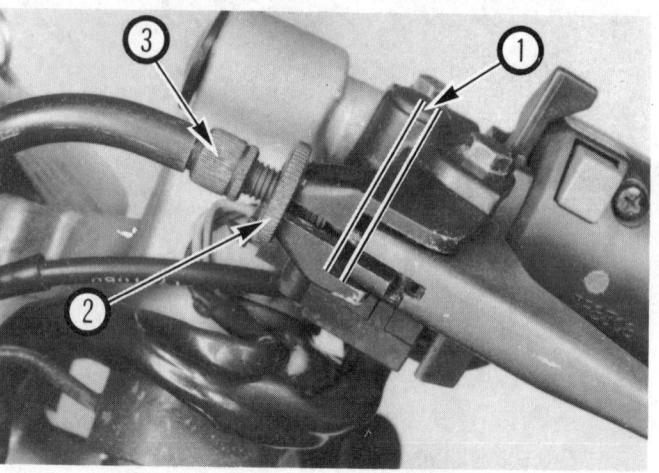

10.2   Pull the clutch lever in until resistance is felt – if the cable is adjusted correctly, there should be about 2 to 3 mm of clearance between the lever and the bracket

1   Clearance   2   Lock wheel   3   Adjuster

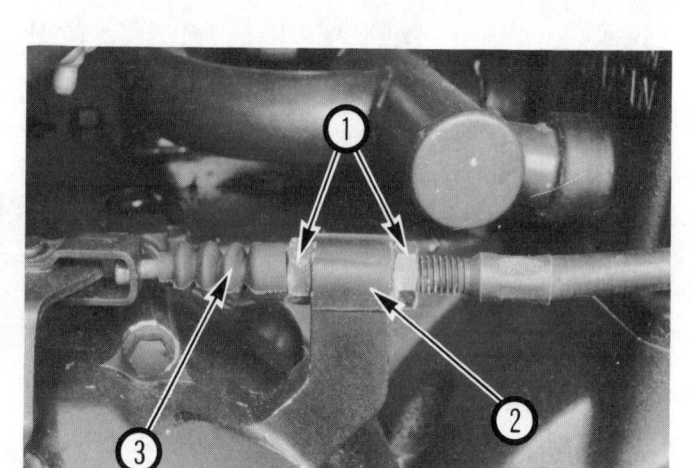

10.5   Details of the lower end of the clutch cable

1   Adjusting nuts   2   Bracket   3   Dust cover

6   Turn out the adjusting nut of the decelerator cable until the inner cable becomes tight, then tighten the locknut.

7   Turn the accelerator adjusting nut until the desired freeplay is obtained, then tighten the locknut. Make sure the throttle linkage lever contacts the idle adjusting screw when the throttle grip is at rest **(see illustration)**.

C models

Refer to illustration 9.9

8   Loosen the locknuts and screw the adjuster in completely at the upper end of the accelerator cable. Tighten the locknut at the upper end of the cable.

9   Loosen the locknut at the lower part of the cable **(see illustration)**. Turn the adjusting nut until the desired freeplay is obtained. Tighten the locknut at the lower part of the cable.

10   If the freeplay is still not adequate, try using the adjuster at the upper end of the cable again.

---

10   Clutch – check and adjustment

Refer to illustrations 10.2, 10.5, 10.6 and 10.8

1   Correct clutch freeplay is necessary to ensure proper clutch operation and reasonable clutch service life. Freeplay normally changes because of

cable stretch and clutch wear, so it should be checked and adjusted periodically.

2   Clutch cable freeplay is checked at the lever on the handlebar. Slowly pull in on the lever until resistance is felt, then note how far the lever has moved away from its bracket at the pivot end **(see illustration)**. Compare this distance with the value listed in this Chapter's Specifications. Too little freeplay may result in the clutch not engaging completely. If there is too much freeplay, the clutch might not release fully.

3   Freeplay adjustments can be made at the clutch lever by loosening the lock wheel and turning the adjuster until the desired freeplay is obtained. Always retighten the lock wheel once the adjustment is complete. If the lever adjuster reaches the end of its travel, try adjusting the cable at its bracket on the engine.

4   On A models, remove the right-side fairing stay (see Chapter 8).

5   Loosen the adjusting nuts at the lower end of the cable completely **(see illustration)**.

6   Loosen the knurled lock wheel at the clutch lever and turn the adjuster in or out until the gap between the adjuster and lock wheel is approximately 5 or 6 mm **(see illustration)**.

7   Pull the clutch cable tight to remove all slack, then tighten the adjusting nuts against the bracket at the lower end of the cable.

8   Turn the adjuster at the clutch lever until the correct freeplay is obtained. When the cable is properly adjusted, the angle between the cable and the release lever should be 80 to 90-degrees **(see illustration)**.

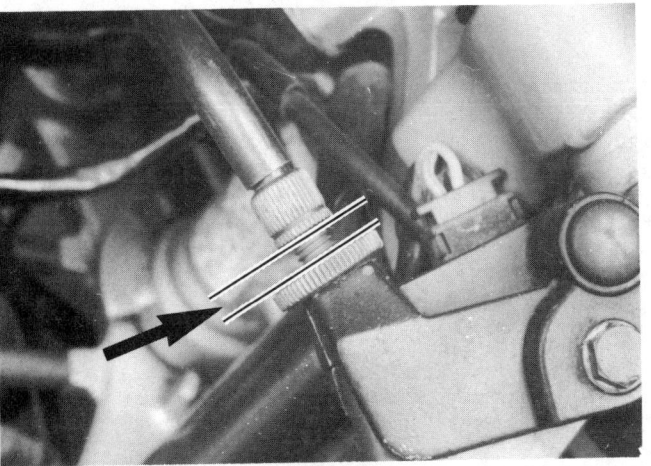

10.6   Turn the adjuster out until the gap between the shoulder of the adjuster and the locknut is 5 to 6 mm, then tighten the lock wheel

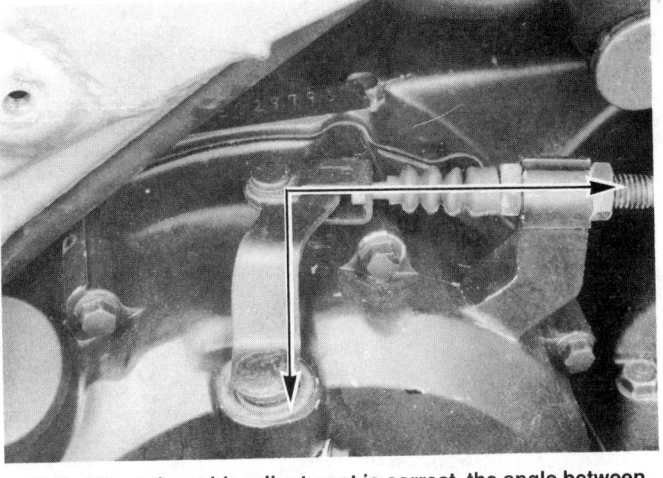

10.8   When the cable adjustment is correct, the angle between the cable and the release lever should be 80 to 90-degrees

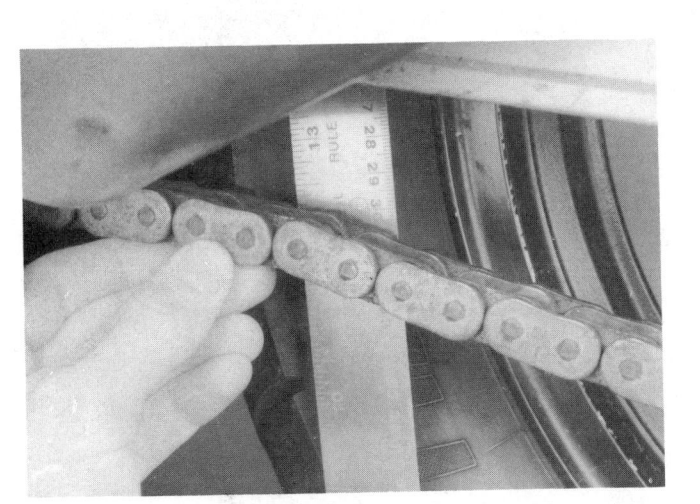

11.3   Push up on the bottom run of the chain and measure how far it deflects – if it's not within the specified limits, adjust the slack in the chain

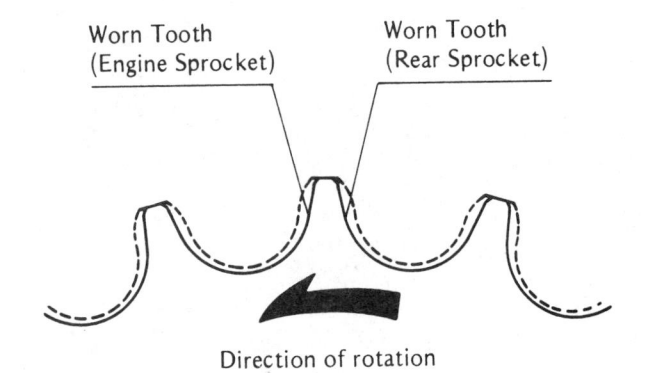

11.5   Check the sprockets in the areas indicated to see if they are worn excessively

9   If the proper amount of freeplay still can't be obtained, the cable must be replaced (see Chapter 2).
10   Install the right-side fairing stay if you're working on an A model.

---

11   Drive chain and sprockets – check, adjustment and lubrication

Check

Refer to illustrations 11.3 and 11.5

1   A neglected drive chain won't last long and can quickly damage the sprockets. Routine chain adjustment and lubrication isn't difficult and will ensure maximum chain and sprocket life.
2   To check the chain, place the bike on its centerstand and shift the transmission into Neutral. Make sure the ignition switch is off.
3   Push up on the bottom run of the chain and measure the slack midway between the two sprockets **(see illustration)**, then compare your measurements to the value listed in this Chapter's Specifications. As wear occurs, the chain will actually stretch, which means adjustment usually involves removing some slack from the chain. In some cases where lubrication has been neglected, corrosion and galling may cause the links to bind and kink, which effectively shortens the chain's length. If the chain is

tight between the sprockets, rusty or kinked, it's time to replace it with a new one.
4   Remove the chain guard (it's held on by two bolts). Check the entire length of the chain for damaged rollers, loose links and pins. Hang a 20-lb weight on the bottom run of the chain and measure the length of 20 links along the top run. Rotate the wheel and repeat this check at several places on the chain, since it may wear unevenly. Compare your measurements with the maximum 20-link length listed in this Chapter's Specifications. If any of your measurements exceed the maximum, replace the chain. **Note:** *Never install a new chain on old sprockets, and never use the old chain if you install new sprockets – replace the chain and sprockets as a set.*
5   Remove the shift lever and engine sprocket cover (see Chapter 6, Section 18). Check the teeth on the engine sprocket and the rear sprocket for wear **(see illustration)**. Refer to Chapter 6 for the sprocket diameter measurement procedure if the sprockets appear to be worn excessively.

Adjustment

Refer to illustrations 11.8, 11.9 and 11.11

6   Rotate the rear wheel until the chain is positioned with the least amount of slack present.
7   Loosen the torque link-to-rear caliper holder bolt.

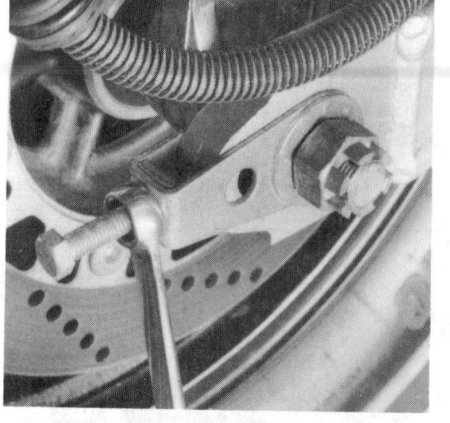

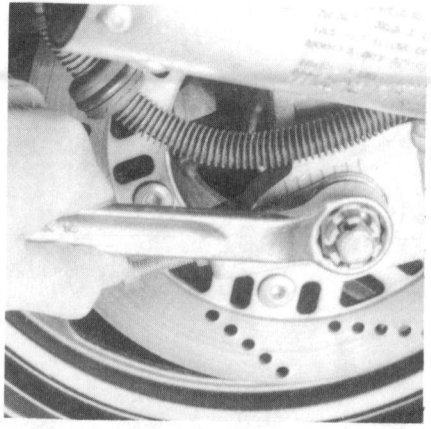

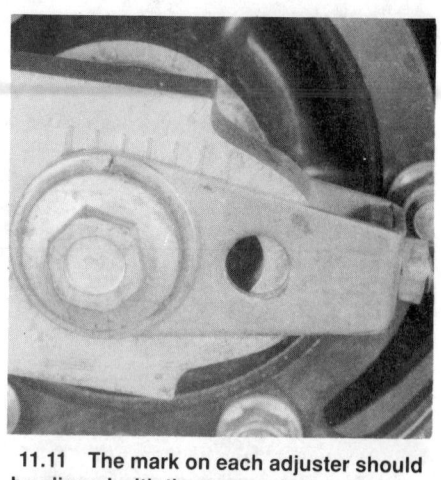

11.8   Loosen the locknuts on the adjusting bolts

11.9   Remove the cotter pin and loosen the axle nut

11.11   The mark on each adjuster should be aligned with the same relative marks on each side of the swingarm – if they aren't, the rear wheel will be out of alignment

11.13   Apply chain lubricant to the joints between the side plates and the rollers – not in the center of the rollers (with the bike on its centerstand, hold the plastic nozzle near the edge of the chain and turn the wheel by hand as the lubricant sprays out – repeat the procedure on the inside edge of the chain)

12.4   The oil drain plug is located in the center of the oil pan, between the exhaust pipes

8   Loosen and back-off the locknuts on the adjuster bolts **(see illustration)**.
9   Remove the cotter pin and loosen the axle nut **(see illustration)**.
10   Turn the axle adjusting bolts on both sides of the swingarm until the proper chain tension is obtained. Be sure to turn the adjusting bolts evenly to keep the rear wheel in alignment. If the adjusting bolts reach the end of their travel, the chain is excessively worn and should be replaced with a new one (see Chapter 6).
11   When the chain has the correct amount of slack, make sure the marks on the adjusters correspond to the same relative marks on each side of the swingarm **(see illustration)**. Tighten the axle nut to the torque listed in the Chapter 7 Specifications, then install a new cotter pin. If necessary, turn the nut an additional amount to line up the cotter pin hole with the castellations in the nut – don't loosen the nut to do this.
12   Tighten the locknuts and the torque link nut securely.

Lubrication

Refer to illustration 11.13
Note: If the chain is extremely dirty, it should be removed and cleaned before it's lubricated (see Chapter 6).

13   The best time to lubricate the chain is after the motorcycle has been ridden. When the chain is warm, the lubricant will penetrate the joints between the side plates, pins, bushings and rollers to provide lubrication of the internal load bearing areas. Use a good quality chain lubricant and ap-

ply it to the area where the side plates overlap – not the middle of the rollers **(see illustration)**. After applying the lubricant, let it soak in a few minutes before wiping off any excess.

---

12   Engine oil/filter – change

Refer to illustrations 12.4, 12.5a, 12.5b, 12.5c, 12.7a, 12.7b and 12.11
1   Consistent routine oil and filter changes are the single most important maintenance procedure you can perform on a motorcycle. The oil not only lubricates the internal parts of the engine, transmission and clutch, but it also acts as a coolant, a cleaner, a sealant, and a protectant. Because of these demands, the oil takes a terrific amount of abuse and should be replaced often with new oil of the recommended grade and type. Saving a little money on the difference in cost between a good oil and a cheap oil won't pay off if the engine is damaged.
2   Before changing the oil and filter, warm up the engine so the oil will drain easily. Be careful when draining the oil, as the exhaust pipes, the engine, and the oil itself can cause severe burns.
3   Put the motorcycle on the centerstand over a clean drain pan. If you're working on an A or B model, remove the lower fairing (see Chapter 8). Remove the oil filler cap to vent the crankcase and act as a reminder that there is no oil in the engine.

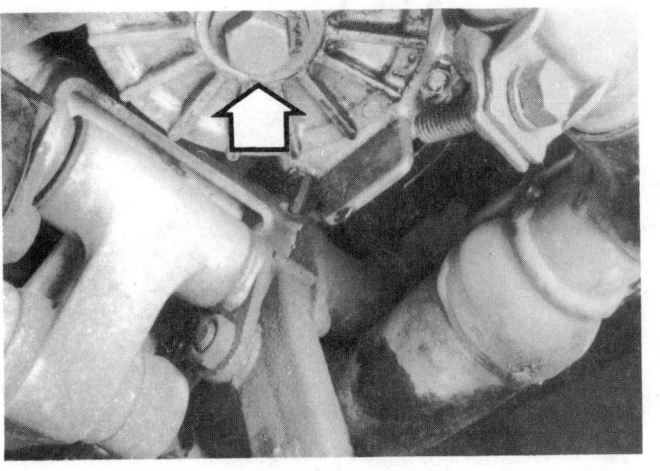

12.5a   Unscrew the oil filter mounting bolt . . .

12.5b   . . . then lower the filter from the crankcase

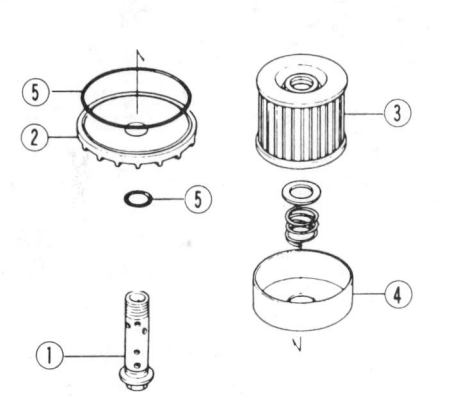

12.5c   Oil filter details

1	Mounting bolt/bypass valve assembly	3	Oil filter
		4	Oil fence
2	Filter cover	5	O-ring

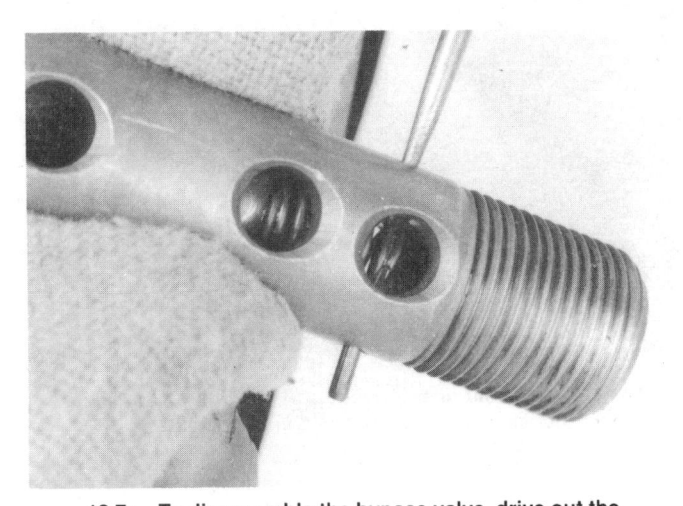

12.7a   To disassemble the bypass valve, drive out the retaining pin . . .

4   Next, remove the drain plug from the engine **(see illustration)** and allow the oil to drain into the pan. Do not lose the sealing washer on the drain plug.

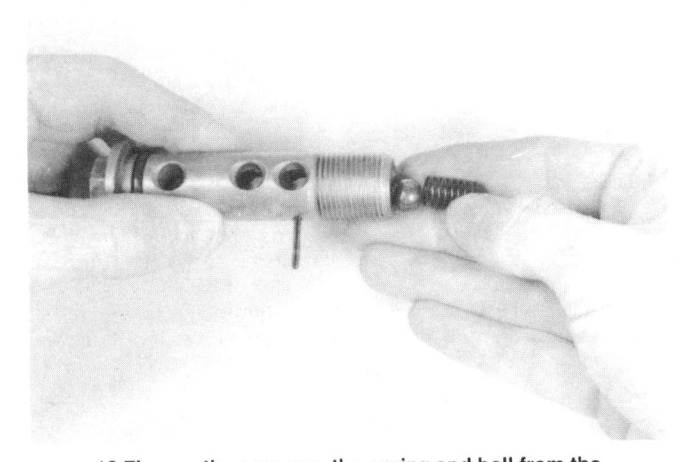

12.7b   . . . then remove the spring and ball from the mounting bolt

5   As the oil is draining, remove the oil filter mounting bolt and lower the filter out of the crankcase **(see illustrations)**. Separate the filter from the mounting bolt, then remove the washer, spring and oil fence **(see illustration)**. If additional maintenance is planned for this time period, check or service another component while the oil is allowed to drain completely.

6   Clean the filter cover and housing with solvent or clean rags. Wipe any remaining oil off the filter cover sealing area of the crankcase.

7   Remove the mounting bolt from the filter cover. The oil filter bypass valve is located inside the mounting bolt. Wash the mounting bolt in solvent and check the bypass valve for damage. If the valve is full of sludge, drive out the retaining pin and remove the spring and steel ball **(see illustrations)**.

8   Clean the components and check them for damage – especially, be sure to check the spring for distortion. If any damage is found, replace the mounting bolt/bypass valve assembly. If the components are okay, reassemble the valve and install the retaining pin.

9   Check the condition of the drain plug threads and the sealing washer. Use a new O-ring on the filter housing when it is installed.

10   Install a new O-ring on the mounting bolt, lubricate the mounting bolt with clean engine oil and insert the bolt through the filter cover. Place the oil fence over the mounting bolt.

11   Install a new O-ring on the filter cover, then install the spring and washer. Twist the new oil filter down the mounting bolt, making sure the

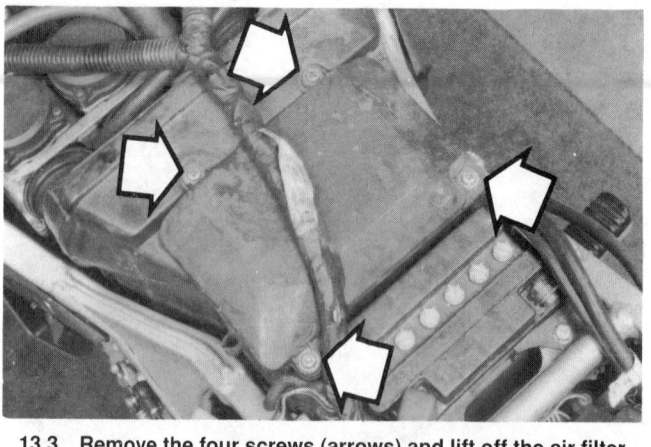

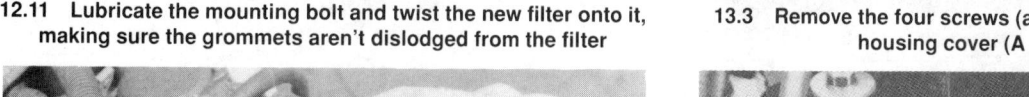

12.11   Lubricate the mounting bolt and twist the new filter onto it, making sure the grommets aren't dislodged from the filter

13.3   Remove the four screws (arrows) and lift off the air filter housing cover (A and B models)

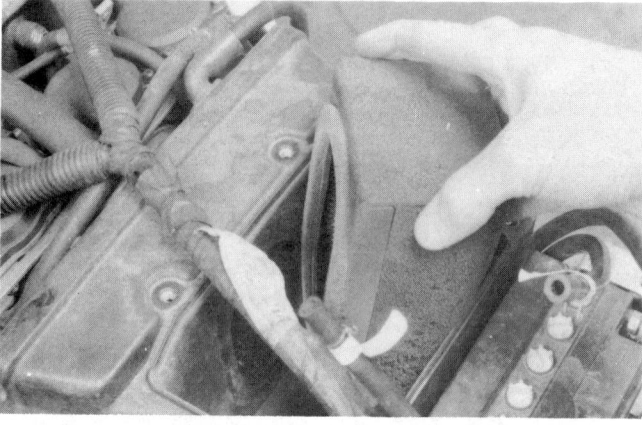

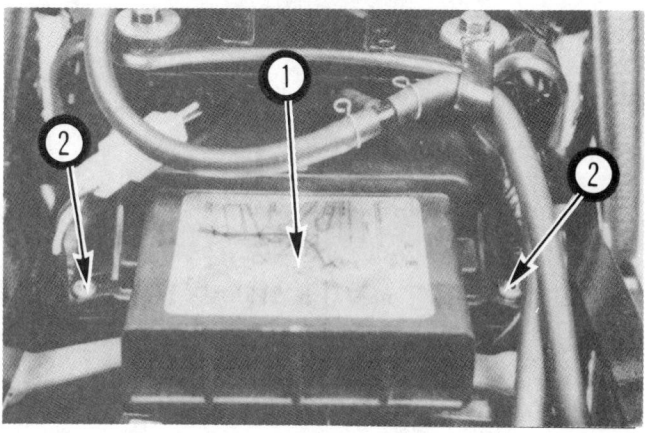

13.4   Detach the air filter element from the front of the filter housing, then lift it out (A and B models)

13.8   The filter housing cover on C models is retained by two screws

1   Cover   2   Screws

rubber grommets on the filter don't slip out of place **(see illustration)**.

12   Guide the oil filter assembly up into the crankcase. Tighten the mounting bolt with your fingers until the filter cover contacts the crankcase, making sure the O-ring on the filter cover stays in its groove and seals properly. Tighten the mounting bolt to the torque listed in this Chapter's Specifications.

13   Slip the sealing washer over the drain plug, then install and tighten the plug. Tighten the drain plug to the torque listed in this Chapter's Specifications. Avoid overtightening, as damage to the engine case will result.

14   Before refilling the engine, check the old oil carefully. If the oil was drained into a clean pan, small pieces of metal or other material can be easily detected. If the oil is very metallic colored, then the engine is experiencing wear from break-in (new engine) or from insufficient lubrication. If there are flakes or chips of metal in the oil, then something is drastically wrong internally and the engine will have to be disassembled for inspection and repair.

15   If there are pieces of fiber-like material in the oil, the clutch is experiencing excessive wear and should be checked.

16   If the inspection of the oil turns up nothing unusual, refill the crankcase to the proper level with the recommended oil and install the filler cap. Start the engine and let it run for two or three minutes. Shut it off, wait a few minutes, then check the oil level. If necessary, add more oil to bring the level up to the Maximum mark. Check around the drain plug and filter housing for leaks.

17   The old oil drained from the engine cannot be reused in its present state and should be disposed of. Oil reclamation centers, auto repair shops and gas stations will normally accept the oil, which can be refined and used again (be sure to check with the repair shop or gas station first). After the oil has cooled, it can be drained into a suitable container (capped

plastic jugs, topped bottles, milk cartons, etc.) for transport to one of these disposal sites.

---

13   Air filter element – servicing

Note: *Replace the air filter element every five cleanings (or more frequently, if the bike is operated in dusty conditions).*

A and B models

Refer to illustrations 13.3 and 13.4

1   Remove the seat and the fuel tank (see Chapter 4).

2   Remove the fuel tank bracket **(see illustration 4.1).**

3   Remove the screws that secure the air filter housing cover, then remove the cover **(see illustration)**.

4   Remove the air filter element **(see illustration)**. Wipe out the housing with a clean rag.

5   Tap the filter element on a solid surface to dislodge dirt and dust from the paper. If compressed air is available, use it to clean the element by blowing from the inside out. If the paper is extremely dirty or torn, replace the element with a new one.

6   Reinstall the filter by reversing the removal procedure. Make sure the element is seated properly in the filter housing before installing the cover. Reinstall the fuel tank bracket, fuel tank and seat.

C models

Refer to illustrations 13.8 and 13.12

7   Remove the seat.

8   Remove the screws that secure the air filter housing cover, then remove the cover **(see illustration)**.

Spark plug maintenance: Checking plug gap with feeler gauges

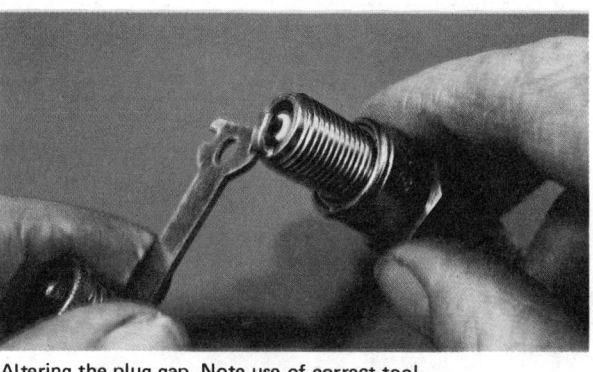

Altering the plug gap. Note use of correct tool

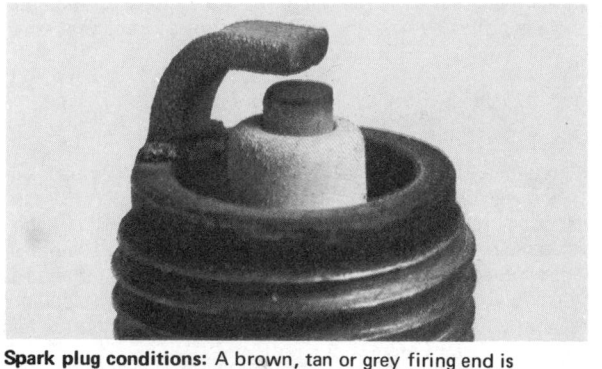

Spark plug conditions: A brown, tan or grey firing end is indicative of correct engine running conditions and the selection of the appropriate heat rating plug

White deposits have accumulated from excessive amounts of oil in the combustion chamber or through the use of low quality oil. Remove deposits or a hot spot may form

1

Black sooty deposits indicate an over-rich fuel/air mixture, or a malfunctioning ignition system. If no improvement is obtained, try one grade hotter plug

Wet, oily carbon deposits form an electrical leakage path along the insulator nose, resulting in a misfire. The cause may be a badly worn engine or a malfunctioning ignition system

A blistered white insulator or melted electrode indicates over-advanced ignition timing or a malfunctioning cooling system. If correction does not prove effective, try a colder grade plug

A worn spark plug not only wastes fuel but also overloads the whole ignition system because the increased gap requires higher voltage to initiate the spark. This condition can also affect air pollution

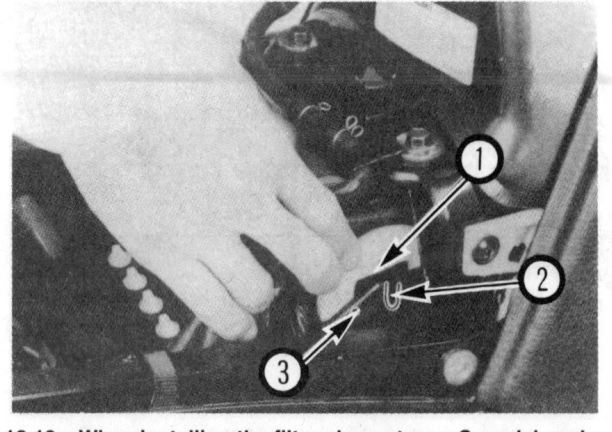

13.12   When installing the filter element on a C model, make sure the pins on the filter frame engage with the grooves in the sides of the housing

1	Frame end	3	Air cleaner
2	Groove		housing

9   Pull the air filter element out of the housing and separate it from the element frame. Wipe out the housing with a clean rag.
10   Wash the filter element with solvent and wring it out. Blow dry it with compressed air, if available.
11   Check the element for holes and tears and replace it if necessary.
12   Install the filter element on the element frame and install it in the filter housing, making sure the pins on the element frame engage with the grooves on the side of the housing **(see illustration)**.
13   Install the seat.

---

14   Cylinder compression – check

Refer to illustration 14.5

1   Among other things, poor engine performance may be caused by leaking valves, incorrect valve clearances, a leaking head gasket, or worn pistons, rings and/or cylinder walls. A cylinder compression check will help pinpoint these conditions and can also indicate the presence of excessive carbon deposits in the cylinder heads.
2   The only tools required are a compression gauge and a spark plug wrench. Depending on the outcome of the initial test, a squirt-type oil can may also be needed.
3   Start the engine and allow it to reach normal operating temperature. Place the motorcycle on the centerstand, remove the fuel tank, then remove the spark plugs (see Section 15, if necessary). Work carefully – don't strip the spark plug hole threads and don't burn your hands.
4   Disable the ignition by unplugging the primary wires from the coils (see Chapter 5). Be sure to mark the locations of the wires before detaching them.
5   Install the compression gauge in one of the spark plug holes **(see illustration)**. Hold or block the throttle wide open.
6   Crank the engine over a minimum of four or five revolutions (or until the gauge reading stops increasing) and observe the initial movement of the compression gauge needle as well as the final total gauge reading. Repeat the procedure for the other cylinders and compare the results to the value listed in this Chapter's Specifications.
7   If the compression in all cylinders built up quickly and evenly to the specified amount, you can assume the engine upper end is in reasonably good mechanical condition. Worn or sticking piston rings and worn cylinders will produce very little initial movement of the gauge needle, but compression will tend to build up gradually as the engine spins over. Valve and valve seat leakage, or head gasket leakage, is indicated by low initial compression which does not tend to build up.
8   To further confirm your findings, add a small amount of engine oil to each cylinder by inserting the nozzle of a squirt-type oil can through the

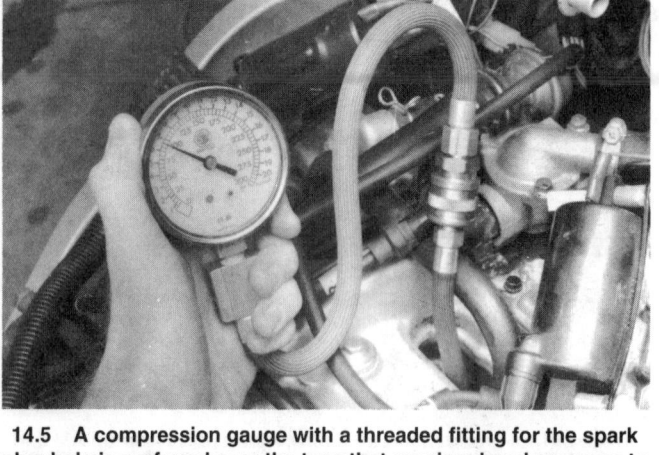

14.5   A compression gauge with a threaded fitting for the spark plug hole is preferred over the type that requires hand pressure to maintain the seal

spark plug holes. The oil will tend to seal the piston rings if they are leaking. Repeat the test for all cylinders.
9   If the compression increases significantly after the addition of the oil, the piston rings and/or cylinders are definitely worn. If the compression does not increase, the pressure is leaking past the valves or the head gasket. Leakage past the valves may be due to insufficient valve clearances, burned, warped or cracked valves or valve seats or valves that are hanging up in the guides.
10   If compression readings are considerably higher than specified, the combustion chambers are probably coated with excessive carbon deposits. It is possible (but not very likely) for carbon deposits to raise the compression enough to compensate for the effects of leakage past rings or valves. Refer to Chapter 2, remove the cylinder head and carefully decarbonize the combustion chambers.

---

15   Spark plugs – replacement

Refer to illustrations 15.2, 15.6a, 15.6b and 15.7

1   This motorcycle is equipped with spark plugs that have 12 mm threads and an 18 mm wrench hex. Make sure your spark plug socket is the correct size before attempting to remove the plugs.
2   Remove the fuel tank (see Chapter 4), then disconnect the spark plug caps from the spark plugs. If available, use compressed air to blow any accumulated debris from around the spark plugs. Remove the plugs **(see illustration)**.

15.2   Use an extension and a deep socket (preferably one with a rubber insert to prevent damage to the plug) to remove the spark plugs

15.6a   Spark plug manufacturers recommend using a wire type gauge when checking the gap – if the wire doesn't slide between the electrodes with a slight drag, adjustment is required

15.6b   To change the gap, bend the side electrode only, as indicated by the arrows, and be very careful not to crack or chip the porcelain insulator surrounding the center electrode

15.7   A length of rubber hose will save time and prevent damaged threads when installing the spark plugs

3   Inspect the electrodes for wear. Both the center and side electrodes should have square edges and the side electrode should be of uniform thickness. Look for excessive deposits and evidence of a cracked or chipped insulator around the center electrode. Compare your spark plugs to the color spark plug reading chart. Check the threads, the washer and the porcelain insulator body for cracks and other damage.

4   If the electrodes are not excessively worn, and if the deposits can be easily removed with a wire brush, the plugs can be regapped and reused (if no cracks or chips are visible in the insulator). If in doubt concerning the condition of the plugs, replace them with new ones, as the expense is minimal.

5   Cleaning spark plugs by sandblasting is permitted, provided you clean the plugs with a high flash-point solvent afterwards.

6   Before installing new plugs, make sure they are the correct type and heat range. Check the gap between the electrodes, as they are not preset. For best results, use a wire-type gauge rather than a flat gauge to check the gap (see illustration). If the gap must be adjusted, bend the side electrode only and be very careful not to chip or crack the insulator nose (see illustration). Make sure the washer is in place before installing each plug.

7   Since the cylinder heads are made of aluminum, which is soft and easily damaged, thread the plugs into the heads by hand. Since the plugs are quite recessed, slip a short length of hose over the end of the plug to use as a tool to thread it into place (see illustration). The hose will grip the plug well enough to turn it, but will start to slip if the plug begins to cross-thread in the hole – this will prevent damaged threads and the accompanying repair costs.

8   Once the plugs are finger tight, the job can be finished with a socket. If a torque wrench is available, tighten the spark plugs to the torque listed in this Chapter's Specifications. If you do not have a torque wrench, tighten the plugs finger tight (until the washers bottom on the cylinder head) then use a wrench to tighten them an additional 1/4 turn. Regardless of the method used, do not over-tighten them.

9   Reconnect the spark plug caps.

16   Lubrication – general

Refer to illustrations 16.3a, 16.3b and 16.3c

1   Since the controls, cables and various other components of a motorcycle are exposed to the elements, they should be lubricated periodically to ensure safe and trouble-free operation.

2   The footpegs, clutch and brake lever, brake pedal, shift lever and side and centerstand pivots should be lubricated frequently. In order for the lubricant to be applied where it will do the most good, the component should be disassembled. However, if chain and cable lubricant is being used, it can be applied to the pivot joint gaps and will usually work its way into the

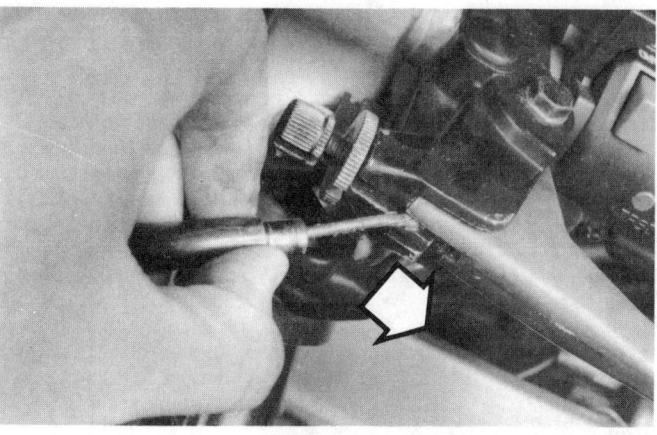

16.3a   To disconnect the clutch cable from the lever and bracket, line-up the slots in the bracket, lock wheel and adjuster, then pull the cable in the direction of the arrow and slide it through the slots

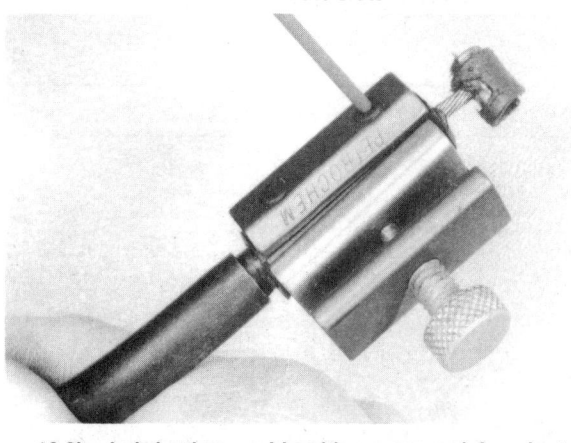

16.3b   Lubricating a cable with a pressure lube adapter (make sure the tool seals around the inner cable)

areas where friction occurs. If motor oil or light grease is being used, apply it sparingly as it may attract dirt (which could cause the controls to bind or wear at an accelerated rate). **Note:** *One of the best lubricants for the control lever pivots is a dry-film lubricant (available from many sources by different names).*

3   The clutch cable should be separated from the handlebar lever and bracket before it is lubricated (see illustration). It should be treated with

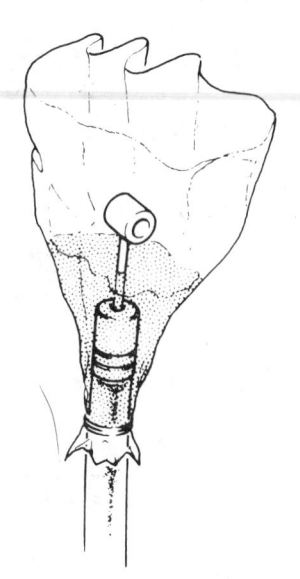

16.3c   Lubricating a control cable with a makeshift funnel and motor oil

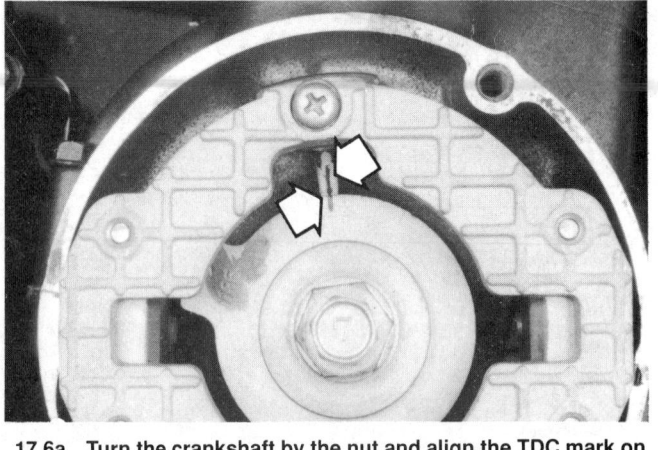

17.6a   Turn the crankshaft by the nut and align the TDC mark on the rotor with the timing mark on the crankcase (arrows)

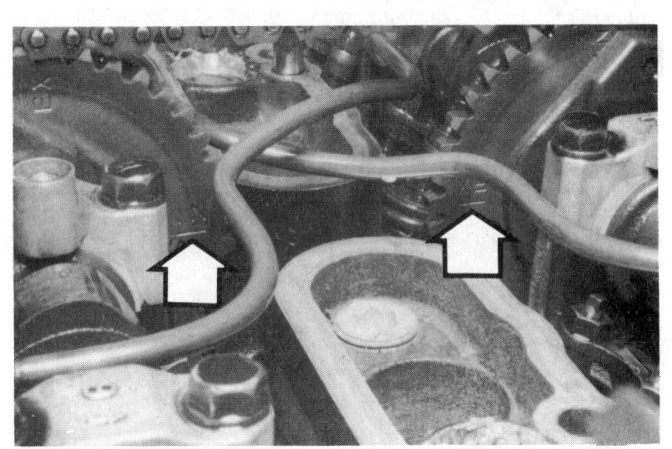

17.6b   The IN and EX marks on the camshaft sprockets will be pointing toward each other if piston no. 1 is positioned at TDC on the compression stroke

motor oil or a commercially available cable lubricant which is specially formulated for use on motorcycle control cables. Small adapters for pressure lubricating the cables with spray can lubricants are available and ensure that the cable is lubricated along its entire length **(see illustration)**. If motor oil is being used, tape a funnel-shaped piece of heavy paper or plastic to the end of the cable, then pour oil into the funnel and suspend the end of the cable upright **(see illustration)**. Leave it until the oil runs down into the cable and out the other end. When attaching the cable to the lever, be sure to lubricate the barrel-shaped fitting at the end with multi-purpose grease.

4   To lubricate the throttle and choke cables, disconnect the cable(s) at the lower end, then lubricate the cable with a pressure lube adapter **(see illustration 16.3b)**. See Chapter 4 for the choke cable removal procedure.

5   Speedometer and tachometer cables should be removed from their housings and lubricated with motor oil or cable lubricant.

6   Refer to Chapter 6 for the swingarm needle bearing and Uni-trak linkage lubrication procedures.

17   Valve clearances – check and adjustment

Refer to illustrations 17.6a, 17.6b, 17.7, 17.8 and 17.12

1   The engine must be completely cool for this maintenance procedure, so let the machine sit overnight before beginning.

2   Disconnect the cable from the negative terminal of the battery.

3   Refer to Chapter 4 and remove the fuel tank.

4   Remove the valve cover (see Chapter 2).

5   Remove the pickup coil cover (see Chapter 5).

6   Position the number 1 piston (on the left side of the engine) at Top Dead Center (TDC) on the compression stroke. Do this by turning the crankshaft, with a wrench placed on the crankshaft nut, until the TDC mark on the rotor is aligned with the timing mark on the crankcase **(see illustration)**. Now, check the position of the camshaft sprockets – the IN and EX marks should be pointing towards each other **(see illustration)**. If they aren't, turn the crankshaft one complete revolution and realign the mark. Piston number 1 is now at TDC compression, which can also be verified by looking at the cam lobes for that cylinder – they should not be depressing the rocker arms for either the intake valves or the exhaust valves.

7   With the engine in this position, all of the valves for cylinder no. 1 can be checked, as well as the exhaust valves for cylinder no. 2 and the intake valves for cylinder no. 3 **(see illustration)**.

Measuring Valves ■

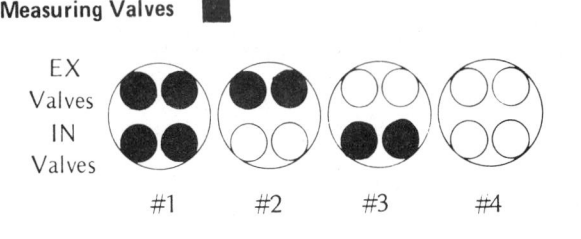

EX Valves
IN Valves

#1   #2   #3   #4

17.7   With cylinder no. 1 at TDC compression, the shaded valves can be adjusted

8   Start with the no. 1 intake valve clearance. Insert a feeler gauge of the thickness listed in this Chapter's Specifications between the valve stem and adjuster screw **(see illustration)**. Pull the feeler gauge out slowly – you should feel a slight drag. If there's no drag or a heavy drag, loosen the adjuster screw locknut (using Kawasaki valve adjusting screw tool no. 57001 – 1217, or equivalent) and turn the adjuster screw in or out, as needed, until you can feel a slight drag on the feeler gauge as you withdraw it.

9   Hold the adjuster screw with the adjusting screw tool (to keep it from turning) and tighten the locknut. Recheck the clearance to make sure it hasn't changed.

17.8   To adjust a valve clearance, loosen the adjuster locknut with a wrench and back off the adjuster screw with a valve adjusting screw tool – slowly tighten the adjuster screw until you feel a slight drag when withdrawing the feeler gauge, then tighten the locknut while still holding the adjuster screw

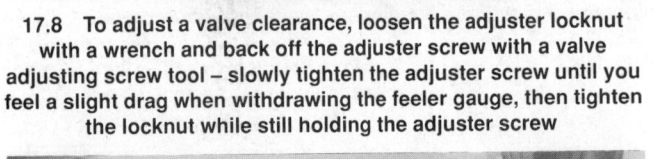

18.3   Turn the idle speed adjusting screw (arrow) in or out until the specified idle is obtained

10   Now adjust the no. 1 exhaust valves, following the same procedure you used for the intake valves. Make sure to use a feeler gauge of the specified thickness.

11   Proceed to adjust the no. 2 exhaust valves and the no. 3 intake valves.

12   Rotate the crankshaft one complete revolution and align the TDC mark on the rotor with the timing mark on the crankcase, which will position piston no. 4 at TDC compression. Adjust all four valves on cylinder no. 4, followed by the no. 3 exhaust valves and the no. 2 intake valves **(see illustration)**.

13   Install the valve cover and all of the components that had to be removed to get it off.

14   Install the fuel tank and reconnect the cable to the negative terminal of the battery.

18   Idle speed – check and adjustment

Refer to illustration 18.3

1   The idle speed should be checked and adjusted after the carburetors are synchronized and when it is obviously too high or too low. Before adjusting the idle speed, make sure the valve clearances and spark plug gaps are correct. Also, turn the handlebars back-and-forth and see if the idle speed changes as this is done. If it does, the throttle cable may not be adjusted correctly, or it may be worn out. Be sure to correct this problem before proceeding.

Measuring Valves ■

EX Valves
IN Valves

#1   #2   #3   #4

17.12   With cylinder no. 4 at TDC compression, the shaded valves can be adjusted

2   The engine should be at normal operating temperature, which is usually reached after 10 to 15 minutes of stop and go riding. Place the motorcycle on the centerstand and make sure the transmission is in Neutral.

3   Turn the throttle stop screw, located on the left side of the bike, just forward of the carburetor for cylinder no. 1 **(see illustration)**, until the idle speed listed in this Chapter's Specifications is obtained.

4   Snap the throttle open and shut a few times, then recheck the idle speed. If necessary, repeat the adjustment procedure.

5   If a smooth, steady idle can't be achieved, the fuel/air mixture may be incorrect. Refer to Chapter 4 for additional carburetor information.

19   Carburetor synchronization – check and adjustment

Refer to illustrations 19.9, 19.13 and 19.15

Warning: *Gasoline is extremely flammable, so take extra precautions when you work on any part of the fuel system. Don't smoke or allow open flames or bare light bulbs near the work area, and don't work in a garage where a natural gas-type appliance (such as a water heater or clothes dryer) is present. If you spill any fuel on your skin, rinse it off immediately with soap and water. When you perform any kind of work on the fuel system, wear safety glasses and have a class B type fire extinguisher on hand.*

1   Carburetor synchronization is simply the process of adjusting the carburetors so they pass the same amount of fuel/air mixture to each cylinder. This is done by measuring the vacuum produced in each cylinder. Carburetors that are out of synchronization will result in decreased fuel mileage, increased engine temperature, less than ideal throttle response and higher vibration levels.

2   To properly synchronize the carburetors, you will need some sort of vacuum gauge setup, preferably with a gauge for each cylinder, or a mercury manometer, which is a calibrated tube arrangement that utilizes columns of mercury to indicate engine vacuum.

3   A manometer can be purchased from a motorcycle dealer or accessory shop and should have the necessary rubber hoses supplied with it for hooking into the vacuum hose fittings on the carburetors.

4   A vacuum gauge setup can also be purchased from a dealer or fabricated from commonly available hardware and automotive vacuum gauges.

5   The manometer is the more reliable and accurate instrument, and for that reason is preferred over the vacuum gauge setup; however, since the mercury used in the manometer is a liquid, and extremely toxic, extra precautions must be taken during use and storage of the instrument.

6   Because of the nature of the synchronization procedure and the need for special instruments, most owners leave the task to a dealer service department or a reputable motorcycle repair shop.

7   Start the engine and let it run until it reaches normal operating temperature, then shut it off.

8   Remove the fuel tank (see Chapter 4).

1

19.9   Detach the vacuum hoses from the fittings on the front of the carburetors – this is where you'll connect the hoses for the vacuum gauges or manometer

19.13   Turn this screw to synchronize the carburetors for cylinders 1 and 2 (the carburetors for cylinders 3 and 4 also have a screw like this between them)

19.15   When the vacuum readings for cylinders 1 and 2 are identical to each other, and the vacuum readings for cylinders 3 and 4 are identical to each other, turn this screw to synchronize carburetors 1 and 2 to carburetors 3 and 4

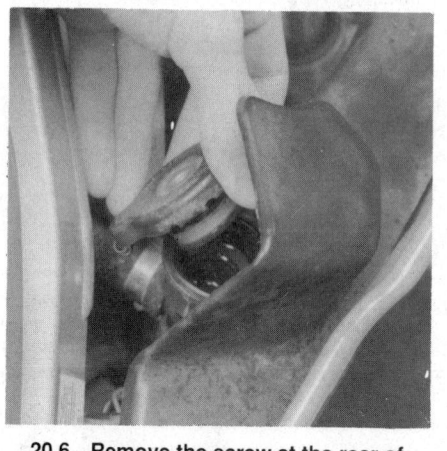

20.6   Remove the screw at the rear of the fairing inner panel to gain access to the radiator cap

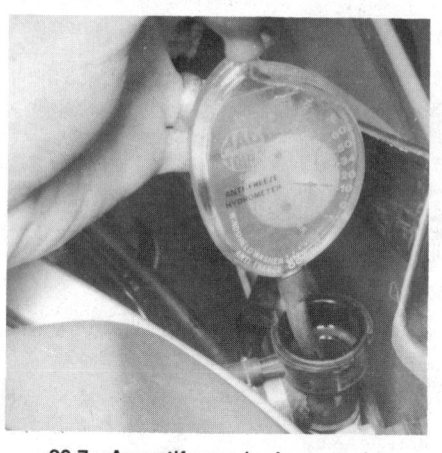

20.7   An antifreeze hydrometer is helpful in determining the condition of the coolant

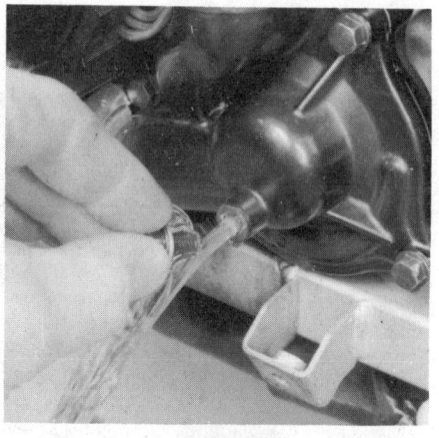

21.3   The drain bolt is located on the water pump – when it's removed, the coolant shoots out quite far – be sure your drain pan is positioned to catch it!

9   Detach the vacuum hoses from the fittings on the carburetors (**see illustration**), then hook up the vacuum gauge set or the manometer according to the manufacturer's instructions. Make sure there are no leaks in the setup, as false readings will result.

10   Reconnect the fuel line to the fuel tank (it's not necessary to hook-up the vacuum line to the fuel tap. Have an assistant hold the fuel tank out of the way, but in such a position that fuel can still be delivered and access to the carburetors is unobstructed. Place the fuel tap lever in the Prime position.

11   Start the engine and make sure the idle speed is correct.

12   The vacuum readings for all of the cylinders should be the same, or at least within the tolerance listed in this Chapter's Specifications. If the vacuum readings vary, adjust as necessary.

13   To perform the adjustment, synchronize the carburetors for cylinders 1 and 2 by turning the butterfly valve adjusting screw between those two carburetors, as needed, until the vacuum is identical or nearly identical for those two cylinders (**see illustration**).

14   Next, synchronize the carburetors for cylinders 3 and 4, using the butterfly valve adjusting screw situated between those two carburetors.

15   Finally, synchronize the carburetors for cylinders 1 and 2 to the carburetors for cylinders 3 and 4 by turning the center adjusting screw (**see illustration**).

16   When the adjustment is complete, recheck the vacuum readings and idle speed, then stop the engine. Remove the vacuum gauge or manometer and attach the hoses to the fittings on the carburetors. Reinstall the fuel tank and seat.

20   Cooling system – check

Refer to illustrations 20.6 and 20.7

Warning: *The engine must be cool before beginning this procedure.*

Note: *Refer to Section 3 and check the coolant level before performing this check.*

1   The entire cooling system should be checked carefully at the recommended intervals. Look for evidence of leaks, check the condition of the coolant, check the radiator for clogged fins and damage and make sure the fan operates when required.

2   Examine each of the rubber coolant hoses along its entire length. Look for cracks, abrasions and other damage. Squeeze each hose at various points. They should feel firm, yet pliable, and return to their original shape when released. If they are dried out or hard, replace them with new ones.

3   Check for evidence of leaks at each cooling system joint. Tighten the hose clamps carefully to prevent future leaks.

4   Check the radiator for evidence of leaks and other damage (remove the fairings if necessary – see Chapter 8). Leaks in the radiator leave tell-

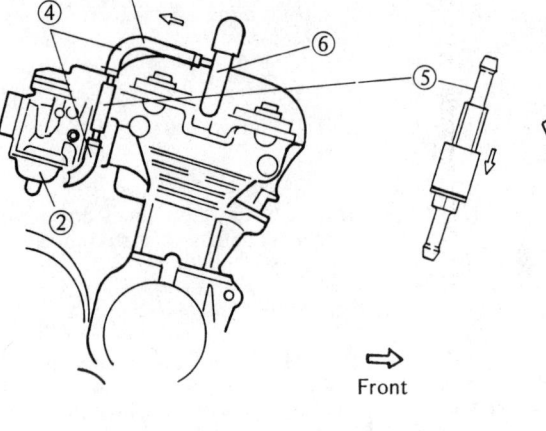

21.6   Coolant filter and check valve details (UK models only)

1 Water pump cover	*3 Check valve*	*5 Coolant filter*
2 Carburetor	*4 Hoses*	*6 Pipes*

tale scale deposits or coolant stains on the outside of the core below the leak. If leaks are noted, remove the radiator (refer to Chapter 3) and have it repaired at a radiator shop or replace it with a new one. **Caution:** *Do not use a liquid leak stopping compound to try to repair leaks.*

5   Check the radiator fins for mud, dirt and insects, which may impede the flow of air through the radiator. If the fins are dirty, force water or low pressure compressed air through the fins from the backside. If the fins are bent or distorted, straighten them carefully with a screwdriver.

6   Remove the radiator cap by turning it counterclockwise until it reaches a stop. If you hear a hissing sound (indicating there is still pressure in the system), Wait until it stops. Now, press down on the cap with the palm of your hand and continue turning the cap counterclockwise until it can be removed **(see illustration)**. Check the condition of the coolant in the radiator. If it is rust colored or if accumulations of scale are visible in the radiator, drain, flush and refill the system with new coolant. Check the cap gaskets for cracks and other damage. Have the cap tested by a dealer service department or replace it with a new one. Install the cap by turning it clockwise until it reaches the first stop, then push down on the cap and continue turning until it can turn no further.

7   Check the antifreeze content of the coolant with an antifreeze hydrometer **(see illustration)**. Sometimes coolant may look like it's in good condition, but might be too weak to offer adequate protection. If the hydrometer indicates a weak mixture, drain, flush and refill the cooling system (see Section 21).

8   Start the engine and let it reach normal operating temperature, then check for leaks again. As the coolant temperature increases, the fan should come on automatically and the temperature should begin to drop. If it does not, refer to Chapter 3 and check the fan and fan circuit carefully.

9   If the coolant level is consistently low, and no evidence of leaks can be found, have the entire system pressure checked by a Kawasaki dealer service department, motorcycle repair shop or service station.

---

21   Cooling system – draining, flushing and refilling

Refer to illustrations 21.3 and 21.6

Warning: *Allow the engine to cool completely before performing this maintenance operation. Also, don't allow antifreeze to come into contact with your skin or painted surfaces of the vehicle. Rinse off spills immediately with plenty of water. Antifreeze is highly toxic if ingested. Never leave antifreeze lying around in an open container or in puddles on the floor; children and pets are attracted by its sweet smell and may drink it. Check with*

local authorities about disposing of used antifreeze. Many communities have collection centers which will see that antifreeze is disposed of safely. Antifreeze is also combustible, so don't store or use it near open flames.

Draining

1   Loosen the radiator cap **(see illustration 20.6).** Place a large, clean drain pan under the left side of the engine.

2   Remove the lower fairing (see Chapter 8).

3   Remove the drain bolt from the side of the water pump cover **(see illustration)** and allow the coolant to drain into the pan. **Note:** *The coolant will rush out with considerable force, so position the drain pan accordingly. Remove the radiator cap completely to ensure that all of the coolant can drain.*

4   Drain the coolant reservoir. On A and B models, remove the cap from the reservoir (it's located in the lower fairing) and pour the coolant into the container. On C models, refer to Chapter 3 for the reservoir removal procedure. Wash the reservoir out with water.

Flushing

5   Flush the system with clean tap water by inserting a garden hose in the radiator filler neck. Allow the water to run through the system until it is clear when it exits the drain bolt hole. If the radiator is extremely corroded, remove it by referring to Chapter 3 and have it cleaned at a radiator shop.

6   On 1988 and later UK models, remove the fuel tank (see Chapter 4) and the knee grip covers (see Chapter 8). Remove the coolant filter from the carburetor coolant hoses **(see illustration)**. Blow compressed air through the filter against the normal direction of flow. Also remove the check valve from the hose that leads from the carburetor to the T-fitting in the lower radiator hose and clean it in the same manner. Be sure to install the filter and the check valve in the proper direction.

7   Check the drain bolt gasket. Replace it with a new one if necessary.

8   Clean the hole, then install the drain bolt and tighten it to the torque listed in this Chapter's Specifications.

9   Fill the cooling system with clean water mixed with a flushing compound. Make sure the flushing compound is compatible with aluminum components, and follow the manufacturer's instructions carefully.

10   Start the engine and allow it to reach normal operating temperature. Let it run for about ten minutes.

11   Stop the engine. Let the machine cool for awhile, then cover the radiator cap with a heavy rag and turn it counterclockwise to the first stop, releasing any pressure that may be present in the system. Once the hissing stops, push down on the cap and remove it completely.

12   Drain the system once again.

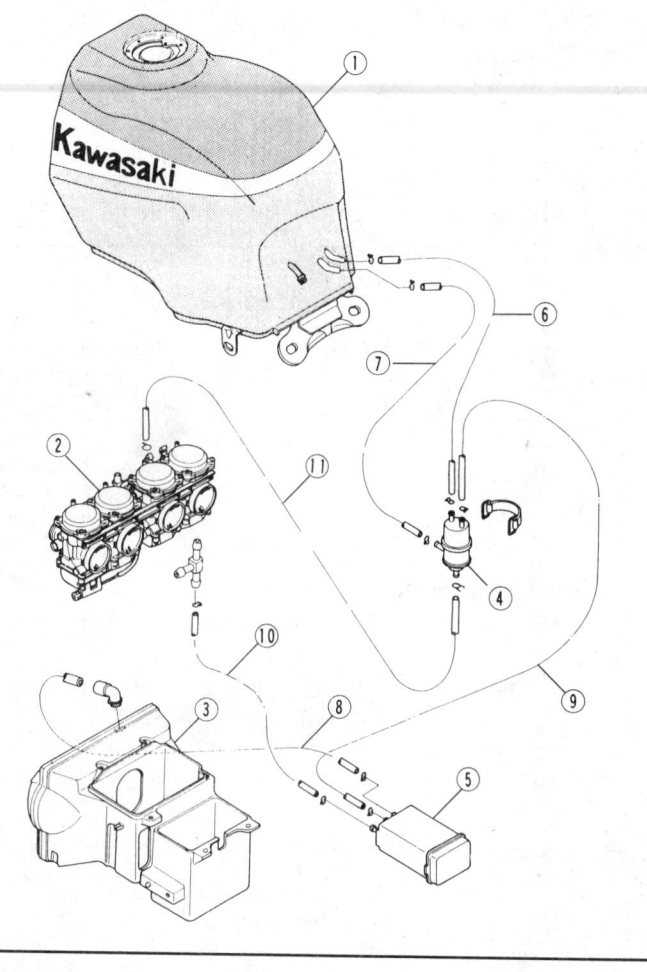

22.2a Evaporative emission control system details (A and B models)

1 *Fuel tank*
2 *Carburetor*
3 *Air cleaner housing*
4 *Liquid/vapor separator*
5 *Canister*
6 *Breather hose (blue)*
7 *Fuel return hose (red)*
8 *Purge hose (green)*
9 *Breather hose (blue)*
10 *Breather hose (yellow)*
11 *Vacuum hose (white)*

13 Fill the system with clean water, then repeat Steps 10, 11 and 12.

Refilling

14 Fill the system with the proper coolant mixture (see this Chapter's Specifications). When the system is full (all the way up to the top of the radiator cap filler neck), install the cap and start the engine. Allow the engine to reach normal operating temperature, then shut it off.

15 Let the engine cool off for awhile, cover the radiator cap with a heavy rag and loosen it to the first stop to allow any pressure in the system to bleed off before the cap is removed completely. Recheck the coolant level in the radiator filler neck. If it's low, add more coolant until it reaches the top of the filler neck. Reinstall the cap.

16 Allow the engine to cool, then check the coolant level in the reservoir (see Section 3). If the coolant level is low, add the specified mixture until it reaches the Hot mark in the reservoir.

17 Check the system for leaks.

18 Do not dispose of the old coolant by pouring it down a drain. Instead, pour it into a heavy plastic container, cap it tightly and take it to an authorized disposal site or a service station.

---

22   Evaporative emission control system (California models only) – check

---

Refer to illustrations 22.2a, 22.2b and 22.3

1   This system, installed on California models to conform to stringent emission control standards, routes fuel vapors from the fuel system into the engine to be burned, instead of letting them evaporate into the atmosphere. When the engine isn't running, vapors are stored in a carbon canister.

Hoses

2   To begin the inspection of the system, remove the seat and side covers (see Chapter 8 if necessary). Inspect the hoses from the fuel tank, carburetor and liquid/vapor separator to the canister for cracking, kinks or other signs of deterioration **(see illustrations)**.

Liquid/vapor separator

3   To check the liquid/vapor separator, label and disconnect the hoses from it **(see illustration)**, then remove it from the machine. Check it closely for cracks or other signs of damage. Reinstall the separator and connect the hoses, except for the breather hose. Using a syringe, inject approximately 20 mL of gasoline into the separator.

4   Disconnect the fuel return hose from the fuel tank and direct the end of the hose into an approved gasoline container. Hold the container level with the top of the fuel tank.

5   Start the engine and allow it to idle. If the fuel that was squirted into the separator comes out of the hose, it's working properly. If fuel doesn't come out of the hose, replace the separator.

Canister

6   Remove the canister from under the passenger's seat and inspect it for cracks or other signs of damage. Tip the canister so the nozzles point down. If fuel runs out of the canister, the liquid/vapor separator is probably bad – check it as described above. The fuel inside the canister has probably caused damage, so it would be a good idea to replace it also.

---

23   Air suction valves – check

Refer to illustrations 23.4 and 23.5

1   The air suction valves, installed on US models only, are one-way check valves that allow fresh air to flow into the exhaust ports. The suction

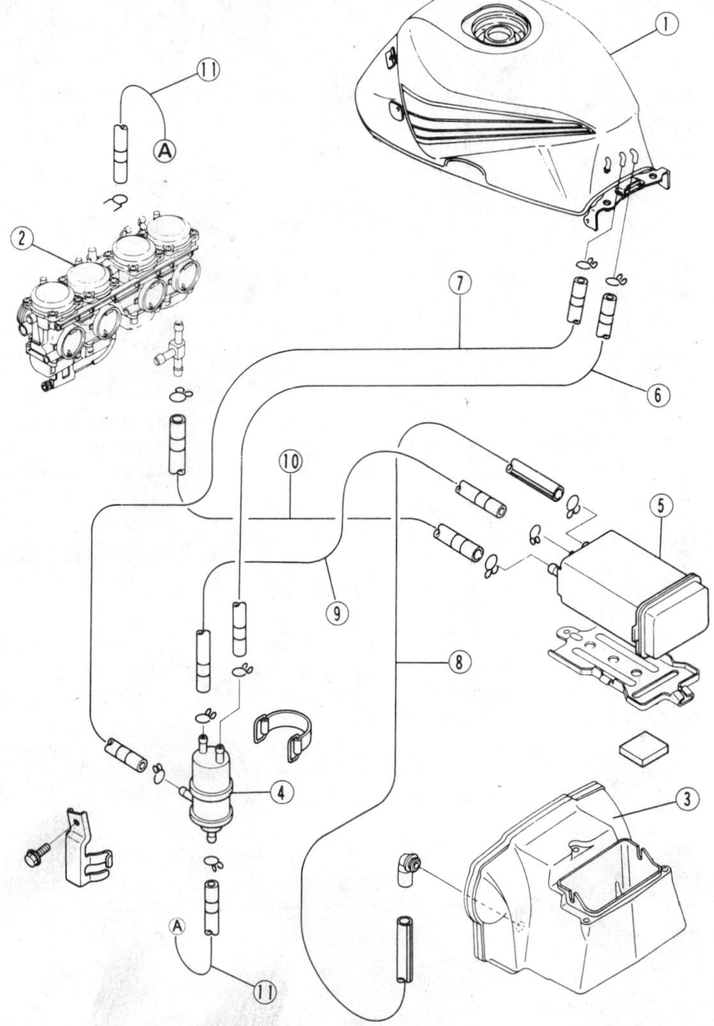

22.2b Evaporative emission control system details (C models)

1 Fuel tank
2 Carburetor
3 Air cleaner housing
4 Liquid/vapor separator
5 Canister
6 Breather hose (blue)
7 Fuel return hose (red)
8 Purge hose (green)
9 Breather hose (blue)
10 Breather hose (yellow)
11 Vacuum hose (white)

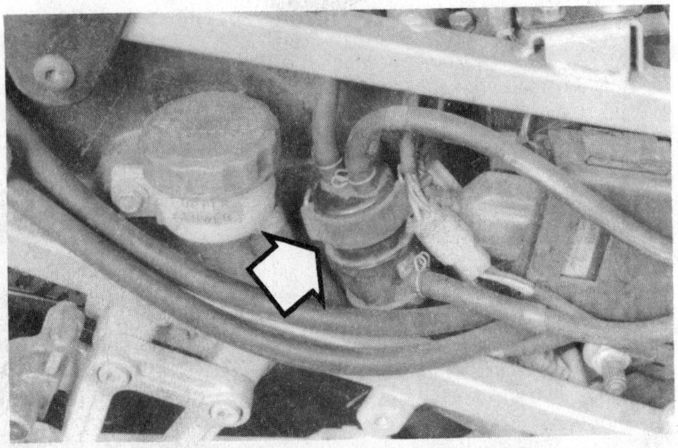

22.3 The liquid/vapor separator (arrow) is retained by a strap

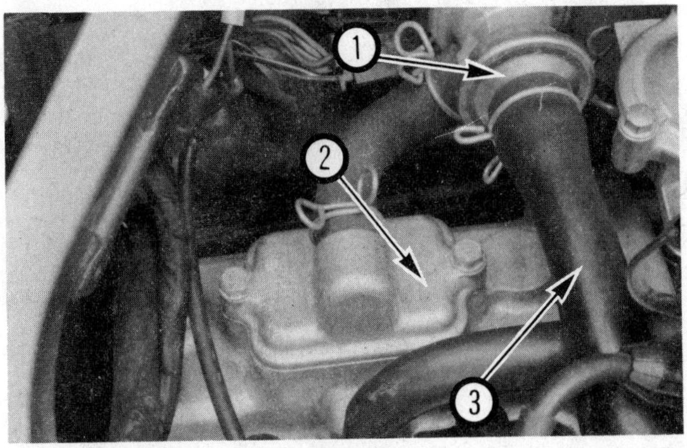

23.4 Details of the air suction valves and hoses

1 Vacuum switching valve   3 Hose to air filter housing
2 Air suction valve

developed by the exhaust pulses pulls the air from the air cleaner, through a hose to the vacuum switch valve, through a pair of hoses and two pairs of reed valves, and finally into the exhaust ports. The introduction of fresh air helps ignite any fuel that may not have been burned by the normal combustion process.

2 Remove the fuel tank (see Chapter 4).
3 Remove the ignition coils (see Chapter 5).
4 Disconnect the hoses from the air suction valves **(see illustration)**. Remove the bolts and lift off the covers.
5 Check the valve for cracks, warping, burning or other damage **(see**

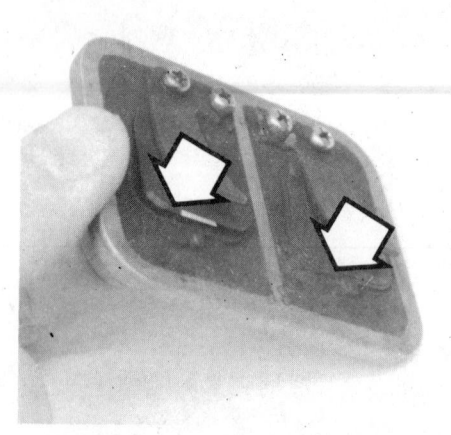

23.5   Check the reeds (arrows) on the air suction valve for damage and carbon build-up

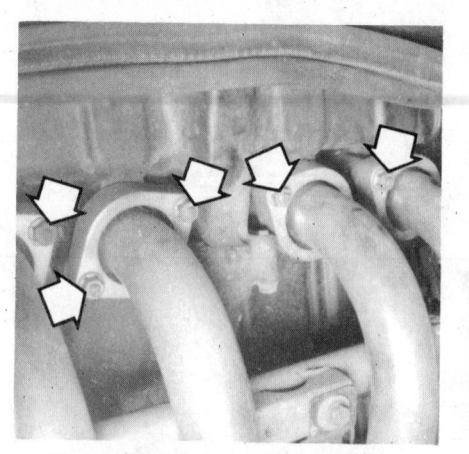

24.2   The exhaust pipe flange bolts (arrows) should be checked frequently and tightened if necessary

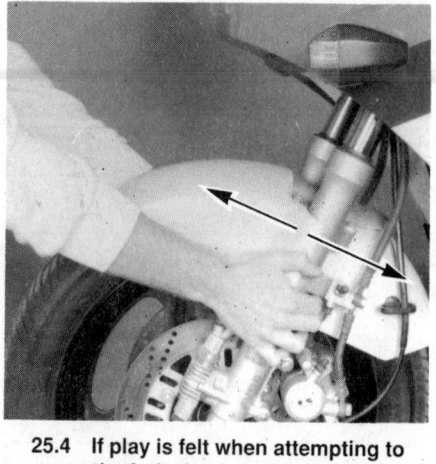

25.4   If play is felt when attempting to move the forks back-and-forth, adjust the steering head bearings

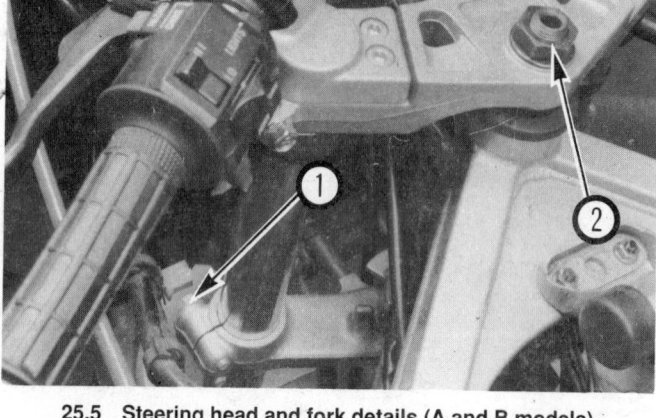

25.5   Steering head and fork details (A and B models)

1	Fork lower pinch bolts	2	Steering head nut

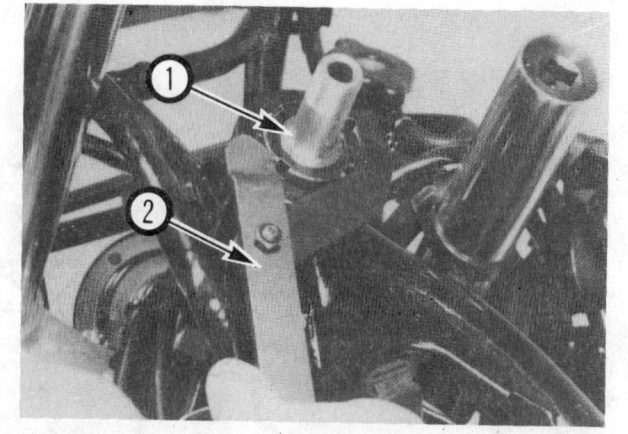

25.6   Tighten the steering stem locknut with a special spanner wrench (C model shown)

1	Stem locknut	2	Spanner wrench (Kawasaki tool no. 57001–1100)

illustration). Check the area where the reeds contact the valve holder for scratches, separation and grooves. If any of these conditions are found, replace the valve.

6   Wash the valves with solvent if carbon has accumulated between the reed and the valve holder.

7   Installation of the valves is the reverse of removal. Be sure to use a new gasket.

24   Exhaust system – check

Refer to illustration 24.2

1   Periodically check all of the exhaust system joints for leaks and loose fasteners. The lower fairing will have to be removed to do this properly (see Chapter 8). If tightening the clamp bolts fails to stop any leaks, replace the gaskets with new ones (a procedure which requires disassembly of the system).

2   The exhaust pipe flange nuts at the cylinder heads **(see illustration)** are especially prone to loosening, which could cause damage to the head. Check them frequently and keep them tight.

25   Steering head bearings – check and adjustment

Refer to illustrations 25.4, 25.5 and 25.6

1   This vehicle is equipped with ball-and-cone type steering head bearings which can become dented, rough or loose during normal use of the machine. In extreme cases, worn or loose steering head bearings can cause steering wobble that is potentially dangerous.

Check

2   To check the bearings, place the motorcycle on the centerstand and block the machine so the front wheel is in the air.

3   Point the wheel straight ahead and slowly move the handlebars from side-to-side. Dents or roughness in the bearing races will be felt and the bars will not move smoothly.

4   Next, grasp the fork legs and try to move the wheel forward and backward **(see illustration)**. Any looseness in the steering head bearings will be felt. If play is felt in the bearings, adjust the steering head as follows:

Adjustment

5   Remove the fuel tank (see Chapter 4). On C models it will be necessary to remove the lower and upper fairings and knee grip covers (see Chapter 8). On A and B models, loosen the fork lower pinch bolts and the steering head nut **(see illustration)**. On C models, remove the steering head nut, the handlebars and the steering head (see Chapter 6). Use a spanner wrench to loosen the steering stem locknut.

6   Carefully tighten the steering stem locknut until the steering head is tight but does not bind when the forks are turned from side-to-side **(see illustration)**.

7   Retighten the steering head nut and the fork pinch bolts, in that order, to the torque values listed in the Chapter 6 Specifications. On C models, make sure the top ends of the fork tubes protrude 15 mm from the upper surface of the fork clamps.

8   Recheck the steering head bearings for play as described above. If necessary, repeat the adjustment procedure. Reinstall all parts previously removed.

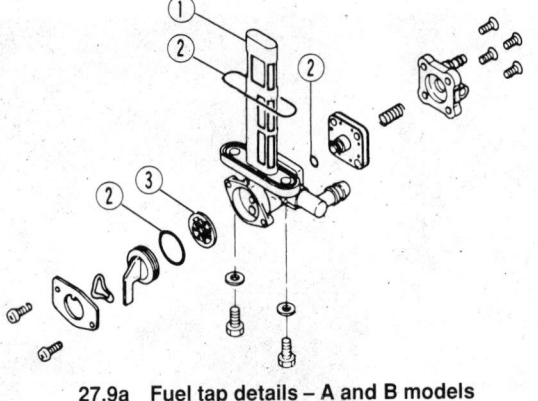

27.9a   Fuel tap details – A and B models

1. Filter   2 O-ring   3 Gasket

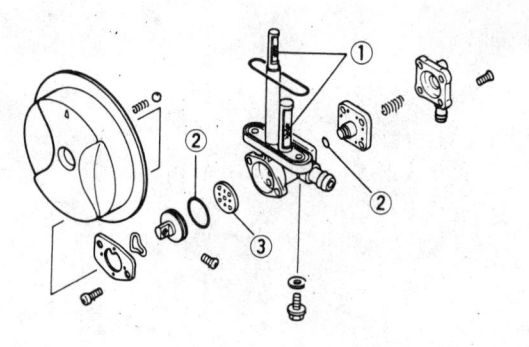

27.9b   Fuel tap details – C models

1   Filter   2   O-ring   3   Gasket

9   Refer to Chapter 6 for steering head bearing lubrication and replacement procedures.

26   Fasteners – check

1   Since vibration of the machine tends to loosen fasteners, all nuts, bolts, screws, etc. should be periodically checked for proper tightness.
2   Pay particular attention to the following:

   Spark plugs
   Engine oil drain plug
   Oil filter cover bolt
   Gearshift lever
   Footpegs and sidestand
   Engine mount bolts
   Shock absorber mount bolts
   Uni-trak linkage bolts
   Front axle and clamp bolt
   Rear axle nut

3   If a torque wrench is available, use it along with the Torque specifications at the beginning of this, or other, Chapters.

27   Fuel system – check and filter cleaning

Refer to illustrations 27.9a and 27.9b
Warning: *Gasoline is extremely flammable, so take extra precautions when you work on any part of the fuel system. Don't smoke or allow open flames or bare light bulbs near the work area, and don't work in a garage where a natural gas-type appliance (such as a water heater or clothes dryer) is present. If you spill any fuel on your skin, rinse it off immediately with soap and water. When you perform any kind of work on the fuel system, wear safety glasses and have a class B type fire extinguisher on hand.*
1   Check the fuel tank, the fuel tap, the lines and the carburetors for leaks and evidence of damage.
2   If carburetor gaskets are leaking, the carburetors should be disassembled and rebuilt by referring to Chapter 4.
3   If the fuel tap is leaking, tightening the screws may help. If leakage persists, the tap should be disassembled and repaired or replaced with a new one.
4   If the fuel lines are cracked or otherwise deteriorated, replace them with new ones.
5   Check the vacuum hose connected to the fuel tap. If it is cracked or otherwise damaged, replace it with a new one.
6   The fuel filter, which is attached to the fuel tap, may become clogged and should be removed and cleaned periodically. In order to clean the filter, the fuel tank must be drained and the fuel tap removed.
7   Remove the fuel tank (see Chapter 4). Drain the fuel into an approved fuel container.

28.3   If oil is leaking past the fork seals (arrow), replace them

8   Once the tank is emptied, loosen and remove the screws that attach the fuel tap to the tank. Remove the tap and filter.
9   Clean the filter **(see illustrations)** with solvent and blow it dry with compressed air. If the filter is torn or otherwise damaged, replace the entire fuel tap with a new one. Check the mounting flange O-ring and the gaskets on the screws. If they are damaged, replace them with new ones.
10   Install the O-ring, filter and fuel tap on the tank, then install the tank. Refill the tank and check carefully for leaks around the mounting flange and screws.

28   Suspension – check

Refer to illustrations 28.3, 28.8a and 28.8b
1   The suspension components must be maintained in top operating condition to ensure rider safety. Loose, worn or damaged suspension parts decrease the vehicle's stability and control.
2   While standing alongside the motorcycle, lock the front brake and push on the handlebars to compress the forks several times. See if they move up-and-down smoothly without binding. If binding is felt, the forks should be disassembled and inspected as described in Chapter 6.
3   Carefully inspect the area around the fork seals for any signs of fork oil leakage **(see illustration)**. If leakage is evident, the seals must be replaced as described in Chapter 6.
4   Check the tightness of all suspension nuts and bolts to be sure none have worked loose.
5   Inspect the shock for fluid leakage and tightness of the mounting nuts. If leakage is found, the shock should be replaced.
6   Set the bike on its centerstand. Grab the swingarm on each side, just ahead of the axle. Rock the swingarm from side to side – there should be no discernible movement at the rear. If there's a little movement or a slight clicking can be heard, Make sure the pivot shaft nuts are tight. If the pivot nuts are tight but movement is still noticeable, the swingarm will have to be removed and the bearings replaced as described in Chapter 6.

1

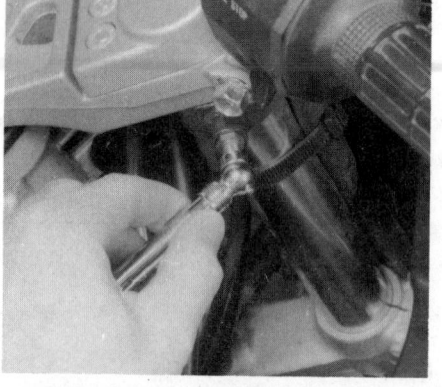

28.8a   A tire pressure gauge can be used to check the air pressure in the front forks if a gauge made for air suspensions isn't available (A and B models only)

28.8b   The Schrader valve for the rear shock absorber (arrow) is located on the right side of the bike, below the igniter

29.4   After the handlebar is removed and the fork upper pinch bolts have been loosened, the top plug can be removed

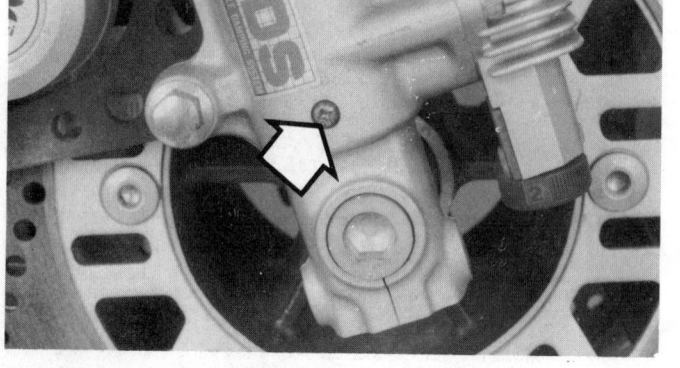

29.5   Fork drain screw location

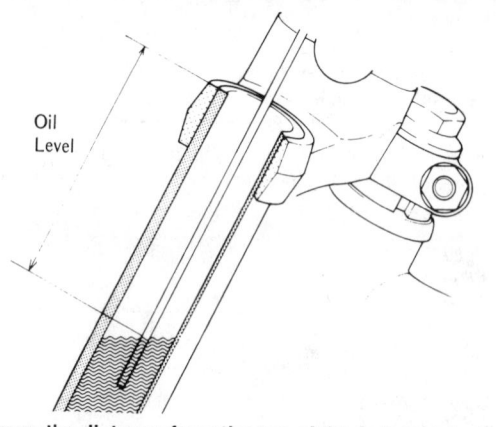

Oil
Level

29.9   Measure the distance from the top of the fork tube to the oil and add or drain oil as necessary until the level is correct

7   Inspect the tightness of the rear suspension nuts and bolts.

8   Check the air pressure in the front forks (A and B models only) and the rear shock absorber **(see illustrations)**. Note: *The manufacturer recommends against the use of a tire pressure gauge – a gauge made especially for air suspensions should be used (a tire pressure gauge may allow too much air to leak out around the Schrader valve, thereby giving you an inaccurate reading). If the special gauge isn't available, however, and the suspension feels too mushy or too firm, a tire pressure gauge can be used to estimate the pressure and avoid a possible hazardous riding condition.* Adjust the air pressures to the values listed in this Chapter's Specifications. Add air a little at a time to avoid over-pressurizing the forks or shock absorber.

9   On C models, the pressure in the front forks should be at atmospheric pressure. Simply remove the valve cap, depress the Schrader valve to equalize the pressure inside the forks, then install the cap.

29   Fork oil – replacement

Refer to illustrations 29.4, 29.5 and 29.9

1   Place the motorcycle on the centerstand. Remove the lower fairing and position a jack with a block of wood on the jack head under the engine to support the motorcycle when the fork cap bolts are removed.

2   Release the air pressure in the forks by depressing the Schrader valve with a small screwdriver.

3   Remove the handlebar from one side (see Chapter 6).

4   Loosen the upper pinch bolts and remove the top plug from the exposed fork tube **(see illustration)**. Pull out the fork spring.

5   Place a drain pan under the fork leg and remove the drain screw **(see illustration)**. **Warning:** *Do not allow the fork oil to contact the brake discs*

or pads. If it does, clean the discs with brake system cleaner and replace the pads with new ones before riding the motorcycle.

6   After most of the oil has drained, slowly compress and release the forks to pump out the remaining oil. An assistant will most likely be required to do this procedure.

7   Check the drain screw gasket for damage and replace it if necessary. Apply sealant to the threads of the drain screw, then install the screw and gasket, tightening it securely.

8   Pour the type and amount of fork oil, listed in this Chapter's Specifications, into the fork tube through the opening at the top. Remove the jack from under the engine and slowly pump the forks a few times to purge the air from the upper and lower chambers.

9   If you're working on an A or B model, raise the front wheel off the ground again. If you're working on a C model, fully compress the front forks (you may need an assistant to do this). Insert a tape measure into the fork tube and measure the distance from the oil to the top of the fork tube **(see illustration)**. Compare your measurement to the value listed in this Chapter's Specifications. drain or add oil, as necessary, until the level is correct.

10   Check the O-rings on the top plug, then coat them with a thin layer of multi-purpose grease. Install the fork spring. Install the top plug and tighten it securely.

11   Tighten the fork tube pinch bolts to the torque listed in the Chapter 6 Specifications. Install the handlebar, tightening the bolts to the torque listed in the Chapter 6 Specifications.

12   Repeat the procedure to the other fork.

13   On A and B models, inject compressed air, a little at a time, until the desired pressure is attained (see this Chapter's Specifications and Section 28). On C models, raise the front wheel off the ground to equalize the pressure in the forks, then reinstall the cap.

14   Install the lower fairing.

Chapter 2 Engine, clutch and transmission

Refer to Chapter 10 for information on the ZX750F model

Contents

Specifications

General

Bore . . . . 2.36 in (60.0 mm)
Stroke . . . . 2.06 in (52.5 mm)
Displacement . . . . 592 cc
Compression ratio
  A and B models . . . . 11.0 : 1
  C models . . . . 11.7 : 1

Camshaft and rocker arms

Lobe height (intake and exhaust) .... 1.42 in (36.06 mm) minimum
Bearing oil clearance
   1985 and 1986
     Standard .... 0.003 to 0.004 in (0.078 to 0.121 mm)
     Maximum .... 0.008 in (0.21 mm)
   1987 on
     Standard
       Outer journals and center journal .... 0.001 to 0.002 in (0.028 to 0.071 mm)
       Other two journals .... 0.003 to 0.004 in (0.078 to 0.121 mm)
     Maximum
       Outer journals and center journal .... 0.006 in (0.16 mm)
       Other two journals .... 0.008 in (0.21 mm)
Journal diameter
   1985 and 1986
     Standard .... 0.902 to 0.903 in (22.900 to 22.922 mm)
     Minimum .... 0.901 in (22.87 mm)
   1987 on
     Standard
       Outer journals and center journal .... 0.904 to 0.905 in (22.950 to 22.972 mm)
       Other two journals .... 0.902 to 0.903 in (22.900 to 22.922 mm)
     Minimum
       Outer journals and center journal .... 0.903 in (22.92 mm)
       Other two journals .... 0.901 in (22.87 mm)
Bearing journal inside diameter
   Standard .... 0.906 to 0.907 in (23.000 to 23.021 mm)
   Maximum .... 0.9073 in (23.03 mm)
Camshaft runout (maximum) .... 0.003 in (0.1 mm)
Camshaft chain 20-link length (maximum) .... 5-5/64 in (128.9 mm)
Rocker arm inside diameter (maximum) .... 0.474 in (12.05 mm)
Rocker shaft diameter (minimum) .... 0.471 in (11.97 mm)

Cylinder head, valves and valve springs

Cylinder head warpage limit .... 0.002 in (0.05 mm)
Valve stem runout limit .... 0.002 in (0.05 mm)
Valve stem diameter
   Intake .... 0.195 to 0.196 in (4.960 to 4.990 mm)
   Exhaust .... 0.194 to 0.195 in (4.940 to 4.970 mm)
Valve guide inside diameter (intake and exhaust) .... 0.197 to 0.1974 in (5.000 to 5.012 mm)
Valve seat width (intake and exhaust) .... 0.020 to 0.040 in (0.5 to 1.0 mm)
Valve spring free length (minimum)
   Inner .... 1-3/16 in (30.0 mm)
   Outer .... 1-5/16 in (33.4 mm)

Cylinder block

Bore diameter (maximum) .... 141.84 in (60.10 mm)
Deck warpage limit .... 0.002 in (0.05 mm)
Taper limit .... 0.002 in (0.05 mm)
Out-of-round limit .... 0.002 in (0.05 mm)

Pistons

Piston diameter .... 2.356 to 2.362 in (59.800 to 59.957 mm)
Piston-to-cylinder clearance .... 0.001 to 0.002 in (0.043 to 0.070 mm)
Oversize pistons and rings .... +0.020 in (+ 0.5 mm) (one oversize only)
Ring side clearance
   Top .... 0.001 to 0.006 in (0.03 to 0.17 mm)
   Second .... 0.0007 to 0.006 in (0.02 to 0.16 mm)
Ring groove width
   Top .... 0.040 to 0.044 in (1.02 to 1.12 mm)
   Second
     1988 and earlier .... 0.047 to 0.102 in (1.21 to 2.60 mm)
     1989 on .... 0.040 to 0.043 in (1.01 to 1.11 mm)
   Oil
     1988 and earlier .... 0.100 to 0.102 in (2.51 to 2.60 mm)
     1989 on .... 0.080 to 0.175 in (2.01 to 2.11 mm)
Ring thickness
   Top .... 0.035 to 0.039 in (0.90 to 0.99 mm)

Second
    1988 and earlier . . . .   0.043 to 0.046 in (1.10 to 1.19 mm)
    1989 on . . . .   0.035 to 0.040 in (0.90 to 0.99 mm)
Ring end gap
    Top . . . .   0.006 to 0.023 in (0.15 to 0.60 mm)
    Second . . . .   0.006 to 0.025 in (0.15 to 0.65 mm)

Crankshaft and bearings

Main bearing oil clearance . . . .   0.0005 to 0.003 in (0.014 to 0.080 mm)
Main bearing journal diameter
    No mark on crank throw . . . .   1.2601 to 1.2604 in (31.984 to 31.992 mm)
    "1" mark on crank throw . . . .   1.2605 to 1.2608 in (31.993 to 32.000 mm)
Connecting rod side clearance . . . .   0.0005 to 0.020 in (0.013 to 0.500 mm)
Connecting rod bearing oil clearance . . . .   0.001 to 0.003 in (0.035 to 0.100 mm)
Connecting rod big-end bore diameter
    No mark on side of rod . . . .   1.4184 to 1.4187 in (36.000 to 36.008 mm)
    "0" mark on side of rod . . . .   1.4187 to 1.4190 in (36.009 to 36.016 mm)
Connecting rod journal diameter
    No mark on crank throw . . . .   1.2995 to 1.2998 in (32.984 to 32.992 mm)
    "0" mark on crank throw . . . .   1.2999 to 1.3002 in (32.993 to 33.000 mm)
Primary chain 20-link length (maximum) . . . .   7-39/64 in (193.4 mm)

Oil pump and relief valve

Oil pressure (warm) . . . .   31 to 40 psi @ 4000 rpm
Relief valve opening pressure . . . .   63 to 85 psi

Clutch

Spring free length (minimum) . . . .   1-1/4 in (31.7 mm)
Friction plate thickness (minimum) . . . .   0.110 in (2.8 mm)
Friction and steel plate warpage limit . . . .   0.019 in (0.3 mm)

Transmission

Gear backlash (maximum) . . . .   0.009 in (0.25 mm)
Shift fork groove width (maximum) . . . .   0.208 in (5.3 mm)
Shift fork ear thickness (minimum) . . . .   0.190 in (4.8 mm)
Shift fork guide pin diameter (minimum) . . . .   0.307 in (7.8 mm)
Shift drum groove width (maximum) . . . .   0.327 in (8.3 mm)

Torque specifications

Valve cover bolts . . . .   87 in-lbs
Camshaft bearing cap bolts . . . .   104 in-lbs
Camshaft gear bolts . . . .   11 ft-lbs
Rocker arm shaft plugs . . . .   87 in-lbs
Oil pipe bolts (on camshaft bearing caps) . . . .   104 in-lbs
Camshaft chain tensioner cap . . . .   18 ft-lbs
Cylinder head nuts . . . .   16.5 ft-lbs
Cylinder block-to-cylinder head bolts
    Initial . . . .   75 in-lbs
    Final . . . .   104 in-lbs
Cylinder block-to-crankcase nuts . . . .   87 in-lbs
Clutch cover bolts . . . .   78 in-lbs
Clutch spring bolts . . . .   78 in-lbs
Clutch hub nut . . . .   100 ft-lbs
Oil pan bolts . . . .   104 in-lbs
Oil pipe-to-cylinder head union bolts . . . .   104 in-lbs
Oil pipe-to-crankcase union bolt . . . .   18 ft-lbs
Relief valve-to-oil pan . . . .   11 ft-lbs
Engine mounting bolt nuts . . . .   25 ft-lbs
Downtube mounting bolts . . . .   18 ft-lbs
Crankcase bolts
    6 mm bolts . . . .   104 in-lbs
    8 mm bolts . . . .   20 ft-lbs
Connecting rod nuts . . . .   27 ft-lbs
Primary chain tensioner bolt . . . .   18 ft-lbs
Chain guide bracket bolts . . . .   104 in-lbs
Secondary shaft nut . . . .   54 ft-lbs
Shift drum guide bolt . . . .   18 ft-lbs
Shift drum positioning bolt . . . .   18 ft-lbs

2

1　General information

The engine/transmission unit is of the water-cooled, in-line, four-cylinder design, installed transversely across the frame. The sixteen valves are operated by double overhead camshafts which are chain driven off the crankshaft. the engine/transmission assembly is constructed from aluminum alloy. The crankcase is divided horizontally.

The crankcase incorporates a wet sump, pressure-fed lubrication system which uses a gear-driven, dual-rotor oil pump, an oil filter and by-pass valve assembly, a relief valve and an oil pressure switch. Also contained in the crankcase is the secondary shaft and the starter motor clutch.

Power from the crankshaft is routed to the transmission via the clutch, which is of the wet, multi-plate type and is chain-driven off the crankshaft. The transmission is a six-speed, constant-mesh unit.

2　Operations possible with the engine in the frame

The components and assemblies listed below can be removed without having to remove the engine from the frame. If, however, a number of areas require attention at the same time, removal of the engine is recommended.

Gear selector mechanism external components
Water pump
Starter motor
Alternator
Clutch assembly
Oil pan, oil pump and relief valve
Valve cover, camshafts and rocker arms
Cam chain tensioner
Cylinder head
Cylinder block and pistons

3　Operations requiring engine removal

It is necessary to remove the engine/transmission assembly from the frame and separate the crankcase halves to gain access to the following components:

Crankshaft, connecting rods and bearings
Transmission shafts
Shift drum and forks
Secondary shaft and starter motor clutch
Camshaft chain
Primary chain

4　Major engine repair – general note

1　It is not always easy to determine when or if an engine should be completely overhauled, as a number of factors must be considered.
2　High mileage is not necessarily an indication that an overhaul is needed, while low mileage, on the other hand, does not preclude the need for an overhaul. Frequency of servicing is probably the single most important consideration. An engine that has regular and frequent oil and filter changes, as well as other required maintenance, will most likely give many miles of reliable service. Conversely, a neglected engine, or one which has not been broken in properly, may require an overhaul very early in its life.
3　Exhaust smoke and excessive oil consumption are both indications that piston rings and/or valve guides are in need of attention. Make sure oil leaks are not responsible before deciding that the rings and guides are bad. Refer to Chapter 1 and perform a cylinder compression check to determine for certain the nature and extent of the work required.
4　If the engine is making obvious knocking or rumbling noises, the connecting rod and/or main bearings are probably at fault.

5　Loss of power, rough running, excessive valve train noise and high fuel consumption rates may also point to the need for an overhaul, especially if they are all present at the same time. If a complete tune-up does not remedy the situation, major mechanical work is the only solution.
6　An engine overhaul generally involves restoring the internal parts to the specifications of a new engine. During an overhaul the piston rings are replaced and the cylinder walls are bored and/or honed. If a rebore is done, then new pistons are also required. The main and connecting rod bearings are generally replaced with new ones and, if necessary, the crankshaft is also replaced. Generally the valves are serviced as well, since they are usually in less than perfect condition at this point. While the engine is being overhauled, other components such as the carburetors and the starter motor can be rebuilt also. The end result should be a like-new engine that will give as many trouble free miles as the original.
7　Before beginning the engine overhaul, read through all of the related procedures to familiarize yourself with the scope and requirements of the job. Overhauling an engine is not all that difficult, but it is time consuming. Plan on the motorcycle being tied up for a minimum of two (2) weeks. Check on the availability of parts and make sure that any necessary special tools, equipment and supplies are obtained in advance.
8　Most work can be done with typical shop hand tools, although a number of precision measuring tools are required for inspecting parts to determine if they must be replaced. Often a dealer service department or motorcycle repair shop will handle the inspection of parts and offer advice concerning reconditioning and replacement. As a general rule, time is the primary cost of an overhaul so it doesn't pay to install worn or substandard parts.
9　As a final note, to ensure maximum life and minimum trouble from a rebuilt engine, everything must be assembled with care in a spotlessly clean environment.

5　Engine – removal and installation

Refer to illustrations 5.14, 5.15, 5.16a, 5.16b, 5.16c, 5.17 and 5.18
Note: *Engine removal and installation should be done with the aid of an assistant to avoid damage or injury that could occur if the engine is dropped. A hydraulic floor jack should be used to support and lower the engine if possible (they can be rented at low cost).*

Removal

1　Set the bike on its centerstand.
2　Remove the seat and the fuel tank (see Chapter 4).
3　Remove the side covers, knee grip covers (C models), fairing side stays (A models) and the upper and lower fairings (see Chapter 8).
4　Drain the coolant and the engine oil (see Chapter 1).
5　Remove the ignition coils (see Chapter 5).
6　Remove the air suction valve and the vacuum switching valve (see Chapter 1).
7　Remove the carburetors (see Chapter 4) and plug the intake openings with rags.
8　Remove the radiator, radiator hoses and oil cooler (see Chapter 3).
9　Remove the horns (see Chapter 9).
10　Remove the exhaust system (see Chapter 4).
11　Disconnect the lower end of the clutch cable from the lever and bracket (see Chapter 1).
12　Remove the engine sprocket cover, unbolt the engine sprocket and detach the sprocket and chain from the engine (see Chapter 6).
13　Mark and disconnect the wires from the oil pressure switch, neutral switch and the starter motor. Unplug the alternator, sidestand and pickup coil electrical connectors (see Chapters 5 and 9).
14　Remove the bolt securing the ground wire to the right rear of the engine case **(see illustration)**.
15　If you're working on a C model, remove the heat guard **(see illustration)**.
16　Remove the engine front mounting bolts/nuts and, on A and B models, the bolts holding the downtubes to the frame **(see illustrations)**.
17　Support the engine with a floor jack and a wood block **(see illustration)**.

5.14   Remove the bolt (arrow) that holds the ground wire to the engine

5.15   The heat guard (A) is retained by two screws (B) (C models only)

5.16a   On A and B models, remove the engine front mounting bolts and nuts and the downtube front mounting bolts (arrows)

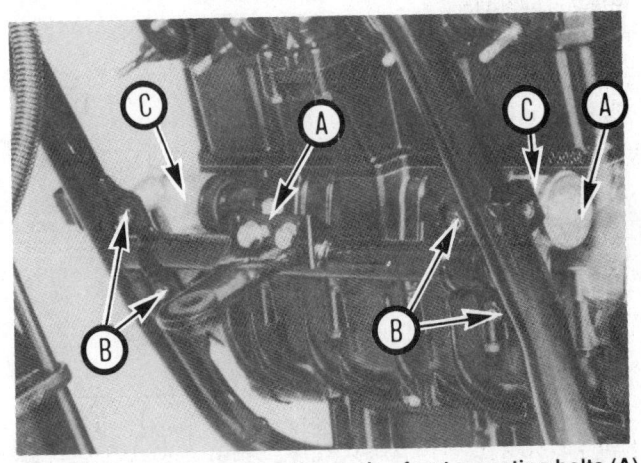

5.16b   On C models, remove the engine front mounting bolts (A), the mount bracket bolts (B), then disconnect the bracket (C)

5.16c   On A and B models, remove the downtube lower mounting bolts (arrows)

5.17   Support the engine with a floor jack, with a wood block as a cushion

2

5.18   Remove the nuts from the engine rear mounting bolts, then pull the bolts out

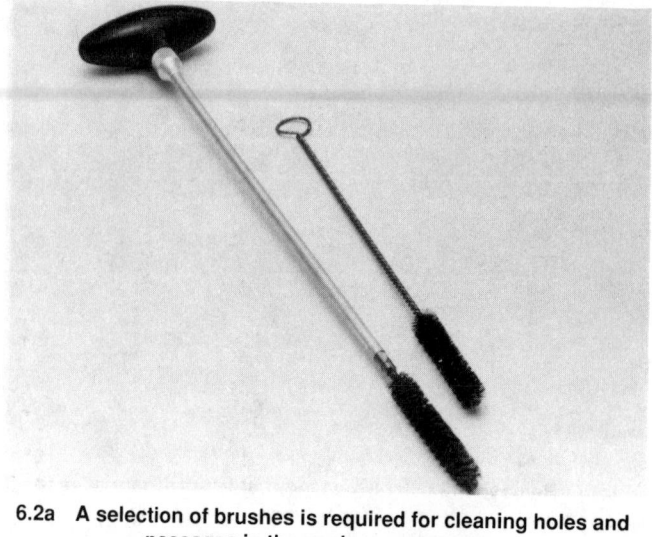

6.2a   A selection of brushes is required for cleaning holes and passages in the engine components

18   Pry the plugs from the holes in the frame and remove the nuts from the rear mounting bolts (see illustration).
19   With the engine supported, pull the rear mounting bolts out. Make sure no wires or hoses are still attached to the engine assembly.
20   On A and B models, slowly and carefully lower the engine assembly to the floor, then guide it out from under the bike.
21   On C models, raise the engine slightly then, with the help of an assistant, slide the engine out to the right. It would be helpful to have another jack, or a small table or platform that is the same height as the bottom frame tube, which the engine can be slid onto as it is removed.

Installation

22   Installation is basically the reverse of removal. Note the following points:

   a) Don't tighten any of the engine mounting bolts until they all have been installed.
   b) Use new gaskets at all exhaust pipe connections.
   c) Make sure all of the wires on the left side of the engine (under the engine sprocket cover) are routed properly.
   d) Tighten the engine mounting bolts and frame downtube bolts to the torque listed in this Chapter's Specifications.
   e) Adjust the drive chain, throttle cables, choke cable and clutch cable following the procedures in Chapter 1.

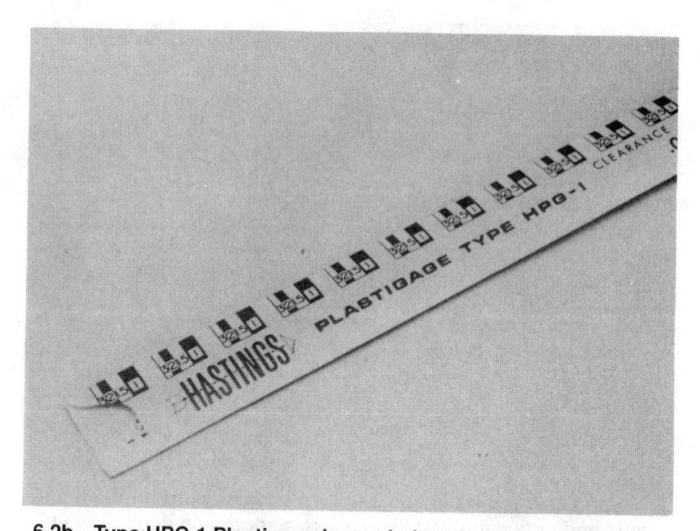

6.2b   Type HPG-1 Plastigage is needed to check the crankshaft, connecting rod and camshaft oil clearances

---

6   Engine disassembly and reassembly – general information

Refer to illustrations 6.2a, 6.2b, 6.3a and 6.3b

1   Before disassembling the engine, clean the exterior with a degreaser and rinse it with water. A clean engine will make the job easier and prevent the possibility of getting dirt into the internal areas of the engine.
2   In addition to the precision measuring tools mentioned earlier, you will need a torque wrench, a valve spring compressor, oil galley brushes, a piston ring removal and installation tool, a piston ring compressor, a pin-type spanner wrench and a clutch holder tool (which is described in Section 19). Some new, clean engine oil of the correct grade and type, some engine assembly lube (or moly-based grease), a tube of Kawasaki Bond liquid gasket (part no. 92104-1003) or equivalent, and a tube of RTV (silicone) sealant will also be required. Although it may not be considered a tool, some Plastigage (type HPG-1) should also be obtained to use for checking bearing oil clearances (see illustrations).
3   An engine support stand make from short lengths of 2 x 4's bolted together will facilitate the disassembly and reassembly procedures (see illustration). The perimeter of the mount should be just big enough to accommodate the engine oil pan. If you have an automotive-type engine

stand, an adapter plate can be made from a piece of plate, some angle iron and some nuts and bolts (see illustration).
4   When disassembling the engine, keep "mated" parts together (including gears, cylinders, pistons, etc. that have been in contact with each other during engine operation). These "mated" parts must be reused or replaced as an assembly.
5   Engine/transmission disassembly should be done in the following general order with reference to the appropriate Sections.

   Remove the cylinder head(s)
   Remove the cylinder block
   Remove the pistons
   Remove the clutch
   Remove the oil pan
   Remove the external shift mechanism
   Remove the alternator rotor/stator coils (see Chapter 9)
   Separate the crankcase halves
   Remove the secondary sprocket, shaft and starter motor clutch
   Remove the crankshaft and connecting rods
   Remove the transmission shafts/gears
   Remove the shift drum/forks

6   Reassembly is accomplished by reversing the general disassembly sequence.

6.3a An engine stand can be made from short lengths of 2 x 4 lumber and lag bolts or nails

6.3b If you have an automotive engine stand, an adapter can be made from a piece of 3/16-inch metal plate, angle iron and some nuts and bolts

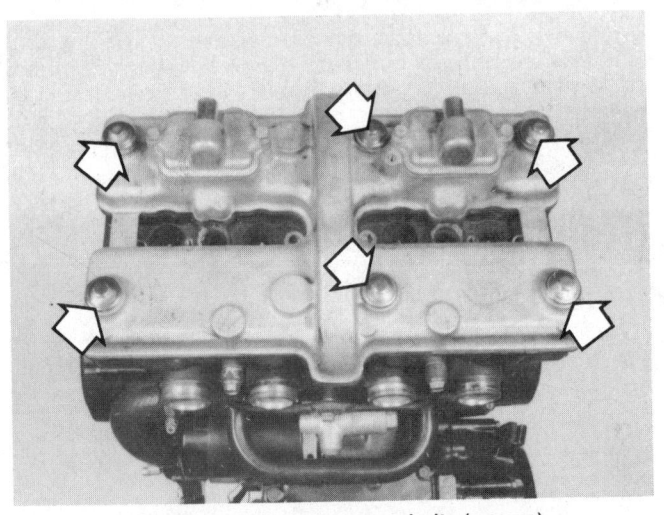

7.9 Remove the valve cover bolts (arrows)

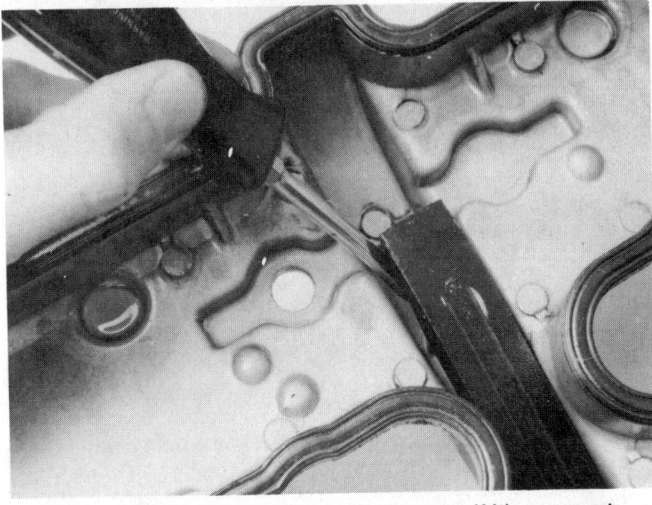

7.10 Pry the chain guide out of the cover if it's worn out

7 Valve cover – removal and installation

Refer to illustrations 7.9, 7.10, 7.11 and 7.12

Note: *The valve cover can be removed with the engine in the frame. If the engine has been removed, ignore the steps which don't apply.*

Removal

1 Set the bike on its centerstand.
2 Drain the engine coolant (see Chapter 1).
3 Remove the fuel tank (see Chapter 4).
4 Remove the upper and lower fairings (see Chapter 8).
5 Remove the Air Suction Valve and the Vacuum Switching Valve (see Chapter 1).
6 Remove the ignition coils and their brackets, along with the spark plug wires (see Chapter 5).
7 Remove the thermostat housing and the upper coolant pipe (see Chapter 3).
8 Remove the baffle plate. On C models, also remove the reserve lighting device (US and Canadian models only)(see Chapter 9).
9 Remove the valve cover bolts **(see illustration)**.
10 Lift the cover off the cylinder head. If it's stuck, don't attempt to pry it off – tap around the sides of it with a plastic hammer to dislodge it. Check the chain guide in the center of the cover – if it's excessively worn, pry it out and install a new one **(see illustration)**.

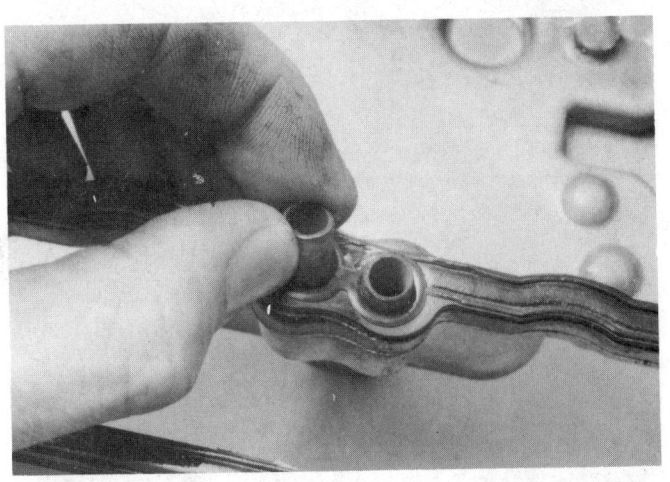

7.11 On US models, be careful not to lose the locating dowels

Installation

11 On US models, remove the locating dowels from the valve cover **(see illustration)**. Peel the rubber gasket from the cover. If it is cracked, hardened, has soft spots or shows signs of general deterioration, replace it with a new one.

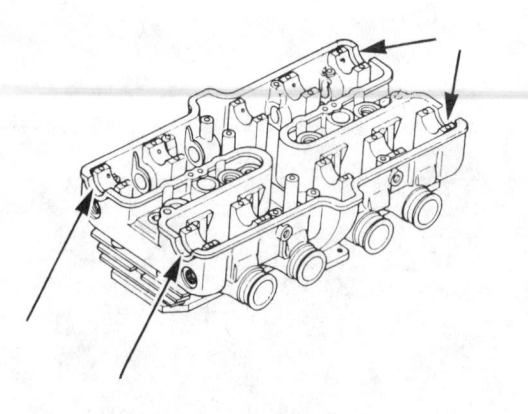

7.12   Apply a thin film of RTV sealant to the half-circle cutouts (arrows)

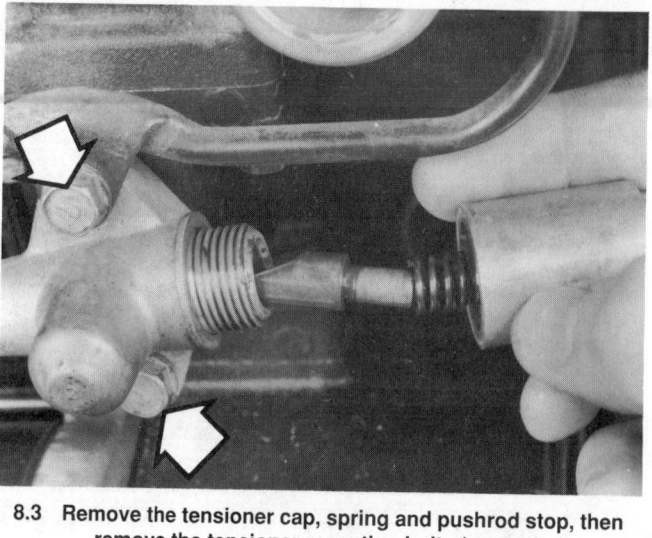

8.3   Remove the tensioner cap, spring and pushrod stop, then remove the tensioner mounting bolts (arrows)

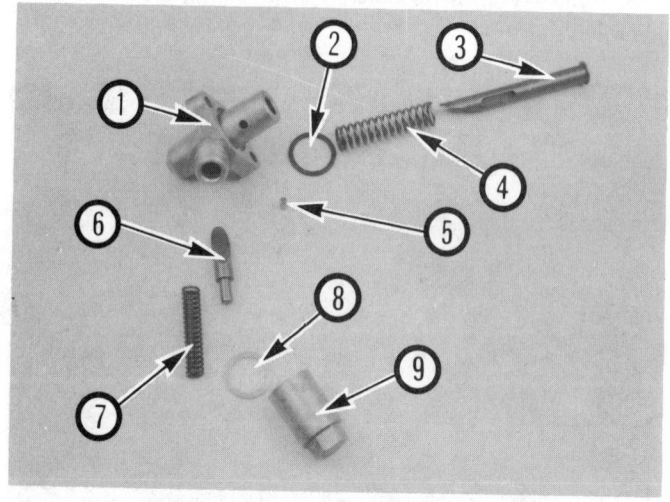

8.5   Components of the camshaft chain tensioner

1	Tensioner body	6	Pushrod stop
2	O-ring	7	Pushrod stop spring
3	Pushrod	8	Sealing washer
4	Pushrod spring	9	Tensioner cap
5	Pin		

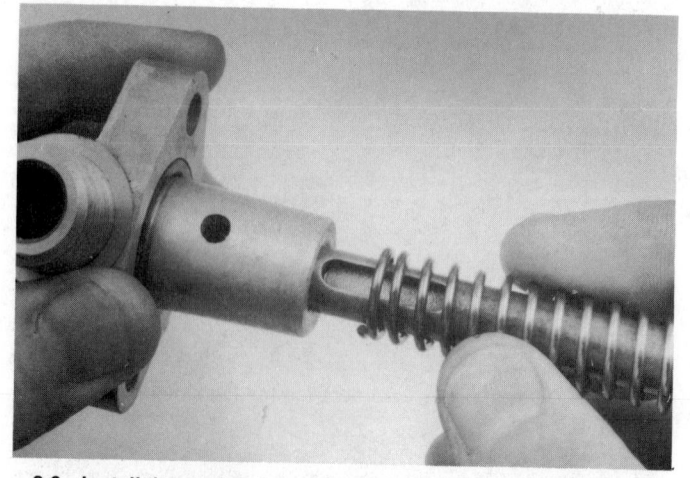

8.6   Install the pushrod and spring part-way into the tensioner body, align the groove in the pushrod with the hole in the tensioner body, depress the pushrod and install the pin

12   Clean the mating surfaces of the cylinder head and the valve cover with lacquer thinner, acetone or brake system cleaner. Apply a thin film of RTV sealant to the half-circle cutouts on each side of the head **(see illustration)**.

13   Install the gasket to the cover. Position the cover on the cylinder head, making sure the gasket doesn't slip out of place.

14   Check the rubber seals on the valve cover bolts, replacing them if necessary. Install the bolts, tightening them evenly, to the torque listed in this Chapter's Specifications.

15   The remainder of installation is the reverse of removal. Fill the cooling system with the recommended type and amount of coolant (see Chapter 1).

8   Camshaft chain tensioner – removal and installation

Refer to illustrations 8.3, 8.5, 8.6 and 8.9
Note: *The camshaft chain tensioner can be removed with the engine in the frame. If the engine has been removed, ignore the steps which don't apply.*

Removal

1   Set the bike on its centerstand.
2   Remove the fuel tank and carburetors (see Chapter 4).
3   Remove the tensioner cap, sealing washer and spring **(see illustration)**.
4   Remove the tensioner mounting bolts and detach it from the cylinder block. If the oil line is in the way, remove the two upper union bolts and carefully guide the tensioner out.
5   Depress the tensioner plunger and pull out the pin. Remove the tensioner components from the tensioner body **(see illustration)** and wash them with solvent.

Installation

6   Lubricate the friction surfaces of the components with moly-based grease. Place the spring on the pushrod and install the pushrod/spring assembly into the tensioner body. Push in on the rod, align the groove in the side of the rod with the pinhole in the side of the tensioner body, then insert the pin into the tensioner body, engaging it with the groove in the pushrod **(see illustration)**.
7   Check the O-ring on the tensioner body for cracks or hardening. It's a good idea to replace this O-ring as a matter of course.
8   Position the tensioner body on the cylinder block and install the bolts, tightening them securely.

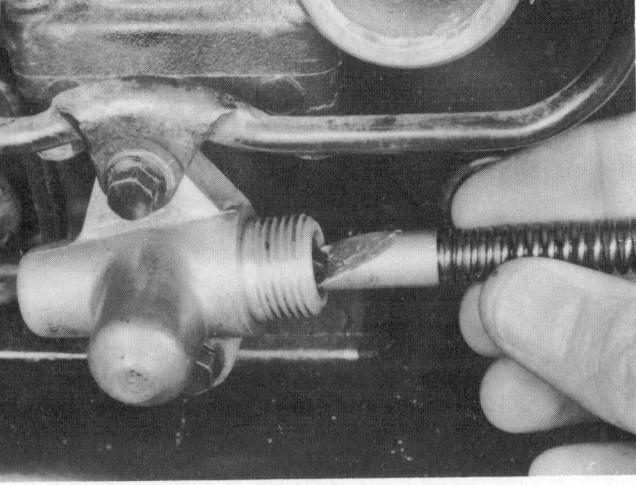

8.9   **Install the pushrod stop like this, so the tapered surface will contact the tapered surface of the pushrod**

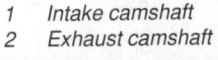

9.5   **Details of the camshafts and related components**

1	Intake camshaft	3	Camshaft bearing caps
2	Exhaust camshaft	4	Oil pipes

9.6   **The camshaft bearing caps have a number cast into them that corresponds to a number cast into the cylinder head (arrows) – make sure the caps are reinstalled in the same positions**

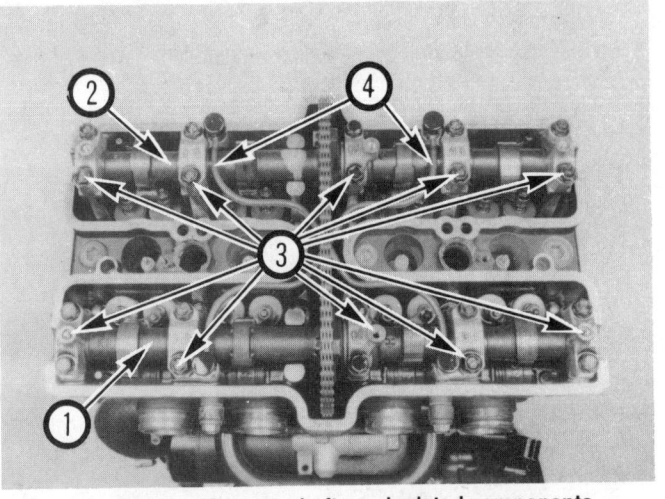

9.7a   **Lift up on the cam chain and carefully guide the camshaft out**

9   Install the pushrod stop into the chain tensioner, so its tapered portion mates with the tapered portion of the pushrod **(see illustration)**. The pushrod stop should protrude approximately 3/16-inch (5 mm) from the end of the tensioner housing. If it sticks out farther than this, the camshaft chain slack hasn't been taken up completely – if this is the case, slowly turn the crankshaft over in the normal direction of rotation (using a wrench placed on the crankshaft bolt under the pickup coil cover – see Chapter 5), pushing the pushrod stop in with your thumb.

10   Slide the spring over the pushrod stop. Install the tensioner cap and sealing washer, tightening it to the torque listed in this Chapter's Specifications.

11   The remainder of installation is the reverse of removal.

---

9   **Camshafts, rocker arm shafts and rocker arms – removal, inspection and installation**

Note: *This procedure can be performed with the engine in the frame.*

Camshafts

Removal

Refer to illustrations 9.5, 9.6, 9.7a, 9.7b and 9.8

1   Remove the valve cover following the procedure given in Section 7.

2   Remove the camshaft chain tensioner (see Section 8).

3   Remove the pickup coil cover (see Chapter 5).

4   Position the engine at Top Dead Center (TDC) for cylinders 1 and 4 (see Chapter 1, *Valve clearances – check and adjustment*, for the TDC locating procedure).

5   Remove the rubber caps and lift the oil pipes from the camshaft bearing caps **(see illustration)**. **Note:** *On early models, the oil pipes are secured by banjo bolts and sealing washers.*

6   Unscrew the bearing cap bolts for one of the camshafts, a little at a time, until they are all loose, then unscrew the bearing cap bolts for the other camshaft. **Caution:** *If the bearing cap bolts aren't loosened evenly, the camshaft may bind. Remove the bolts and lift off the bearing caps. Note the numbers on the bearing caps which correspond to the numbers on the cylinder head* **(see illustration)**. *When you reinstall the caps, be sure to install them in the correct positions.*

7   Pull up on the camshaft chain and carefully guide the camshaft out **(see illustrations)**. With the chain still held taut, remove the other camshaft. Look for marks on the camshafts. The intake camshaft should have an IN mark and the exhaust camshaft should have an EX mark. If you can't find these marks, label the camshafts to ensure they are installed in their original locations. **Note:** *Don't remove the sprockets from the camshafts unless absolutely necessary.*

2

9.7b   Exploded view of the camshafts and related components

1   Air suction valve cover
2   Air suction valve
3   Gasket
4   Valve cover
5   Valve cover bolt
6   Cap
7   Seal
8   Gasket
9   Locating dowels
10 Exhaust camshaft
11 Intake camshaft
12 Camshaft sprockets
13 Camshaft chain
14 Chain guides
15 Chain guide bracket
16 Tensioner pushrod
17 Tensioner spring
18 O-ring
19 Tensioner body
20 Tensioner pushrod stop
21 Spring
22 Sealing washer
23 Tensioner cap
24 Plug
25 O-ring
26 Locating pin
27 Rocker arm shafts
28 Valve adjusting screws
29 Rocker arms
30 Retaining springs
31 Intake valve and related components
32 Exhaust valve and related components

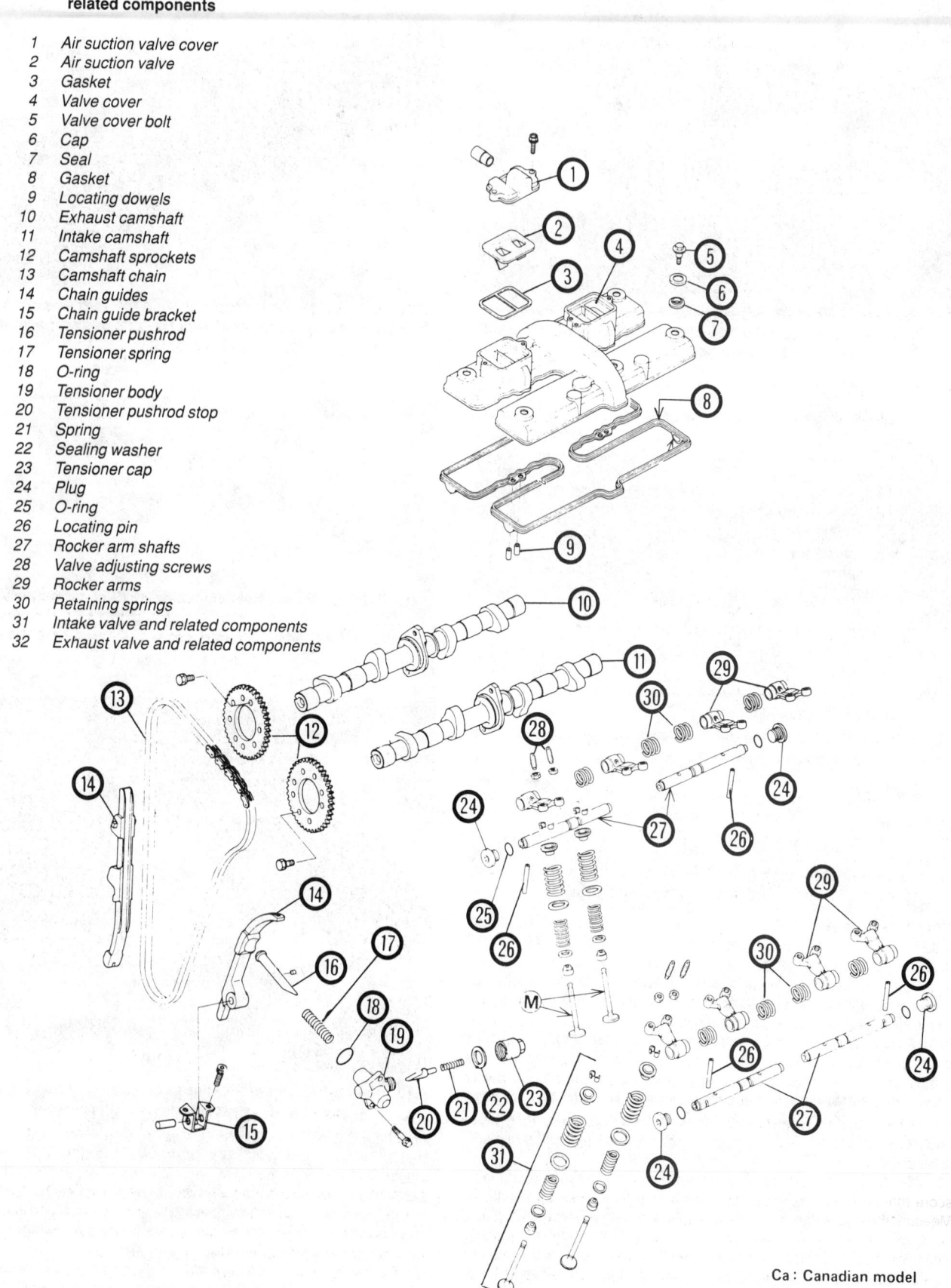

Ca : Canadian model

9.8 While the camshafts are out, wire the cam chain to another component to keep tension on it

9.10a Check the lobes of the camshaft for wear – here's a good example of damage which will require replacement (or repair) of the camshaft

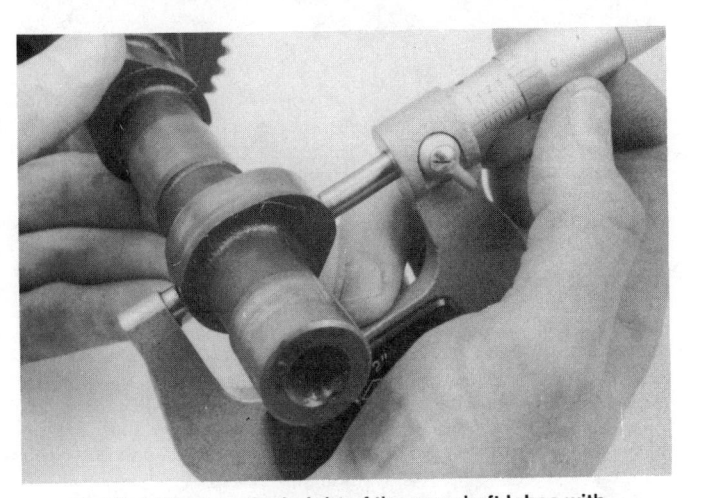

9.10b Measure the height of the camshaft lobes with a micrometer

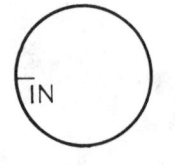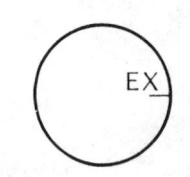

9.11 When installing the camshafts, the IN and EX marks on the camshaft sprockets should be positioned like this, with the marks aligned with the machined surface of the cylinder head

2

8   While the camshafts are out, don't allow the chain to go slack – if you do, it will become detached from the gear on the crankshaft and may bind between the crankshaft and case, which could cause damage to these components. Wire the chain to another component to prevent it from dropping down **(see illustration)**. Also, cover the top of the cylinder head with a rag to prevent foreign objects from falling into the engine.

Inspection
Refer to illustrations 9.10a, 9.10b, 9.11, 9.12, 9.13, 9.15a and 9.15b

Note: *Before replacing camshafts or the cylinder head and bearing caps because of damage, check with local machine shops specializing in motorcycle engine work. In the case of the camshafts, it may be possible for cam lobes to be welded, reground and hardened, at a cost far lower than that of a new camshaft. If the bearing surfaces in the cylinder head are damaged, it may be possible for them to be bored out to accept bearing inserts. Due to the cost of a new cylinder head it is recommended that all options be explored before condemning it as trash!*

9   Inspect the cam bearing surfaces of the head and the bearing caps. Look for score marks, deep scratches and evidence of spalling (a pitted appearance).

10   Check the camshaft lobes for heat discoloration (blue appearance), score marks, chipped areas, flat spots and spalling **(see illustration)**. Measure the height of each lobe with a micrometer **(see illustration)** and compare the results to the minimum lobe height listed in this Chapter's Specifications. If damage is noted or wear is excessive, the camshaft must be replaced. Also, be sure to check the condition of the rocker arms, as described later in this Section.

9.12 Position a strip of Plastigage on each cam bearing journal, parallel with the centerline of the camshaft

11   Next, check the camshaft bearing oil clearances. Clean the camshafts, the bearing surfaces in the cylinder head and the bearing caps with a clean, lint-free cloth, then lay the cams in place in the cylinder head, with the IN and EX marks on the gears facing away from each other and level with the valve cover gasket surface of the cylinder head **(see illustration)**. Engage the cam chain with the cam gears, so the camshafts don't turn as the bearing caps are tightened.

12   Cut ten strips of Plastigage (type HPG-1) and lay one piece on each bearing journal, parallel with the camshaft centerline **(see illustration)**.

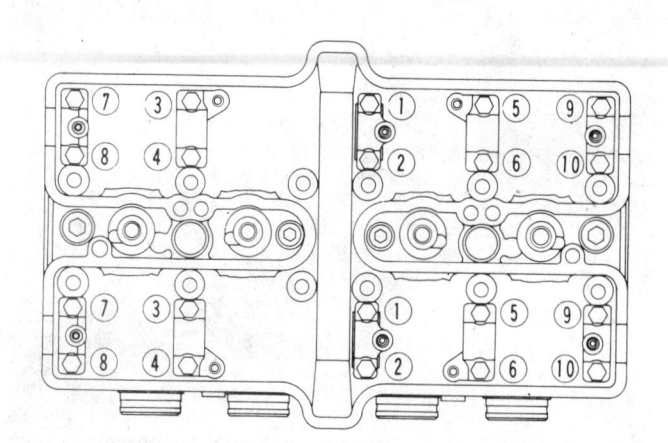

9.13   Camshaft bearing cap tightening sequence

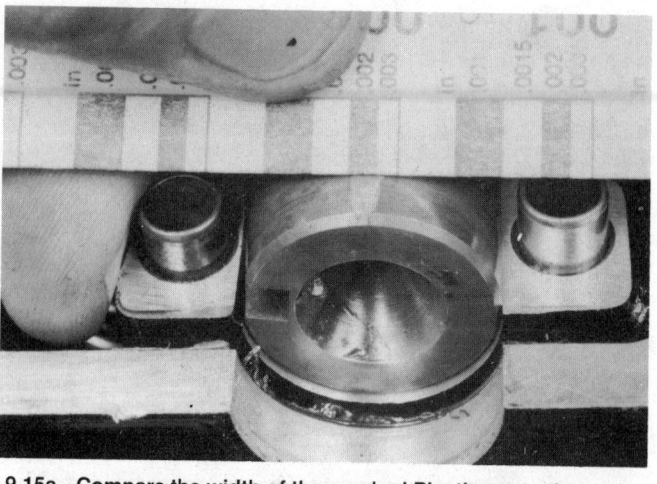

9.15a   Compare the width of the crushed Plastigage to the scale on the Plastigage container to obtain the clearance

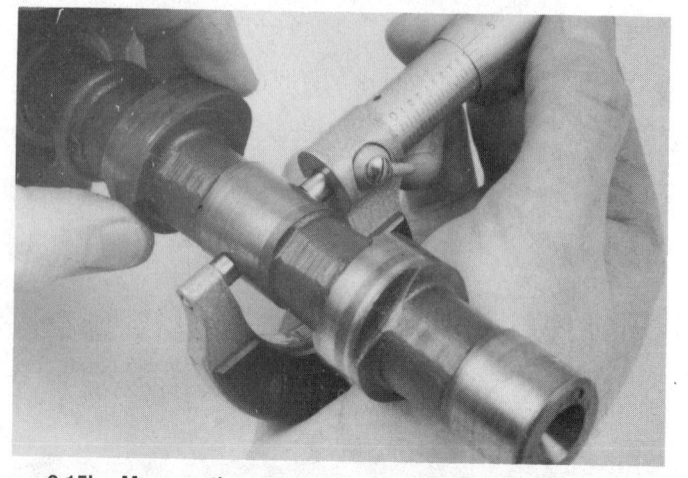

9.15b   Measure the cam bearing journal with a micrometer

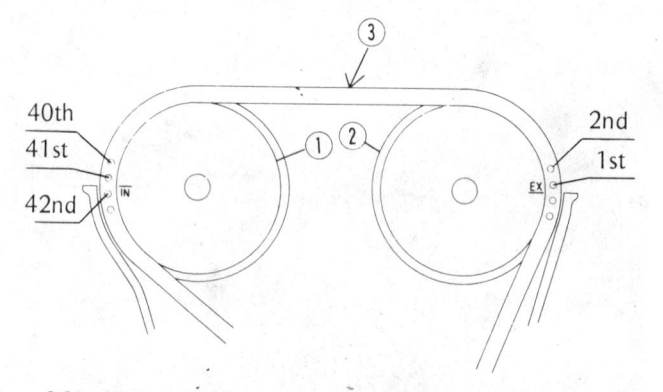

9.21   With no slack in the camshaft chain, there should be forty-one link pins present between the EX and IN marks on the cam sprockets

1   Intake sprocket
2   Exhaust sprocket
3   There should be no slack in this area when counting the link pins

13   Install the bearing caps in their proper positions (the arrows on the caps must face toward the front of the engine and the numbers on the caps must correspond with the numbers on the cylinder head) and install the bolts. Tighten the bolts in three steps, following the recommended sequence **(see illustration)**, to the torque listed in this Chapter's Specifications. While doing this, Do not let the camshafts rotate!

14   Now unscrew the bolts, a little at a time, and carefully lift off the bearing caps.

15   To determine the oil clearance, compare the crushed Plastigage (at its widest point) on each journal to the scale printed on the Plastigage container **(see illustration)**. Compare the results to this Chapter's Specifications. If the oil clearance is greater than specified, measure the diameter of the cam bearing journal with a micrometer **(see illustration)**. If the journal diameter is less than the specified limit, replace the camshaft with a new one and recheck the clearance. If the clearance is still too great, replace the cylinder head and bearing caps with new parts (see the Note that precedes Step 9).

16   Except in cases of oil starvation, the camshaft chain wears very little.. If the chain has stretched excessively, which makes it difficult to maintain proper tension, replace it with a new one (see Section 28).

17   Check the sprockets for wear, cracks and other damage, replacing them if necessary. If the sprockets are worn, the chain is also worn, and also the sprocket on the crankshaft (which can only be remedied by replacing the crankshaft). If wear this severe is apparent, the entire engine should be disassembled for inspection.

18   Check the chain guides for wear or damage. If they are worn or damaged, the chain is worn out or improperly adjusted. Replacement of the guides requires removal of the cylinder head and cylinder block.

Installation

Refer to illustration 9.21

19   Make sure the bearing surfaces in the cylinder head and the bearing caps are clean, then apply a light coat of engine assembly lube or moly-based grease to each of them.

20   Apply a coat of moly-based grease to the camshaft lobes. Make sure the camshaft bearing journals are clean, then lay the camshafts in the cylinder head (do not mix them up), ensuring the marks on the cam sprockets are aligned properly **(see illustration 9.11)**.

21   Make sure the timing marks are aligned as described in Step 11, then mesh the chain with the camshaft sprockets. Count the number of chain link pins between the EX mark and the IN mark **(see illustration)**. There should be no slack in the chain between the two sprockets.

22   Carefully set the bearing caps in place (arrows pointing toward the front of the engine and in their proper positions) **(see illustration 9.6)** and install the bolts. Tighten them in three steps, in the recommended sequence **(see illustration 9.13)**, to the torque listed in this Chapter's Specifications.

23   Insert your finger or a wood dowel into the cam chain tensioner hole and apply pressure to the cam chain. Check the timing marks to make sure they are aligned (see Step 11) and there are still the correct number of link pins between the EX and IN marks on the cam sprockets. If necessary, change the position of the sprocket(s) on the chain to bring all of the marks

9.28 Remove the rocker arm shaft locating pin

9.29 Unscrew the rocker arm shaft plug – be sure to check the condition of the O-ring under the head of the plug

9.30 Thread a bolt of the proper size and thread pitch into the rocker arm shaft and use it as a handle to pull the shaft out

9.31 After the shaft has been removed, remove the rocker arm and retaining spring – note how the springs are nearer to the center of the cylinder head

into alignment. **Caution:** *If the marks are not aligned exactly as described, the valve timing will be incorrect and the valves may contact the pistons, causing extensive damage to the engine.*

24 Remove the cap, spring and pushrod stop from the cam chain tensioner, then install the tensioner as described in Section 8.

25 Adjust the valve clearances (see Chapter 1).

26 The remainder of installation is the reverse of removal.

Rocker arm shafts and rocker arms

Removal

Refer to illustrations 9.28, 9.29, 9.30, 9.31, 9.33, 9.34a, 9.34b, 9.34c and 9.36

27 Remove the camshafts following the procedure given above. Be sure to keep tension on the camshaft chain.

28 Remove the rocker arm shaft locating pins **(see illustration)**.

29 Remove the rocker shaft plugs **(see illustration)**.

30 Thread a bolt (8M x 1.8 x 30 mm) into the end of one of the rocker arm shafts and use it as a handle to pull the shaft out **(see illustration)**.

31 Remove the rocker arms and springs **(see illustration)**.

32 Repeat the above Steps to remove the other rocker arm shafts and rocker arms. Keep all of the parts in order so they can be reinstalled in their original locations.

Inspection

Refer to illustrations 9.33, 9.34a, 9.34b and 9.34c

33 Clean all of the components with solvent and dry them off. Blow through the oil passages in the rocker arms with compressed air, if avail-

able. Inspect the rocker arm faces for pits, spalling, score marks and rough spots **(see illustration)**. Check the rocker arm-to-shaft contact areas and the adjusting screws, as well. Look for cracks in each rocker arm. If the faces of the rocker arms are damaged, the rocker arms and the camshafts should be replaced as a set.

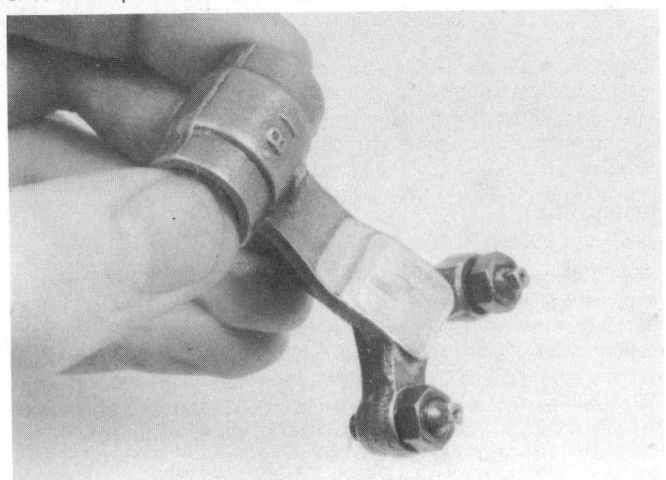

9.33 Inspect the rocker arms, especially the faces that contact the cam lobes, for wear

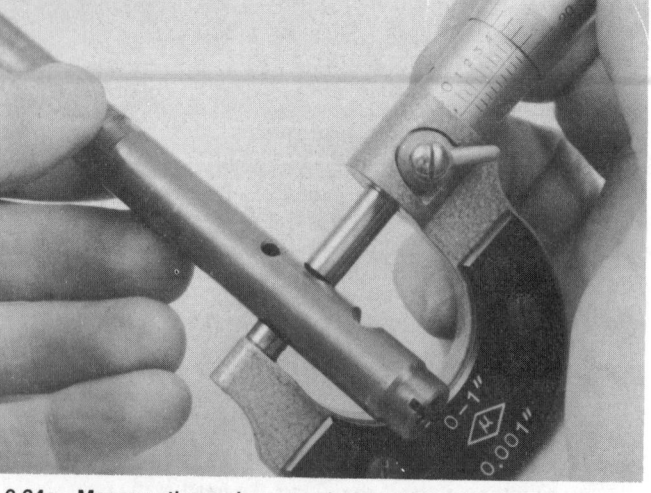

9.34a   Measure the rocker arm shafts with a micrometer, in the area where the rocker arms ride

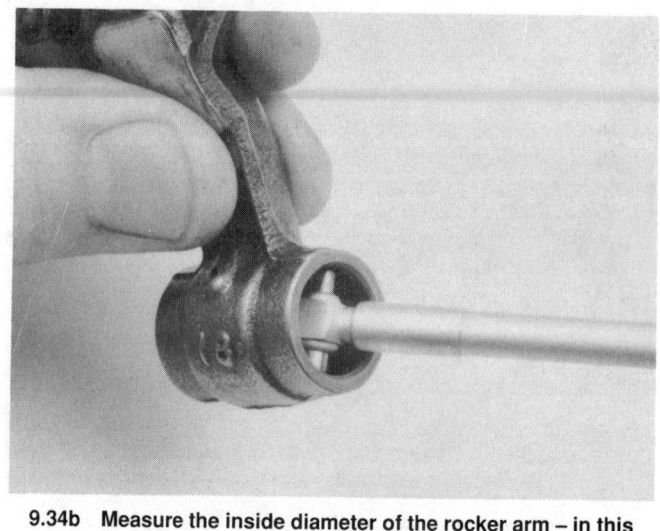

9.34b   Measure the inside diameter of the rocker arm – in this case, a telescoping gauge is expanded against the bore of the rocker arm, then locked . . .

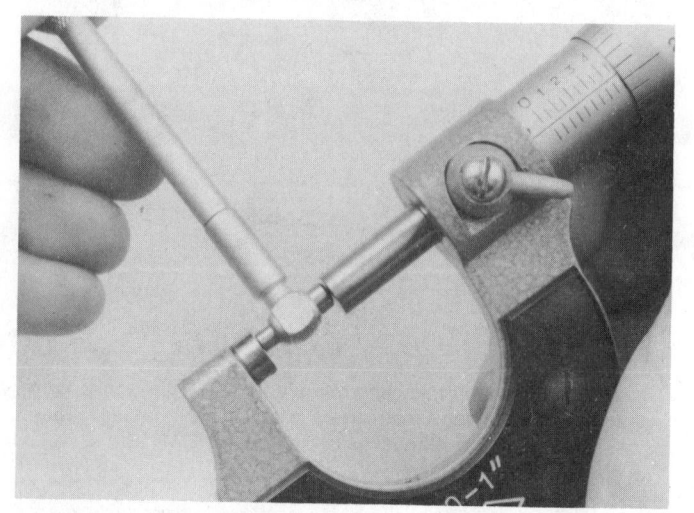

9.34c   . . . and a micrometer is used to measure the gauge

9.36   When installing the rocker arm shafts, align the notch in the shaft with the locating pin hole in the cylinder head (arrows)

34   Measure the diameter of the rocker arm shafts, in the area where the rocker arms ride, and compare the results with this Chapter's Specifications **(see illustration)**. Also measure the inside diameter of the rocker arms **(see illustrations)** and compare the results with this Chapter's Specifications. If either the shaft or the rocker arms are worn beyond the specified limits, replace them as a set.

Installation

Refer to illustration 9.36

35   Position a rocker arm and spring in the cylinder head, with the spring toward the center of the cylinder head **(see illustration 9.31)**.
36   Lubricate the rocker arm shaft with engine oil and slide it into the cylinder head and through the rocker arm and spring. Make sure the notch is aligned with the locating pin hole **(see illustration)**. Install the locating pin.
37   Check the O-ring under the head of the rocker arm shaft plug, replacing it if necessary. Install the plug, tightening it to the torque listed in this Chapter's Specifications.
38   Repeat Steps 35, 36 and 37 to install the remaining rocker arms and shafts.
39   Install the camshafts following the procedure described earlier in this Section.

10   Cylinder head – removal and installation

Caution: *The engine must be completely cool before beginning this procedure, or the cylinder head may become warped.*
Note: *This procedure can be performed with the engine in the frame. If the engine has been removed, ignore the steps which don't apply.*

Removal

Refer to illustrations 10.6 and 10.8
1   Set the bike on its centerstand.
2   Remove the valve cover following the procedure given in Section 7.
3   Remove the radiator (see Chapter 3).
4   Remove the exhaust system (see Chapter 4).
5   Remove the camshafts (see Section 9).
6   Remove the cylinder block-to-cylinder head bolts **(see illustration)**. There are two on the rear side of the cylinder head and two on the front side of the cylinder head.
7   Loosen the cylinder head nuts, a little at a time, using the reverse order of the tightening sequence **(see illustration 10.17)**.
8   Remove the oil pipe banjo bolts and washers from the rear of the cylinder head **(see illustration)**.

10.6   Remove the cylinder block-to-cylinder head bolts (arrows)
(rear bolts shown)

10.8   Remove the oil pipe banjo bolts (arrows)

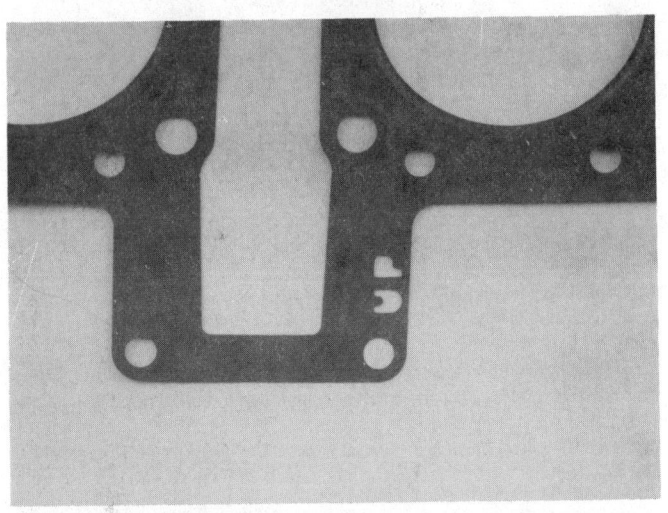

10.14   When installing the cylinder head gasket, make sure the
UP mark is situated on the right-hand side of the engine (by the
no. 3 cylinder)

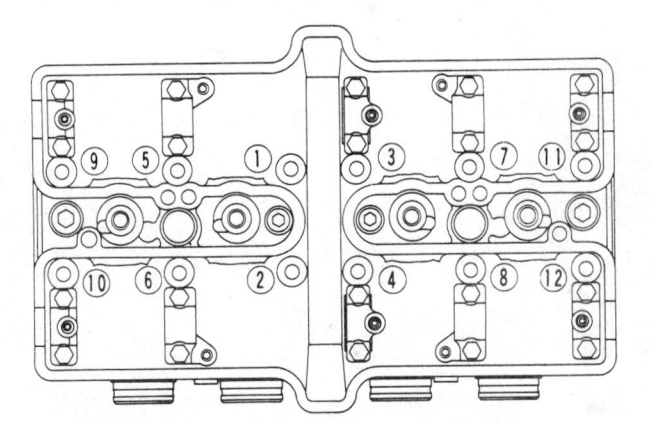

10.17   Cylinder head nut tightening sequence

9   Pull the cylinder head off the cylinder block. If the head is stuck, tap around the side of the head with a rubber mallet to jar it loose, or use two wooden dowels inserted into the intake or exhaust ports to lever the head off. Don't attempt to pry the head off by inserting a screwdriver between the head and the cylinder block – you'll damage the sealing surfaces.

10   Stuff a clean rag into the cam chain tunnel to prevent the entry of debris. Remove all of the washers from their seats, using a pair of needle-nose pliers.

11   Remove the two dowel pins from the cylinder block (see illustration).

12   Check the cylinder head gasket and the mating surfaces on the cylinder head and block for leakage, which could indicate warpage. Refer to Section 12 and check the flatness of the cylinder head.

13   Clean all traces of old gasket material from the cylinder head and block. Be careful not to let any of the gasket material fall into the crankcase, the cylinder bores or the water passages.

Installation

Refer to illustrations 10.14 and 10.17

14   Install the two dowel pins over their studs, then lay the new gasket in place on the cylinder block. Make sure the UP mark on the gasket is positioned on the right-hand side of the engine (see illustration). Never reuse the old gasket and don't use any type of gasket sealant.

15   Carefully lower the cylinder head over the studs. It is helpful to have an assistant support the camshaft chain with a piece of wire so it doesn't

fall and become kinked or detached from the crankshaft. When the head is resting against the cylinder block, wire the cam chain to another component to keep tension on it.

16   Lubricate both sides of the head nut washers with engine oil and place them over the head studs.

17   Install the head nuts. Using the proper sequence (see illustration), tighten the nuts to approximately half the torque listed in this Chapter's Specifications.

18   Using the same sequence, tighten the nuts to the torque listed in this Chapter's Specifications.

19   Install the four cylinder block-to-head bolts, tightening them to the initial torque, then to the final torque listed in this Chapter's Specifications.

20   Install the camshafts and the valve cover (see Sections 9 and 7).

21   Change the engine oil (see Chapter 1)

11   Valves/valve seats/valve guides – servicing

1   Because of the complex nature of this job and the special tools and equipment required, servicing of the valves, the valve seats and the valve guides (commonly known as a valve job) is best left to a professional.

2   The home mechanic can, however, remove and disassemble the head, do the initial cleaning and inspection, then reassemble and deliver the head to a dealer service department or properly equipped motorcycle repair shop for the actual valve servicing. Refer to Section 12 for those procedures.

12.7a   Compressing the valve springs with a valve spring compressor

12.7b   Remove the keepers with needle-nose pliers or tweezers

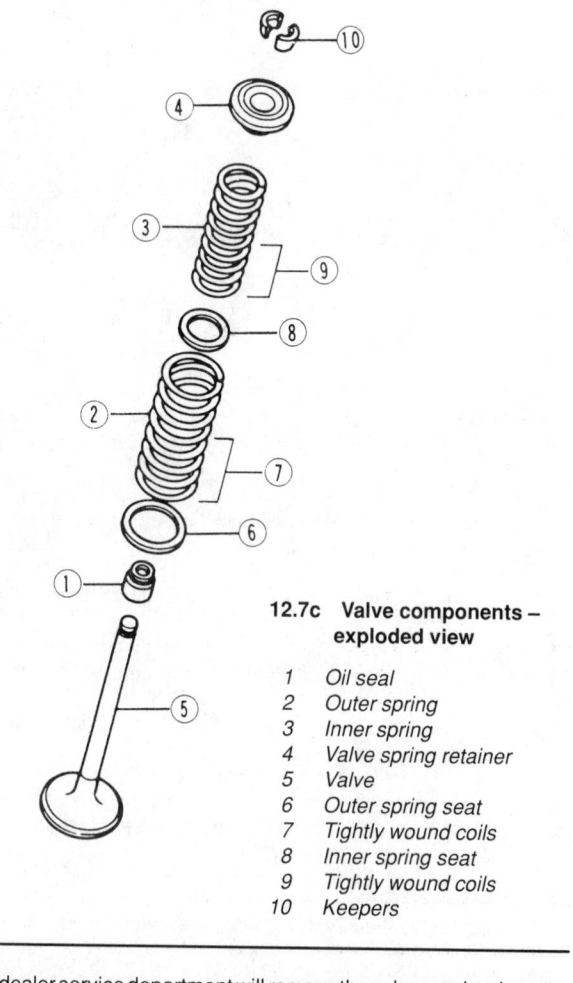

12.7c   Valve components – exploded view

1   *Oil seal*
2   *Outer spring*
3   *Inner spring*
4   *Valve spring retainer*
5   *Valve*
6   *Outer spring seat*
7   *Tightly wound coils*
8   *Inner spring seat*
9   *Tightly wound coils*
10   *Keepers*

3   The dealer service department will remove the valves and springs, recondition or replace the valves and valve seats, replace the valve guides, check and replace the valve springs, spring retainers and keepers (as necessary), replace the valve seals with new ones and reassemble the valve components.

4   After the valve job has been performed, the head will be in like-new condition. When the head is returned, be sure to clean it again very thoroughly before installation on the engine to remove any metal particles or

abrasive grit that may still be present from the valve service operations. Use compressed air, if available, to blow out all the holes and passages.

---

12   Cylinder head and valves – disassembly, inspection and reassembly

1   As mentioned in the previous Section, valve servicing and valve guide replacement should be left to a dealer service department or motorcycle repair shop. However, disassembly, cleaning and inspection of the valves and related components can be done (if the necessary special tools are available) by the home mechanic. This way no expense is incurred if the inspection reveals that service work is not required at this time.

2   To properly disassemble the valve components without the risk of damaging them, a valve spring compressor is absolutely necessary. If the special tool is not available, have a dealer service department or motorcycle repair shop handle the entire process of disassembly, inspection, service or repair (if required) and reassembly of the valves.

Disassembly

Refer to illustrations 12.7a, 12.7b, 12.7c and 12.7d

3   Remove the rocker arm shafts and rocker arms (see Section 9). Store the components in such a way that they can be returned to their original locations without getting mixed up (labeled plastic bags work well).

4   Before the valves are removed, scrape away any traces of gasket material from the head gasket sealing surface. Work slowly and do not nick or gouge the soft aluminum of the head. Gasket removing solvents, which work very well, are available at most motorcycle shops and auto parts stores.

5   Carefully scrape all carbon deposits out of the combustion chamber area. A hand held wire brush or a piece of fine emery cloth can be used once the majority of deposits have been scraped away. Do not use a wire brush mounted in a drill motor, or one with extremely stiff bristles, as the head material is soft and may be eroded away or scratched by the wire brush.

6   Before proceeding, arrange to label and store the valves along with their related components so they can be kept separate and reinstalled in the same valve guides they are removed from (again, plastic bags work well for this).

7   Compress the valve spring on the first valve with a spring compressor, then remove the keepers (**see illustrations**) and the retainer from the valve assembly. Do not compress the springs any more than is absolutely necessary. Carefully release the valve spring compressor and remove the springs and the valve from the head (**see illustration**). If the valve binds in the guide (won't pull through), push it back into the head and deburr the area around the keeper groove with a very fine file or whetstone (**see illustration**).

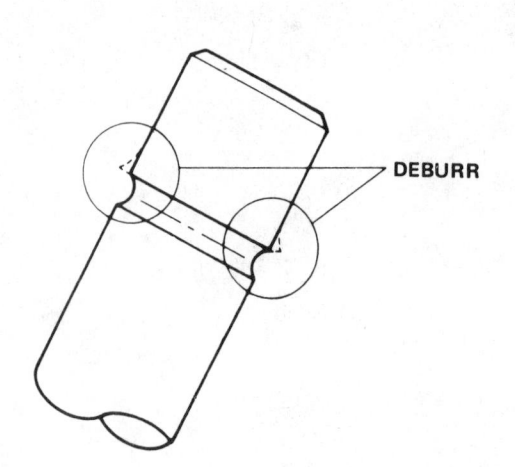

12.7d   If the valve binds in the guide, deburr the area above the keeper groove

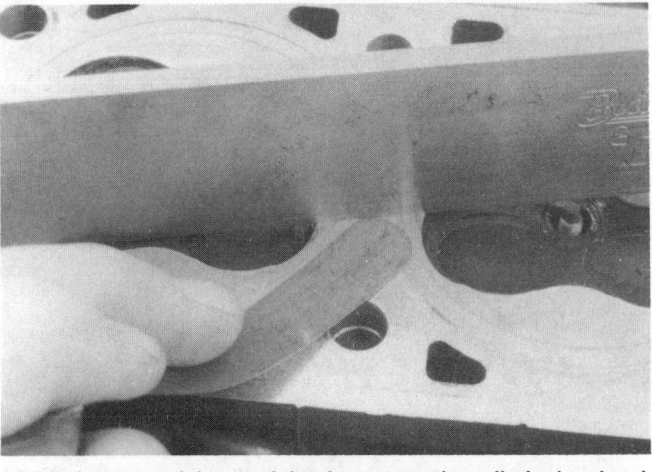

12.14   Lay a precision straightedge across the cylinder head and try to slide a feeler gauge of the specified thickness (equal to the maximum allowable warpage) under it

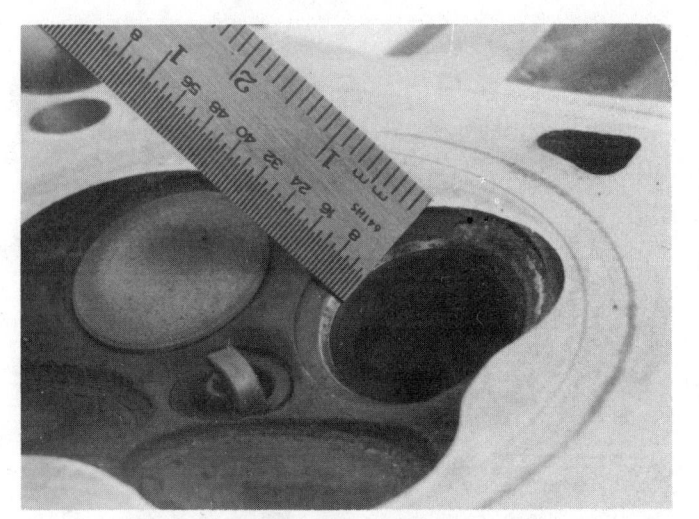

12.15   Measuring the valve seat width

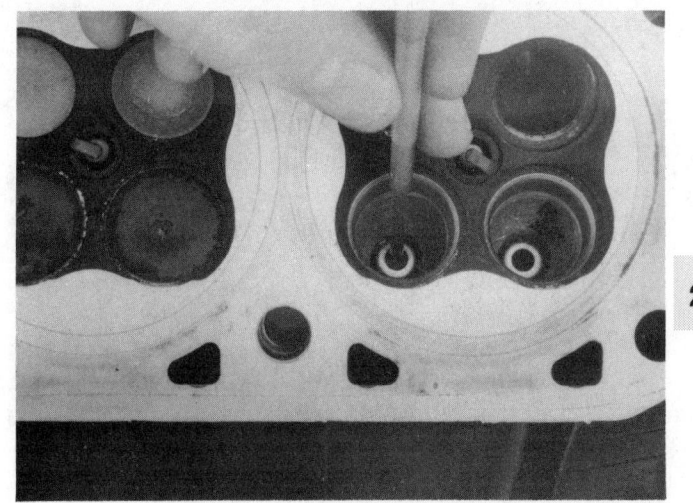

12.16a   Insert a small hole gauge into the valve guide and expand it so there is a slight drag when it's pulled out

2

8   Repeat the procedure for the remaining valves. Remember to keep the parts for each valve together so they can be reinstalled in the same location.

9   Once the valves have been removed and labeled, pull off the valve stem seals with pliers and discard them (the old seals should never be reused), then remove the spring seats.

10   Next, clean the cylinder head with solvent and dry it thoroughly. Compressed air will speed the drying process and ensure that all holes and recessed areas are clean.

11   Clean all of the valve springs, keepers, retainers and spring seats with solvent and dry them thoroughly. Do the parts from one valve at a time so that no mixing of parts between valves occurs.

12   Scrape off any deposits that may have formed on the valve, then use a motorized wire brush to remove deposits from the valve heads and stems. Again, make sure the valves do not get mixed up.

Inspection

Refer to illustrations 12.14, 12.15, 12.16a, 12.16b, 12.17, 12.18a, 12.18b, 12.19a and 12.19b

13   Inspect the head very carefully for cracks and other damage. If cracks are found, a new head will be required. Check the cam bearing surfaces for wear and evidence of seizure. Check the camshafts and rocker arms for wear as well (see Section 9).

14   Using a precision straightedge and a feeler gauge, check the head

gasket mating surface for warpage. Lay the straightedge lengthwise, across the head and diagonally (corner-to-corner), intersecting the head bolt holes, and try to slip a 0.002 in (0.05 mm) feeler gauge under it, on either side of each combustion chamber **(see illustration)**. If the feeler gauge can be inserted between the head and the straightedge, the head is warped and must either be machined or, if warpage is excessive, replaced with a new one.

15   Examine the valve seats in each of the combustion chambers. If they are pitted, cracked or burned, the head will require valve service that is beyond the scope of the home mechanic. Measure the valve seat width **(see illustration)** and compare it to this Chapter's Specifications. If it is not within the specified range, or if it varies around its circumference, valve service work is required.

16   Clean the valve guides to remove any carbon buildup, then measure the inside diameters of the guides (at both ends and the center of the guide) with a small hole gauge and a 0-to-1-inch micrometer **(see illustrations)**. Record the measurements for future reference. These measurements, along with the valve stem diameter measurements, will enable you to compute the valve stem-to-guide clearance. This clearance, when compared to the Specifications, will be one factor that will determine the extent of the valve service work required. The guides are measured at the ends and at the center to determine if they are worn in a bell-mouth pattern (more wear at the ends). If they are, guide replacement is an absolute must.

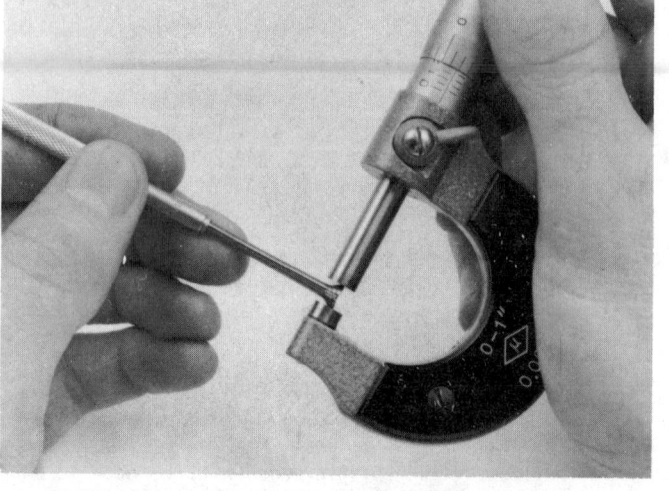

12.16b   Measure the small hole gauge with a micrometer

12.17   Check the valve face, stem and keeper groove for signs of wear and damage

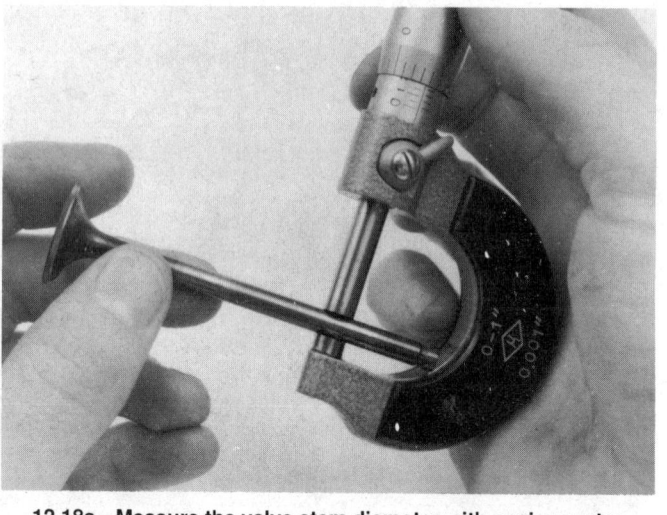

12.18a   Measure the valve stem diameter with a micrometer

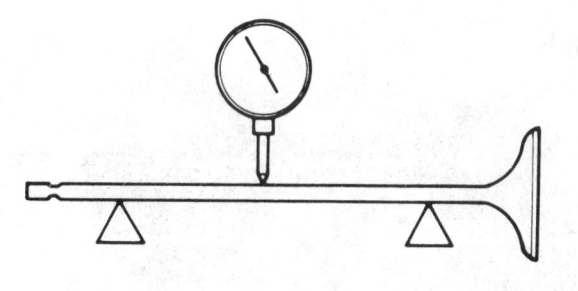

12.18b   Check the valve stem for bends with a V-block (or blocks, as shown here) and a dial indicator

Reassembly

Refer to illustrations 12.23, 12.24a, 12.24b, 12.24c and 12.27

17   Carefully inspect each valve face for cracks, pits and burned spots. Check the valve stem and the keeper groove area for cracks **(see illustration)**. Rotate the valve and check for any obvious indication that it is bent. Check the end of the stem for pitting and excessive wear and make sure the bevel is the specified width. The presence of any of the above conditions indicates the need for valve servicing.

18   Measure the valve stem diameter **(see illustration)**. By subtracting the stem diameter from the valve guide diameter, the valve stem-to-guide clearance is obtained. If the stem-to-guide clearance is greater than listed in this Chapter's Specifications, the guides and valves will have to be replaced with new ones. Also check the valve stem for bending. Set the valve in a V-block with a dial indicator touching the middle of the stem **(see illustration)**. Rotate the valve and note the reading on the gauge. If the stem runout exceeds the value listed in this Chapter's Specifications, replace the valve.

19   Check the end of each valve spring for wear and pitting. Measure the free length **(see illustration)** and compare it to this Chapter's Specifications. Any springs that are shorter than specified have sagged and should not be reused. Stand the spring on a flat surface and check it for squareness **(see illustration)**.

20   Check the spring retainers and keepers for obvious wear and cracks. Any questionable parts should not be reused, as extensive damage will occur in the event of failure during engine operation.

21   If the inspection indicates that no service work is required, the valve components can be reinstalled in the head.

22   Before installing the valves in the head, they should be lapped to ensure a positive seal between the valves and seats. This procedure requires fine valve lapping compound (available at auto parts stores) and a valve lapping tool. If a lapping tool is not available, a piece of rubber or plastic hose can be slipped over the valve stem (after the valve has been installed in the guide) and used to turn the valve.

23   Apply a small amount of fine lapping compound to the valve face **(see illustration)**, then slip the valve into the guide. **Note:** *Make sure the valve is installed in the correct guide and be careful not to get any lapping compound on the valve stem.*

24   Attach the lapping tool (or hose) to the valve and rotate the tool between the palms of your hands. Use a back-and-forth motion rather than a circular motion **(see illustration)**. Lift the valve off the seat and turn it at regular intervals to distribute the lapping compound properly. Continue the lapping procedure until the valve face and seat contact area is of uniform width and unbroken around the entire circumference of the valve face and seat **(see illustrations)**.

25   Carefully remove the valve from the guide and wipe off all traces of lapping compound. Use solvent to clean the valve and wipe the seat area thoroughly with a solvent soaked cloth. Repeat the procedure for the remaining valves.

26   Lay the spring seats in place in the cylinder head, then install new valve stem seals on each of the guides. Use an appropriate size deep socket to push the seals into place until they are properly seated. Don't twist or cock them, or they will not seal properly against the valve stems. Also, don't remove them again or they will be damaged.

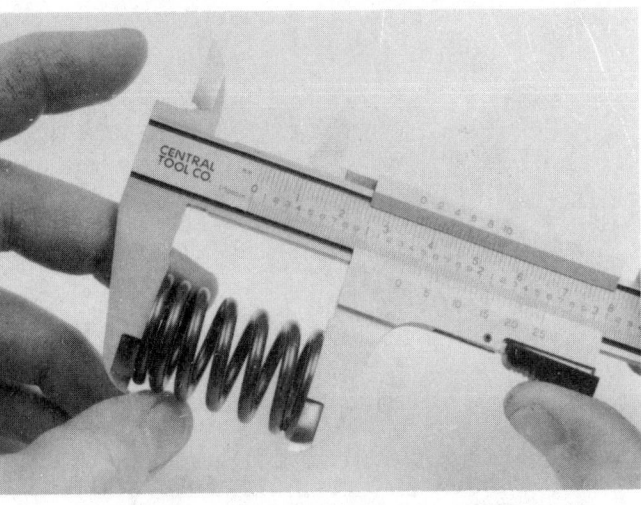

12.19a Measure the free length of the valve springs

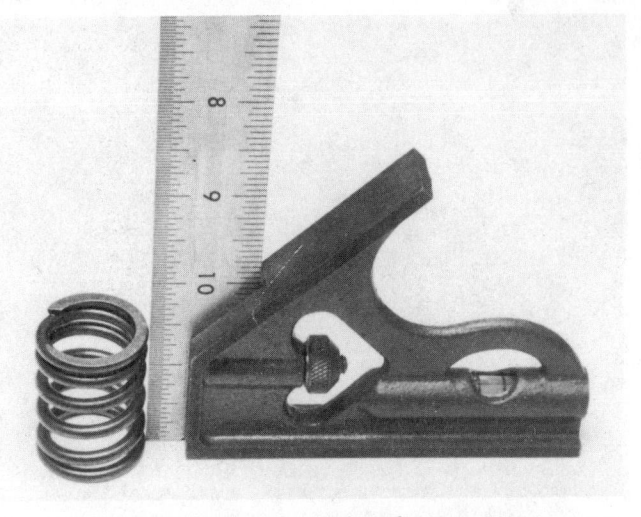

12.19b Check the valve springs for squareness

12.23 Apply the lapping compound very sparingly, in small dabs, to the valve face only

12.24a A hose, pushed over the end of the valve, can be used to turn the valve back and forth

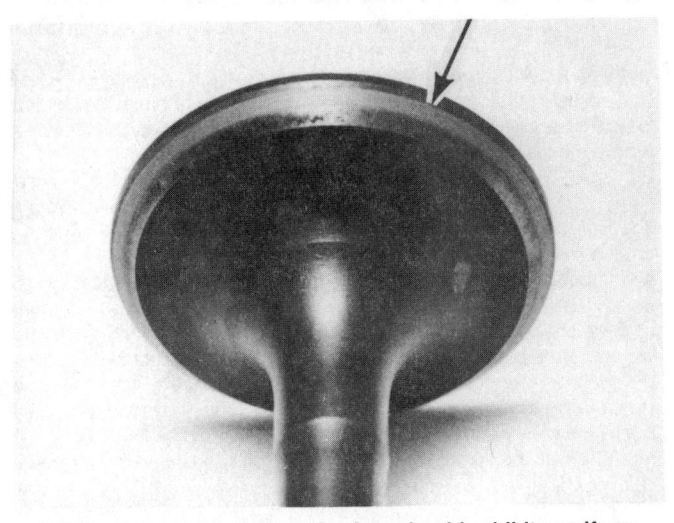

12.24b After lapping, the valve face should exhibit a uniform, unbroken contact pattern (arrow) . . .

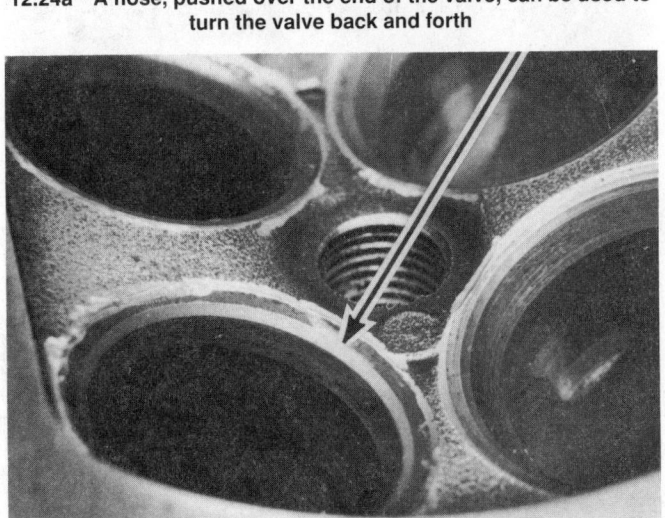

12.24c . . . and the seat should be the specified width (arrow), with a smooth, unbroken appearance

2

12.27   A small dab of grease will help hold the keepers in place on the valve while the spring is released

13.3   Remove the oil pipe bolt and the cylinder block-to-crankcase nuts (arrows)

13.4   Lift the cam chain front guide out

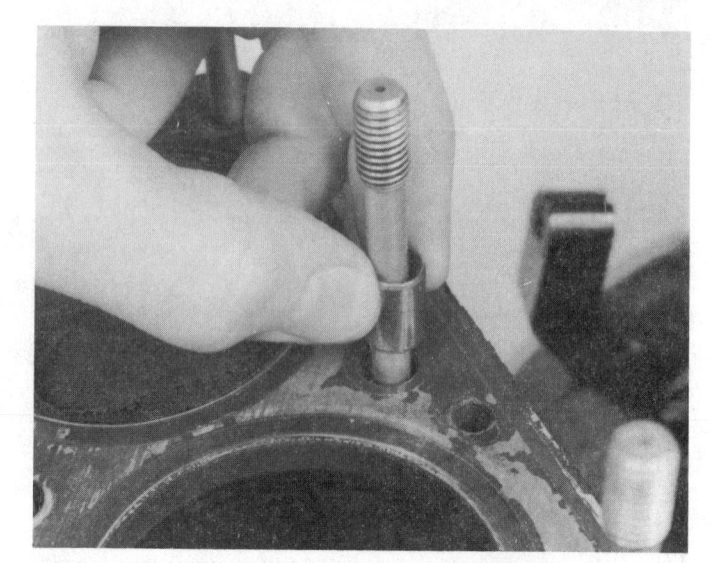

13.6   Remove the dowel pins from the crankcase

27   Coat the valve stems with assembly lube or moly-based grease, then install one of them into its guide. Next, install the springs and retainers, compress the springs and install the keepers. **Note:** *Install the springs with the tightly wound coils at the bottom (next to the spring seat). When compressing the springs with the valve spring compressor, depress them only as far as is absolutely necessary to slip the keepers into place. Apply a small amount of grease to the keepers* **(see illustration)** *to help hold them in place as the pressure is released from the springs. Make certain that the keepers are securely locked in their retaining grooves.*
28   Support the cylinder head on blocks so the valves can't contact the workbench top, then very gently tap each of the valve stems with a soft-faced hammer. This will help seat the keepers in their grooves.
29   Once all of the valves have been installed in the head, check for proper valve sealing by pouring a small amount of solvent into each of the valve ports. If the solvent leaks past the valve(s) into the combustion chamber area, disassemble the valve(s) and repeat the lapping procedure, then re-install the valve(s) and repeat the check. Repeat the procedure until a satisfactory seal is obtained.

---

13   Cylinder block – removal, inspection and installation

Removal

Refer to illustrations 13.3, 13.4 and 13.6

1   Following the procedure given in Section 10, remove the cylinder head. Make sure the crankshaft is positioned at Top Dead Center (TDC) for cylinders 1 and 4.
2   Remove the water pipe from the rear of the cylinder head (see Chapter 3).
3   Remove the oil pipe mounting bolt and the cylinder block-to-crankcase nuts **(see illustration)**.
4   Lift out the camshaft chain front guide **(see illustration)**.
5   Lift the cylinder block straight up to remove it. If it's stuck, tap around its perimeter with a soft-faced hammer. Don't attempt to pry between the block and the crankcase, as you will ruin the sealing surfaces.
6   Remove the dowel pins from the mating surface of the crankcase **(see illustration)**. Be careful not to let these drop into the engine. Stuff rags around the pistons and remove the gasket and all traces of old gasket material from the surfaces of the cylinder block and the cylinder head.

Inspection

Refer to illustration 13.8

Caution: *Don't attempt to separate the liners from the cylinder block.*

7   Check the cylinder walls carefully for scratches and score marks.
8   Using the appropriate precision measuring tools, check each cylinder's diameter near the top, center and bottom of the cylinder bore, parallel

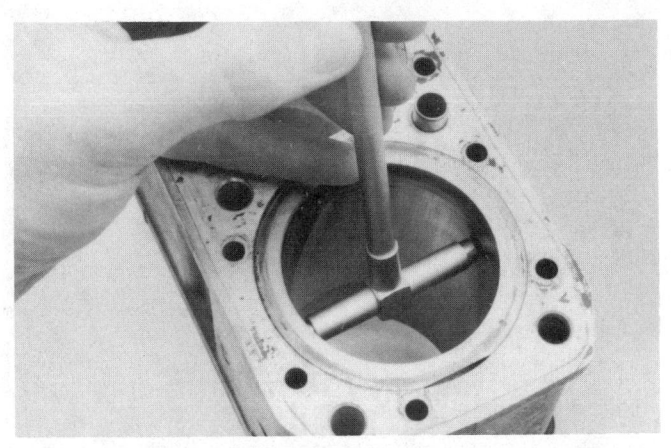

13.8   Measure the cylinder bore with a telescoping gauge (then measure the gauge with a micrometer)

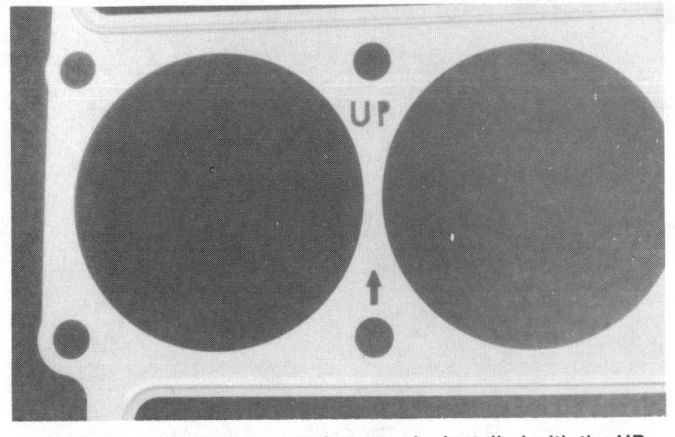

13.14   The cylinder base gasket must be installed with the UP mark on the right and the arrow pointing to the front of the engine

13.15   Slide rods under the pistons to support them as the cylinder block is lowered down

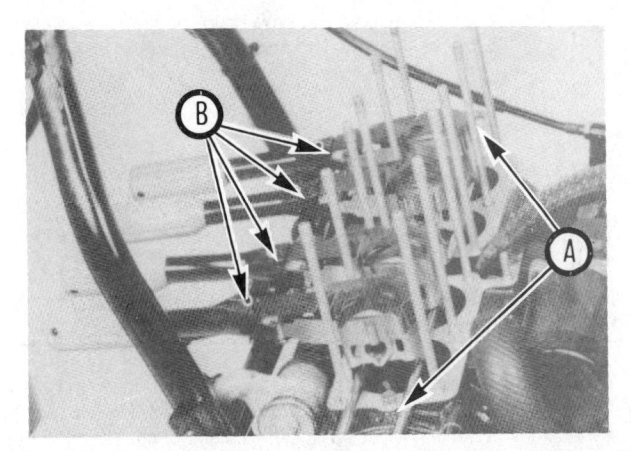

13.16   Compress the piston rings with piston ring compressors (shown here) or large hose clamps

A   Piston base (57001 – 147)   B   Piston ring compressor
                                          assembly (57001 – 1094

to the crankshaft axis **(see illustration)**. Next, measure each cylinder's diameter at the same three locations across the crankshaft axis. Compare the results to this Chapter's Specifications. If the cylinder walls are tapered, out-of-round, worn beyond the specified limits, or badly scuffed or scored, have them rebored and honed by a dealer service department or a motorcycle repair shop. If a rebore is done, oversize pistons and rings will be required as well. **Note:** *Kawasaki supplies pistons in one oversize only – +0.020 in (+0.5 mm).*

9   As an alternative, if the precision measuring tools are not available, a dealer service department or motorcycle repair shop will make the measurements and offer advice concerning servicing of the cylinders.

10   If they are in reasonably good condition and not worn to the outside of the limits, and if the piston-to-cylinder clearances can be maintained properly (see Section 14), then the cylinders do not have to be rebored; honing is all that is necessary.

11   To perform the honing operation you will need the proper size flexible hone with fine stones, or a "bottle brush" type hone, plenty of light oil or honing oil, some shop towels and an electric drill motor. Hold the cylinder block in a vise (cushioned with soft jaws or wood blocks) when performing the honing operation. Mount the hone in the drill motor, compress the stones and slip the hone into the cylinder. Lubricate the cylinder thoroughly, turn on the drill and move the hone up and down in the cylinder at a pace which will produce a fine crosshatch pattern on the cylinder wall with the crosshatch lines intersecting at approximately a 60-degree angle. Be sure to use plenty of lubricant and do not take off any more material than is absolutely necessary to produce the desired effect. Do not withdraw the hone from the cylinder while it is running. Instead, shut off the drill and continue moving the hone up and down in the cylinder until it comes to a complete stop, then compress the stones and withdraw the hone. Wipe

the oil out of the cylinder and repeat the procedure on the remaining cylinder. Remember, do not remove too much material from the cylinder wall. If you do not have the tools, or do not desire to perform the honing operation, a dealer service department or motorcycle repair shop will generally do it for a reasonable fee.

12   Next, the cylinders must be thoroughly washed with warm soapy water to remove all traces of the abrasive grit produced during the honing operation. Be sure to run a brush through the bolt holes and flush them with running water. After rinsing, dry the cylinders thoroughly and apply a coat of light, rust-preventative oil to all machined surfaces.

Installation

Refer to illustrations 13.14, 13.15, 13.16 and 13.19

13   Lubricate the cylinder bores with plenty of clean engine oil. Apply a thin film of moly-based grease to the piston skirts.

14   Install the dowel pins, then lower a new cylinder base gasket over the studs, with the UP mark on the right-hand side of the engine. Some gaskets also have an arrow, which must point to the front of the engine **(see illustration)**.

15   Slowly rotate the crankshaft until all of the pistons are at the same level. Slide lengths of welding rod or pieces of a straightened-out coat hanger under the pistons, on both sides of the connecting rods **(see illustration)**. This will help keep the pistons level as the cylinder block is lowered onto them.

16   Attach four piston ring compressors to the pistons and compress the piston rings **(see illustration)**. Large hose clamps can be used instead – just make sure they don't scratch the pistons, and don't tighten them too much.

2

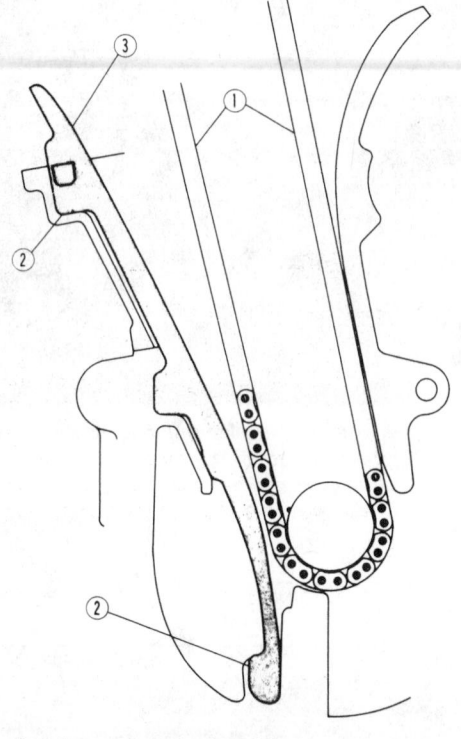

13.19 Pull the cam chain tight (1), then install the chain guide (3), making sure it fits correctly at each end (2)

17 Install the cylinder block over the studs and carefully lower it down until the piston crowns fit into the cylinder liners. while doing this, pull the camshaft chain up, using a hooked tool or a piece of coat hanger. Push down on the cylinder block, making sure the pistons don't get cocked sideways, until the bottom of the cylinder liners slide down past the piston rings. A wood or plastic hammer handle can be used to gently tap the block down, but don't use too much force or the pistons will be damaged.
18 Remove the piston ring compressors or hose clamps, being careful not to scratch the pistons. Remove the rods from under the pistons.
19 Install the cam chain front guide **(see illustration)**.
20 Install the cylinder head and tighten the nuts (see Section 10).
21 Tighten the cylinder block-to-crankcase nuts to the torque listed in this Chapter's Specifications.
22 The remainder of installation is the reverse of removal

14 Pistons – removal, inspection and installation

1 The pistons are attached to the connecting rods with piston pins that are a slip fit in the pistons and rods.
2 Before removing the pistons from the rods, stuff a clean shop towel into each crankcase hole, around the connecting rods. This will prevent the circlips from falling into the crankcase if they are inadvertently dropped.

Removal

Refer to illustrations 14.3a, 14.3b, 14.3c and 14.4
3 Using a sharp scribe, scratch the number of each piston into its crown **(see illustration)**. Each piston should also have an arrow pointing toward the front of the engine. If not, scribe an arrow into the piston crown before removal. Support the first piston, grasp the circlip with needle-nose pliers and remove it from the groove **(see illustration)**. If the pin won't come out, use a special piston pin removal tool (Kawasaki tool no. 57001-910) **(see illustration)**.
4 Push the piston pin out from the opposite end to free the piston from

14.3a Using a sharp scribe, scratch the cylinder numbers into the piston crowns – also note the arrow, which must point to the front

the rod. You may have to deburr the area around the groove to enable the pin to slide out (use a triangular file for this procedure). Repeat the procedure for the remaining pistons. Use large rubber bands to support the connecting rods **(see illustration)**.

Inspection

Refer to illustrations 14.6, 14.11, 14.13 and 14.14
5 Before the inspection process can be carried out, the pistons must be cleaned and the old piston rings removed.
6 Using a piston ring installation tool, carefully remove the rings from the pistons **(see illustration)**. Do not nick or gouge the pistons in the process.
7 Scrape all traces of carbon from the tops of the pistons. A hand-held wire brush or a piece of fine emery cloth can be used once the majority of the deposits have been scraped away. Do not, under any circumstances, use a wire brush mounted in a drill motor to remove deposits from the pistons; the piston material is soft and will be eroded away by the wire brush.
8 Use a piston ring groove cleaning tool to remove any carbon deposits from the ring grooves. If a tool is not available, a piece broken off the old ring will do the job. Be very careful to remove only the carbon deposits. Do not remove any metal and do not nick or gouge the sides of the ring grooves.
9 Once the deposits have been removed, clean the pistons with solvent and dry them thoroughly. Make sure the oil return holes below the oil ring grooves are clear.
10 If the pistons are not damaged or worn excessively and if the cylinders are not rebored, new pistons will not be necessary. Normal piston wear appears as even, vertical wear on the thrust surfaces of the piston and slight looseness of the top ring in its groove. New piston rings, on the other hand, should always be used when an engine is rebuilt.
11 Carefully inspect each piston for cracks around the skirt, at the pin bosses and at the ring lands **(see illustration)**.
12 Look for scoring and scuffing on the thrust faces of the skirt, holes in the piston crown and burned areas at the edge of the crown. If the skirt is scored or scuffed, the engine may have been suffering from overheating and/or abnormal combustion, which caused excessively high operating temperatures. The oil pump and cooling system should be checked thoroughly. A hole in the piston crown, an extreme to be sure, is an indication that abnormal combustion (pre-ignition) was occurring. Burned areas at the edge of the piston crown are usually evidence of spark knock (detonation). If any of the above problems exist, the causes must be corrected or the damage will occur again.
13 Measure the piston ring-to-groove clearance by laying a new piston ring in the ring groove and slipping a feeler gauge in beside it **(see illustration)**. Check the clearance at three or four locations around the groove. Be sure to use the correct ring for each groove; they are different. If the clearance is greater then specified, new pistons will have to be used when the engine is reassembled.

14.3b   Use needle-nose pliers and remove the piston pin circlips
(note the rag used to keep foreign objects out of the crankcase)

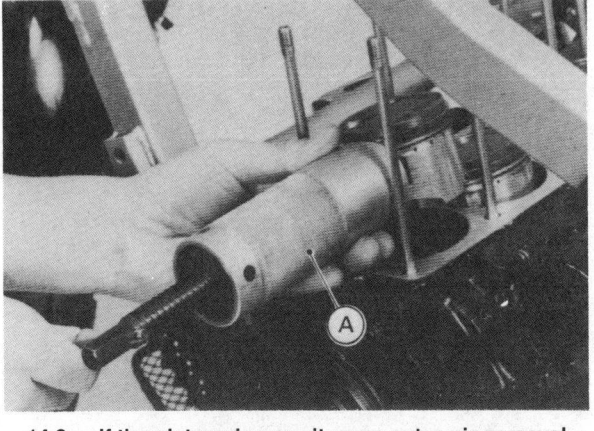

14.3c   If the piston pins won't come out, a pin removal
tool will have to be used – if you don't have access to
one of these, one can be fabricated from a threaded rod,
nuts, washers and a piece of pipe

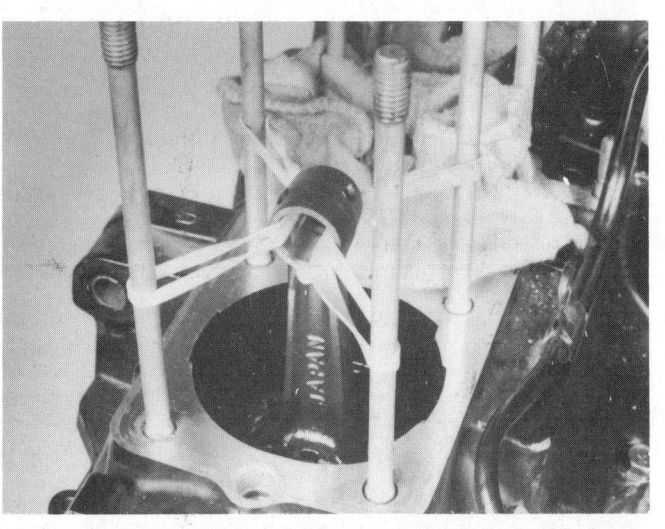

14.4   Use large rubber bands to keep the connecting rods from
flopping around after the pistons are removed

14.6   Remove the piston rings with a ring removal and
installation tool

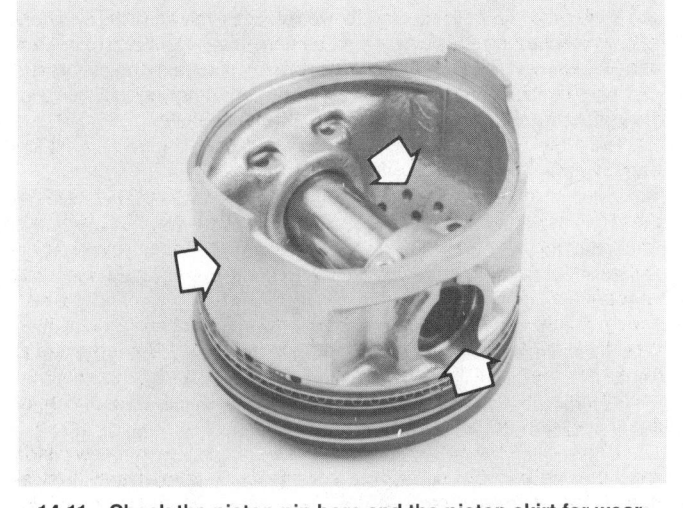

14.11   Check the piston pin bore and the piston skirt for wear,
and make sure the oil holes are clear (arrows)

14.13   Measure the piston ring-to-groove clearance with a
feeler gauge

2

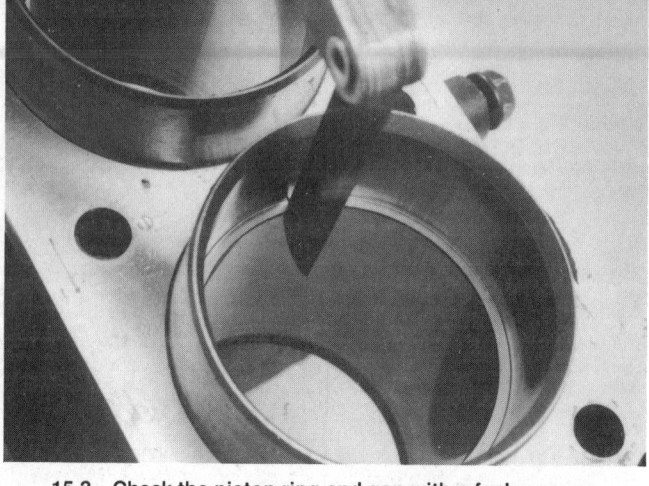

14.14   Measure the piston diameter with a micrometer

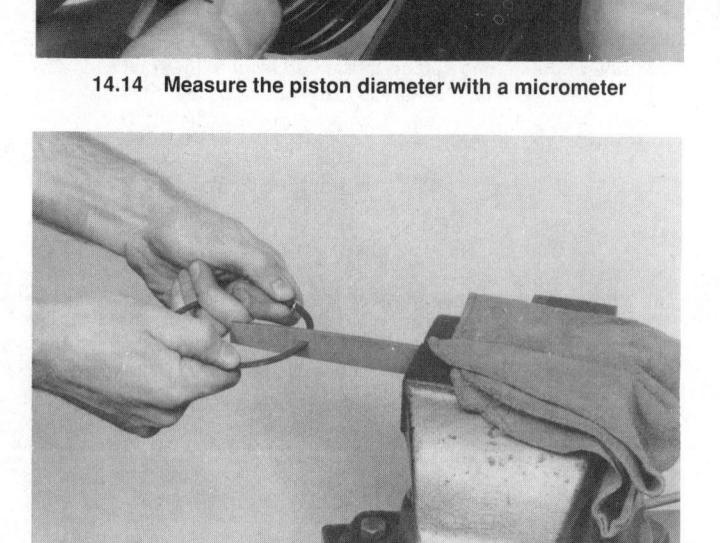

15.5   If the end gap is too small, clamp a file in a vise and file the ring ends (from the outside in only) to enlarge the gap slightly

14   Check the piston-to-bore clearance by measuring the bore (see Section 13) and the piston diameter. Make sure that the pistons and cylinders are correctly matched. Measure the piston across the skirt on the thrust faces at a 90-degree angle to the piston pin, about 1/2-inch (13 mm) up from the bottom of the skirt **(see illustration)**. Subtract the piston diameter from the bore diameter to obtain the clearance. If it is greater than specified, the cylinders will have to be rebored and new oversized pistons and rings installed. If the appropriate precision measuring tools are not available, the piston-to-cylinder clearances can be obtained, though not quite as accurately, using feeler gauge stock. Feeler gauge stock comes in 12-inch lengths and various thicknesses and is generally available at auto parts stores. To check the clearance, select a 0.002 in (0.07 mm) feeler gauge and slip it into the cylinder along with the appropriate piston. The cylinder should be upside down and the piston must be positioned exactly as it normally would be. Place the feeler gauge between the piston and cylinder on one of the thrust faces (90-degrees to the piston pin bore). The piston should slip through the cylinder (with the feeler gauge in place) with moderate pressure. If it falls through, or slides through easily, the clearance is excessive and a new piston will be required. If the piston binds at the lower end of the cylinder and is loose toward the top, the cylinder is tapered, and if tight spots are encountered as the piston/feeler gauge is rotated in the cylinder, the cylinder is out-of-round. Repeat the procedure for the remaining pistons and cylinders. Be sure to have the cylinders and pistons checked by a dealer service department or a motorcycle repair shop to confirm your findings before purchasing new parts.

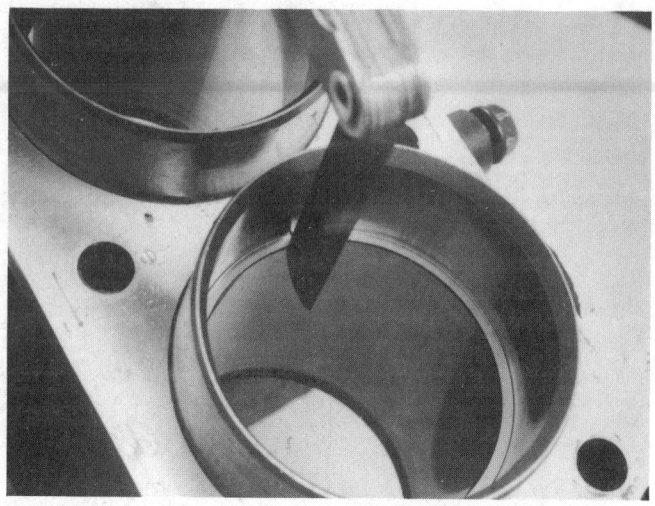

15.3   Check the piston ring end gap with a feeler gauge

15   Apply clean engine oil to the pin, insert it into the piston and check for freeplay by rocking the pin back-and-forth. If the pin is loose, new pistons and possibly new pins must be installed.
16   Refer to Section 15 and install the rings on the pistons.

Installation

Note: *When installing the pistons, install the pistons for cylinders 2 and 3 first.*

17   Install the pistons in their original locations with the arrows pointing to the front of the engine. Lubricate the pins and the rod bores with clean engine oil. Install new circlips in the grooves in the inner sides of the pistons (don't reuse the old circlips). Push the pins into position from the opposite side and install new circlips. Compress the circlips only enough for them to fit in the piston. Make sure the clips are properly seated in the grooves.

---

15   Piston rings – installation

Refer to illustrations 15.3, 15.5, 15.9a, 15.9b, 15.11, 15.12 and 15.15

1   Before installing the new piston rings, the ring end gaps must be checked.
2   Lay out the pistons and the new ring sets so the rings will be matched with the same piston and cylinder during the end gap measurement procedure and engine assembly.
3   Insert the top (No. 1) ring into the bottom of the first cylinder and square it up with the cylinder walls by pushing it in with the top of the piston. The ring should be about one inch above the bottom edge of the cylinder. To measure the end gap, slip a feeler gauge between the ends of the ring **(see illustration)** and compare the measurement to the Specifications.
4   If the gap is larger or smaller than specified, double check to make sure that you have the correct rings before proceeding.
5   If the gap is too small, it must be enlarged or the ring ends may come in contact with each other during engine operation, which can cause serious damage. The end gap can be increased by filing the ring ends very carefully with a fine file **(see illustration)**. When performing this operation, file only from the outside in.
6   Excess end gap is not critical unless it is greater than 0.040 in (1 mm). Again, double check to make sure you have the correct rings for your engine.
7   Repeat the procedure for each ring that will be installed in the first cylinder and for each ring in the remaining cylinder. Remember to keep the rings, pistons and cylinders matched up.
8   Once the ring end gaps have been checked/corrected, the rings can be installed on the pistons.
9   The oil control ring (lowest on the piston) is installed first. It is composed of three separate components. Slip the expander into the groove, then install the upper side rail **(see illustrations)**. Do not use a

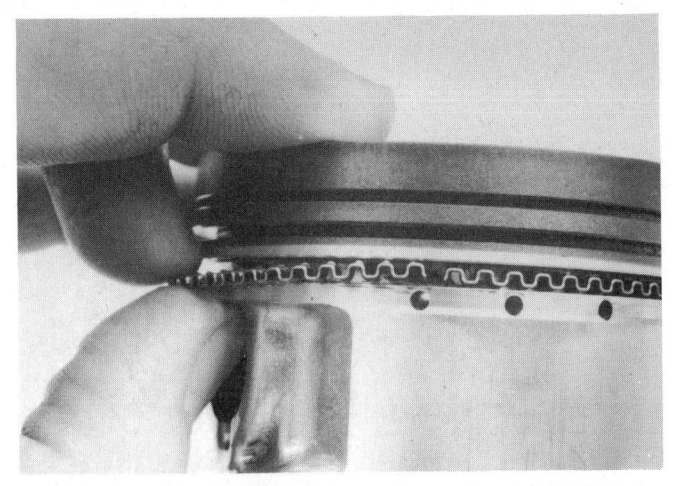

15.9a   Installing the oil ring expander – make sure the ends don't overlap

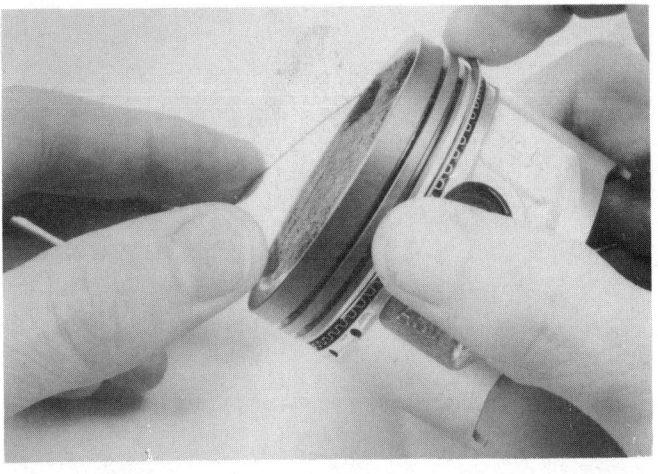

15.9b   Installing an oil ring side rail – don't use a ring installation tool to do this

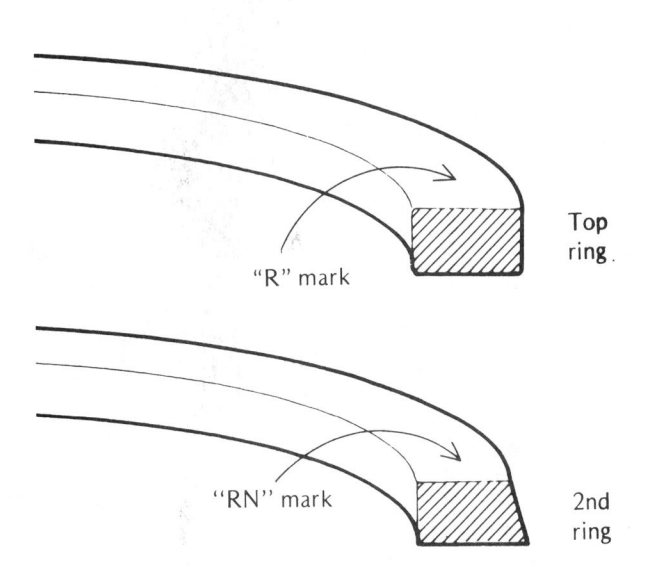

15.11   Don't confuse the top ring with the middle ring

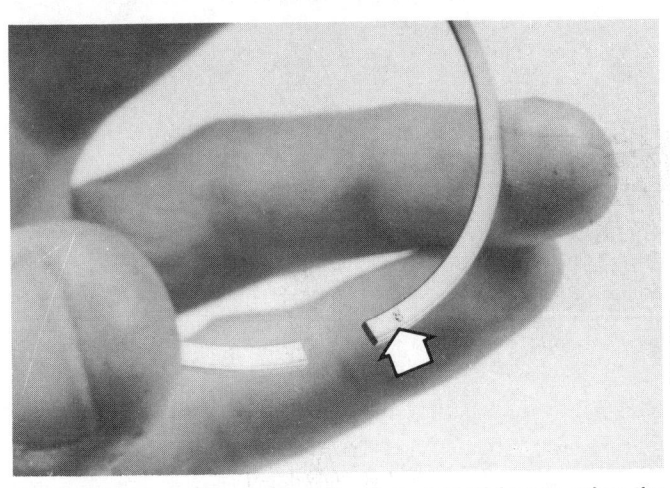

15.12   Make sure the marks on the rings (arrow) face up when the rings are installed on the pistons

piston ring installation tool on the oil ring side rails as they may be damaged. Instead, place one end of the side rail into the groove between the spacer expander and the ring land. Hold it firmly in place and slide a finger around the piston while pushing the rail into the groove. Next, install the lower side rail in the same manner.

10   After the three oil ring components have been installed, check to make sure that both the upper and lower side rails can be turned smoothly in the ring groove.

11   Install the no. 2 (middle) ring next. It can be readily distinguished from the top ring by its cross-section shape and the RN mark on it **(see illustration)**. Do not mix the top and middle rings.

12   To avoid breaking the ring, use a piston ring installation tool and make sure that the identification mark is facing up **(see illustration)**. Fit the ring into the middle groove on the piston. Do not expand the ring any more than is necessary to slide it into place.

13   Finally, install the no. 1 (top) ring in the same manner. Make sure the identifying mark is facing up.

14   Repeat the procedure for the remaining piston and rings. Be very careful not to confuse the no. 1 and no. 2 rings.

15   Once the rings have been properly installed, stagger the end gaps, including those of the oil ring side rails **(see illustration)**.

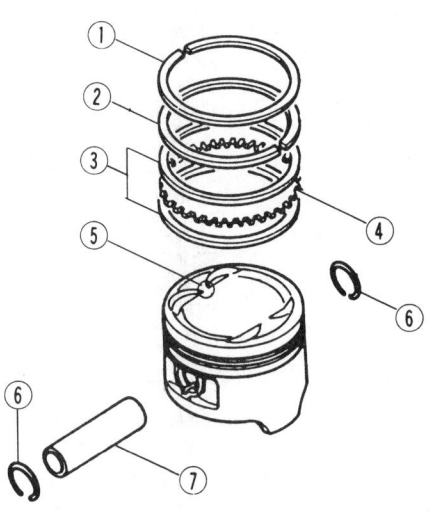

15.15   Piston and piston ring details – when installing the oil ring side rails, stagger them approximately 30 to 40-degrees on either side of the top compression ring

1 Top compression ring	5 Arrow mark
2 Second compression ring	6 Circlip
3 Oil ring side rails	7 Piston pin
4 Oil ring expander	

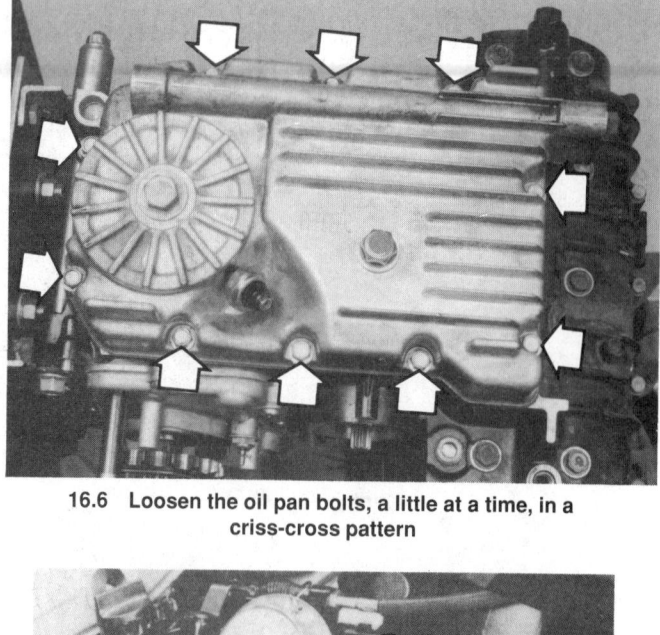

16.6   Loosen the oil pan bolts, a little at a time, in a criss-cross pattern

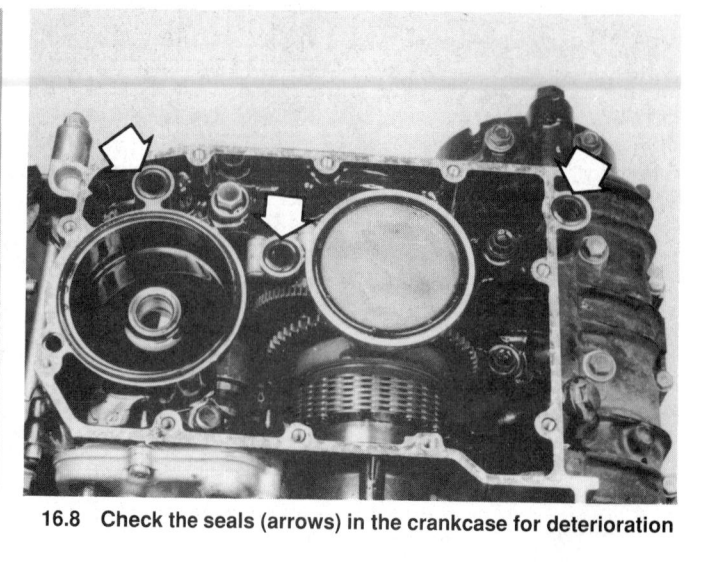

16.8   Check the seals (arrows) in the crankcase for deterioration

9   Position a new gasket on the oil pan. A thin film of RTV sealant can be used to hold the gasket in place. Install the oil pan and bolts, tightening the bolts to the torque listed in this Chapter's Specifications, using a criss-cross pattern.

10   The remainder of installation is the reverse of removal. Install a new filter and fill the crankcase with oil (see Chapter 1), then run the engine and check for leaks.

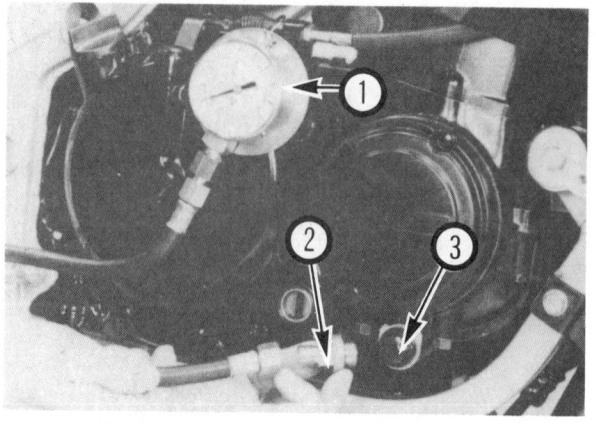

17.2   To check the oil pressure, remove the plug and connect an oil pressure gauge using the proper adapter

    1   Oil pressure gauge   3   Plug
    2   Adapter

---

17   Oil pump – pressure check, removal, inspection and installation

Note: *The oil pump can be removed with the engine in the frame.*

Check

Refer to illustration 17.2

Warning: *If the oil passage plug is removed when the engine is hot, hot oil will drain out – wait until the engine is cold before beginning this check (it must be cold to preform the relief valve opening pressure check, anyway).*

1   If you're working on an A or B model, remove the lower fairing (see Chapter 8).

2   Remove the plug at the bottom of the crankcase on the right-hand side and install an oil pressure gauge **(see illustration)**.

3   Start the engine and watch the gauge while varying the engine rpm. The pressure should stay within the relief valve opening pressure listed in this Chapter's Specifications. If the pressure is too high, the relief valve is stuck closed. To check it, see Section 18.

4   If the pressure is lower than the standard, either the relief valve is stuck open, the oil pump is faulty, or there is other engine damage. Begin diagnosis by checking the relief valve (see Section 18), then the oil pump. If those items check out okay, chances are the bearing oil clearances are excessive and the engine needs to be overhauled.

5   If the pressure reading is in the desired range, allow the engine to warm up to normal operating temperature and check the pressure again, at the specified engine rpm. Compare your findings with this Chapter's Specifications.

6   If the pressure is significantly lower than specified, check the relief valve and the oil pump.

Removal

Refer to illustration 17.9

7   Remove the oil pan (see Section 16).

8   Remove the clutch assembly (see Section 19).

9   Remove the mounting bolt and screws, then detach the bearing stop **(see illustration)**.

10   Slide the oil pump toward the crankcase and remove it.

---

16   Oil pan – removal and installation

Refer to illustrations 16.6 and 16.8
Note: *The oil pan can be removed with the engine in the frame.*

Removal

1   Set the bike on its centerstand.

2   Drain the engine oil and remove the oil filter (see Chapter 1).

3   Remove the exhaust system (see Chapter 4).

4   Remove the banjo bolts that attach the oil cooler lines to the oil pan (see Chapter 3).

5   Remove the small screw and disconnect the wire from the oil pressure switch (see Chapter 9).

6   Remove the oil pan bolts and detach the pan from the crankcase **(see illustration)**.

7   Remove all traces of old gasket material from the mating surfaces of the oil pan and crankcase.

Installation

8   Check the small O-rings in the oil passages in the crankcase and the large O-ring around the oil filter hole (in the pan) for cracking and general deterioration **(see illustration)**. Replace them if necessary. The flat side of the O-rings must face the crankcase.

17.9   **Remove the bearing stop screws and detach the stop, then remove the oil pump bolt**

1   Bearing stop screws   4   Secondary shaft gear
2   Bolt   5   Oil pump
3   Bearing stop

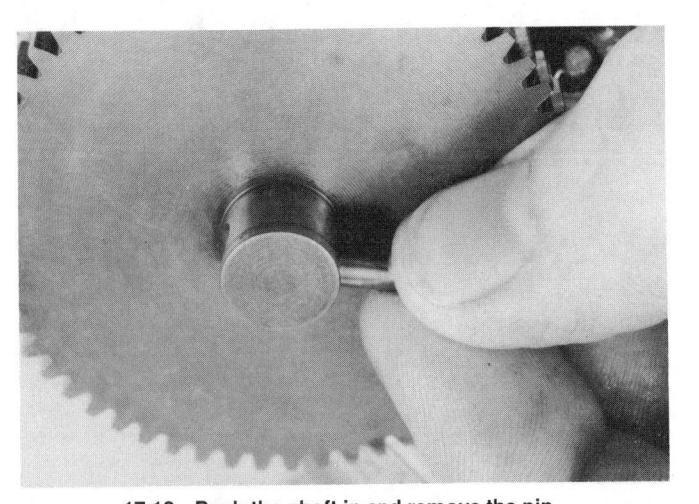

17.12   **Push the shaft in and remove the pin**

Inspection

Refer to illustrations 17.11, 17.12 and 17.14

11   Remove the snap-ring from the pump shaft **(see illustration)** and lift off the washer.

12   Push the shaft into the pump gear just far enough to remove the pin, then detach the gear from the shaft **(see illustration)**.

13   Remove the oil pump cover screws and lift off the cover. clean all traces of gasket material from the mating surfaces.

14   Remove the oil pump shaft, pin, inner rotor and outer rotor from the pump **(see illustration)**. Mark the rotors so they can be installed in the same relative positions.

15   Wash all the components in solvent, then dry them off. Check the pump body, the rotors and the cover for scoring and wear. Make sure the pick-up screen isn't clogged. Kawasaki doesn't publish clearance specifications, so if any damage or uneven or excessive wear is evident, replace the pump. If you are rebuilding the engine, it's a good idea to install new oil pump.

16   Reassemble the pump by reversing the removal steps, but before installing the cover, pack the cavities between the rotors with petroleum jelly – this will ensure the pump develops suction quickly and begins oil circulation as soon as the engine is started. Be sure to use a new gasket.

17.11   **Remove the snap-ring with snap-ring pliers**

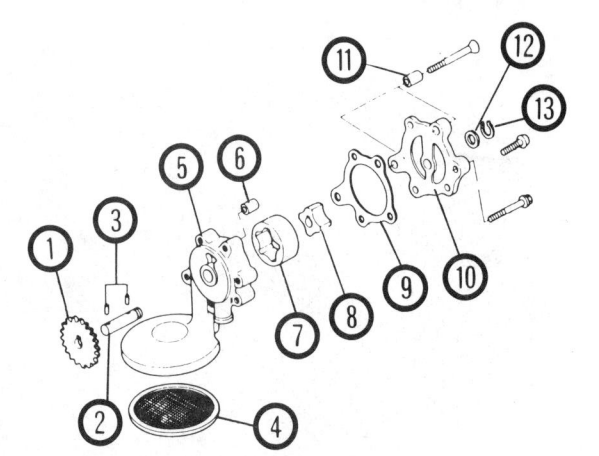

17.14   **Exploded view of the oil pump**

1   Gear   6   Dowel pin   10   Cover
2   Shaft   7   Outer rotor   11   Dowel pin
3   Pins   8   Inner rotor   12   Washer
4   Screen   9   Gasket   13   Snap-ring
5   Oil pump body

17.17   **Stake the screws to prevent them from loosening**

Installation

17   Installation is the reverse of removal. Make sure the two dowel pins are in place before installing the bearing stop and screws. After tightening the mounting screws, stake them with a hammer and punch **(see illustration)**.

2

18.2   Location of the oil pressure relief valve (arrow)

19.4   Remove the clutch cover bolts (arrows)

19.5a   Loosen the clutch spring bolts a little at a time, in a criss-cross pattern – a screwdriver wedged between a bolt and the clutch housing will prevent it from turning

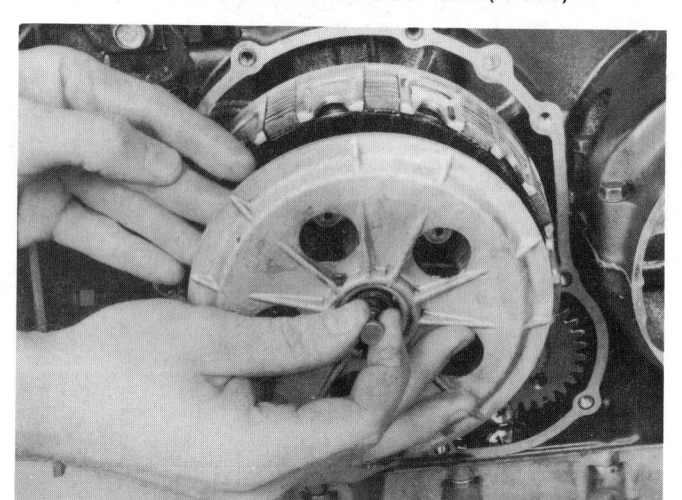

19.5b   Remove the spring plate and pushrod

18   Oil pressure relief valve – removal, inspection and installation

Refer to illustration 18.2

Removal

1   Remove the oil pan (see Section 16).
2   Unscrew the relief valve from the crankcase **(see illustration)**.

Inspection

3   Clean the valve with solvent and dry it, using compressed air if available.
4   Using a wood or plastic tool, depress the steel ball inside the valve and see if it moves smoothly. Make sure it returns to its seat completely. If it doesn't, replace it with a new one (don't attempt to disassemble and repair it).

Installation

5   Apply a non-hardening thread locking compound to the threads of the valve and install it into the case, tightening it to the torque listed in this Chapter's Specifications.
6   The remainder of installation is the reverse of removal.

19   Clutch – removal, inspection and installation

Note: *The clutch can be removed with the engine in the frame.*

Removal

Refer to illustrations 19.4, 19.5a, 19.5b, 19.6, 19.7a, 19.7b, 19.8a and 19.8b

1   Set the bike on its centerstand. Remove the lower fairing (see Chapter 8).
2   Drain the engine oil (see Chapter 1).
3   Completely loosen the rear adjustment nut on the clutch cable at its bracket on the clutch cover. Pull the cable out of the bracket, then detach the cable end from the lever.
4   Remove the clutch cover bolts and take the cover off **(see illustration)**. If the cover is stuck, tap around its perimeter with a soft-face hammer.
5   Remove the clutch spring bolts **(see illustration)**. To prevent the assembly from turning, thread one of the cover mounting bolts into the case and wedge a screwdriver between the bolt and the clutch housing. Remove the clutch spring plate, bearing and pushrod **(see illustration)**.
6   Remove the clutch friction and steel plates from the clutch housing **(see illustration)**.
7   Remove the clutch hub nut, using a special holding tool (Kawasaki tool no. 57001-305 or 1243) to prevent the clutch housing from turning **(see illustration)**. An alternative to this tool can be fabricated from some

19.6   Remove the clutch friction and steel plates

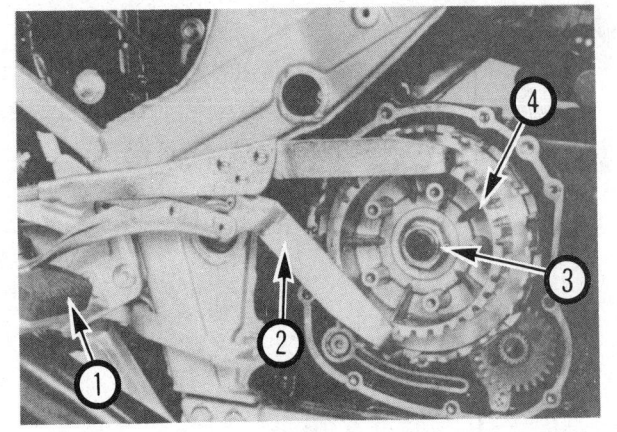

19.7a   The clutch hub must be prevented from rotating
so the hub nut can be removed – in this photo, the
special Kawasaki tool is shown

1	Footpeg (the tool rests against it)	3	Hub nut
2	Clutch hub holding tool (no. 57001-305, or equivalent)	4	Clutch hub

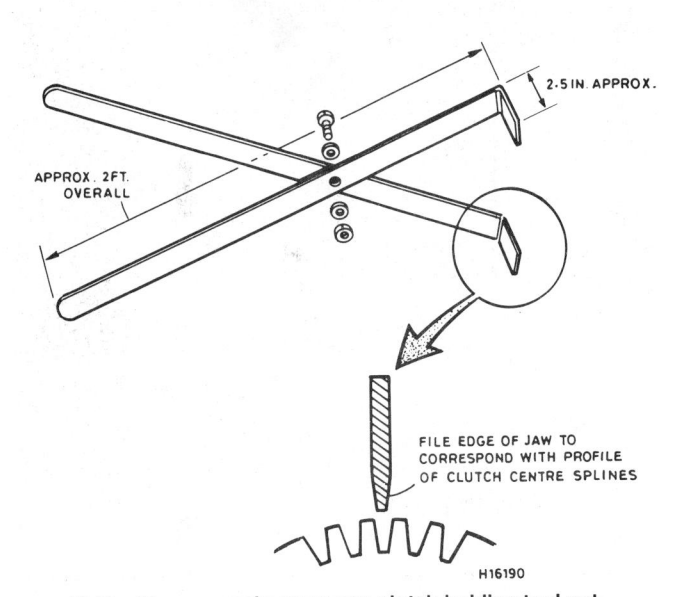

APPROX. 2 FT.
OVERALL

2.5 IN. APPROX.

FILE EDGE OF JAW TO
CORRESPOND WITH PROFILE
OF CLUTCH CENTRE SPLINES

H16190

19.7b   You can make your own clutch holding tool out
of steel strap

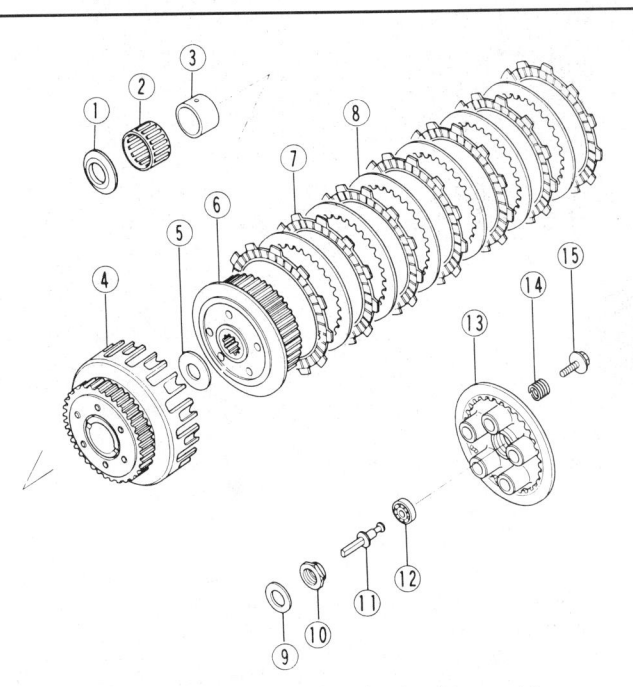

19.8a   Exploded view of the clutch assembly

1	Spacer	9	Washer
2	Needle bearing	10	Hub nut
3	Collar	11	Pushrod
4	Clutch housing	12	Bearing
5	Washer	13	Spring plate
6	Clutch hub	14	Clutch spring
7	Friction plate	15	Bolt
8	Steel plate		

steel strap, bent at the ends and bolted together in the middle **(see illustration)**.

8   Remove the thrust washer, clutch hub, washer, clutch housing, needle bearing, collar and spacer **(see illustrations)**.

Inspection

Refer to illustrations 19.9, 19.10, 19.11, 19.12 and 19.14

9   Examine the splines on both the inside and the outside of the clutch hub **(see illustration)**. If any wear is evident, replace the hub with a new one.

10   Measure the free length of the clutch springs **(see illustration)** and compare the results to this Chapter's Specifications. If the springs have sagged, or if cracks are noted, replace them with new ones as a set.

11   If the lining material of the friction plates smells burnt or if it is glazed, new parts are required. If the metal clutch plates are scored or discolored, they must be replaced with new ones. Measure the thickness of each friction plate **(see illustration)** and compare the results to this Chapter's Specifications. Replace with new parts any friction plates that are near the wear limit.

12   Lay the metal plates, one at a time, on a perfectly flat surface (such as a piece of plate glass) and check for warpage by trying to slip a 0.019-inch feeler gauge between the flat surface and the plate. Do this at several

places around the plate's circumference. If the feeler gauge can be slipped under the plate, it is warped and should be replaced with a new one.

13   Check the tabs on the friction plates for excessive wear and mushroomed edges. They can be cleaned up with a file if the deformation is not severe.

14   Check the edges of the slots in the clutch housing for indentations made by the friction plate tabs. If the indentations are deep they can prevent clutch release, so the housing should be replaced with a new one. If

2

19.8b   Remove the collar, bearing and spacer from the mainshaft

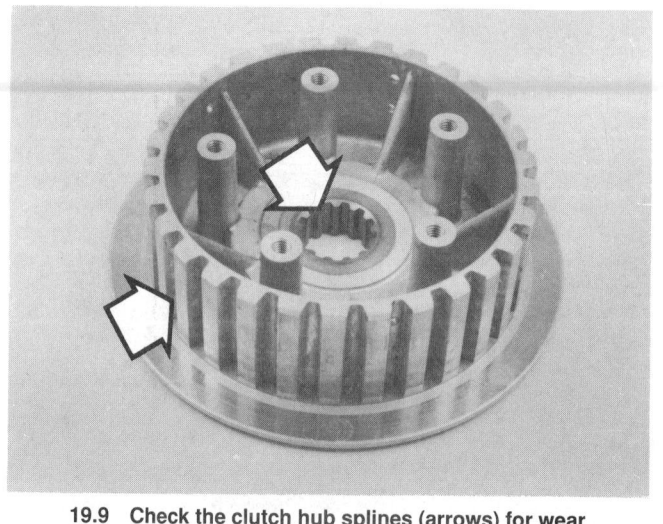

19.9   Check the clutch hub splines (arrows) for wear and distortion

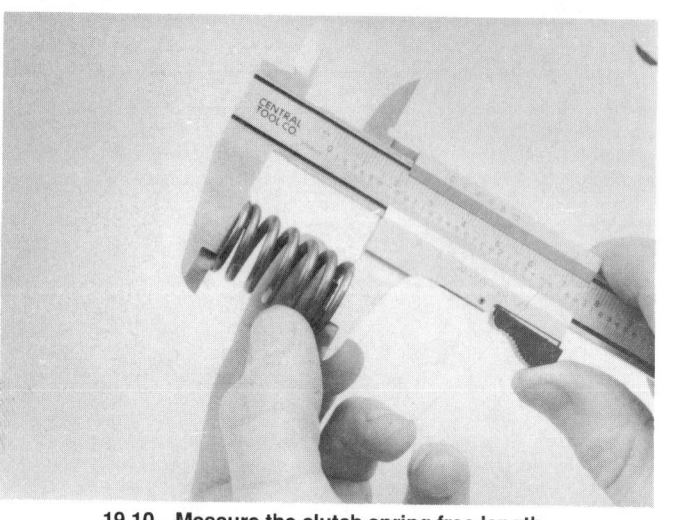

19.10   Measure the clutch spring free length

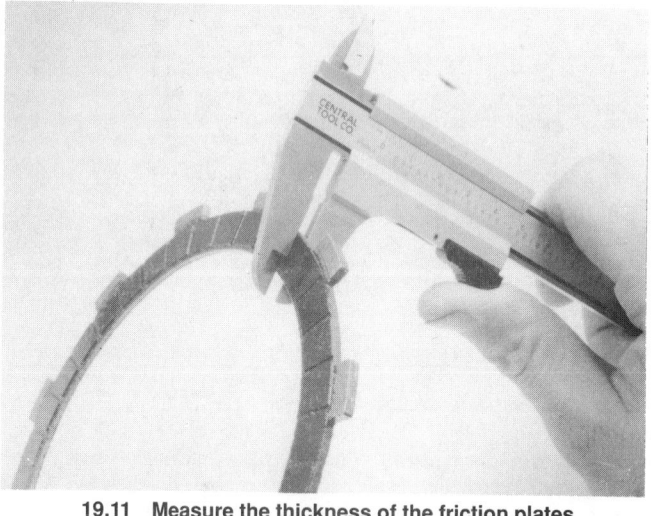

19.11   Measure the thickness of the friction plates

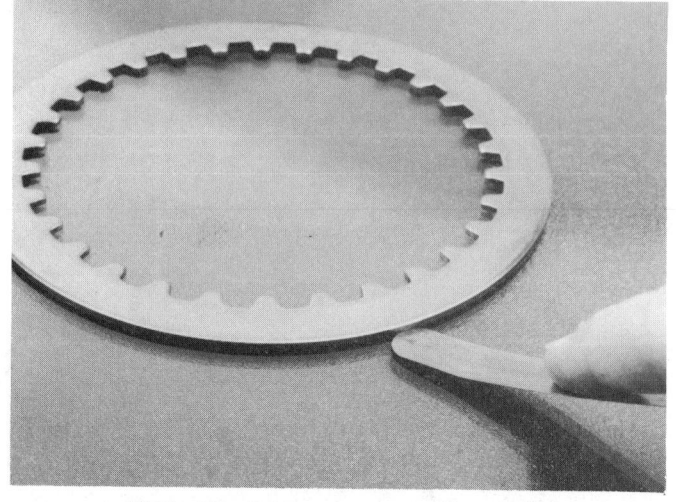

19.12   Check the metal plates for warpage

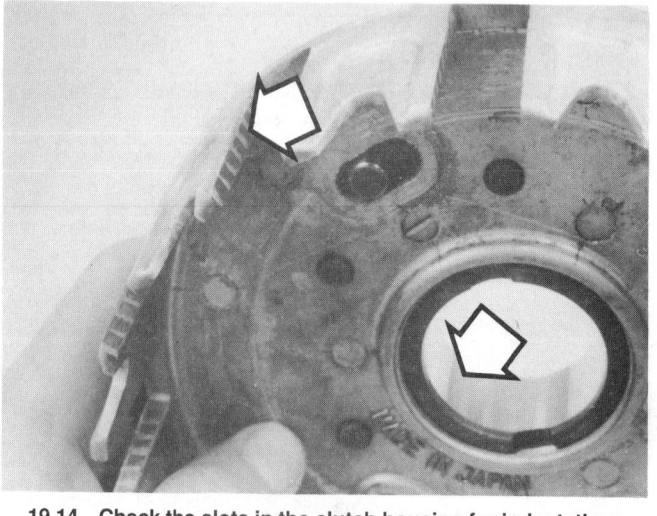

19.14   Check the slots in the clutch housing for indentations (minor damage can be removed with a file) and check the bearing for wear (arrows)

21.3 Remove the shift mechanism screws (arrows)

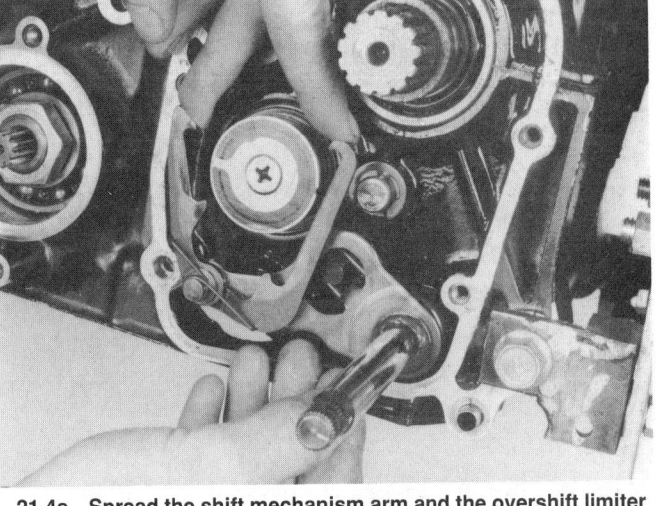

21.4a Spread the shift mechanism arm and the overshift limiter apart, then remove the mechanism

the indentations can be removed easily with a file, the life of the housing can be prolonged to an extent. Also, check the primary gear teeth for cracks, chips and excessive wear. If the gear is worn or damaged, the clutch housing must be replaced with a new one. Check the bearing for score marks, scratches and excessive wear.

15 Check the bearing journal on the transmission mainshaft for score marks, heat discoloration and evidence of excessive wear. Check the clutch spring plate for wear and damage and make sure the pushrod is not bent (roll it on a perfectly flat surface or use V-blocks and a dial indicator).

16 Clean all traces of old gasket material from the clutch cover. If the release shaft seal has been leaking, it can be replaced by removing the positioning bolt on the outside of the housing and pulling out the shaft. The seal can then be pried out and a new one driven in, using a hammer and a socket with an outside diameter slightly smaller than that of the seal.

Installation

17 Install the spacer over the transmission mainshaft, with the chamfered side facing in.

18 Lubricate the collar and the needle bearing with engine oil and slide them over the mainshaft.

19 Install the clutch housing, washer and the clutch hub. Install a new hub nut and tighten it to the torque listed in this Chapter's Specifications. Use the technique described in Step 7 to prevent the hub from turning.

20 Coat the clutch friction plates with engine oil. Install the clutch plates, starting with a friction plate and alternating them. There are seven friction plates and six steel plates.

21 Lubricate the pushrod and install it through the spring plate. Mount the spring plate to the clutch assembly and install the springs and bolts, tightening them to the torque listed in this Chapter's Specifications in a criss-cross pattern.

22 Install the clutch cover and bolts, using a new gasket. Tighten the bolts, in a criss-cross pattern, to the torque listed in this Chapter's Specifications.

23 Connect the clutch cable to the release lever and adjust the freeplay (see Chapter 1).

24 Fill the crankcase with the recommended type and amount of engine oil (see Chapter 1).

---

20 Clutch cable – replacement

1 Disconnect the upper end of the clutch cable from the lever (see Chapter 1, illustration 16.3a).

2 Fully loosen the rear adjusting nut at the lower end of the clutch cable (see Chapter 1, Section 10 if necessary). Pull the cable through the bracket on the clutch cover, then detach the cable end from the release lever.

21.4b Be sure not to pull on the shift rod (arrow) – if you do, you'll have to separate the crankcase halves to reinstall the shift forks!

3 Before removing the cable from the bike, tape the lower end of the new cable to the upper end of the old cable. Slowly pull the lower end of the old cable out, guiding the new cable down into position. Using this method will ensure the cable is routed correctly.

4 Lubricate the cable (see Chapter 1, Section 16). Reconnect the ends of the cable by reversing the removal procedure, then adjust the cable following the procedure given in Chapter 1, Section 10.

---

21 External shift mechanism – removal, inspection and installation

Removal

Refer to illustrations 21.3, 21.4a and 21.4b

1 Set the bike on its centerstand.

2 Remove the shift lever, engine sprocket cover and the engine sprocket (see Chapter 6).

3 Position a drain pan under the shift mechanism cover. Remove the screws (**see illustration**) and detach the cover from the crankcase.

4 Spread the shift mechanism arm and overshift limiter to clear the shift drum, then pull the mechanism and shaft off (**see illustration**). **Caution:** *Don't pull the shift rod out of the crankcase – the shift forks will fall into the oil pan, and the crankcase will have to be separated to reinstall them.*

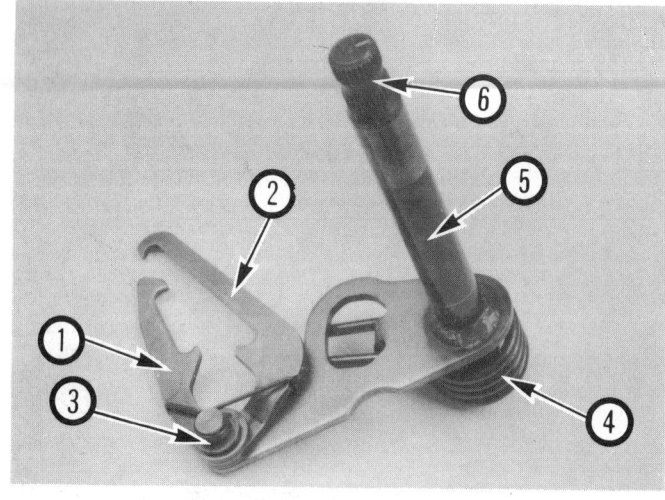

21.5 Shift mechanism details

1	Shift mechanism arm	4	Return spring
2	Overshift limiter	5	Shift shaft
3	Pawl spring	6	Splines

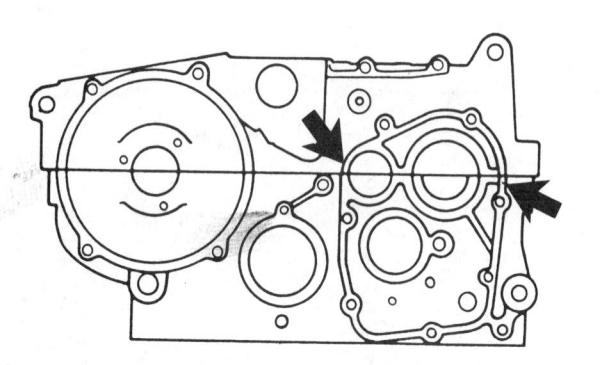

21.12 Apply RTV sealant to the shaded areas (arrows)

21.9 New seals can be driven into the cover with a socket having an outside diameter slightly smaller than the seal

22.3 Hold the rotor from turning and loosen the secondary shaft nut

Inspection

Refer to illustrations 21.5 and 21.9

5   Check the shift shaft for bends and damage to the splines **(see illustration)**. If the shaft is bent, you can attempt to straighten it, but if the splines are damaged it will have to be replaced.

6   Check the condition of the return spring and the pawl spring. Replace them if they are cracked or distorted.

7   Check the shift mechanism arm and the overshift limiter for cracks, distortion and wear. If any of these conditions are found, replace the shift mechanism.

8   Make sure the return spring pin isn't loose. If it is, unscrew it, apply a non-hardening locking compound to the threads, then reinstall it and tighten it securely.

9   Check the condition of the seals in the cover. If they have been leaking, drive them out with a hammer and punch. New seals can be installed by driving them in with a socket **(see illustration)**.

Installation

Refer to illustration 21.12

10   Slide the external shift mechanism into place, spreading the shift arm and the overshift limiter to clear the shift drum. Make sure the springs are positioned correctly.

11   Apply high-temperature grease to the lips of the seals. Wrap the splines of the shift shaft with electrical tape, so the splines won't damage the seal as the cover is installed.

12   Apply a thin coat of RTV sealant to the cover mating areas on the crankcase, where the halves of the crankcase join **(see illustration)**.

13   Carefully guide the cover into place and install the screws, tightening them securely.

14   Install the engine sprocket and chain, engine sprocket cover and the shift lever (see Chapter 6).

15   Check the engine oil level and add some, if necessary (see Chapter 1).

22   Crankcase – disassembly and reassembly

1   To examine and repair or replace the crankshaft, connecting rods, bearings, transmission components and secondary shaft/starter motor clutch, the crankcase must be split into two parts.

2   Before this can be done, the water pump and coolant pipe (on the cylinder block) (see Chapter 3), the external shift mechanism (see Section 21), the starter motor, the alternator cover, the timing rotor and the pick-up coil (see Chapter 9) must be removed.

Disassembly

Refer to illustrations 22.3, 22.8, 22.12, 22.15a, 22.15b and 22.16

3   Using a special alternator rotor holder or a pin-type spanner, hold the rotor stationary and loosen the secondary shaft nut **(see illustration)**.

4   Remove the alternator rotor and the stator (see Chapter 9).

5   If the crankcase is being separated to remove the crankshaft, remove the cylinder head, cylinder block and pistons (see Sections 10, 13 and 14).

22.8 Loosen the upper crankcase half bolts (arrows), a little at a time, then remove them

22.12 Remove the primary chain tensioner bolt, spring and pin

22.15a Loosen the lower crankcase half bolts (arrows), a little at a time, then remove them

22.15b Pry the crankcase apart only on the corners, in the areas provided for this purpose

6   Remove the clutch if you are separating the crankcase halves to disassemble the transmission main drive shaft (see Section 19).

7   If the engine is bolted to a mounting stand that fastens to the rear mounting bolt holes (upper and lower), remove it from the stand and fabricate a holder that will support the crankcase upside down, with the seam level.

8   Remove the twelve upper crankcase half bolts **(see illustration)**.

9   Turn the engine upside-down and remove the oil filter (see Chapter 1, if necessary).

10   Remove the oil pan (see Section 16) and retrieve the O-rings from the oil passages.

11   Remove the oil pump (see Section 17).

12   Remove the primary chain tensioner bolt **(see illustration)**.

13   Remove the secondary shaft nut.

14   Remove the secondary shaft from the case (see Section 27).

15   Remove the lower crankcase half bolts **(see illustration)**. Carefully pry the crankcase apart. Pry ONLY on the corners, in the areas indicated **(see illustration)**.

16   Lift the starter motor clutch/secondary sprocket assembly **(see illustration)**.

17   Refer to Sections 23 through 31 for information on the internal components of the crankcase.

22.16 Lift up on the primary chain and remove the secondary sprocket, shaft and starter motor clutch assembly

Lower Crankcase Half

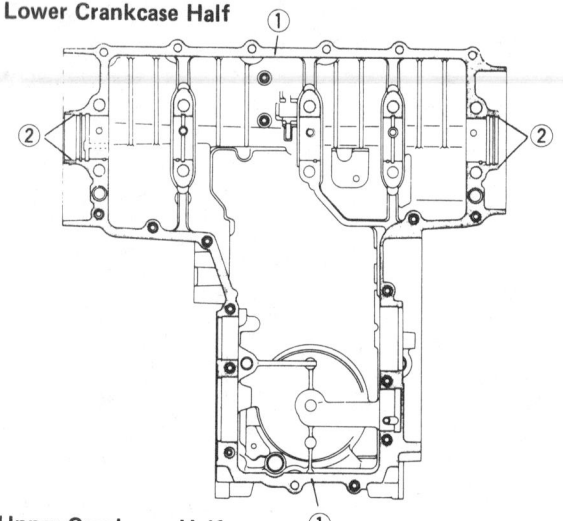

Upper Crankcase Half

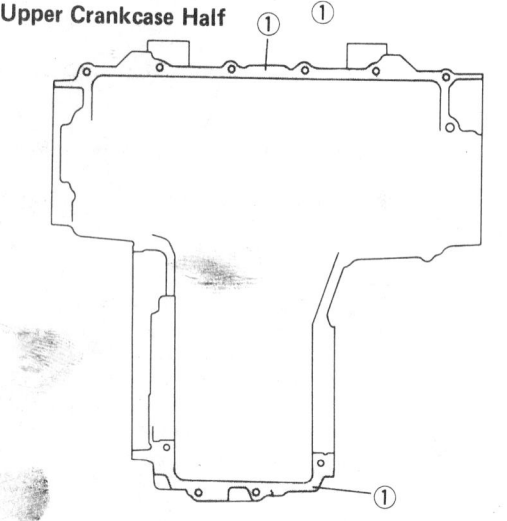

22.22   Apply Kawasaki Bond sealant to the shaded areas (1), and a thin film of RTV sealant to the areas on the sides of the crankshaft seal (2)

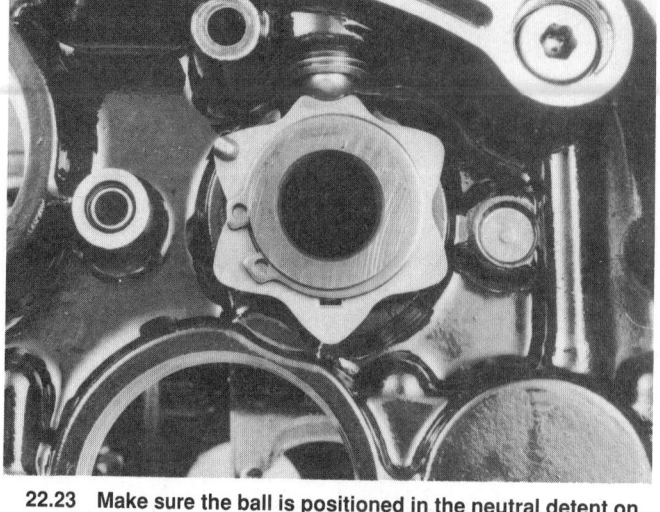

22.23   Make sure the ball is positioned in the neutral detent on the operating plate

22.24   When assembling the case halves, make sure the shift forks fit into their gear grooves (arrows) and the breather tube fits into its hole in the lower case half

Reassembly

Refer to illustrations 22.22, 22.23, 22.24 and 22.26

18   Remove all traces of sealant from the crankcase mating surfaces. Be careful not to let any fall into the case as this is done.

19   Check to make sure the two dowel pins are in place in their holes in the mating surface of the upper crankcase half.

20   Insert the starter motor clutch gear into the secondary sprocket. Lift the primary chain up and guide the secondary sprocket/starter motor clutch assembly into place, making sure the chain meshes properly with the gear (see Section 27).

21   Pour some engine oil over the transmission gears, the crankshaft main bearings and the shift drum. Don't get any oil on the crankcase mating surface.

22   Apply a thin, even bead of Kawasaki Bond sealant (part no. 92104-1003) to the indicated areas of the crankcase mating surfaces **(see illustration)**. Also apply RTV sealant to the areas near the ends of the crankshaft seal areas (lay it over the Kawasaki Bond). **Caution:** *Don't apply an excessive amount of either type of sealant, as it will ooze out when the case halves are assembled and may obstruct oil passages.*

23   Check the position of the shift drum – make sure it's in the neutral position **(see illustration)**.

24   Carefully place the lower crankcase half onto the upper crankcase half. While doing this, make sure the shift forks fit into their gear grooves, and guide the breather tube into its hole in the lower crankcase half **(see illustration)**.

25   Install the lower crankcase half bolts and tighten them so they are just snug.

26   In two steps, tighten the larger bolts (8 mm), in the indicated sequence, to the torque listed in this Chapter's Specifications **(see illustration)**.

27   Turn the case over and install the upper crankcase half bolts, tightening them to the torque listed in this Chapter's Specifications.

28   Turn the case over again and install the smaller (6 mm) bolts in the lower crankcase half, tightening them to the torque listed in this Chapter's Specifications.

29   Install the washer and sleeve on the secondary shaft, if they were removed. Lubricate the secondary shaft and install it through the case and the secondary sprocket/starter motor clutch assembly.

30   Turn the main drive shaft and the output shaft to make sure they turn freely. Install the shift lever on the shift shaft and, while turning the output shaft, shift the transmission through the gears, first through sixth, then back to first. If the transmission doesn't shift properly, the case will have to be separated again to correct the problem. Also make sure the crankshaft turns freely.

31   The remainder of installation is the reverse of removal.

Lower Crankcase Half

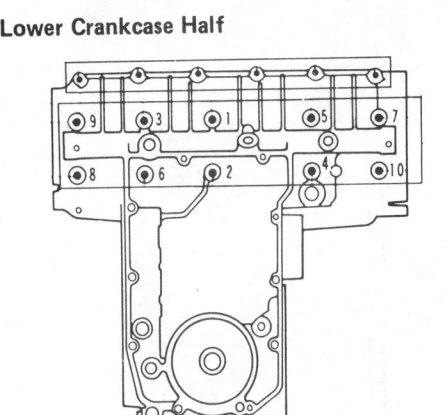

22.26 Tighten the larger (8 mm) bolts in the indicated sequence, in two passes, to the torque listed in this Chapter's Specifications

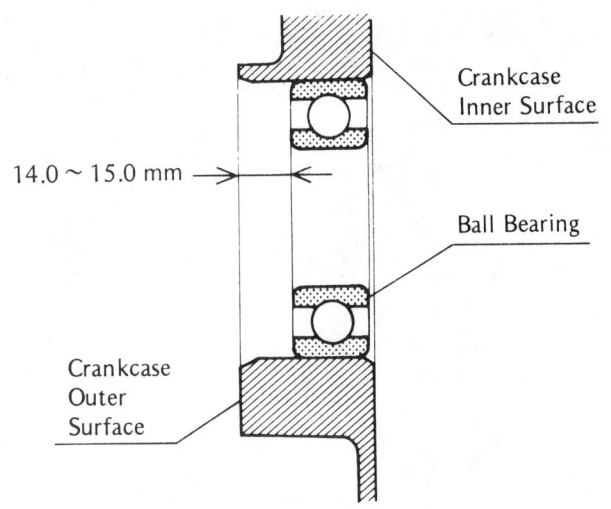

23.3 When installing the secondary shaft bearing in the left side of the case, drive it in to the depth shown

23 Crankcase components – inspection and servicing

Refer to illustration 23.3

1   After the crankcases have been separated and the crankshaft, shift drum and forks and transmission components removed, the crankcases should be cleaned thoroughly with new solvent and dried with compressed air. All oil passages should be blown out with compressed air and all traces of old gasket sealant should be removed from the mating surfaces. **Caution:** *Be very careful not to nick or gouge the crankcase mating surfaces or leaks will result. Check both crankcase sections very carefully for cracks and other damage.*

2   Check the primary chain guides for wear – one is in the upper case half and the other is in the lower case half. If they appear to be worn excessively, replace them.

3   Check the ball and needle bearings in the case. If they don't turn smoothly, drive them out with a bearing driver or a socket having an outside diameter slightly smaller than that of the bearing. Before installing them, allow them to sit in the freezer overnight, and about fifteen-minutes before installation, place the case half in an oven, set to about 200-degrees F, and allow it to heat up. The bearings are an interference fit, and this will ease installation. If you are installing the secondary shaft ball bearing on the left side of the lower case half, drive it in so it's recessed approximately 9/16 to 19/32-inch (14 to 15 mm) **(see illustration)**. **Warning:** *Before heating the case, wash it thoroughly with soap and water so no explosive fumes are present. Also, don't use a flame to heat the case.*

4   Check all the studs in the case for damaged threads or bending. To replace a stud, thread two nuts onto it and tighten them against each other, then unscrew the stud, using a wrench on the lower nut. Before installing a stud, apply a non-hardening thread locking compound to the threads.

5   If any damage is found that can't be repaired, replace the crankcase halves as a set.

24 Main and connecting rod bearings – general note

1   Even though main and connecting rod bearings are generally replaced with new ones during the engine overhaul, the old bearings should be retained for close examination as they may reveal valuable information about the condition of the engine.

2   Bearing failure occurs mainly because of lack of lubrication, the presence of dirt or other foreign particles, overloading the engine and/or corrosion. Regardless of the cause of bearing failure, it must be corrected before the engine is reassembled to prevent it from happening again.

3   When examining the bearings, remove the main bearings from the case halves and the rod bearings from the connecting rods and caps and lay them out on a clean surface in the same general position as their location on the crankshaft journals. This will enable you to match any noted bearing problems with the corresponding side of the crankshaft journal.

4   Dirt and other foreign particles get into the engine in a variety of ways. It may be left in the engine during assembly or it may pass through filters or breathers. It may get into the oil and from there into the bearings. Metal chips from machining operations and normal engine wear are often present. Abrasives are sometimes left in engine components after reconditioning operations such as cylinder honing, especially when parts are not thoroughly cleaned using the proper cleaning methods. Whatever the source, these foreign objects often end up imbedded in the soft bearing material and are easily recognized. Large particles will not imbed in the bearing and will score or gouge the bearing and journal. The best prevention for this cause of bearing failure is to clean all parts thoroughly and keep everything spotlessly clean during engine reassembly. Frequent and regular oil and filter changes are also recommended.

5   Lack of lubrication or lubrication breakdown has a number of interrelated causes. Excessive heat (which thins the oil), overloading (which squeezes the oil from the bearing face) and oil leakage or throw off (from excessive bearing clearances, worn oil pump or high engine speeds) all contribute to lubrication breakdown. Blocked oil passages will also starve a bearing and destroy it. When lack of lubrication is the cause of bearing failure, the bearing material is wiped or extruded from the steel backing of the bearing. Temperatures may increase to the point where the steel backing and the journal turn blue from overheating.

6   Riding habits can have a definite effect on bearing life. Full throttle low speed operation, or lugging the engine, puts very high loads on bearings, which tend to squeeze out the oil film. These loads cause the bearings to flex, which produces fine cracks in the bearing face (fatigue failure). Eventually the bearing material will loosen in pieces and tear away from the steel backing. Short trip driving leads to corrosion of bearings, as insufficient engine heat is produced to drive off the condensed water and corrosive gases produced. These products collect in the engine oil, forming acid and sludge. As the oil is carried to the engine bearings, the acid attacks and corrodes the bearing material.

7   Incorrect bearing installation during engine assembly will lead to bearing failure as well. Tight fitting bearings which leave insufficient bearing oil clearances result in oil starvation. Dirt or foreign particles trapped behind a bearing insert result in high spots on the bearing which lead to failure.

8   To avoid bearing problems, clean all parts thoroughly before reassembly, double check all bearing clearance measurements and lubricate the new bearings with engine assembly lube or moly-based grease during installation.

25.1   Measure the endplay with a feeler gauge inserted between the no. 2 crank journal and the case web – if the endplay isn't as listed in this Chapter's Specifications, the case halves must be replaced

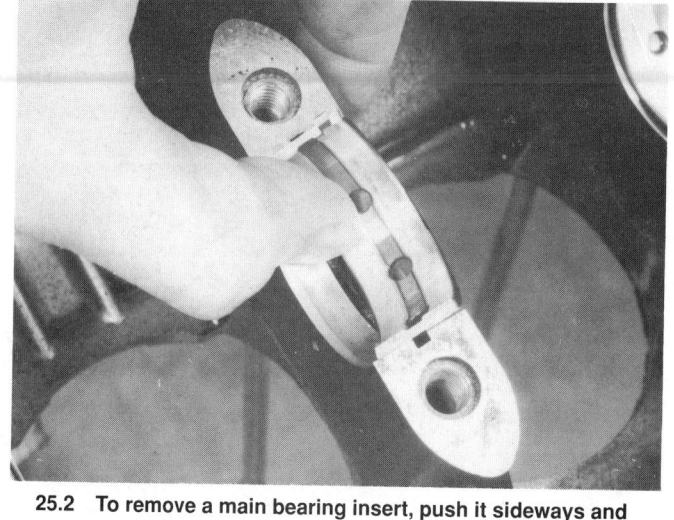

25.2   To remove a main bearing insert, push it sideways and lift it out

Inspection

3   Mark and remove the connecting rods from the crankshaft (see Section 26).

4   Clean the crankshaft with solvent, using a rifle-cleaning brush to scrub out the oil passages. If available, blow the crank dry with compressed air. Check the main and connecting rod journals for uneven wear, scoring and pits. Rub a penny across the journal several times – if a journal picks up copper from the penny, it's too rough. Replace the crankshaft.

5   Check the camshaft chain gear and the primary chain gear on the crankshaft for chipped teeth and other wear. If any undesirable conditions are found, replace the crankshaft. Check the chains as described in Section 28.

6   Check the rest of the crankshaft for cracks and other damage. It should be magnafluxed to reveal hidden cracks – a dealer service department or motorcycle machine shop will handle the procedure.

7   Set the crankshaft on V-blocks and check the runout with a dial indicator touching the center main journal, comparing your findings with this Chapter's Specifications. If the runout exceeds the limit, replace the crank.

Main bearing selection

Refer to illustrations 25.8, 25.10, 25.13, 25.15, 25.16 and 25.17

8   To check the main bearing oil clearance, clean off the bearing inserts (and reinstall them, if they've been removed from the case) and lower the crankshaft into the upper half of the case. Cut five pieces of Plastigage (type HPG-1) and lay them on the crankshaft main journals, parallel with journal axis **(see illustrations)**.

9   Very carefully, guide the lower case half down onto the upper case half. Install the large (8 mm) bolts and tighten them, using the recommended sequence, to the torque listed in this Chapter's Specifications (see Section 22). Don't rotate the crankshaft!

10   Now, remove the bolts and carefully lift the lower case half off. Compare the width of the crushed Plastigage on each journal to the scale printed on the Plastigage envelope to obtain the main bearing oil clearance **(see illustration)**. Write down your findings, then remove all traces of Plastigage from the journals, using your fingernail or the edge of a credit card.

11   If the oil clearance falls into the specified range, no bearing replacement is required (provided they are in good shape). If the clearance is within 0.0015-inch (0.038 mm) and the service limit (0.003-inch [0.08 mm]), replace the bearing inserts with inserts that have blue paint marks, then check the oil clearance once again. Always replace all of the inserts at the same time.

12   The clearance might be slightly greater than the standard clearance, but that doesn't matter, as long as it isn't greater than the maximum clearance or less than the minimum clearance.

13   If the clearance is greater than the service limit listed in this Chapter's

25.8   Lay the Plastigage strips (arrow) on the journals, parallel to the crankshaft centerline

---

25   Crankshaft and main bearings – removal, inspection, main bearing selection and installation

---

Removal

Refer to illustrations 25.1 and 25.2

1   Crankshaft removal is a simple matter of lifting it out of place once the crankcase has been separated and the starter motor clutch/secondary sprocket assembly has been removed. Before removing the crankshaft check the endplay. This can be done with a dial indicator mounted in-line with the crankshaft, or feeler gauges inserted between the no. 2 crankcase main journal **(see illustration)**. Compare your findings with this Chapter's Specifications. If the endplay is excessive, the case halves must be replaced.

2   The main bearing inserts can be removed from their saddles by pushing their centers to the side, then lifting them out **(see illustration)**. Keep the bearing inserts in order. The main bearing oil clearance should be checked, however, before removing the inserts (see Step 8).

25.10 Measuring the width of the crushed Plastigage (be sure to use the correct scale – standard and metric are included)

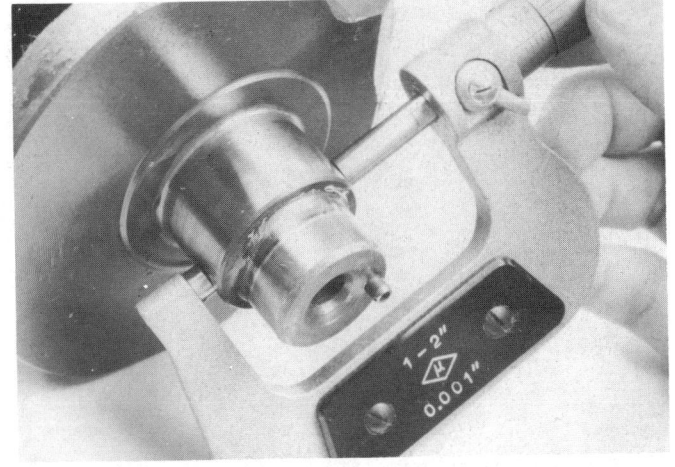

25.13 Measure the diameter of each crankshaft journal at several points to detect taper and out-of-round conditions

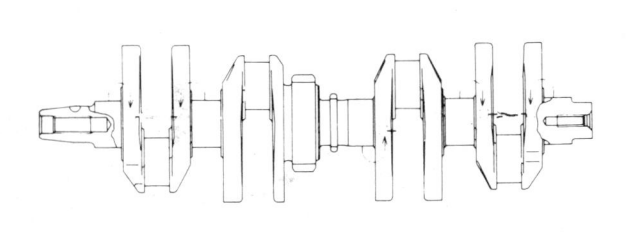

25.15 Use the marks ("1" or none) on the crankshaft (arrows) . . .

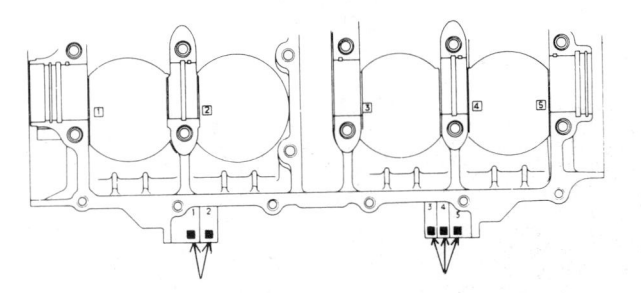

25.16 . . . in conjunction with the marks ("0" or none) on the upper case half (arrows) . . .

25.17 . . . to determine the proper main bearing sizes

Crankcase Main Bearing Bore Diameter Marking	Crankshaft Main Journal Diameter Marking	Bearing Insert*		
		Size Color	Part Number	Journal Nos.
○	1	Brown	13034-1016	2, 4
			13034-1066	1, 3, 5
○	None	Black	13034-1017	2, 4
None	1		13034-1065	1, 3, 5
None	None	Blue	13034-1018	2, 4
			13034-1064	1, 3, 5

Specifications, measure the diameter of the crankshaft journals with a micrometer (**see illustration**) and compare your findings with this Chapter's Specifications. Also, by measuring the diameter at a number of points around each journal's circumference, you'll be able to determine whether or not the journal is out-of-round. Take the measurement at each end of the journal, near the crank throws, to determine if the journal is tapered.

14 If any crank journal has worn down past the service limit, replace the crankshaft.

15 If the diameters of the journals aren't less than the service limit but differ from the original markings on the crankshaft (**see illustration**), apply new marks with a hammer and punch.

If the journal measures between 1.2601 to 1.2604-inch (31.984 to 31.992 mm) don't make any marks on the crank (there shouldn't be any marks there, anyway).

If the journal measures between 1.2605 to 1.2608-inch (31.993 to 32.000 mm), make a "1" mark on the crank in the area indicated (if it's not already there).

16 Remove the main bearing inserts and assemble the case halves (see Section 22). Using a telescoping gauge and a micrometer, measure the diameters of the main bearing bores, then compare the measurements with the marks on the upper case half (**see illustration**).

If the bores measure between 1.4184 to 1.4187-inch (36.000 to 36.008 mm), there should be a "0" mark in the indicated areas.

If the bores measure between 1.4187 to 1.4190-inch (36.009 to 36.016 mm), there shouldn't be any marks in the indicated areas.

17 Using the marks on the crank and the marks on the case, determine the bearing sizes required by referring to the accompanying bearing selection chart (**see illustration**).

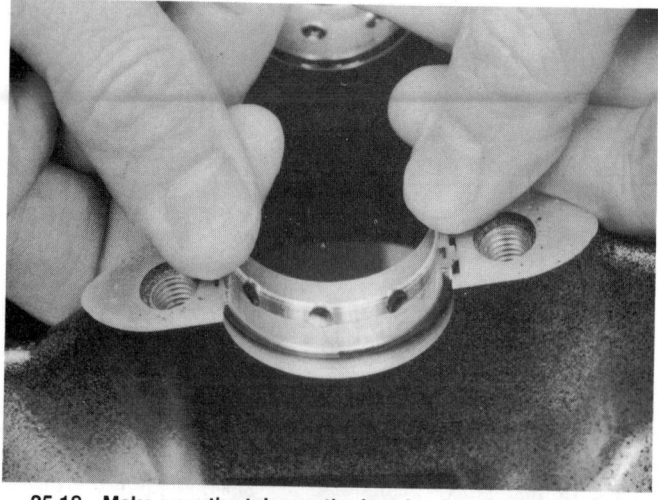

25.18   Make sure the tabs on the bearing inserts fit into the notches in the web

25.23   When installing the crankshaft, make sure the ribs on each seal seat in the grooves in the case (arrows)

26.1   Check the connecting rod side clearance with a feeler gauge

26.2   Using a hammer and a punch, make matching cylinder number marks on the connecting rod and its cap

Installation

Refer to illustrations 25.18 and 25.23

18   Separate the case halves once again. Clean the bearing saddles in the case halves, then install the bearing inserts in their webs in the case **(see illustration)**. The bearing inserts for journals 2 and 4 have oil grooves. When installing the bearings, use your hands only – don't tap them into place with a hammer.

19   Lubricate the bearing inserts with engine assembly lube or moly-based grease.

20   Install the connecting rods, if they were removed (see Section 26).

21   Install new oil seals to the ends of the crankshaft (the lips of the seal must face the crankshaft. Be sure to lubricate the lips of the seals with high-temperature grease before sliding them into place.

22   Loop the camshaft chain and the primary chain over the crankshaft and lay them onto their gears.

23   Carefully lower the crankshaft into place, making sure the ribs on the seal outer diameters seat in the grooves in the case **(see illustration)**.

24   Assemble the case halves (see Section 22) and check to make sure the crankshaft and the transmission shaft turns freely.

---

26   **Connecting rods and bearings – removal, inspection, bearing selection and installation**

Removal

Refer to illustrations 26.1 and 26.2

1   Before removing the connecting rods from the crankshaft, measure the side clearance of each rod with a feeler gauge **(see illustration)**. If the clearance on any rod is greater than that listed in this Chapter's Specifications, that rod will have to be replaced with a new one.

2   Using a center punch, mark the position of each rod and cap, relative to its position on the crankshaft **(see illustration)**.

3   Unscrew the bearing cap nuts, separate the cap from the rod, then detach the rod from the crankshaft. If the cap is stuck, tap on the ends of the rod bolts with a soft face hammer to free them.

4   Separate the bearing inserts from the rods and caps, keeping them in order so they can be reinstalled in their original locations. Wash the parts in solvent and dry them with compressed air, if available.

Inspection

Refer to illustration 26.5

5   Check the connecting rods for cracks and other obvious damage. Lubricate the piston pin for each rod, install it in the proper rod and check for play **(see illustration)**. If it is loose, replace the connecting rod and/or the pin.

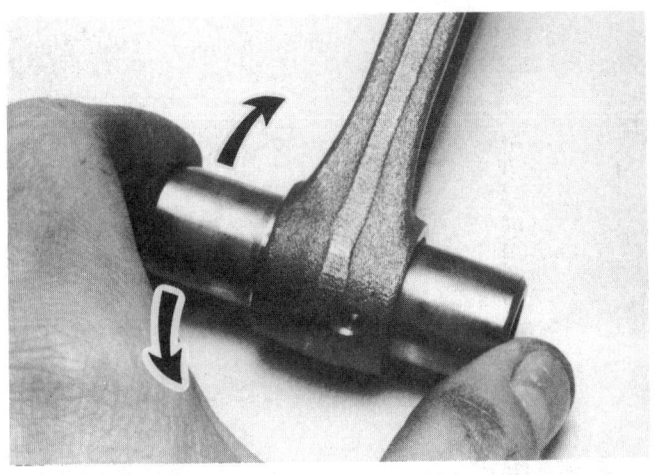

26.5 Checking the piston pin and connecting rod bore for wear

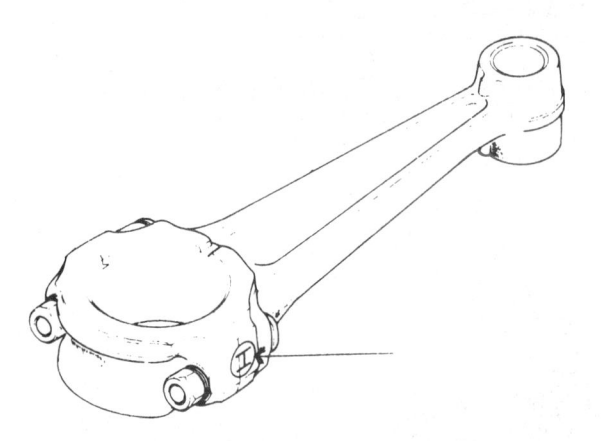

26.18 The marks on the crank throws (arrows) should coincide with the diameters of the connecting rod journals

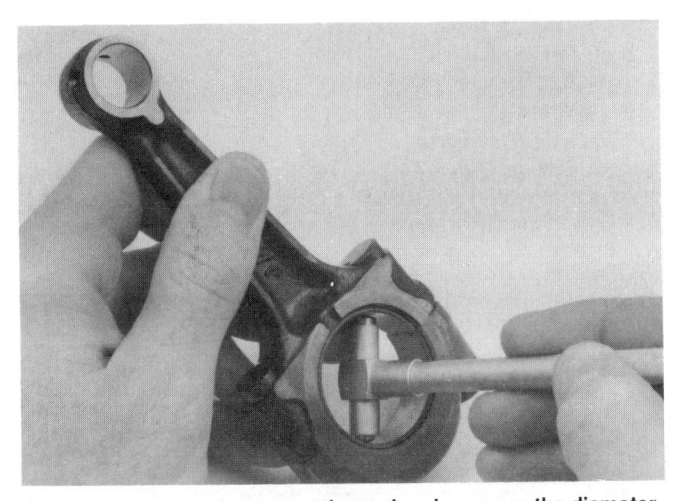

26.20a Assemble the connecting rod and measure the diameter of the bore with a telescoping gauge – then measure the gauge with a micrometer

6   Refer to Section 24 and examine the connecting rod bearing inserts. If they are scored, badly scuffed or appear to have been seized, new bearings must be installed. Always replace the bearings in the connecting rods as a set. If they are badly damaged, check the corresponding crankshaft journal. Evidence of extreme heat, such as discoloration, indicates that lubrication failure has occurred. Be sure to thoroughly check the oil pump and pressure relief valve as well as all oil holes and passages before reassembling the engine.

7   Have the rods checked for twist and bending at a dealer service department or other motorcycle repair shop.

Bearing selection

Refer to illustrations 26.18, 26.20a, 26.20b and 26.21

8   If the bearings and journals appear to be in good condition, check the oil clearances as follows:

9   Start with the rod for the number one cylinder. Wipe the bearing inserts and the connecting rod and cap clean, using a lint-free cloth.

10   Install the bearing inserts in the connecting rod and cap. Make sure the tab on the bearing engages with the notch in the rod or cap.

11   Wipe off the connecting rod journal with a lint-free cloth. Lay a strip of Plastigage (type HPG-1) across the top of the journal, parallel with the journal axis **(see illustration 25.8)**.

12   Position the connecting rod on the bottom of the journal, then install the rod cap and nuts. Tighten the nuts to the torque listed in this Chapter's Specifications, but don't allow the connecting rod to rotate at all.

13   Unscrew the nuts and remove the connecting rod and cap from the journal, being very careful not to disturb the Plastigage.

26.20b The mark (or lack of a mark) on the connecting rod (arrow), in conjunction with the mark on the crank throw . . .

Compare the width of the crushed Plastigage to the scale printed in the Plastigage envelope **(see illustration 25.10)** to determine the bearing oil clearance.

14   If the clearance is within the range listed in this Chapter's Specifications and the bearings are in perfect condition, they can be reused. If the clearance is within 0.0023-inch (0.059 mm) and the service limit (0.0039 in [0.10 mm]), replace the bearing inserts with inserts that have blue paint marks, then check the oil clearance once again. Always replace all of the inserts at the same time.

15   The clearance might be slightly greater than the standard clearance, but that doesn't matter, as long as it isn't greater than the maximum clearance or less than the minimum clearance.

16   If the clearance is greater than the service limit listed in this Chapter's Specifications, measure the diameter of the connecting rod journal with a micrometer and compare your findings with this Chapter's Specifications. Also, by measuring the diameter at a number of points around the journal's circumference, you'll be able to determine whether or not the journal is out-of-round. Take the measurement at each end of the journal to determine if the journal is tapered.

17   If any journal has worn down past the service limit, replace the crankshaft.

18   If the diameter of the journal isn't less than the service limit but differs from the original markings on the crankshaft **(see illustration)**, apply new marks with a hammer and punch.

> *If the journal measures between 1.2995 to 1.2998-inch (32.984 to 32.992 mm) don't make any marks on the crank (there shouldn't be one there anyway).*
>
> *If the journal measures between 1.2999 to 1.3002-inch (32.993 to 33.000 mm), make a "0" mark on the crank in the area indicated (if not already there).*

19   Remove the bearing inserts from the connecting rod and cap, then assemble the cap to the rod. Tighten the nuts to the torque listed in this Chapter's Specifications.

20   Using a telescoping gauge and a micrometer, measure the inside diameter of the connecting rod **(see illustration)**. The mark on the connect-

2

Con-rod Big End Bore Diameter Marking	Crankpin Diameter Marking	Bearing Insert	
		Size Color	Part Number
○	None	Blue	13034-1067
○	○	Black	13034-1068
None	None		
None	○	Brown	13034-1069

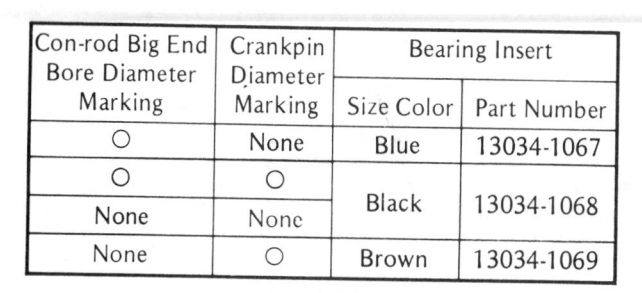

26.21 ... can be used, along with this chart, to determine the correct connecting rod bearing inserts to install

26.24   When installing the connecting rods, make sure your matchmarks are on the same side and the JAPAN casting points toward the tapered end of the crankshaft – the letter (arrow) is a weight grade mark

and they don't all have the same letter on them, two rods with the same letter should be installed on one side of the crank, and the letters on the other two rods should match each other. This will minimize vibration.

25 When you're sure the rods are positioned correctly, tighten the nuts to the torque listed in this Chapter's Specifications.

26 Turn the rods on the crankshaft. If any of them feel tight, tap on the bottom of the connecting rod caps with a hammer – this should relieve stress and free them up. If it doesn't, recheck the bearing clearance.

27 As a final step, recheck the connecting rod side clearances (see Step 1). If the clearances aren't correct, find out why before proceeding with engine assembly.

27.5   Use a plastic hammer to drive the secondary shaft from the case

ing rod (if any) should coincide with the measurement, but if it doesn't, make a new mark **(see illustration)**.

> If the inside diameter measures between 1.4184 to 1.4187-inch (36.000 to 36.008 mm), don't make any mark on the rod (there shouldn't be any there anyway).
> If the inside diameter measures between 1.4187 to 1.4190-inch (36.009 to 36.016 mm), make a 0 mark on the rod (it should already be there).

21 By referring to the accompanying chart **(see illustration)**, select the correct connecting rod bearing inserts.

22 Repeat the bearing selection procedure for the remaining connecting rods.

Installation

Refer to illustration 26.24

23 Wipe off the bearing inserts and connecting rods and caps. Install the inserts into the rods and caps, using your hands only, making sure the tabs on the inserts engage with the notches in the rods and caps. When all the inserts are installed, lubricate them with engine assembly lube or moly-based grease. Don't get any lubricant on the mating surfaces of the rod or cap.

24 Assemble each connecting rod to its proper journal, making sure the previously applied matchmarks correspond to each other and the JAPAN casting points to the alternator rotor end of the crankshaft (the tapered end) **(see illustration)**. Also, the letter present at the rod/cap seam on one side of the connecting rod is a weight mark. If new rods are being installed

27   Secondary sprocket, shaft and starter motor clutch – removal, inspection and installation

Removal

Refer to illustrations 27.5, 27.6 and 27.7

1 Drain the cooling system and the engine oil (see Chapter 1). Remove the water pump (see Chapter 3). Also remove the water pump base – it's fastened to the crankcase with two bolts.

2 Remove the alternator cover. Using a special alternator rotor holder or a pin-type spanner, hold the rotor stationary and loosen the secondary shaft nut **(see illustration 22.3)**.

3 Remove the engine (see Section 5).

4 Separate the crankcase halves (see Section 22).

5 Remove the nut from the secondary shaft. Using a soft face hammer, tap the secondary shaft out, toward the right side of the case, until the bearing on the right side of the case is free **(see illustration)**.

6 Hold the starter motor clutch assembly and pull the secondary shaft out of the case **(see illustration)**. There is a sleeve on the shaft that fits into the ball bearing on the left side of the case – be careful not to lose it. There's also a washer on the shaft.

7 Detach the primary chain from the starter motor clutch/secondary sprocket remove the clutch assembly **(see illustration)**.

Inspection

Starter motor clutch

Refer to illustrations 27.8 and 27.9

8 Hold the starter motor clutch and attempt to turn the starter motor clutch gear back and forth **(see illustration)**. It should only turn in one direction.

27.6 Hold the secondary sprocket/starter motor clutch assembly and pull the secondary shaft out – be careful not to lose the sleeve that fits into the bearing in the left side of the case, or the washer on the shaft

27.7 Lift the primary chain and remove the secondary sprocket/starter motor clutch assembly

27.8 Try to turn the starter motor clutch gear back and forth – it should only turn in one direction

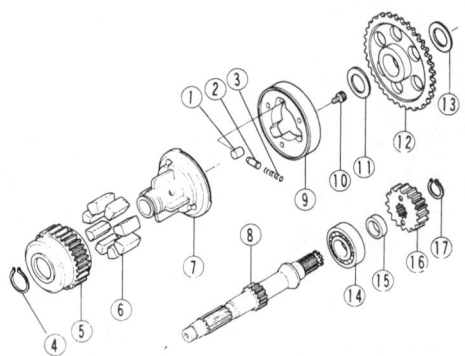

27.9 Exploded view of the secondary sprocket/starter motor clutch and shaft assembly

1	Roller	9	Starter motor clutch
2	Spring cap	10	Allen bolts
3	Spring	11	Thrust washer
4	Snap-ring	12	Starter motor clutch gear
5	Secondary sprocket	13	Thrust washer
6	Rubber dampers	14	Ball bearing assembly
7	Inner coupling	15	Collar
8	Secondary shaft	16	Secondary shaft gear
		17	Snap-ring

9   If the starter motor clutch turns freely in both directions, or if it's locked up, disassemble it and inspect the components **(see illustration)**. To do this, remove the snap-ring and pull off the secondary sprocket, remove the Allen-head bolts and detach the inner coupling from the clutch.

10   Check the springs for wear, the rollers for scoring and pitting, and the rubber dampers for deterioration. Check the teeth on the sprockets for cracks and chips. Check the bushing in the starter motor clutch gear for scoring or heat discoloration. Replace parts as necessary.

Starter motor idler gear
Refer to illustration 27.11

11   Inspect the teeth on the starter motor idler gear for cracks and chips **(see illustration)**. Turn the idler gear to make sure it spins freely. If the idler gear exhibits any undesirable conditions, replace it. To remove the idler, pry the clip from the idler shaft, slide the shaft out and remove the gear. Coat the shaft with engine assembly lube or moly-based grease before installing it.

Secondary shaft and bearings
Refer to illustration 27.13 and 27.14

12   Check the splines, gear and threads on the shaft for wear or damage.

27.11 If it's necessary to remove the idler gear from the case, remove the clip (arrow), slide the shaft out and lift the gear from the case

27.13   Use a bearing puller setup like this to remove the bearing from the shaft (it can also be used to pull the gear off the shaft, if it's turned around)

27.14   Remove the snap-ring from the end of the shaft with snap-ring pliers

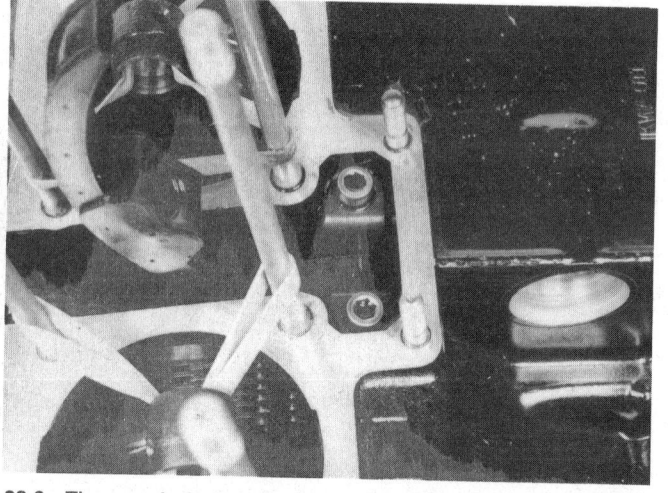

28.6   The camshaft chain rear guide is retained to the crankcase by two Allen-head bolts

13   Turn the bearing and feel for tight spots and roughness. If necessary, pull the bearing off the shaft, using a bearing puller **(see illustration)**. The new bearing can be tapped onto the shaft, using a piece of pipe with an inside diameter large enough to fit over the shaft and contact the inner race of the bearing.

14   If the gear needs to be replaced, remove the snap-ring from the end of the shaft **(see illustration)** and pull the gear off, using the same setup described in Step 13 **(see illustration 27.13)**. Don't lose the collar on the shaft. When installing the gear, lubricate the splines on the shaft with engine oil and carefully tap the gear into place using a section of pipe.

15   Check the secondary shaft bearing in the right side of the lower case half. If it turns roughly or feels tight, replace it by referring to Section 23.

Installation

16   Lubricate the rollers in the starter motor clutch with engine oil and assemble the clutch gear to it. Make sure the washer is present between the two components.

17   Lift the primary chain and guide the starter motor clutch assembly into place.

18   Lubricate the secondary shaft with engine oil and install the washer and sleeve. Guide the shaft into the case and through the secondary sprocket/starter clutch assembly.

19   Using a soft-face hammer, tap the shaft into the case until the bearing is completely seated. Install the secondary shaft nut, hold the alternator rotor stationary and tighten the nut to the torque listed in this Chapter's Specifications. You may want to wait until the engine is mounted in the frame before you tighten this nut, unless you have an assistant to help you.

20   The remainder of installation is the reverse of the removal procedure. Be sure to fill the cooling system with the proper coolant mixture and the crankcase with the recommended engine oil (see Chapter 1).

---

28   Primary chain, camshaft chain and guides – removal, inspection and installation

---

Removal

Primary chain and camshaft chain
1   Remove the engine (see Section 5).
2   Separate the crankcase halves (see Section 22).
3   Remove the crankshaft (see Section 25).
4   Remove the chains from the crankshaft.

Chain guides
Refer to illustrations 28.6 and 28.8

5   The cam chain front guide can be lifted from the cylinder block after the head has been removed (see Section 13).

6   The cam chain rear guide is fastened to the crankcase with a bracket and two bolts **(see illustration)**. Remove the bolts and detach the guide and bracket from the case.

7   The primary chain guide in the lower case half is removed in a similar manner.

8   The primary chain guide in the upper case half is secured by two Allen-head bolts **(see illustration)**.

Inspection

Primary chain and camshaft chain
Refer to illustration 28.9

9   The primary chain and camshaft chains are checked in a similar manner. Pull the chain tight to eliminate all slack and measure the length of twenty links, pin-to-pin **(see illustration)**. Compare your findings to this Chapter's Specifications.

10   Also check the chains for binding and obvious damage.

11   If the twenty-link length is not as specified, or there is visible damage, replace the chain.

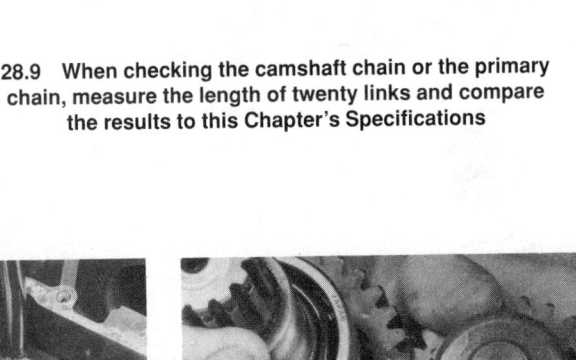

28.9 When checking the camshaft chain or the primary chain, measure the length of twenty links and compare the results to this Chapter's Specifications

28.8 The chain guide in the upper case half is secured to the case with two Allen-head bolts

29.2 With the plunger of the dial indicator contacting a gear tooth, move the gear back-and-forth within its freeplay while holding its companion gear still

29.5 Make sure the set pins and rings (arrows) are installed in their proper positions

29.6 When lowering the shafts into place, the hole in the needle bearing outer race must fit over the set pin, and groove in the ball bearing outer race must fit over the set ring (arrows)

2

Chain guides

12 Check the guides for deep grooves, cracking and other obvious damage, replacing them if necessary.

Installation

13 Installation of these components is the reverse of the removal procedure. When installing the brackets for the cam chain rear guide and the primary chain guides, apply a non-hardening thread locking compound to the threads of the bolts. Tighten the bolts to the torque listed in this Chapter's Specifications. Apply engine oil to the faces of the guides and to the chains.

---

29 Transmission shafts – removal and installation

Refer to illustrations 29.2, 29.5 and 29.6

Removal

1 Remove the engine and clutch, then separate the case halves (see Sections 5, 19 and 22).
2 Before removing either shaft, check the backlash of each set of gears.

To do this, mount a dial indicator with the plunger of the indicator touching a tooth on one of the gears, then move the gear back and forth within its freeplay, holding its companion gear stationary **(see illustration)**. Check each set of gears, recording the measurements, and compare the results to this Chapter's Specifications. If the backlash between any pair of gears exceeds the limit, replace both gears (see Section 30).
3 The shafts can simply be lifted out of the upper half of the case. If they are stuck, use a soft-face hammer and gently tap on the bearings on the ends of the shafts to free them. The shaft nearest the rear of the case is the output shaft – the other shaft is the main drive shaft.
4 Refer to Section 30 for information pertaining to transmission shaft service and Section 31 for information pertaining to the shift drum and forks.

Installation

5 Check to make sure the set pins and rings are present in the upper case half, where the shaft bearings seat **(see illustration)**.
6 Carefully lower each shaft into place. The holes in the needle bearing outer races must engage with the set pins, and the grooves in the ball bearing outer races must engage with the set rings **(see illustration)**.
7 The remainder of installation is the reverse of removal.

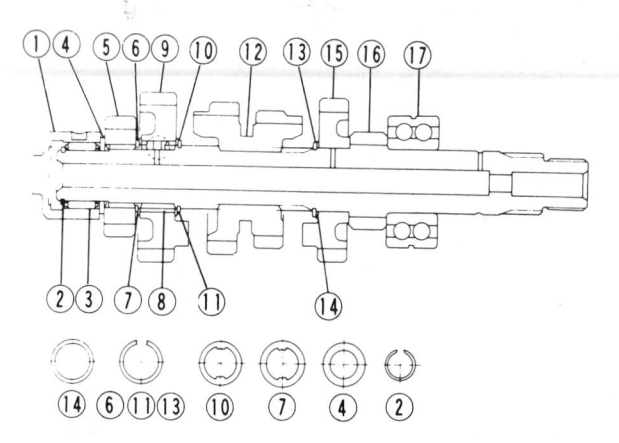

30.2a Details of the transmission main drive shaft

1	Bearing outer race	10	Toothed washer
2	Snap-ring	11	Snap-ring
3	Needle bearing	12	Third/fourth gear
4	Thrust washer	13	Snap-ring
5	Second gear	14	Washer
6	Snap-ring	15	Fifth gear
7	Toothed washer	16	Drive shaft (first gear)
8	Bushing	17	Ball bearing
9	Sixth gear		

30.2b Remove the snap-ring from the end of the shaft and slide the needle bearing off

30.4a Remove the snap-ring . . .

30.3 Slide the thrust washer and second gear from the shaft

4   Remove the snap-ring **(see illustration)**, toothed washer, sixth gear and bushing **(see illustration)**.
5   Slide the next toothed washer off and remove the snap-ring **(see illustration)**.
6   Remove the third/fourth gear cluster from the shaft **(see illustration)**.
7   Remove the next snap-ring, then slide the washer and and fifth gear off the shaft **(see illustration)**.

Inspection

Refer to illustrations 30.9 and 30.11

8   Wash all of the components in clean solvent and dry them off. Rotate the ball bearing on the shaft, feeling for tightness, rough spots, excessive looseness and listening for noises. If any of these conditions are found, replace the bearing. This will require the use of a hydraulic press or a bearing puller setup. If you don't have access to these tools, take the shaft and bearing to a Kawasaki dealer or other motorcycle repair shop and have them press the old bearing off the shaft and install the new one.
9   Measure the shift fork groove between third and fourth gears **(see illustration)**. If the groove width exceeds the figure listed in this Chapter's Specifications, replace the third/fourth gear assembly, and also check the third/fourth gear shift fork (see Section 31).
10   Check the gear teeth for cracking and other obvious damage. Check the bushing surface in the inner diameter of sixth gear for scoring or heat discoloration. If it's damaged, replace it (check with your Kawasaki dealer – they may be able to replace the bushing insert).
11   Inspect the dogs and the dog holes on the gears for excessive wear **(see illustration)**. Replace the paired gears as a set if necessary.
12   Check the needle bearing and race for wear or heat discoloration and replace them if necessary.

30 Transmission shafts – disassembly, inspection and reassembly

Note: *When disassembling the transmission shafts, place the parts on a long rod or thread a wire through them to keep them in order and facing the proper direction.*
1   Remove the shafts from the case (see Section 29).

Main drive shaft

Disassembly
Refer to illustrations 30.2a, 30.2b, 30.3, 30.4a, 30.4b, 30.5, 30.6 and 30.7
2   Remove the needle bearing outer race, then remove the snap-ring from the end of the shaft and slide the needle bearing off **(see illustrations)**.
3   Remove the thrust washer and slide second gear off the shaft **(see illustration)**.

30.4b . . . followed by the washer, sixth gear and bushing

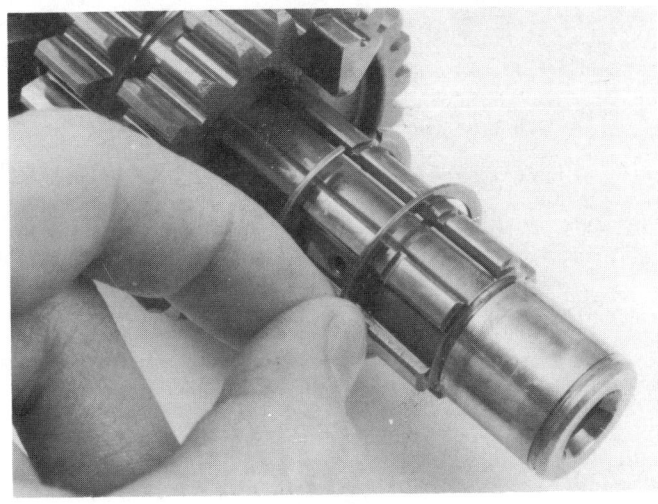

30.5 Remove the toothed washer and snap-ring from the shaft . . .

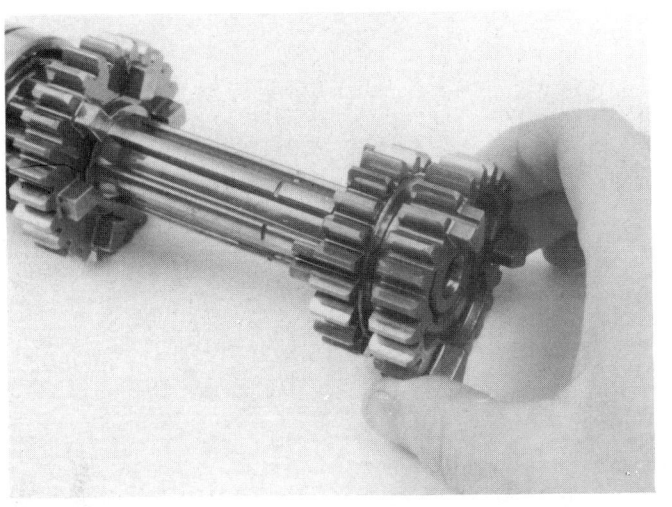

30.6 . . . then slide the third/fourth gear cluster off the shaft

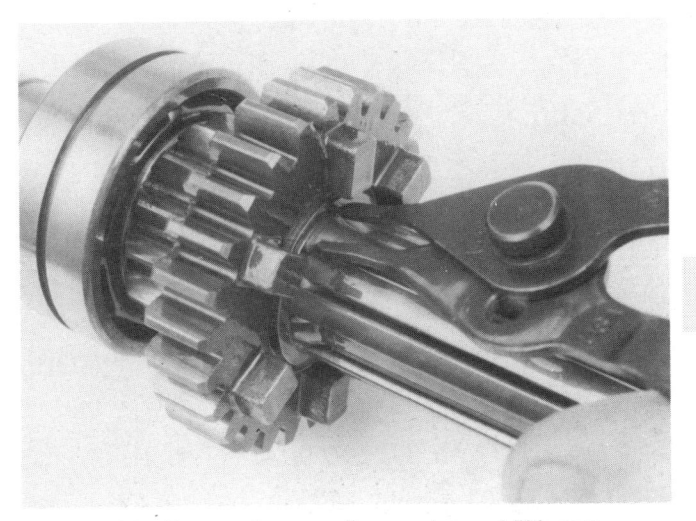

30.7 Remove the snap-ring, washer and fifth gear

2

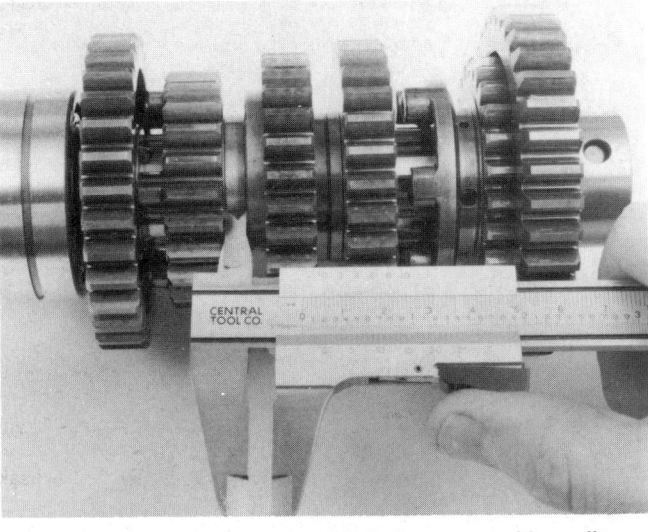

30.9 Measure the width of the shift fork grooves with a caliper

30.11 If the gear dogs and dog holes (arrows) show signs of excessive wear, replace the gears as a set

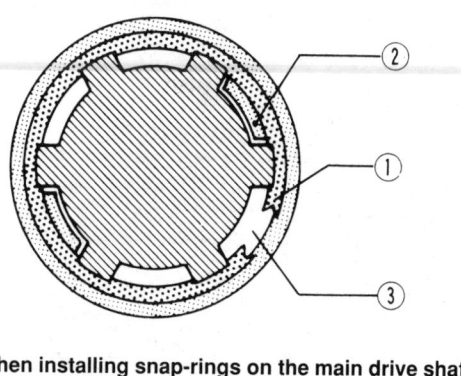

30.13a   When installing snap-rings on the main drive shaft, align the opening in the snap-ring with a spline groove

1   Snap-ring
2   Tab on toothed washer
3   Spline groove

30.13b   Align the oil hole in the bushing with the hole in the shaft (arrows)

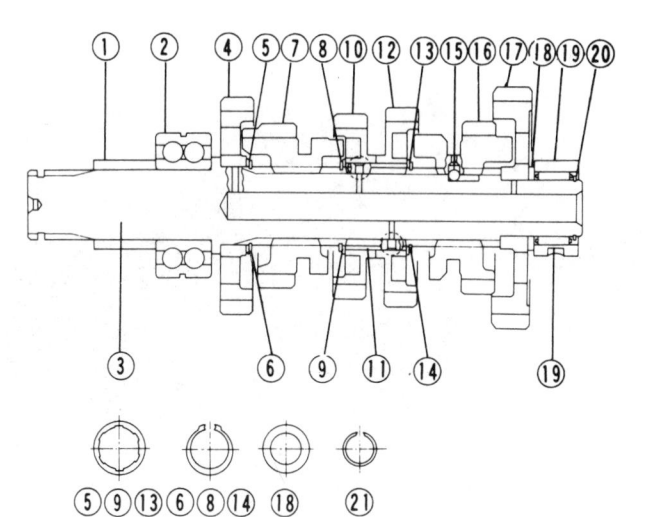

30.14   Details of the transmission output shaft

1	*Collar*	*12*	*Third gear*
2	*Ball bearing*	*13*	*Toothed washer*
3	*Output shaft*	*14*	*Snap-ring*
4	*Second gear*	*15*	*Steel ball*
5	*Toothed washer*	*16*	*Fifth gear*
6	*Snap-ring*	*17*	*First gear*
7	*Sixth gear*	*18*	*Thrust washer*
8	*Snap-ring*	*19*	*Needle bearing*
9	*Toothed washer*	*20*	*Bearing outer race*
10	*Fourth gear*	*21*	*Snap-ring*
11	*Bushing*		

30.15   Remove the snap-ring from the end of the shaft and slide the needle bearing off

Reassembly

Refer to illustrations 30.13a and 30.13b

13   Reassembly is the basically the reverse of the disassembly procedure, but take note of the following points:

a)   Always use new snap-rings and align the opening of the ring with a spline groove **(see illustration)**

b)   When installing the bushing for sixth gear to the shaft, align the oil hole on the shaft with the oil hole in the bushing **(see illustration)**.

c)   Lubricate the components with engine oil before assembling them.

Output shaft

Disassembly

Refer to illustrations 30.14, 30.15, 30.16, 30.17, 30.18 and 30.19

14   Remove the needle bearing outer race **(see illustration)**.

15   Remove the snap-ring from the end of the shaft and slide the needle bearing off **(see illustration)**.

16   Remove the washer, first gear and fifth gear from the shaft. Fifth gear has three steel balls in it for the positive neutral finder mechanism. To remove the gear, grasp third gear and hold the shaft in a vertical position with one hand, and with the other hand, spin the shaft back and forth, holding onto fifth gear and pulling up **(see illustration)**. **Caution:** *Don't pull the gear up too hard or fast – the balls will fly out of the gear.*

17   Remove the snap-ring, toothed washer, third gear, bushing and fourth gear from the shaft **(see illustration)**.

18   Remove the toothed washer, snap-ring and sixth gear **(see illustration)**.

19   Remove the next snap-ring, toothed washer and second gear.

30.16   Hold the output shaft vertically and spin fifth gear (which will also turn the shaft) while pulling up

30.17   Remove the snap-ring, toothed washer, third gear, bushing and fourth gear

30.18   Remove the washer, snap-ring and sixth gear

30.19   Remove the snap-ring, washer and second gear

Inspection

20   Refer to Steps 8 through 12 for the inspection procedures. They are the same, except when checking the shift fork groove width you'll be checking it on fifth gear and sixth gears.

Reassembly

Refer to illustration 30.21

21   Reassembly is the basically the reverse of the disassembly procedure, but take note of the following points:

   a) Always use new snap-rings and align the opening of the ring with a spline groove (**see illustration**).

   b) When installing the bushing for third and fourth gear, align the oil hole in the bushing with the hole in the shaft.

   c) When installing fifth gear, don't use grease to hold the balls in place – to do so would impair the positive neutral finder mechanism. Just set the balls in their holes (the holes that they can't pass through), keep the gear in a vertical position and carefully set it on the shaft (engine oil will help keep them in place). The spline grooves that contain the holes with the balls must be aligned with the slots in the shaft spline grooves.

   d) Lubricate the components with engine oil before assembling them.

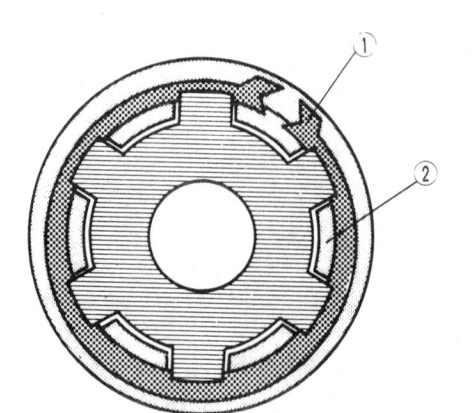

30.21   Install the snap-rings so the opening in the ring is aligned with a spline groove

31.2   Hold the shift forks and pull the shift rod out

31.3   Remove the shift drum positioning bolt and lift out the spring and pin

31.4   Remove the guide bolt

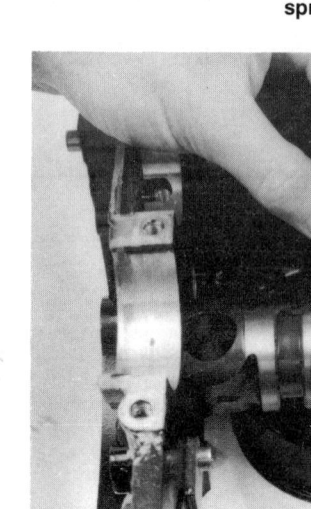

31.5   Remove the cotter pin and guide pin

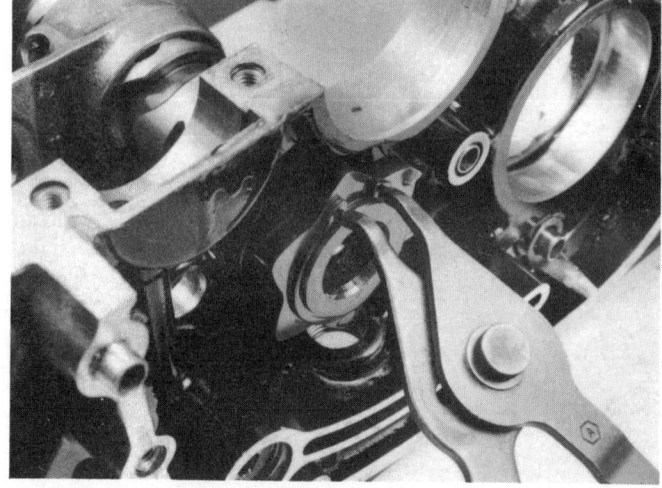

31.6   Remove the snap-ring and slide the operating plate off the shift drum

---

31   Shift drum and forks – removal, inspection and installation

Removal

Refer to illustrations 31.2, 31.3, 31.4, 31.5, 31.6 and 31.7

1   Remove the engine and separate the crankcase halves (see Sections 5 and 22).

2   Support the shift forks and pull the shift rod out to the left **(see illustration)**.

3   Remove the shift drum positioning bolt and remove the spring and pin **(see illustration)**.

4   Straighten the lock tab on the shift drum guide bolt, then remove the bolt and tab **(see illustration)**.

5   Remove the cotter pin and pull out the guide pin **(see illustration)**.

6   Remove the operating plate snap-ring from the end of the shift drum, then slide the shift drum off **(see illustration)**.

7   Pull the shift drum out of the case far enough to remove the fifth/sixth shift fork **(see illustration)**, then slide the shift drum out of the case.

31.7   Pull the shift drum out slightly and remove the fifth/sixth gear shift fork

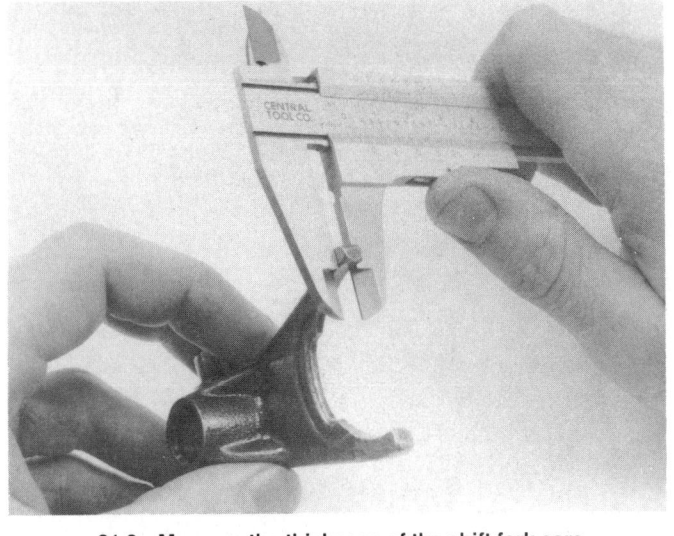

31.9   Measure the thickness of the shift fork ears

Inspection

Refer to illustration 31.9

8   Check the edges of the grooves in the drum for signs of excessive wear. Measure the widths of the grooves and compare your findings to this Chapter's Specifications.

9   Check the shift forks for distortion and wear, especially at the fork ears. Measure the thickness of the fork ears and compare your findings with this Chapter's Specifications **(see illustration)**. If they are discolored or severely worn they are probably bent. If damage or wear is evident, check the shift fork groove in the corresponding gear as well. Inspect the guide pins and the shaft bore for excessive wear and distortion and replace any defective parts with new ones.

10   Check the shift fork shafts for evidence of wear, galling and other damage. Make sure the shift forks move smoothly on the shafts. If the shafts are worn or bent, replace them with new ones.

Installation

Refer to illustration 31.11

11   Installation is the reverse of removal, noting the following points:
   a) Install the shift drum part-way into the case and install the fifth/sixth shift fork (the long end goes onto the drum first).
   b) Be sure to use a new cotter pin and install it correctly **(see illustration)**.
   c) Lubricate all parts with engine oil before installing them.
   d) Tighten the guide bolt and the positioning bolt to the torque listed in this Chapter's Specifications.

---

32   Initial start-up after overhaul

Note: *Make sure the cooling system is checked carefully (especially the coolant level) before starting and running the engine.*

1   Make sure the engine oil level is correct, then remove the spark plugs from the engine. Place the engine STOP switch in the Off position and unplug the primary (low tension) wires from the coil.

2   Turn on the key switch and crank the engine over with the starter until the oil pressure indicator light goes off (which indicates that oil pressure exists). Reinstall the spark plugs, connect the wires and turn the switch to On.

3   Make sure there is fuel in the tank, then turn the fuel tap to the Prime position and operate the choke.

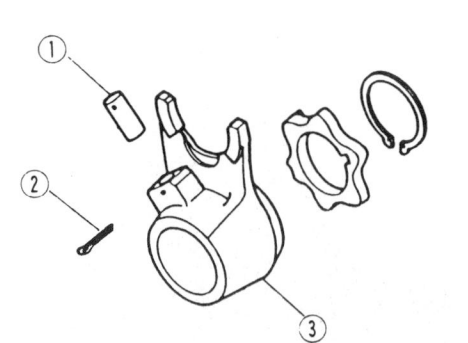

31.11   When installing the cotter pin, insert it from the side shown

| 1 | Shift fork | 2 | Cotter pin |
| | guide pin | 3 | Shift fork |

---

4   Start the engine and allow it to run at a moderately fast idle until it reaches operating temperature. **Warning:** *If the oil pressure indicator light doesn't go off, or it comes on while the engine is running, stop the engine immediately.*

5   Check carefully for oil leaks and make sure the transmission and controls, especially the brakes, function properly before road testing the machine. Refer to Section 33 for the recommended break-in procedure.

6   Upon completion of the road test, and after the engine has cooled down completely, recheck the valve clearances (see Chapter 1).

---

33   Recommended break-in procedure

---

1   Any rebuilt engine needs time to break-in, even if parts have been installed in their original locations. For this reason, treat the machine gently for the first few miles to make sure oil has circulated throughout the engine and any new parts installed have started to seat.

2   Even greater care is necessary if the engine has been rebored or a new crankshaft has been installed. In the case of a rebore, the engine will have to be broken in as if the machine were new. This means greater use

of the transmission and a restraining hand on the throttle until at least 500 miles have been covered. There's no point in keeping to any set speed limit – the main idea is to keep from lugging the engine and to gradually increase performance until the 500 mile mark is reached. These recommendations can be lessened to an extent when only a new crankshaft is installed. Experience is the best guide, since it's easy to tell when an engine is running freely.

3   If a lubrication failure is suspected, stop the engine immediately and try to find the cause. If an engine is run without oil, even for a short period of time, irreparable damage will occur.

Chapter 3   Cooling system

Refer to Chapter 10 for information on the ZX750F model

3

Contents

Specifications

General

Coolant type .... See Chapter 1
Mixture ratio .... See Chapter 1
Radiator cap pressure rating .... 14 to 18 psi
Thermostat rating
  Opening temperature
    A and B models .... 157 to 163-degrees F (69.5 to 72.5-degrees C)
    C models .... 177 to 182-degrees F (80.5 to 83.5-degrees C)
  Fully open at:
    A and B models .... 185-degrees F (85-degrees C)
    C models .... 203-degrees F (95-degrees C)
  Valve travel (when fully open) .... Not less then 5/16-in (8 mm)

Torque specifications

Thermostatic fan switch-to-radiator .... 69 in-lbs
Coolant temperature sending unit-to-thermostat housing .... 69 in-lbs
Oil cooler hose union bolts .... 18 ft-lbs

1   General information

Refer to illustrations 1.1a and 1.1b

The models covered by this manual are equipped with a liquid cooling system which utilizes a water/antifreeze mixture to carry away excess heat produced during the combustion process **(see illustrations)**. The cylinders are surrounded by water jackets, through which the coolant is circulated by the water pump. The pump is mounted to the left side of the crankcase and is driven by a gear mounted on the secondary shaft. The coolant passes up through a flexible hose and a coolant pipe, which distributes to water around the four cylinders. It flows through the water passages in the cylinder head, through another pipe (or hoses) and into the thermostat housing. The hot coolant then flows down into the radiator (which is mounted on the frame downtubes to take advantage of maximum air flow), where it is cooled by the passing air, through another hose and back to the water pump, where the cycle is repeated.

An electric fan, mounted behind the radiator and automatically controlled by a thermostatic switch, provides a flow of cooling air through the radiator when the motorcycle is not moving. Under certain conditions, the fan may come on even after the engine is stopped, and the ignition switch is off, and may run for several minutes.

The coolant temperature sending unit, threaded into the thermostat housing, senses the temperature of the coolant and controls the coolant temperature gauge on the instrument cluster.

The entire system is sealed and pressurized. The pressure is controlled by a valve which is part of the radiator cap. By pressurizing the coolant, the boiling point is raised, which prevents premature boiling of the coolant. An overflow hose, connected between the radiator and reservoir tank, directs coolant to the tank when the radiator cap valve is opened by excessive pressure. The coolant is automatically siphoned back to the radiator as the engine cools.

Many cooling system inspection and service procedures are considered part of routine maintenance and are included in Chapter 1.

On later UK models, the coolant is also used to warm the carburetor bodies via an arrangement of small hoses. The coolant travels from the rear of the cylinder block, through a filter, through the carburetor castings and then rejoins the main cooling system at the water pump. A check valve is fitted above the water pump to ensure the correct flow of coolant.

Warning: *Do not allow antifreeze to come in contact with your skin or painted surfaces of the vehicle. Rinse off spills immediately with plenty of water. Antifreeze is highly toxic if ingested. Never leave antifreeze lying around in an open container or in puddles on the floor; children and pets are attracted by it's sweet smell and may drink it. Check with local authorities about disposing of used antifreeze. Many communities have collection centers which will see that antifreeze is disposed of safely.*

Caution: *Do not remove the radiator cap when the engine and radiator are hot. Scalding hot coolant and steam may be blown out under pressure, which could cause serious injury. To open the radiator cap, remove the rear screw from the right side panel on the inside of the fairing (if equipped). When the engine has cooled, lift up the panel and place a thick rag, like a towel, over the radiator cap; slowly rotate the cap counterclockwise to the first stop. This procedure allows any residual pressure to escape. When the steam has stopped escaping, press down on the cap while turning counterclockwise and remove it.*

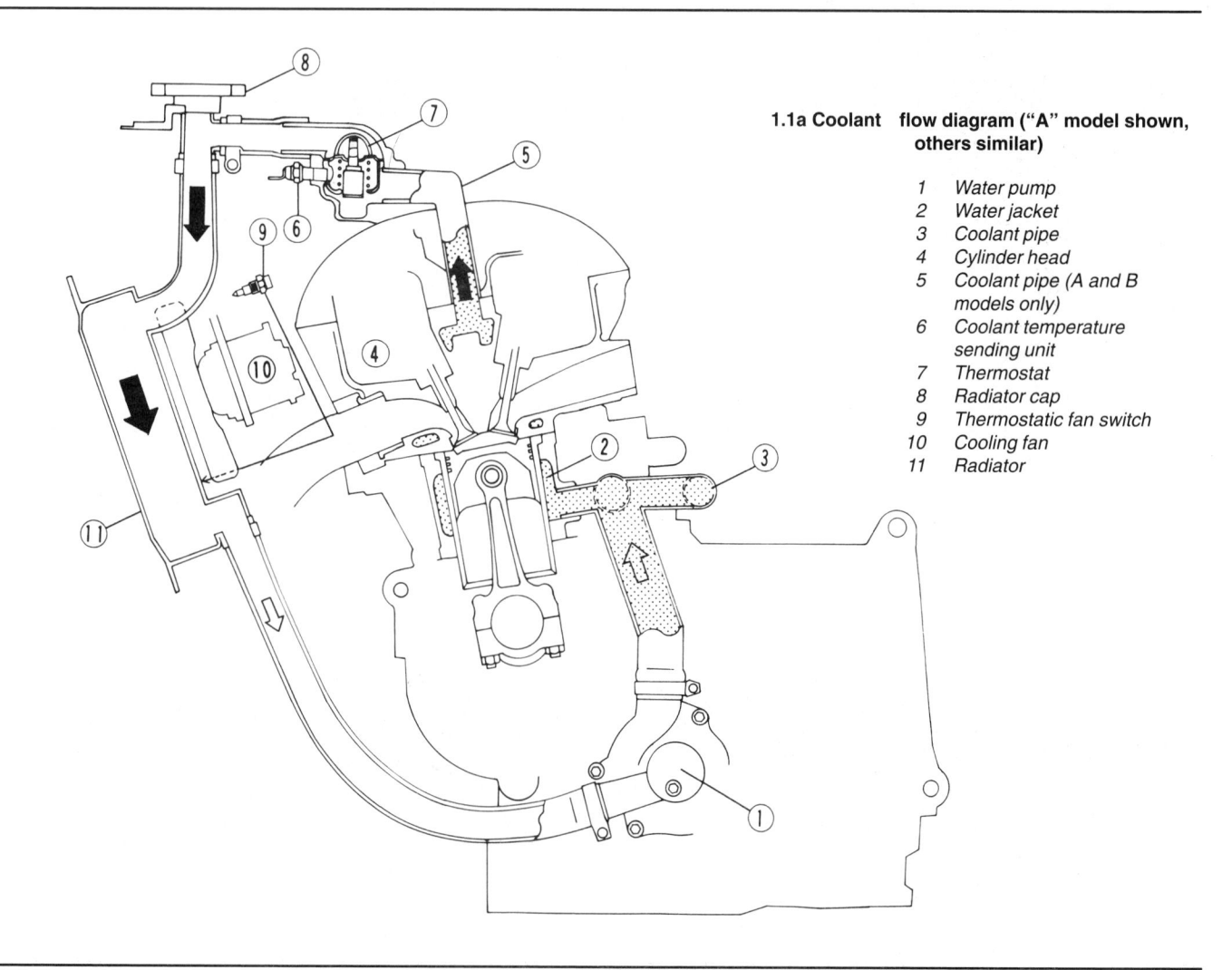

1.1a Coolant   flow diagram ("A" model shown, others similar)

1. Water pump
2. Water jacket
3. Coolant pipe
4. Cylinder head
5. Coolant pipe (A and B models only)
6. Coolant temperature sending unit
7. Thermostat
8. Radiator cap
9. Thermostatic fan switch
10. Cooling fan
11. Radiator

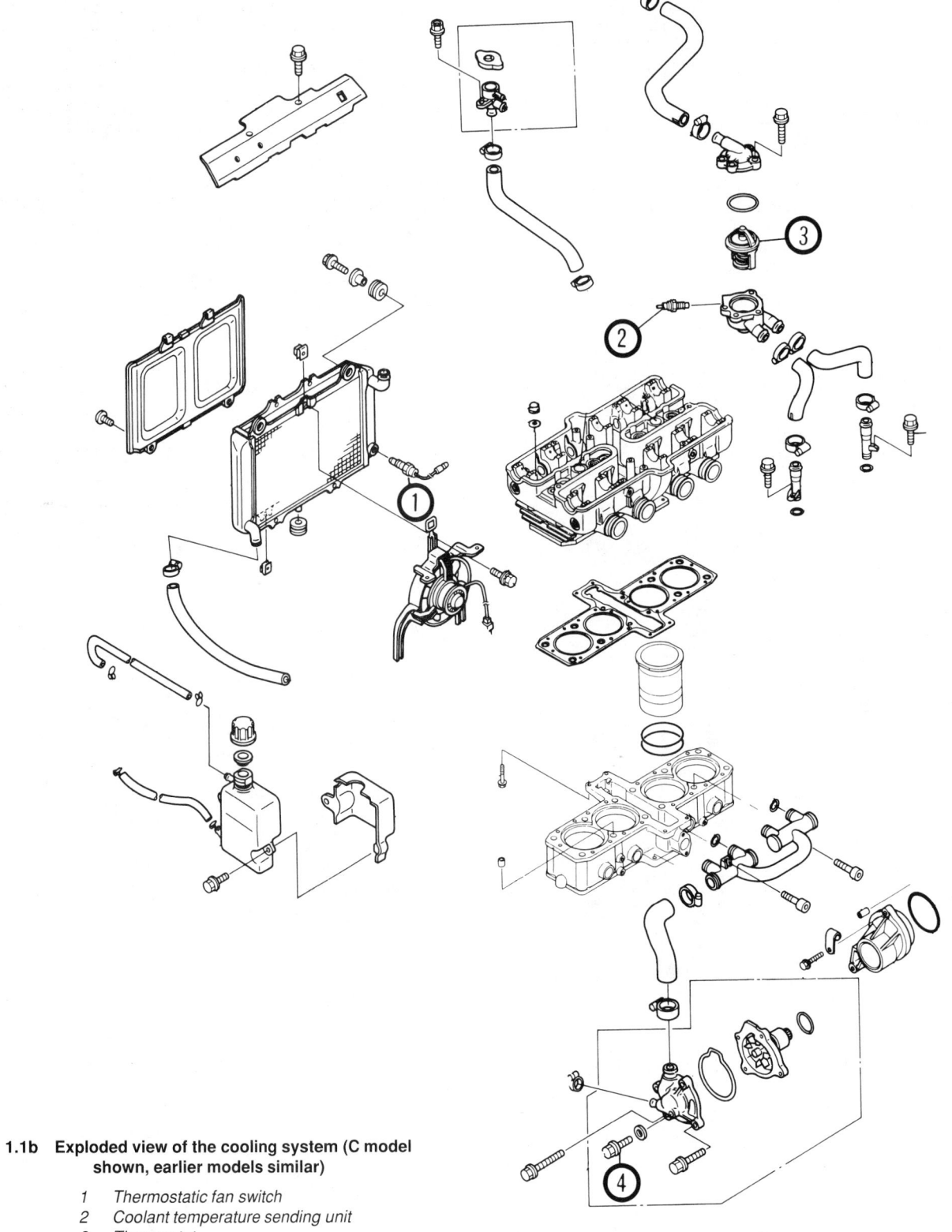

**1.1b Exploded view of the cooling system (C model
shown, earlier models similar)**

1   Thermostatic fan switch
2   Coolant temperature sending unit
3   Thermostat
4   Coolant drain plug

3

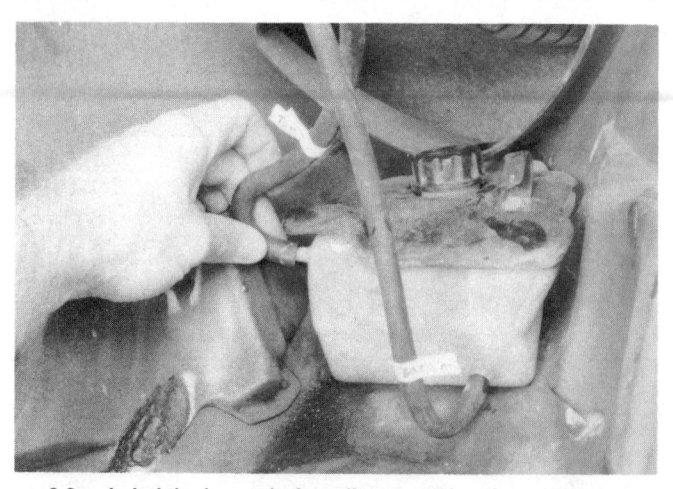

3.2a Label the hoses before disconnecting them from the reservoir (lower fairing-mounted reservoir shown)

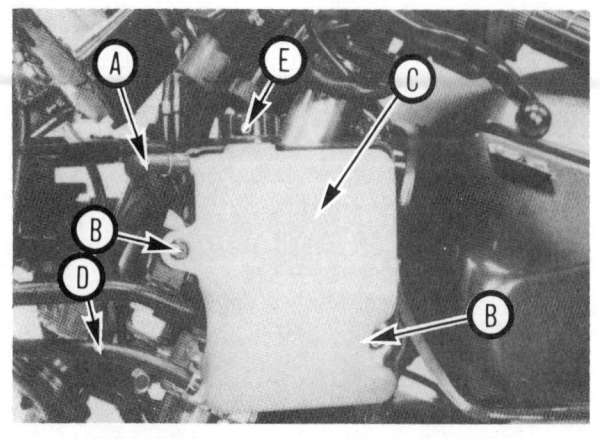

3.2b Coolant reservoir details – C models

A	Vent hose	D	Reservoir tank hose
B	Mounting bolts	E	Cap
C	Reservoir		

2   Radiator cap – check

If problems such as overheating and loss of coolant occur, check the entire system as described in Chapter 1. The radiator cap opening pressure should be checked by a dealer service department or service station equipped with the special tester required to do the job. If the cap is defective, replace it with a new one.

3   Coolant reservoir – removal and installation

Refer to illustrations 3.2a and 3.2b

1   If you're working on an A model or B model, remove the lower fairing (see Chapter 8). If you're working on a C model, remove the upper fairing (see Chapter 8).
2   Disconnect the hose(s) from the reservoir **(see illustrations)**. It's a good idea to mark the positions of the hoses so they aren't attached to the wrong fitting when the reservoir is installed.
3   Remove the reservoir retaining screws and detach the reservoir from the lower fairing (early models) or the frame (later models).
4   Installation is the reverse of the removal procedure.

4   Cooling fan and thermostatic fan switch – check and replacement

Check

Refer to illustrations 4.1 and 4.2

1   If the engine is overheating and the cooling fan isn't coming on, first remove the seat and check the fuses. If a fuse is blown, check the fan circuit for a short to ground (see the Wiring diagrams at the end of this book). If the fuses are all good, remove the lower and upper fairings (see Chapter 8) and unplug the fan electrical connector **(see illustration)**. Using two jumper wires, apply battery voltage to the terminals in the fan motor side of the electrical connector. If the fan doesn't work, replace the motor.
2   If the fan does come on, the problem lies in the thermostatic fan switch, the fan relay, or the wiring that connects the components. Remove the jumper wires and plug in the electrical connector to the fan. Unplug the electrical connector to the thermostatic fan switch, attach a jumper wire to the wiring harness side of the electrical connector and ground the other end of the jumper wire **(see illustration)**. If the fan comes on, the circuit to the motor is okay, and the thermostatic fan switch is defective (see Step 10).
3   If the fan still doesn't work, place your hand on the junction block (fuse box). Repeatedly touch the jumper wire to ground – if you feel a clicking inside the junction block, the relay is probably good. If it's not clicking,

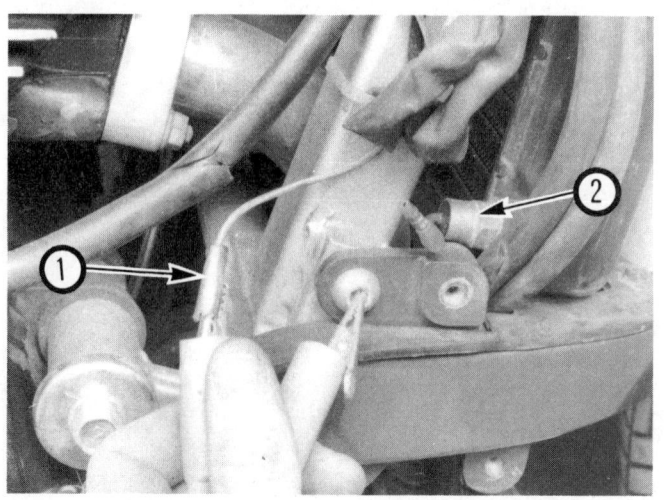

4.1 Location of the fan motor electrical connector (arrow)

4.2 Using a jumper wire, ground the fan circuit wiring harness – the fan motor will run if the circuit and motor are okay

1   Electrical connector
2   Thermostatic fan switch

4.6   Remove the fan bracket-to-radiator bolts and separate the bracket from the radiator

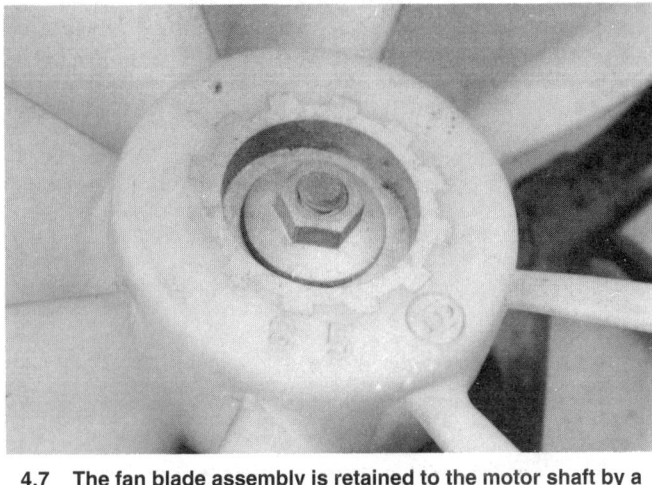

4.7   The fan blade assembly is retained to the motor shaft by a single nut

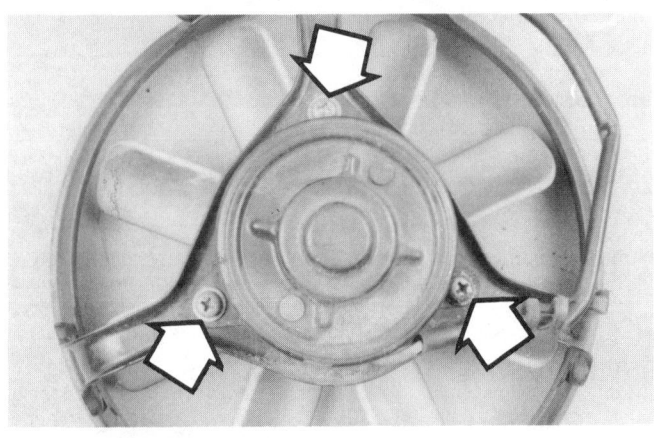

4.8   Remove the three screws that secure the motor to the bracket, then detach the motor

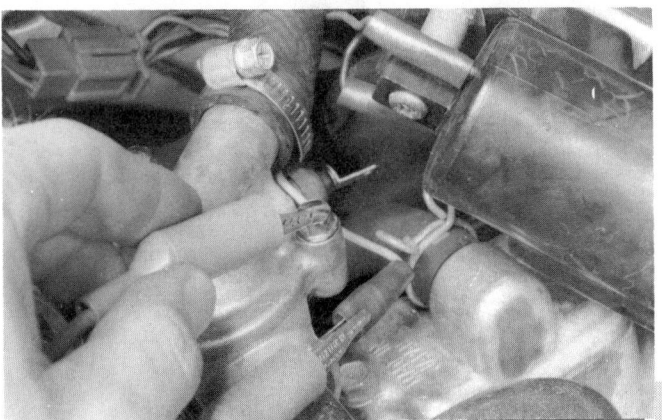

5.3   When the wire to the sending unit is grounded, the needle on the gauge should move all the way past the Hot mark

3

check the wiring from the thermostatic fan switch to the junction block. If it is clicking, check the wiring from the junction block to the fan motor. If the wiring checks out okay, the fan relay is most likely the problem, in which case the junction block must be replaced (the relays aren't replaceable individually). Refer to Chapter 9 for further junction block checks.

Replacement
Fan motor
Refer to illustrations 4.6, 4.7 and 4.8

Warning: *The engine must be completely cool before beginning this procedure.*

4   Disconnect the cable from the negative terminal of the battery.
5   Remove the radiator (see Section 8).
6   Remove the three bolts securing the fan bracket to the radiator **(see illustration)**, noting which bolt the ground wire is attached to. Separate the fan and bracket from the radiator.
7   Remove the nut that retains the fan blades to the fan motor shaft **(see illustration)** and remove the fan blade assembly from the motor.
8   Remove the screws that secure the fan motor to the bracket **(see illustration)** and detach the motor from the bracket.
9   Installation is the reverse of the removal procedure. Be sure to reinstall the ground wire under the bracket-to-radiator bolt.

Thermostatic fan switch
Warning: *The engine must be completely cool before beginning this procedure.*

10   Prepare the new switch by wrapping the threads with Teflon tape or by coating the threads with RTV sealant.

11   Unscrew the switch from the radiator **(see illustration 4.2 for switch location)** and quickly install the new switch, tightening it to the torque listed in this Chapter's Specifications.
12   Plug in the electrical connector to the switch.
13   Check and, if necessary, add coolant to the system (see Chapter 1).

---

5   Coolant temperature gauge and sending unit – check and replacement

---

Refer to illustration 5.3

Check
1   If the engine has been overheating but the coolant temperature gauge hasn't been indicating a hotter than normal condition, begin with a check of the coolant level (see Chapter 1). If it's low, add the recommended type of coolant and be sure to locate the source of the leak.
2   Remove the seat and the fuel tank (see Chapter 4). Locate the coolant temperature sending unit, which is screwed into the thermostat housing. Unplug the electrical connector from the sending unit, turn the ignition key to the Run position (don't crank the engine over) and note the temperature gauge – it should read Cold.
3   With the ignition key still in the run position, connect one end of a jumper wire to the sending unit wire and ground the other end **(see illustration)**. The needle on the temperature gauge should swing over past the Hot mark. **Caution:** *Don't ground the wire any longer than necessary or the gauge may be damaged.*
4   If the gauge passes both of these tests, but doesn't operate correctly under normal riding conditions, the temperature sending unit is defective and must be replaced.

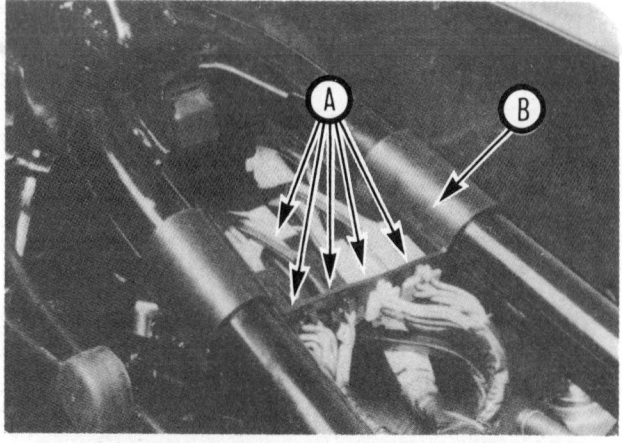

6.3   On C models, unplug the electrical connectors (A) and remove the wiring harness bracket (B) from between the frame tubes

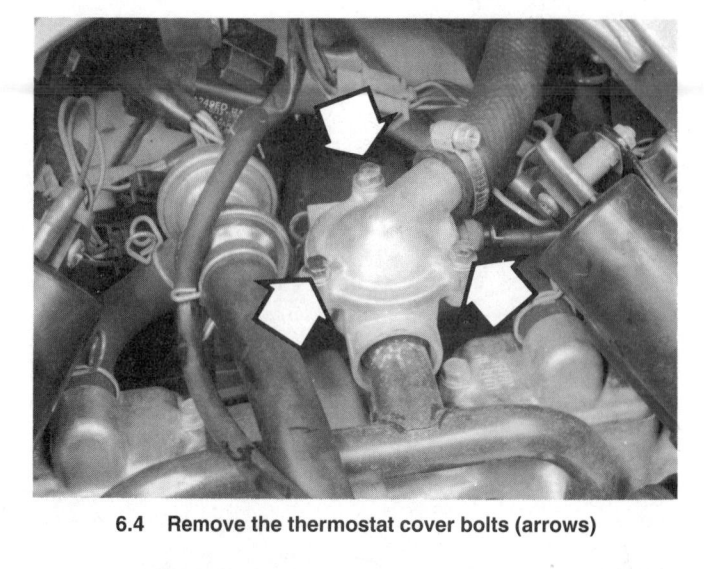

6.4   Remove the thermostat cover bolts (arrows)

6.5a   Remove the thermostat from the housing, noting how it is installed

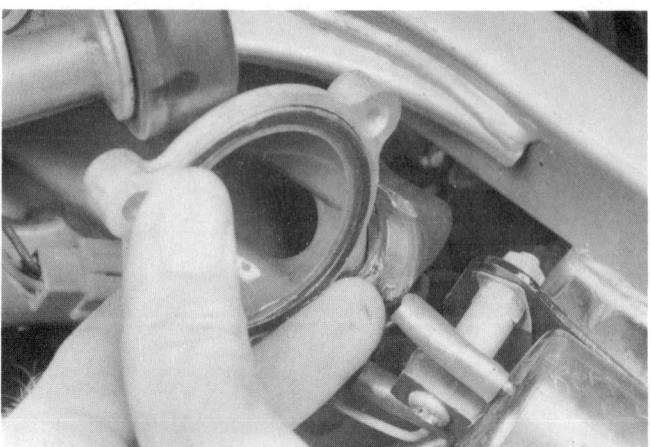

6.5b   Remove the O-ring from the groove in the thermostat cover

5   If the gauge didn't respond to the tests properly, either the wire to the gauge is bad or the gauge itself is defective.

Replacement

Sending unit
Warning: *The engine must be completely cool before beginning this procedure.*

6   Prepare the new sending unit by wrapping the threads with Teflon tape or by coating the threads with RTV sealant.
7   Unscrew the sending unit from the thermostat housing and quickly install the new unit, tightening it to the torque listed in this Chapter's Specifications.
8   Reconnect the electrical connector to the sending unit. Check and, if necessary, add coolant to the system (see Chapter 1).

Coolant temperature gauge
9   Refer to Chapter 9 for the coolant temperature gauge replacement procedure.

---

6   Thermostat – removal, check and installation

Refer to illustrations 6.3, 6.4, 6.5a and 6.5b
Warning: *The engine must be completely cool before beginning this procedure.*

Removal
1   If the thermostat is functioning properly, the coolant temperature gauge should rise to the normal operating temperature quickly and then stay there, only rising above the normal position occasionally when the engine gets unusually hot. If the engine does not reach normal operating temperature quickly, or if it overheats, the thermostat should be removed and checked, or replaced with a new one.
2   Refer to Chapter 1 and drain the cooling system. Remove the seat and the fuel tank (see Chapter 4).
3   If you're working on a C model, unplug the electrical connectors and remove the wiring harness bracket **(see illustration)**.
4   Remove the three bolts securing the thermostat cover **(see illustration)** and remove the cover (it's not necessary to disconnect the hose from the cover).
5   Withdraw the thermostat from the housing and remove the O-ring from the cover **(see illustrations)**.

Check
6   Remove any coolant deposits, then visually check the thermostat for corrosion, cracks and other damage. If it was open when it was removed, it is defective. Check the O-ring for cracks and other damage.
7   To check the thermostat operation, submerge it in a container of water along with a thermometer. **Warning:** *Antifreeze is poisonous. Don't use a cooking pan.* The thermostat should be suspended so it does not touch the container.
8   Gradually heat the water in the container with a hotplate or stove and check the temperature when the thermostat first starts to open.

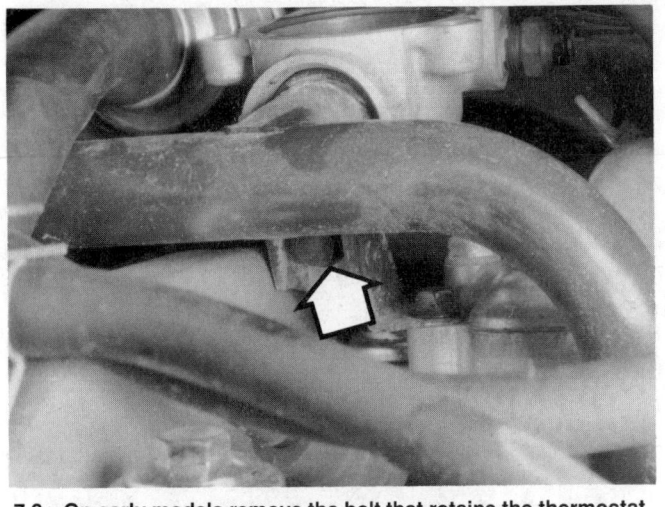

7.3   On early models remove the bolt that retains the thermostat housing to the coolant pipe (arrow)

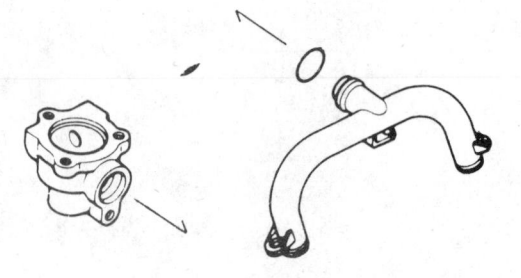

7.6   Be sure to install a new O-ring on the coolant pipe before installing the thermostat housing

9   Continue heating the water and check the temperature when the thermostat is fully open.
10   Lift the fully open thermostat out of the water and measure the distance the valve has opened.
11   Compare the opening temperature, the fully open temperature and the valve travel to the values listed in this Chapter's Specifications.
12   If these specifications are not met, or if the thermostat does not open while the water is heated, replace it with a new one.

Installation

13   Install the thermostat into the housing with the spring pointing down **(see illustration 6.5a)**.
14   Install a new O-ring in the groove in the thermostat cover.
15   Place the cover on the housing and install the bolts, tightening them securely.
16   The remainder of installation is the reverse of the removal procedure. Fill the cooling system with the recommended coolant (see Chapter 1).

---

7   Thermostat housing – removal and installation

Refer to illustrations 7.3 and 7.6
Warning: *The engine must be completely cool before beginning this procedure.*

Removal

1   Refer to Steps 2 and 3 of Section 6.
2   Detach the hose(s) from the housing.
3   On A and B models, remove the bolt securing the thermostat housing to the upper coolant pipe **(see illustration)**. On C models remove the thermostat housing mounting bolts.
4   Mark and disconnect any wires or hoses that may interfere with the removal of the thermostat housing.
5   Remove the thermostat housing. On A and B models slide the housing forward, off the coolant pipe. Remove the O-ring from the coolant pipe.

Installation

6   On A and B models, install a new O-ring to the coolant pipe **(see illustration)**. Lubricate the O-ring with a little engine oil.
7   Place the thermostat housing in position and install the bolt(s), tightening them securely.
8   Connect the hose(s) to the thermostat housing.
9   The remainder of installation is the reverse of the removal procedure. Fill the cooling system with the recommended coolant (see Chapter 1).

8.6   Remove the bolts that attach the baffle plate to the fan bracket (left side shown)

---

8   Radiator – removal and installation

Refer to illustrations 8.6, 8.8, 8.9, 8.10 and 8.11
Warning: *The engine must be completely cool before beginning this procedure.*

Removal

1   Set the bike on its centerstand. Disconnect the cable from the negative terminal of the battery.
2   Remove the upper and lower fairings (see Chapter 8).
3   Drain the coolant (see Chapter 1).
4   Unplug the electrical connectors for the fan motor and the thermostatic fan switch **(see illustrations 4.1 and 4.2)**.
5   Loosen the hose clamps on both radiator hoses (one on each side of the radiator). Detach the hoses. On some models it may be easier to detach the left side hose at the water pump, instead of the radiator.
6   Remove the baffle plate bolts **(see illustration)**.
7   On C models, unplug the electrical connectors from the horn and detach the horn wires from the guide on the radiator. Detach any other wiring that may interfere with radiator removal.

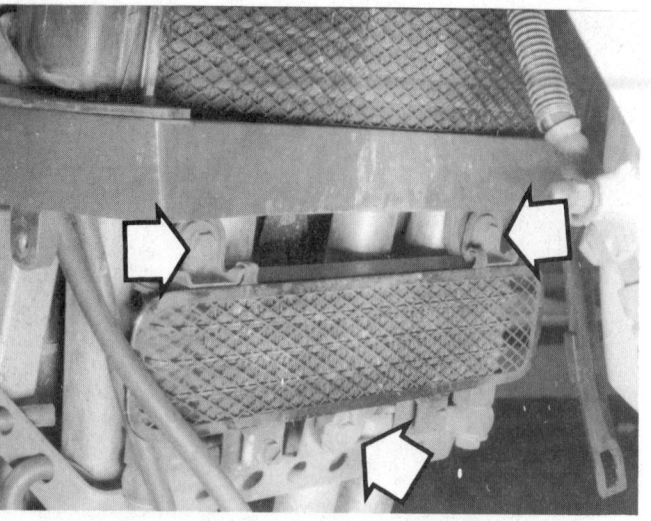

8.8   Remove the three oil cooler mounting bolts (arrows)

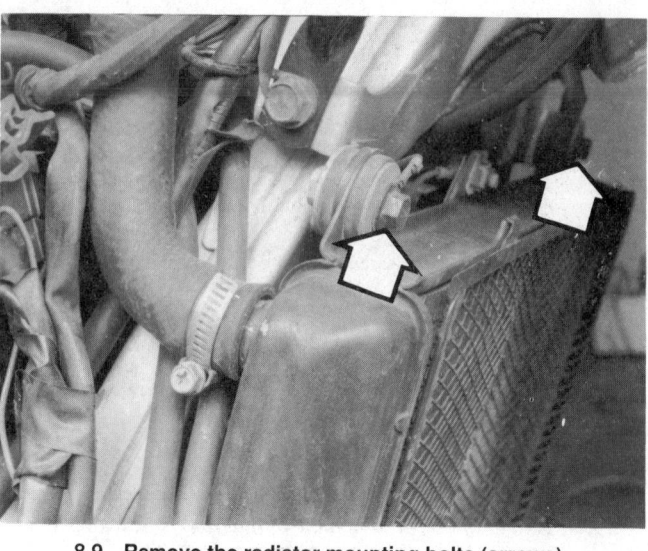

8.9   Remove the radiator mounting bolts (arrows)

8.10   Remove the fairing stay bolts (arrows) from both sides

8   On A and B models, remove the oil cooler mounting bolts **(see illustration)**.
9   Remove the radiator mounting bolts **(see illustration)**.
10   On A and B models, remove the bolts from each side of the frame stay **(see illustration)**.
11   Lift the top of the radiator forward and up, then remove the fairing stay (if equipped) along with the radiator **(see illustration)**. Be sure to check the rubber bushing in the fairing stay and replace it if it's worn.
12   If the radiator is to be repaired, pressure checked or replaced, detach the cooling fan (see Section 4).
13   Carefully examine the radiator for evidence of leaks and damage. It is recommended that any necessary repairs be performed by a reputable radiator repair shop.
14   If the radiator is clogged, or if large amounts of rust or scale have formed, the repair shop will also do a thorough cleaning job.
15   Make sure the spaces between the cooling tubes and fins are clear. If necessary, use compressed air or running water to remove anything that may be clogging them. If the fins are bent or flattened, straighten them very carefully with a small screwdriver.

Installation

16   Installation is the reverse of the removal procedure. Be sure to replace the hoses if they are deteriorated, and refill the cooling system with the recommended coolant (see Chapter 1).

---

9   Water pump – check, removal and installation

Warning: *The engine must be completely cool before beginning this procedure.*
Note: *The water pump on these models can't be overhauled – it must be replaced as a unit.*

Check

Refer to illustrations 9.6, 9.7 and 9.9

1   Visually check around the area of the water pump for coolant leaks. Try to determine if the leak is simply the result of a loose hose clamp or deteriorated hose.
2   Set the bike on its centerstand.
3   Remove the lower fairing (see Chapter 8).
4   Drain the engine coolant following the procedure in Chapter 1.
5   Loosen the hose clamps and detach the hoses from the water pump cover.

8.11   Lift the radiator up with the fairing stay and carefully guide it out

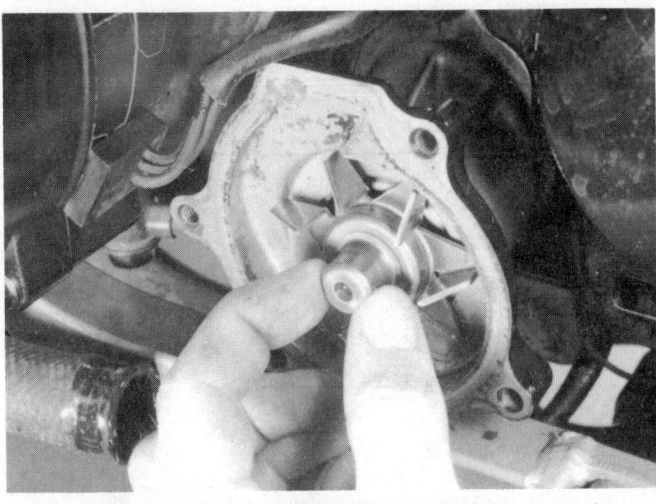

9.6   Detach the hoses then remove the bolts that secure the water pump cover to the pump body

9.7   If you can wiggle the impeller or pull it in-and-out, the pump is defective

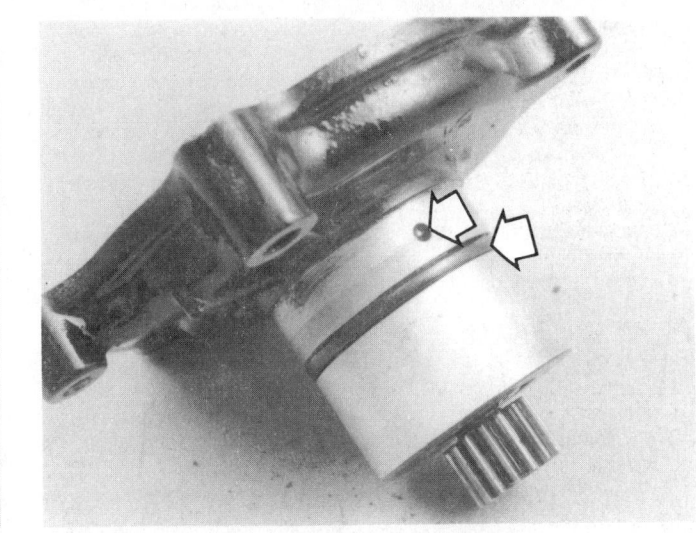

9.9   If the cover O-ring is cracked or deteriorated, replace it – make sure the new one seats in the groove fully

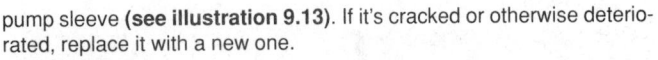

9.13   Check the hole in the sleeve for coolant residue – also check the O-ring for deterioration

6   Remove the cover bolts (**see illustration**) and separate the cover from the water pump body.

7   Try to wiggle the water pump impeller back-and-forth and in-and-out (**see illustration**). If you can feel movement, the water pump must be replaced.

8   Check the impeller blades for corrosion. If they are heavily corroded, replace the water pump and flush the system thoroughly (it would also be a good idea to check the internal condition of the radiator).

9   If the cause of the leak was just a defective cover O-ring, remove the old O-ring (**see illustration**) and install a new one.

Removal

Refer to illustration 9.13

10   Drain the coolant and remove the hoses from the pump (if the cover hasn't already been removed).

11   Drain the engine oil (see Chapter 1).

12   Remove any bolts still retaining the pump. Pull the pump straight out to remove it.

13   Check the hole in the sleeve of the pump, just below the pump body (**see illustration**). If there is coolant residue around it, the water pump is defective.

14   If the original water pump is to be installed, check the O-ring on the

pump sleeve (**see illustration 9.13**). If it's cracked or otherwise deteriorated, replace it with a new one.

Installation

15   Installation is basically the reverse of the removal procedure. Before installing the pump, smear a little engine oil on the sleeve O-ring. Be sure to tighten the pump cover bolts securely. Fill the cooling system with the recommended coolant and the crankcase with the specified type and amount of engine oil (see Chapter 1).

---

10   Coolant pipe(s) – removal and installation

Warning: *The engine must be completely cool before beginning this procedure.*

1   Place the bike on its centerstand.

2   Remove the lower fairing (see Chapter 8).

3   Drain the engine coolant (see Chapter 1).

Upper coolant pipe (A and B models only)

Refer to illustration 10.5

4   Remove the thermostat housing (see Section 7).

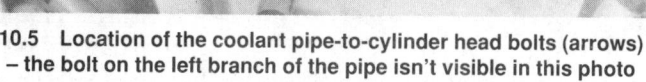

10.5   Location of the coolant pipe-to-cylinder head bolts (arrows)
– the bolt on the left branch of the pipe isn't visible in this photo

10.12   Remove the bolts retaining the lower coolant pipe to the
engine (left side shown)

5   Remove the coolant pipe-to-cylinder head bolts **(see illustration)**
and separate the pipe from the cylinder head.
6   Remove the O-rings from the ends of the pipe and install new ones. If
one of the ends doesn't have an O-ring, be sure to retrieve it from the thermostat housing or one of the holes in the cylinder head.
7   Check the holes in the head and in the thermostat housing for corrosion, and remove all traces of corrosion if any exists.
8   Install new O-rings on the pipe ends, lubricating them with a little
clean engine oil.
9   Install the ends of the coolant pipe into the holes in the cylinder head.
Install the mounting bolts, tightening them securely.
10   Install the thermostat housing (see Section 7).

Lower coolant pipe

Refer to illustration 10.12
11   Detach the hose from the left side of the coolant pipe.
12   Remove the two coolant pipe-to-engine bolts **(see illustration)**.
13   Pull the pipe out of the water jacket. Make sure all the O-rings come
out with the pipe – if not, be sure to retrieve them.
14   Check the pipe ends and the holes in the water jacket for corrosion,
and remove all traces of corrosion if any exists.
15   Install new O-rings on the pipe ends, lubricating them with a little
clean engine oil.
16   Install the ends of the coolant pipe into the holes in the water jacket.
Install the mounting bolts, tightening them securely.

Upper and lower coolant pipes

17   Fill the cooling system with the recommended coolant (see Chapter 1) and check for leaks.
18   The remainder of installation is the reverse of the removal procedure.

---

11   Oil cooler – removal and installation

Refer to illustrations 11.3 and 11.4
Note: *Wait until the engine is cool before beginning this procedure.*
1   Set the bike on its centerstand and drain the engine oil (see Chapter 1).
2   Remove the lower fairing (see Chapter 8).
3   Place a drain pan under the front of the crankcase and remove the oil
cooler hose-to-crankcase union bolts **(see illustration)**. Retrieve the
sealing washers.
4   Remove the oil cooler mounting bolts and the bracket-to-frame bolts
(see illustration).
5   Installation is the reverse of removal. Be sure to use new sealing
washers if the old ones were leaking or damaged, and fill the crankcase
with the recommended type and amount of oil (see Chapter 1). Tighten the
union bolts to the torque listed in this Chapter's Specifications.

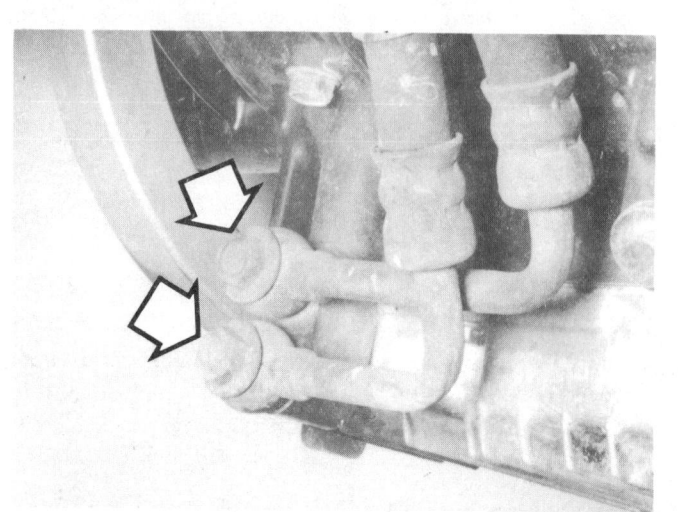

11.3   Remove the union bolts (arrows)

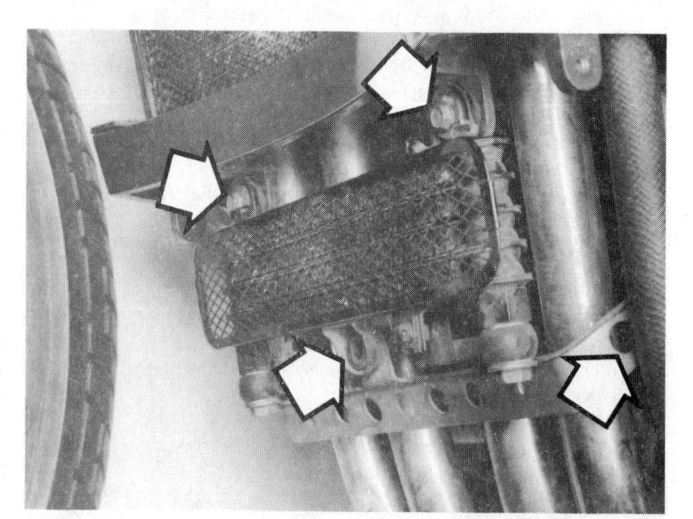

11.4   Remove the cooler mounting bolts and the bracket-to-frame
bolts (arrows)

Chapter 4   Fuel and exhaust systems

Refer to Chapter 10 for information on the ZX750F model

Contents

Specifications

General
Carburetor type . . . .   Keihin CVK32 (four)

4

Jet sizes
1988 and earlier A and B models
  Main jet
    Cyls. 1 and 4
      California models   108
      All others   105
    Cyls. 2 and 3   108
  Main air jet   100
  Jet needle N27L
  Pilot jet   38
  Pilot air jet   145
  Pilot screw setting . . . .   2 turns out
  Choke jet
    California models   42
    All others   45
1988 C1 models
  Main jet   105
  Main air jet   100
  Jet needle
    California models N52T
    All others N52Q
  Pilot jet   35
  Pilot air jet
    California models   160
    All others   150
  Pilot screw setting . . . .   2 turns out
  Choke jet
    California models   48
    All others   52

1989 A5 models

Main jet	102 (all cylinders)
Main air jet	100
Jet needle	N52N
Pilot jet	35
Pilot air jet	160
Pilot screw setting	2-1/8 to 2-1/4 turns out
Choke jet	
California models	52
All others	45

1989-on C2, C3, C4, C5, C6, C7 models

Main jet	
C2 models	105
C3, C4, C5, C6, C7 models	102
Main air jet	100
Jet needle	
California models	N52T
All others	N52Q
Pilot jet	35
Pilot air jet	
California models	160
All others	150
Pilot screw setting	1-3/4 to 2 turns out
Choke jet	
California models	48
All others	52

Carburetor adjustments

Float height	17 mm
Fuel level	0.5 ± 1 mm above the bottom edge of the carburetor body

---

1   General information

The fuel system consists of the fuel tank, the fuel tap and filter, the carburetors and the connecting lines, hoses and control cables.

The carburetors used on these motorcycles are four constant vacuum Keihins with butterfly-type throttle valves. For cold starting, an enrichment circuit is actuated by a cable and the choke lever mounted on the left handlebar.

The exhaust system is a four-into-two design with a crossover pipe.

Many of the fuel system service procedures are considered routine maintenance items and for that reason are included in Chapter 1.

2   Fuel tank – removal and installation

Refer to illustrations 2.4, 2.5 and 2.6

Warning: *Gasoline is extremely flammable, so take extra precautions when you work on any part of the fuel system. Don't smoke or allow open flames or bare light bulbs near the work area, and don't work in a garage where a natural gas-type appliance (such as a water heater or clothes dryer) is present. If you spill any fuel on your skin, rinse it off immediately with soap and water. When you perform any kind of work on the fuel system, wear safety glasses and have a class B type fire extinguisher on hand.*

1   The fuel tank is held in place at the forward end by two cups, one on each side of the tank, which slide over two rubber dampers on the frame. The rear of the tank is fastened to a bracket by two bolts and rubber insulators, which fit through a flange projecting from the tank.

2   Remove the seat and disconnect the cable from the negative terminal of the battery. On A and B models, remove the side covers. On C models, remove the screw securing the fuel tap knob, then remove the knee grip covers (see Chapter 8, if necessary).

3   Mark and disconnect the breather hose and, on California models, the evaporative emission control system hoses from the rear of the tank.

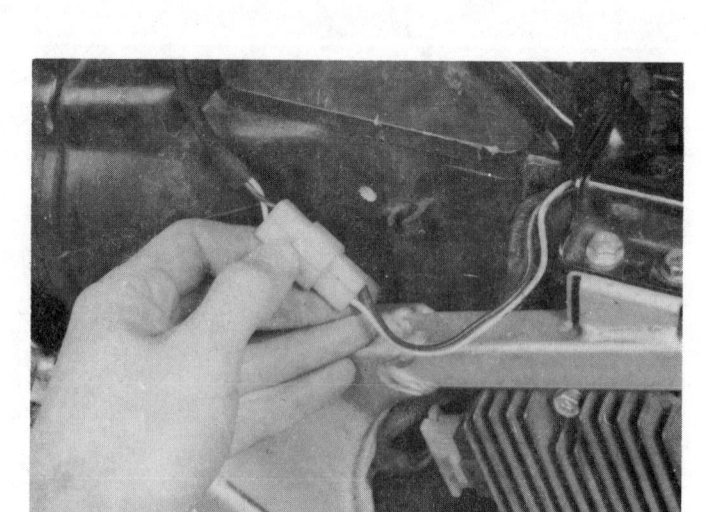

2.4   Unplug the fuel gauge electrical connector

4   Disconnect the electrical connector for the fuel gauge sending unit **(see illustration)**.

5   Remove the two bolts securing the rear of the tank to the bracket **(see illustration)**.

6   Turn the fuel tap to the On or Reserve position, lift the rear of the tank up, slide back the hose clamps and pull the fuel and vacuum lines **(see illustration)** off the fuel tap.

7   Slide the tank to the rear to disengage the front of the tank from the rubber dampers, then carefully lift the tank away from the machine.

8   Before installing the tank, check the condition of the rubber mounting dampers – if they're hardened, cracked, or show any other signs of deterioration, replace them.

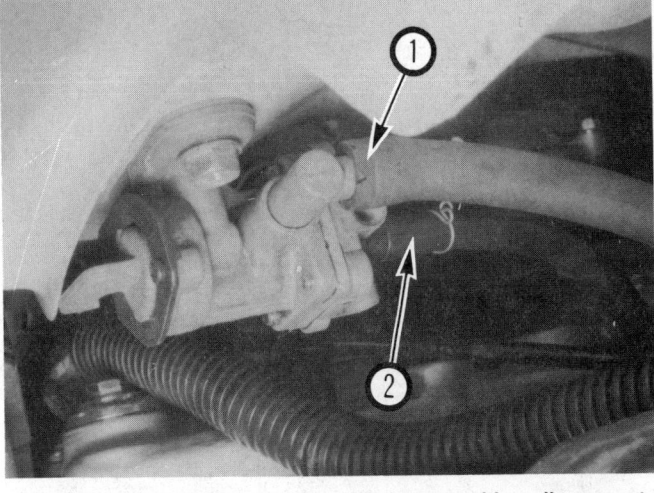

2.5 Disconnect the hoses and remove the fuel tank mounting bolts

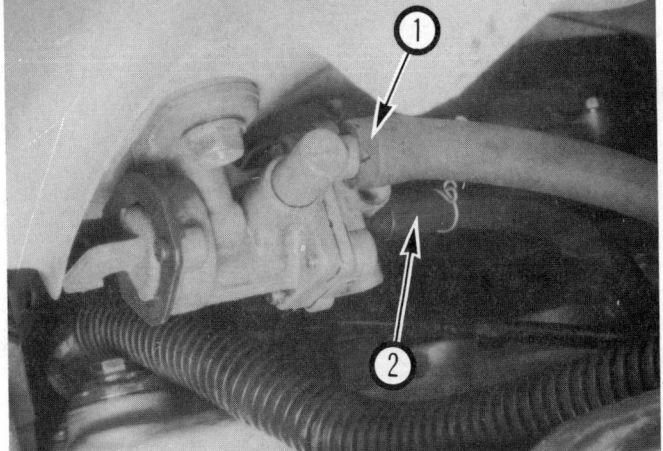

2.6 With the fuel tap in the On or Reserve position, disconnect the vacuum hose and the fuel line from the tap fittings

1 *Fuel line*   2 *Vacuum hose*

9   When replacing the tank, reverse the above procedure. Make sure the tank seats properly and does not pinch any control cables or wires. If difficulty is encountered when trying to slide the tank cups onto the dampers, a small amount of light oil should be used to lubricate them.

3   Fuel tank – cleaning and repair

1   All repairs to the fuel tank should be carried out by a professional who has experience in this critical and potentially dangerous work. Even after cleaning and flushing of the fuel system, explosive fumes can remain and ignite during repair of the tank.
2   If the fuel tank is removed from the vehicle, it should not be placed in an area where sparks or open flames could ignite the fumes coming out of the tank. Be especially careful inside garages where a natural gas-type appliance is located, because the pilot light could cause an explosion.

4   Idle fuel/air mixture adjustment – general information

1   Due to the increased emphasis on controlling motorcycle exhaust emissions, certain governmental regulations have been formulated which directly affect the carburetion of this machine. In order to comply with the regulations, the carburetors on some models have a metal sealing plug pressed into the hole over the pilot screw (which controls the idle fuel/air mixture) on each carburetor, so they can't be tampered with. These should only be removed in the event of a complete carburetor overhaul, and even then the screws should be returned to their original settings. The pilot screws on other models are accessible, but the use of an exhaust gas analyzer is the only accurate way to adjust the idle fuel/air mixture and be sure the machine doesn't exceed the emissions regulations.
2   If the engine runs extremely rough at idle or continually stalls, and if a carburetor overhaul does not cure the problem, take the motorcycle to a Kawasaki dealer service department or other repair shop equipped with an exhaust gas analyzer. They will be able to properly adjust the idle fuel/ air mixture to achieve a smooth idle and restore low speed performance.

5   Carburetor overhaul – general information

1   Poor engine performance, hesitation, hard starting, stalling, flooding and backfiring are all signs that major carburetor maintenance may be required.
2   Keep in mind that many so-called carburetor problems are really not carburetor problems at all, but mechanical problems within the engine or

ignition system malfunctions. Try to establish for certain that the carburetors are in need of maintenance before beginning a major overhaul.
3   Check the fuel tap filter, the fuel lines, the gas tank cap vent, the intake manifold hose clamps, the vacuum hoses, the air filter element, the cylinder compression, the spark plugs, and the carburetor synchronization before assuming that a carburetor overhaul is required.
4   Most carburetor problems are caused by dirt particles, varnish and other deposits which build up in and block the fuel and air passages. Also, in time, gaskets and O-rings shrink or deteriorate and cause fuel and air leaks which lead to poor performance.
5   When the carburetor is overhauled, it is generally disassembled completely and the parts are cleaned thoroughly with a carburetor cleaning solvent and dried with filtered, unlubricated compressed air. The fuel and air passages are also blown through with compressed air to force out any dirt that may have been loosened but not removed by the solvent. Once the cleaning process is complete, the carburetor is reassembled using new gaskets, O-rings and, generally, a new inlet needle valve and seat.
6   Before disassembling the carburetors, make sure you have a carburetor rebuild kit (which will include all necessary O-rings and other parts), some carburetor cleaner, a supply or rags, some means of blowing out the carburetor passages and a clean place to work. It is recommended that only one carburetor be overhauled at a time to avoid mixing up parts.

6   Carburetors – removal and installation

Refer to illustrations 6.5, 6.7, 6.8a and 6.8b
Warning: *Gasoline is extremely flammable, so take extra precautions when you work on any part of the fuel system. Don't smoke or allow open flames or bare light bulbs near the work area, and don't work in a garage where a natural gas-type appliance (such as a water heater or clothes dryer) is present. If you spill any fuel on your skin, rinse it off immediately with soap and water. When you perform any kind of work on the fuel system, wear safety glasses and have a class B type fire extinguisher on hand.*

Removal

1   Remove the fuel tank (see Section 2). On C models, remove the side covers (see Chapter 8, if necessary).
2   Pull the large hose leading to the vacuum switch out of the front of the air filter housing and secure it out of the way.
3   Disconnect the choke cable from the carburetor assembly (see Section 10).
4   Loosen the lockwheel on the throttle cable adjuster at the handlebar and turn the adjuster in all the way.

4

6.5   Loosen the clamps on the intake manifold tubes

6.6   Mark and disconnect the vacuum hoses from the carburetors

6.7   Push the spring bands back, toward the air cleaner housing

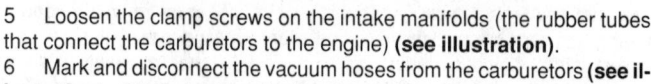

6.8a   Gently pull the assembly to the rear, detaching the carburetors from the intake manifold tubes

6.8b   Raise the carburetors up, then align the throttle cables with the slots in the throttle pulley and pass the cables through

5   Loosen the clamp screws on the intake manifolds (the rubber tubes that connect the carburetors to the engine) **(see illustration)**.

6   Mark and disconnect the vacuum hoses from the carburetors **(see illustration)**. Disconnect and plug the coolant hoses on models so equipped.

7   Slide the spring bands on the ducts from the air filter housings away from the carburetors **(see illustration)**. On A and B models, remove the air filter housing (see Section 11).

8   Pull the carburetor assembly to the rear, clear of the intake manifold tubes **(see illustration)**. Raise the assembly up far enough to disconnect the throttle cables from the throttle pulley **(see illustration)**, then remove the carburetors from the machine.

9   After the carburetors have been removed, stuff clean rags into the intake manifold tubes to prevent the entry of dirt or other objects.

Installation

10   Position the assembly over the intake manifold tubes. Lightly lubricate the ends of the throttle cables with multi-purpose grease and attach them to the throttle pulley. Make sure the accelerator and decelerator cables are in their proper positions.

11   Tilt the front of the assembly down and insert the fronts of the carburetors into the intake manifold tubes. Push the assembly forward and tighten the clamps.

12   Install the air filter housing (see Section 11).

13   Make sure the ducts from the air cleaner housing are seated properly, then slide the spring bands into position.

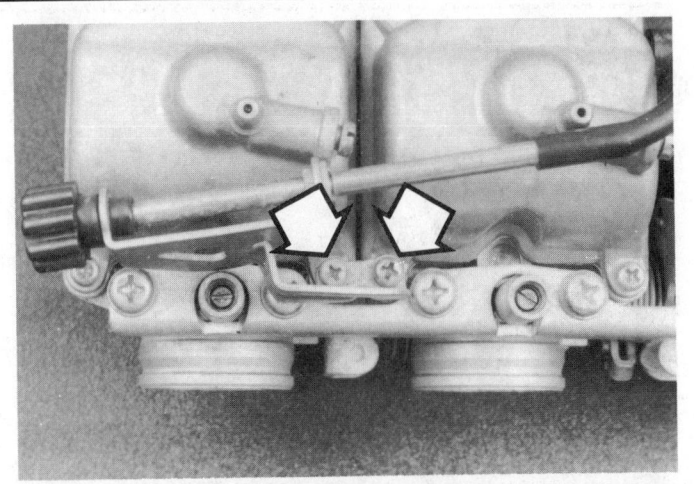

7.2b The idle adjusting screw holder is retained by two screws

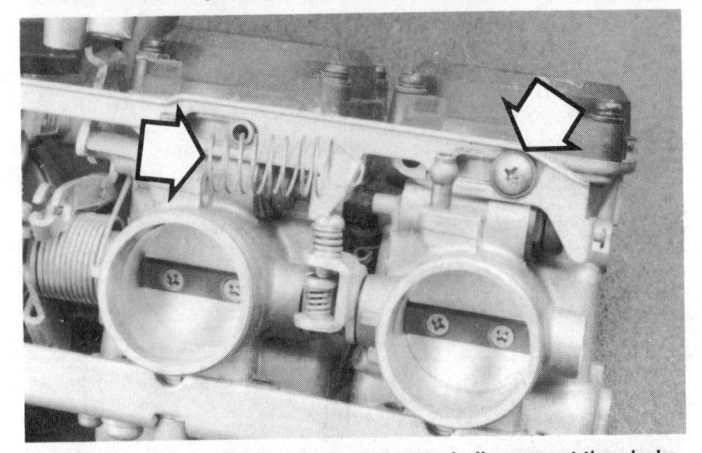

7.2c If the carburetors are to be separated, disconnect the choke spring, remove the three choke lever screws and detach the lever

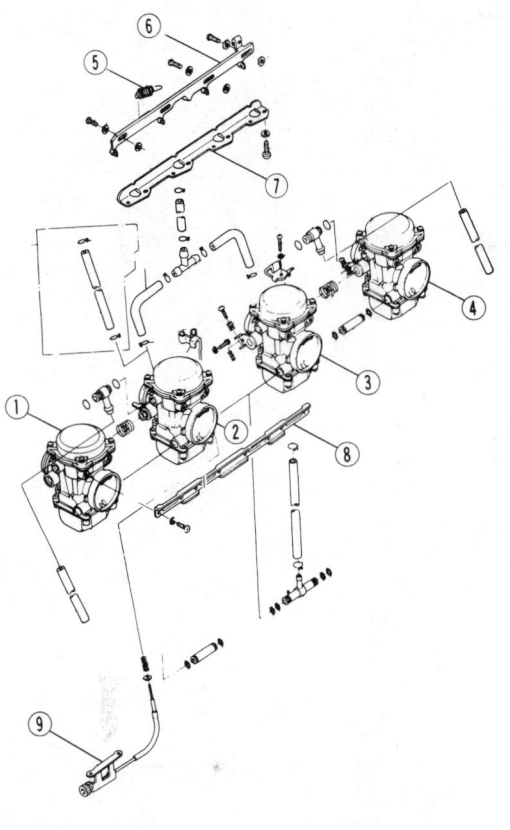

7.2a Exploded view of the carburetors

1	No. 1 carburetor	6	Choke lever
2	No. 2 carburetor	7	Upper mounting plate
3	No. 3 carburetor	8	Lower mounting plate
4	No. 4 carburetor	9	Idle adjusting screw holder
5	Choke lever spring		

14 Connect the choke cable to the assembly and adjust it (see Section 10).

15 Connect the large hose from the vacuum switch to the air filter housing. On models so equipped, connect the coolant lines to the carburetors. Connect the other vacuum hoses that were previously disconnected.

16 Adjust the throttle grip freeplay (see Chapter 1).

17 Install the fuel tank, turn the fuel tap to PRI and check for leaks.

18 Check and, if necessary, adjust the idle speed and carburetor synchronization (see Chapter 1).

19 Install the seat and side covers.

---

7 Carburetors – disassembly, cleaning and inspection

Warning: *Gasoline is extremely flammable, so take extra precautions when you work on any part of the fuel system. Don't smoke or allow open flames or bare light bulbs near the work area, and don't work in a garage where a natural gas-type appliance (such as a water heater or clothes dryer) is present. If you spill any fuel on your skin, rinse it off immediately with soap and water. When you perform any kind of work on the fuel system, wear safety glasses and have a class B type fire extinguisher on hand.*

Disassembly

Refer to illustrations 7.2a, 7.2b, 7.2c, 7.2d, 7.2e, 7.3, 7.4, 7.5a, 7.5b, 7.7, 7.8, 7.9, 7.10, 7.11 and 7.12

1 Remove the carburetors from the machine as described in Section 6. Set the assembly on a clean working surface. Note: *Unless the O-rings on*

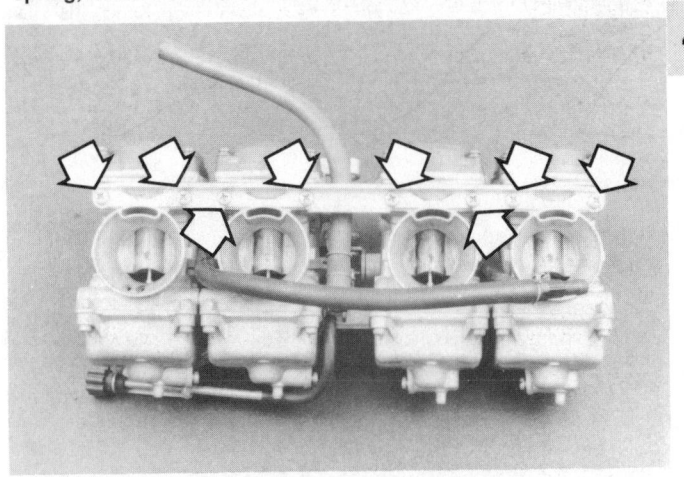

7.2d Rear view of the carburetor assembly, showing the upper mounting plate screws (arrows)

the fuel, vent and (if applicable) coolant fittings between the carburetors are leaking, don't detach the carburetors from their mounting brackets. Also, work on one carburetor at a time to avoid getting parts mixed up.

2 If the carburetors must be separated from each other (during a complete overhaul, for example) remove the idle adjusting screw assembly **(see illustrations)**, being careful not to lose the spring and washer on the end of the screw. Disconnect the fuel hoses. Remove the choke lever spring and choke lever by removing the three screws and six plastic washers (two washers per screw, one on each side of the lever) **(see illustration)**, then remove the screws securing the upper and lower mounting

4

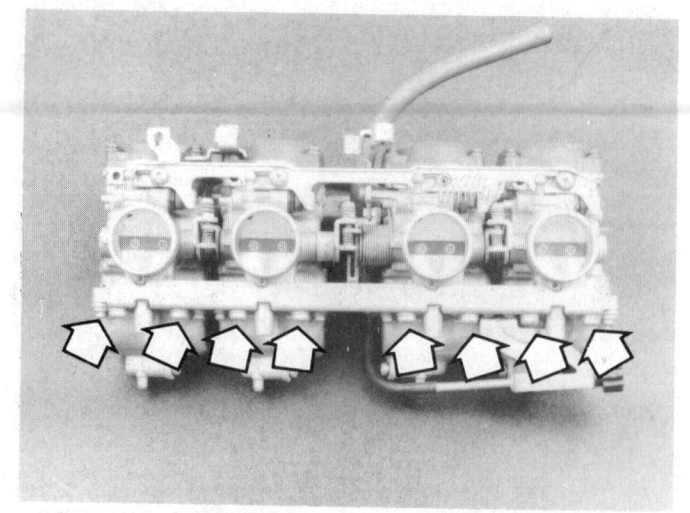

7.2e   Front view of the carburetor assembly, showing the lower mounting plate screws (arrows)

plates to the carburetors (**see illustrations**). Mark the position of each carburetor and gently separate them, noting how the throttle linkage is connected, and being careful not to lose any springs or fuel, vent and coolant (where applicable) fittings that are present between the carburetors.
3   Remove the four screws securing the top cover to the carburetor body. Lift the cover off and remove the piston spring (**see illustration**).
4   Peel the diaphragm away from its groove in the carburetor body, being careful not to tear it. Lift out the diaphragm/piston assembly (**see illustration**).
5   Remove the piston spring seat and separate the needle from the piston (**see illustrations**).
6   Remove the four screws retaining the float bowl to the carburetor body, then detach the bowl (**see illustration 7.3**).
7   Push the float pivot pin out and detach the float (and fuel inlet valve needle) from the carburetor body (**see illustration**). Detach the valve needle from the float.
8   Unscrew the main jet from the needle jet holder (**see illustration**).
9   Unscrew the needle jet holder/air bleed pipe (**see illustration**).
10   Using a wood or plastic tool, push the needle jet out of the carburetor body (**see illustration**).
11   Using a small, flat-bladed screwdriver, remove the pilot jet (**see illustration**).
12   The pilot (idle mixture) screw is located in the bottom of the carburetor body (**see illustration**). On US models, this screw is hidden behind a plug which will have to be removed if the screw is to be taken out. To do this, punch a hole in the plug with an awl or a scribe, then pry it out. On all models, turn the pilot screw in, counting the number of turns until it bottoms lightly. Record that number for use when installing the screw. Now remove the pilot screw along with its spring, washer and O-ring.
13   The choke plunger can be removed by unscrewing the nut that retains it to the carburetor body (**see illustration 7.3**), if the carburetors have been separated from each other (see Step 2).

Cleaning

Caution: *Use only a carburetor cleaning solution that is safe for use with plastic parts (be sure to read the label on the container).*

14   Submerge the metal components in the carburetor cleaner for approximately thirty minutes (or longer, if the directions recommend it).
15   After the carburetor has soaked long enough for the cleaner to loosen and dissolve most of the varnish and other deposits, use a brush to remove the stubborn deposits. Rinse it again, then dry it with compressed air. Blow out all of the fuel and air passages in the main and upper body.
Caution: *Never clean the jets or passages with a piece of wire or a drill bit, as they will be enlarged, causing the fuel and air metering rates to be upset.*

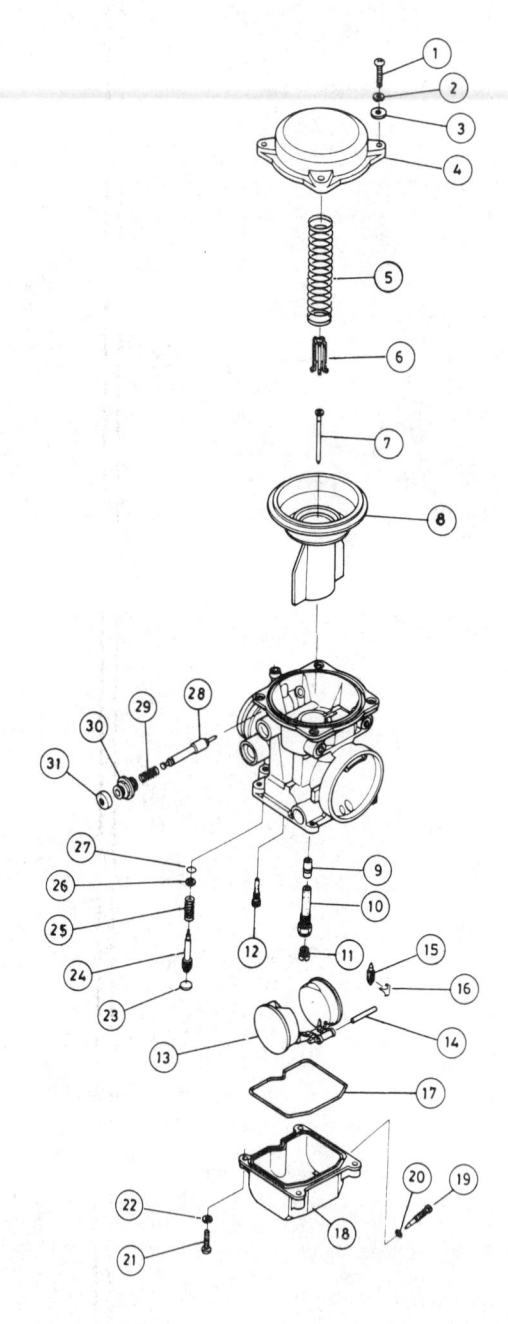

7.3   Carburetor – exploded view

1	Screw	16	Clip
2	Spring washer	17	O-ring
3	Washer	18	Float bowl
4	Top cover	19	Drain screw
5	Piston spring	20	O-ring
6	Spring seat	21	Screw
7	Jet needle	22	Spring washer
8	Diaphragm/vacuum	23	Sealing plug
	piston assembly		(US models only)
9	Needle jet	24	Pilot screw
10	Needle jet holder/air	25	Spring
	bleed pipe	26	Washer
11	Main jet	27	O-ring
12	Pilot jet	28	Choke plunger
13	Float assembly	29	Spring
14	Pivot pin	30	Nut
15	Fuel inlet valve needle	31	Cap

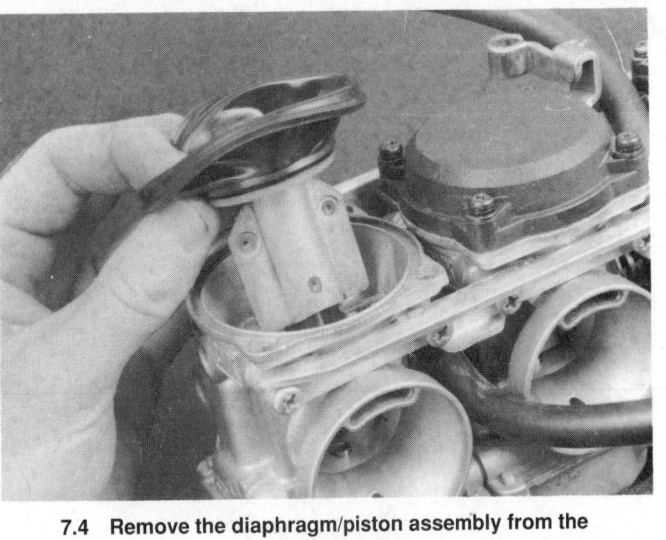

7.4 Remove the diaphragm/piston assembly from the carburetor body

7.5a Remove the vacuum piston spring seat from the piston

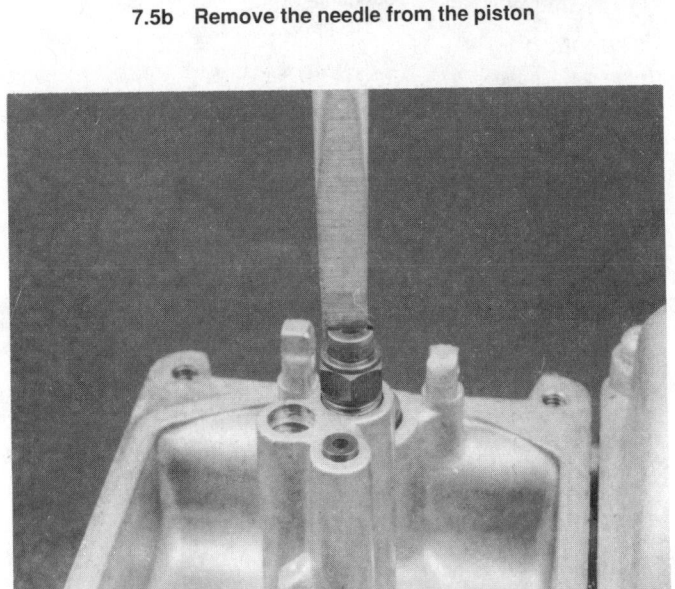

7.5b Remove the needle from the piston

7.7 Push the float pivot pin out, then remove the float and valve needle assembly

4

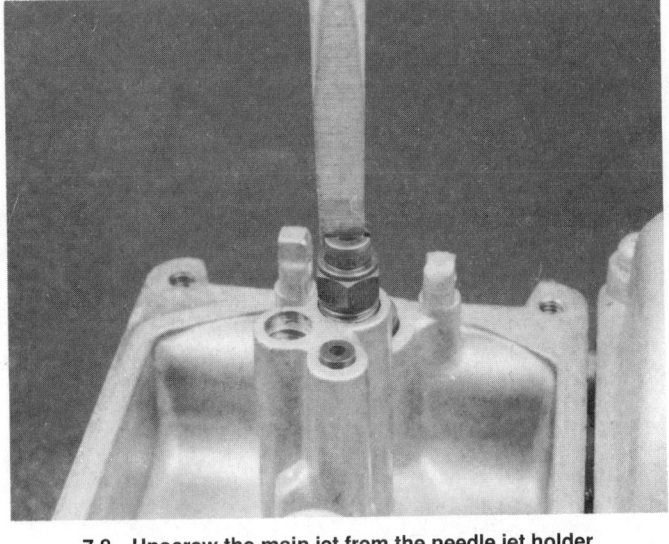

7.8 Unscrew the main jet from the needle jet holder

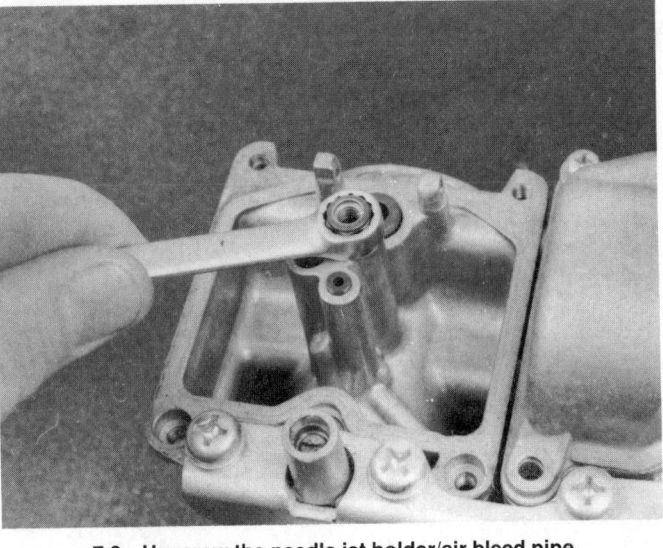

7.9 Unscrew the needle jet holder/air bleed pipe

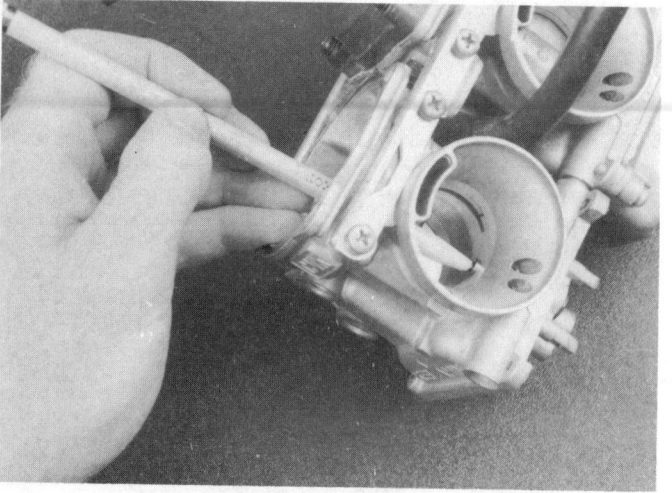

7.10   Working from the top of the carburetor, push the needle jet out with a wood or plastic tool

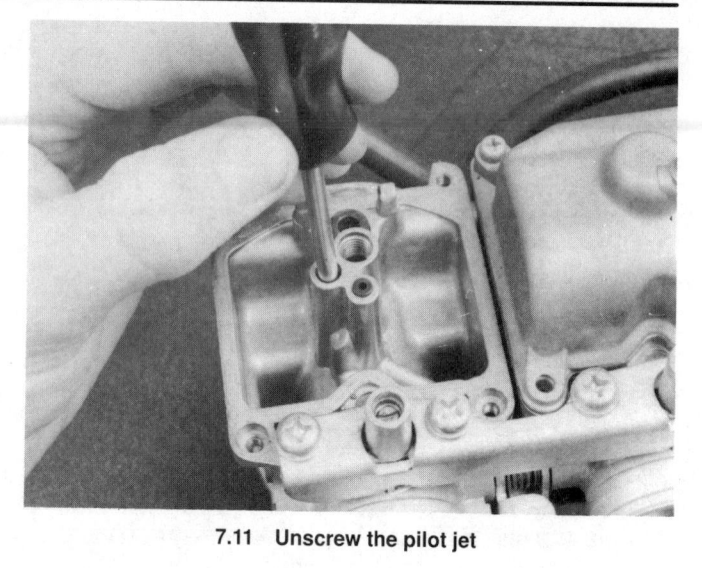

7.11   Unscrew the pilot jet

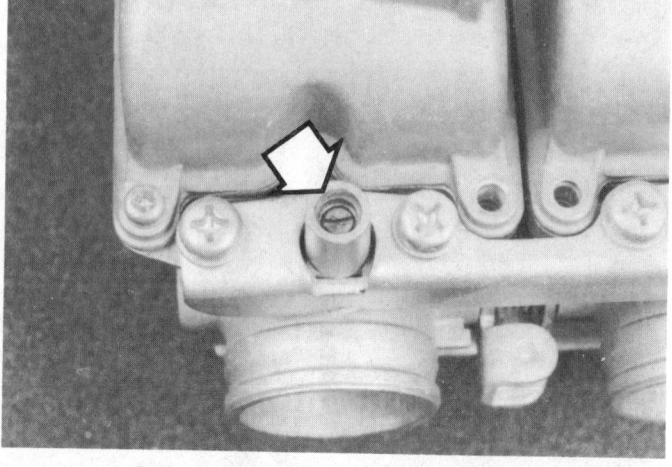

7.12   Location of the pilot screw (arrow)

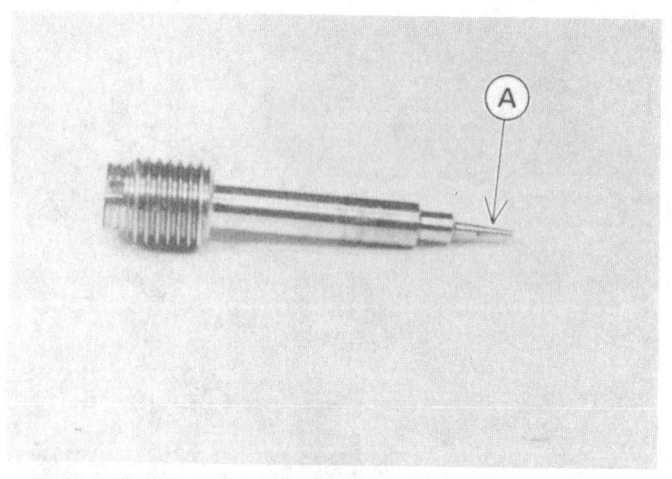

7.17   Check the tapered portion of the pilot screw for wear or damage

Inspection

Refer to illustrations 7.17 and 7.22

16   Check the operation of the choke plunger. If it doesn't move smoothly, replace it, along with the return spring.

17   Check the tapered portion of the pilot screw for wear or damage **(see illustration)**. Replace the pilot screw if necessary.

18   Check the carburetor body, float bowl and top cover for cracks, distorted sealing surfaces and other damage. If any defects are found, replace the faulty component, although replacement of the entire carburetor will probably be necessary (check with your parts supplier for the availability of separate components).

19   Check the diaphragm for splits, holes and general deterioration. Holding it up to a light will help to reveal problems of this nature.

20   Insert the vacuum piston in the carburetor body and see that it moves up-and-down smoothly. Check the surface of the piston for wear. If it's worn excessively or doesn't move smoothly in the bore, replace the carburetor.

21   Check the jet needle for straightness by rolling it on a flat surface (such as a piece of glass). Replace it if it's bent or if the tip is worn.

22   Check the tip of the fuel inlet valve needle. If it has grooves or scratches in it, it must be replaced. Push in on the rod in the other end of the needle, then release it – if it doesn't spring back, replace the valve needle **(see illustration)**.

23   Check the O-rings on the float bowl and the drain plug (in the float bowl). Replace them if they're damaged.

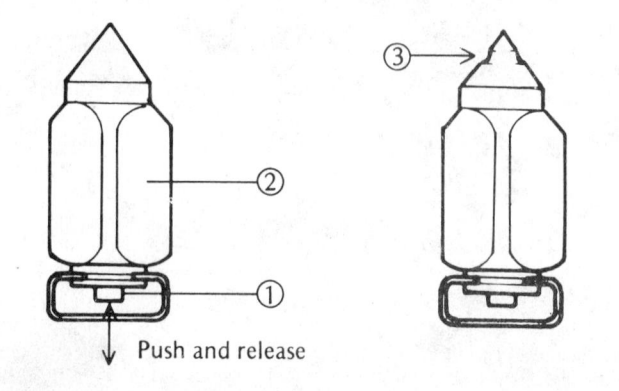

7.22   Check the tip of the fuel inlet valve needle for grooves or scratches – also make sure the rod in the end of the needle pops back out quickly after it's pushed in

| 1 | Rod | 3 | Groove in tip |
| 2 | Valve needle | | |

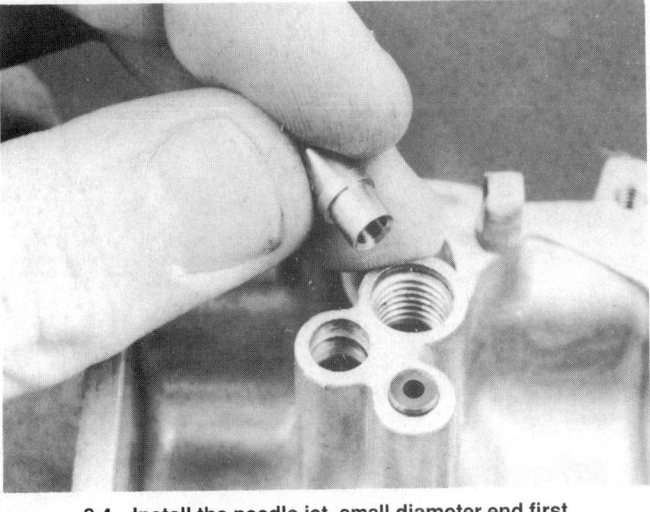

8.4   Install the needle jet, small diameter end first

8.8   Make sure the bead of the vacuum diaphragm seats in its groove, and that the diaphragm isn't distorted

24   Operate the throttle shaft to make sure the throttle butterfly valve opens and closes smoothly. If it doesn't, replace the carburetor.
25   Check the floats for damage. This will usually be apparent by the presence of fuel inside one of the floats. If the floats are damaged, they must be replaced.

8   Carburetors – reassembly and fuel level adjustment

Caution: *When installing the jets, be careful not to over-tighten them – they're made of soft material and can strip or shear easily.*
Note: *When reassembling the carburetors, be sure to use the new O-rings, gaskets and other parts supplied in the rebuild kit.*

Reassembly
Refer to illustrations 8.4, 8.8, 8.10, 8.15 and 8.16
1   If the choke plunger was removed, install it in its bore, followed by its spring and nut. Tighten the nut securely and install the cap.
2   Install the pilot screw (if removed) along with its spring, washer and O-ring, turning it in until it seats lightly. Now, turn the screw out the number of turns that was previously recorded. If you're working on a US model, install a new metal plug in the hole over the screw. Apply a little bonding agent around the circumference of the plug after it has been seated.
3   Install the pilot jet, tightening it securely.
4   Turn the carburetor body upside-down and install the needle jet into its hole, small diameter first **(see illustration)**.
5   Install the needle jet holder/air bleed pipe, tightening it securely.
6   Install the main jet into the needle jet holder/air bleed pipe, tightening it securely.
7   Drop the jet needle down into its hole in the vacuum piston and install the spring seat over the needle. Make sure the spring seat doesn't cover the hole at the bottom of the vacuum piston – reposition it if necessary.
8   Install the diaphragm/vacuum piston assembly into the carburetor body. Lower the spring into the piston. Seat the bead of the diaphragm into the groove in the top of the carburetor body, making sure the diaphragm isn't distorted or kinked **(see illustration)**. This is not always an easy task. If the diaphragm seems too large in diameter and doesn't want to seat in the groove, place the top cover over the carburetor diaphragm, insert your finger into the throat of the carburetor and push up on the vacuum piston. Push down gently on the top cover – it should drop into place, indicating the diaphragm has seated in its groove.
9   Install the top cover, tightening the screws securely. If you're working on the no. 3 carburetor, don't forget to install the choke cable bracket on the right front corner.
10   Invert the carburetor. Attach the fuel inlet valve needle to the float. Set the float into position in the carburetor, making sure the valve needle seats

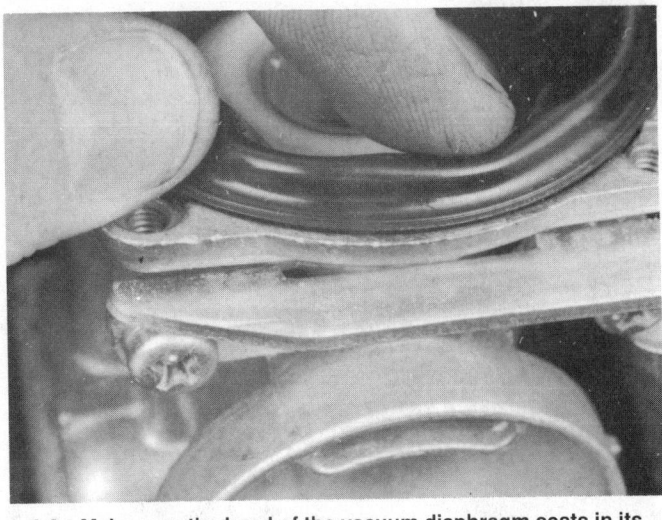

8.10   Float height adjustment details

1	*Carburetor body*	3	*Float*
2	*Float valve needle rod*	4	*Float height*

correctly. Install the float pivot pin. To check the float height, hold the carburetor so the float hangs down, then tilt it back until the valve needle is just seated (the rod in the end of the valve shouldn't be compressed). Measure the distance from the carburetor body to the top of the float **(see illustration)** and compare your measurement to the float height listed in this Chapter's Specifications. If it isn't as specified, carefully bend the tang that contacts the valve needle up or down until the float height is correct.
11   Install the O-ring into the groove in the float bowl. Place the float bowl on the carburetor and install the screws, tightening them securely.
12   If the carburetors were separated, install new O-rings on the fuel, vent and (if applicable) coolant fittings. Lubricate the O-rings on the fittings with a light film of oil and install them into their respective holes, making sure they seat completely **(see illustration 7.3)**.
13   Position the coil springs between the carburetors, gently push the carburetors together, then make sure the throttle linkages are correctly engaged. Check the fuel, vent and coolant (if applicable) fittings to make sure they engage properly also.
14   Install the upper and lower mounting plates and install the screws, but don't tighten them completely yet. Set the carburetors on a sheet of glass,

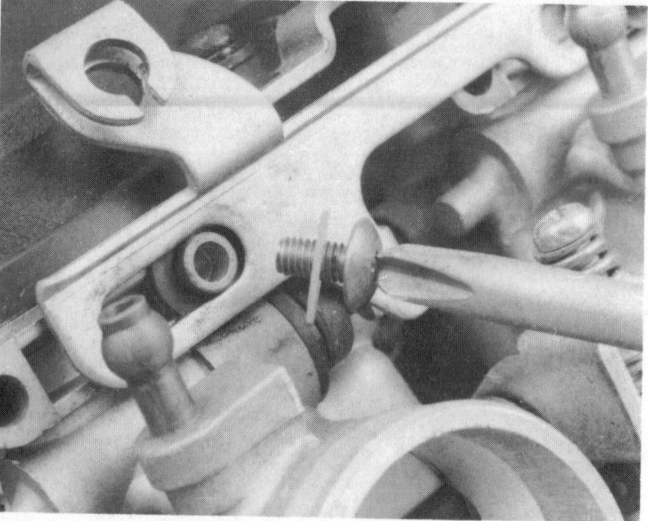

8.15   Make sure to install a plastic washer on each side of the choke lever when installing the screws

8.16   Install the throttle linkage springs

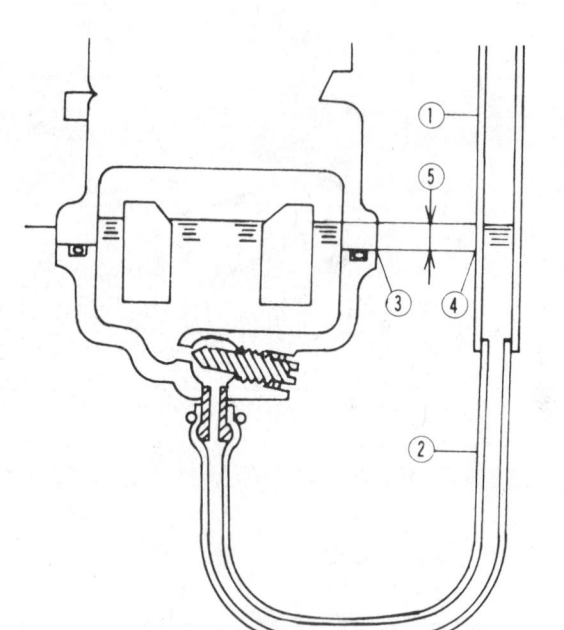

8.18   Checking the fuel level in a carburetor

1   Kawasaki tool no. 57001-1017
2   Fuel hose
3   Bottom edge of carburetor body
4   Zero line
5   Fuel level

then align them with a straightedge placed along the edges of the bores. When the centerlines of the carburetors are all in horizontal and vertical alignment, tighten the mounting plate screws securely.

15   Install the choke lever, making sure it engages correctly with all the choke plungers. Position a plastic washer on each side of the choke lever **(see illustration)** and install the screws, tightening them securely. Install the lever return spring, then make sure the choke mechanism operates smoothly.

16   Install the throttle linkage springs **(see illustration)**. Visually synchronize the throttle butterfly valves, turning the adjusting screws on the throttle linkage, if necessary, to equalize the clearance between the but-

terfly valve and throttle bore of each carburetor. Check to ensure the throttle operates smoothly.

Fuel level adjustment

Refer to illustration 8.18

Warning: *Gasoline is extremely flammable, so take extra precautions when you work on any part of the fuel system. Don't smoke or allow open flames or bare light bulbs near the work area, and don't work in a garage where a natural gas-type appliance (such as a water heater or clothes dryer) is present. If you spill any fuel on your skin, rinse it off immediately with soap and water. When you perform any kind of work on the fuel system, wear safety glasses and have a class B type fire extinguisher on hand.*

17   Lightly clamp the carburetor assembly in the jaws of a vise. Make sure the vise jaws are lined with wood. Set the fuel tank next to the vise, but at an elevation that is higher than the carburetors (resting on a box, for example). Connect a hose from the fuel tap to the fuel inlet fitting on the carburetor assembly – make sure the fuel tap is in the On or Reserve position.

18   Attach Kawasaki service tool no. 57001-1017 to the drain fitting on the bottom of one of the carburetor float bowls (all four will be checked) **(see illustration)**. This is a clear plastic tube graduated in millimeters. An alternative is to use a length of clear plastic tubing and an accurate ruler. Hold the graduated tube (or the free end of the clear plastic tube) against the carburetor body, as shown in the accompanying illustration. If the Kawasaki tool is being used, raise the zero mark to a point several millimeters above the bottom edge of the carburetor main body. If a piece of clear plastic tubing is being used, make a mark on the tubing at a point several millimeters above the bottom edge of the carburetor main body.

19   Unscrew the drain screw at the bottom of the float bowl a couple of turns, then turn the fuel tap to the Prime position – fuel will flow into the tube. Wait for the fuel level to stabilize, then slowly lower the tube until the zero mark is level with the bottom edge of the carburetor body. **Note:** *Don't lower the zero mark below the bottom edge of the carburetor then bring it back up – the reading won't be accurate.*

20   Measure the distance between the mark and top of the fuel level in the tube or gauge. This distance is the fuel level – write it down on a piece of paper, screw in the drain screw, turn the fuel tap to the On or Reserve position, then move on to the next carburetor and check it the same way.

21   Compare your fuel level readings to the value listed in this Chapter's Specifications. If the fuel level in any carburetor is not correct, remove the float bowl and bend the tang up or down (see Step 10), as necessary, then recheck the fuel level. **Note:** *Bending the tang up increases the float height and lowers the fuel level – bending it down decreases the float height and raises the fuel level.*

22   After the fuel level for each carburetor has been adjusted, install the carburetor assembly (see Section 6).

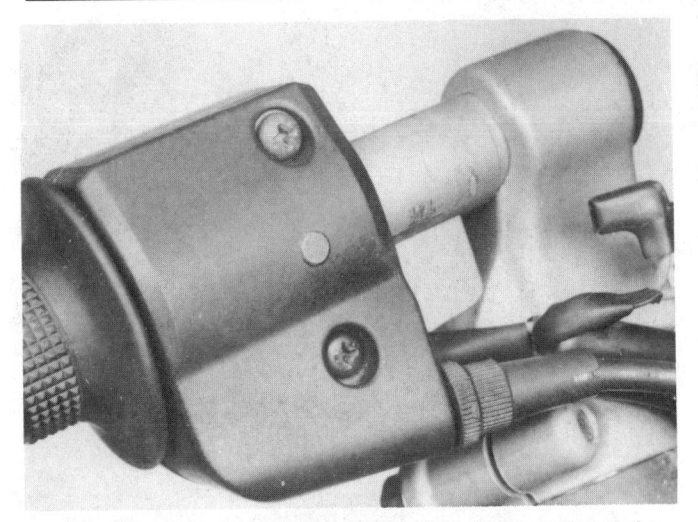

9.4   Remove the screws from the cable/switch housing and detach the front half of the housing

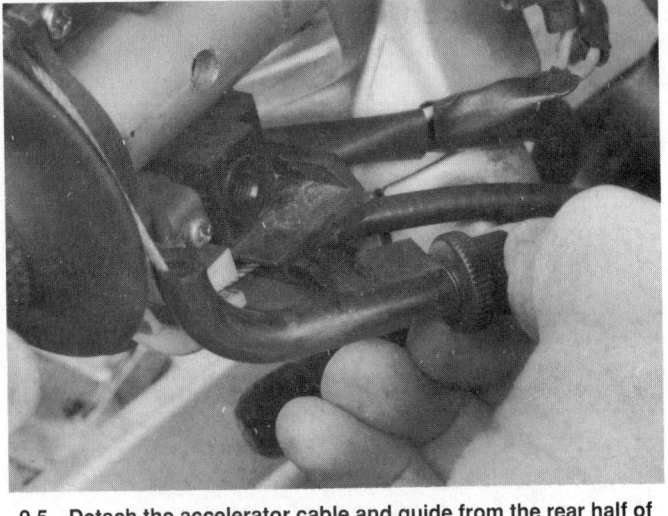

9.5   Detach the accelerator cable and guide from the rear half of the housing

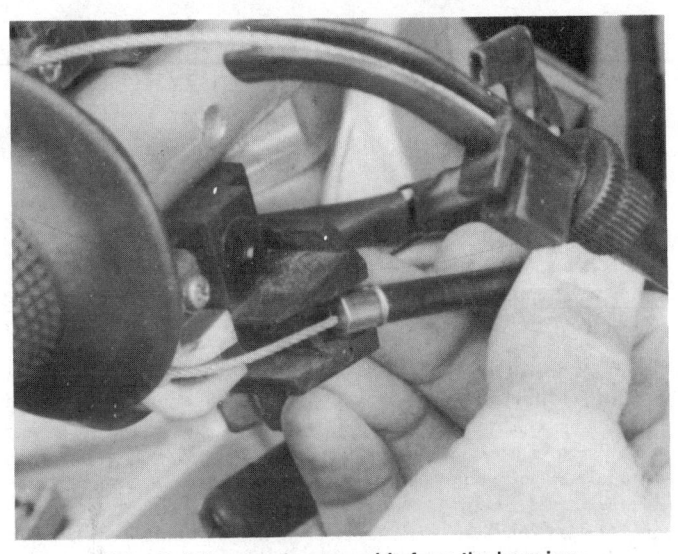

9.6   Pull the decelerator cable from the housing

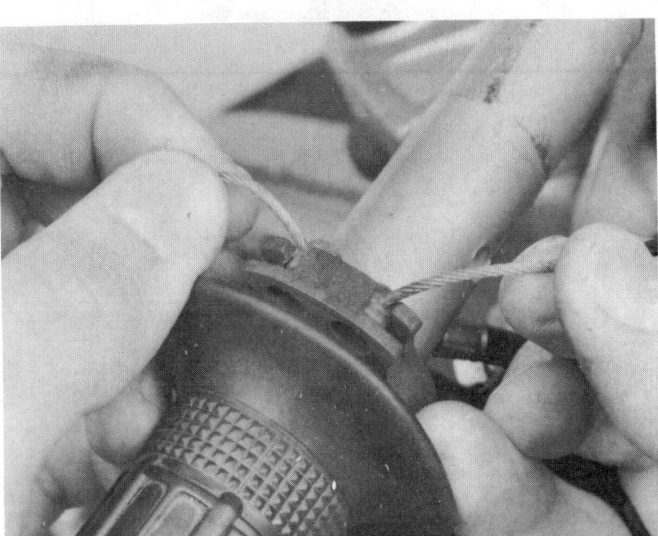

9.7   Align the cables with the slots in the throttle grip pulley, then slide the cable ends out

4

9   Throttle cables and grip – removal, installation and adjustment

Throttle cables

Refer to illustrations 9.4, 9.5, 9.6, 9.7, 9.8 and 9.9

Removal

1   Remove the fuel tank (see Section 2).

2   Detach the front brake master cylinder from the handlebar and position it out of the way (see Chapter 7).

3   Loosen the accelerator cable lockwheel and screw the cable adjuster in.

4   Remove the cable/switch housing screws **(see illustration)** and remove the front half of the housing.

5   Detach the accelerator cable and guide from the cable/switch housing **(see illustration)**.

6   Pull the decelerator cable from the rear half of the cable/switch housing **(see illustration)**.

7   Remove the rear half of the cable/switch housing from the handlebar. Detach both cables from the throttle grip pulley **(see illustration)**.

8   Detach the decelerator cable from the throttle pulley at the carburetor assembly **(see illustration)**.

9.8   Detach the decelerator cable from the carburetor throttle pulley

9.9   Rotate the throttle pulley at the carburetor assembly to full throttle, then detach the cable from the pulley

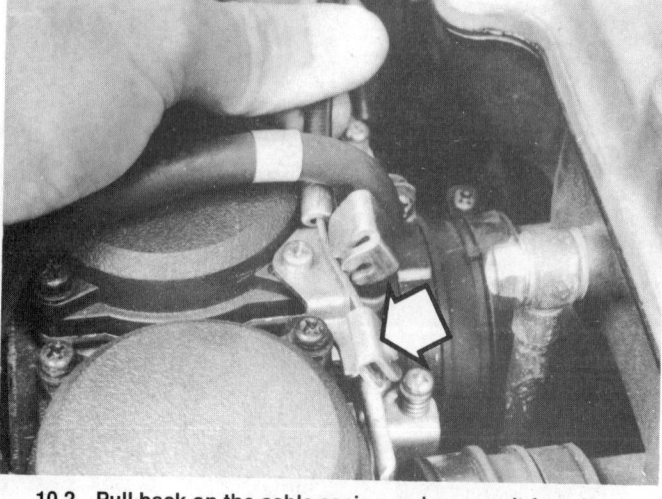

10.2   Pull back on the cable casing and remove it from its bracket, then detach the cable end from the choke lever (arrow)

9   Rotate the throttle pulley at the carburetor and detach the accelerator cable from the pulley **(see illustration)**.
10   Remove the cables, noting how they are routed.

Installation

11   Route the cables into place. Make sure they don't interfere with any other components and aren't kinked or bent sharply.
12   Lubricate the end of the accelerator cable with multi-purpose grease and connect it to the throttle pulley at the carburetor. Pass the inner cable through the slot in the bracket, then seat the cable housing in the bracket.
13   Repeat the previous step to connect the decelerator cable.
14   Route the decelerator cable around the backside of the handlebar and connect it to the rear hole in the throttle grip pulley.
15   From the front side of the handlebar, connect the accelerator cable to the forward hole in the throttle grip pulley.
16   Attach the rear half of the cable/switch housing to the handlebar, seating the decelerator cable in the groove in the housing as it's installed.
17   Hold the rear half of the cable/switch housing to the handlebar, then push the accelerator cable guide into place, making sure the notched portion is correctly engaged with the housing.
18   Install the front half of the cable/switch housing, making sure the locating pin engages with the hole in the handlebar. If necessary, rotate the housing back and forth, until the locating pin drops into the hole and the housing halves mate together. Install the screws and tighten them securely.
19   Install the master cylinder (see Chapter 7).

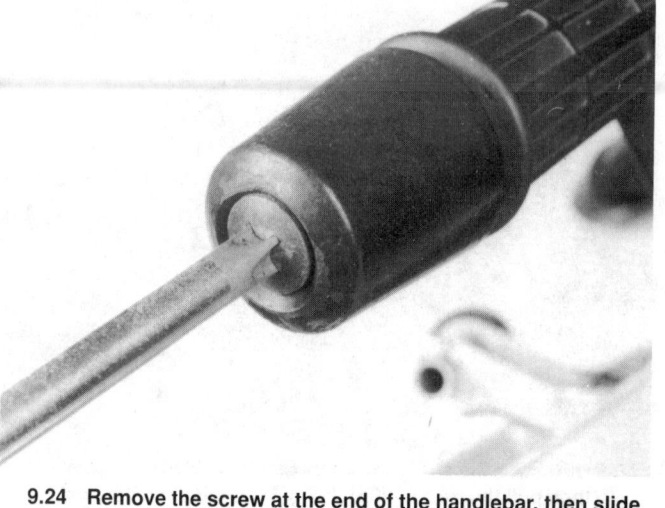

9.24   Remove the screw at the end of the handlebar, then slide the end and throttle grip off

Adjustment

20   Follow the procedure outlined in Chapter 1, Throttle operation/grip freeplay – check and adjustment, to adjust the cables.
21   Turn the handlebars back and forth to make sure the cables don't cause the steering to bind.
22   Install the fuel tank.

Throttle grip

Refer to illustration 9.24

Removal

23   Follow Steps 2 through 7 to detach the upper ends of the throttle cables from the throttle grip pulley.
24   Remove the screw retaining the handlebar end **(see illustration)** and remove the end. Slide the throttle grip off the handlebar.

Installation

25   Clean the handlebar and apply a light coat of multi-purpose grease.
26   If it is necessary to replace the rubber grip itself, slice the old grip lengthwise with a sharp knife and remove it. Lubricate the new grip and handlebar with soapy water or a commercially available grip cement (which acts as a lubricant and then dries, bonding the rubber to the handlebar or twist grip) and push the grip on.
27   Push the twist grip on and install the handlebar end. Apply a non-hardening thread locking compound to the screw and tighten it securely.
28   Attach the cables following Steps 14 through 19, then adjust the cables following the procedure outlined in Chapter 1, Throttle operation/grip freeplay – check and adjustment.

---

10   Choke cable – removal, installation and adjustment

Removal

Refer to illustrations 10.2 and 10.3

1   Remove the seat and fuel tank (see Section 2).
2   Pull the choke cable casing away from its mounting bracket at the carburetor assembly, pass the inner cable through the opening in the bracket **(see illustration)**. Detach the cable end from the choke lever by the no. 4 carburetor.
3   Remove the two screws securing the choke cable/switch housing halves to the left handlebar **(see illustration)**. Pull the front half of the housing off and separate the choke cable from the lever.
4   Remove the cable, noting how it's routed.

Installation

Refer to illustration 10.5

5   Route the cable into position. Connect the upper end of the cable to the choke lever. Make sure the cable guide seats properly in the housing

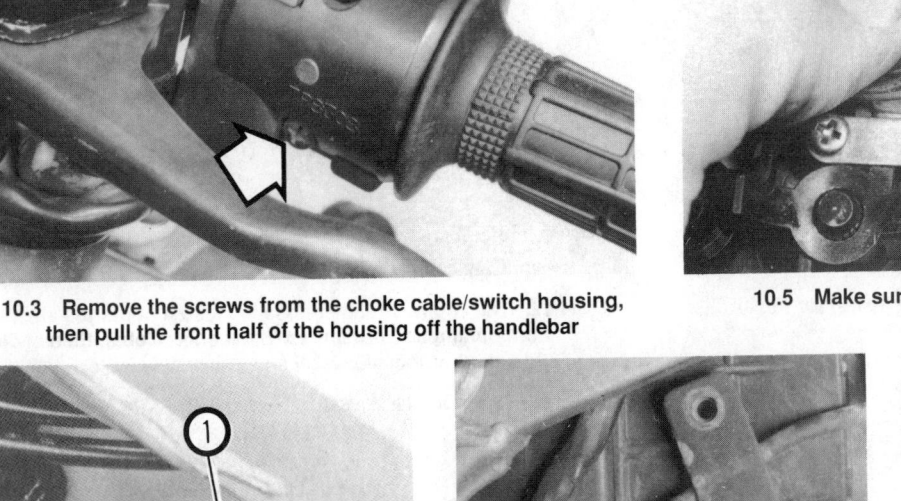

10.3 Remove the screws from the choke cable/switch housing, then pull the front half of the housing off the handlebar

10.5 Make sure the choke cable guide seats in the housing properly

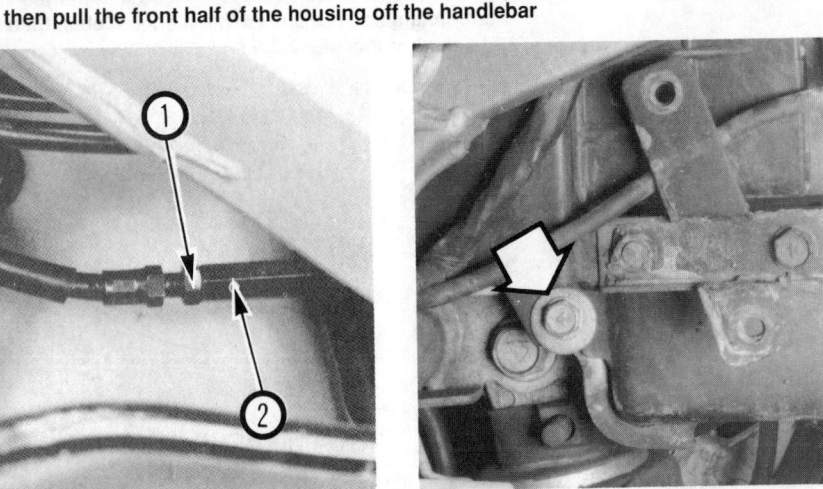

10.8 To adjust the choke cable, loosen the locknut (1) and turn the adjusting nut (2) in or out until the freeplay at the choke lever is about 2 or 3 millimeters (1/8-inch)

11.7 Once the voltage regulator/rectifier has been detached from its bracket, the left-side mounting bolt (arrow) for the air filter housing can be removed (A and B models)

11.8 The right-side mounting bolt for the air filter housing (arrow) is located in front of the igniter unit (A and B models)

4

(see illustration). Place the housing up against the handlebar, making sure the pin in the housing fits into the hole in the handlebar. Install the screws, tightening them securely.

6 Connect the lower end of the cable to the choke lever. Pull back on the cable casing and connect it to the bracket on the no. 3 carburetor.

Adjustment

Refer to illustration 10.8

7 Check the freeplay at the lever on the handlebar. It should move about two to three millimeters (1/8-inch).

8 If the freeplay isn't as specified, loosen the cable adjusting locknut **(see illustration)** and turn the adjusting nut in or out, as necessary, until the freeplay at the lever is correct. Tighten the locknut.

9 Install the fuel tank and all of the other components that were previously removed.

11 Air filter housing – removal and installation

Refer to illustrations 11.7, 11.8, 11.9, 11.12, 11.14 and 11.15

1 Remove the seat. On C models, remove the knee grip covers.

2 Remove the side covers (see Chapter 8 if necessary).

3 Remove the fuel tank (see Section 2).

4 Remove the fuel tank rear mount.

5 On A and B models, disconnect the cables from the battery (negative cable first), then remove the battery.

6 On A and B models, remove the voltage regulator/rectifier (see Chapter 9) and its bracket.

7 On A and B models, remove the left-side mounting bolt **(see illustration)**.

8 On A and B models, remove the right-side mounting bolt **(see illustration)**.

9 On A and B models, remove the rear mounting bolts **(see illustration)**.

10 Slide the spring bands that attach the ducts to the carburetors toward the air filter housing.

11 On C models, remove the carburetor assembly (see Section 6).

12 Using a pair of pliers, squeeze the hose clamp on the crankcase breather hose (underneath the air filter housing) and detach the hose from the crankcase **(see illustration)**.

13 Detach the evaporative emission control system hose from the air cleaner housing (if equipped).

14 On A and B models, lift the air filter housing up and out of the frame **(see illustration)**.

15 On C models, remove the air ducts from the front of the air filter housing. Lift up the air filter housing far enough to disengage the lug on the bottom of the housing from the hole in the frame **(see illustration)**. Slide the housing forward and remove it out the left or right side of the machine.

16 Installation is the reverse of removal.

11.9   Location of the rear mounting bolts (arrows) for the air filter housing (A and B models)

11.12   The engine breather hose is located under the air filter housing and is secured to the engine by a hose clamp (C model shown, A and B models similar)

1   Breather hose   *2   Clamp*

11.14   Lift the housing out of the frame, front side first (A and B models)

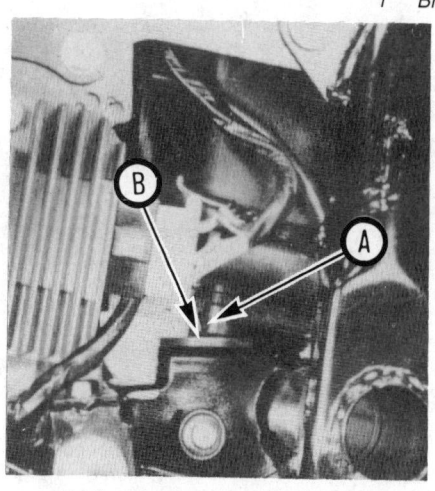

11.15   On C models, lift the air filter housing up to detach the lug (A) from the hole in the frame (B), slide the housing forward and remove it out from the side of the bike

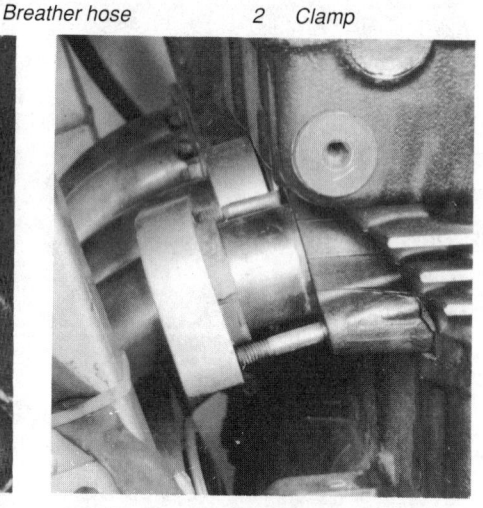

12.5   Remove the nuts and slide the exhaust pipe holders away from the cylinder head

12.6   Remove the muffler mounting bolts from the passenger footpeg bracket on each side

12   Exhaust system – removal and installation

Refer to illustrations 12.5 and 12.6

1   Remove the lower fairing (see Chapter 8).

2   Drain the coolant (see Chapter 1).

3   Remove the radiator (see Chapter 3).

4   Loosen the clamps securing the connecting pipe to the right and left side exhaust pipes (it's located under the engine).

5   Remove the exhaust pipe holder nuts and slide the holders off the mounting studs **(see illustration)**. If the split keepers didn't come off with the holders, remove them from the pipes.

6   Remove the muffler mounting bolts at the footpeg brackets **(see illustration)**.

7   Pull the exhaust system forward, separate the right side pipes from the left side pipes and remove the system from the machine.

8   Installation is the reverse of removal, but be sure to install a new gasket at the connecting pipe.

Chapter 5 Ignition system

Refer to Chapter 10 for information on the ZX750F model

Contents

Specifications

Ignition coil

Primary resistance
  A and B models .... 1.8 to 2.8 ohms
  C models .... 2.61 to 3.19 ohms
Secondary resistance
  A and B models .... 10 to 16 k-ohms
  C models .... 13.5 to 16.5 k-ohms
Arcing distance .... 1/4 in (7 mm) or more

Pickup coil resistance .... 360 to 440 ohms

Ignition timing .... Not adjustable

Torque specifications

	In-lbs
Pickup coil cover bolts	43

1 General information

This motorcycle is equipped with a battery operated, fully transistorized, breakerless ignition system. The system consists of the following components:

Pickup coils
IC igniter unit
Battery and fuse
Ignition coils
Spark plugs
Stop and main (key) switches
Primary and secondary circuit wiring

The transistorized ignition system functions on the same principle as a conventional DC ignition system with the pickup unit and igniter performing the tasks normally associated with the breaker points and mechanical advance system. As a result, adjustment and maintenance of ignition components is eliminated (with the exception of spark plug replacement).

Because of their nature, the individual ignition system components can be checked but not repaired. If ignition system troubles occur, and the faulty component can be isolated, the only cure for the problem is to replace the part with a new one. Keep in mind that most electrical parts, once purchased, can't be returned. To avoid unnecessary expense, make very sure the faulty component has been positively identified before buying a replacement part.

2 Ignition system – check

Refer to illustrations 2.3, 2.5, 2.13 and 2.14
Warning: *Because of the very high voltage generated by the ignition system, extreme care should be taken when these checks are performed.*
1 If the ignition system is the suspected cause of poor engine performance or failure to start, a number of checks can be made to isolate the problem.
2 Make sure the ignition stop switch is in the Run or On position.

2.3   With the wire attached, ground a spark plug to the engine and operate the starter – bright blue sparks should be visible

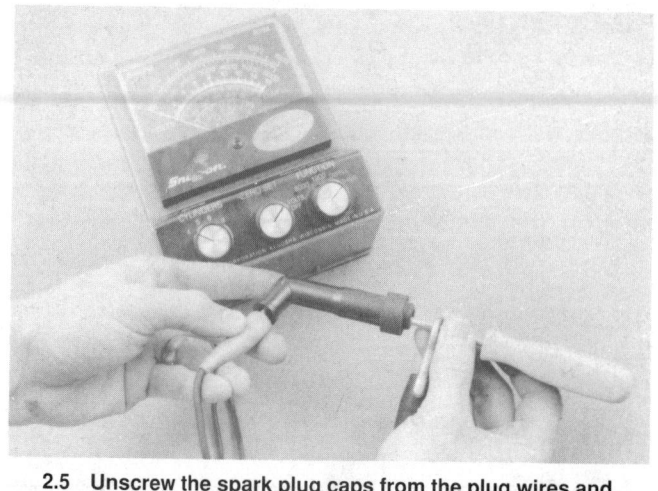

2.5   Unscrew the spark plug caps from the plug wires and measure their resistance with an ohmmeter

2.13   A simple spark gap testing fixture can be made from a block of wood, a large alligator clip, two nails, a screw and a piece of wire

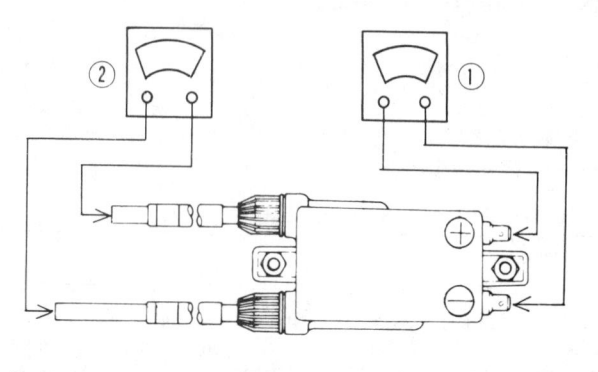

2.14   Connect the tester to a good ground and attach one of the spark plug wires – when the engine is cranked, sparks should jump the gap between the nails

Engine will not start

3   Remove the fuel tank (see Chapter 4). Disconnect one of the spark plug wires, connect the wire to a spare spark plug and lay the plug on the engine with the threads contacting the engine. If necessary, hold the spark plug with an insulated tool **(see illustration)**. Crank the engine over and make sure a well-defined, blue spark occurs between the spark plug electrodes. **Warning:** *Don't remove one of the spark plugs from the engine to perform this check – atomized fuel being pumped out of the open spark plug hole could ignite, causing severe injury!*

4   If no spark occurs, the following checks should be made:

5   Unscrew a spark plug cap from a plug wire and check the cap resistance with an ohmmeter **(see illustration)**. If the resistance is infinite, replace it with a new one. Repeat this check on the remaining plug caps.

6   Make sure all electrical connectors are clean and tight. Check all wires for shorts, opens and correct installation.

7   Check the battery voltage with a voltmeter and the specific gravity with a hydrometer (see Chapter 1). If the voltage is less than 12-volts or if the specific gravity is low, recharge the battery.

8   Check the ignition fuse and the fuse connections. If the fuse is blown, replace it with a new one; if the connections are loose or corroded, clean or repair them.

9   Refer to Section 3 and check the ignition coil primary and secondary resistance.

10   Refer to Section 4 and check the pickup coil resistance.

11   If the preceding checks produce positive results but there is still no spark at the plug, remove the IC igniter and have it checked by a Kawasaki

3.4   To check the resistance of the primary windings, connect the leads of the ohmmeter to the primary terminals (1) – to check the resistance of the secondary windings, attach the leads of the ohmmeter to the spark plug wires of that coil (2)

dealer service department or other repair shop equipped with the special tester required.

Engine starts but misfires

12   If the engine starts but misfires, make the following checks before deciding that the ignition system is at fault.

13   The ignition system must be able to produce a spark across a seven

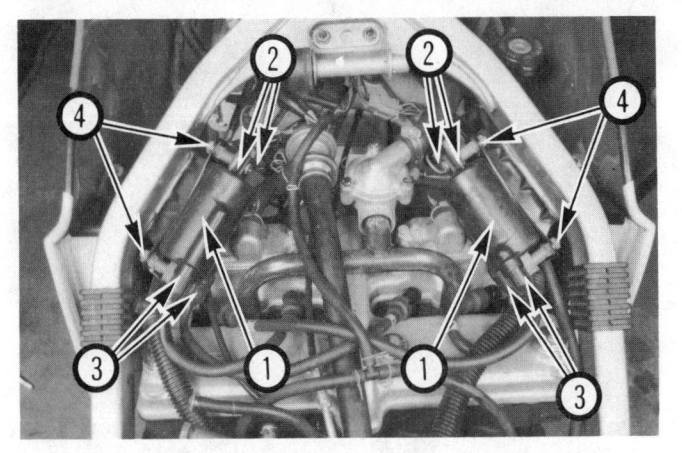

3.10a   Ignition coil installation details – A and B models

1	Ignition coils	3	Spark plug wire caps
2	Primary wires	4	Coil mounting nuts

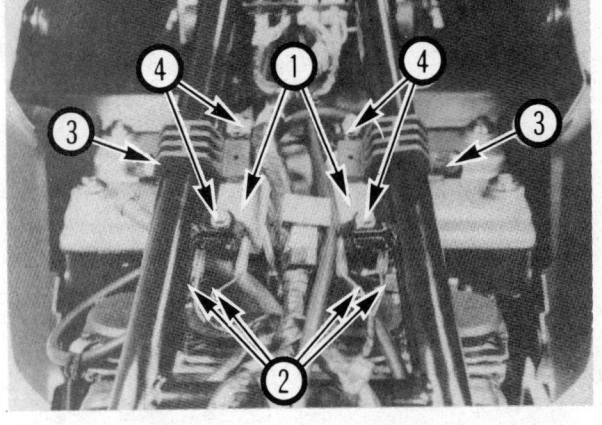

3.10b   Ignition coil installation details – C models

1	Ignition coils	3	Spark plug wire caps
2	Primary wires	4	Coil mounting nuts

millimeter (1/4-inch) gap (minimum). A simple test fixture **(see illustration)** can be constructed to make sure the minimum spark gap can be jumped. Make sure the fixture electrodes are positioned seven millimeters apart.

14   Connect one of the spark plug wires to the protruding test fixture electrode, then attach the fixture's alligator clip to a good engine ground **(see illustration)**.

15   Crank the engine over (it will probably start and run on the remaining cylinders) and see if well-defined, blue sparks occur between the test fixture electrodes. If the minimum spark gap test is positive, the ignition coil for that cylinder (and its companion cylinder) is functioning properly. Repeat the check on one of the spark plug wires that is connected to the other coil. If the spark will not jump the gap during either test, or if it is weak (orange colored), refer to Paragraphs 5 through 11 of this Section and perform the component checks described.

---

3   Ignition coils – check, removal and installation

Refer to illustrations 3.4, 3.10a and 3.10b

Check

1   In order to determine conclusively that the ignition coils are defective, they should be tested by an authorized Kawasaki dealer service department which is equipped with the special electrical tester required for this check.

2   However, the coils can be checked visually (for cracks and other damage) and the primary and secondary coil resistances can be measured with an ohmmeter. If the coils are undamaged, and if the resistances are as specified, they are probably capable of proper operation.

3   To check the coils for physical damage, they must be removed (see Step 9). To check the resistances, simply remove the fuel tank (see Chapter 4), unplug the primary circuit electrical connectors from the coil(s) and remove the spark plug wires from the plugs that are connected to the coil being checked. Mark the locations of all wires before disconnecting them.

4   To check the coil primary resistance, attach one ohmmeter lead to one of the primary terminals and the other ohmmeter lead to the other primary terminal **(see illustration)**.

5   Place the ohmmeter selector switch in the Rx1 position and compare the measured resistance to the value listed in this Chapter's Specifications.

6   If the coil primary resistance is as specified, check the coil secondary resistance by disconnecting the meter leads from the primary terminals and attaching them to the spark plug wire terminals **(see illustration 3.4)**.

7   Place the ohmmeter selector switch in the Rx100 position and compare the measured resistance to the values listed in this Chapter's Specifications.

8   If the resistances are not as specified, unscrew the spark plug wire retainers from the coil, detach the wires and check the resistance again. If

4.2   Depress the tang and unplug the electrical connector for the pickup coils

it is now within specifications, one or both of the wires are bad. If it's still not as specified, the coil is probably defective and should be replaced with a new one.

Removal and installation

9   To remove the coils, refer to Chapter 4 and remove the fuel tank, then disconnect the spark plug wires from the plugs. After labeling them with tape to aid in reinstallation, unplug the coil primary circuit electrical connectors.

10   Support the coil with one hand and remove the coil mounting nuts **(see illustrations)**, then withdraw the coil from its bracket. If necessary, detach the bracket from the frame – it's secured by two bolts.

11   Installation is the reverse of removal. If a new coil is being installed, unscrew the spark plug wire terminals from the coil, pull the wires out and transfer them to the new coil. Make sure the primary circuit electrical connectors are attached to the proper terminals. Just in case you forgot to mark the wires, the black and red wires connect to the no. 1 and 4 ignition coil (red to positive, black to negative) and the red and green wires attach to the no. 2 and 3 coil (red to positive, green to negative).

---

4   Pickup coils – check, removal and installation

Refer to illustrations 4.2, 4.6, 4.7a, 4.7b, 4.8 and 4.10

Check

1   Remove the right side cover.

2   Disconnect the electrical connector for the pickup coil **(see illustration)**.

5

4.6   Remove the screws that secure the pickup coil cover

4.7a   Remove the screws (arrows) and detach the pickup coil

4.7b   Detach the wiring harness from the clamps (arrows) below the clutch housing

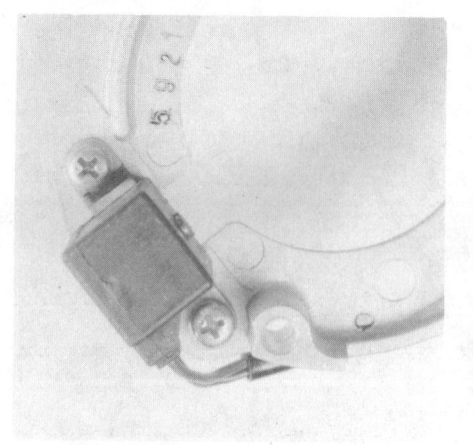

4.8   Each pickup coil is secured to the mounting plate with two screws

4.10   The notch in the pickup coil cover serves as a drain for moisture – make sure it's positioned on the bottom

5.2   To remove the igniter, simply pull it from its mounting bracket and detach the electrical connector

3   Probe each pair of terminals in the pickup coil connector with an ohmmeter (the black and yellow wire terminals, then the blue and black/white wire terminals) and compare the resistance reading with the value listed in this Chapter's Specifications.

4   Set the ohmmeter on the highest resistance range. Measure the resistance between a good ground and each terminal in the electrical connector. The meter should read infinity.

5   If the pickup coils fail either of the above tests, they must be replaced.

Removal

6   Remove the screws that secure the pickup coil cover to the engine case **(see illustration)** and detach the cover from the engine.

7   Unscrew the pickup coil assembly mounting screws and remove the pickup coils **(see illustration)**. Detach the wiring harness from the clamps beneath the clutch housing **(see illustration)**.

Installation

8   If the new pickup coils don't come with a mounting plate, remove the screws and detach the pickup coils from the plate, noting how they're installed **(see illustration)**. Place the new pickup coils on the plate and install the screws, tightening them securely.

9   Position the pickup coil assembly on the engine and install the screws, tightening them securely. Be sure to seat the grommet on the wiring harness into the notch in the case.

10   Install the pickup coil cover, making sure the notch in the cover is positioned on the lower side **(see illustration)**. Tighten the cover bolts to the torque listed in this Chapter's Specifications.

11   Attach the harness to the clamps on the bottom of the clutch housing **(see illustration 4.7b)**.

12   Plug in the electrical connector and install the side cover.

---

5   IC igniter – removal, check and installation

Refer to illustration 5.2

Removal

1   Remove the right side cover.

2   Pull the igniter from its bracket **(see illustration)**. Unplug the electrical connector.

Check

3   A special tester is required to accurately measure the resistance values across the various terminals of the IC igniter. Take the unit to a Kawasaki dealer service department or other repair shop equipped with this tester.

Installation

4   If a new igniter is being installed, slide the rubber cover off the old one and transfer it to the new one.

5   Plug in the electrical connector and push the igniter into its bracket, making sure the slots of the rubber cover are engaged properly with the tabs on the bracket.

6   Install the side cover.

Chapter 6   Frame, suspension and final drive

Refer to Chapter 10 for information on the ZX750F model

Contents

6

Specifications

Fork spring length

A and B models
  Standard . . . .   18 53/64 in (478 mm)
  Minimum . . . .   18 7/16 in (468 mm)
C models
  Standard . . . .   18 61/64 in (481 mm)
  Minimum . . . .   18 19/32 in (472 mm)

Rear sprocket

Runout (maximum) . . . .   0.020 in (0.5 mm)
Diameter
  Standard . . . .   7.368 to 7.388 in (187.02 to 187.52 mm)
  Minimum . . . .   7.355 in (186.7 mm)

Torque specifications
Ft-lbs (unless otherwise indicated)

Frame rear section mounting bolts (C models only)
  Lower bolts   33
  Upper bolts   14
Frame downtube bolts   18

Torque specifications (continued)

Ft-lbs (unless otherwise indicated)

Handlebar-to-upper triple clamp bolts	16.5
Handlebar tube-to-mount bolt (C models only)	16.5
Brake plunger bolts (A and B models only)	61 in-lbs
Anti-dive unit-to-fork leg bolts (A and B models only)	61 in-lbs
ESCS-to-fork leg bolts (C models only)	61 in-lbs
Damper rod bolt	
A and B models	22
C models	29
Fork top plug	16.5
Steering stem nut	29
Fork clamp bolts	15
Rear shock absorber mounting bolts/nuts	
A and B models	39
C models	36
Tie-rod-to-rocker arm bolt/nut	
A and B models	39
C models	36
Tie-rod-to-swingarm bolts/nuts	
A and B models	39
C models	36
Rocker arm pivot shaft nut	
A and B models	39
C models	36
Swingarm pivot shaft nut	
A and B models	65
C models	69
Engine sprocket cover bolts	78 in-lbs
Rear sprocket-to-wheel coupling nuts	54
Engine sprocket holding plate bolts	87 in-lbs

1   General information

Refer to illustrations 1.1, 1.2 and 1.5

The machines covered by this manual use two different frame designs. On A and B models, the frame is of the full cradle design, constructed of square tubing; steel for the A models and aluminum alloy for the B models **(see illustration)**. The down tubes on these models are detachable, which allows for easy engine removal. B models have integral frame members where the removable plastic side stays are on A models.

The frame on C models is fabricated from round steel tubing and is of the diamond design **(see illustration)**. The down tubes aren't detachable, but the rear section of the frame is.

The front forks are of the conventional coil spring, hydraulically-damped telescopic type. On A and B models they are air-assisted. C models are designed to run at atmospheric pressure.

A and B models use a variable damping system, controlled by a knob at the lower end of each fork leg, on the AVDS units. A brake valve mounted to the top of these units firms-up the damping characteristics of the forks during braking, which reduces fork compression. On C models, all this is controlled electrically by the Electric Suspension Control System (ESCS); note that this system is not fitted to ZX600C6-on UK models.

The rear suspension is Kawasaki's Uni-trak design, which consists of a single shock absorber, a rocker arm, two tie-rods and a square-section aluminum swingarm **(see illustration)**. The shock absorber has four damping settings and is also air adjustable.

The final drive uses an endless chain (which means it doesn't have a master link). A rubber damper is installed between the rear wheel coupling and the wheel.

2   Frame – inspection and repair

1   The frame should not require attention unless accident damage has occurred. In most cases, frame replacement is the only satisfactory reme-

dy for such damage. A few frame specialists have the jigs and other equipment necessary for straightening the frame to the required standard of accuracy, but even then there is no simple way of assessing to what extent the frame may have been overstressed.

2   After the machine has accumulated a lot of miles, the frame should be examined closely for signs of cracking or splitting at the welded joints. Rust corrosion can also cause weakness at these joints. Loose engine mount bolts can cause ovaling or fracturing of the mounting tabs. Minor damage can often be repaired by welding, depending on the extent and nature of the damage.

3   Remember that a frame which is out of alignment will cause handling problems. If misalignment is suspected as the result of an accident, it will be necessary to strip the machine completely so the frame can be thoroughly checked.

3   Frame rear section (C models only) – removal and installation

1   Remove the rider's seat.

2   Remove the knee grip covers and the side covers (see Chapter 8).

3   Remove the passenger seat and tailpiece (see Chapter 8).

4   Detach the air valve (see Chapter 1), the starter solenoid and voltage regulator/rectifier (see Chapter 9) and the rear brake fluid reservoir (see Chapter 7) from the frame.

5   Remove the rear section of the rear fender (see Chapter 8).

6   Detach any wiring harness clamps or other components which may interfere with removal of the frame rear section.

7   Unscrew the bolts and detach the frame rear section **(see illustration 1.2)**.

8   If necessary, unbolt the passenger footpeg brackets, the seat lock and the helmet lock from the frame section.

9   Installation is the reverse of the removal procedure. Be sure to tighten the bolts to the torque listed in this Chapter's Specifications.

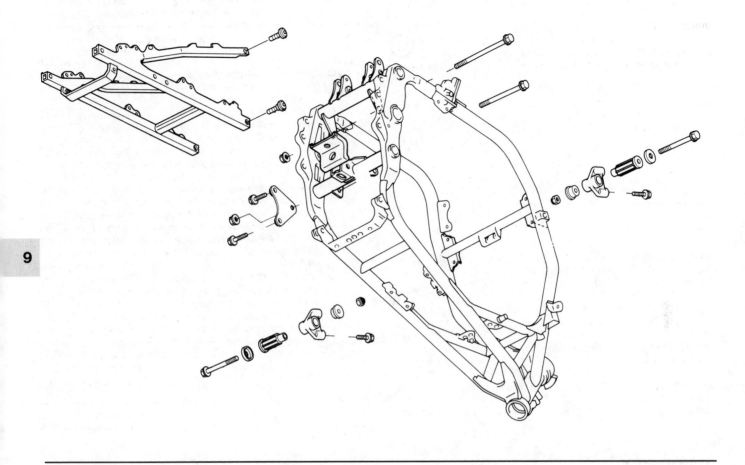

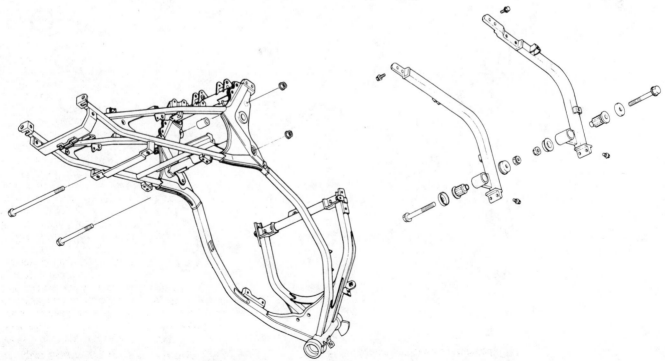

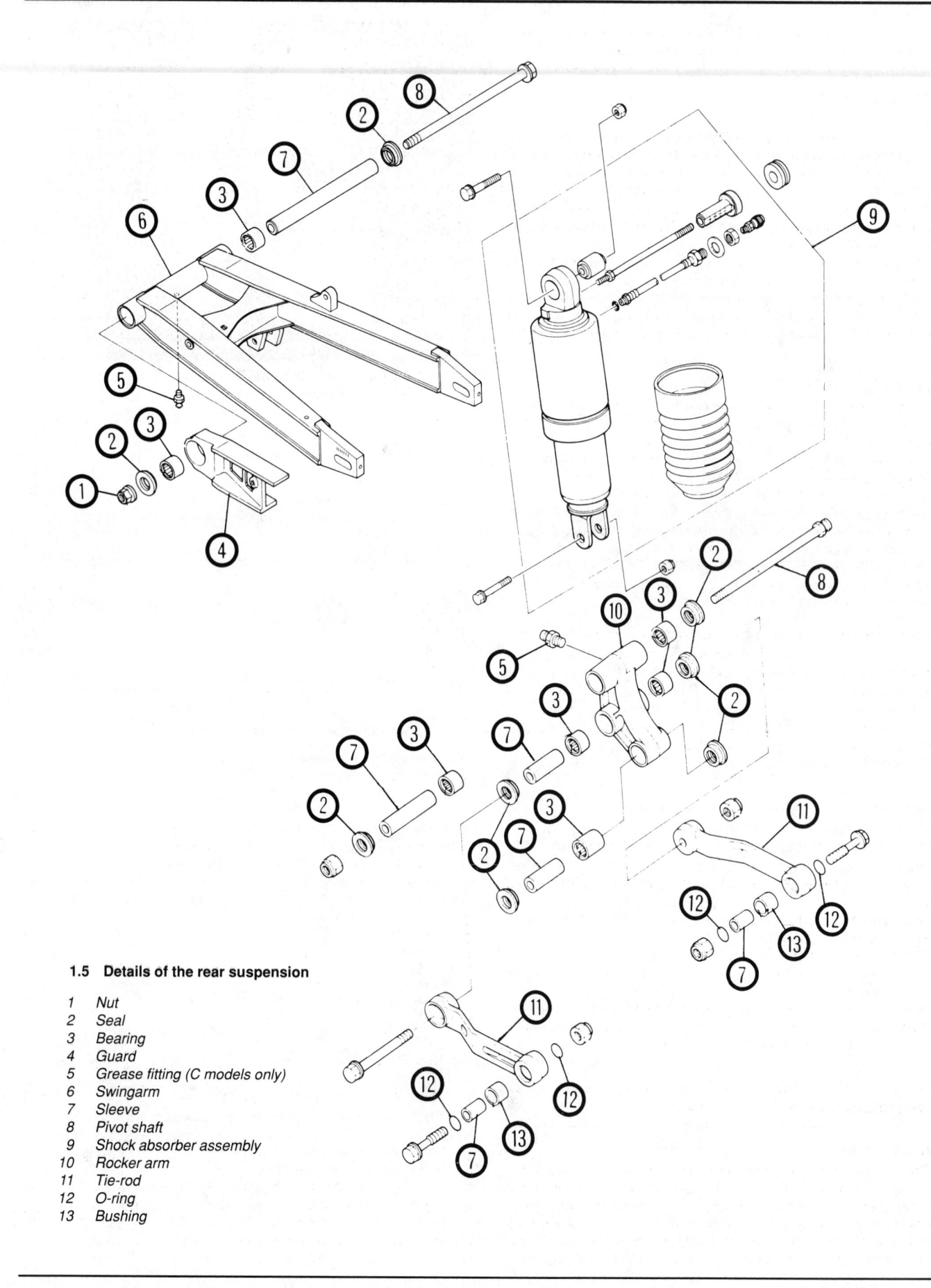

1.5   Details of the rear suspension

1   Nut
2   Seal
3   Bearing
4   Guard
5   Grease fitting (C models only)
6   Swingarm
7   Sleeve
8   Pivot shaft
9   Shock absorber assembly
10   Rocker arm
11   Tie-rod
12   O-ring
13   Bushing

4   Footpegs and brackets – removal and installation

Rider's left side

Refer to illustration 4.1

1   If it's only necessary to detach the footpeg from the bracket, pry the C-clip off the pivot pin **(see illustration)**, slide out the pin and detach the footpeg from the bracket. Be careful not to lose the spring. Installation is the reverse of removal, but be sure to install the spring correctly.

2   If it's necessary to remove the entire bracket from the frame, mark the relationship of the shift lever to the shift shaft, then remove the clamp bolt. Slide the lever off the shaft.

3   Unscrew the shift lever pivot bolt and the bracket-to-frame bolt and separate the footpeg and bracket from the frame.

4   Installation is the basically the reverse of removal. Apply a thin coat of grease to the shift pedal pivot bolt, and be sure to line up the matchmarks on the shift lever and shift shaft. The link rod should be parallel to the shift pedal.

Rider's right side

5   If it's only necessary to detach the footpeg from the bracket, pry the C-clip off the pivot pin **(see illustration 4.1)**, slide out the pin and detach the footpeg from the bracket. Be careful not to lose the spring. Installation is the reverse of removal, but be sure to install the spring correctly.

6   If it's necessary to remove the entire bracket from the frame, unplug the electrical connector for the rear brake light switch.

7   Remove the cotter pin from the clevis pin that attaches the brake pedal to the master cylinder, then remove the clevis pin (see Chapter 9).

8   Unbolt the master cylinder from the bracket.

9   Remove the Allen-head bolts that secure the bracket to the frame, then detach the footpeg and bracket.

10   Installation is the reverse of removal.

Passenger footpegs and brackets (either side)

11   If it's only necessary to detach the footpeg from the bracket, pry the C-clip off the pivot pin **(see illustration 4.1)**, slide out the pin and detach the footpeg from the bracket. Be careful not to lose the spring. Installation is the reverse of removal, but be sure to install the spring correctly.

12   If it's necessary to remove the entire bracket, unscrew the two Allen head bolts and detach the bracket from the frame.

13   Installation is the reverse of removal.

5   Side and centerstand – maintenance

1   The centerstand pivots on two bolts attached to the frame. Periodically, remove the pivot bolts and grease them thoroughly to avoid excessive wear.

2   Make sure the return spring is in good condition. A broken or weak spring is an obvious safety hazard.

3   The sidestand is attached to a bracket bolted to the frame. An extension spring anchored to the bracket ensures that the stand is held in the retracted position.

4   Make sure the pivot bolt is tight and the extension spring is in good condition and not overstretched. An accident is almost certain to occur if the stand extends while the machine is in motion.

6   Handlebars – removal and installation

Refer to illustration 6.1

1   The handlebars are individual assemblies that slip over the tops of the fork tubes, each being retained to the steering head by two Allen-head bolts. If the handlebars must be removed for access to other components, such as the forks or the steering head, simply remove the bolts and slip the handlebar(s) off the fork tubes **(see illustration)**. It's not necessary to disconnect the cables, wires or hoses, but it is a good idea to support the

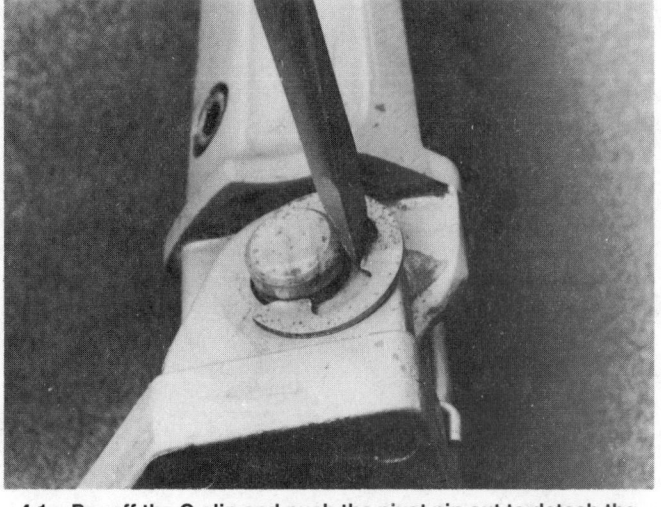

4.1   Pry off the C-clip and push the pivot pin out to detach the footpeg from the bracket

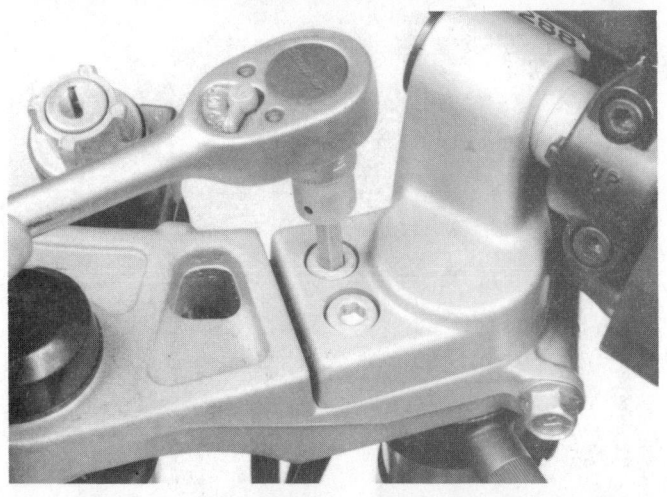

6.1   To detach a handlebar, remove the two bolts and slide the assembly off the fork tube – if it's stuck, wiggle it back and forth while pulling up

assembly with a piece of wire or rope, to avoid unnecessary strain on the cables, wires and (on the right side) the brake hose.

2   If the handlebars are to be removed completely, refer to Chapter 9 for the master cylinder removal procedure, Chapter 4 for the throttle grip removal procedure and Chapter 9 for the switch removal procedure.

3   Check the handlebars for cracks and distortion and replace them if any undesirable conditions are found. When installing the handlebars, tighten the bolts to the torque listed in this Chapter's Specifications.

7   Forks – removal and installation

Refer to illustrations 7.9, 7.11, 7.12a, 7.12b, 7.13 and 7.16

Removal

1   Set the bike on its centerstand.

2   Remove the upper fairing (see Chapter 8).

3   If you're working on an A or B model, release the air pressure from the forks.

4   Remove the front fender (see Chapter 8).

5   Remove the wheel (see Chapter 7).

6   Remove the handlebars (see Section 6). Support them so the cables, wires and brake hose aren't strained or kinked.

7   Unbolt the brake calipers (see Chapter 7) and hang them with pieces of wire or rope. On A and B models, unbolt the junction blocks from the fork tubes.

7.9   On A and B models, unbolt the brake plungers from the anti-dive units – don't disconnect the brake lines

7.11   If the forks are going to be disassembled, loosen the upper clamp bolt, then loosen the top plug with a 1/2 inch drive ratchet

7.12a   Loosen the fork lower clamp bolts

7.12b   Slide the forks down a little, pull the sleeves of the air connecting tube up and, using a small screwdriver, pry the retaining rings out of their grooves (A and B models only)

8   If you're removing the right side fork on a C model, detach the ESCS electrical connector from the ESCS unit.

9   If you're working on an A or B model, unbolt the brake plungers from the anti-dive units **(see illustration)**.

10   Remove any wiring harness clamps or straps from the fork tubes.

11   If the forks will be disassembled after removal, loosen the upper triple clamp bolts, then loosen the top plugs **(see illustration)**.

12   Loosen the fork upper and lower triple clamp bolts **(see illustration)**, then slide the fork tubes down slightly, using a twisting motion, then retighten the lower clamp bolts. Remove the retaining rings from their grooves **(see illustration)**.

13   Loosen the lower clamp bolts again and slide the fork tube down (one at a time) and out of the steering stem. If you're working on an A or B model, hold the sleeve of the air connecting pipe stationary so the pipe doesn't bend or break **(see illustration)**.

14   If you're working on an A or B model, stick a piece of tape over the air holes to prevent oil loss.

Installation

15   Slide each fork leg into the lower triple clamp. On A and B models, install the retaining rings, then lubricate the O-rings in the sleeves of the air connecting pipe assembly with the recommended fork oil (see Chapter 1). Install the the air connecting pipe assembly over the tops of the fork tubes.

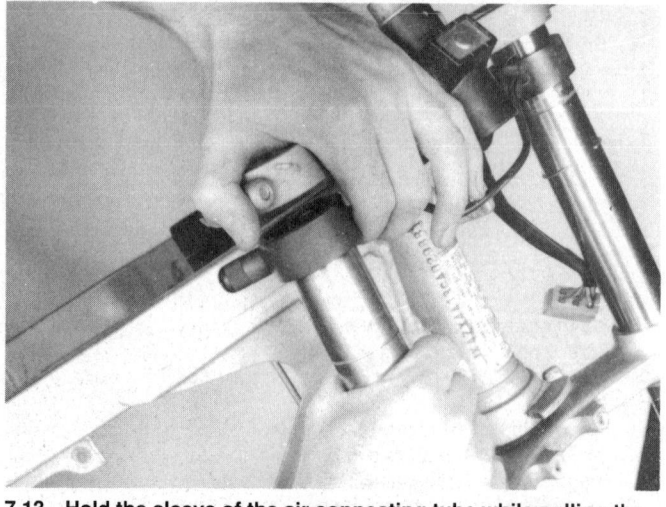

7.13   Hold the sleeve of the air connecting tube while pulling the fork tube down, so the air connecting tube doesn't break (A and B models only)

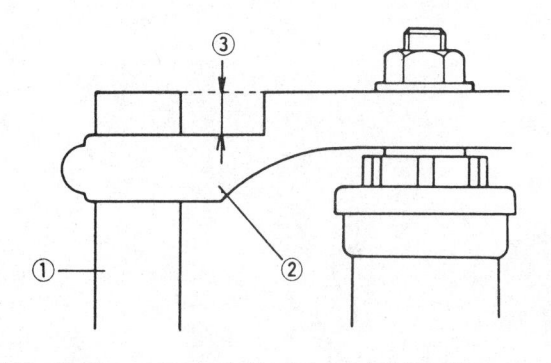

7.16   On C models, push the fork tube (1) into the upper clamp (2) until approximately 5/8 to 11/16 inch (16 to 17.5 mm) of the fork tube is protruding (3), then tighten the clamp bolts

16   Slide the fork legs up, installing the tops of the tubes into the upper triple clamp. On A and B models, align the air holes in the fork tubes with the pipes on the sleeves. Push the forks up until the sleeves of the air connecting pipe assembly contact the retaining rings. On C models, push the forks into the upper clamp until 5/8 to 11/16 inch (16.0 to 17.5 mm) of the fork tubes protrude past the upper surface of the upper clamp **(see illustration)**.
17   The remainder of installation is the reverse of the removal procedure. Be sure to tighten the clamp bolts and the brake plunger bolts (A and B models) to the torque listed in this Chapter's Specifications. Tighten the caliper mounting bolts to the torque listed in the Chapter 7 Specifications.
18   If you're working on an A or B model, charge the forks with the recommended air pressure (see Chapter 1).
19   Pump the front brake lever several times to bring the pads into contact with the discs.

---

8   Forks – disassembly, inspection and reassembly

Disassembly

Refer to illustrations 8.3a, 8.3b, 8.3c, 8.3d, 8.4, 8.5a, 8.5b, 8.6, 8.7, 8.8, 8.9 and 8.11

1   Remove the forks following the procedure in Section 7. Work on one fork leg at a time to avoid mixing up the parts.
2   Remove the axle clamp bolts. If you're working on the left fork leg of an A or B model, remove the axle nut. If you're working on the right fork leg on a C model, remove the axle clamp bolt.
3   Remove the top plug and washer (it should have been loosened before the forks were removed), spacer and spring guide (C models only) and spring **(see illustrations)**. When removing the plug, exert downward pressure on it to counteract the pressure from the fork spring – this will help to prevent damage to the threads.
4   Invert the fork assembly over a container and allow the oil to drain out. Be careful not to let the Travel Control Valve (TCV) fall out (A and B models only). Gently tap the fork leg with a rubber mallet until the valve comes out – be ready to catch it **(see illustration)**.
5   Prevent the damper rod from turning using a holding handle (Kawasaki tool no. 57001-183) and adapter (Kawasaki tool no. 57001-1057). Unscrew the Allen bolt at the bottom of the outer tube and retrieve the copper washer. **Note:** *If you don't have access to these special tools, you can fabricate your own using a bolt with a 23 mm head, two nuts, a socket (to fit on the nuts), a long extension and a ratchet. Thread the two nuts onto the bolt and tighten them against each other* **(see illustration)**. *Insert the assembly into the socket and tape it into place* **(see illustration)**. *Now, insert the tool into the fork tube and engage the bolt head (or the special Kawasaki tool) into the hex recess in the damper rod.*
6   Pull out the damper rod and the rebound spring **(see illustration)**.

8.3a   Remove the top plug, then pull out the fork spring

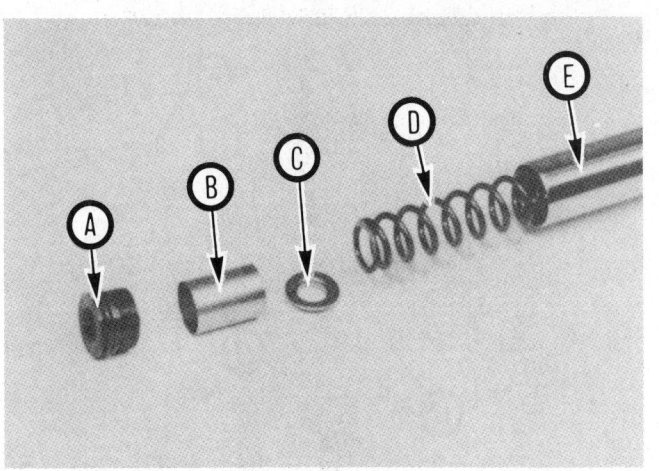

8.3b   On C models, a spacer and spring guide must also be removed

A	Top plug	D	Spring
B	Spacer	E	Inner fork tube
C	Spring guide		

Don't remove the Teflon ring from the damper rod unless a new one will be installed.
7   Pry the dust seal from the outer tube **(see illustration)**.
8   Pry the retaining ring from its groove in the outer tube **(see illustration)**. Remove the ring and the washer that's present underneath it.
9   Hold the inner tube and, using a dead-blow plastic mallet, tap the outer tube off (be careful not to let it fall) **(see illustration)**. An alternative method is to hold the outer tube and yank the inner tube upward, repeatedly (like a slide hammer), until the seal and outer tube guide bushing pop loose.
10   Slide the seal, washer and outer tube guide bushing from the inner tube.
11   Invert the outer tube and remove the damper rod base and the washers **(see illustration)**. **Note:** *On C models, only the right fork leg has washers.*

Inspection

12   Clean all parts in solvent and blow them dry with compressed air, if available. Check the inner and outer fork tubes, the guide bushings and the damper rod for score marks, scratches, flaking of the chrome and excessive or abnormal wear. Look for dents in the tubes and replace them if any are found. Check the fork seal seat for nicks, gouges and scratches. If damage is evident, leaks will occur around the seal-to-outer tube junction. Replace worn or defective parts with new ones.

6

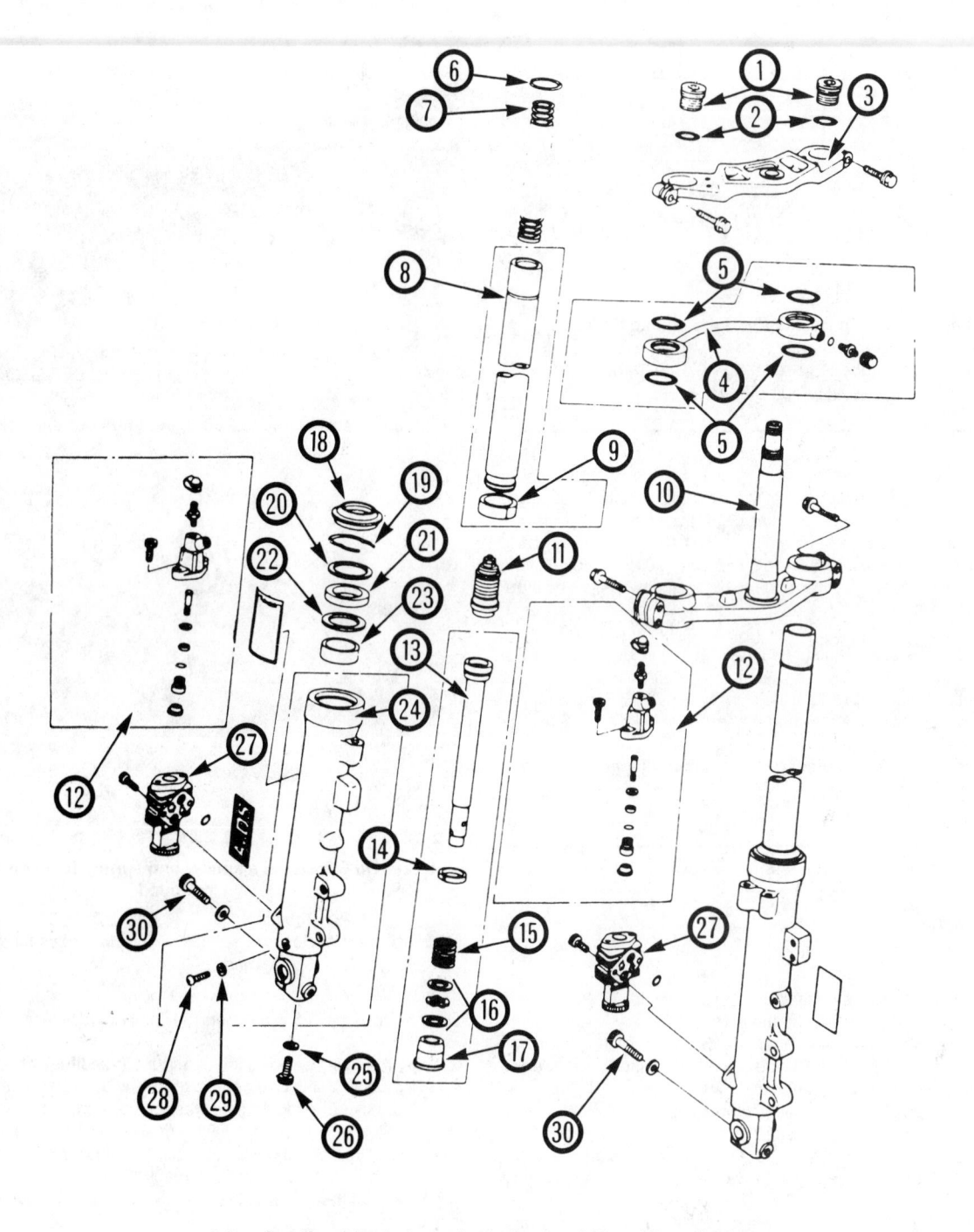

8.3c   Details of the forks and steering head (A and B models)

1	Top plug	11	Travel Control Valve	21	Oil seal
2	O-ring	12	Brake plunger assembly	22	Washer
3	Upper clamp	13	Damper rod	23	Outer guide bushing
4	Air connecting pipe	14	Teflon ring	24	Fork tube (outer)
5	O-rings	15	Rebound spring	25	Copper washer
6	Washer	16	Washers	26	Allen-head bolt
7	Fork spring	17	Damper rod base	27	Anti-dive unit
8	Fork tube (inner)	18	Dust seal	28	Drain screw
9	Inner guide bushing	19	Retaining ring	29	Gasket
10	Steering stem/lower clamp assembly	20	Washer	30	Axle clamp bolt

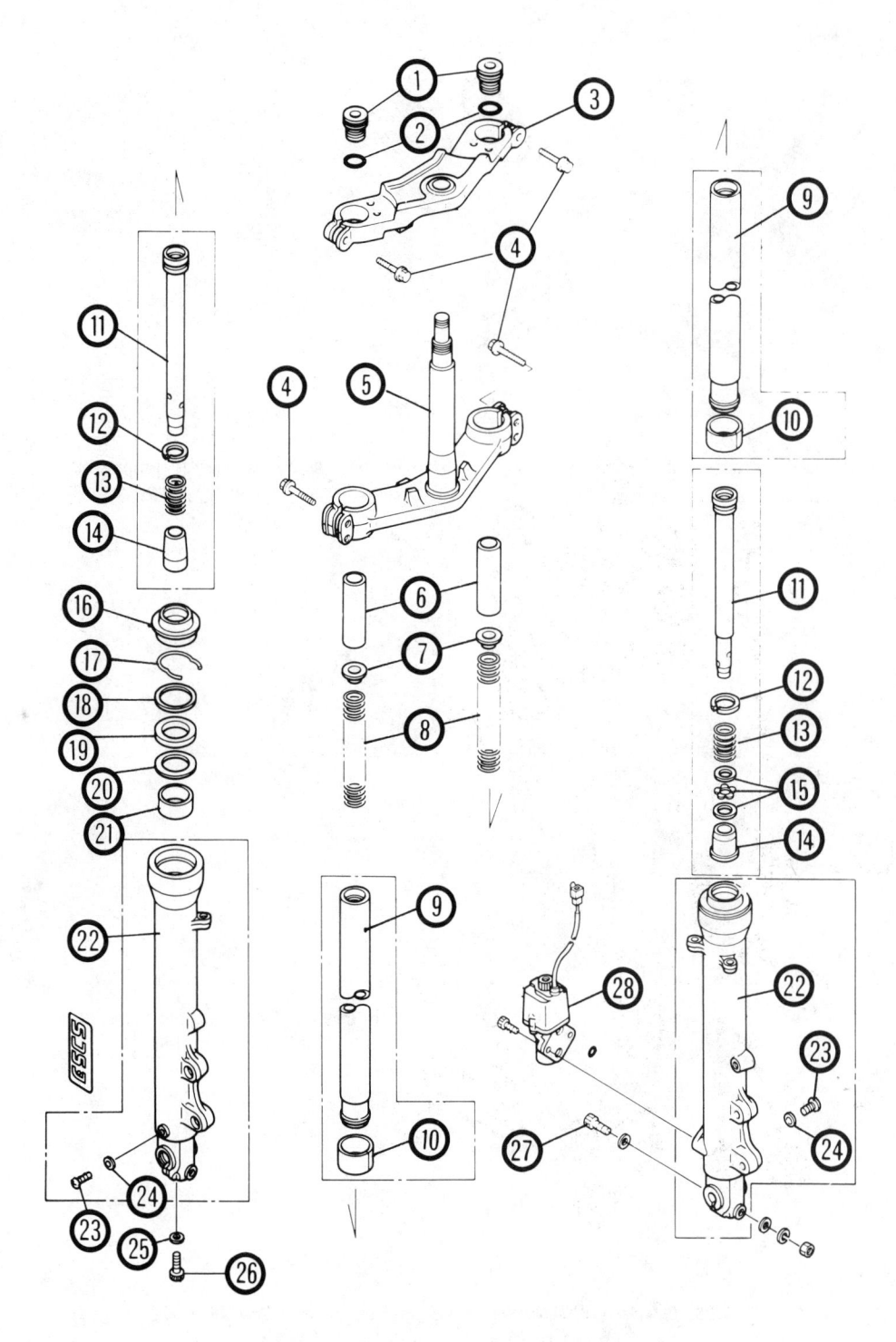

8.3d   Details of the forks and steering head (C models)

1	Top plug	8	Fork spring	15	Washers (right fork only)	22	Fork tube (outer)

1   Top plug
2   O-ring
3   Upper clamp
4   Clamp bolts
5   Steering stem/lower clamp
6   Spacer
7   Spring guide

8   Fork spring
9   Fork tube (inner)
10 Inner guide bushing
11 Damper rod
12 Teflon ring
13 Rebound spring
14 Damper rod base

15 Washers (right fork only)
16 Dust seal
17 Retaining ring
18 Washer
19 Oil seal
20 Washer
21 Outer guide bushing

22 Fork tube (outer)
23 Drain screw
24 Gasket
25 Copper washer
26 Allen-head bolt
27 Axle clamp bolt
28 Electric Suspension Control
     System (ESCS) adjuster

8.4   Remove the TCV from the inner tube

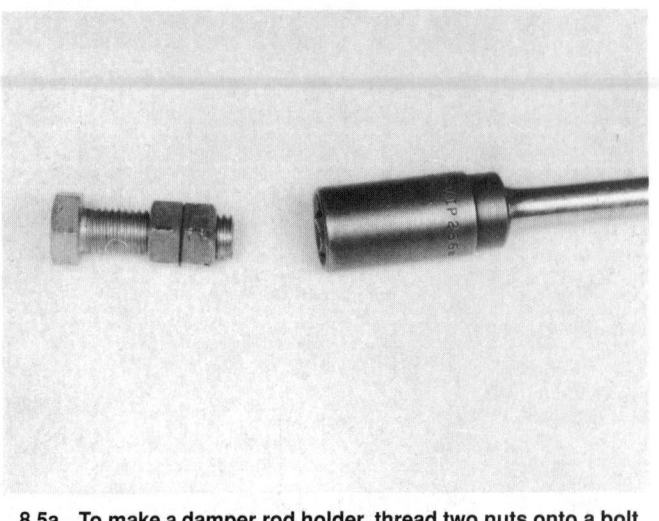

8.5a   To make a damper rod holder, thread two nuts onto a bolt with a 23 mm head and tighten the nuts against each other . . .

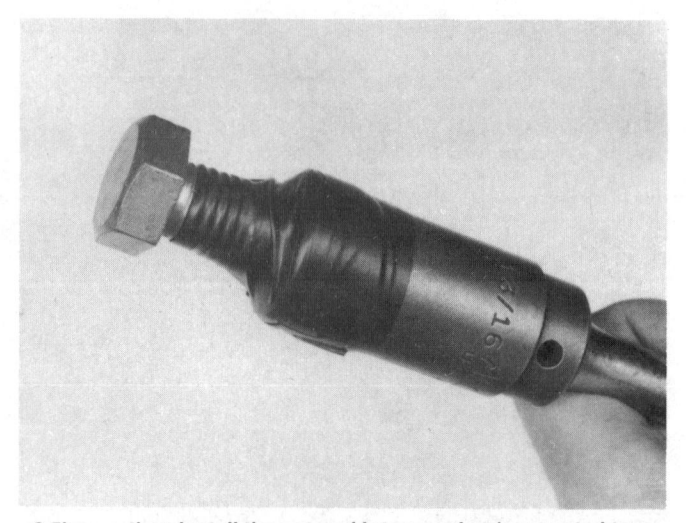

8.5b   . . . then install the nut-end into a socket (connected to a long extension) and tape it into place

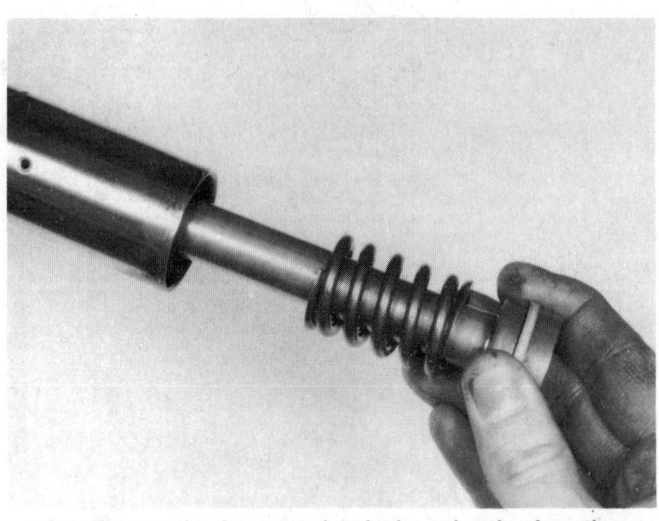

8.6   Remove the damper rod and rebound spring from the inner tube

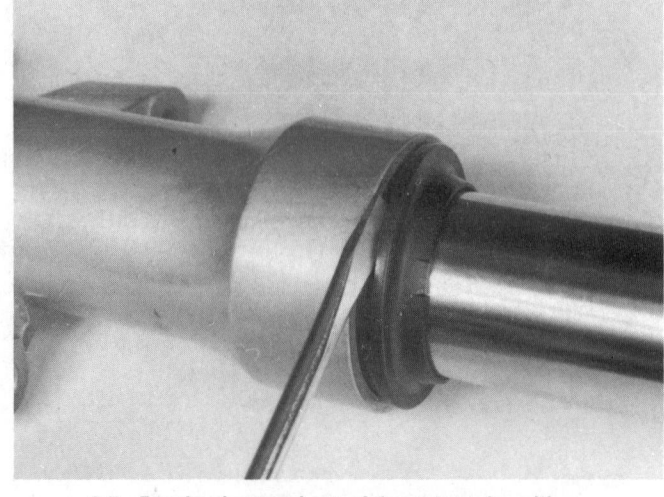

8.7   Pry the dust seal out of the outer tube with a small screwdriver

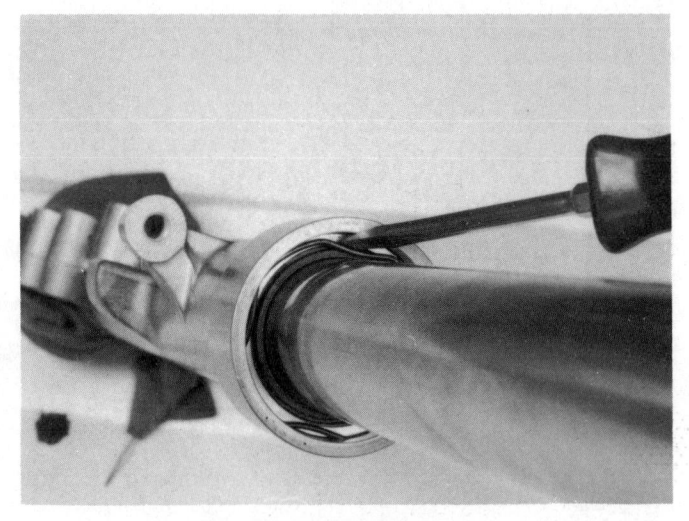

8.8   Pry out the retaining ring

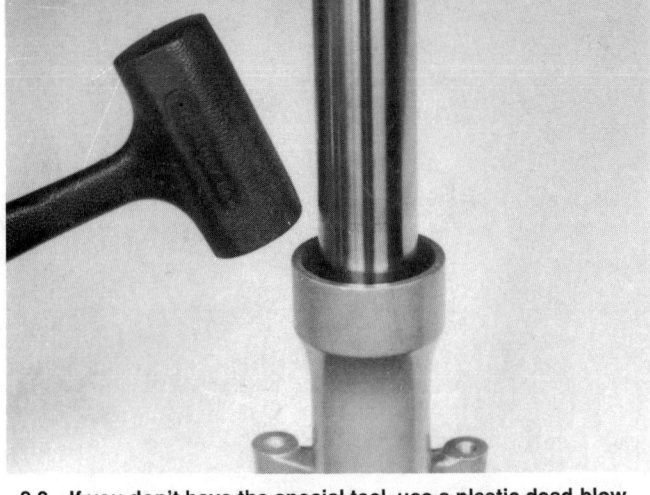

8.9   If you don't have the special tool, use a plastic dead-blow hammer to tap the outer tube from the inner tube

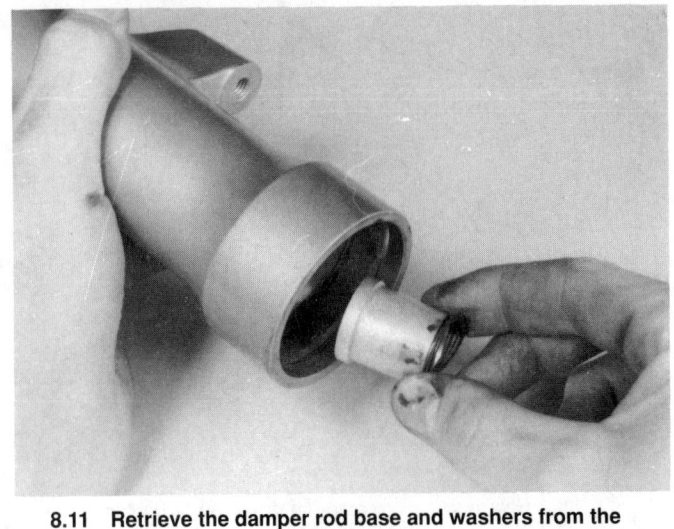

8.11   Retrieve the damper rod base and washers from the outer tube

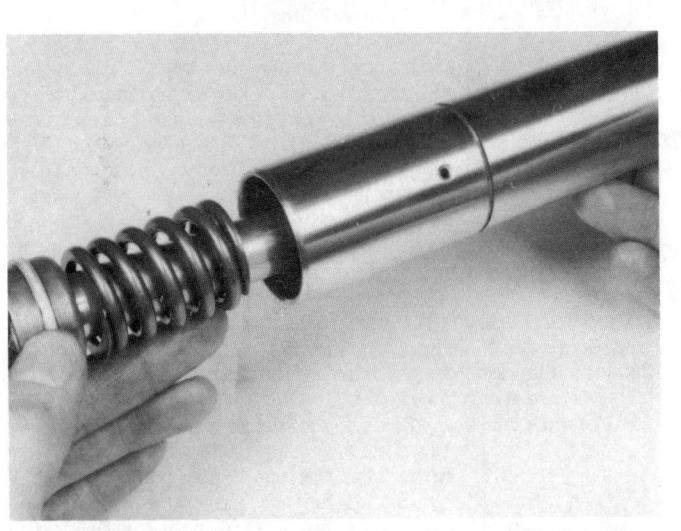

8.17   Install the damper rod/rebound spring assembly into the inner tube

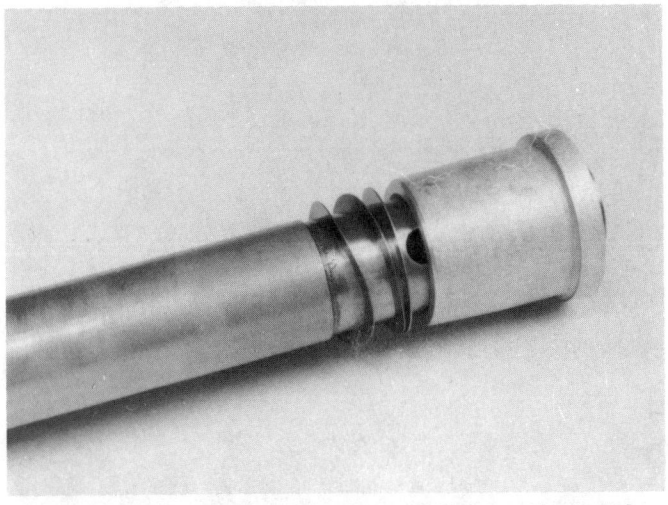

8.18   Install the damper rod washers and base on the end of the damper rod – the flat washer should be between the two spring washers

6

13   Have the fork inner tube checked for runout at a dealer service department or other repair shop. **Warning:** *If it is bent, it should not be straightened; replace it with a new one.*

14   Measure the overall length of the long spring and check it for cracks and other damage. Compare the length to the minimum length listed in this Chapter's Specifications. If it's defective or sagged, replace both fork springs with new ones. Never replace only one spring.

15   Check the TCV for any signs of damage and replace it if necessary (A and B models only). Don't attempt to disassemble it.

Reassembly

Refer to illustrations 8.17, 8.18, 8.19, 8.20a, 8.20b an 8.22

16   If it's necessary to replace the inner guide bushing (the one that won't come off that's on the bottom of the inner tube), pry it apart at the slit and slide it off. Make sure the new one seats properly.

17   Place the rebound spring over the damper rod, slide the rod assembly into the inner fork tube until it protrudes from the lower end of the tube **(see illustration)**.

18   Install the damper rod washers and base onto the end of the damper rod **(see illustration)**. **Note:** *Remember, only the right fork leg on C models has these washers.*

19   Insert the inner tube/damper rod assembly into the outer tube **(see illustration)** until the Allen-head bolt (with copper washer) can be

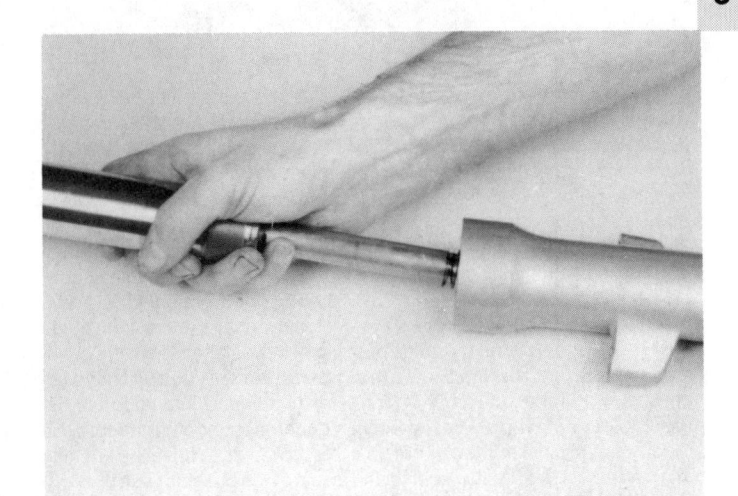

8.19   Install the inner tube/damper rod assembly into the outer tube

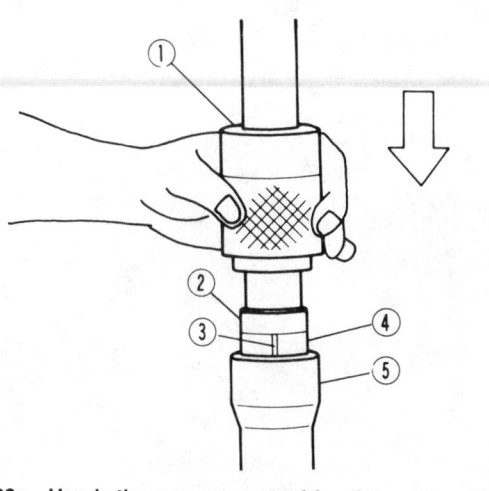

8.20a   Here's the proper way to drive the outer guide bushing into place

1   *Tool no. 57001-1104 (this is the tool for*
    A and B models; tool for C models is similar)
2   *Used guide bushing*
3   *Slit – this must face to the left or right*
4   *New guide bushing*
5   *Outer tube*

8.22   Install the oil seal

threaded into the damper rod from the lower end of the outer tube. **Note:** *Apply a non-permanent thread locking compound to the threads of the bolt. Keep the two tubes fairly horizontal so the damper rod base and washers don't fall off. Using the tool described in Step 5, hold the damper rod and tighten the Allen-head bolt to the torque listed in this Chapter's Specifications.*

20   Slide the outer guide bushing down the inner tube. the slit in the bushing must point to the left or right – not to the front or rear. Using a special bushing driver (Kawasaki tool no. 57001-1104 or equivalent for A and B models, or no. 57001-1219 or equivalent for C models) and a used guide bushing placed on top of the guide bushing being installed, drive the bushing into place until it is fully seated **(see illustration)**. If you don't have access to one of these tools, it is highly recommended that you take the assembly to a Kawasaki dealer service department or other motorcycle repair shop to have this done. It is possible, however, to drive the bushing into place using a section of tubing and an old guide bushing **(see illustration)**. Wrap tape around the ends of the tubing to prevent it from scratching the fork tube.

21   Slide the washer down the inner tube, into position over the guide bushing.

8.20b   If you don't have the proper tool, a section of pipe can be used the same way the special tool would be used – as a slide hammer (be sure to tape the ends of the pipe so it doesn't scratch the fork tube

22   Lubricate the lips and the outer diameter of the fork seal with the recommended fork oil (see Chapter 1) and slide it down the inner tube, with the lips facing down **(see illustration)**. Drive the seal into place with a special seal driver (Kawasaki tool no. 57001-1104 or equivalent for A and B models, or no. 57001-1219 or equivalent for C models). If you don't have access to one of these, it is recommended that you take the assembly to a Kawasaki dealer service department or other motorcycle repair shop to have the seal driven in. If you are very careful, the seal can be driven in with a hammer and a drift punch. Work around the circumference of the seal, tapping gently on the outer edge of the seal until it's seated. Be careful – if you distort the seal, you'll have to disassemble the fork again and end up taking it to a dealer anyway!

23   Install the washer and the retaining ring, making sure the ring is completely seated in its groove.

24   Install the dust seal, making sure it seats completely.

25   Install the drain screw and a new gasket, if it was removed.

26   Install the TCV, with the nuts at the top (A and B models only).

27   On A and B models, extend the fork fully and add the recommended type and amount of fork oil (see Chapter 1). On C models, this should be done with the forks fully compressed.

28   Install the fork spring, with the closer-wound springs at the top. On C models, install the spring guide and spacer.

29   Check the O-ring on the top plug – if it's deteriorated, replace it. Lubricate the O-ring with fork oil and install the top plug. Tighten it to the torque listed in this Chapter's Specifications after the fork has been installed.

30   Install the fork by following the procedure outlined in Section 7. If you won't be installing the fork right away, store it in an upright position and stick a piece of tape over the air hole at the top, to prevent leakage.

---

9   Brake plunger unit (A and B models only) – check and overhaul

---

Refer to illustrations 9.3, 9.7 and 9.8

Check

1   Unbolt the brake plunger from the anti-dive unit **(see illustration 7.9)**. Don't disconnect the brake line.

2   Unbolt the junction block from the fork leg (so it doesn't get bent).

3   Gently squeeze the front brake lever and watch the plunger – it should come out about 2 mm **(see illustration)**.

4   Let go of the brake lever and push on the plunger with your finger – it should retract without having to apply much pressure.

5   If the plunger doesn't perform as described, proceed to the next step.

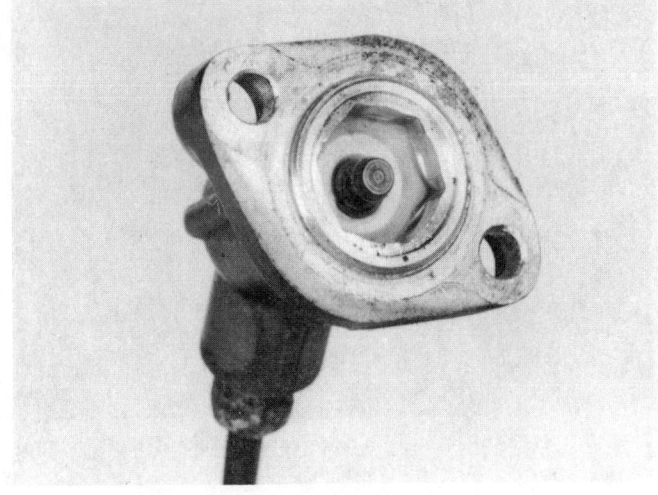

9.3 When the brake lever is squeezed, the plunger should extend approximately 2 mm

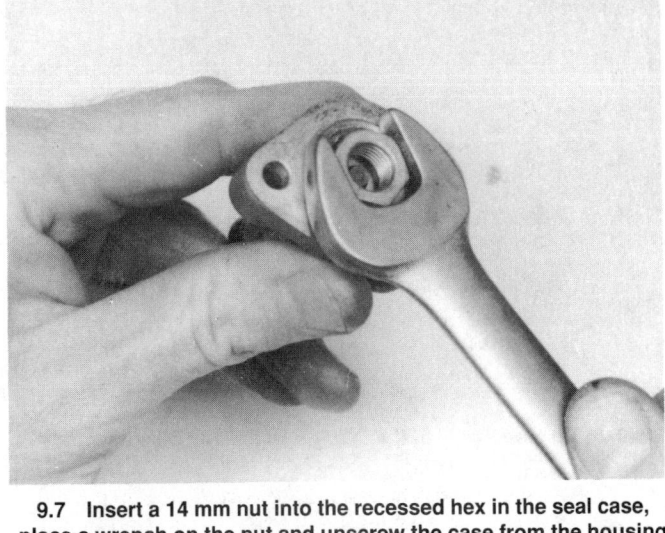

9.7 Insert a 14 mm nut into the recessed hex in the seal case, place a wrench on the nut and unscrew the case from the housing

Overhaul

6   Disconnect the brake line from the plunger unit. You may have to bolt it to the anti-dive unit if the fitting is very tight. Also, use a flare nut wrench, if available, to prevent rounding off the fitting.
7   Remove the rubber cap and unscrew the seal case from the plunger housing **(see illustration)**.
8   Remove the O-rings from the seal case **(see illustration)**.
9   Check the bore of the plunger housing for corrosion and scoring. If either of these conditions are found, replace the brake plunger assembly.
10   If the bore is okay, reassemble the valve using a new seal ring and O-ring. Lubricate the components with clean brake fluid and tighten the seal case securely.
11   Installation is the reverse of removal, but be sure to tighten the mounting bolts to the torque listed in this Chapter's Specifications and bleed the front brakes following the procedure in Chapter 7.

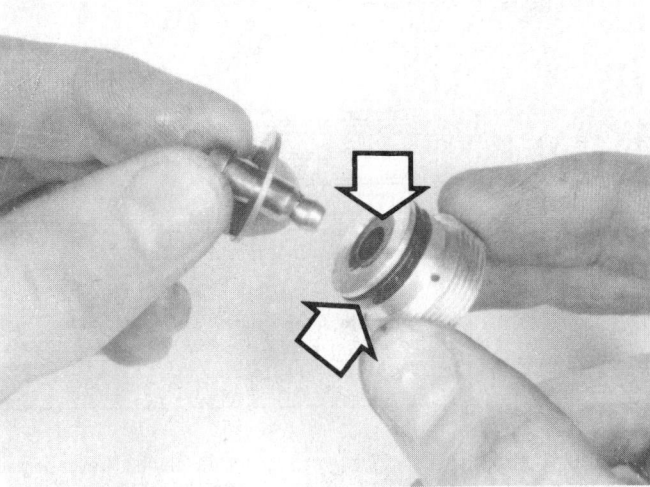

9.8 Pull the plunger and washer out of the seal case, then remove the O-rings (arrows)

10 Anti-dive valve assembly (A and B models only) – check, removal and installation

Refer to illustrations 10.4 and 10.9

Check

1   The forks must be removed from the machine to check the operation of the anti-dive units. Remove the handlebar (see Section 6), loosen the top plug, then refer to Section 7 and remove one fork leg at a time.
2   Remove the top plug and pull out the fork spring.
3   Hold the fork leg upright and compress it (be careful not to let any oil spill out). The stroke should be smooth and shouldn't offer too much resistance.
4   Extend the fork. Depress the rod on the anti-dive valve with your thumb and compress the fork again **(see illustration)**. The fork should offer more resistance than the first time.
5   If the valve doesn't change the damping characteristics of the fork when depressed, replace it. Don't attempt to disassemble the valve – it isn't serviceable.

Removal and installation

6   Relieve the air pressure in the forks and drain the fork oil (see Chapter 1).
7   Unbolt the brake plunger from the anti-dive unit **(see illustration 7.9)**.
8   Remove the two Allen-head bolts and detach the anti-dive unit from the fork leg .

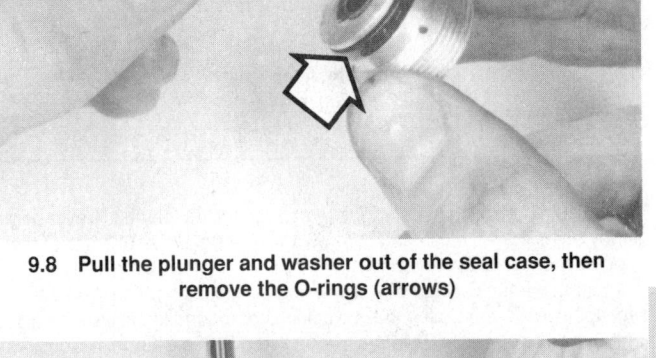

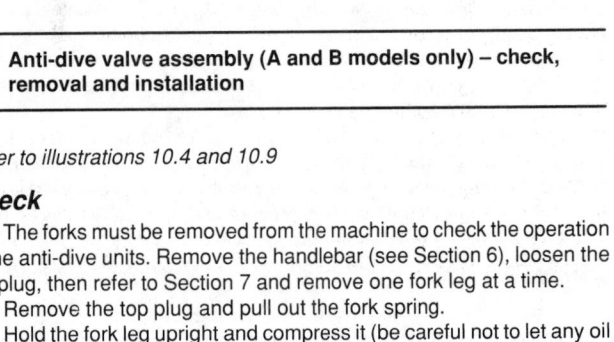

10.4 The fork should be harder to compress when the rod on the anti-dive unit is depressed

6

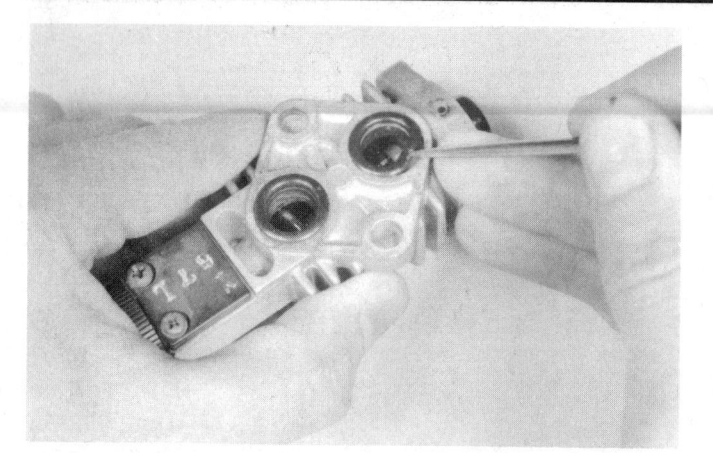

10.9   Be sure to check the O-rings on the anti-dive unit and replace them if necessary

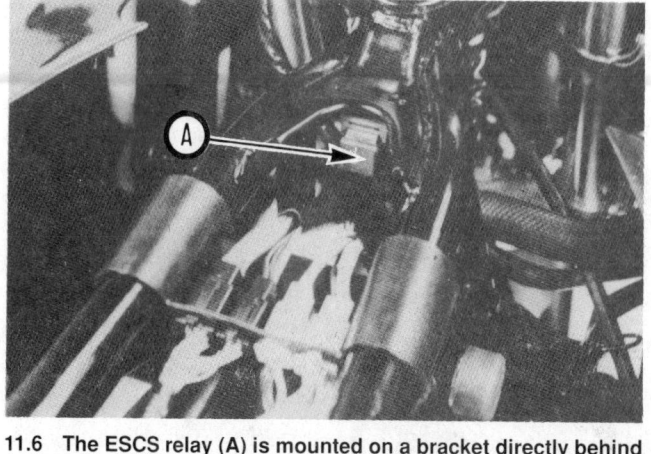

11.6   The ESCS relay (A) is mounted on a bracket directly behind the steering head

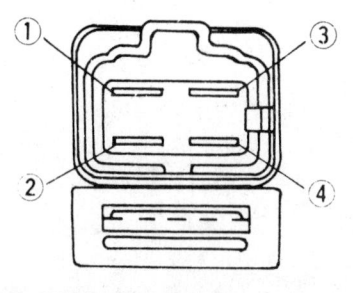

11.7   ESCS relay terminal identification

1   *Brown wire terminal*
2   *Brown/red wire terminal*
3   *Black/yellow wire terminal*
4   *Blue/red wire terminal*

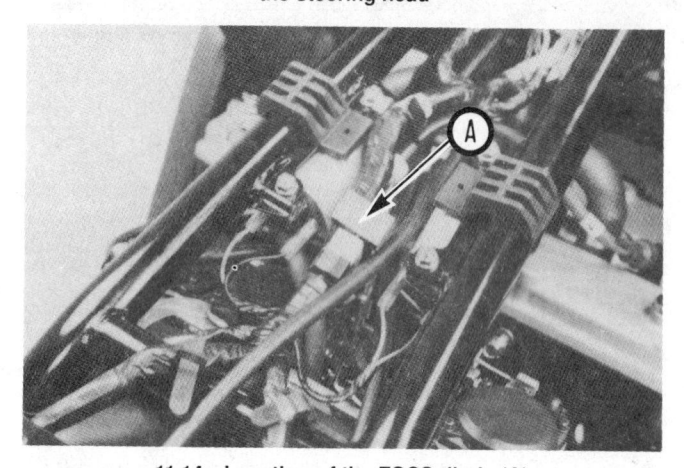

11.14   Location of the ESCS diode (A)

9   If you're installing the original unit, check the condition of the O-rings. If they are cracked, hardened or show any signs of general deterioration, replace them **(see illustration)**.
10   Lubricate the O-rings with clean fork oil. Position the unit on the fork leg, apply a non-hardening thread locking compound to the threads of the bolts and tighten the bolts to the torque listed in this Chapter's Specifications.
11   Install the fork (if removed) following the procedure described in Section 7. Fill the fork with the recommended type and amount of fork oil, then charge the fork with the recommended amount of air pressure (see Chapter 1).

11   Electric Suspension Control System (ESCS) (C models only) – check and component replacement

Refer to illustrations 11.6, 11.7 and 11.14

Circuit check

1   Turn the ignition switch to the On position.
2   Squeeze the front brake lever and listen for a click coming from the ESCS unit, which is mounted under the fuel tank.
3   If no click is heard, check the front brake light switch (see Chapter 9), the ESCS relay and the ESCS unit.
4   If a click is heard, depress the rear brake pedal – you shouldn't hear a click. If you do, check the ESCS diode. If no click is heard, operation is normal.

ESCS relay

5   Remove the fuel tank (see Chapter 4).
6   Remove the ESCS relay from its bracket **(see illustration)** and unplug the electrical connector.
7   Using an ohmmeter, check the resistance between the terminal for the blue/red wire and the terminal for the black/yellow wire **(see illustration)**. The reading should be 90 to 100 ohms.
8   Using two jumper wires, connect battery voltage to the two terminals that were checked in Step 7. Set the ohmmeter on the R x 1 range and connect the leads across the remaining terminals (the ones for the brown/red wire and the solid brown wire). This should cause the relay to click.
9   If the relay fails either test, replace it.

ESCS unit

10   Remove the fuel tank, if you haven't already done so (see Chapter 4).
11   Unplug the electrical connector from the ESCS unit.
12   Using jumper wires, apply battery voltage to the terminals of the ESCS unit. The wire from the positive terminal of the battery must be connected to the white wire terminal, and the wire from the negative terminal must be connected to the black wire terminal. When the connection is made, the ESCS unit should click. If it doesn't, replace it.

ESCS diode

13   Remove the fuel tank, if you haven't already done so (see Chapter 4).
14   Remove the ESCS diode **(see illustration)** and unplug the electrical connector.
15   Using an ohmmeter set on the R x 10 or R x 100 scale, check the resistance across the terminals of the diode, reverse the ohmmeter leads and check the resistance again. The resistance of the diode should be low in one direction and more than ten times as much in the other direction. If not, replace the diode.

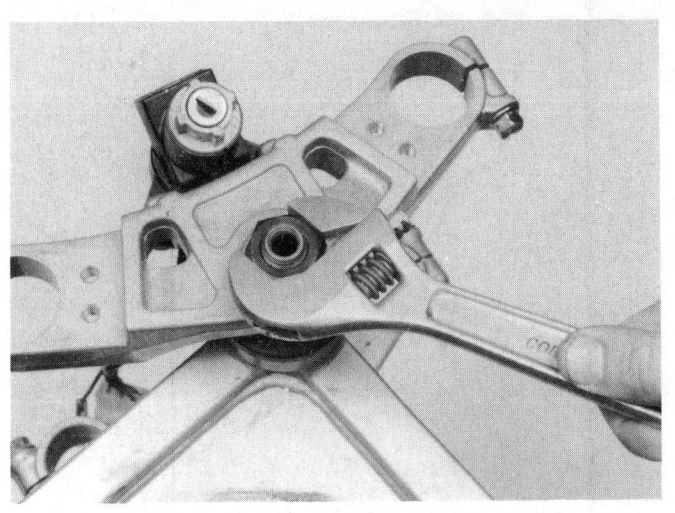

12.3   Unscrew the steering stem nut and lift off the upper triple clamp

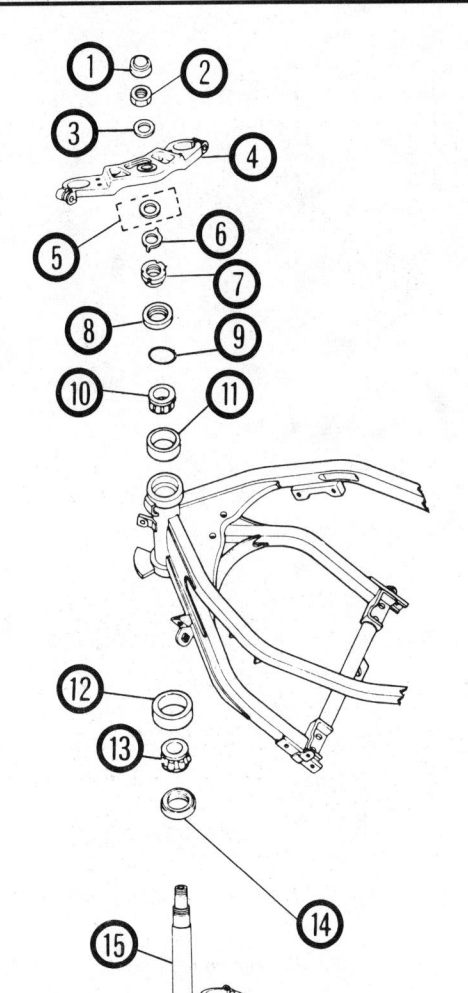

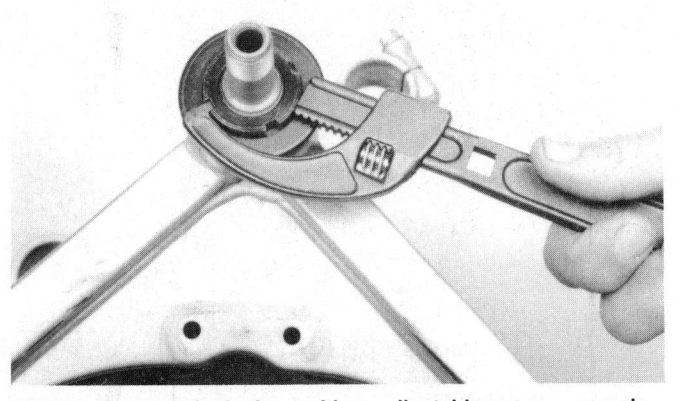

12.4b   Unscrew the locknut with an adjustable spanner wrench

ESCS adjuster

16   Remove the front wheel (see Chapter 7).
17   Remove the right handlebar (see Section 6) and unscrew the top plug. Pull out the spacer, spring guide and the fork spring.
18   Compress the fork leg slowly (be careful not to spill any fork oil – it would be a good idea to cover the fuel tank and bodywork before doing this). The fork shouldn't offer much resistance. Allow the fork to extend.
19   Turn the ignition to the On position. Squeeze the brake lever and compress the fork again – it should be much harder to compress that before.
20   If it isn't harder to compress, and all of the ESCS components check out okay, replace the ESCS adjuster. Follow Steps 6, 8, 9, 10 and 11 of Section 10 for the replacement procedure.

---

12   Steering head bearings – replacement

Refer to illustrations 12.3, 12.4a, 12.4b, 12.5, 12.6, 12.9a, 12.9b, 12.11, 12.15, 12.16

1   If the steering head bearing check/adjustment (see Chapter 1) does not remedy excessive play or roughness in the steering head bearings, the entire front end must be disassembled and the bearings and races replaced with new ones.
2   Refer to Chapter 4 and remove the fuel tank. Refer to Section 7 and remove the front forks.

12.4a   Exploded view of the steering head

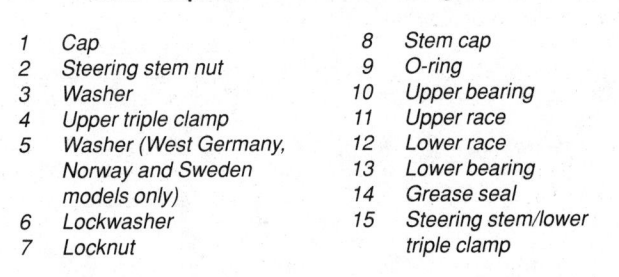

1	Cap	8	Stem cap
2	Steering stem nut	9	O-ring
3	Washer	10	Upper bearing
4	Upper triple clamp	11	Upper race
5	Washer (West Germany,	12	Lower race
	Norway and Sweden	13	Lower bearing
	models only)	14	Grease seal
6	Lockwasher	15	Steering stem/lower
7	Locknut		triple clamp

---

3   Remove the steering stem nut **(see illustration)**, then lift off the upper triple clamp (sometimes called the fork bridge or crown).
4   Remove the lockwasher from the stem locknut **(see illustration)**. Using an adjustable spanner wrench, remove the stem locknut/stem cap assembly **(see illustration)** while supporting the steering head from the bottom. Lift off the nut and race cover.
5   Remove the steering stem and lower triple clamp assembly **(see illustration)**. If it's stuck, gently tap on the top of the steering stem with a plastic mallet or a hammer and a wood block.
6   Remove the upper bearing and O-ring **(see illustration)**.
7   Clean all the parts with solvent and dry them thoroughly, using compressed air, if available. If you do use compressed air, don't let the bearings spin as they're dried – it could ruin them. Wipe the old grease out of the frame steering head and bearing races.

6

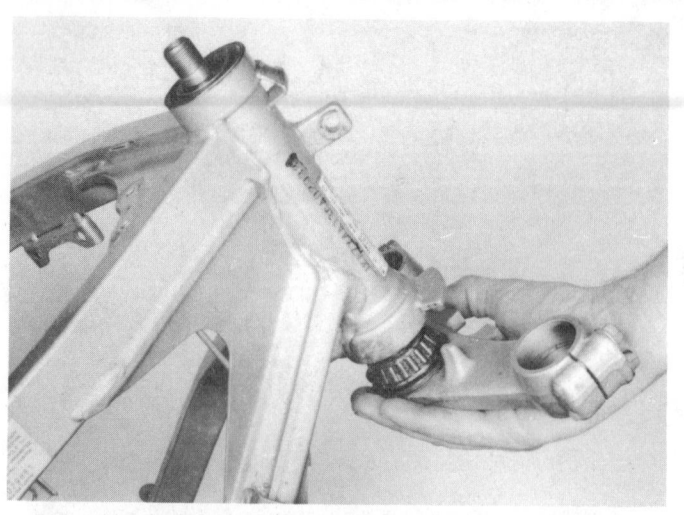

12.5 Pull the steering stem/lower triple clamp out – if it's stuck, tap gently on the steering stem with a soft-face hammer

12.6 Lift out the O-ring and the upper bearing

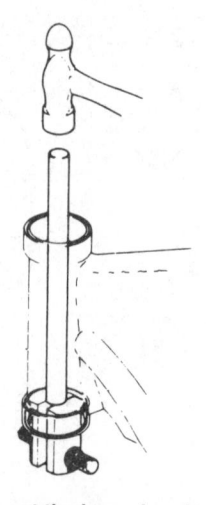

12.9a Driving out the lower bearing race with the special Kawasaki tool

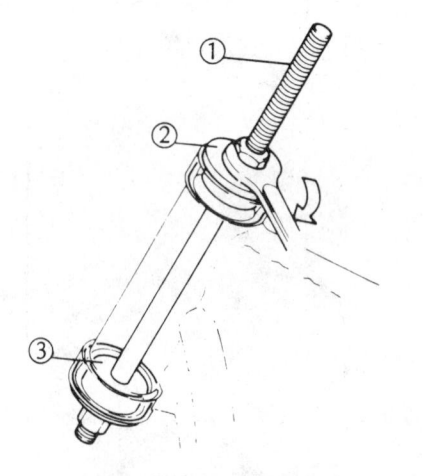

12.9b Using the special Kawasaki tool to press the outer races into the frame

1 Driver press shaft (tool no. 57001-1075)
2 Driver (tool no. 57001-1106)
3 Driver (tool no. 57001-1076)

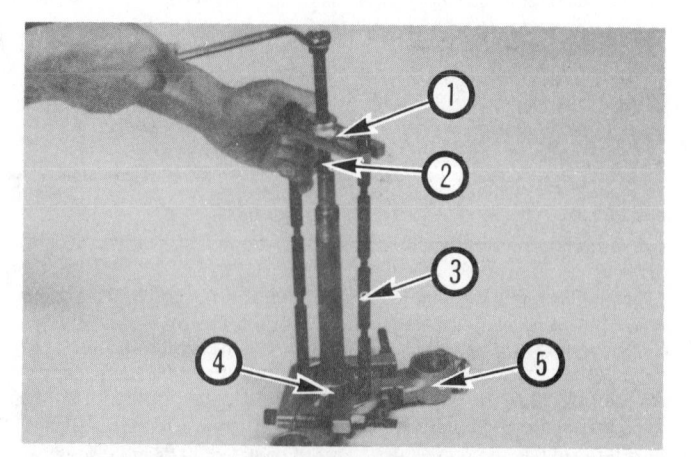

12.11 Using the special Kawasaki tools to pull the lower bearing off the steering stem

1 Bearing puller (tool no. 57001-158)
2 Adapter (tool no. 57001-317)
3 Pole (tool no. 57001-1190)
4 Bearing inner race
5 Lower triple clamp

8 Examine the races in the steering head for cracks, dents, and pits. If even the slightest amount of wear or damage is evident, the races should be replaced with new ones.

9 To remove the races, drive them out of the steering head with Kawasaki tool no. 57001-1107 or equivalent **(see illustration)**. A slide hammer with the proper internal-jaw puller will also work. Since the races are an interference fit in the frame, installation will be easier if the new races are left overnight in a refrigerator. this will cause them to contract and slip into place in the frame with very little effort. When installing the races, use Kawasaki press shaft no. 57001-1075 and drivers no. 57001-1106 and 57001-1076 **(see illustration)**, or tap them gently into place with a hammer and punch or a large socket. Do not strike the bearing surface or the race will be damaged.

10 Check the bearings for wear. Look for cracks, dents, and pits in the races and flat spots on the bearings. Replace any defective parts with new ones. If a new bearing is required, replace both of them as a set.

11 To remove the lower bearing from the steering stem, use a bearing puller (Kawasaki tool no. 57001-158 or equivalent, combined with adapter no. 57001-317 and pole no. 57001-1190) **(see illustration)**. Don't remove this bearing unless it, or the grease seal underneath, must be replaced.

12 Check the grease seal under the lower bearing and replace it with a new one if necessary.

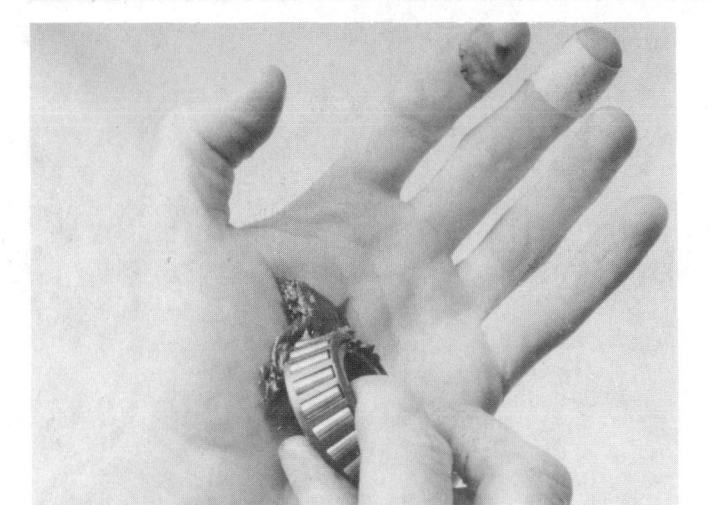

12.15   Work the grease completely into the rollers

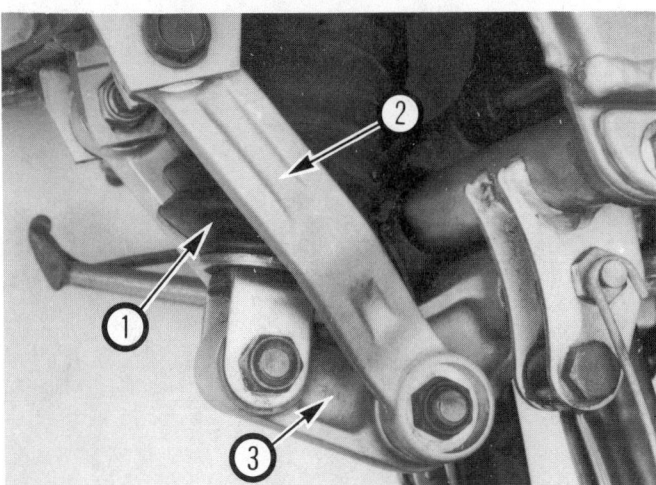

12.16   Driving the lower bearing onto the steering stem with the special Kawasaki tools (a piece of tubing, with a diameter the same as the inner race of the bearing can be used instead)

1   *Stem bearing driver (tool no. 57001-137)*
2   *Adapter (tool no. 57001-1074)*

13.7   Loosen the shock absorber upper nut (arrow)

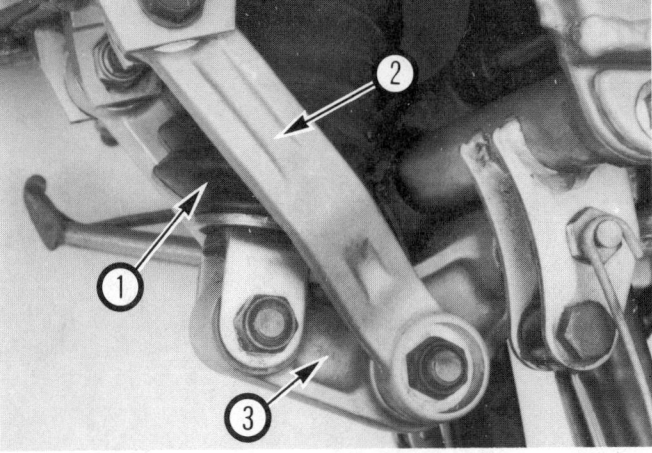

13.8   Suspension linkage details

1   *Shock absorber*   3   *Rocker arm*
2   *Tie-rod (right)*

13   Inspect the steering stem/lower triple clamp for cracks and other damage. Do not attempt to repair any steering components. Replace them with new parts if defects are found.
14   Check the rubber portion of the stem locknut/stem cap assembly – if it's worn or deteriorated, replace it.
15   Pack the bearings with high-quality grease (preferably a moly-based grease) **(see illustration)**. Coat the outer races with grease also.
16   Install the grease seal and lower bearing onto the steering stem. Drive the lower bearing onto the steering stem using Kawasaki stem bearing driver no. 57001-137 and adapter no. 57001-1074 **(see illustration)**. If you don't have access to these tools, a section of pipe with a diameter the same as the inner race of the bearing can be used. Drive the bearing on until it is fully seated.
17   Insert the steering stem/lower triple clamp into the frame head. Install the upper bearing, O-ring and the stem locknut/stem cap assembly. Using the adjustable spanner, tighten the locknut while moving the lower triple clamp back and forth. Continue to tighten the nut (to approximately 30 ft-lbs) until the steering head becomes tight, then back off until there is some play in the bearings. Now, turn the locknut until there is no more play, and tighten the nut just a fraction of a turn from that point (not too much, though, or the steering will be too tight). Make sure the steering head turns smoothly.
18   Install the lockwasher on the locknut, then install the upper triple clamp on the steering stem. Install the washer and nut, tightening the nut to the torque listed in this Chapter's Specifications.
19   The remainder of installation is the reverse of removal.

6

---

13   Rear shock absorber – removal and installation

Refer to illustrations 13.7 and 13.8
1   Set the bike on its centerstand.
2   Remove the side covers.
3   Unscrew the nut and detach the Schrader (air) valve from its bracket.
4   Unscrew the damper adjusting knob.
5   Remove the IC igniter from its bracket and position it out of the way. Remove the screw and detach the bracket from the frame.
6   Loosen the locknut and unscrew the adjusting rod.
7   Loosen the shock absorber upper nut **(see illustration)**. Don't remove it yet.
8   Remove the shock absorber lower nut and bolt and the tie-rod lower nut and bolt **(see illustration)**.
9   Remove the upper nut and bolt. Pull the tie-rods back and lower the shock absorber to the ground.
10   Installation is the reverse of the removal procedure. Tighten the shock absorber and tie-rod nuts to the torque values listed in this Chapter's Specifications.

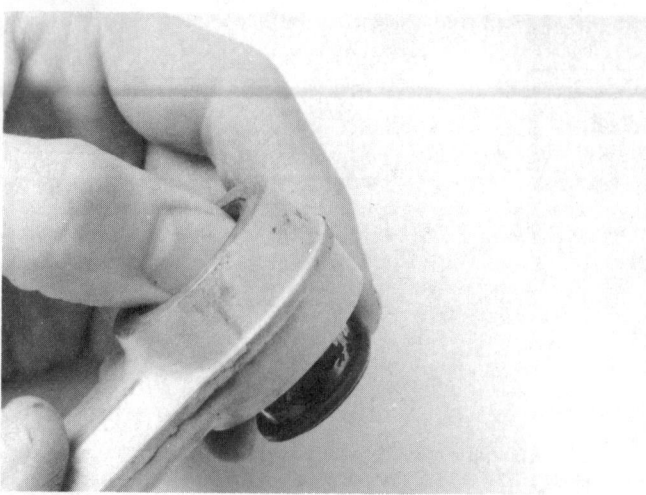

14.4   Push the sleeve out of the end of the tie-rod and remove the O-rings

14.11   Remove the nut (arrow) then push the rocker arm pivot shaft out

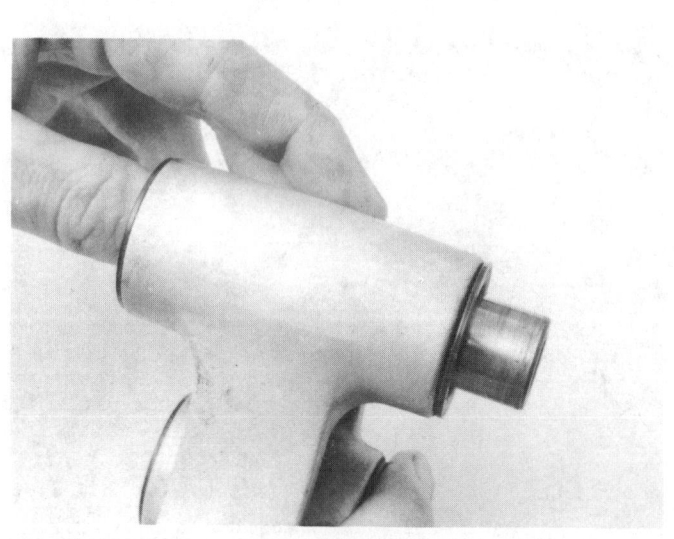

14.12a   To check the condition of the needle bearings, push the sleeves out of the rocker arm

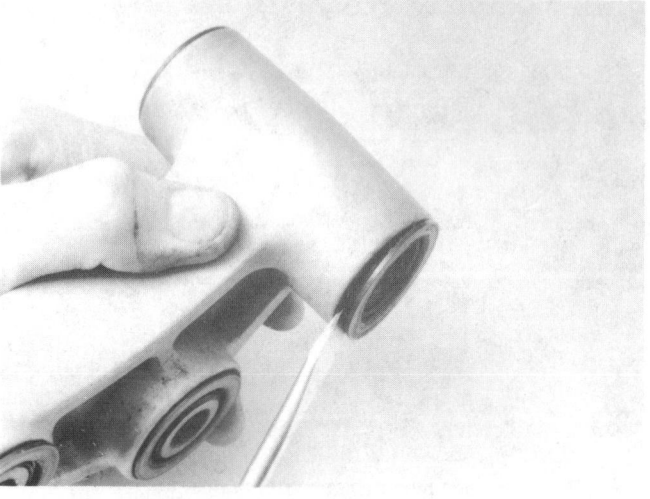

14.12b   Pry out the grease seals for access to the bearings

14.13a   To replace the bearings, knock them out with a hammer and punch . . .

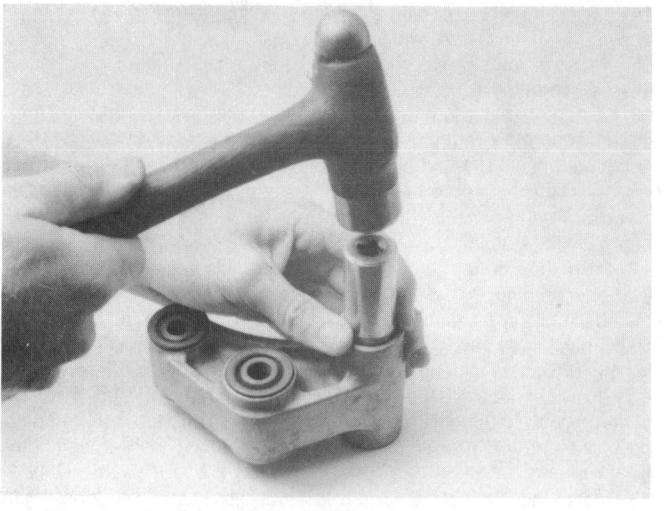

14.13b   . . . then drive them in with a socket that just fits into the bore of the rocker arm

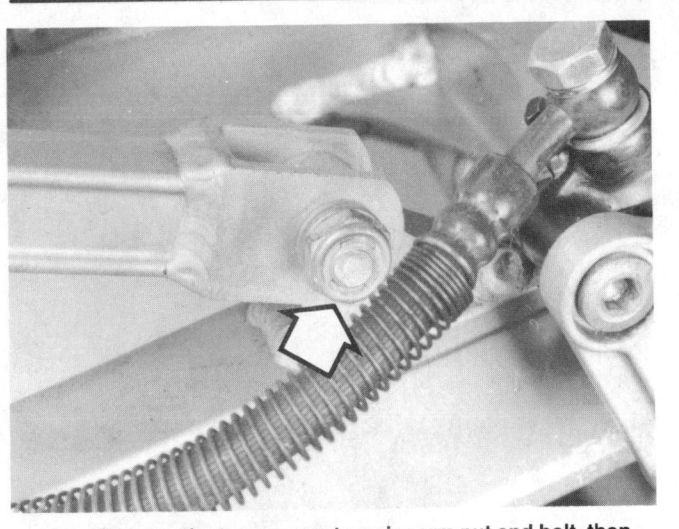

16.3   Remove the torque arm-to-swingarm nut and bolt, then support the brake caliper and torque arm with wire or rope

16.4   The swingarm pivot shaft nut is located on the left side of the frame – pry out the plug for access

14   Rear suspension linkage – removal, check and installation

1   Set the bike on its centerstand.

Tie-rod(s)

Refer to illustration 14.4

2   Remove the tie-rod lower nut and bolt (see illustrations 1.5 and 13.8).
3   Remove the nut(s) and bolt(s) that secure the tie-rods to the swingarm and remove the tie-rod(s).
4   Push the sleeve out of the tie-rod (see illustration). Check the O-rings for cracking and general deterioration and replace them if necessary. Check the bushing in the tie-rod and the outer surface of the sleeve for wear, replacing them if necessary. Note: *A bushing driver will be required if the bushing is to be replaced.*
5   Apply a thin coat of moly-based grease to the bushing and sleeve and install the sleeve in the bushing. Press the O-rings into place around the sleeve.
6   Installation is the reverse of removal. Tighten the bolts to the torque listed in this Chapter's Specifications.

Rocker arm

Refer to illustrations 14.11, 14.12a, 14.12b, 14.13a and 14.13b

7   Remove the lower fairing (see Chapter 8).
8   Support the bike with a floor jack, with a piece of wood on the jack head, positioned underneath the engine. It would be a good idea to have an assistant steady the bike during this procedure.
9   Retract the centerstand and disconnect the spring.
10   Disconnect the shock absorber and the tie-rods from the rocker arm (see illustration 13.8). Support the swingarm with a rope or piece of wire so it doesn't fall.
11   Remove the nut and pull out the rocker arm pivot bolt (see illustration). Detach the rocker arm from the frame.
12   Push the sleeves out of the rocker arm (see illustration). Check the needle bearings for dryness and discoloration. If necessary, pry out the grease seal (see illustration), clean the bearings with solvent, dry and re-pack them with moly-based grease.
13   If the bearings are deteriorated, drive them out of the rocker arm with a hammer and punch (see illustration). Install new bearing sets by driving them in with a hammer and a socket of the appropriate size (see illustration).
14   Coat the bearings with grease, install the grease seals and slide the bushings into place.

15   The remainder of installation is the reverse of the removal procedure. Tighten the nut of the rocker arm pivot bolt, the shock absorber-to-rocker arm bolt/nut and the tie-rod-to-rocker arm bolt/nut to the torque values listed in this Chapter's Specifications.

15   Swingarm bearings – check

1   Refer to Chapter 7 and remove the rear wheel, then refer to Section 13 and remove the rear shock absorber.
2   Grasp the rear of the swingarm with one hand and place your other hand at the junction of the swingarm and the frame. Try to move the rear of the swingarm from side-to-side. Any wear (play) in the bearings should be felt as movement between the swingarm and the frame at the front. The swingarm will actually be felt to move forward and backward at the front (not from side-to-side). If any play is noted, the bearings should be replaced with new ones (see Section 17).
3   Next, move the swingarm up and down through its full travel. It should move freely, without any binding or rough spots. If it does not move freely, refer to Section 17 for servicing procedures.

16   Swingarm – removal and installation

Refer to illustrations 16.3 and 16.4

1   Raise the bike and set it on its centerstand.
2   Remove the rear wheel (see Chapter 7).
3   Detach the torque arm from the swingarm (see illustration). Support the rear brake caliper and torque arm with a piece of rope or wire – don't let them hang by the brake hose.
4   Remove the swingarm pivot nut (see illustration). Don't remove the pivot shaft yet.
5   Detach the tie-rods and the shock absorber from the rocker arm (see illustration 13.8). Support the swingarm while doing this.
6   Support the swingarm and pull the pivot shaft out. Remove the swingarm. If necessary, remove the bolts and detach the tie-rods from the swingarm.
7   Check the pivot bearings in the swingarm for dryness or deterioration. If they're in need of lubrication or replacement, refer to Section 17.
8   Installation is the reverse of the removal procedure. Be sure the bearing seals are in position before installing the pivot shaft. Tighten the pivot shaft nut and the shock absorber and tie-rod lower mounting bolts/nuts to the torque values listed in this Chapter's Specifications. Adjust the chain as described in Chapter 1.

6

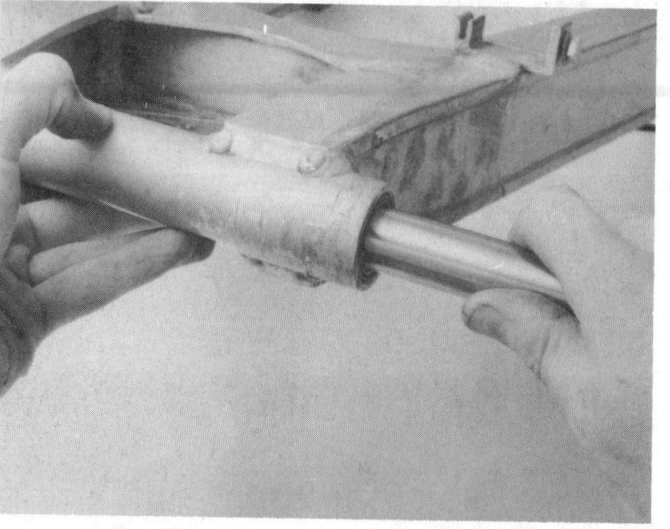

17.2   Slide the sleeve out of the front of the swingarm

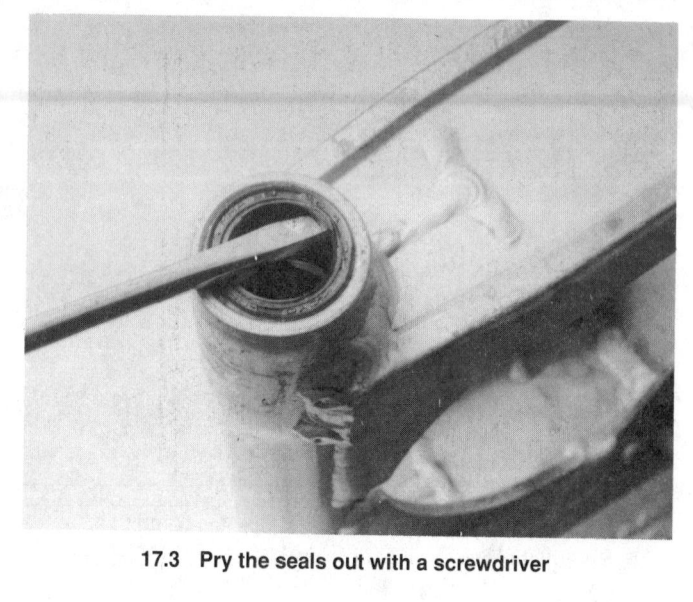

17.3   Pry the seals out with a screwdriver

18.1   Mark the relationship of the shift lever to the shift shaft so it can be reinstalled in the same position

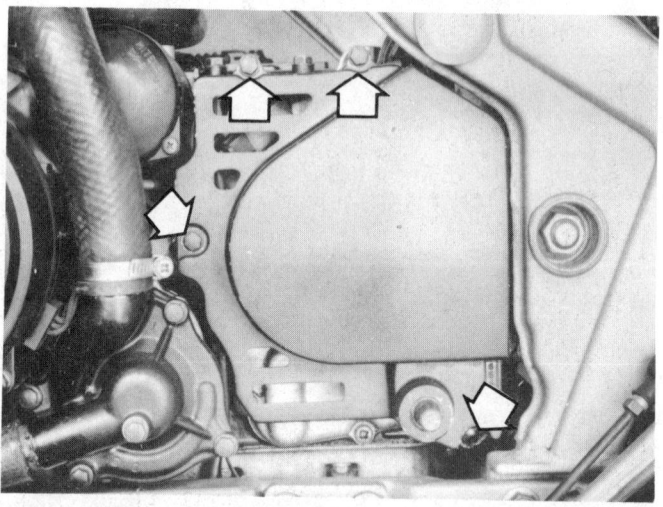

18.2   Remove the engine sprocket cover bolts (arrows) and slide the cover off

17   Swingarm bearings – replacement

Refer to illustrations 17.2 and 17.3

1   Remove the swingarm (see Section 16).
2   Slide the sleeve out **(see illustration)**.
3   Pry out the seals **(see illustration)**.
4   Refer to Section 14, Steps 12, 13 and 14 for the bearing service procedures.

18   Drive chain – removal, cleaning and installation

Refer to illustrations 18.1, 18.2 and 18.5

Removal

1   Mark the relationship of the shift lever to the shift shaft **(see illustration)**. Remove the shift lever pinch bolt and slide the lever off the shaft.
2   Remove the bolts securing the engine sprocket cover to the engine case **(see illustration)**. Slide the sprocket cover off.
3   Remove the rear wheel (see Chapter 7).

4   Lift the chain off the engine sprocket.
5   Detach the swingarm from the frame by following the first few Steps of Section 16. Pull the swingarm back far enough to allow the chain to slip between the frame and the front of the swingarm **(see illustration)**.

Cleaning

6   Soak the chain in kerosene or diesel fuel for approximately five or six minutes. **Caution:** *Don't use gasoline or other cleaning fluids. Remove the chain, wipe it off then blow dry it with compressed air immediately. The entire process shouldn't take longer than ten minutes – if it does, the O-rings in the chain rollers could be damaged.*

Installation

7   Installation is the reverse of the removal procedure. Tighten the suspension fasteners and the engine sprocket cover bolts to the torque values listed in this Chapter's Specifications. Tighten the rear axle nut to the torque listed in the Chapter 7 Specifications.
8   Connect the shift lever to the shift shaft, lining up the marks. If it's installed correctly, the link rod should be parallel to the shift pedal.
9   Lubricate the chain following the procedure described in Chapter 1.

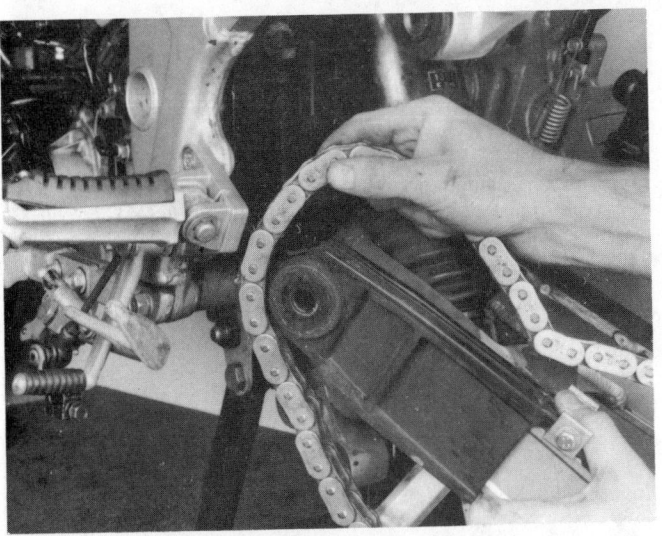

18.5   Pull the swingarm back and pass the chain between the frame and the swingarm

19.4   Check the runout of the rear sprocket with a dial indicator

19.6   Remove the holding plate bolts and slide the sprocket and chain off the shaft

19.8   Measure the diameter of the rear sprocket and replace it, the engine sprocket and the chain if it has worn past the minimum diameter

19   Sprockets – check and replacement

Refer to illustrations 19.4, 19.6, 19.8 and 19.9

1   Set the bike on its centerstand.

2   Whenever the drive chain is inspected, the sprockets should be inspected also. If you are replacing the chain, replace the sprockets as well. Likewise, if the sprockets are in need of replacement, install a new chain also.

3   Remove the engine sprocket cover following the procedure outlined in the previous Section.

4   Attach a dial indicator to the swingarm, with the plunger of the indicator touching the sprocket near its outer diameter **(see illustration)**. Turn the wheel and measure the runout. If the runout exceeds the maximum runout listed in this Chapter's Specifications, replace the rear sprocket. As stated before, it's a good idea to replace the chain and the sprockets as a set. However, if the components are relatively new or in good condition, but the sprocket is warped, you may be able to get away with just replacing the rear sprocket.

5   Check the wear pattern on the sprockets **(see Chapter 1, illustration 11.5)**. If the sprocket teeth are worn excessively, replace the chain and sprockets.

6   If you're planning to remove the engine sprocket, place the transmission in first gear, have an assistant apply the rear brake and loosen the holding plate bolts **(see illustration)**.

7   Remove the rear wheel (see Chapter 7).

8   Using vernier calipers, measure the diameter of the rear sprocket **(see illustration)**. If the diameter of the sprocket is less than the minimum diameter listed in this Chapter's Specifications, replace the chain and sprockets.

9   To replace the rear sprocket, unscrew the nuts holding it to the wheel coupling and lift the sprocket off. When installing the sprocket, apply a non-hardening thread locking compound to the threads of the studs. Tighten the nuts to the torque listed in this Chapter's Specifications. Also, check the condition of the rubber damper under the rear wheel coupling (see Section 20).

10   Remove the holding plate and pull the engine sprocket and chain off the shaft, then separate the sprocket from the chain.

11   When installing the engine sprocket, engage it with the chain, making sure the IN mark, or recess, faces the engine case. Install the holding plate, apply a non-hardening thread locking compound to the bolts, then tighten the bolts to the torque listed in this Chapter's Specifications.

12   Install the engine sprocket cover and shift lever (see Section 18).

6

20.3   Replace the rubber damper if it shows signs of deterioration

20   Rear wheel coupling/rubber damper – check and replacement

Refer to illustration 20.3

1   Remove the rear wheel (see Chapter 7).

2   Lift the collar and rear sprocket/rear wheel coupling from the wheel **(see Chapter 7, illustrations 13.4a and 13.4b)**.

3   Lift the rubber damper from the wheel **(see illustration)** and check it for cracks, hardening and general deterioration. Replace it with a new one if necessary.

4   Checking and replacement procedures for the coupling bearing are similar to those described for the wheel bearings. Refer to Chapter 7, Section 13.

5   Installation is the reverse of the removal procedure.

Chapter 7   Brakes, wheels and tires

Refer to Chapter 10 for information on the ZX750F model

Contents

Specifications

Brakes

Brake fluid type	See Chapter 1
Brake disc minimum thickness	See Chapter 1

Disc thickness
  A and B models
    Front
      Standard . . . .   0.189 to 0.2 in (4.8 to 5.1 mm)
      Minimum* . . . .   0.177 in (4.5 mm)
    Rear
      Standard . . . .   0.228 to 0.240 in (5.8 to 6.1 mm)
      Minimum* . . . .   0.217 in (5.5 mm)
  C models
    Front
      Standard . . . .   0.170 to 0.181 in (4.3 to 4.6 mm)
      Minimum* . . . .   0.157 in (4.0 mm)
    Rear
      Standard . . . .   0.228 to 0.240 in (5.8 to 6.1 mm)
      Minimum* . . . .   0.217 in (5.5 mm)

* Refer to marks stamped into the disc (they supersede information printed here)

Disc runout (maximum, front and rear, all models) . . . .   0.012 in (0.3 mm)

Wheels and tires

Wheel runout
  Axial (side-to-side) . . . .   0.020 in (0.5 mm)
  Radial (out-of-round) . . . .   0.031 in (0.8 mm)
Rear axle runout . . . .   0.007 in (0.2 mm)
Tire pressures . . . .   See Chapter 1
Tire sizes
  A and B models
    Front 110/90V16
    Rear 130/90V16
  C models
    Front 110/80V16
    Rear 130/90V16

Torque specifications

Ft-lbs (unless otherwise indicated)

Caliper mounting bolts   24
Banjo fitting bolts   18
Brake disc-to-wheel bolts 16.5
Master cylinder mounting bolts
  Front . . . .   78 in-lbs
  Rear 16.5
Front axle   66
Front axle clamp bolt   15
Rear axle nut   80

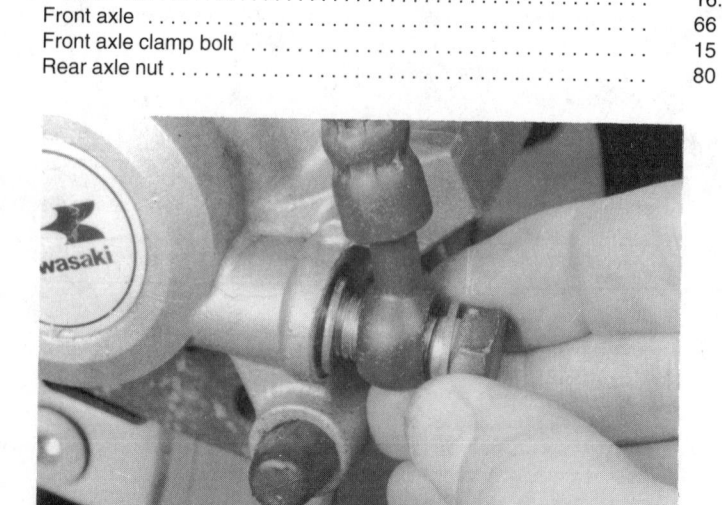

2.3a   Unscrew the banjo fitting bolt, . . .

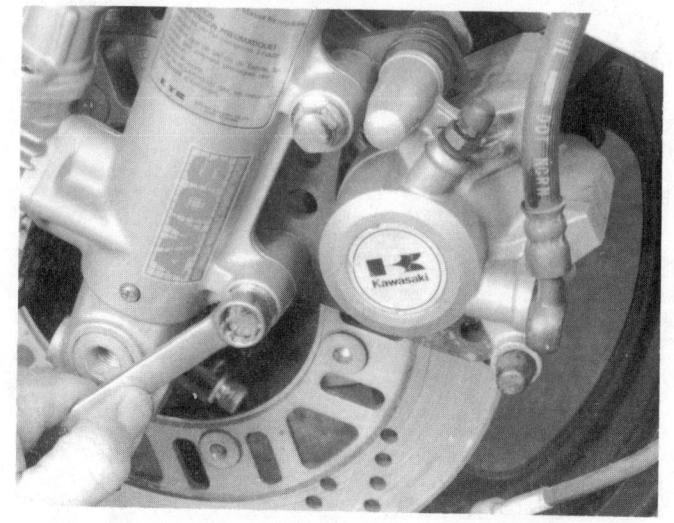

2.3b   . . . then remove the caliper mounting bolts

1   General information

The models covered by this manual are equipped with hydraulic disc brakes on the front and rear. All A and B models employ single piston calipers, while all C models use dual piston calipers.

All models are equipped with cast aluminum wheels, which require very little maintenance and allow tubeless tires to be used.

Caution: *Disc brake components rarely require disassembly. Do not disassemble components unless absolutely necessary. If any hydraulic brake line connection in the system is loosened, the entire system should be disassembled, drained, cleaned and then properly filled and bled upon reassembly. Do not use solvents on internal brake components. Solvents will cause seals to swell and distort. Use only clean brake fluid or alcohol for cleaning. Use care when working with brake fluid as it can injure your eyes and it will damage painted surfaces and plastic parts.*

2   Brake caliper – removal, overhaul and installation

Warning: *If a front caliper indicates the need for an overhaul (usually due to leaking fluid or sticky operation), BOTH front calipers should be overhauled and all old brake fluid flushed from the system. Also, the dust created by the brake system may contain asbestos, which is harmful to your health. Never blow it out with compressed air and don't inhale any of it. An approved filtering mask should be worn when working on the brakes. Do not, under any circumstances, use petroleum-based solvents to clean brake parts. Use brake cleaner or denatured alcohol only!*

Note: *If you are removing the caliper only to replace or inspect the brake pads, don't disconnect the hose from the caliper.*

Removal

Refer to illustrations 2.3a and 2.3b

1   Place the bike on its centerstand.
2   If you're removing the left front caliper, disconnect the lower end of the speedometer cable from the hub.
3   **Note:** *Remember, if you're just removing the caliper to inspect or replace the brake pads, ignore this step.* Disconnect the brake hose from the caliper. Remove the brake hose banjo fitting bolt (except on models with a

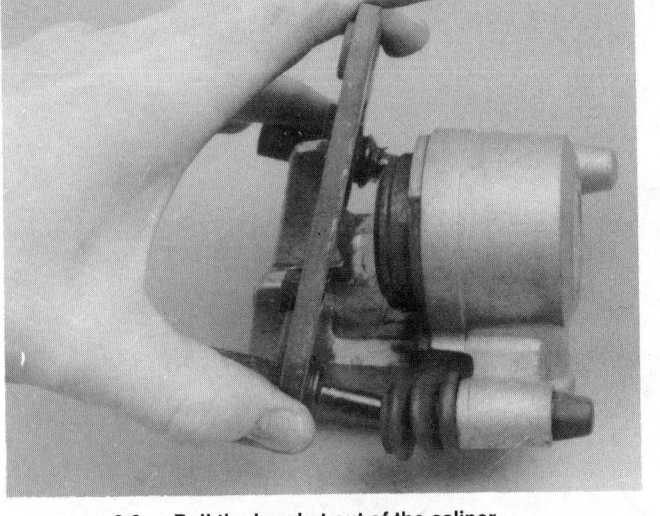

2.6a Pull the bracket out of the caliper . . .

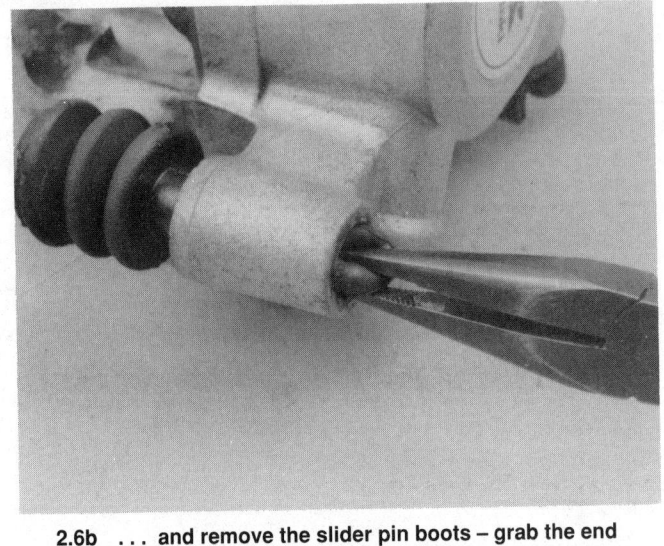

2.6b . . . and remove the slider pin boots – grab the end with a pair of needle-nose pliers, twist, then push the boot through the hole

threaded fitting) and separate the hose from the caliper **(see illustration)**. Discard the sealing washers. If a threaded fitting (tube nut) is used instead of a banjo fitting, use a flare-nut wrench to unscrew it. If equipped, remove the hose support bolt from the caliper bracket. Plug the end of the hose or wrap a plastic bag tightly around it to prevent excessive fluid loss and contamination. Unscrew the caliper mounting bolts **(see illustration)**.

4   Lift off the caliper, being careful not to strain or twist the brake hose. If you're removing the rear caliper, detach the brake hose from the clip on the swingarm.

Overhaul
Refer to illustrations 2.6a, 2.6b, 2.6c, 2.6d, 2.6e, 2.6f, 2.7, 2.9, 2.15, 2.16 and 2.17

5   Remove the brake pads and anti-rattle spring from the caliper (see Section 3, if necessary). Clean the exterior of the caliper with denatured alcohol or brake system cleaner.

6   Remove the caliper bracket and the slider pin boots from the caliper **(see illustrations)**.

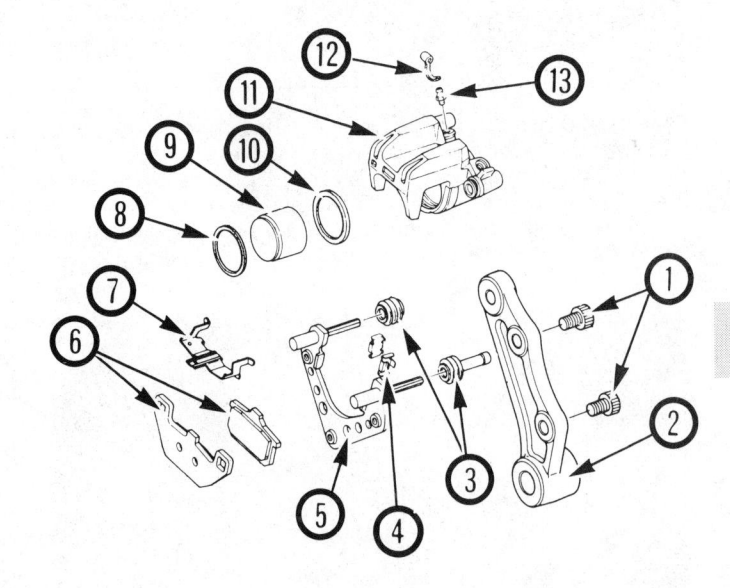

2.6c   Single piston front caliper – exploded view

1	Caliper mounting bolts	7	Piston seal
2	Caliper bracket	8	Slider pin boots
3	Pad support clips	9	Caliper body
4	Brake pads	10	Anti-rattle spring
5	Dust seal	11	Bleeder valve
6	Piston	12	Bleeder valve cap

2.6d   Single piston rear caliper – exploded view

1	Caliper mounting bolts	7	Anti-rattle spring
2	Caliper holder	8	Dust seal
3	Slider pin boots	9	Piston
4	Pad support clips	10	Piston seal
5	Caliper bracket	11	Caliper body
6	Brake pads	12	Bleeder valve cap
		13	Bleeder valve

7

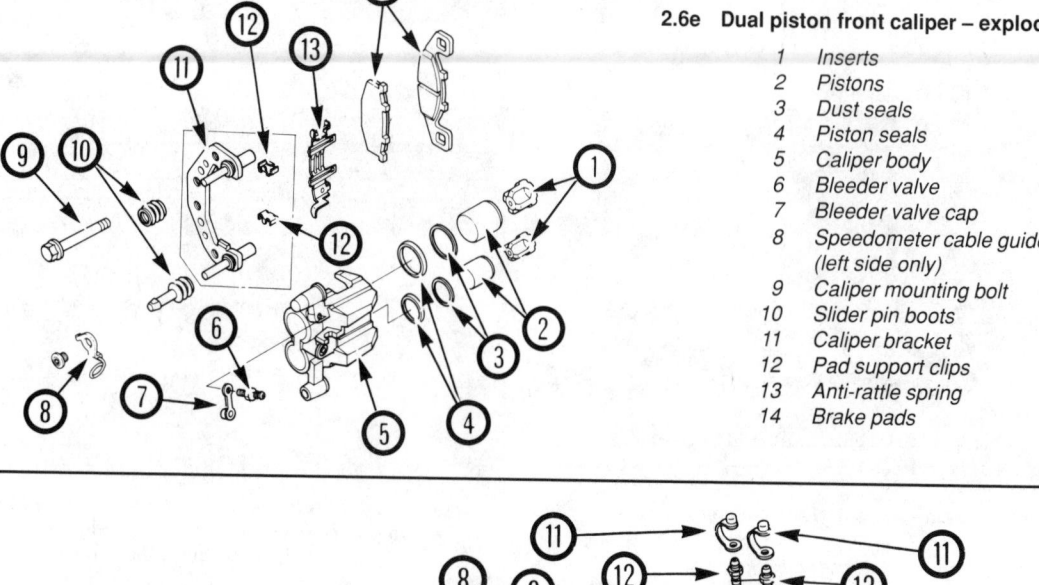

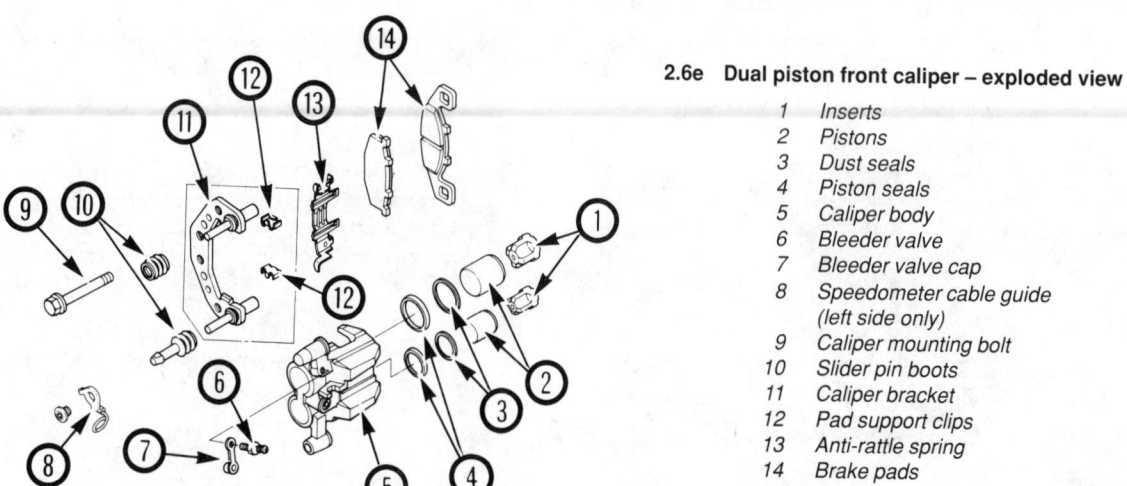

2.6e Dual piston front caliper – exploded view

1   Inserts
2   Pistons
3   Dust seals
4   Piston seals
5   Caliper body
6   Bleeder valve
7   Bleeder valve cap
8   Speedometer cable guide
    (left side only)
9   Caliper mounting bolt
10 Slider pin boots
11 Caliper bracket
12 Pad support clips
13 Anti-rattle spring
14 Brake pads

2.6f Dual piston rear caliper – exploded view

1   Pad support clips
2   Caliper bracket
3   Brake pads
4   Anti-rattle spring
5   Dust seals
6   Inserts
7   Pistons
8   Piston seals
9   Slider pin boots
10 Caliper body
11 Bleeder valve caps
12 Bleeder valves

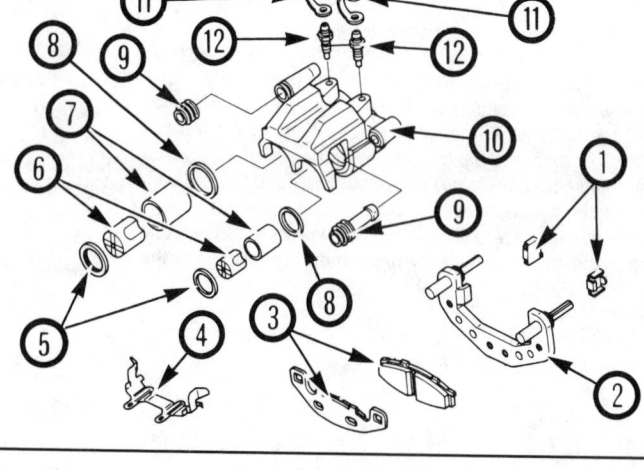

7   Place a few rags between the piston(s) and the caliper frame to act as a cushion, then use compressed air, directed into the fluid inlet, to remove the piston(s) **(see illustration)**. Use only enough air pressure to ease the piston(s) out of the bore. If a piston is blown out, even with the cushion in place, it may be damaged. **Warning:** *Never place your fingers in front of the piston in an attempt to catch or protect it when applying compressed*

air, as serious injury could occur.
8   If compressed air isn't available, reconnect the caliper to the brake hose and pump the brake lever or pedal until the piston(s) is/are free.
9   Using a wood or plastic tool, remove the dust seal(s) **(see illustration)**. Metal tools may cause bore damage.
10   Using a wood or plastic tool, remove the piston seal(s) from the

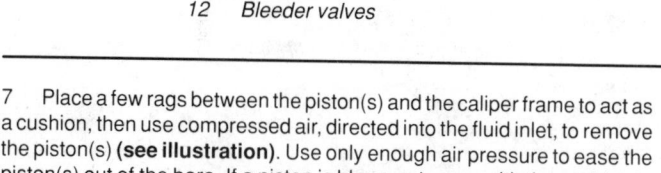

2.7   With a rag placed between the piston and caliper frame, use compressed air to ease the piston out of the bore

2.9   The dust seal should be removed with a plastic or wooden tool to avoid damage to the bore and seal groove (a pencil works well) – remove the piston seal the same way

2.15   Bottom the piston in the caliper bore – make sure it goes in straight

2.16   Install the slider pin boots

2.17   Apply a thin coat of the specified grease to the slider pins on the caliper bracket

groove in the caliper bore.

11   Clean the piston(s) and the bore(s) with denatured alcohol, clean brake fluid or brake system cleaner and blow dry them with filtered, unlubricated compressed air. Inspect the surfaces of the piston(s) for nicks and burrs and loss of plating. Check the caliper bore(s), too. If surface defects are present, the caliper must be replaced. If the caliper is in bad shape, the master cylinder should also be checked.

12   Temporarily reinstall the caliper bracket. Make sure it slides smoothly in-and-out of the caliper. If it doesn't, check the slider pins for burrs or excessive wear. also check the slider pin bores in the caliper for wear and scoring. Replace the caliper bracket, the caliper, or both if necessary.

13   Lubricate the piston seal(s) with clean brake fluid and install it in its groove in the caliper bore. Make sure it isn't twisted and seats completely.

14   Lubricate the dust seal(s) with clean brake fluid and install it in its groove, making sure it seats correctly.

15   Lubricate the piston(s) with clean brake fluid and install it into the caliper bore. Using your thumbs, push the piston all the way in (**see illustration**), making sure it doesn't get cocked in the bore.

16   Install the slider pin boots (**see illustration**).

17   Apply a thin coat of PBC (poly butyl cuprysil) grease, or silicone grease designed for high-temperature brake applications, to the slider pins on the caliper bracket (**see illustration**). Install the caliper bracket to the caliper and seat the boots over the lips on the bracket.

Installation

18   Install the anti-rattle spring and the brake pads (see Section 3).

19   Install the caliper, tightening the mounting bolts to the torque listed in this Chapter's Specifications.

20   Connect the brake hose to the caliper, using new sealing washers on each side of the fitting. Tighten the banjo fitting bolt to the torque listed in this Chapter's Specifications. If a threaded fitting (tube nut) is used instead of a banjo bolt, tighten it securely with a flare-nut wrench.

21   Reconnect the speedometer cable.

22   Fill the master cylinder with the recommended brake fluid (see Chapter 1) and bleed the system (see Section 8). Check for leaks.

23   Check the operation of the brakes carefully before riding the motorcycle.

---

3   Brake pads – replacement

Refer to illustrations 3.3, 3.4, 3.5 and 3.6

Warning: *When replacing the front brake pads always replace the pads in BOTH calipers – never just on one side. Also, the dust created by the brake system may contain asbestos, which is harmful to your health. Never blow it out with compressed air and don't inhale any of it. An approved filtering mask should be worn when working on the brakes.*

1   Set the bike on its centerstand.

2   Remove the caliper following the procedure in Section 2, but don't disconnect the brake hose.

3   Remove the inner brake pad from the caliper bracket (**see illustration**).

4   Push the caliper bracket in (toward the piston) until the pins on the bracket clear the holes in the pad backing plate, then remove the outer pad (**see illustration**).

5   Remove the anti-rattle spring (**see illustration**). If it appears damaged, replace it.

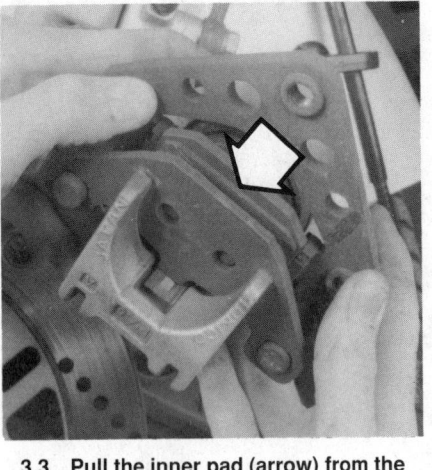

3.3   Pull the inner pad (arrow) from the caliper bracket

3.4   Push the caliper bracket towards the piston and remove the outer pad

3.5   Remove the anti-rattle spring and check it for distortion, replacing it if necessary

7

3.6   Also check the pad support clips (arrow) on the caliper bracket – replace them if they're damaged

4.3   Use a dial indicator to check disc runout – if the reading exceeds the specified limit, the disc will have to be replaced

6   Check the pad support clips on the caliper bracket (**see illustration**). If they are missing or distorted, replace them.

7   Check the condition of the brake disc(s) (see Section 4). If they are in need of machining or replacement, follow the procedure in that Section to remove them. If they are okay, deglaze them with sandpaper or emery cloth, using a swirling motion.

8   Remove the cap from the master cylinder reservoir and siphon out some fluid. Push the piston into the caliper as far as possible, while checking the master cylinder reservoir to make sure it doesn't overflow. If you can't depress the piston with thumb pressure, try using a C-clamp. If the piston sticks, remove the caliper and overhaul it as described in Section 2.

9   Install the anti-rattle spring in the caliper.

10   Install the outer pad in the caliper and pull the caliper bracket out, so the pins on the bracket engage with the holes in the pad backing plate.

11   Install the inner pad in the caliper bracket.

12   Install the caliper, tightening the mounting bolts to the torque listed in this Chapter's Specifications.

13   Refill the master cylinder reservoir (see Chapter 1) and install the diaphragm and cap.

14   Operate the brake lever or pedal several times to bring the pads into contact with the disc. Check the operation of the brakes carefully before riding the motorcycle.

4   Brake disc(s) – inspection, removal and installation

Inspection

Refer to illustrations 4.3, 4.4a and 4.4b

1   Set the bike on its centerstand.

2   Visually inspect the surface of the disc(s) for score marks and other damage. Light scratches are normal after use and won't affect brake operation, but deep grooves and heavy score marks will reduce braking efficiency and accelerate pad wear. If the discs are badly grooved they must be machined or replaced.

3   To check disc runout, mount a dial indicator to a fork leg or the swingarm, with the plunger on the indicator touching the surface of the disc about 1/2-inch from the outer edge (**see illustration**). Slowly turn the wheel (if you're checking the front discs, have an assistant sit on the seat to raise the front wheel off the ground) and watch the indicator needle, comparing your reading with the limit listed in this Chapter's Specifications. If the runout is greater than allowed, check the hub bearings for play (see Chapter 1). If the bearings are worn, replace them and repeat this check. If the disc runout is still excessive, it will have to be replaced.

4   The disc must not be machined or allowed to wear down to a thick-

4.4a   Use a micrometer to measure the thickness of the disc at several points

4.4b   The minimum allowable thickness is stamped into the disc

4.6 Loosen the disc retaining bolts a little at a time to prevent distortion

5.4 Use a six-point box-end wrench to remove the banjo bolt from the master cylinder – be prepared for spillage

ness less than the minimum allowable thickness, listed in this Chapter's Specifications. The thickness of the disc can be checked with a micrometer **(see illustration)**. If the the thickness of the disc is less than the minimum allowable, it must be replaced. The minimum thickness is also stamped into the disc **(see illustration)**.

Removal

Refer to illustration 4.6

5   Remove the wheel (see Section 11 for front wheel removal or Section 12 for rear wheel removal). **Caution:** *Don't lay the wheel down and allow it to rest on one of the discs – the disc could become warped.* Set the wheel on wood blocks so the disc doesn't support the weight of the wheel.

6   Mark the relationship of the disc to the wheel, so it can be installed in the same position. Remove the Allen head bolts that retain the disc to the wheel **(see illustration)**. Loosen the bolts a little at a time, in a criss-cross pattern, to avoid distorting the disc.

7   Take note of any paper shims that may be present where the disc mates to the wheel. If there are any, mark their position and be sure to include them when installing the disc.

Installation

8   Position the disc on the wheel, aligning the previously applied matchmarks (if you're reinstalling the original disc). Make sure the arrow (stamped on the disc) marking the direction of rotation is pointing in the proper direction.

9   Apply a non-hardening thread locking compound to the threads of the bolts. Install the bolts, tightening them a little at a time, in a criss-cross pattern, until the torque listed in this Chapter's Specifications is reached. Clean off all grease from the brake disc(s) using acetone or brake system cleaner.

10   Install the wheel.

11   Operate the brake lever or pedal several times to bring the pads into contact with the disc. Check the operation of the brakes carefully before riding the motorcycle.

---

5   Front brake master cylinder – removal, overhaul and installation

1   If the master cylinder is leaking fluid, or if the lever does not produce a firm feel when the brake is applied, and bleeding the brakes does not help, master cylinder overhaul is recommended. Before disassembling the master cylinder, read through the entire procedure and make sure that you

have the correct rebuild kit. Also, you will need some new, clean brake fluid of the recommended type, some clean rags and internal snap-ring pliers. **Note:** *To prevent damage to the paint from spilled brake fluid, always cover the gas tank when working on the master cylinder.*

2   **Caution:** *Disassembly, overhaul and reassembly of the brake master cylinder must be done in a spotlessly clean work area to avoid contamination and possible failure of the brake hydraulic system components.*

Removal

Refer to illustrations 5.4, 5.5, 5.6 and 5.7

3   Loosen, but do not remove, the screws holding the reservoir cover in place.

4   Pull back the rubber boot, loosen the banjo fitting bolt **(see illustration)** and separate the brake hose from the master cylinder. Wrap the end of the hose in a clean rag and suspend the hose in an upright position or bend it down carefully and place the open end in a clean container. The objective is to prevent excess loss of brake fluid, fluid spills and system contamination.

5   Remove the locknut from the underside of the lever pivot bolt, then unscrew the bolt **(see illustration)**.

7

5.5 Remove the locknut then unscrew the brake lever pivot bolt

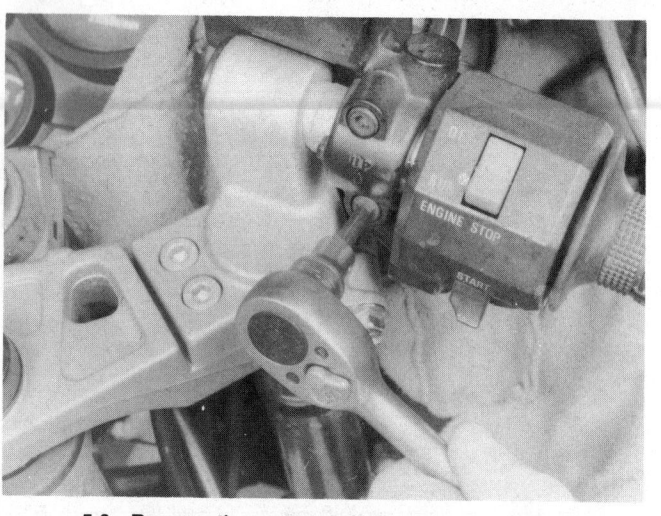

5.6   Remove the master cylinder mounting bolts

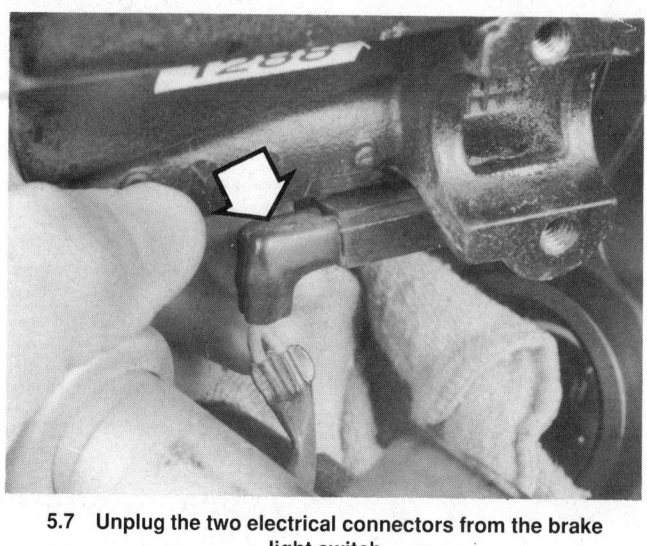

5.7   Unplug the two electrical connectors from the brake light switch

6   Remove the master cylinder mounting bolts **(see illustration)** and separate the master cylinder from the handlebar. **Caution:** *Do not tip the master cylinder upside down or brake fluid will run out.*

7   Disconnect the electrical connectors from the brake light switch **(see illustration).**

Overhaul

Refer to illustrations 5.9, 5.10a, 5.10b and 5.12

8   Detach the top cover and the rubber diaphragm, then drain the brake fluid into a suitable container. Wipe any remaining fluid out of the reservoir with a clean rag.

9   Carefully remove the rubber dust boot from the end of the piston **(see illustration).**

10   Using snap-ring pliers, remove the snap-ring **(see illustrations)** and slide out the piston, the cup seals and the spring. Lay the parts out in the proper order to prevent confusion during reassembly.

11   Clean all of the parts with brake system cleaner (available at auto parts stores), isopropyl alcohol or clean brake fluid. **Caution:** *Do not, under any circumstances, use a petroleum-based solvent to clean brake parts. If compressed air is available, use it to dry the parts thoroughly (make sure it's filtered and unlubricated). Check the master cylinder bore for corrosion, scratches, nicks and score marks. If damage is evident, the master cylinder must be replaced with a new one. If the master cylinder is*

in poor condition, then the calipers should be checked as well.

12   Remove the old cup seals from the piston and spring and install the new ones. Make sure the lips face away from the lever end of the piston **(see illustration).** If a new piston is included in the rebuild kit, use it regardless of the condition of the old one.

13   Before reassembling the master cylinder, soak the piston and the rubber cup seals in clean brake fluid for ten or fifteen minutes. Lubricate the master cylinder bore with clean brake fluid, then carefully insert the piston and related parts in the reverse order of disassembly. Make sure the lips on the cup seals do not turn inside out when they are slipped into the bore.

14   Depress the piston, then install the snap-ring (make sure the snap-ring is properly seated in the groove with the sharp edge facing out). Install the rubber dust boot (make sure the lip is seated properly in the piston groove).

Installation

15   Attach the master cylinder to the handlebar and tighten the bolts to the torque listed in this Chapter's Specifications. The arrow and the word "up" on the master cylinder clamp should be pointing up and readable. Install the brake lever and tighten the pivot bolt locknut.

16   Connect the brake hose to the master cylinder, using new sealing washers. Tighten the banjo fitting bolt to the torque listed in this Chapter's Specifications. Refer to Section 8 and bleed the air from the system.

5.9   Remove the rubber boot from the end of the master cylinder piston, . . .

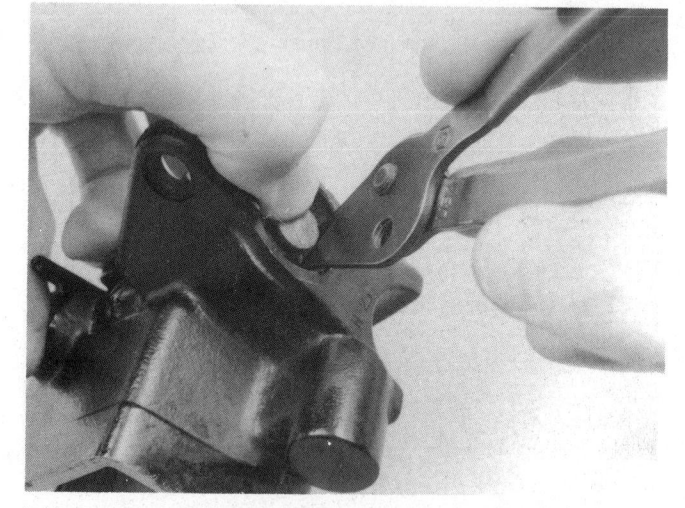

5.10a   . . . then depress the piston and remove the snap-ring with a pair of snap-ring pliers

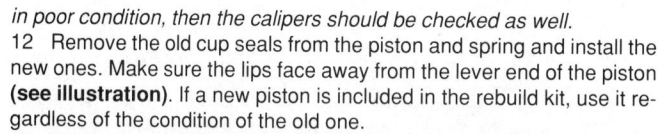

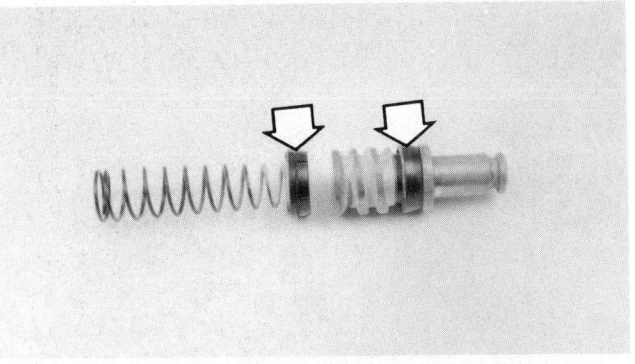

5.12   Make sure the lips of the piston cups (arrows) are facing away from the lever end of the piston

2   **Caution:** *Disassembly, overhaul and reassembly of the brake master cylinder must be done in a spotlessly clean work area to avoid contamination and possible failure of the brake hydraulic system components.*

Removal

Refer to illustrations 6.4 and 6.5

3   Set the bike on its centerstand. Remove the right side cover (see Chapter 8 if necessary).

4   Remove the cotter pin from the clevis pin on the master cylinder push-rod **(see illustration)**. Remove the clevis pin.

5   Have a container and some rags ready to catch spilling brake fluid. Using a pair of pliers, slide the clamp up the fluid feed hose and detach the hose from the master cylinder **(see illustration)**. Direct the end of the hose into the container, unscrew the cap on the master cylinder reservoir and allow the fluid to drain.

6   Using a six-point box-end wrench, unscrew the banjo fitting bolt from the top of the master cylinder **(see illustration 6.5)**. Discard the sealing washers on either side of the fitting.

7   Remove the two master cylinder mounting bolts and detach the cylinder from the bracket.

Overhaul

Refer to illustrations 6.8a, 6.8b, 6.9a, 6.9b, 6.10a, 6.10b, 6.12 and 6.15

8   Using a pair of snap-ring pliers, remove the snap-ring from the fluid

---

5.10b   Exploded view of the master cylinder

1	Pivot bolt	6	Secondary cup	11	Brake light switch
2	Brake lever	7	Piston	12	Master cylinder
3	Locknut	8	Primary cup		body
4	Dust boot	9	Bolt	13	Diaphragm
5	Snap-ring	10	Clamp	14	Cover

6   Rear brake master cylinder – removal, overhaul and installation

1   If the master cylinder is leaking fluid, or if the pedal does not produce a firm feel when the brake is applied, and bleeding the brakes does not help, master cylinder overhaul is recommended. Before disassembling the master cylinder, read through the entire procedure and make sure that you have the correct rebuild kit. Also, you will need some new, clean brake fluid of the recommended type, some clean rags and internal snap-ring pliers.

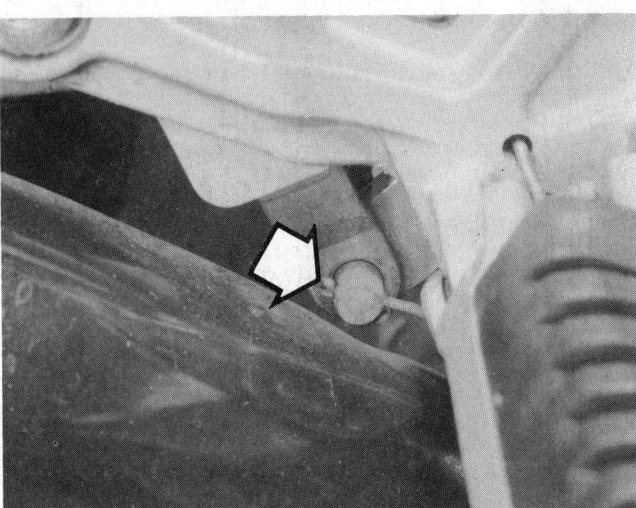

6.4   Remove the cotter pin (arrow) from the clevis pin

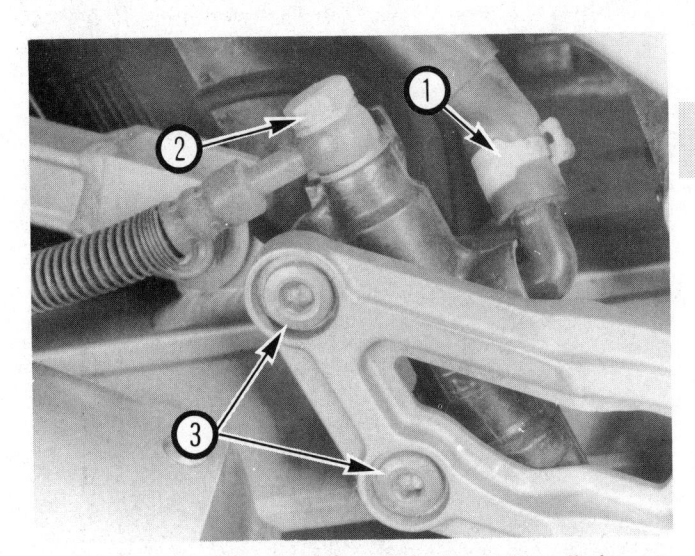

6.5   Mounting details of the rear brake master cylinder

1	Fluid feed hose	3	Master cylinder
2	Banjo fitting bolt		mounting bolts

7

6.8a   Remove the snap-ring that secures the fluid inlet fitting

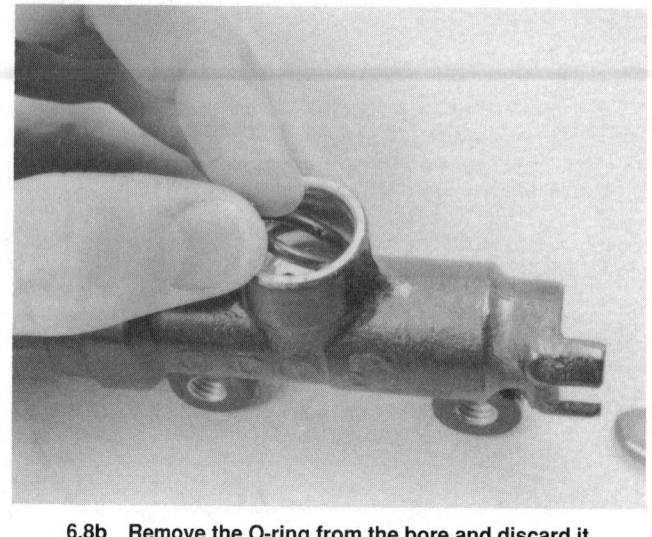

6.8b   Remove the O-ring from the bore and discard it

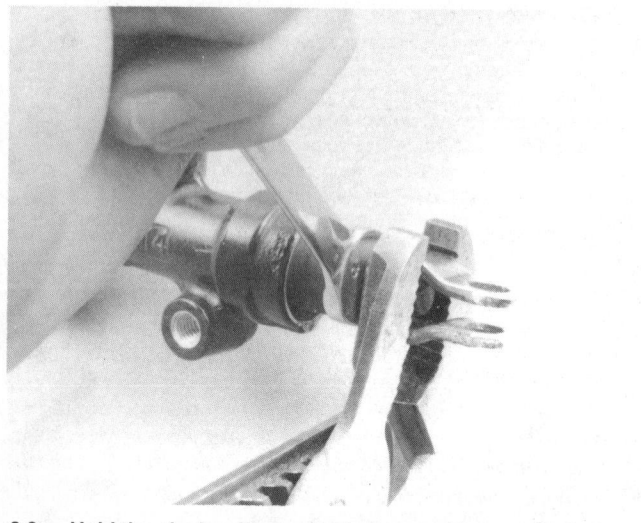

6.9a   Hold the clevis with a pair of pliers and loosen the locknut

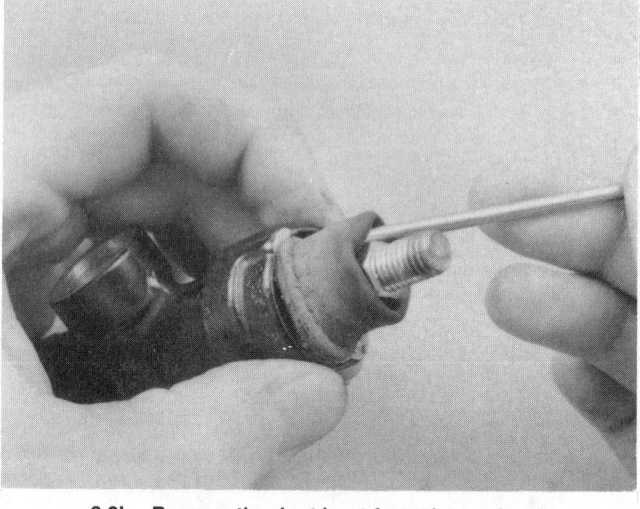

6.9b   Remove the dust boot from the pushrod

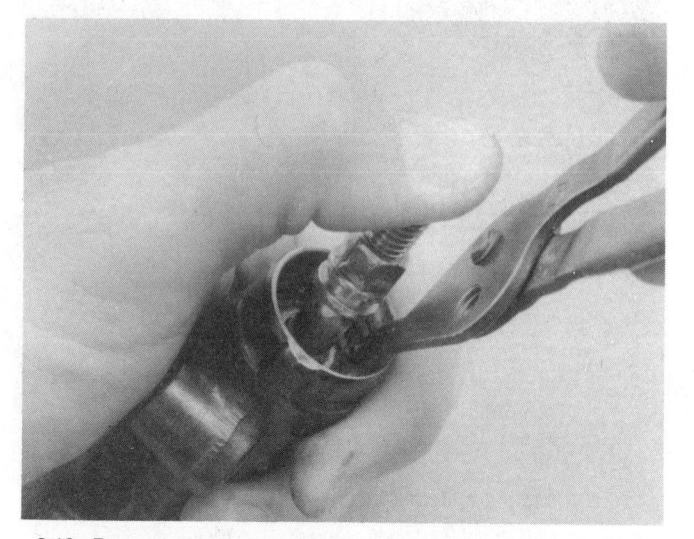

6.10a Depress the pushrod and remove the snap-ring from the cylinder bore

inlet fitting (**see illustration**) and detach the fitting from the master cylinder. Remove the O-ring from the bore (**see illustration**).

9   Hold the clevis with a pair of pliers and loosen the locknut (**see illustration**). Carefully remove the rubber dust boot from the pushrod (**see illustration**).

10   Depress the pushrod and, using snap-ring pliers, remove the snap-ring (**see illustrations**). Slide out the piston, the cup seal and spring. Lay the parts out in the proper order to prevent confusion during reassembly.

11   Clean all of the parts with brake system cleaner (available at auto parts stores), isopropyl alcohol or clean brake fluid. **Caution:** *Do not, under any circumstances, use a petroleum-based solvent to clean brake parts.* If compressed air is available, use it to dry the parts thoroughly (make sure it's filtered and unlubricated). Check the master cylinder bore for corrosion, scratches, nicks and score marks. If damage is evident, the master cylinder must be replaced with a new one. If the master cylinder is in poor condition, then the caliper should be checked as well.

12   Remove the old cup seals from the piston and spring and install the new ones. Make sure the lips face away from the pushrod end of the piston (**see illustration**). If a new piston is included in the rebuild kit, use it regardless of the condition of the old one.

13   Before reassembling the master cylinder, soak the piston and the rubber cup seals in clean brake fluid for ten or fifteen minutes. Lubricate the master cylinder bore with clean brake fluid, then carefully insert the parts in

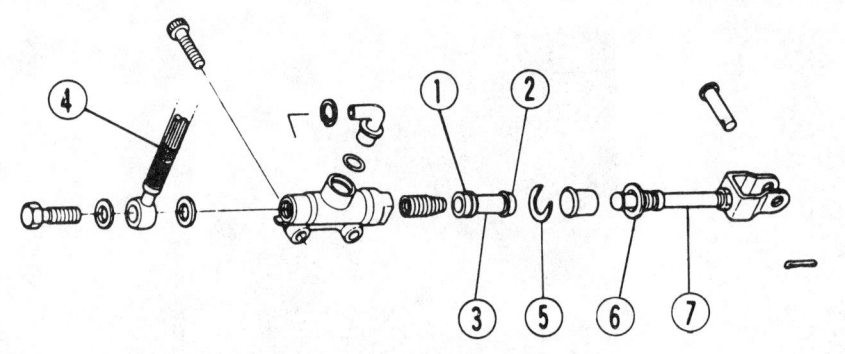

6.10b **Exploded view of the rear brake master cylinder**

1 *Primary cup*   5 *Retainer*
2 *Secondary cup*   6 *Piston stop*
3 *Piston*   7 *Pushrod*
4 *Brake hose*

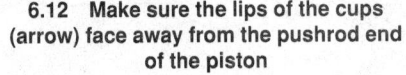

6.12   **Make sure the lips of the cups (arrow) face away from the pushrod end of the piston**

the reverse order of disassembly. Make sure the lips on the cup seals do not turn inside out when they are slipped into the bore.

14   Lubricate the end of the pushrod with PBC (poly butyl cuprysil) grease, or silicone grease designed for brake applications, and install the pushrod and stop washer into the cylinder bore. Depress the pushrod, then install the snap-ring (make sure the snap-ring is properly seated in the groove with the sharp edge facing out). Install the rubber dust boot (make sure the lip is seated properly in the groove in the piston stop nut).

15   Install the clevis to the end of the pushrod, leaving about 3.5 to 5.5 mm of the end of the pushrod exposed past the adjusting nut **(see illustration)**, then tighten the locknut This will ensure the brake pedal will be positioned correctly.

16   Install the feed hose fitting, using a new O-ring. Install the snap-ring, making sure it seats properly in its groove.

Installation

17   Position the master cylinder on the frame and install the bolts, tightening them to the torque listed in this Chapter's Specifications.

18   Connect the banjo fitting to the top of the master cylinder, using new sealing washers on each side of the fitting. Tighten the banjo fitting bolt to the torque listed in this Chapter's Specifications.

19   Connect the fluid feed hose to the inlet fitting and install the

hose clamp.

20   Connect the clevis to the brake pedal and secure the clevis pin with a new cotter pin.

21   Fill the fluid reservoir with the specified fluid (see Chapter 1) and bleed the system following the procedure in Section 8. Install the side cover.

22   Check the position of the brake pedal (see Chapter 1) and adjust it if necessary. Check the operation of the brakes carefully before riding the motorcycle.

---

7   Brake hoses and lines – inspection and replacement

Inspection

Refer to illustration 7.2

1   Once a week, or if the motorcycle is used less frequently, before every ride, check the condition of the brake hoses and the metal lines that feed the brake fluid to the anti-dive units on the front forks.

2   Twist and flex the rubber hoses **(see illustration)** while looking for cracks, bulges and seeping fluid. Check extra carefully around the areas where the hoses connect with the banjo fittings, as these are common areas for hose failure.

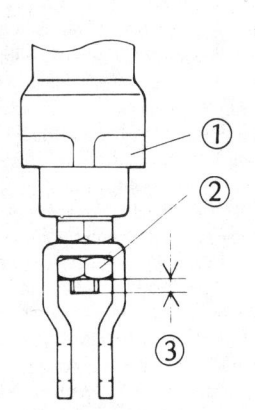

6.15   **Allow 3.5 to 5.5 mm of the pushrod to protrude past the adjusting nut, then tighten the locknut**

1 *Master cylinder*   3 *Rod position*
2 *Adjusting nut*

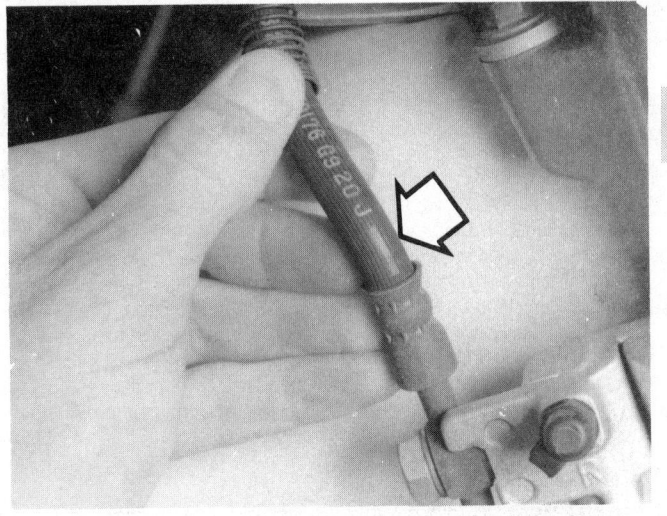

7.2   **Flex the brake hoses and check for cracks, bulges and leaking fluid**

7

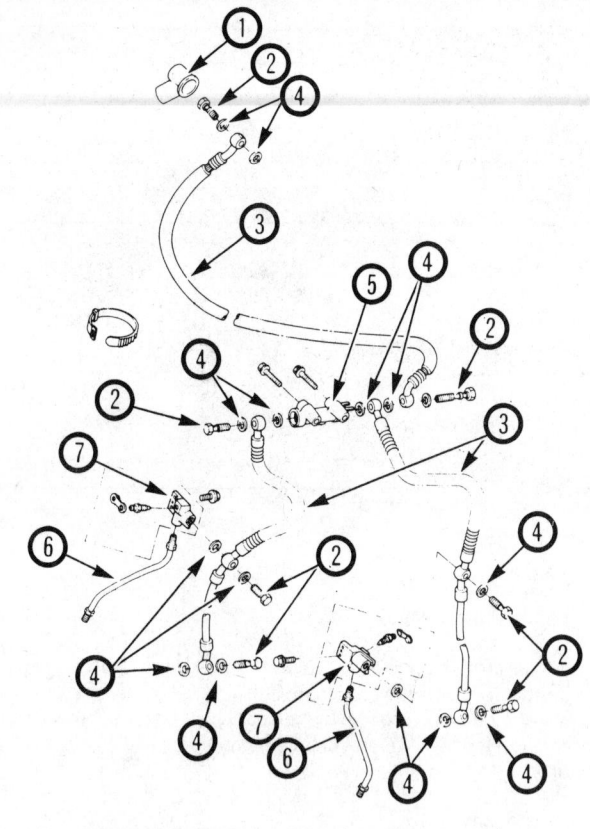

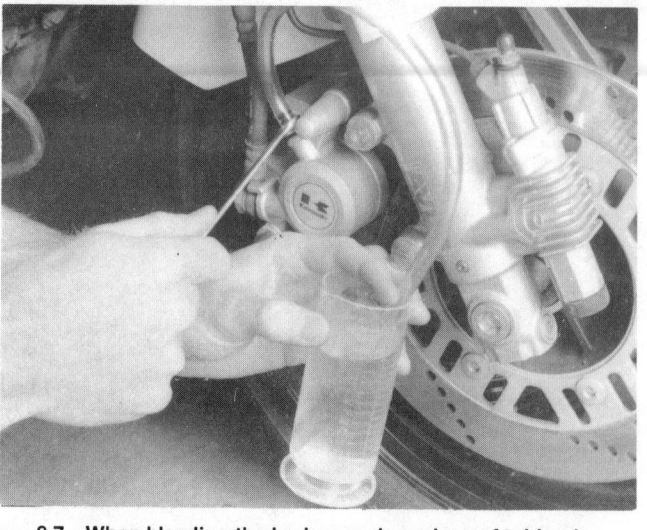

8.7   When bleeding the brakes, a clear piece of tubing is attached to the bleeder valve and submerged in brake fluid – the air bubbles can easily be seen in the tube and container (when no more bubbles appear, the air has been purged from the caliper or wheel cylinder)

7.4   Front brake hose installation details (typical)

1	*Rubber boot*	5	*Connector*
2	*Banjo fitting bolt*	6	*Brake line junction*
3	*Brake hose*		*block-to-antidive unit*
4	*Sealing washers*	7	*Junction block*

3   Inspect the metal lines connected to the anti-dive units on the front forks. If the plating on the lines is chipped or scratched, the lines may rust. If the lines are rusted, scratched or cracked, replace them.

Replacement

Refer to illustration 7.4

4   Most brake hoses have banjo fittings on each end of the hose **(see illustration)**. Cover the surrounding area with plenty of rags and unscrew the banjo bolts on either end of the hose. If a threaded fitting is used instead of a banjo bolt, use a flare nut wrench to loosen it. Detach the hose from any clips that may be present and remove the hose.

5   Position the new hose, making sure it isn't twisted or otherwise strained, between the two components. Make sure the metal tube portion of the banjo fitting is located between the casting protrusions on the component it's connected to, if equipped. Install the banjo bolts, using new sealing washers on both sides of the fittings, and tighten them to the torque listed in this Chapter's Specifications. If a threaded fitting is used instead of a banjo bolt, tighten it securely, again using a flare nut wrench.

6   Flush the old brake fluid from the system, refill the system with the recommended fluid (see Chapter 1) and bleed the air from the system (see Section 8). Check the operation of the brakes carefully before riding the motorcycle.

8   Brake system bleeding

Refer to illustrations 8.7, 8.9a and 8.9b

1   Bleeding the brake is simply the process of removing all the air

bubbles from the brake fluid reservoir, the lines and the brake caliper. Bleeding is necessary whenever a brake system hydraulic connection is loosened, when a component or hose is replaced, or when the master cylinder or caliper is overhauled. Leaks in the system may also allow air to enter, but leaking brake fluid will reveal their presence and warn you of the need for repair.

2   To bleed the brake, you will need some new, clean brake fluid of the recommended type (see Chapter 1), a length of clear vinyl or plastic tubing, a small container partially filled with clean brake fluid, some rags and a wrench to fit the brake caliper bleeder valve.

3   Cover the gas tank and other painted components to prevent damage in the event that brake fluid is spilled.

4   Remove the reservoir cap or cover and slowly pump the brake lever or pedal a few times, until no air bubbles can be seen floating up from the the holes at the bottom of the reservoir. Doing this bleeds the air from the master cylinder end of the line. Reinstall the reservoir cap or cover.

5   Attach one end of the clear vinyl or plastic tubing to the brake caliper bleeder valve and submerge the other end in the brake fluid in the container.

6   Remove the reservoir cap or cover and check the fluid level. Do not allow the fluid level to drop below the lower mark during the bleeding process.

7   Carefully pump the brake lever or pedal three or four times and hold it while opening the caliper bleeder valve **(see illustration)**. When the valve is opened, brake fluid will flow out of the caliper into the clear tubing and the lever will move toward the handlebar or the pedal will move down.

8   Retighten the bleeder valve, then release the brake lever or pedal gradually. Repeat the process until no air bubbles are visible in the brake fluid leaving the caliper and the lever or pedal is firm when applied. **Note:** *The rear calipers on later models have two bleeder valves – air must be bled from both, one after the other. Remember to add fluid to the reservoir as the level drops.* Use only new, clean brake fluid of the recommended type. Never reuse the fluid lost during bleeding.

9   If you're bleeding the front brakes, repeat this procedure to the other caliper, then bleed both anti-dive units on the lower ends of the forks, followed by the junction blocks about half-way up the forks **(see illustrations)**. **Note:** *Later models don't have bleeder valves on the anti-dive units or the junction blocks.* Be sure to check the fluid level in the master cylinder reservoir frequently.

10   Replace the reservoir cover, wipe up any spilled brake fluid and check the entire system for leaks. **Note:** *If bleeding is difficult, it may be neces-*

8.9a After bleeding the front calipers, bleed the anti-dive units. . .

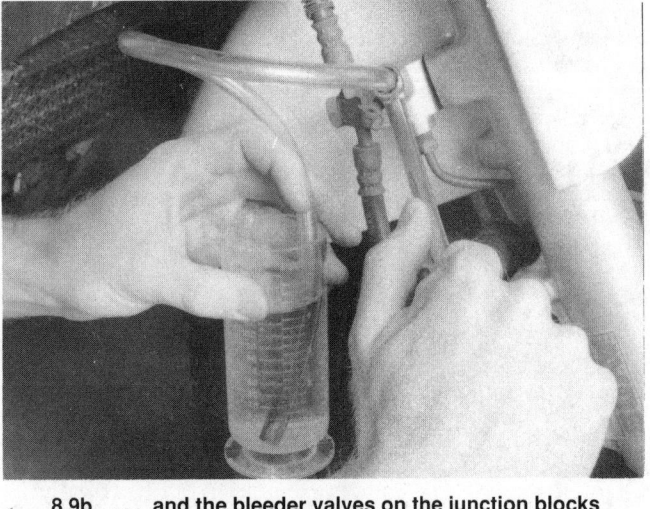

8.9b . . . and the bleeder valves on the junction blocks

sary to let the brake fluid in the system stabilize for a few hours (it may be aerated). Repeat the bleeding procedure when the tiny bubbles in the system have settled out.

9 Wheels – inspection and repair

Refer to illustration 9.2

1   Place the motorcycle on the centerstand, then clean the wheels thoroughly to remove mud and dirt that may interfere with the inspection procedure or mask defects. Make a general check of the wheels and tires as described in Chapter 1.

2   With the motorcycle on the centerstand and the wheel in the air, attach a dial indicator to the fork slider or the swingarm and position the stem against the side of the rim **(see illustration)**. Spin the wheel slowly and check the side-to-side (axial) runout of the rim, then compare your readings with the value listed in this Chapter's Specifications. In order to accurately check radial runout with the dial indicator, the wheel would have to be removed from the machine and the tire removed from the wheel. With the axle clamped in a vise, the wheel can be rotated to check the runout.

3   An easier, though slightly less accurate, method is to attach a stiff wire pointer to the fork slider or the swingarm and position the end a fraction of an inch from the wheel (where the wheel and tire join). If the wheel is true, the distance from the pointer to the rim will be constant as the wheel is rotated. Repeat the procedure to check the runout of the rear wheel. **Note:** *If wheel runout is excessive, refer to the appropriate Section in this Chapter and check the wheel bearings very carefully before replacing the wheel.*

4   The wheels should also be visually inspected for cracks, flat spots on the rim and other damage. Since tubeless tires are involved, look very closely for dents in the area where the tire bead contacts the rim. Dents in this area may prevent complete sealing of the tire against the rim, which leads to deflation of the tire over a period of time.

5   If damage is evident, or if runout in either direction is excessive, the wheel will have to be replaced with a new one. Never attempt to repair a damaged cast aluminum wheel.

10 Wheels – alignment check

1   Misalignment of the wheels, which may be due to a cocked rear wheel or a bent frame or triple clamps, can cause strange and possibly serious handling problems. If the frame or triple clamps are at fault, repair by a frame specialist or replacement with new parts are the only alternatives.

2   To check the alignment you will need an assistant, a length of string or a perfectly straight piece of wood and a ruler graduated in 1/64 inch increments. A plumb bob or other suitable weight will also be required.

9.2 Axial runout of the wheel can be checked with a dial indicator mounted to a fork tube (front) or the swingarm (rear)

3   Place the motorcycle on the centerstand, then measure the width of both tires at their widest points. Subtract the smaller measurement from the larger measurement, then divide the difference by two. The result is the amount of offset that should exist between the front and rear tires on both sides.

4   If a string is used, have your assistant hold one end of it about half way between the floor and the rear axle, touching the rear sidewall of the tire.

5   Run the other end of the string forward and pull it tight so that it is roughly parallel to the floor. Slowly bring the string into contact with the front sidewall of the rear tire, then turn the front wheel until it is parallel with the string. Measure the distance from the front tire sidewall to the string.

6   Repeat the procedure on the other side of the motorcycle. The distance from the front tire sidewall to the string should be equal on both sides.

7   As was previously pointed out, a perfectly straight length of wood may be substituted for the string. The procedure is the same.

8   If the distance between the string and tire is greater on one side, or if the rear wheel appears to be cocked, refer to Chapter 6, Swingarm bearings – check, and make sure the swingarm is tight.

9   If the front-to-back alignment is correct, the wheels still may be out of alignment vertically.

10   Using the plumb bob, or other suitable weight, and a length of string, check the rear wheel to make sure it is vertical. To do this, hold the string

7

11.4a   Loosen the axle clamp bolt at the bottom of the right fork leg (it isn't necessary to remove it completely)

11.4b   On early models the axle can be unscrewed with a 12 mm Allen wrench

11.5   Support the wheel and pull out the axle

against the tire upper sidewall and allow the weight to settle just off the floor. When the string touches both the upper and lower tire sidewalls and is perfectly straight, the wheel is vertical. If it is not, place thin spacers under one leg of the centerstand.

11   Once the rear wheel is vertical, check the front wheel in the same manner. If both wheels are not perfectly vertical, the frame and/or major suspension components are bent.

11   Front wheel – removal and installation

Refer to illustrations 11.4a, 11.4b and 11.5

Removal

1   Remove the lower portion of the fairing (see Chapter 8). Place the motorcycle on the centerstand, then raise the front wheel off the ground by placing a floor jack, with a wood block on the jack head, under the engine.
2   Disconnect the speedometer cable from the drive unit.
3   Remove one of the brake calipers and support it with a piece of wire. Don't disconnect the brake hose from the caliper.
4   Loosen the right side axle clamp bolt **(see illustration)**. On early models unscrew the axle **(see illustration)**. On later models, the axle nut on the left side must be removed.
5   Support the wheel, then pull out the axle **(see illustration)** and carefully lower the wheel until the brake disc clears the caliper that is still in-

stalled. It will probably be necessary to tilt the wheel to one side to allow removal. Don't lose the spacer that fits into the right side of the hub. **Caution:** *Don't lay the wheel down and allow it to rest on one of the discs – the disc could become warped. Set the wheel on wood blocks so the disc doesn't support the weight of the wheel.* If the axle is corroded, remove the corrosion with fine emery cloth. **Note:** *Do not operate the front brake lever with the wheel removed.*
6   Check the condition of the wheel bearings (see Section 13).

Installation

7   Installation is the reverse of removal. Apply a thin coat of grease to the seal lip, then slide the collar into the right side of the hub. Position the speedometer drive unit in place in the left side of the hub, then slide the wheel into place. Make sure the notches in the speedometer drive housing line up with the lugs in the wheel. If the disc will not slide between the brake pads, remove the wheel and carefully pry them apart with a piece of wood.
8   Slip the axle into place, then tighten the axle (early models) or the axle nut (later models) to the torque listed in this Chapter's Specifications. Tighten the right side axle clamp bolt to the torque listed in this Chapter's Specifications.
9   Apply the front brake, pump the forks up and down several times and check for binding and proper brake operation.

12   Rear wheel – removal and installation

Refer to illustrations 12.3, 12.4, 12.6 and 12.8

Removal

1   Set the bike on its centerstand.
2   Remove the chain guard (see Chapter 6 if necessary).
3   Remove the cotter pin from the axle nut **(see illustration)** and remove the nut.
4   Loosen the torque link nut **(see illustration)**.
5   Loosen the chain adjusting bolt locknuts (see Chapter 1) and fully loosen both adjusting bolts.
6   Push the rear wheel as far forward as possible. Lift the top of the chain up off the rear sprocket and pull it to the left while rotating the wheel backwards **(see illustration)**. This will disengage the chain from the sprocket. **Warning:** *Don't let your fingers slip between the chain and the sprocket.*
7   Support the wheel and slide the axle out. Lower the wheel and remove it from the swingarm, being careful not to lose the spacers on either side of the hub. **Caution:** *Don't lay the wheel down and allow it to rest on the disc or the sprocket – they could become warped. Set the wheel on wood blocks so the disc or the sprocket doesn't support the weight of the wheel. Do not operate the brake pedal with the wheel removed.*

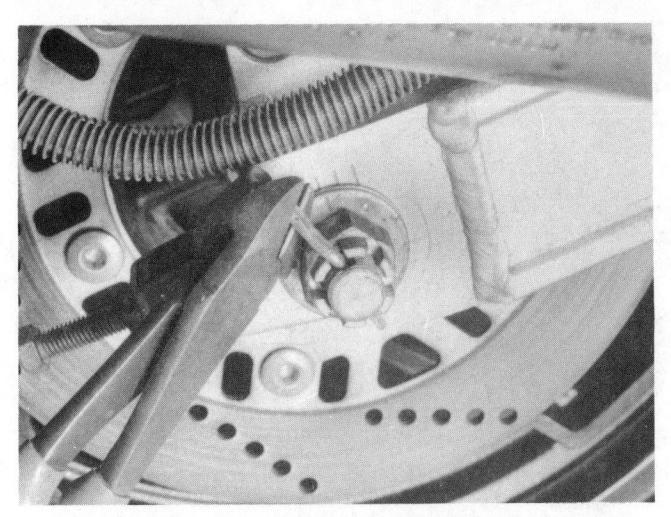

12.3   Remove the cotter pin from the axle nut

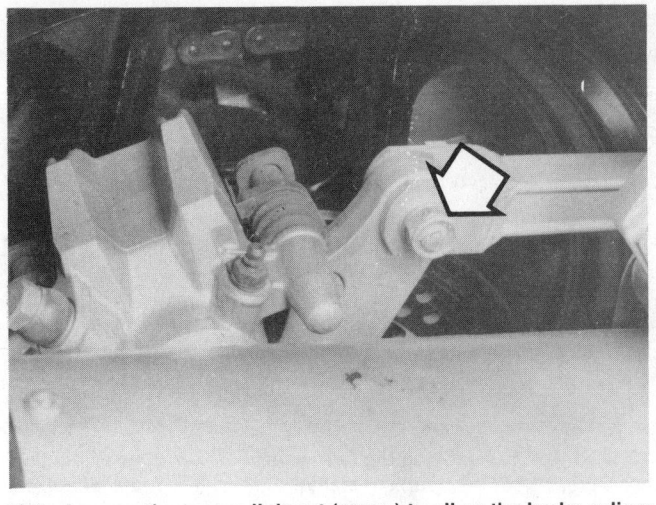

12.4   Loosen the torque link nut (arrow) to allow the brake caliper to swing to the rear as the wheel is removed

12.6   Push the wheel forward and detach the chain from the sprocket

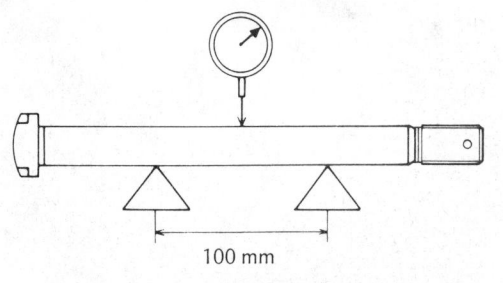

12.8   Check the axle for runout using a dial indicator and V-blocks

100 mm

8   Before installing the wheel, check the axle for straightness. If the axle is corroded, first remove the corrosion with fine emery cloth. Set the axle on V-blocks and check it for runout using a dial indicator **(see illustration)**. If the axle exceeds the maximum allowable runout limit listed in this Chapter's Specifications, it must be replaced.
9   Check the condition of the wheel bearings (see Section 13).

Installation

10   Apply a thin coat of grease to the seal lips, then slide the spacers into their proper positions on the sides of the hub.
11   Slide the wheel into place, making sure the brake disc slides between the brake pads. If it doesn't, spread the pads apart with a piece of wood.
12   Pull the chain up over the sprocket, raise the wheel and install the axle and axle nut. Don't tighten the axle nut at this time.
13   Adjust the chain slack (see Chapter 1) and tighten the adjuster locknuts.
14   Tighten the axle nut to the torque listed in this Chapter's Specifications. Install a new cotter pin, tightening the axle nut an additional amount, if necessary, to align the hole in the axle with the castellations on the nut.
15   Tighten the torque link nut to the torque listed in the Chapter 6 Specifications.
16   Check the operation of the brakes carefully before riding the motorcycle.

13.3   If you're removing the front wheel bearings, remove the snap-ring that secures the speedometer drive, then remove the drive (arrow)

13   Wheel bearings – inspection and maintenance

Refer to illustrations 13.3, 13.4a, 13.4b, 13.5, 13.7, 13.10 and 13.11
1   Set the bike on its centerstand and remove the wheel (see Section 11 (front wheel) or 12 (rear wheel).
2   Set the wheel on blocks so as not to allow the weight of the wheel rest on the brake disc or sprocket.
3   If you're removing the front wheel bearings, remove the snap-ring securing the speedometer drive **(see illustration)**. Remove the speedometer drive from the hub.

7

13.4a   If you're removing the rear wheel bearings, lift out the coupling sleeve, . . .

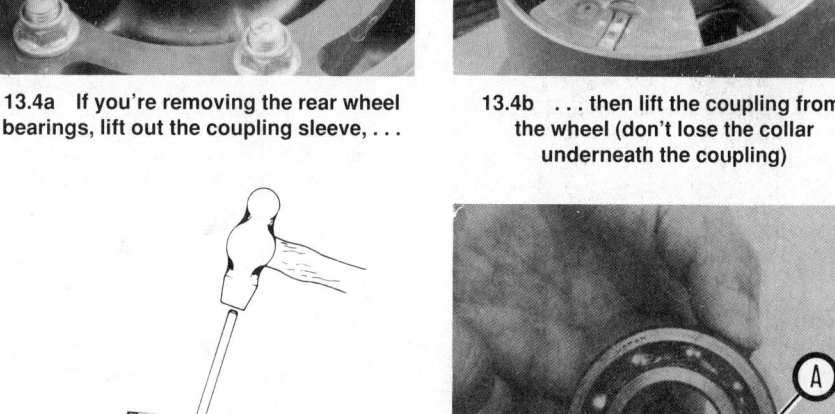

13.4b   . . . then lift the coupling from the wheel (don't lose the collar underneath the coupling)

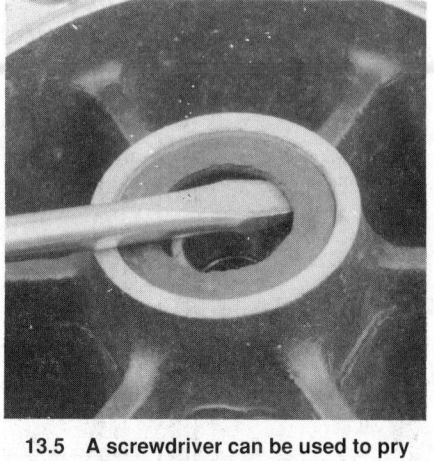

13.5   A screwdriver can be used to pry out the grease seal

13.7   Once the snap-rings have been removed, drive the bearings from the hub with a metal rod and a hammer

13.10   Press grease into the open side of the bearing until it's full

13.11   A socket of the appropriate diameter can be used to drive the bearing into the hub

4   If you're removing the rear wheel bearings, lift off the coupling sleeve, rear wheel coupling and coupling collar **(see illustrations)**.

5   Pry out the grease seal **(see illustration)**.

6   Remove the snap-ring from the other side of the hub.

7   Using a metal rod (preferably a brass drift punch) inserted through the center of the hub bearing, tap evenly around the inner race of the opposite bearing to drive it from the hub **(see illustration)**. The bearing spacer will also come out.

8   Lay the wheel on its other side and remove the remaining bearing using the same technique.

9   Clean the bearings with a high flash-point solvent (one which won't leave any residue) and blow them dry with compressed air (don't let the bearing spin as you dry them). Apply a few drops of oil to the bearing. Hold the outer race of the bearing and rotate the inner race – if the bearing doesn't turn smoothly, has rough spots or is noisy, replace it with a new one.

10   If the bearing checks out okay and will be reused, wash it in solvent once again and dry it, then pack the bearing from the open side with high-quality bearing grease **(see illustration)**.

11   Thoroughly clean the hub area of the wheel. Install the bearing into the recess in the hub, with the marked or shielded side facing out. Using a bearing driver or a socket large enough to contact the outer race of the bearing, drive it in **(see illustration)** until the snap-ring groove is visible. Install the snap-ring.

12   Turn the wheel over and install the bearing spacer and bearing, driving the bearing into place as described in Step 10, then install the snap-ring. Install the speedometer drive (if you're working on the front wheel)

and the snap-ring.

13   Install a new grease seal, using a seal driver, large socket or a flat piece of wood to drive it into place.

14   If you're working on the rear wheel, press a little grease into the bearing in the rear wheel coupling. Install the coupling to the wheel, making sure the coupling collar is located in the inside of the inner race (between the wheel and the coupling).

15   Clean off all grease from the brake disc(s) using acetone or brake system cleaner. Install the wheel.

---

14   Tubeless tires – general information

1   Tubeless tires are used as standard equipment on this motorcycle. They are generally safer than tube-type tires but if problems do occur they require special repair techniques.

2   The force required to break the seal between the rim and the bead of the tire is substantial, and is usually beyond the capabilities of an individual working with normal tire irons.

3   Also, repair of the punctured tire and replacement on the wheel rim requires special tools, skills and experience that the average do-it-yourselfer lacks.

4   For these reasons, if a puncture or flat occurs with a tubeless tire, the wheel should be removed from the motorcycle and taken to a dealer service department or a motorcycle repair shop for repair or replacement of the tire.

Chapter 8 Fairing and bodywork

Refer to Chapter 10 for information on the ZX750F model

Contents

8

1   General information

Refer to illustrations 1.1a, 1.1b, 1.1c and 1.1d

This Chapter covers the procedures necessary to remove and install the fairing and other body parts **(see illustrations)**. Since many service and repair operations on these motorcycles require removal of the fairing and/or other body parts, the procedures are grouped here and referred to from other Chapters.

In the case of damage to the fairing or other body part, it is usually necessary to remove the broken component and replace it with a new (or used) one. The material that the fairing and other body parts is composed of doesn't lend itself to conventional repair techniques. There are, however, some shops that specialize in "plastic welding", so it would be advantageous to check around first before throwing the damaged part away.

Note that the fairing and body parts from A and B models aren't interchangeable with similar components on C models, and vice-versa.

2   Lower fairing – removal and installation

Refer to illustration 2.2

1   Set the bike on its centerstand.
2   Support the lower fairing and remove the mounting screws **(see illustration)**.
3   Carefully maneuver the fairing out from under the bike. On A and B models, mark and disconnect the hoses from the coolant reservoir (see Chapter 3).
4   Installation is the reverse of removal. On A and B models, check the coolant level and add some, if necessary (see Chapter 1).

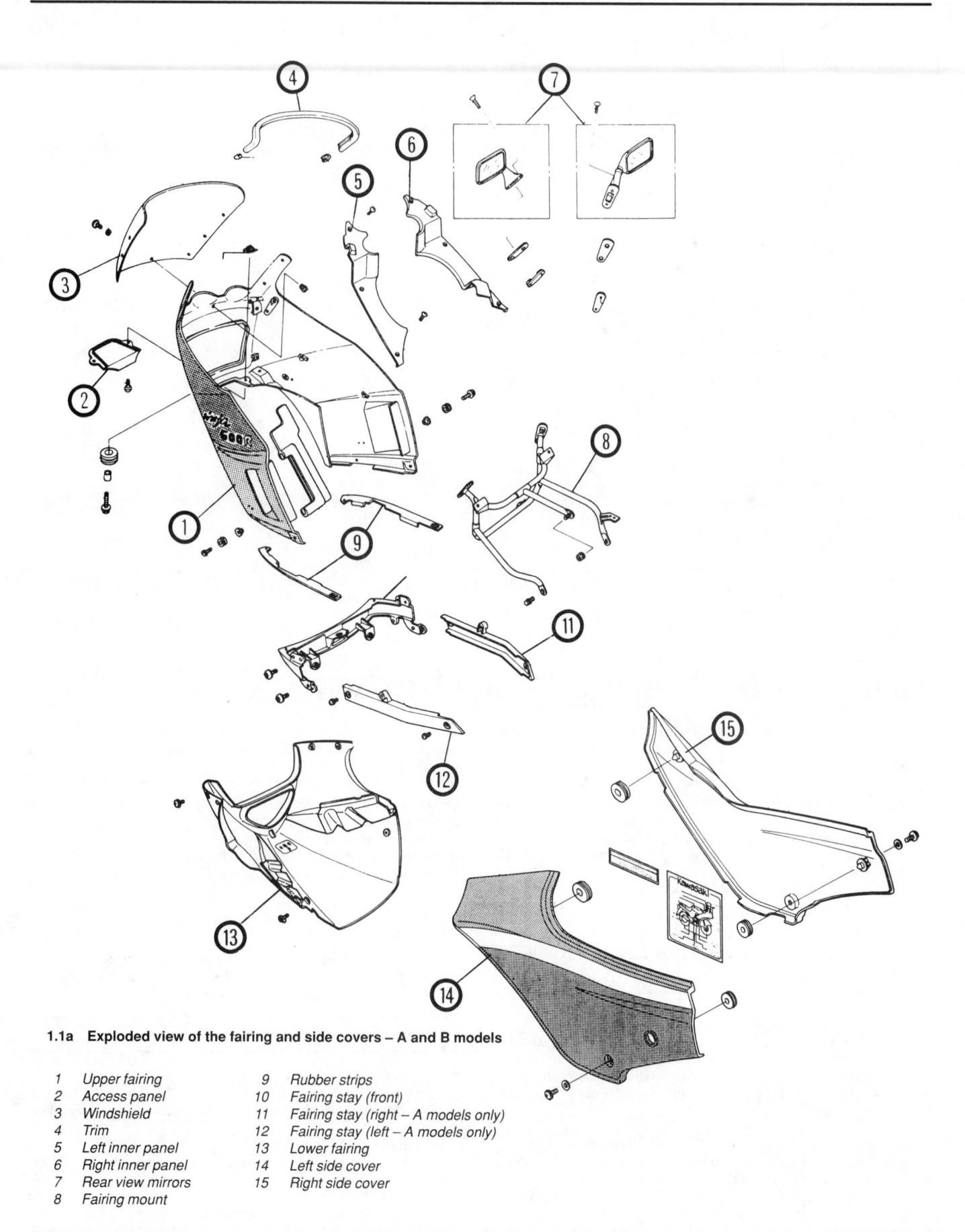

1.1a   Exploded view of the fairing and side covers – A and B models

1	Upper fairing	9	Rubber strips
2	Access panel	10	Fairing stay (front)
3	Windshield	11	Fairing stay (right – A models only)
4	Trim	12	Fairing stay (left – A models only)
5	Left inner panel	13	Lower fairing
6	Right inner panel	14	Left side cover
7	Rear view mirrors	15	Right side cover
8	Fairing mount		

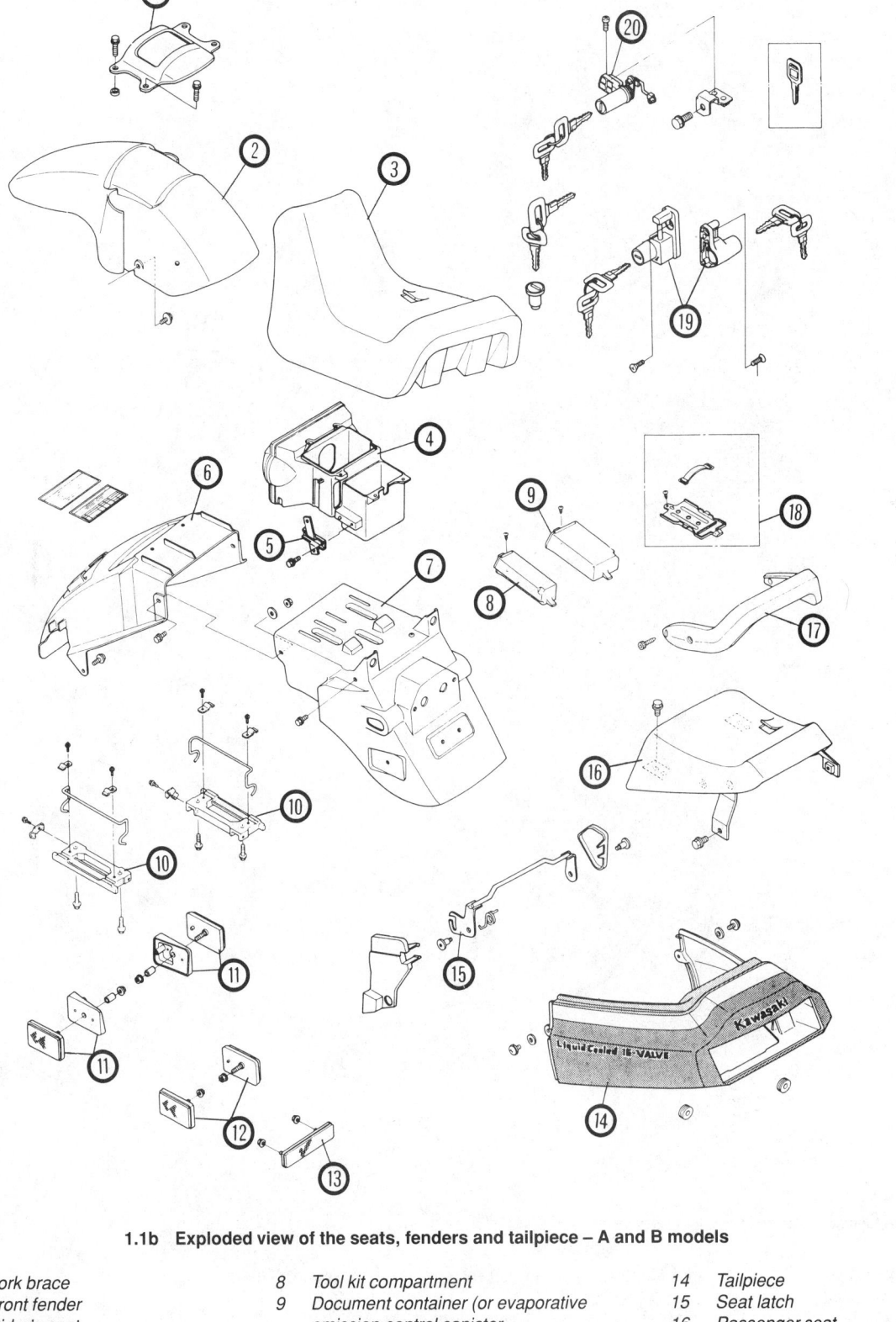

1.1b Exploded view of the seats, fenders and tailpiece – A and B models

1	Fork brace	8	Tool kit compartment	14	Tailpiece
2	Front fender	9	Document container (or evaporative	15	Seat latch
3	Rider's seat		emission control canister –	16	Passenger seat
4	Air filter housing		California models)	17	Grab handle
5	Voltage regulator/rectifier	10	Tie-down hook and bracket	18	Canister mount
	mounting bracket	11	Upper fairing reflectors		(California models only)
6	Rear fender (front section)	12	Rear fender side reflectors	19	Helmet locks
7	Rear fender (rear section)	13	Rear reflector	20	Seat latch lock

8

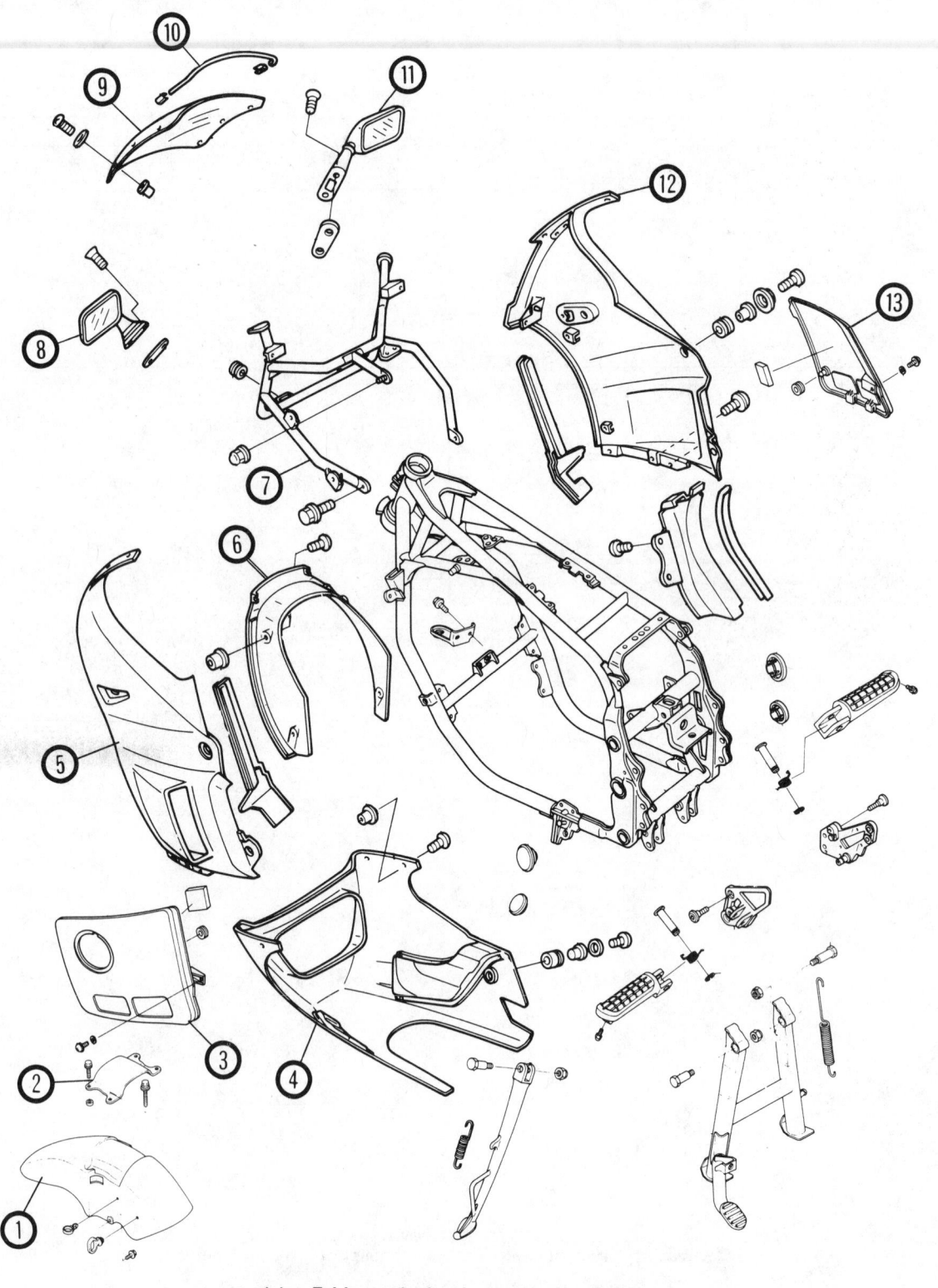

1.1c   Fairing and related components – C models

1	Front fender	8	Rear view mirror (left side)
2	Fender brace	9	Windshield
3	Knee grip cover (left side)	10	Trim
4	Lower fairing	11	Rear view mirror (right side)
5	Upper fairing (left side)	12	Upper fairing (right side)
6	Headlight lower cover	13	Knee grip cover (right side)
7	Fairing mount		

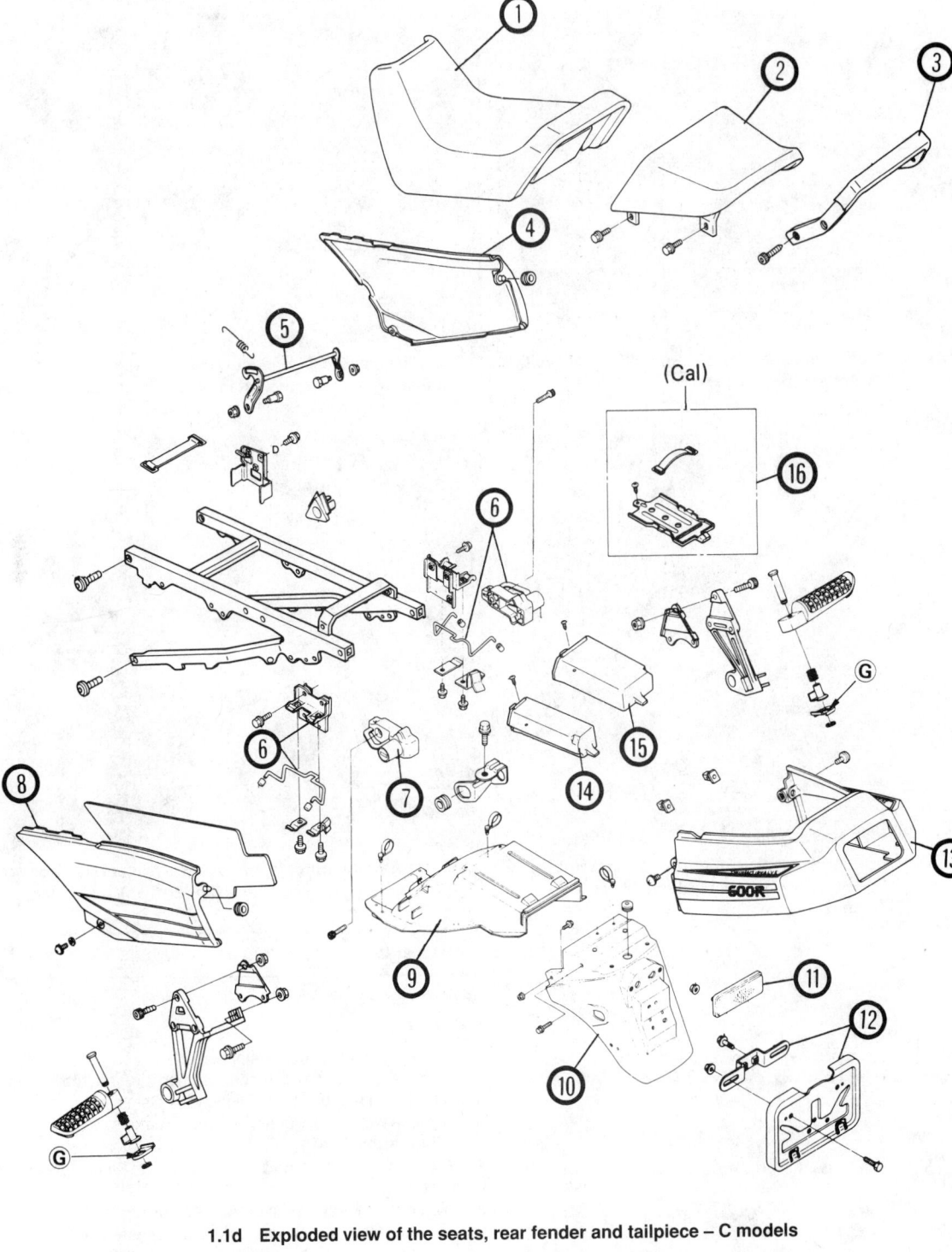

1.1d   Exploded view of the seats, rear fender and tailpiece – C models

1	Rider's seat	10	Rear fender (rear section)
2	Passenger seat	11	Rear reflector
3	Grab handle	12	License plate bracket and mount
4	Right side cover	13	Tailpiece
5	Seat latch	14	Tool kit compartment
6	Tie-down hook and bracket	15	Document container (or evaporative
7	Helmet lock		emission control canister – California models)
8	Left side cover	16	Canister mount (California models only)
9	Rear fender (front section)		

8

2.2   Remove these screws from each side of the fairing (A model shown, others similar)

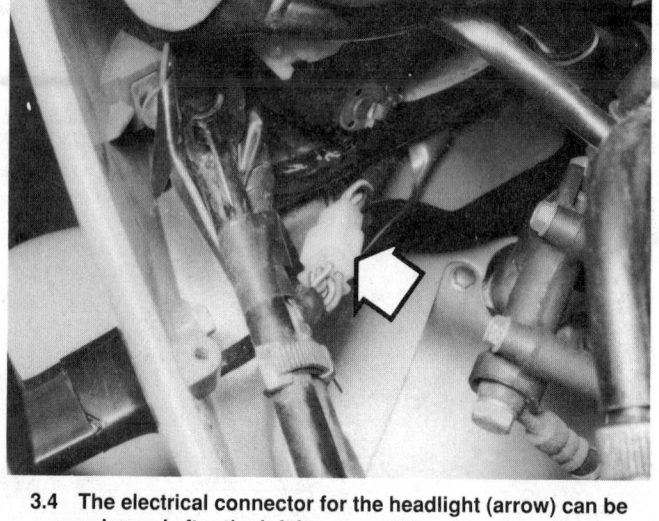

3.4   The electrical connector for the headlight (arrow) can be unplugged after the left inner panel has been removed

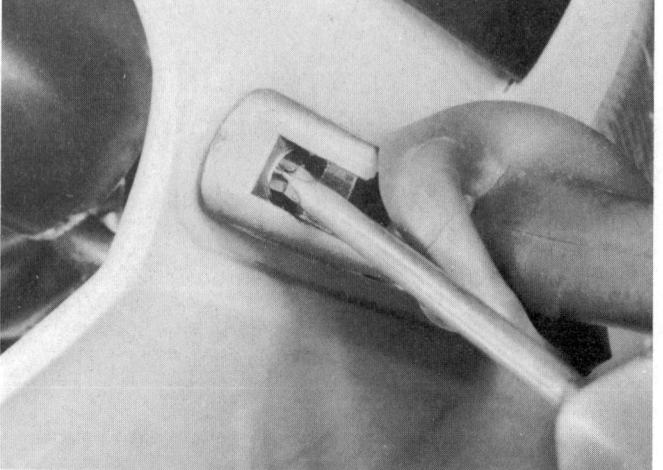

3.5   Each rear view mirror serves as an upper mounting point for the fairing, and is retained by two screws hidden under the mirror cover

3.6a   On A and B models, remove the two screws from each side of the fairing (arrows)

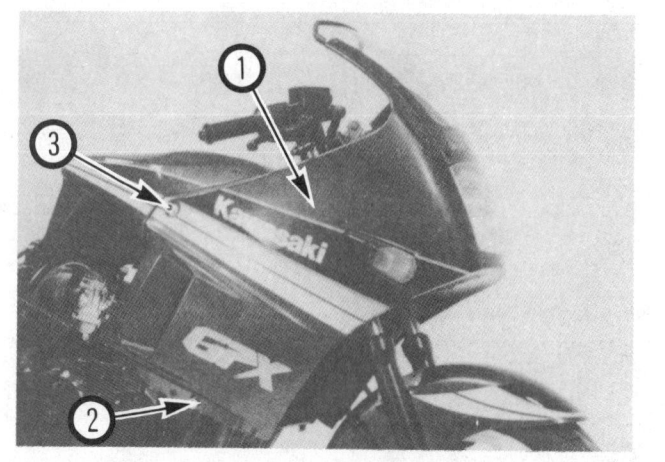

3.6b   On C models, remove the screw and the Allen bolt from each side of the fairing

1 Fairing	3 Allen bolt
2 Screw	

3   Upper fairing and mount – removal and installation

Refer to illustrations 3.4, 3.5, 3.6a, 3.6b and 3.7

Upper fairing

1   Set the bike on its centerstand.
2   If you're working on a C model, remove the seat, the knee grip covers (see Section 7) and the lower fairing (see Section 2).
3   If you're working on an A or B model, remove the fairing inner panels **(see illustration 1.1a)**.
4   On A and B models, unplug the headlight electrical connector **(see illustration)**.
5   Remove the rear view mirrors **(see illustration)**.
6   Remove the side mounting screws/bolts **(see illustrations)**. If you're working on a C model, be sure to support the fairing as this is done.
7   On A and B models, support the fairing and remove the two front mounting bolts **(see illustration)**.
8   Carefully pull the fairing forward and off the bike. It may be necessary to spread the lower sides of the fairing to clear the frame as you do this. If you're working on a C model, unplug the electrical connector for the headlight.
9   If it is necessary to disassemble the fairing (C models only), refer to illustration 1.1c.
10   Installation is the reverse of removal.

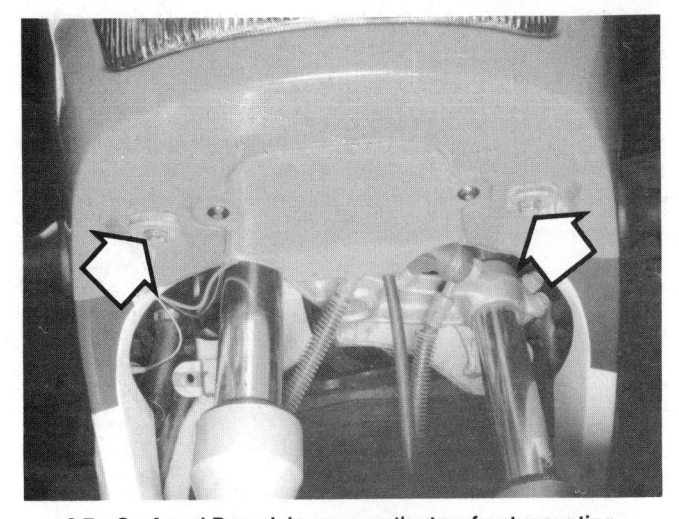

3.7   On A and B models, remove the two front mounting bolts (arrows)

3.14   Unbolt the radiator filler neck from the fairing mount, then remove the right mounting bolt (arrows)

3.15   Location of the fairing mount-to-steering head bolt (arrow)

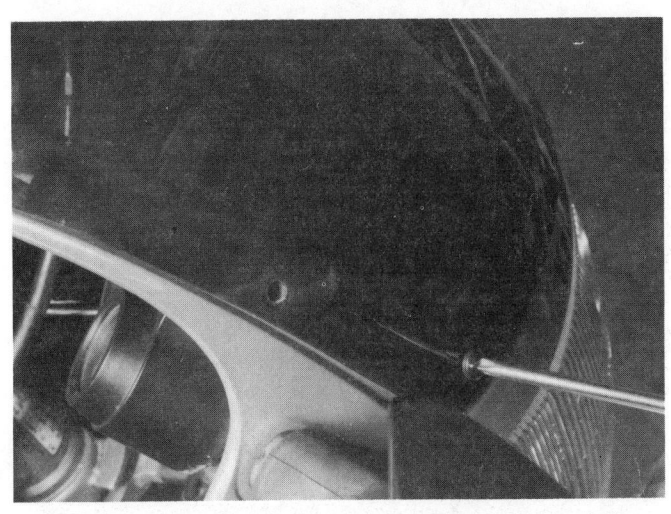

4.1   Remove the windshield screws and carefully detach the windshield from the upper fairing

Mount

11   Remove the upper fairing, if you haven't already done so.
12   Detach the electrical connectors to the instrument cluster, noting how the harnesses are routed.
13   Detach the upper end of the speedometer cable from the speedometer. On C models, remove the coolant reservoir (see Chapter 3).
14   On A and B models, unbolt the radiator filler neck from the mount, then remove the right mounting bolt **(see illustration)**.
15   Remove the mount-to-steering head bolt **(see illustration)**.
16   Remove the left side mounting bolt and detach the mount from the frame. If it is necessary to remove the instrument cluster from the mount, refer to Chapter 9.
17   Installation is the reverse of removal.

---

4   Windshield – removal and installation

Refer to illustration 4.1

1   Remove the screws securing the windshield to the fairing **(see illustration)**.
2   Carefully separate the windshield from the fairing. If it sticks, don't attempt to pry it off – just keep applying steady pressure with your fingers.

3   Installation is the reverse of the removal procedure. Be sure each screw has a plastic washer under its head. Tighten the screws securely, but be careful not to overtighten them, as the windshield might crack.

---

5   Rear view mirrors – removal and installation

Refer to Section 3, Step 5 – removing the rear view mirrors is part of the upper fairing removal procedure

---

6   Fairing stays – removal and installation

Side stays (A models only)

1   Remove the rear mounting screw from each side of the upper fairing **(see illustration 3.6a)**.
2   Remove the screw from each end of the side stay. Remove the stay and separate the boss for the upper fairing mounting bolt from the rubber strip.
3   Installation is the reverse of removal.

Front stay

4   Refer to Chapter 3, Section 8, Step 10 for the front fairing stay removal procedure.

8

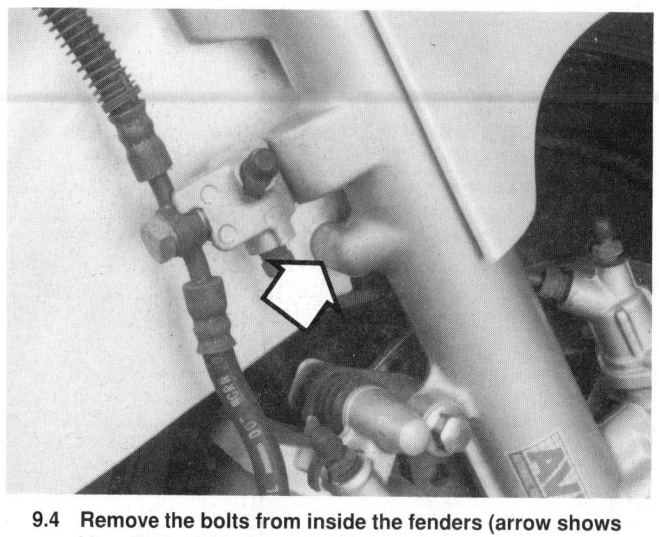

8.2   The side covers are retained by a single screw (arrow) – A model shown, others similar

9.4   Remove the bolts from inside the fenders (arrow shows general location), right above the brake calipers (there's one bolt per side)

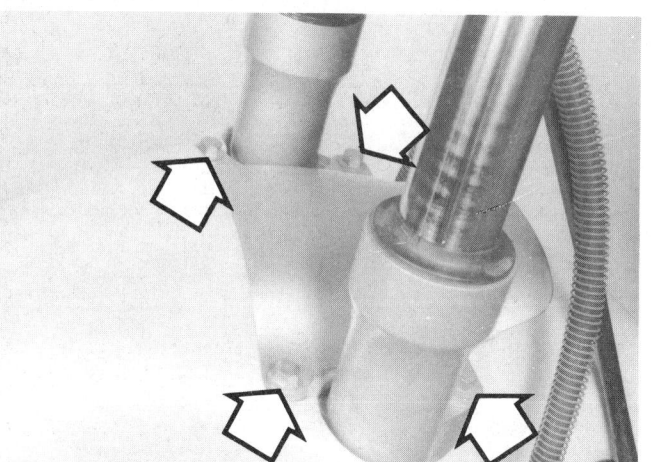

9.5   Remove the four bolts retaining the fork brace (arrows)

7   Knee grip covers (C models only) – removal and installation

1   If you're removing the left side knee grip cover, remove the screw from the fuel tap knob and pull the knob off.
2   Remove the seat.
3   Remove the screw from the rear edge of the knee grip cover **(see illustration 1.1c)**, then carefully pull the cover off. The resistance that will be felt is the lug on the front part of the cover pulling out of its rubber grommet.
4   Installation is the reverse of removal.

8   Side covers – removal and installation

Refer to illustration 8.2
1   Remove the seat.
2   Remove the side cover mounting screw **(see illustration)**.
3   Carefully pull the side cover from the bike. There's a lug that fits into a rubber bushing on the fuel tank, so apply a little extra force there (be careful not to break it off, though).
4   Installation is the reverse of the removal procedure.

9   Front fender – removal and installation

Refer to illustrations 9.4 and 9.5
1   Set the bike on its centerstand.
2   Disconnect the speedometer from the speedometer drive.
3   On C models, cut the guides that secure the brake hoses and ESCS wires to the fender.
4   Remove the bolts from inside the fender **(see illustration)**.
5   Remove the bolts from the fork brace **(see illustration)**. Remove the brace, being careful not to lose the spacers that sit in the front two holes. Remove the fender toward the front.
6   Installation is the reverse of removal. On C models, install new guides for the brake hoses and ESCS wires.

10   Tailpiece and passenger seat – removal and installation

Refer to illustrations 10.2 and 10.4
1   Remove the riders seat, then remove the side covers (see Section 8).
2   Remove the two screws securing the tailpiece to the frame **(see illustration)**.

10.2   The tailpiece is secured to the frame by a screw on each side

10.4   The passenger seat is retained to the frame by four
bolts (arrows)

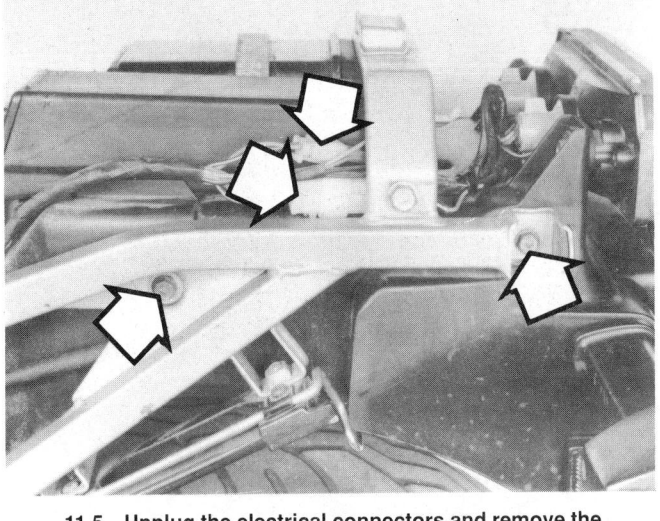

11.5   Unplug the electrical connectors and remove the
bolts (arrows)

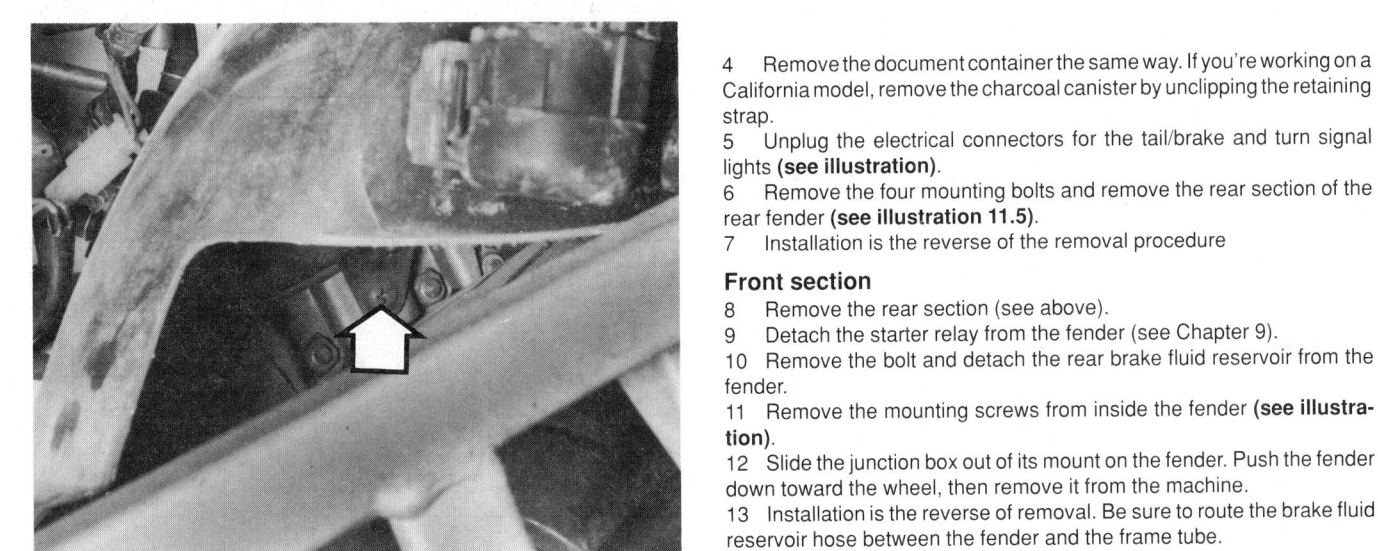

11.11   Location of the mounting screws for the fender front
section (arrow)

3   Slide the tailpiece to the rear to remove it.
4   To remove the passenger seat, remove the four bolts that secure the seat to the frame **(see illustration)**, then lift it off.
5   Installation is the reverse of removal.

---

11   Rear fender – removal and installation

A and B models

Refer to illustrations 11.5 and 11.11

Rear section

1   Set the bike on its centerstand.
2   Remove the riders seat, the tailpiece and the passenger seat (see Section 10).
3   Open the tool compartment and remove the mounting screw. Slide the compartment forward and remove it.

4   Remove the document container the same way. If you're working on a California model, remove the charcoal canister by unclipping the retaining strap.
5   Unplug the electrical connectors for the tail/brake and turn signal lights **(see illustration)**.
6   Remove the four mounting bolts and remove the rear section of the rear fender **(see illustration 11.5)**.
7   Installation is the reverse of the removal procedure

Front section

8   Remove the rear section (see above).
9   Detach the starter relay from the fender (see Chapter 9).
10   Remove the bolt and detach the rear brake fluid reservoir from the fender.
11   Remove the mounting screws from inside the fender **(see illustration)**.
12   Slide the junction box out of its mount on the fender. Push the fender down toward the wheel, then remove it from the machine.
13   Installation is the reverse of removal. Be sure to route the brake fluid reservoir hose between the fender and the frame tube.

C models

Refer to illustration 11.19

Rear section

14   Remove the riders seat and knee grip covers (see Section 7).
15   Remove the fuel tank (see Chapter 4) and side covers (see Section 8).
16   Remove the tailpiece and passenger seat (see Section 10).
17   Remove the tool kit compartment and document container by removing the screw inside the door of each one. If you're working on a California model, remove the charcoal canister.
18   Unplug the electrical connectors for the tail/brake, turn signal and license plate lights.
19   Remove the mounting bolts and remove the rear fender section **(see illustration)**.
20   Installation is the reverse of removal.

Front section

21   Remove the rear section (see above).
22   Detach the turn signal relay and the starter relay from the left side of the fender (see Chapter 9).
23   Detach the brake fluid reservoir and the air valve mounting bracket from the right side of the fender.
24   Remove the battery (see Chapter 9).

8

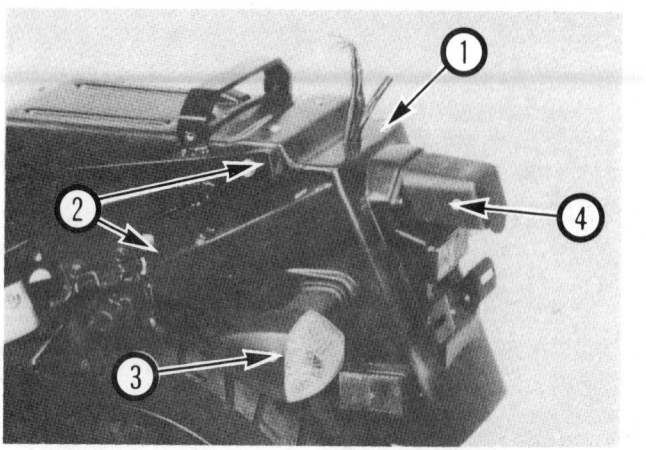

11.19   Fender rear section mounting details (C models)

1	*Fender rear section*	*3*	*Turn signal*
2	*Mounting bolts*	*4*	*License plate light*

25   Slide the junction box out of its mount (see Chapter 9).
26   Detach any breather hoses that might interfere with fender removal.
27   Slide the fender to the rear and remove it.
28   Installation is the reverse of the removal procedure.

Chapter 9 Electrical system

Refer to Chapter 10 for information on the ZX750F model

Contents

Specifications

Battery

Type	12 volt, 12Ah (amp hours)
Specific gravity	
Fully charged	1.280 at 68-degrees F
Minimum	1.260 at 68-degrees F

Charging system

Charging voltage	14.5 ± 0.5 volts at 4000 rpm
Stator coil resistance	0.1 to 0.8 ohms

Starter motor

Brush length	
Standard	15/32 in (12 mm)
Minimum	15/64 in (6 mm)
Commutator diameter	
Standard	1-7/64 in (28 mm)
Minimum	1-1/16 in (27 mm)

Circuit fuse ratings

Taillight	10A
Accessory	10A
Headlight relay	10A
Main fuse	30A

Torque specifications

Alternator rotor bolt	110 ft-lbs
Alternator stator bolts	104 in-lbs
Alternator cover bolts	43 in-lbs
Neutral switch	132 in-lbs

1   General information

The machines covered by this manual are equipped with a 12-volt electrical system. The components include a crankshaft mounted permanent magnet alternator and a solid state voltage regulator/rectifier unit.

The regulator maintains the charging system output within the specified range to prevent overcharging. The rectifier converts the AC output of the alternator to DC current to power the lights and other components and to charge the battery.

The alternator consists of a multi-coil stator (bolted to the left-hand engine case) and a permanent magnet rotor.

An electric starter mounted to the engine case behind the bank of the cylinders is standard equipment. The starting system includes the motor, the battery, the solenoid, the starter circuit relay (part of the junction box) and the various wires and switches. If the engine STOP switch and the main key switch are both in the On position, the circuit relay allows the starter motor to operate only if the transmission is in Neutral (Neutral switch on) or the clutch lever is pulled to the handlebar (clutch switch on) and the sidestand is up (sidestand switch on).

Note: *Keep in mind that electrical parts, once purchased, can't be returned. To avoid unnecessary expense, make very sure the faulty component has been positively identified before buying a replacement part.*

2   Electrical troubleshooting

A typical electrical circuit consists of an electrical component, the switches, relays, etc. related to that component and the wiring and connectors that hook the component to both the battery and the frame. To aid in locating a problem in any electrical circuit, complete wiring diagrams of each model are included at the end of this Chapter.

Before tackling any troublesome electrical circuit, first study the appropriate diagrams thoroughly to get a complete picture of what makes up that individual circuit. Trouble spots, for instance, can often be narrowed down by noting if other components related to that circuit are operating properly or not. If several components or circuits fail at one time, chances are the fault lies in the fuse or ground connection, as several circuits often are routed through the same fuse and ground connections.

Electrical problems often stem from simple causes, such as loose or corroded connections or a blown fuse. Prior to any electrical troubleshooting, always visually check the condition of the fuse, wires and connections in the problem circuit.

If testing instruments are going to be utilized, use the diagrams to plan where you will make the necessary connections in order to accurately pinpoint the trouble spot.

The basic tools needed for electrical troubleshooting include a test light or voltmeter, a continuity tester (which includes a bulb, battery and set of test leads) and a jumper wire, preferably with a circuit breaker incorporated, which can be used to bypass electrical components. Specific checks described later in this Chapter may also require an ammeter or ohmmeter.

Voltage checks should be performed if a circuit is not functioning properly. Connect one lead of a test light or voltmeter to either the negative battery terminal or a known good ground. Connect the other lead to a connector in the circuit being tested, preferably nearest to the battery or fuse. If the bulb lights, voltage is reaching that point, which means the part of the circuit between that connector and the battery is problem-free. Continue checking the remainder of the circuit in the same manner. When you reach a point where no voltage is present, the problem lies between there and the last good test point. Most of the time the problem is due to a loose connection. Keep in mind that some circuits only receive voltage when the ignition key is in the On position.

One method of finding short circuits is to remove the fuse and connect a test light or voltmeter in its place to the fuse terminals. There should be no load in the circuit. Move the wiring harness from side-to-side while watching the test light. If the bulb lights, there is a short to ground somewhere in that area, probably where insulation has rubbed off a wire. The same test can be performed on other components in the circuit, including the switch.

A ground check should be done to see if a component is grounded properly. Disconnect the battery and connect one lead of a self-powered test light (such as a continuity tester) to a known good ground. Connect the other lead to the wire or ground connection being tested. If the bulb lights, the ground is good. If the bulb does not light, the ground is not good.

A continuity check is performed to see if a circuit, section of circuit or individual component is capable of passing electricity through it. Disconnect the battery and connect one lead of a self-powered test light (such as a continuity tester) to one end of the circuit being tested and the other lead to the other end of the circuit. If the bulb lights, there is continuity, which means the circuit is passing electricity through it properly. Switches can be checked in the same way.

Remember that all electrical circuits are designed to conduct electricity from the battery, through the wires, switches, relays, etc. to the electrical component (light bulb, motor, etc.). From there it is directed to the frame (ground) where it is passed back to the battery. Electrical problems are basically an interruption in the flow of electricity from the battery or back to it.

3   Battery – inspection and maintenance

1   Most battery damage is caused by heat, vibration, and/or low electrolyte levels, so keep the battery securely mounted, check the electrolyte level frequently and make sure the charging system is functioning properly.
2   Refer to Chapter 1 for electrolyte level and specific gravity checking procedures.
3   Check around the base inside of the battery for sediment, which is the result of sulfation caused by low electrolyte levels. These deposits will cause internal short circuits, which can quickly discharge the battery. Look for cracks in the case and replace the battery if either of these conditions is found.
4   Check the battery terminals and cable ends for tightness and corrosion. If corrosion is evident, remove the cables from the battery and clean the terminals and cable ends with a wire brush or knife and emery paper. Reconnect the cables and apply a thin coat of petroleum jelly to the connections to slow further corrosion.
5   The battery case should be kept clean to prevent current leakage, which can discharge the battery over a period of time (especially when it sits unused). Wash the outside of the case with a solution of baking soda and water. Do not get any baking soda solution in the battery cells. Rinse the battery thoroughly, then dry it.
6   If acid has been spilled on the frame or battery box, neutralize it with the baking soda and water solution, dry it thoroughly, then touch up any damaged paint. Make sure the battery vent tube is directed away from the frame and is not kinked or pinched.
7   If the motorcycle sits unused for long periods of time, disconnect the cables from the battery terminals. Refer to Section 4 and charge the battery approximately once every month.

4   Battery – charging

1   If the machine sits idle for extended periods or if the charging system malfunctions, the battery can be charged from an external source.
2   To properly charge the battery, you will need a charger of the correct rating, a hydrometer, a clean rag and a syringe for adding distilled water to the battery cells.
3   The maximum charging rate for any battery is 1/10 of the rated amp/hour capacity. As an example, the maximum charging rate for the 14 amp/hour battery would be 1.4 amps. If the battery is charged at a higher rate, it could be damaged.
4   Do not allow the battery to be subjected to a so-called quick charge (high rate of charge over a short period of time) unless you are prepared to buy a new battery.

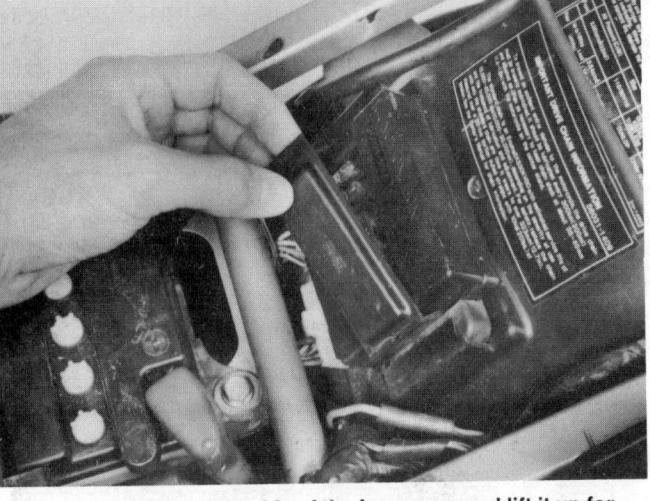

5.1   Unlatch the right side of the fuse cover and lift it up for access to the fuses

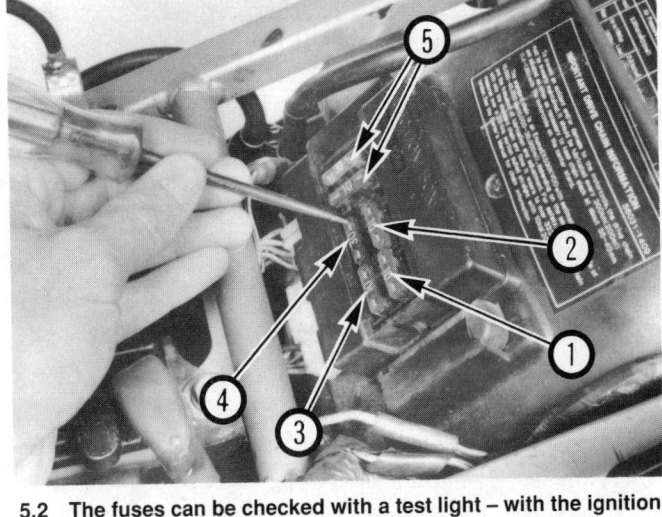

5.2   The fuses can be checked with a test light – with the ignition On, each fuse should have voltage available on both sides

1	Taillight fuse (10A)	4	Main fuse (30A)
2	Accessory fuse (10A)	5	Spare fuses (10A and 30A)
3	Headlight relay fuse (10A)		

5   When charging the battery, always remove it from the machine and be sure to check the electrolyte level before hooking up the charger. Add distilled water to any cells that are low.

6   Loosen the cell caps, hook up the battery charger leads (red to positive, black to negative), cover the top of the battery with a clean rag, then, and only then, plug in the battery charger. **Warning:** *Remember, the gas escaping from a charging battery is explosive, so keep open flames and sparks well away from the area. Also, the electrolyte is extremely corrosive and will damage anything it comes in contact with.*

7   Allow the battery to charge until the specific gravity is as specified (refer to Chapter 1 for specific gravity checking procedures). The charger must be unplugged and disconnected from the battery when making specific gravity checks. If the battery overheats or gases excessively, the charging rate is too high. Either disconnect the charger or lower the charging rate to prevent damage to the battery.

8   If one or more of the cells do not show an increase in specific gravity after a long slow charge, or if the battery as a whole does not seem to want to take a charge, it is time for a new battery.

9   When the battery is fully charged, unplug the charger first, then disconnect the leads from the battery. Install the cell caps and wipe any electrolyte off the outside of the battery case.

5   Fuses – check and replacement

Refer to illustrations 5.1, 5.2 and 5.3

1   The fuses are located under the seat, on the junction box **(see illustration)**. The fuses are protected by a plastic cover, which snaps into place. It contains fuses (and spares) which protect the main, headlight, taillight and accessory circuit wiring and components from damage caused by short circuits.

2   If you have a test light, the fuses can be checked without removing them. Turn the ignition to the On position, connect one end of the test light to a good ground, then probe each terminal on top of the fuse **(see illustration)**. If the fuse is good, there will be voltage available at both terminals. If the fuse is blown, there will only be voltage present at one of the terminals.

3   The fuses can be removed and checked visually. If you can't pull the fuse out with your fingertips, use a pair of needle-nose pliers. A blown fuse is easily identified by a break in the element **(see illustration)**.

4   If a fuse blows, be sure to check the wiring harnesses very carefully for evidence of a short circuit. Look for bare wires and chafed, melted or burned insulation. If a fuse is replaced before the cause is located, the new fuse will blow immediately.

5   Never, under any circumstances, use a higher rated fuse or bridge the fuse block terminals, as damage to the electrical system could result.

| Normal | Failed |

5.3   A blown fuse can be identified by a broken element – be sure to replace a blown fuse with one of the same amperage rating

6   Occasionally a fuse will blow or cause an open circuit for no obvious reason. Corrosion of the fuse ends and fuse block terminals may occur and cause poor fuse contact. If this happens, remove the corrosion with a wire brush or emery paper, then spray the fuse end and terminals with electrical contact cleaner.

6   Junction box – check

1   Aside from serving as the fuse block, the junction box also houses three relays – the fan relay, the starter circuit relay (not the starter solenoid) and the headlight relay. None of these relays are replaceable individually. If one of them fails, the junction box must be replaced.

2   In addition to the relay checks, the fuse circuits and diode circuits should be checked also, to rule out the possibility of an open circuit condition or blown diode within the junction block as the cause of an electrical problem. Schematics of the junction box can be found in the Wiring diagrams at the end of this Chapter.

Fuse circuit check

Refer to illustration 6.4

3   Remove the junction box by sliding it out of its holder. Unplug the electrical connectors from the box.

9

Fuse Circuit Inspection

Meter Connection	Meter Reading (Ω)
1 — 2	0
1 — 3A	0
6 — 7	0
6 — 17	0
1 — 7	∞
3A — 8	∞
8 — 17	∞

6.4   Using an ohmmeter, check the conductivity across the indicated pairs of terminals

	Meter Connection	Battery Connection + −	Meter Reading (Ω)
Fan	2 — 5	2 — 4	0
Headlight	*7 — 8	9 — 13	0
Starter	11 — 13	11 — 12	0

6.10b   Use jumper wires to connect battery voltage to the indicated terminals, then check the conductivity across the corresponding terminals – the resistance should be zero

US and Canadian models only

4   If the terminals are dirty or bent, clean and straighten them. Using the accompanying table as a guide, check the continuity across the indicated terminals with an ohmmeter – some should have no resistance and others should have infinite resistance **(see illustration)**.
5   If the resistance values are not as specified, replace the junction box.

Diode circuit check

6   Remove the junction box by sliding it out of its holder. Unplug the electrical connectors from the box.
7   Using an ohmmeter, check the resistance across the following pairs of terminals, then write down the readings.
   Here are the terminal pairs to be checked:
   13 and 8 (US and Canadian models only)
   13 and 9 (US and Canadian models only)
   12 and 14
   15 and 14
   16 and 14
8   Now, reverse the ohmmeter leads and check the resistances again, writing down the readings. The resistances should be low in one direction and more than ten times as much in the other direction. If the readings for any pair of terminals are low or high in both directions, a diode is defective and the junction box must be replaced.

Relay checks

Refer to illustrations 6.10a and 6.10b

9   Remove the junction box by sliding it out of its holder. Unplug the electrical connectors from the box.
10   Using an ohmmeter, check the conductivity across the terminals indicated in the accompanying table **(see illustration)**. Then, energize each relay by applying battery voltage across the indicated terminals and check the conductivity across the corresponding terminals shown on the table **(see illustration)**.
11   If the junction box fails any of these tests, it must be replaced.

	Meter Connection	Meter Reading (Ω)
Fan Relay	2 — 5	∞
	4 — 5	∞
Headlight Relay	*7 — 8	∞
	*7 — 13	∞
Starter Relay	11 — 13	∞
	12 — 13	∞

6.10a   With the junction box unplugged, there should be infinite resistance between the indicated terminals

US and Canadian models only

7   Lighting system – check

1   The battery provides power for operation of the headlight, taillight, brake light, license plate light and instrument cluster lights. If none of the lights operate, always check battery voltage before proceeding. Low battery voltage indicates either a faulty battery, low battery electrolyte level or a defective charging system. Refer to Chapter 1 for battery checks and Section 30 and 31 for charging system tests. Also, check the condition of the fuses and replace any blown fuses with new ones.

Headlight

Refer to illustrations 7.2 and 7.3

2   If the headlight is out with the engine running (US and Canadian models) or with the lighting switch in the On position (UK models), check the fuse first with the key On (see Section 5), then unplug the electrical connector for the headlight **(see illustration)** and use jumper wires to connect the bulb directly to the battery terminals. If the light comes on, the problem lies in the wiring or one of the switches in the circuit. Refer to Sections 20 and 21 for the switch testing procedures, and also the wiring diagrams at the end of this Chapter.
3   US and Canadian models use an additional relay in the system, called the reserve lighting device. On these models, the headlight doesn't come on when the ignition switch is first turned on, but comes on when the starter button is pressed and stays on until the ignition is turned off. The light will go out whenever the starter is operated after the engine has stalled (this prevents excessive strain on the battery). The reserve lighting device is located behind the steering head, mounted to a bracket that is bolted to the frame **(see illustration)**.

Taillight/license plate light

4   If the taillight fails to work, check the bulbs and the bulb terminals first, then check for battery voltage at the red wire in the taillight. If voltage is present, check the ground circuit for an open or poor connection.
5   If no voltage is indicated, check the wiring between the taillight and the main (key) switch, then check the switch.

Brake light

6   See Section 14 for the brake light circuit checking procedure.

Neutral indicator light

7   If the neutral light fails to operate when the transmission is in Neutral, check the fuses and the bulb (see Section 18 for bulb removal procedures). If the bulb and fuses are in good condition, check for battery voltage at the green wire attached to the neutral switch on the left side of the engine. If battery voltage is present, refer to Section 23 for the neutral switch check and replacement procedures.
8   If no voltage is indicated, check the brown wire between the junction box and the bulb, and the light green wire between the junction box and the switch and between the switch and the bulb for open circuits and poor connections.

7.2   Unplug the headlight electrical connector and apply battery voltage to the red/yellow wire and ground the black/yellow wire – the light should come on

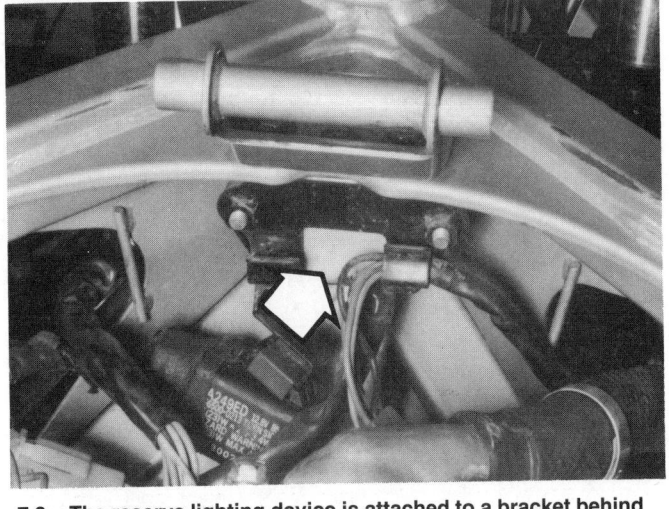

7.3   The reserve lighting device is attached to a bracket behind the steering head (arrow)

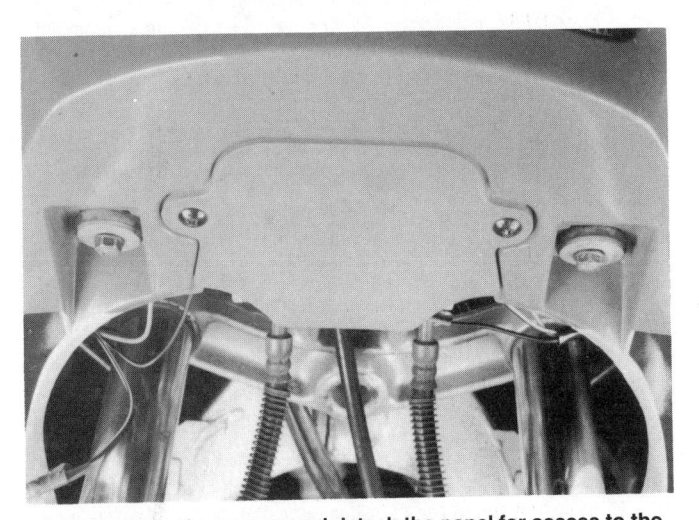

8.1   Remove the screws and detach the panel for access to the headlight bulb (A and B models)

Oil pressure warning light

9   See Section 19 for the oil pressure warning light circuit check.

8   Headlight bulb – replacement

Refer to illustrations 8.1, 8.2 and 8.3

1   On A and B models, remove the access cover from the underside of the upper fairing **(see illustration)**. On C models, remove the headlight lower cover screws and remove the cover (the piece that joins the two halves of the upper fairing together).

2   Unplug the electrical connector from the headlight, then remove the dust cover **(see illustration)**.

3   Lift up the retaining clip and swing it out of the way **(see illustration)**. Remove the bulb holder.

4   When installing the new bulb, reverse the removal procedure. Be sure not to touch the bulb with your fingers – oil from your skin will cause the bulb to overheat and fail prematurely. If you do touch the bulb, wipe it off with a clean rag dampened with rubbing alcohol.

5   The parking (or city) light on UK models is positioned in the base of the headlight unit. Peel back the rubber dust cover and pull the bulbholder out of the grommet in the headlight. Twist the bulb counterclockwise to release it.

8.2   The dust cover can be removed after the electrical connector is unplugged (fairing removed for clarity)

8.3   Unsnap the headlight retaining clip, then pull the bulb holder out of the headlight housing (fairing removed for clarity)

9

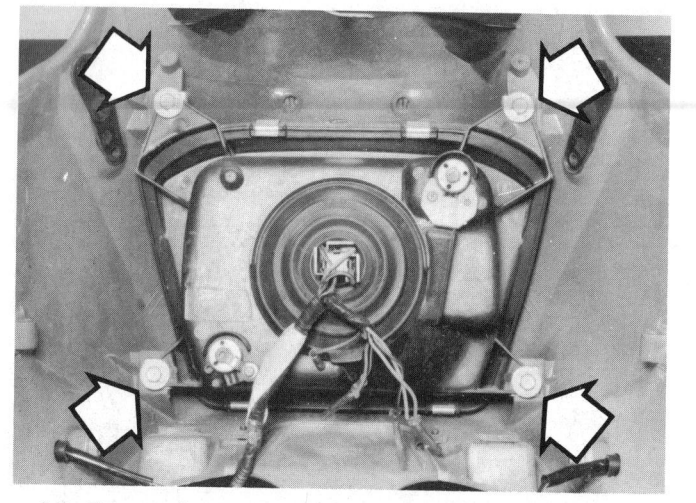

9.2   Remove the screws (arrows) and separate the headlight assembly from the fairing

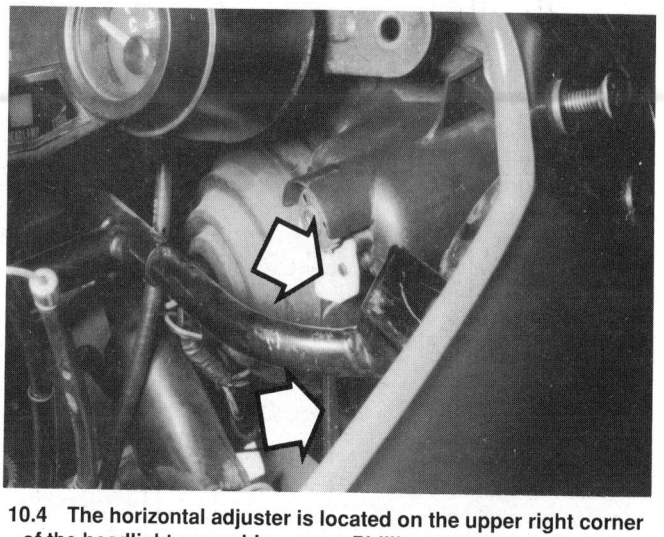

10.4   The horizontal adjuster is located on the upper right corner of the headlight assembly – use a Phillips screwdriver (arrow), inserted from below

10.5   The vertical adjuster is located on the lower left corner of the headlight housing

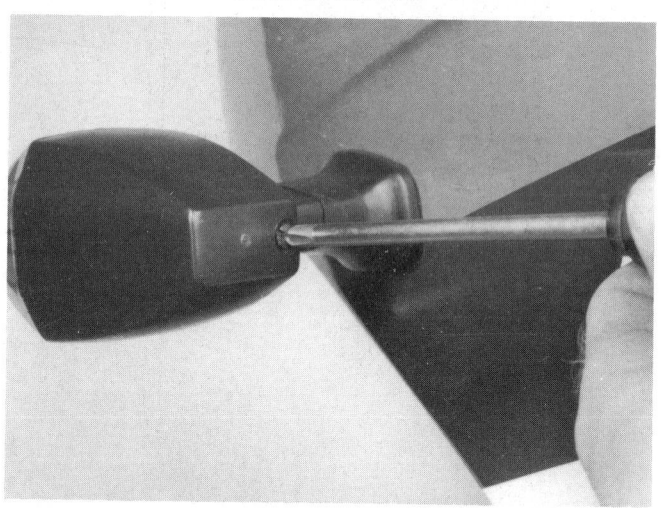
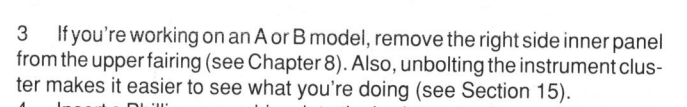

11.2   Remove the screw securing the turn signal lens/reflector assembly to the turn signal housing, then pull the lens/reflector assembly out

9   Headlight assembly – removal and installation

Refer to illustration 9.2

1   Remove the upper fairing (see Chapter 8).
2   Remove the screws holding the headlight assembly to the fairing **(see illustration)**. Separate the headlight assembly from the fairing.
3   Installation is the reverse of removal. Be sure to adjust the headlight aim (see Section 10).

10   Headlight aim – check and adjustment

Refer to illustrations 10.4 and 10.5

1   An improperly adjusted headlight may cause problems for oncoming traffic or provide poor, unsafe illumination of the road ahead. Before adjusting the headlight, be sure to consult with local traffic laws and regulations.
2   The headlight beam can be adjusted both vertically and horizontally. Before performing the adjustment, make sure the fuel tank has at least a half tank of gas, and have an assistant sit on the seat.

3   If you're working on an A or B model, remove the right side inner panel from the upper fairing (see Chapter 8). Also, unbolting the instrument cluster makes it easier to see what you're doing (see Section 15).
4   Insert a Phillips screwdriver into the horizontal adjuster guide **(see illustration)**, then turn the adjuster as necessary to center the beam.
5   To adjust the vertical position of the beam, insert the screwdriver into the vertical adjuster guide **(see illustration)** and turn the adjuster as necessary to raise or lower the beam.
6   Install the right side inner panel into the upper fairing, if you're working on an A or B model. Install the instrument cluster if it was removed.

11   Turn signal and taillight bulbs – replacement

Turn signal bulbs

Refer to illustrations 11.2 and 11.3

1   Bulb replacement for the turn signals is the same for the front and rear.
2   Remove the screw that holds the lens/reflector assembly to the turn signal housing **(see illustration)**. Pull out the lens/reflector assembly.
3   Remove the screws securing the lens to the reflector **(see illustration)**.

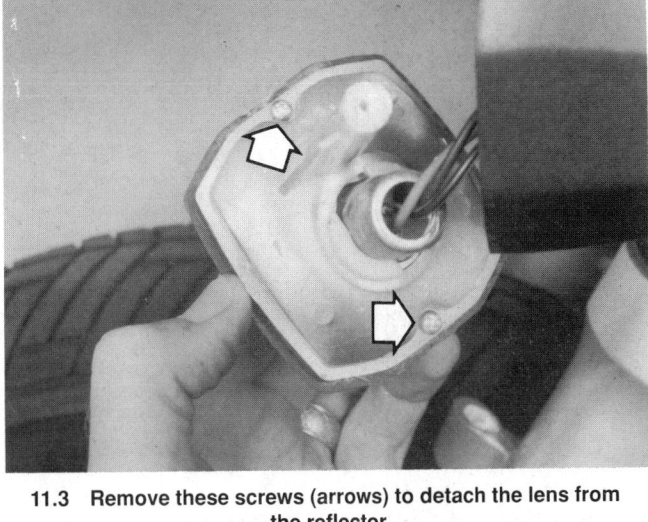

11.3   Remove these screws (arrows) to detach the lens from the reflector

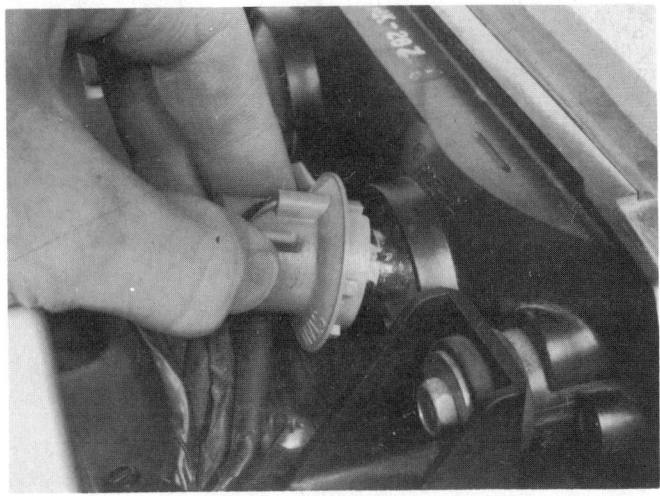

11.8   Turn the bulb holder counterclockwise until it stops, then pull it out of the taillight housing

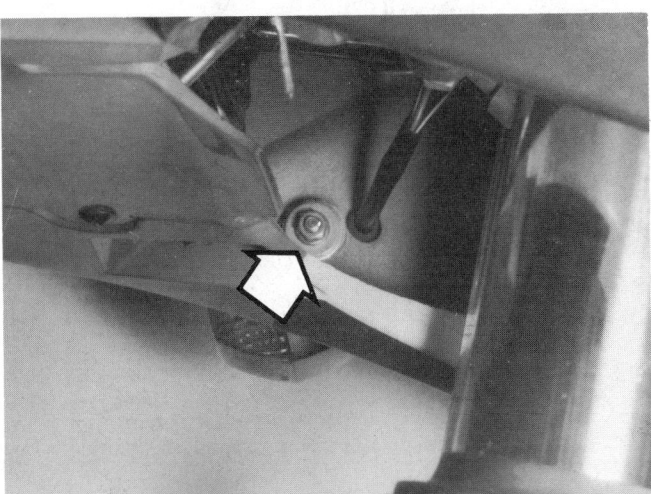

12.3a   Front turn signal nut (arrow)

12.3b   Rear turn signal nut (arrow)

4   Push the bulb in and turn it counterclockwise to remove it. Check the socket terminals for corrosion and clean them if necessary. Line up the pins on the new bulb with the slots in the socket, push in and turn the bulb clockwise until it locks in place. **Note:** *The pins on the bulb are offset so it can only be installed one way. It is a good idea to use a paper towel or dry cloth when handling the new bulb to prevent injury if the bulb should break and to increase bulb life.*

5   Position the lens on the reflector and install the screws. Be careful not to overtighten them.

6   Place the lens/reflector assembly into the housing and install the screw, tightening it securely.

Taillight bulbs

Refer to illustration 11.8

7   To remove the taillight bulbs, remove the tail section and the passenger seat (see Chapter 8).

8   Turn the bulb holders counterclockwise **(see illustration)** until they stop, then pull straight out to remove them from the taillight housing. The bulbs can be removed from the holders by turning them counterclockwise and pulling straight out.

9   Check the socket terminals for corrosion and clean them if necessary. Line up the pins on the new bulb with the slots in the socket, push in and turn the bulb clockwise until it locks in place. **Note:** *The pins on the bulb are offset so it can only be installed one way. It is a good idea to use a paper towel or dry cloth when handling the new bulb to prevent injury if the bulb*

should break and to increase bulb life.

10   Make sure the rubber gaskets are in place and in good condition, then line up the tabs on the holder with the slots in the housing and push the holder into the mounting hole. Turn it clockwise until it stops to lock it in place. **Note:** *The tabs and slots are two different sizes so the holders can only be installed one way.*

11   Reinstall the seat and the tail section.

---

12   Turn signal assemblies – removal and installation

Refer to illustrations 12.3a and 12.3b

1   The turn signal assemblies can be removed individually in the event of damage or failure.

2   To remove a turn signal assembly, first follow the wiring harness from the turn signal to its electrical connectors. Mark the wires with pieces of numbered tape then unplug the electrical connectors.

3   Unscrew the nut that secures the turn signal to the fairing or rear fender **(see illustrations)**. If you're removing a rear turn signal, don't lose the spring plate.

4   Detach the turn signal from the fairing or fender. If you're installing a new turn signal, separate the stalk trim from the old stalk and transfer it to the new one.

5   Installation is the reverse of the removal procedure.

13.3   Location of the turn signal flasher (arrow)

14.6   The brake light switch mounted on the brake lever is retained by a screw

13   Turn signal circuit – check

Refer to illustration 13.3

1   The battery provides power for operation of the signal lights, so if they do not operate, always check the battery voltage and specific gravity first. Low battery voltage indicates either a faulty battery, low electrolyte level or a defective charging system. Refer to Chapter 1 for battery checks and Sections 30 and 31 for charging system tests. Also, check the fuses (see Section 5).

2   Most turn signal problems are the result of a burned out bulb or corroded socket. This is especially true when the turn signals function properly in one direction, but fail to flash in the other direction. Check the bulbs and the sockets (see Section 11).

3   If the bulbs and sockets check out okay, check for power at the brown wire to the turn signal flasher **(see illustration)** with the ignition On. If there's no power at the brown wire, check the junction box (see Section 6).

4   If the junction box is okay, check the wiring between the turn signal flasher and the turn signal lights (see the wiring diagrams at the end of this Chapter).

5   If the wiring checks out okay, replace the turn signal flasher.

14   Brake light switches – check and replacement

Refer to illustration 14.6, 14.9 and 14.10

Circuit check

1   Before checking any electrical circuit, check the fuses (see Section 5).

2   Using a test light connected to a good ground, check for voltage to the brown wire at the brake light switch. If there's no voltage present, check the brown wire between the switch and the junction box (see the wiring diagrams at the end of this Chapter).

3   If voltage is available, touch the probe of the test light to the other terminal of the switch, then pull the brake lever or depress the brake pedal – if the test light doesn't light up, replace the switch.

4   If the test light does light, check the wiring between the switch and the brake lights (see the wiring diagrams at the end of this Chapter).

Switch replacement

Brake lever switch

5   Unplug the electrical connectors from the switch.

6   Remove the mounting screw **(see illustration)** and detach the switch from the brake lever bracket/front master cylinder.

7   Installation is the reverse of the removal procedure. The brake lever switch isn't adjustable.

Brake pedal switch

8   Unplug the electrical connector in the switch harness.

9   Disconnect the spring from the brake pedal spring **(see illustration)**.

10   Loosen the adjuster nut **(see illustration)** and unscrew the switch.

11   Install the switch by reversing the removal procedure, then adjust the switch by following the procedure described in Chapter 1, Section 6.

15   Instrument cluster – removal and installation

Refer to illustrations 15.2 and 15.3

1   If you're working on a C model, remove the lower and upper fairings (see Chapter 8). This will also make removal of the instrument cluster easier on A and B models, although it isn't absolutely necessary.

2   Detach the speedometer cable from the speedometer and unplug the electrical connectors from the cluster harness **(see illustration)**.

3   Remove the instrument cluster mounting bolts **(see illustration)** and detach the cluster from the upper fairing mount.

4   Installation is the reverse of the removal procedure.

16   Meters and gauges – check and replacement

Refer to illustrations 16.4, 16.5 and 16.6

Fuel gauge

1   To check the operation of the fuel gauge, unplug the electrical connector from the fuel level sending unit (see Chapter 4, Fuel tank – removal and installation).

2   Turn the ignition switch to the On position. Using a jumper wire, ground the female sending unit wire (on the wiring harness side – not the wires that lead back to the fuel tank). If the fuel level gauge is working properly, the needle will swing past the full mark on the gauge. **Caution:** *Don't leave the wire grounded longer than necessary to perform this check. If you do, the gauge could be damaged. With the wire disconnected, the needle should fall to the empty mark.*

3   If the gauge doesn't respond as described, either the wiring is defective or the gauge itself is malfunctioning. If the gauge does pass the above test, the fuel level sensor is defective (see Section 17).

4   If it's necessary to replace the gauge, remove the instrument cluster (see Section 15). Remove the fasteners that secure the cluster mounting bracket to the cluster **(see illustration)** and detach the bracket.

5   Remove the three screws that secure the instrument cluster cover **(see illustration)**. Detach the cover. **Caution:** *Always store the cluster with the gauges facing up or in a horizontal position – otherwise, the unit could be damaged.*

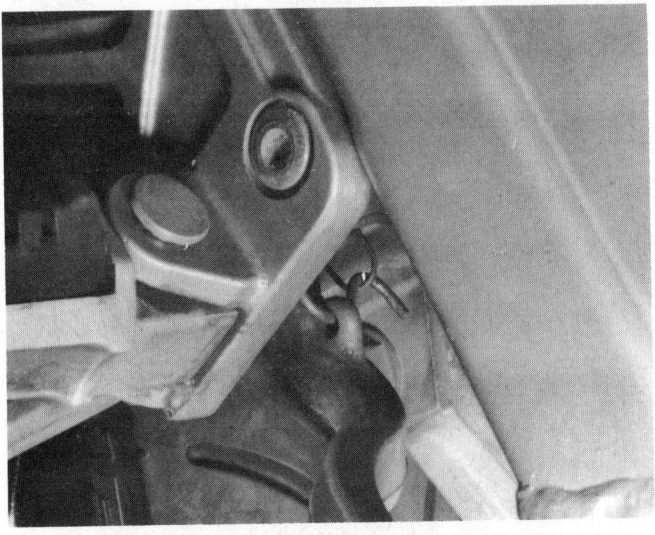

14.9 Unhook the spring from the brake pedal spring . . .

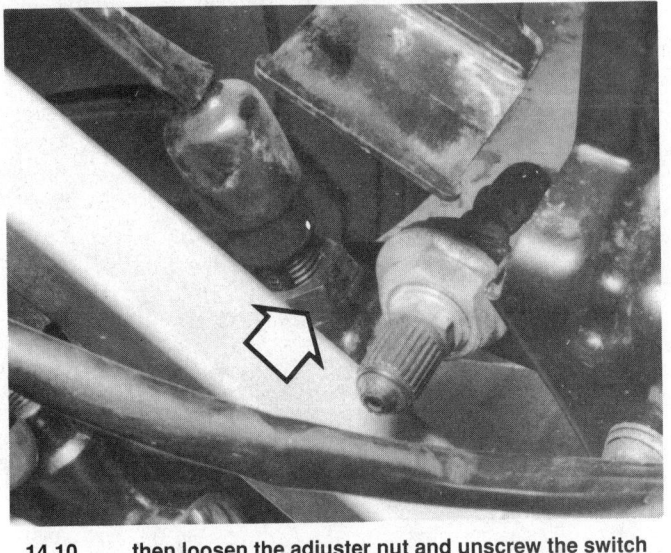

14.10 . . . then loosen the adjuster nut and unscrew the switch

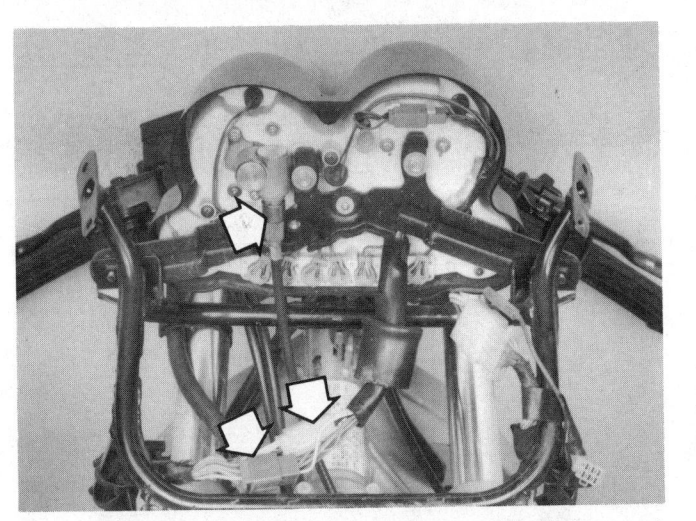

15.2 Unplug the electrical connectors in the cluster harness and unscrew the speedometer cable end from the speedometer (arrows) (fairing removed for clarity)

15.3 The instrument cluster is retained by two bolts (arrows)

16.4 The instrument cluster mounting bracket is secured by two nuts and a screw (arrows) on A and B models (on C models it's retained by three nuts)

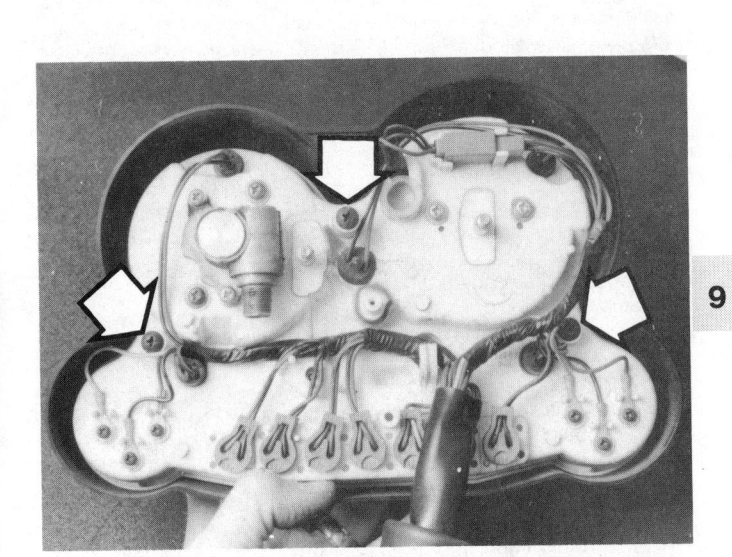

16.5 To remove the cover from the instrument cluster, remove these three screws and carefully lift the cover off

9

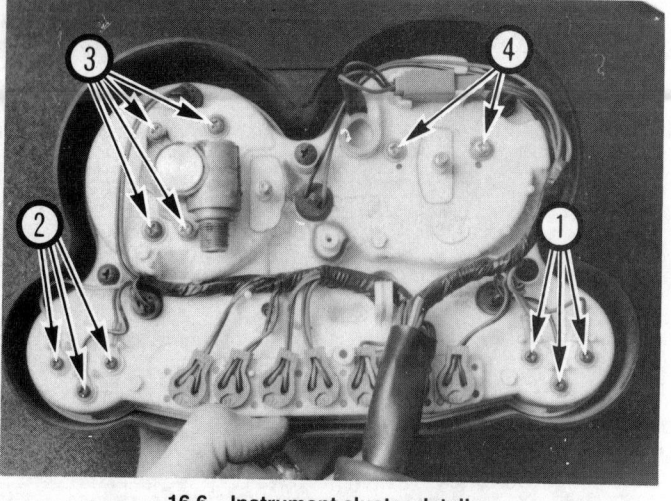

16.6   Instrument cluster details

1	*Fuel gauge screws*	3	*Speedometer screws*
2	*Temperature gauge screws*	4	*Tachometer screws*

6   Mark the positions of the wires and remove the small screws that secure the gauge to the cluster housing **(see illustration)**.

7   Detach the gauge from the housing, being careful not to disturb the other components.

8   Installation is the reverse of the removal procedure.

Temperature gauge

9   Refer to Chapter 3 for the temperature gauge checking procedure.

10   To replace the gauge, follow steps 4 through 8.

Tachometer and speedometer

11   Special instruments are required to properly check the operation of these meters. Take the instrument cluster to a Kawasaki dealer service department or other qualified repair shop for diagnosis.

12   The replacement procedure for either of these meters is essentially the same as the gauge replacement procedure. Follow Steps 4 through 8.

---

17   Fuel level sensor – check and replacement

Refer to illustration 17.3

Warning: *Gasoline is extremely flammable, so take extra precautions when you work on any part of the fuel system. Don't smoke or allow open flames or bare light bulbs near the work area, and don't work in a garage where a natural gas-type appliance (such as a water heater or clothes dryer) is present. If you spill any fuel on your skin, rinse it off immediately with soap and water. When you perform any kind of work on the fuel system, wear safety glasses and have a class B type fire extinguisher on hand.*

1   Remove the fuel tank (see Chapter 4). Drain the fuel into an approved fuel container.

2   Unscrew the sending unit fasteners and remove the sending unit from the tank.

3   Using an ohmmeter, measure the resistance across the terminals of the sensor electrical connector. With the float in the full position **(see illustration)**, the resistance should be 4 to 10 ohms (A and B models) and 2 to 8 ohms (C models). With the float in the empty position, the reading should be 90 to 100 ohms.

4   If the sensor fails either test, replace it.

---

18   Instrument and warning light bulbs – replacement

Refer to illustration 18.2

1   Remove the instrument cluster (see Section 15).

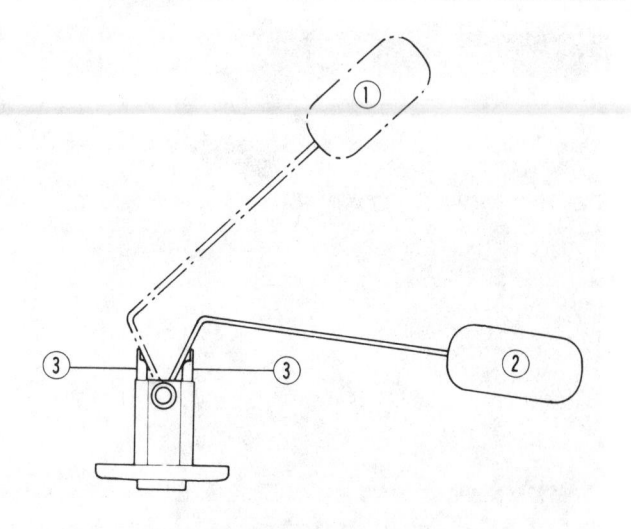

17.3   Fuel level sensor details

1   Full position
2   Empty position
3   Float arm stop

2   To replace a bulb, pull the appropriate rubber socket out of the back of the instrument cluster housing **(see illustration)**, then pull the bulb out of the socket. If the socket contacts are dirty or corroded, they should be scraped clean and sprayed with electrical contact cleaner before new bulbs are installed.

3   Carefully push the new bulb into position, then push the socket into the cluster housing.

---

19   Oil pressure sending unit – check and replacement

Refer to illustration 19.2

1   If the oil pressure warning light fails to operate properly, check the oil level and make sure it is correct.

2   If the oil level is correct, disconnect the wire from the oil pressure sending unit, which is located on the bottom of the engine. Turn the main switch On and ground the end of the wire **(see illustration)**. If the light comes on, the oil pressure sending unit is defective and must be replaced with a new one (only after draining the engine oil).

3   If the light does not come on, check the oil pressure warning light bulb, the wiring between the oil pressure sending unit and the light, and between the light and the junction box (see the wiring diagrams at the end of this Chapter).

4   To replace the sending unit, drain the engine oil (see Chapter 1) and unscrew the sending unit from the case. Wrap the threads of the new sending unit with Teflon tape or apply a thin coat of sealant on them, then screw the unit into its hole, tightening it securely.

5   Fill the crankcase with the recommended type and amount of oil (see Chapter 1) and check for leaks.

---

20   Ignition main (key) switch – check and replacement

Refer to illustrations 20.2 and 20.7

Check

1   Remove the upper fairing (see Chapter 8). This isn't absolutely necessary, but it sure makes access to the switch electrical connector easier.

2   Using an ohmmeter, check the continuity of the terminal pairs indicated in the accompanying table **(see illustration)**. Continuity should exist between the terminals connected by a solid line when the switch is in the indicated position.

3   If the switch fails any of the tests, replace it.

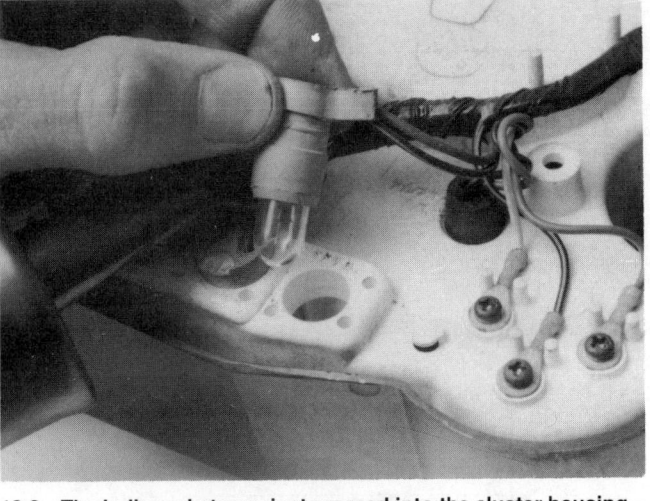

18.2 The bulb sockets are just pressed into the cluster housing – sometimes they're tough to remove and have to be pried out with a small screwdriver

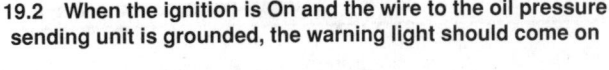

19.2 When the ignition is On and the wire to the oil pressure sending unit is grounded, the warning light should come on

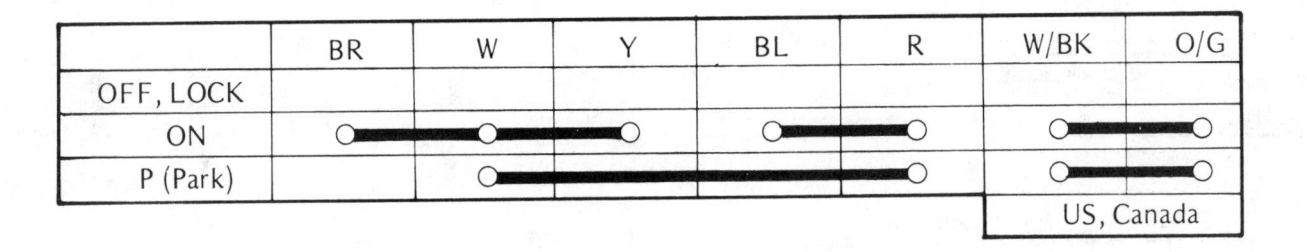

	BR	W	Y	BL	R	W/BK	O/G
OFF, LOCK							
ON	●———●———●			●———●		●———●	
P (Park)		●———————————●				●———●	
						US, Canada	

20.2 Check the continuity of the ignition switch in the different switch positions across the indicated terminals

Replacement

4   Remove the upper fairing, if you haven't already done so (see Chapter 8).

5   Remove the instrument cluster (see Section 15).

6   Unplug the switch electrical connector.

7   The switch is held to the upper clamp with two shear-head bolts **(see illustration)**. Using a hammer and a sharp punch, knock the shear-head bolts in a counterclockwise direction to unscrew them. If they're too tight and won't turn, carefully drill holes through the centers of the bolts and unscrew them using a screw extractor (E-Z out). If necessary, remove the fairing mount for better access to the bolts. Detach the switch from the upper clamp.

8   Hold the new switch in position and install the new shear-head bolts. Tighten the bolts until the heads break off.

9   The remainder of installation is the reverse of the removal procedure.

21   Handlebar switches – check

Refer to illustration 21.4

1   Generally speaking, the switches are reliable and trouble-free. Most troubles, when they do occur, are caused by dirty or corroded contacts, but wear and breakage of internal parts is a possibility that should not be overlooked. If breakage does occur, the entire switch and related wiring harness will have to be replaced with a new one, since individual parts are not usually available.

2   The switches can be checked for continuity with an ohmmeter or a continuity test light. Always disconnect the battery ground cable, which will prevent the possibility of a short circuit, before making the checks.

20.7 The shear bolts (arrows) must be carefully drilled and removed with a screw extractor or knocked in a counterclockwise direction using a hammer and punch

3   Trace the wiring harness of the switch in question and unplug the electrical connectors.

4   Using the ohmmeter or test light, check for continuity between the terminals of the switch harness with the switch in the various positions **(see illustration)**. Continuity should exist between the terminals connected by a solid line when the switch is in the indicated position.

9

Starter Lockout Switch Connections

	BK/Y	Y/G (BK)	LG (BK/R)
When clutch lever is pulled in	O	O	
When clutch lever is released		O	O

( ): Late Model

Dimmer Switch Connections (US, Canada)

	BL/Y	BL/O	R/Y	R/BK
HI	O			O
HI		O	O	
LO	O		O	
LO		O		O

Engine Stop Switch Connections

	R	Y/R
OFF		
RUN	O	O

Dimmer Switch Connections (Other than US, Canada)

	R/BK	BL/Y	R/Y
HI	O	O	
LO		O	O

Starter Button Connections

	BK (BK/R)	BK (BK/R)
Free		
Push on	O	O

( ): Late Model

Turn Signal Switch Connections

	GY	O	G
R	O	O	
N			
L		O	O

Headlight Switch Connections (Other than US, Canada)

	R/W	R/BL	BL	BL/Y
OFF				
■	O	O		
ON	O	O	O	O

Hazard Switch Connections

	GY	O	G
Off			
On	O	O	O

Front Brake Light Switch Connections

	BR (BK)	BL or BL/R (BK)
When brake lever is pulled in	O	O

( ): Late Model

Passing Button Connections (Other than US, Canada)

	BR	R/BK
Free		
Push on	O	O

Horn Button Connections

	BK/W	BK/Y
Free		
Push on	O	O

21.4 Continuity tables for the handlebar switches

23.1 Mark the relationship of the shift lever to the shift shaft so it can be installed in the same position

23.2 Remove the engine sprocket cover bolts and slide the cover off

23.3 If the switch is working properly, the meter should read 0 ohms when the transmission is in neutral

5   If the continuity check indicates a problem exists, refer to Section 22, disassemble the switch and spray the switch contacts with electrical contact cleaner. If they are accessible, the contacts can be scraped clean with a knife or polished with crocus cloth. If switch components are damaged or broken, it will be obvious when the switch is disassembled.

22   Handlebar switches – removal and installation

1   The handlebar switches are composed of two halves that clamp around the bars. They are easily removed for cleaning or inspection by taking out the clamp screws and pulling the switch halves away from the handlebars.
2   To completely remove the switches, the electrical connectors in the wiring harness should be unplugged. The right side switch must be separated from the throttle cables, also.
3   When installing the switches, make sure the wiring harnesses are properly routed to avoid pinching or stretching the wires.

23   Neutral switch – check and replacement

Refer to illustrations 23.1, 23.2 and 23.3

Check

1   Mark the position of the shift lever to the shift lever shaft **(see illustration)**. Remove the shift lever pinch bolt and slide the lever off the shaft.
2   Remove the bolts securing the engine sprocket cover to the engine case **(see illustration)**. Slide the sprocket cover off.
3   Disconnect the wire from the neutral switch. Connect one lead of an ohmmeter to a good ground and the other lead to the post on the switch **(see illustration)**.
4   When the transmission is in neutral, the ohmmeter should read 0 ohms – in any other gear, the meter should read infinite.
5   If the switch doesn't check out as described, replace it.

Replacement

6   Unscrew the neutral switch from the case.
7   Wrap the threads of the new switch with Teflon tape or apply a thin coat of RTV sealant to them. Install the switch in the case and tighten it to the torque listed in this Chapter's Specifications.

24   Sidestand switch – check and replacement

Check

1   Following Steps 1 and 2 of Section 23, remove the engine sprocket cover.
2   Follow the wiring harness from the switch to the connector, then unplug the connector. Connect the leads of an ohmmeter to the brown and black/yellow wire terminals. With the sidestand in the up position, there should be continuity through the switch (0 ohms).
3   Connect the leads of the ohmmeter to the black/yellow and green/white wires. With the sidestand in the down position, the meter should indicate continuity.
4   If the switch fails either of these tests, replace it.

Replacement

5   Remove the engine sprocket cover, if you haven't already done so.
6   Unscrew the two countersunk Phillips head screws and remove the switch. Disconnect the switch electrical connector.
7   Installation is the reverse of the removal procedure.

9

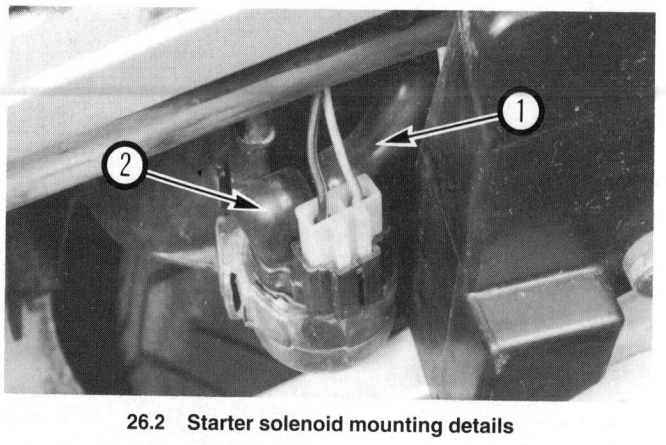

26.2   Starter solenoid mounting details

1   Battery positive cable   2   Cable to starter motor

25.5   Horn installation details (radiator and exhaust system removed for clarity)

1   Horn bracket-to-frame bolt   3   Electrical connectors
2   Horn-to-bracket nut

26   Starter solenoid – check and replacement

Refer to illustration 26.2

Check

1   Remove the left side cover.
2   Disconnect the battery positive cable and the starter wire from the terminals on the starter solenoid **(see illustration)**. **Caution:** *Don't let the battery positive cable make contact with anything, as it would be a direct short to ground.*
3   Connect the leads of an ohmmeter to the terminals of the starter solenoid. Press the starter button – the solenoid should click and the ohmmeter should indicated 0 ohms.
4   If the solenoid clicks but the ohmmeter doesn't indicate zero ohms, replace the solenoid.
5   If the solenoid doesn't click, it may be defective or there may be a problem in the starter circuit. To determine which, disconnect the electrical connector from the solenoid and connect a voltmeter or 12-volt test lamp between the terminals of the black/yellow and yellow/red wires in the wiring harness. Press the starter button again – the voltmeter should indicate approximately 12 volts or the test lamp should light.
   a) If the voltmeter indicates 12 volts or the test lamp lights, the circuit is good. Replace the solenoid.
   b) If the voltmeter indicates no voltage or the test lamp stays out, check all wiring connections in the starter circuit (refer to the Wiring diagrams at the end of this book). Also test the starter circuit relay in the junction box, the starter lockout switch, starter switch (button), engine stop switch and ignition switch.

Replacement

6   Disconnect the cable from the negative terminal of the battery.
7   Detach the battery positive cable, the starter cable and two wire electrical connector from the solenoid **(see illustration 26.2)**.
8   Slide the solenoid off its mounting tabs.
9   Installation is the reverse of removal. Reconnect the negative battery cable after all the other electrical connections are made.

27   Starter motor – removal and installation

Refer to illustrations 27.5, 27.6 and 27.7

Removal

1   Remove the lower fairing (see Chapter 8).
2   Disconnect the cable from the negative terminal of the battery.
3   Drain the engine oil and cooling system (see Chapter 1).
4   Remove the coolant hose from the water pump to the lower coolant pipe. Remove the lower coolant pipe (see Chapter 3).

27.5   Remove the nut that retains the starter wire (arrow) and detach the wire

25   Horn – check, replacement and adjustment

Refer to illustration 25.5

Check

1   Remove the lower fairing.
2   Unplug the electrical connectors from the horn. Using two jumper wires, apply battery voltage directly to the terminals on the horn. If the horn sounds, check the switch (see Section 21) and the wiring between the switch and the horn (see the wiring diagrams at the end of this Chapter).
3   If the horn doesn't sound, replace it. If it makes noise, but sounds "sick", try adjusting the tone as described below.

Replacement

4   Remove the lower fairing, if you haven't already done so.
5   Unbolt the horn bracket from the frame **(see illustration)** and detach the electrical connectors.
6   Unbolt the horn from the bracket and transfer the bracket to the new horn.
7   Installation is the reverse of removal.

Adjustment

8   Loosen the locknut on the adjustment screw **(see illustration 25.5)**. Have an assistant operate the horn. Turn the adjustment screw in or out until the tone is satisfactory. Tighten the locknut.

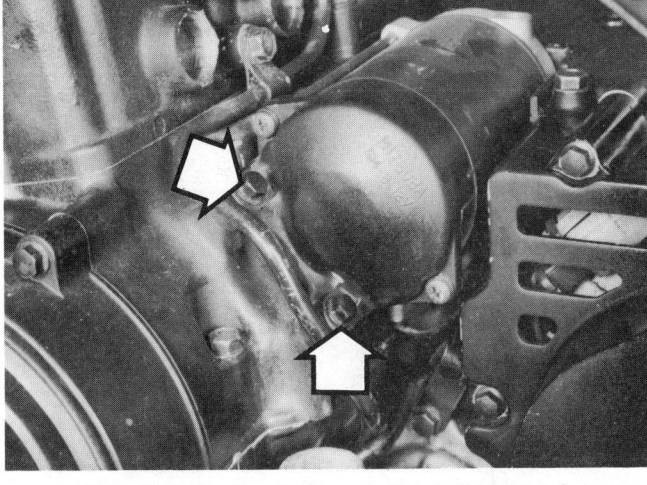

27.6 Remove the starter mounting bolts (arrows)

27.7 Lift the left end of the starter up slightly, then pull the starter out

5   Remove the nut retaining the starter wire to the starter (see illustration).

6   Remove the starter mounting bolts (see illustration).

7   Lift the outer end of the starter up a little bit and slide the starter out of the engine case (see illustration).

8   Check the condition of the O-ring on the end of the starter and replace it if necessary.

Installation

9   Remove any corrosion or dirt from the mounting lugs on the starter and the mounting points on the crankcase.

10   Apply a little engine oil to the O-ring and install the starter by reversing the removal procedure. Refill the cooling system and the engine crankcase following the procedures outlined in Chapter 1.

28 Starter motor – disassembly, inspection and reassembly

1   Remove the starter motor (see Section 27).

Disassembly

Refer to illustrations 28.2, 28.4 and 28.5

2   Mark the position of the housing to each end cover. Remove the two long screws and detach both end covers (see illustration).

3   Pull the armature out of the housing (toward the pinion gear side).

4   Remove the brush plate from the housing (see illustration).

5   Remove the nut and push the terminal bolt through the housing. Remove the two brushes with the plastic holder from the housing (see illustration).

Inspection

Refer to illustrations 28.6, 28.7, 28.8a, 28.8b, 28.9 and 28.10

6   The parts of the starter motor that most likely will require attention are the brushes. Measure the length of the brushes and compare the results to the brush length listed in this Chapter's Specifications (see illustration). If any of the brushes are worn beyond the specified limits, replace the brush holder assembly with a new one. If the brushes are not worn excessively, cracked, chipped, or otherwise damaged, they may be reused.

7   Inspect the commutator (see illustration) for scoring, scratches and discoloration. The commutator can be cleaned and polished with crocus cloth, but do not use sandpaper or emery paper. After cleaning, wipe away any residue with a cloth soaked in an electrical system cleaner or denatured alcohol. Measure the commutator diameter and compare it to the diameter listed in this Chapter's Specifications. If it is less than the service limit, the motor must be replaced with a new one.

8   Using an ohmmeter or a continuity test light, check for continuity between the commutator bars (see illustration). Continuity should exist be-

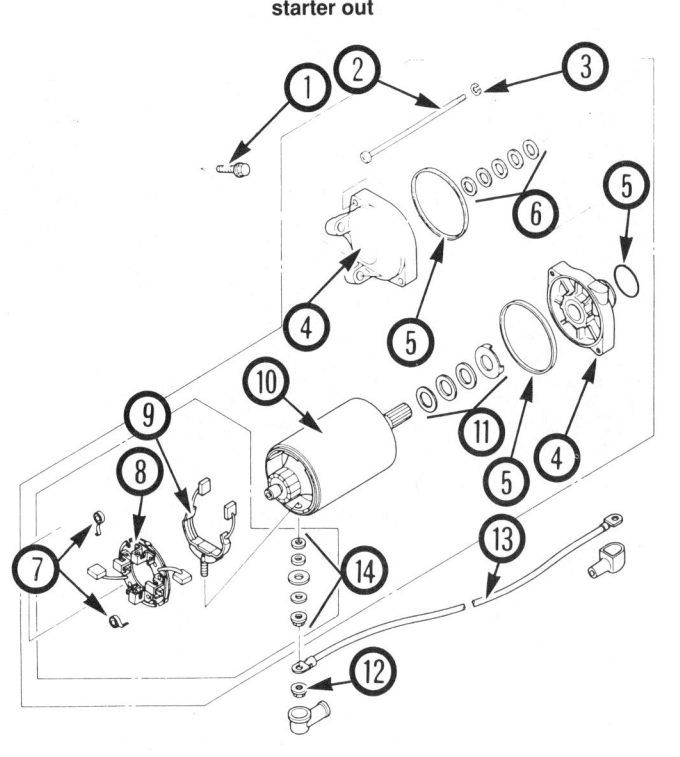

28.2 Exploded view of the starter motor

1	Bolt	8	Brush plate
2	Screw	9	Plastic holder and
3	Lockwasher		starter wire terminal
4	End cover	10	Armature and housing
5	O-ring	11	Washers
6	Washers	12	Nut
7	Spring	13	Starter wire
		14	Washers

tween each bar and all of the others. Also, check for continuity between the commutator bars and the armature shaft (see illustration). There should be no continuity between the commutator and the shaft. If the checks indicate otherwise, the armature is defective.

9   Check for continuity between the brush plate and the brushes (see illustration). The meter should read close to 0 ohms. If it doesn't, the brush plate has an open and must be replaced.

9

28.4   Remove the brush plate from the housing (four-brush starter shown; two-brush similar)

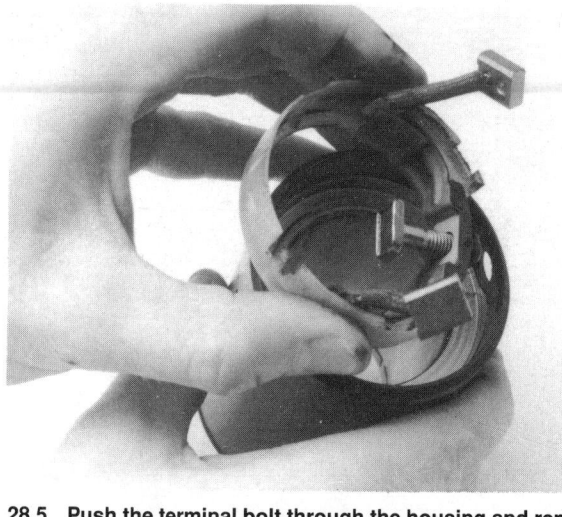

28.5   Push the terminal bolt through the housing and remove the plastic brush holder

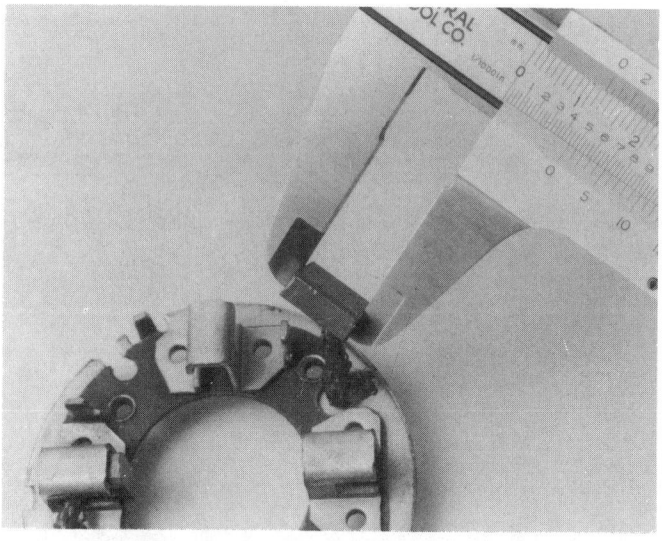

28.6   Measure the length of the brushes and compare the length of the shortest brush with the length listed in this Chapter's Specifications

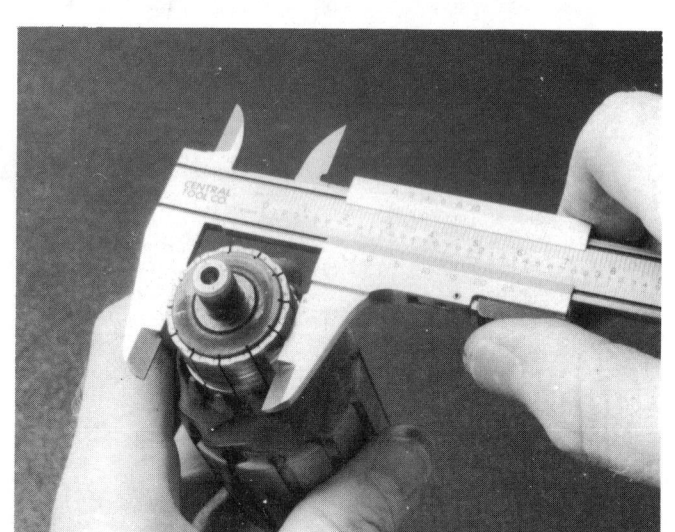

28.7   Check the commutator for cracks and discoloring, then measure the diameter and compare it with the minimum diameter listed in this Chapter's Specifications

10   Using the highest range on the ohmmeter, measure the resistance between the brush holders and the brush plate **(see illustration)**. The reading should be infinite. If there is any reading at all, replace the brush plate.

11   Check the starter pinion gear for worn, cracked, chipped and broken teeth. If the gear is damaged or worn, replace the starter motor.

Reassembly

Refer to illustrations 28.12, 28.13, 28.14a and 28.14b

12   Install the plastic brush holder into the housing. Make sure the terminal bolt and washers are assembled correctly **(see illustration)**. Tighten the terminal nut securely.

13   Detach the brush springs from the brush plate (this will make armature installation mush easier). Install the brush plate into the housing, routing the brush leads into the notches in the plate **(see illustration)**. Make sure the tongue on the brush plate fits into the notch in the housing.

14   Install the brushes into their holders and slide the armature into place. Install the brush springs **(see illustrations)**.

15   Install any washers that were present on the end of the armature shaft. Install the end covers, aligning the previously applied matchmarks. Install the two long screws and tighten them securely.

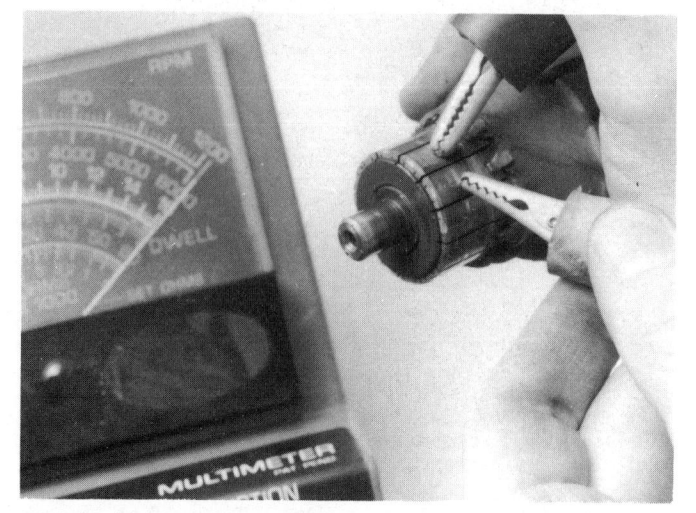

28.8a   Continuity should exist between the commutator bars

28.8b   There should be no continuity between the commutator bars and the armature shaft

28.9   There should be almost no resistance (0 ohms) between the brushes and the brush plate

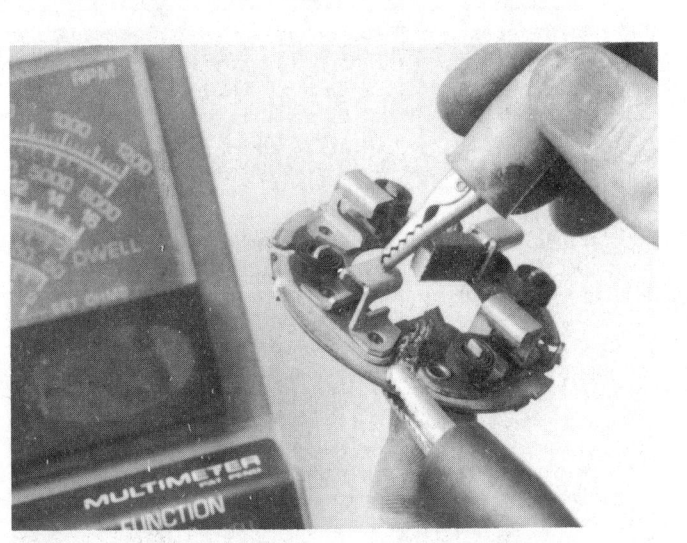

28.10   There should be no continuity between the brush plate and the brush holders (the resistance reading should be infinite)

28.12   Install the washers on the starter terminal as shown

28.13   When installing the brush plate, make sure the brush leads fit into the notches in the plate (arrow) – also, make sure the tongue on the plate fits into the notch in the housing (arrows)

28.14a   Install each brush spring on the post in this position . . .

9

28.14b ... then pull the end of the spring 1/2 turn clockwise and seat the end of it in the groove in the end of the brush

32.3 The alternator cover is retained by four bolts – when installing it, make sure the notch (2) is at the bottom

29 Charging system testing – general information and precautions

1   If the performance of the charging system is suspect, the system as a whole should be checked first, followed by testing of the individual components (the alternator and the voltage regulator/rectifier). **Note:** *Before beginning the checks, make sure the battery is fully charged and that all system connections are clean and tight.*

2   Checking the output of the charging system and the performance of the various components within the charging system requires the use of special electrical test equipment. A voltmeter and ammeter or a multimeter are the absolute minimum tools required. In addition, an ohmmeter is generally required for checking the remainder of the system.

3   When making the checks, follow the procedures carefully to prevent incorrect connections or short circuits, as irreparable damage to electrical system components may result if short circuits occur. Because of the special tools and expertise required, it is recommended that the job of checking the charging system be left to a dealer service department or a reputable motorcycle repair shop.

30 Charging system – output test

Caution: *Never disconnect the battery cables from the battery while the engine is running. If the battery is disconnected, the alternator and regulator/rectifier will be damaged.*

1   To check the charging system output, you will need a voltmeter or a multimeter with a voltmeter function.

2   The battery must be fully charged (charge it from an external source if necessary) and the engine must be at normal operating temperature to obtain an accurate reading.

3   Attach the positive (red) voltmeter lead to the positive (+) battery terminal and the negative (black) lead to the battery negative (-) terminal. the voltmeter selector switch (if so equipped) must be in a DC volt range greater than 15 volts.

4   Start the engine.

5   The charging system output should be 14.5 $\pm$ 0.5 volts at 4000 or more rpm.

6   If the output is as specified, the alternator is functioning properly. If the charging system as a whole is not performing as it should, refer to Section 33 and check the voltage regulator/rectifier.

7   Low voltage output may be the result of damaged windings in the alternator stator coils, loss of magnetism in the alternator rotor or wiring problems. Make sure all electrical connections are clean and tight, then refer to Section 31 and check the alternator stator coil windings and leads for continuity.

31 Alternator stator coil – continuity test

1   If charging system output is low or non-existent, the alternator stator coil windings and leads should be checked for proper continuity. The test can be made with the stator in place on the machine.

2   To gain access to the stator coil wiring harness connector, remove engine sprocket cover (see Section 23).

3   Locate the stator coil electrical connector and unplug it (the connector contains three yellow wires on the chassis side of the harness and three black wires on the alternator side of the harness).

4   Using an ohmmeter (preferred) or a continuity test light, check for continuity between each of the wires coming from the alternator stator. Continuity should exist between any one wire and each of the others (Kawasaki actually specifies a resistance of 0.1 to 0.8 ohms).

5   Check for continuity between each of the wires and the engine. No continuity should exist between any of the wires and the case.

6   If there is no continuity between any two of the wires, or if there is continuity between the wires and an engine ground, an open circuit or a short exists within the stator coils. Since repair of the stator is not feasible, it must be replaced with a new one.

32 Alternator – removal and installation

Removal

Refer to illustrations 32.3, 32.4, 32.5 and 32.6

1   Disconnect the cable from the negative terminal of the battery.

2   Remove the lower fairing.

3   Remove the alternator cover **(see illustration)**. Remove the engine sprocket cover (see Section 23, Steps 1 and 2).

4   Prevent the alternator rotor from turning by holding it with Kawasaki tool no. 57001-308 or a pin spanner wrench. Remove the rotor bolt **(see illustration)**.

5   Hold the rotor from turning again, and using tool no. 57001-1216 or equivalent, remove the rotor from the crankshaft **(see illustration)**.

6   To remove the stator coil, follow the wiring harness back from the stator and disconnect the electrical connector. Remove the three Allen bolts and detach the stator from the engine **(see illustration)**.

Installation

Refer to illustration 32.8

7   Position the stator coil on the engine and install the bolts, tightening them to the torque listed in this Chapter's Specifications. Install the wiring harness grommet in the slot in the case. Route the wiring harness into position, making sure it's secured by the clamp behind the water pump, then plug in the electrical connector.

32.4 A pin spanner wrench can be used to hold the rotor stationary while the bolt is loosened

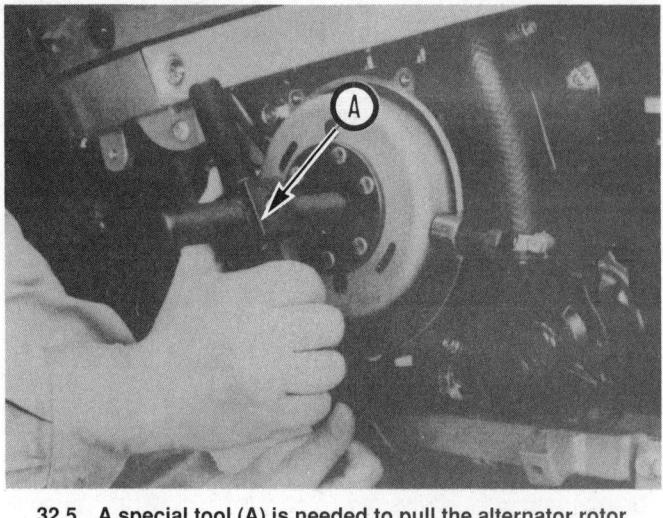

32.5 A special tool (A) is needed to pull the alternator rotor off – the rotor must be held stationary while doing this, also

32.6 The alternator stator is retained by three Allen head bolts (arrows)

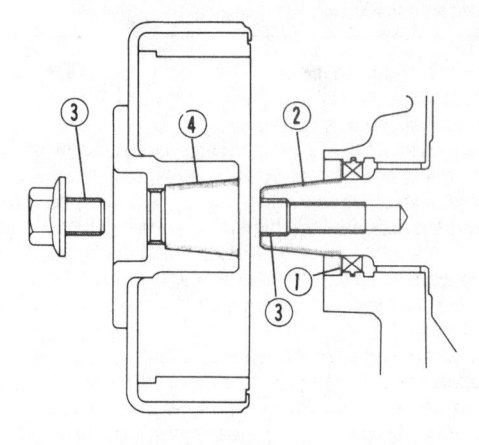

32.8 Clean the areas indicated before installing the alternator rotor

1   The surface of the crankshaft oil seal
2   The tapered portion of the crankshaft
3   The alternator rotor bolt and the threads in the crankshaft
4   The tapered portion of the rotor

8   Clean the end of the crankshaft, the rotor bolt, the threads in the crankshaft and the tapered portion of the rotor with an oil-less cleaning solvent (brake system cleaner works well, as it leaves no residue) **(see illustration)**.

9   Install the rotor and the bolt. Prevent the rotor from turning using the method described in Step 4, and tighten the rotor bolt to the torque listed in this Chapter's Specifications.

10   Install the alternator cover, making sure the notch in the edge of the cover is at the bottom (it serves as a drain for moisture).

11   Install the engine sprocket cover.

12   Install the lower fairing and connect the cable to the negative terminal of the battery.

33   Voltage regulator/rectifier – check and replacement

Refer to illustrations 33.2 and 33.3

1   Remove the riders seat and the left side cover.

2   Remove the two bolts securing the regulator/rectifier to its bracket, then detach the electrical connector **(see illustration)**.

33.2 The voltage regulator/rectifier is held to its bracket by two bolts

9

33.3   Rectifier circuit diode test table

No.	Connections		Reading	Meter Range
---	Meter (+) to	Meter (−) to		
1	Y_1			
2	Y_2	W	∞	
3	Y_3			
4	Y_1			x 10 Ω or x 100 Ω
5	Y_2	Bk/Y		
6	Y_3		½ scale	
7		Y_1		
8	W	Y_2		
9		Y_3		
10		Y_1		
11	Bk/Y	Y_2	∞	
12		Y_3		

3   Using an ohmmeter, check the resistance across the terminals indicated in the accompanying table (see illustration). If the meter readings are not as specified, replace the regulator.

4   This check, combined with the charging system output test described in Section 30 and the alternator stator coil test outlined in Section 31, should diagnose most charging system problems. If the voltage regulator/rectifier passes the test described in Step 3, and the stator coil passes the test in Section 31, take the regulator/rectifier to a dealer service department or other repair shop for further checks, or substitute a known good unit and recheck the charging system output.

34   Wiring diagrams

Prior to troubleshooting a circuit, check the fuses to make sure they're in good condition. Make sure the battery is fully charged and check the cable connections.

When checking a circuit, make sure all connectors are clean, with no broken or loose terminals or wires. When unplugging a connector, don't pull on the wires – pull only on the connector housings themselves. *Refer to the accompanying table for the wire color codes.*

Wiring diagram color code key

BK	Black	LG	Light green
BL	Blue	O	Orange
BR	Brown	P	Pink
CH	Chocolate	PU	Purple
DG	Dark Green	R	Red
G	Green	W	White
GY	Gray	Y	Yellow
LB	Light blue		

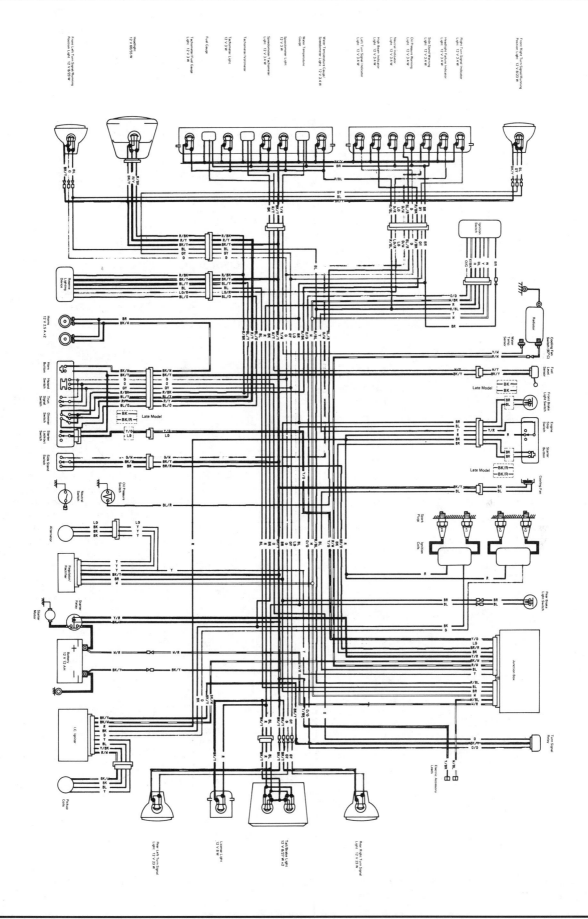

Wiring diagram for ZX600-A1, A2, A3, A4 and B1 models (US and Canada)

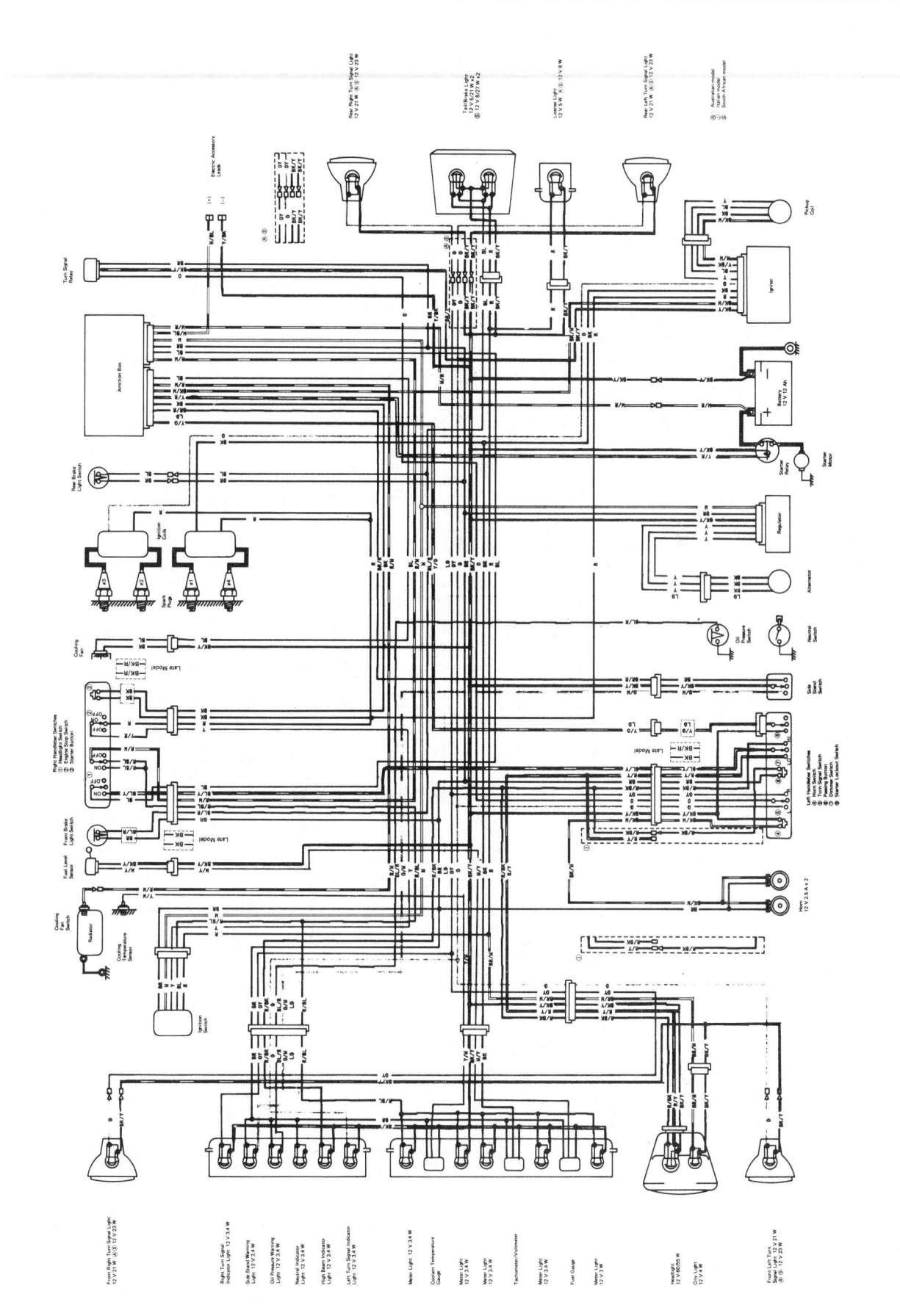

Wiring diagram for ZX600-A1, A2, A3 and A4 models (other than US and Canada)

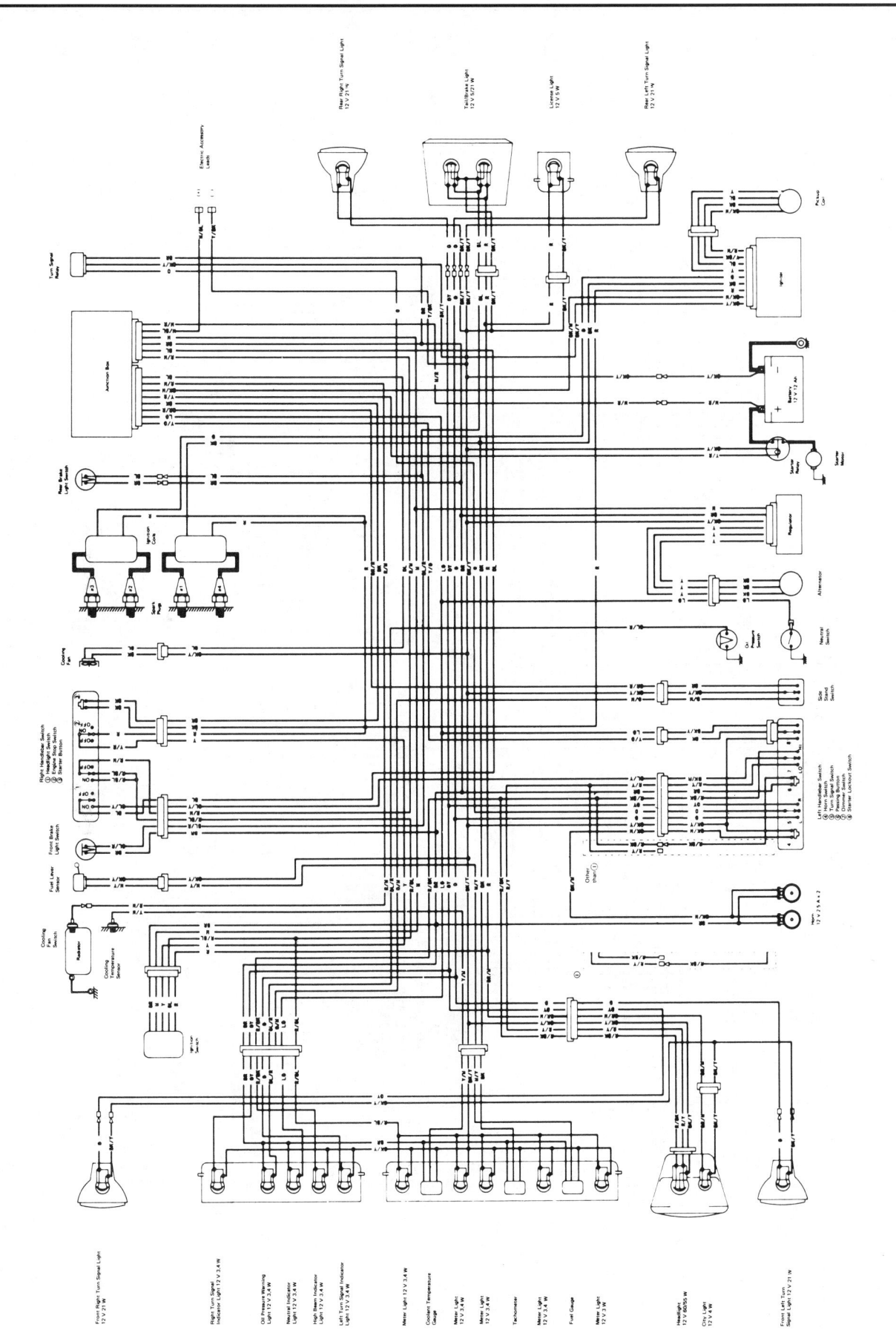

Wiring diagram for ZX600-A5 models (other than US and Canada)

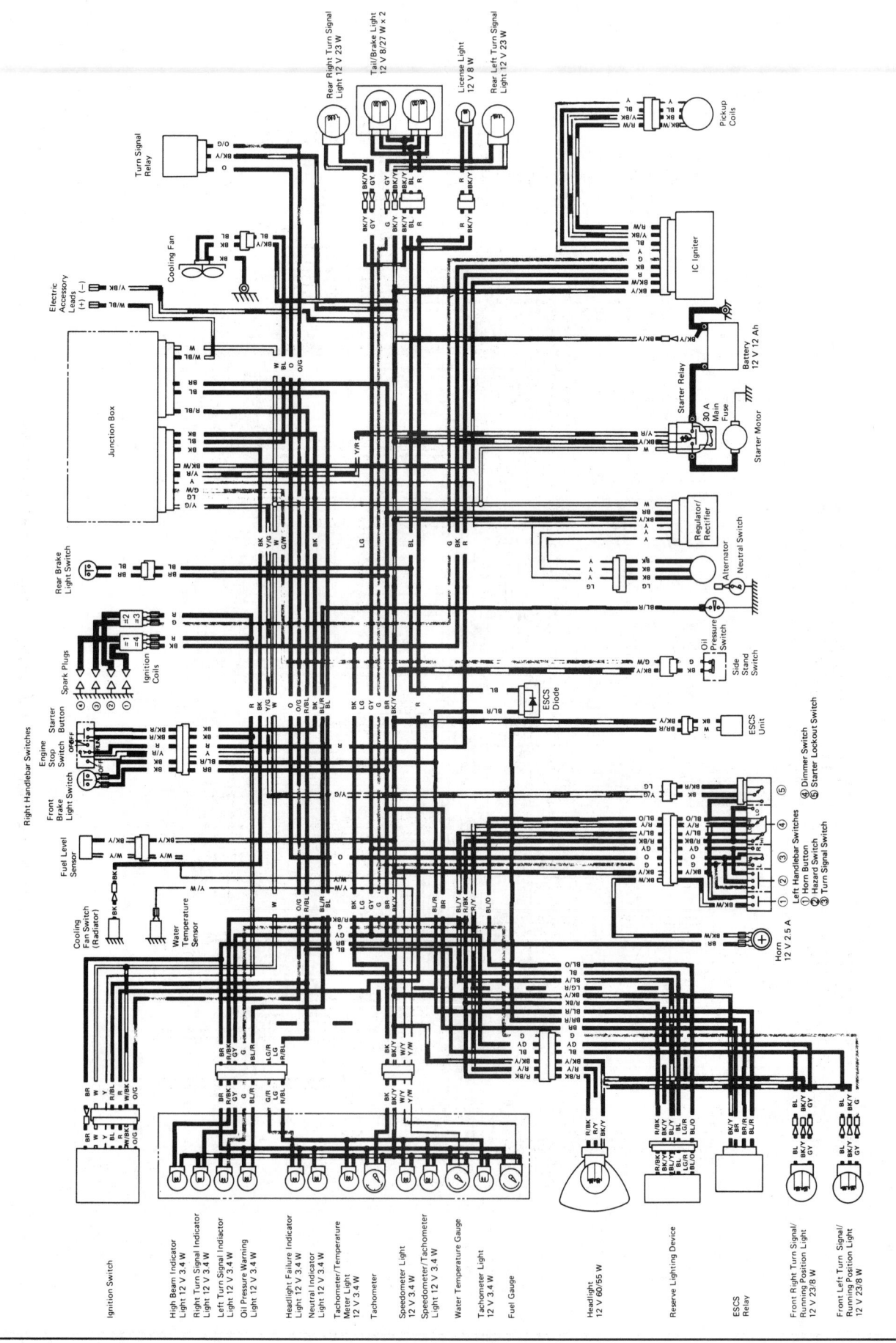

Wiring diagram for ZX600-C1 models (US and Canada)

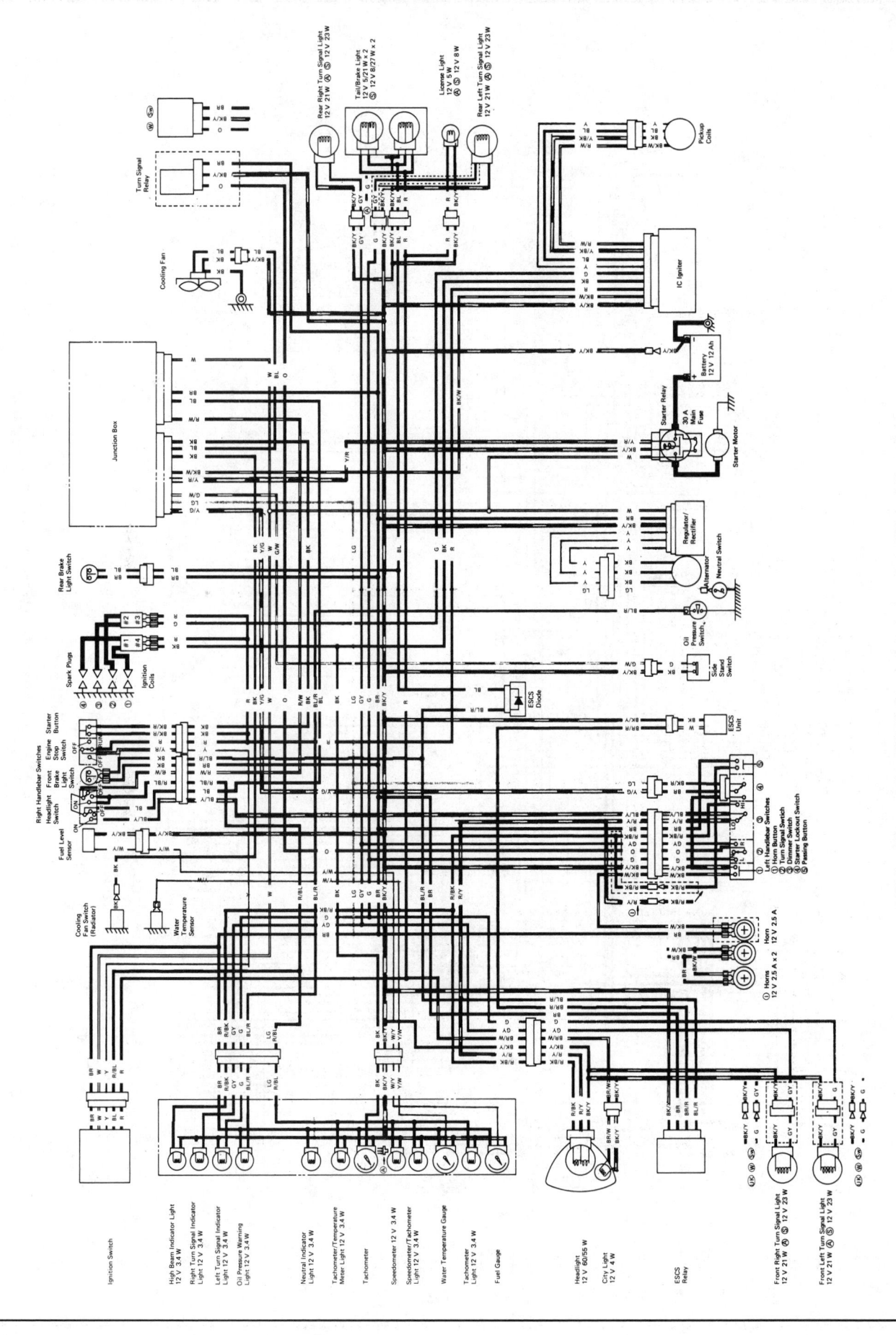

Wiring diagram for ZX600-C1 models (other than US and Canada)

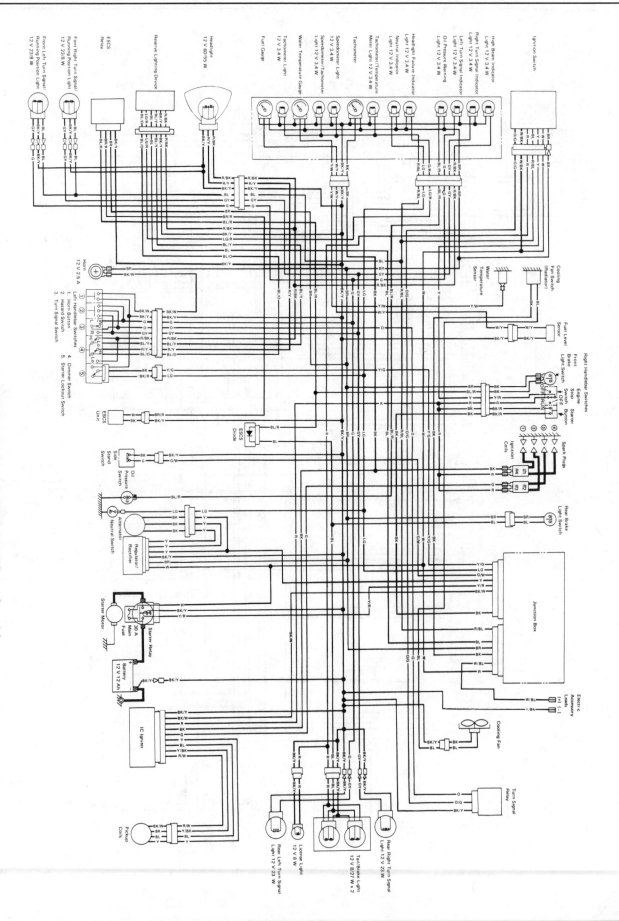

Wiring diagram for ZX600-C2 through C7 models (US and Canada)

Wiring diagram for ZX600-C2 through C7 models (other than US and Canada)

6

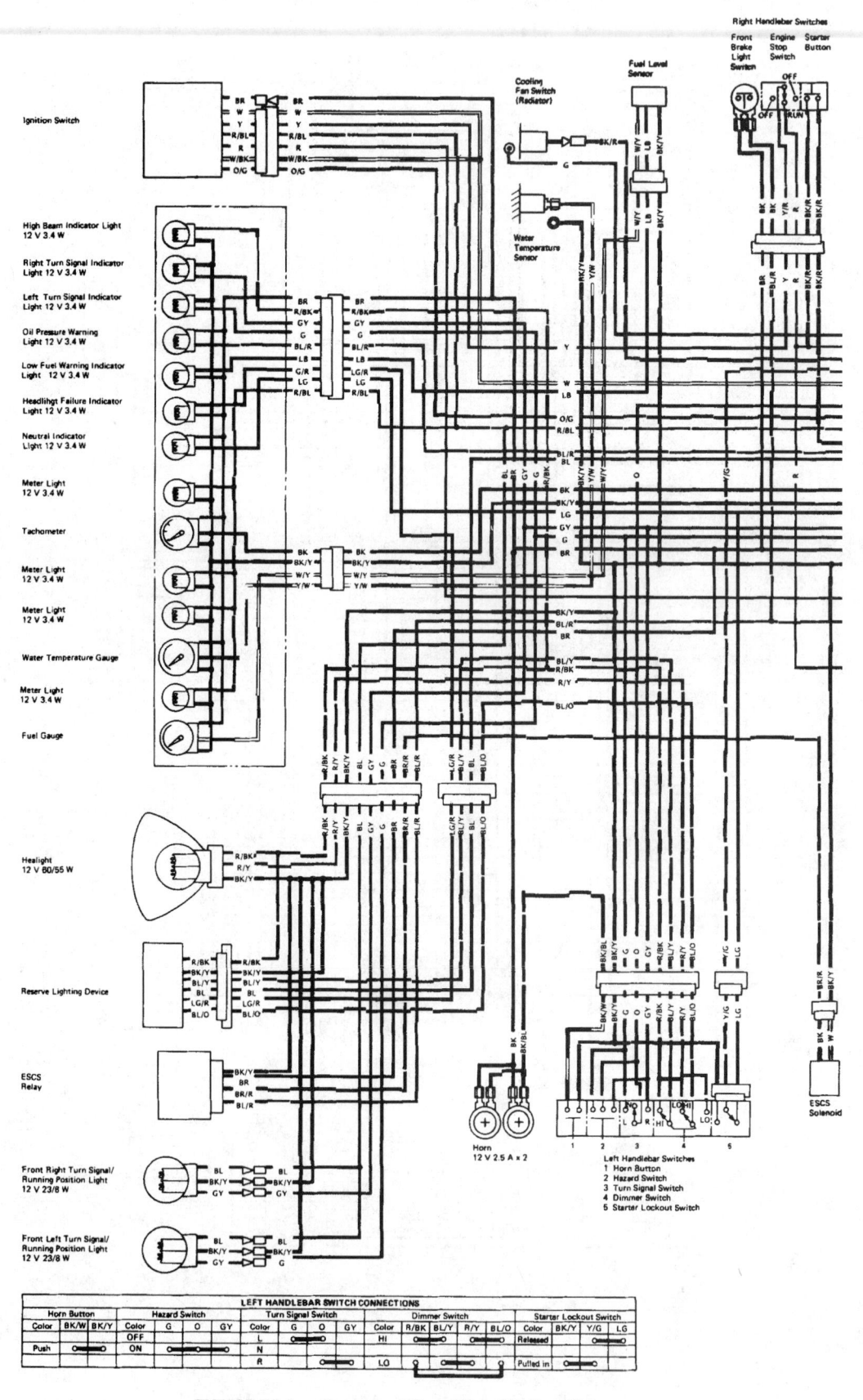

ZX750F Wiring diagram - US and Canada (1 of 2)

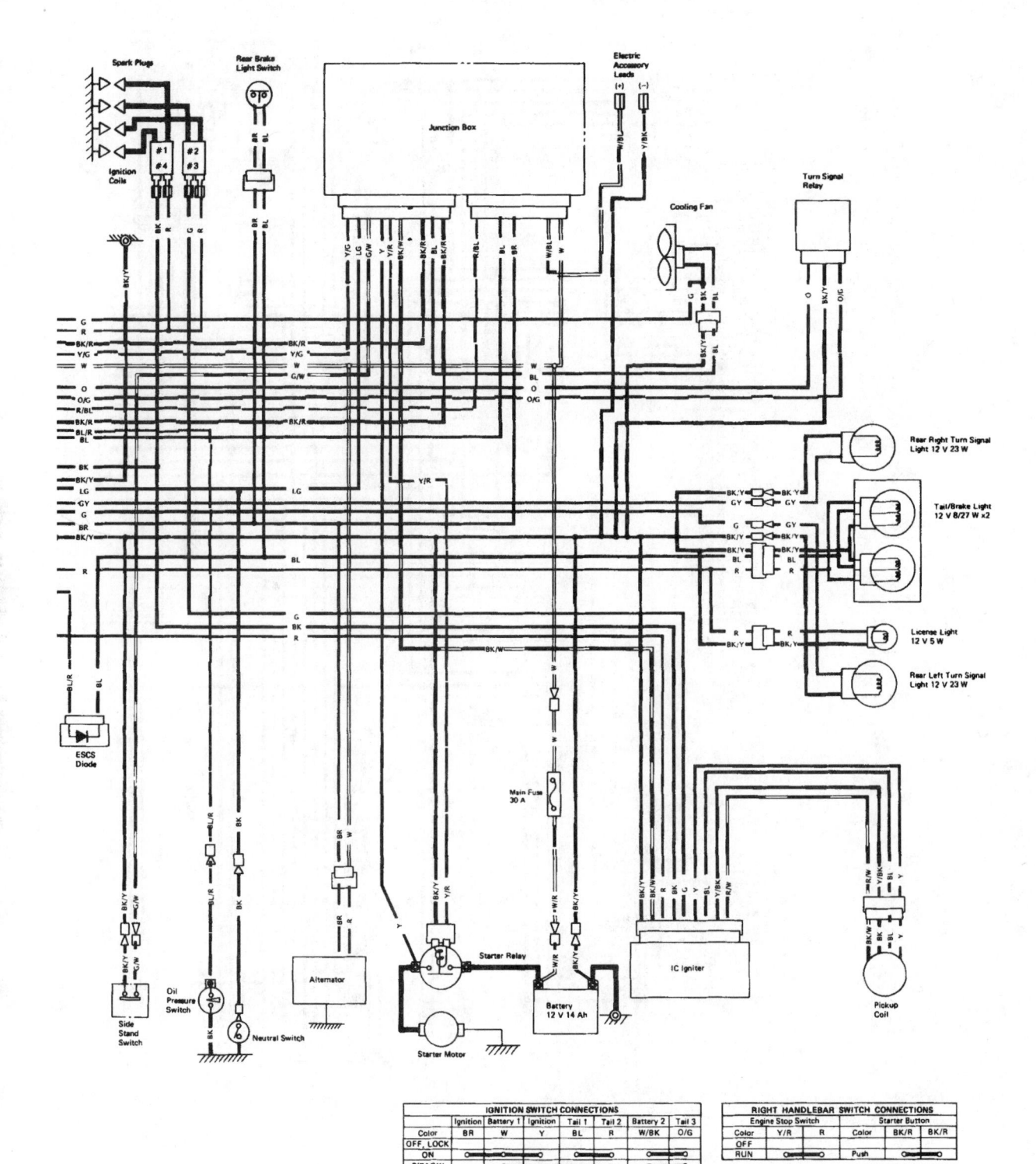

9

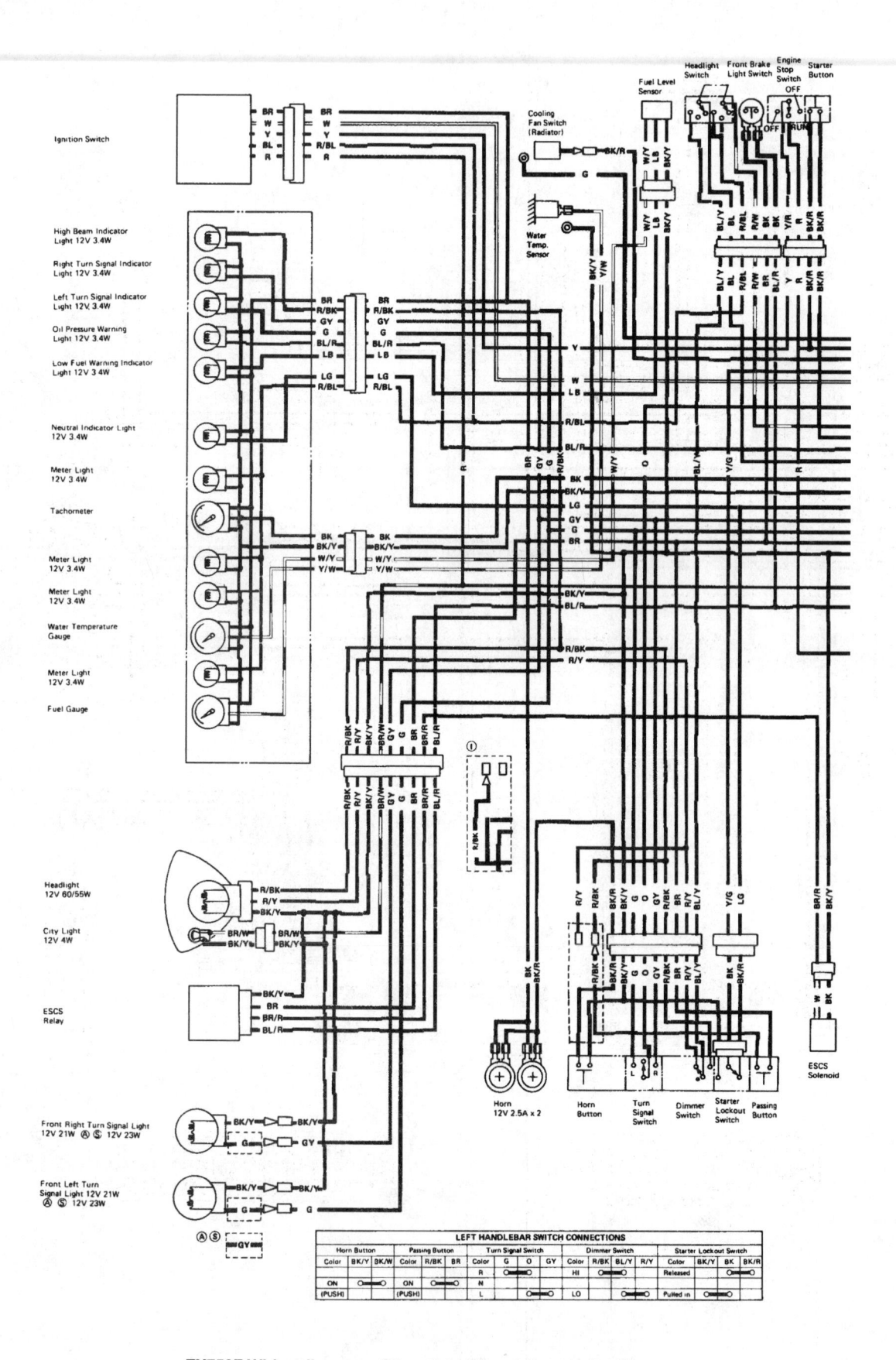

ZX750F Wiring diagram - Other than US and Canada (1 of 2)

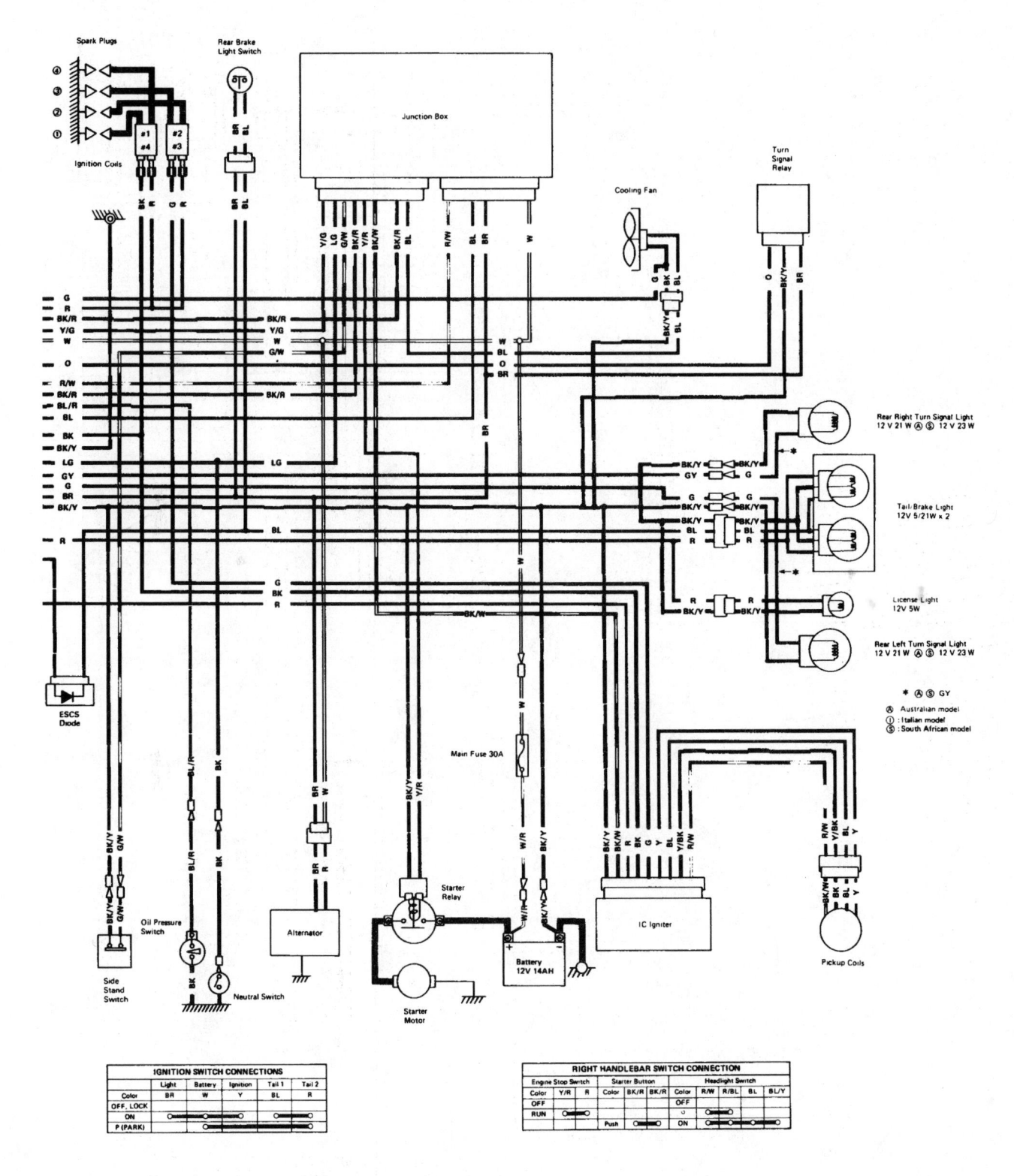

Chapter 10 The ZX750 models

Contents

10

Specifications

Unless given below, specifications for the ZX750 models are the same as for the 600C models.

General specifications

Frame and suspension

Wheelbase	1460 mm (57.48 inches)
Overall length	
US	2115 mm (83.28 inches)
UK	2170 mm (85.43 inches)
Overall width	715 mm (28.15 inches)
Overall height	1185 mm (46.65 inches)
Seat height	775 mm (30.51 inches)
Dry weight	
Except California	195 kg (429 lbs)
California	195.5 kg (430.1 lbs)
Front suspension	Telescopic fork
Rear suspension	Uni-Trak
Front brake	Dual hydraulic discs
Rear brake	Single hydraulic disc
Fuel capacity	21 liters (5.4 US gal, 4.6 Imp gal)

Engine

Type	Liquid-cooled, 4-stroke, DOHC inline four
Bore	2.677 in (68.0 mm)
Stroke	2.027 in (51.5 mm)
Displacement	748 cc
Compression ratio	11.2 : 1
Ignition system	Transistorized
Carburetor type	Four 34 mm Keihin carburetors
Clutch	Wet, multi-plate
Transmission	6-speed, constant mesh

Specifications relating to Chapter 1

Engine

Spark plugs	
Type - US	
Standard plug	NGK D8EA or ND X24ES-U
For racing	NGK D9EA or ND X27ES-U
For cold operation	NGK D7EA or ND X22ES-U
Canada	
Standard plug	NGK DR8ES-L or ND X24ESR-U
For racing	NGK DR8ES or ND X27ESR-U
For cold operation	NGK DR7ES or ND X22ESR-U
Type - UK	
Standard and racing plug	NGK DR8ES or ND X27ESR-U
For cold operation	NGK DR8ES-L or DR7ES. ND X24ESR-U or X22ESR-U
Gap	0.024 to 0.028 in (0.6 to 0.7 mm)
Engine idle speed	
All except California models	950 to 1050 rpm
California models	1200 to 1300 rpm
Valve clearances (COLD engine)	
Intake	0.0031 to 0.0051 in (0.08 to 0.13 mm)
Exhaust	0.0047 to 0.0066 in (0.12 to 0.17 mm)
Cylinder compression pressure	
Acceptable range	139 to 213 psi (9.58 to 14.67 Bars)
Maximum difference between cylinders	Not specified
Carburetor synchronization	
(vacuum difference between cylinders)	Less than 0.391 in (2 cm) Hg
Cylinder numbering (from left side to right side of bike)	1-2-3-4
Firing order	1-2-4-3

Miscellaneous

Brake pad minimum thickness	0.040 in (1.0 mm)
Throttle grip freeplay	0.08 to 0.12 in (2 to 3 mm)
Drive chain	
Slack	1.38 to 1.57 in (35 to 40 mm)
20-link length	12.73 in (323 mm) maximum
Battery electrolyte specific gravity	1.280 at 68-degrees F (20-degrees C)
Minimum tire tread depth	
Front	0.040 in (1.0 mm)
Rear	
Up to 80 mph (130 kph)	0.079 in (2.0 mm)
Above 80 mph (130 kph)	0.118 in (3.0 mm)

Tire pressures (cold)
  Front
    Up to 215 lbs (97.5 kg) load.. 32 psi
    215 to 401 lbs (97.5 to 182 kg) load .... 36 psi
    Above 130 mph (210 kph)... 36 psi
  Rear
    Up to 215 lbs (97.5 kg) load.. 36 psi
    215 to 401 lbs (97.5 to 182 kg) load .... 41 psi
    Above 130 mph (210 kph)... 41 psi

Torque specifications   **Ft-lb** (unless otherwise indicated)
Oil drain plug 14.5
Oil filter mounting bolt 14.5
Coolant drain bolt .... 69 in-lbs
Spark plugs... 120 in-lbs
Valve cover bolts .... 87 in-lbs

Recommended lubricants and fluids
Engine/transmission oil
  Type .... API grade SG multi-grade and fuel efficient oil
  Viscosity
    In cold climates... SAE 10W40 or 10W50
    In warm climates... SAE 20W40 or 20W50
  Capacity
    With filter change .... 3.4 US qt (3.2 liters)
    Oil change only .... 3.2 US qt (3.0 liters)
Coolant
  Type .... 50/50 mixture of ethylene glycol based antifreeze and soft water
  Capacity .... 2.1 US qt (2.0 liters)
Brake and clutch fluid.. DOT 4
Fork oil
  Type .... SAE 10W20 - fork oil
  Amount
    Dry fill .... 380 ± 4 cc
    At oil change .... Approximately 325 cc
  Oil level (forks fully compressed - no spring)
    Left fork tube .... 4.724 +/- 0.079 in (120 +/- 2 mm)
    Right fork tube .... 5.866 +/- 0.079 in (149 +/- 2 mm)

Specifications relating to Chapter 2

Camshaft and rocker arms
Lobe height (intake and exhaust)
  Standard.. 1.324 to 1.328 in (33.623 to 33.731 mm)
  Minimum... 1.319 in (33.52 mm)
Bearing oil clearance
  Journals 1 and 4
    Standard .... 0.0011 to 0.0027 in (0.028 to 0.071 mm)
    Maximum .... 0.0063 in (0.16 mm)
  Journals 2 and 3
    Standard .... 0.0030 to 0.0047 in (0.078 to 0.121 mm)
    Maximum .... 0.008 in (0.21 mm)
Journal diameter
  Journals 1 and 4
    Standard .... 0.9429 to 0.9437 in (23.950 to 23.972 mm)
    Minimum .... 0.9417 in (23.92 mm)
  Journals 2 and 3
    Standard .... 0.9409 to 0.9418 in (23.900 to 23.922 mm)
    Minimum .... 0.9397 in (23.87 mm)
Bearing journal inside diameter
  Standard .... 0.9448 to 0.9457 in (24.000 to 24.021 mm)
  Maximum.. 0.9480 in (24.08 mm)
Camshaft runout
  Standard.. 0.0007 in (0.02 mm)
  Maximum.. 0.0039 in (0.1 mm)
Camshaft chain 20-link length
  Standard.. 5.000 to 5.015 in (127.0 to 127.4 mm)
  Maximum.. 5.074 in (128.9 mm)

Cylinder head, valves and valve springs
Cylinder head warpage.. 0.002 in (0.05 mm) maximum
  Maximum.. 0.002 in (0.05 mm)
Valve stem runout limit .... 0.0008 in (0.02 mm)
Valve stem diameter
  Intake
    Standard .... 0.1958 to 0.1964 in (4.975 to 4.990 mm)
    Minimum .... 0.1952 in (4.96 mm)

10

Cylinder head, valves and valve springs (continued)
Exhaust
    Standard .... 0.1950 to 0.1956 in (4.955 to 4.970 mm)
    Minimum .... 0.1944 in (4.94 mm)
Valve guide inside diameter (intake and exhaust)
    Standard .... 0.1968 to 0.1974 in (5.000 to 5.012 mm)
    Maximum .... 0.2 in (5.08 mm)
Valve seat width (intake and exhaust) .... 0.020 to 0.040 in (0.5 to 1.0 mm)
Valve spring free length (inner)
    Standard .... 1.429 in (36.3 mm)
    Minimum .... 1.378 in (35.0 mm)
Valve spring free length (outer)
    Standard .... 1.590 in (40.4 mm)
    Minimum .... 1.535 in (39 mm)

Cylinder block
Bore diameter
    Standard .... 2.677 to 2.6776 in (68.000 to 68.012 mm)
    Maximum .... 2.681 in (68.1 mm)
Taper limit .... 0.002 in (0.05 mm)
Out-of-round limit .... 0.002 in (0.05 mm)

Pistons
Piston diameter
    Standard .... 2.6748 to 2.6755 in (67.942 to 67.958 mm)
    Minimum .... 2.6688 in (67.79 mm)
Piston-to-cylinder clearance .... 0.001 to 0.002 in (0.042 to 0.070 mm)
Top ring side clearance
    Standard .... 0.001 to 0.003 in (0.03 to 0.07 mm)
    Maximum .... 0.006 in (0.17 mm)
Second ring side clearance
    Standard .... 0.0007 to 0.0023 in (0.02 to 0.06 mm)
    Maximum .... 0.006 in (0.16 mm)
Top ring groove width
    Standard .... 0.0410 to 0.0409 in (1.02 to 1.04 mm)
    Maximum .... 0.044 in (1.12 mm)
Second ring groove width
    Standard .... 0.0397 to 0.0405 in (1.01 to 1.093 mm)
    Maximum .... 0.0437 in (1.11 mm)
Oil ring groove width
    Standard .... 0.0988 to 0.0996 in (2.51 to 2.53 mm)
    Maximum .... 0.1023 in (2.60 mm)
Top and second ring thickness
    Standard .... 0.0381 to 0.0389 in (0.97 to 0.99 mm)
    Minimum .... 0.035 in (0.90 mm)
Top and second ring end gap
    Standard .... 0.0078 to 0.0137 in (0.20 to 0.35 mm)
    Maximum .... 0.0275 in (0.7 mm)

Crankshaft and bearings
Main bearing oil clearance
    Standard .... 0.0008 to 0.0017 in (0.020 to 0.044 mm)
    Maximum .... 0.0031 in (0.08 mm)
Main bearing journal diameter
    No mark on crank throw .... 1.3379 to 1.3382 in (33.984 to 33.992 mm)
    "1" mark on crank throw .... 1.3383 to 1.3385 in (33.993 to 34.000 mm)
Connecting rod side clearance
    Standard .... 0.0005 to 0.0118 in (0.013 to 0.300 mm)
    Maximum .... 0.0196 in (0.50 mm)
Connecting rod bearing oil clearance
    Standard .... 0.0018 to 0.0029 in (0.046 to 0.076 mm)
    Maximum .... 0.0043 in (0.11 mm)
Connecting rod big-end bore diameter
    No mark on side of rod .... 1.496 to 1.4963 in (38.000 to 38.008 mm)
    "0" mark on side of rod .... 1.4964 to 1.4966 in (38.009 to 38.016 mm)
Connecting rod journal (crankpin) diameter
    No mark on crank throw .... 1.3773 to 1.3776 in (34.984 to 34.992 mm)
    "0" mark on crank throw .... 1.3776 to 1.3779 in (34.993 to 35.000 mm)

Oil pump and relief valve
Oil pressure (warm) .... 43 to 57 psi @ 4000 rpm
Relief valve opening pressure .... 63 to 85 psi

Clutch
Spring free length
    Standard .... 1.433 in (36.4 mm)
    Minimum .... 1.381 in (35.1 mm)

Friction plate thickness
    Standard.. 0.114 to 0.122 in (2.9 to 3.1 mm)
    Minimum... 0.110 in (2.8 mm)
Friction and steel plate warpage
    Standard.. 0.008 in (0.2 mm)
    Maximum... 0.012 in (0.3 mm)

Transmission
Shift fork groove width in gears
    Standard.. 0.1988 to 0.2027 in (5.05 to 5.15 mm)
    Maximum... 0.2086 in (5.3 mm)
Shift fork ear thickness
    Standard.. 0.1929 to 0.1968 in (4.9 to 5.0 mm)
    Minimum... 0.1889 in (4.8 mm)
Shift fork guide pin diameter
    Standard.. 0.2322 to 0.2362 in (5.9 to 6.0 mm)
    Maximum... 0.2283 in (5.8 mm)
Shift drum groove width
    Standard.. 0.2381 to 0.2440 in (6.05 to 6.20 mm)
    Maximum... 0.2480 in (6.3 mm)

Torque specifications
Valve cover bolts .... 87 in-lbs
Camshaft bearing cap bolts .... 104 in-lbs
Camshaft gear bolts .... 11 ft-lbs*
Camshaft chain tensioner cap.. 43 in-lbs
Camshaft chain tensioner mounting bolts...................................... 104 in-lbs
Camshaft chain tensioner rear guide bracket bolts .... 104 in-lbs
Cylinder head bolts... 29 ft-lbs**
Clutch damper bolts .... 87 in-lbs
Clutch spring bolts .... 87 in-lbs
Clutch hub nut .... 100 ft-lbs
Clutch master cylinder clamp bolts.. 78 in-lbs
Clutch slave cylinder bleed valve .... 69 in-lbs
Clutch line banjo bolts.. 22 ft-lbs
Oil pan bolts .... 104 in-lbs
Oil pipe-to-cylinder head union bolts .... 104 in-lbs
Oil pipe-to-oil cooler union bolts .... 18 ft-lbs
Relief valve-to-oil pan .... 11 ft-lbs
Long engine mounting bolts.. 33 ft-lbs
Short engine mounting bolts .... 13.5 ft-lbs
Crankcase bolts
    6 mm bolts marked "12" on head (F4 models) .... 16 ft-lbs
    6 mm bolts not marked "12" on head.. 104 in-lbs
    8 mm bolts .... 20 ft-lbs
Connecting rod nuts .... 27 ft-lbs
Chain guide bracket bolts .... 104 in-lbs*
Shift drum mounting plate bolt... Not specified*
*Apply a non-permanent thread locking agent to the threads.
**Apply clean engine oil to both sides of the head bolt washers. Tighten the bolts evenly in the proper sequence (see text).

Specifications relating to Chapter 3

Thermostat rating
Opening temperature... 176 to 183-degrees F (80 to 84-degrees C)
Fully open at .... 203-degrees F (95-degrees C)
Valve travel (when fully open) .... Not less than 5/16-in (8 mm)

Specifications relating to Chapter 4

Carburetor type .... Keihin CVK34 (four)

Jet sizes
Main jet
    California models 118
    All others 112
Main air jet .... Not specified
Jet needle N53L
Pilot jet .... Not specified
Pilot air jet .... Not specified
Pilot screw setting
    US models.. Preset
    UK models.. 2 turns out
Choke jet .... Not specified

Specifications relating to Chapter 5

Ignition coil
Primary resistance .... 1.8 to 2.8 ohms
Secondary resistance .... 10 to 16 k-ohms

10

Specifications relating to Chapter 5 (continued)

Arcing distance... 1/4 in (7 mm) or more
Pickup coil resistance.. 390 to 590 ohms
Pickup coil air gap .... 0.020 in (0.5 mm)

Ignition timing .... Not adjustable

Torque specifications
Pickup coil cover screws... Not specified

Specifications relating to Chapter 6
Fork spring length
Standard... 16.26 in (413 mm)
Minimum... 15.94 in (405 mm)

Rear sprocket
Runout (maximum) .... 0.020 in (0.5 mm)
Diameter .... Not specified

Torque specifications
Rear shock absorber mounting bolts/nuts.................................... **Ft-lbs** (unless otherwise indicated)
Rear shock absorber mounting bolts/nuts.................................... 43
Tie-rod-to-rocker arm bolt/nut 43
Swingarm pivot shaft nut... 65
Engine sprocket nut... 72
Engine sprocket cover screws .... Not specified

Specifications relating to Chapter 7
Brakes
Front disc thickness
  Standard... 0.189 to 0.2 in (4.8 to 5.1 mm)
  Minimum*... 0.177 in (4.5 mm)
Rear disc thickness
  Standard... 0.228 to 0.240 in (5.8 to 6.1 mm)
  Minimum*... 0.217 in (5.5 mm)
*Refer to marks stamped into the disc (they supersede information printed here)

Wheels and tires
Tire sizes
  US and Canada (except F3 models)
    Front.. 110/90 V16
    Rear .... 140/70 V18 or 140/70 VB18
  All UK and US/Canada F3 models
    Front.. 110/90 V16/V250
    Rear .... 140/70 V18/V250, 140/70 VR18, 140/70 VB18 or 140/70 V18

Torque specifications
Front axle.. **Ft-lbs** (unless otherwise indicated)
Front axle.. 65

Specifications relating to Chapter 9
Charging system
Charging voltage .... 13.5 volts at 4000 rpm (minimum)
Stator coil resistance... Less than 1.0 ohm
Slip ring diameter
  Standard... 0.567 in (14.4 mm)
  Minimum... 0.551 in (14.0 mm)
Alternator brush length
  Standard... 0.413 in (10.5 mm)
  Minimum... 0.177 in (4.5 mm)
Starter motor
Brush length
  Standard... 0.472 in (12 mm)
  Minimum... 0.335 in (8.5 mm)
Circuit fuse ratings
Taillight 10A
Accessory.. 10A
Fan... 10A
Headlight 10A
Main fuse 30A

Torque specifications
Alternator mounting bolts .... **Ft-lbs** (unless otherwise noted)
Alternator mounting bolts 29
Alternator belt cover bolts .... 43 in-lbs
Alternator pulley nut 80
Neutral switch.. 11
Timing rotor Allen bolt 18

1   Identification numbers

Year	Model code	Frame number range	Engine number range
1987	ZX750-F1	US JKAZXDF1 HA000001-016200* US JKAZXDF1 HB500001-504300** UK ZX750F-000001-016200	ZX750FE000001-018000
1988	ZX750-F2	US JKAZXDF1 JA016201-020200* US JKAZXDF1 JB504301-506699** UK ZX750F-016201-020200	ZX750FE018001-024000
1989 (US), 1989 to 1991 (UK)	ZX750-F3	US JKAZXDF1 KB506700-on UK ZX750F-020201-on	ZX750FE024001-on
1990 (US only)	ZX750-F4	JKAZXDF1 LB508401-on	ZX750FE024001-on

*Manufactured in Japan.
**Manufactured in US.

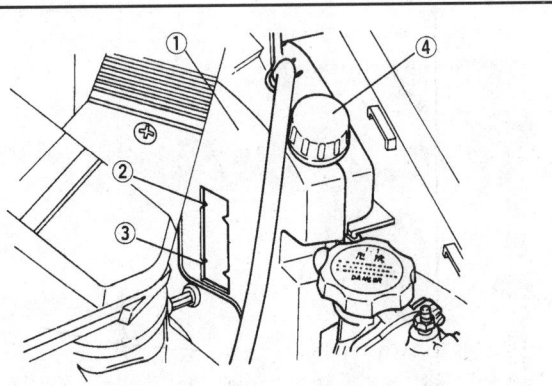

3.2 Check the coolant level through the window in the fairing

1   Coolant reservoir
2   Full mark
3   Low mark
4   Reservoir cap

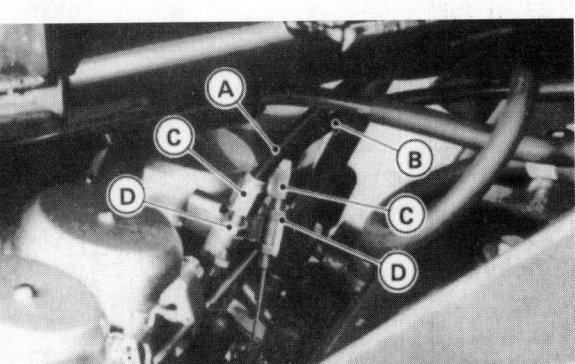

3.3 Throttle cable lower adjusting nuts

A   Accelerator cable
B   Decelerator cable
C   Adjusting nuts
D   Lock nuts

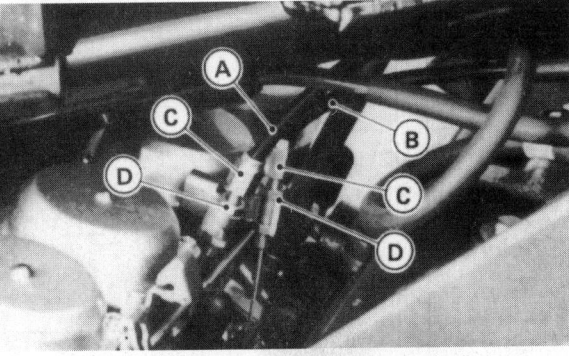

3.6 Remove the drain plug from the coolant tube

A   Water pump cover
B   Drain hole with tube attached
C   Coolant tube

2   Introduction

This Chapter covers the ZX750-F models from 1987 through 1990 (US) or 1991 (UK), giving information where it differs from that in Chapters 1 to 9 of this manual. If no mention is made of a procedure, it can be assumed that it is the same as for the ZX600C models.

3   Tune-up and routine maintenance (Chapter 1) - modified procedures

Routine maintenance intervals

Periodic maintenance for ZX750 models includes all the maintenance procedures for the ZX600, plus hydraulic clutch fluid level check and adjustment of the alternator drive belt every 10,000 km (6000 miles) (see below).

Clutch fluid check

1   The hydraulic clutch used on these models has a master cylinder similar to the brake master cylinder. Fluid level is checked at the window on the reservoir; top up the clutch master cylinder in the same manner as the brake master cylinder if it's low. Clutch and brakes use the same type of hydraulic fluid.

Coolant level check

Refer to illustration 3.2
2   Check coolant level through the window in the right inner fairing **(see illustration)**.

Throttle operation/grip freeplay - check and adjustment

Refer to illustration 3.3
3   The check and adjustment procedures are the same as for 600C models; the lower adjusting nuts are located at the carburetor ends of the cables, rather than midway along the cable housings **(see illustration)**.

Clutch - check and adjustment

4   These models are equipped with a hydraulic clutch. Lever play is automatically adjusted by the clutch hydraulic system. No means of manual adjustment is provided.

Valve clearances - check and adjustment

5   The procedure is the same as for 600 models, except that there's a separate adjuster for each valve. The adjuster screw head differs on 750 models, so if you use the service tool note that pt. no. 57001-1232 will be required.

Cooling system - draining, flushing and refilling

Refer to illustration 3.6
6   The procedure is the same as for 600 models, with two exceptions. The drain plug is in the bottom of the water pump inlet tube **(see illustration)**. The reservoir tank is drained by blowing air into its

10

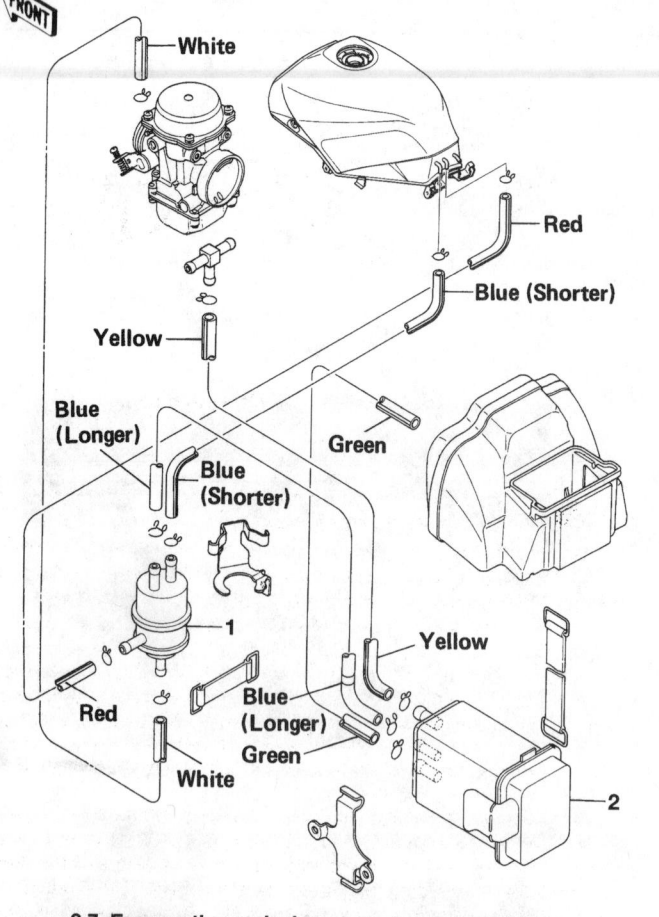

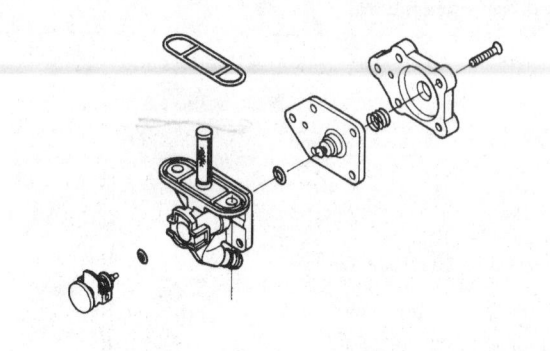

3.8 Fuel tap details

**3.10 Note which of the marks on the scale (A) aligns
with the pointer (B)**

3.7 Evaporative emission control system details

1 *Liquid-vapor separator*	2 *Canister*

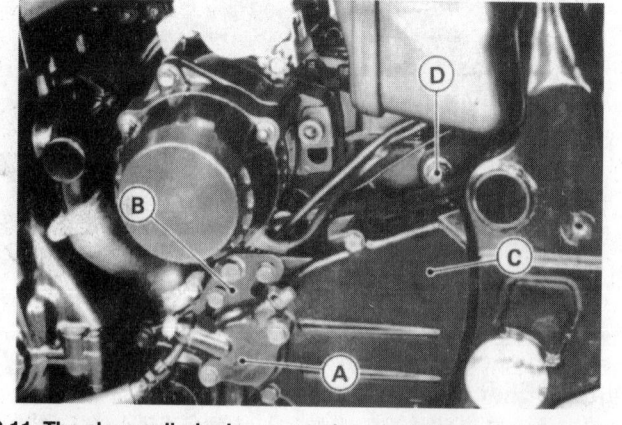

3.11 The slave cylinder is mounted on the left side of the engine

A	*Slave cylinder*	*C*	*Engine sprocket cover*
B	*Bracket*	*D*	*Engine mounting bolt*

overflow tube. **Warning**: *Antifreeze is poisonous. If you blow air into
the overflow tube by mouth, slip a clean hose over the overflow tube so
your mouth doesn't contact the overflow tube.*

Evaporative emission control system (California models only) - check

Refer to illustration 3.7

7   The procedure is the same as for 600 models; the arrangement of
components differs slightly **(see illustration)**.

Fuel system - check and filter cleaning

Refer to illustration 3.8

8   The procedure is the same as for 600 models. The design of the
fuel tap differs slightly **(see illustration)**.

Alternator belt - check and adjustment

Refer to illustrations 3.10, 3.11, 3.12a and 3.12b

9   The belt must be adjusted with the engine cold (at room temperature). The procedure requires a special tool and two torque wrenches,
so it may be more practical to have a Kawasaki dealer adjust the belt
for you.

10   Note which of the adjustment marks on the alternator scale aligns
with the pointer **(see illustration)**. Write this down.

11   Remove the clutch slave cylinder (see Section 23). Remove the alternator bracket, engine sprocket cover and the upper rear engine
mounting bolt **(see illustration)**.

12   Insert the alternator tension wrench (Kawasaki tool no. 57001-
1235) into the engine mounting bolt hole and place the tool lever
against the alternator belt **(see illustrations)**.

13   Loosen the alternator mounting bolts. Push the alternator down
against the crankcase, then retighten the alternator mounting bolts
with an Allen bolt bit. To get the correct torque for this stage of the procedure, turn the Allen bolt bit with a thumb and two fingers (don't use a
ratchet handle).

14   Attach a torque wrench to the special tool and apply 16 Nm (11.5
ft-lbs) torque.

15   While holding the first torque wrench at the setting specified in
Step 14, tighten the alternator mounting bolts to the torque listed in
this Chapter's Specifications.

16   Check the position of the pointer relative to the adjustment marks
on the scale. It should be at the same position or higher. If it's lower,
readjust the belt tension.

3.12a Use the alternator tension wrench (A) to set belt tension

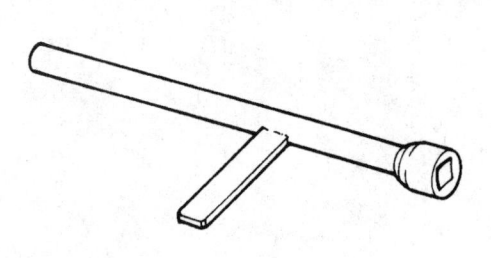

3.12b Alternator tension wrench

4 Engine general information - 750 models

The ZX750 engine/transmission unit is of the water-cooled, in-line, four-cylinder design, installed transversely across the frame. The sixteen valves are operated by double overhead camshafts which are chain driven off the crankshaft. Separate rocker arms are used for each valve.

The engine/transmission assembly is constructed from aluminum alloy. The crankcase is divided horizontally.

The crankcase incorporates a wet sump, pressure-fed lubrication system which uses a chain-driven, dual-rotor oil pump, an oil filter and by-pass valve assembly, a relief valve and an oil pressure switch. Also contained in the crankcase is the idler shaft and the starter motor clutch. The idler shaft turns the alternator pulley, which in turn drives the alternator through a ribbed belt.

Power from the crankshaft is routed to the transmission via the clutch, which is of the wet, multi-plate type and is gear-driven off the crankshaft. The transmission is a six-speed, constant-mesh unit.

5 Operations possible with the engine in the frame (ZX750 models)

The components and assemblies listed below can be removed without having to remove the engine from the frame. If, however, a number of areas require attention at the same time, removal of the engine is recommended.

Gear selector mechanism external components
Water pump
Starter motor
Alternator
Clutch assembly and slave cylinder
Oil pan, oil pump and relief valve
Valve cover, camshafts and rocker arms
Cam chain tensioner
Cylinder head
Cylinder block and pistons

6 Operations requiring engine removal (ZX750 models)

It is necessary to remove the engine/transmission assembly from the frame and separate the crankcase halves to gain access to the following components:

Crankshaft, connecting rods and bearings
Transmission shafts
Shift drum and forks
Idler shaft and starter motor clutch
Camshaft chain
Alternator/starter chain

7 Major engine repair - general note

1   It is not always easy to determine when or if an engine should be completely overhauled, as a number of factors must be considered.
2   High mileage is not necessarily an indication that an overhaul is needed, while low mileage, on the other hand, does not preclude the need for an overhaul. Frequency of servicing is probably the single most important consideration. An engine that has regular and frequent oil and filter changes, as well as other required maintenance, will most likely give many miles of reliable service. Conversely, a neglected engine, or one which has not been broken in properly, may require an overhaul very early in its life.
3   Exhaust smoke and excessive oil consumption are both indications that piston rings and/or valve guides are in need of attention. Make sure oil leaks are not responsible before deciding that the rings and guides are bad. Refer to Chapter 1 and perform a cylinder compression check to determine for certain the nature and extent of the work required.
4   If the engine is making obvious knocking or rumbling noises, the connecting rod and/or main bearings are probably at fault.
5   Loss of power, rough running, excessive valve train noise and high fuel consumption rates may also point to the need for an overhaul, especially if they are all present at the same time. If a complete tune-up does not remedy the situation, major mechanical work is the only solution.
6   An engine overhaul generally involves restoring the internal parts to the specifications of a new engine. During an overhaul the piston rings are replaced and the cylinder walls are bored and/or honed. If a rebore is done, then new pistons are also required. The main and connecting rod bearings are generally replaced with new ones and, if necessary, the crankshaft is also replaced. Generally the valves are serviced as well, since they are usually in less than perfect condition at this point. While the engine is being overhauled, other components such as the carburetors and the starter motor can be rebuilt also. The end result should be a like-new engine that will give as many trouble free miles as the original.
7   Before beginning the engine overhaul, read through all of the related procedures to familiarize yourself with the scope and requirements of the job. Overhauling an engine is not all that difficult, but it is time consuming. Plan on the motorcycle being tied up for a minimum of two (2) weeks. Check on the availability of parts and make sure that any necessary special tools, equipment and supplies are obtained in advance.
8   Most work can be done with typical shop hand tools, although a number of precision measuring tools are required for inspecting parts to determine if they must be replaced. Often a dealer service department or motorcycle repair shop will handle the inspection of parts and offer advice concerning reconditioning and replacement. As a general rule, time is the primary cost of an overhaul so it doesn't pay to install worn or substandard parts.
9   As a final note, to ensure maximum life and minimum trouble from a rebuilt engine, everything must be assembled with care in a spotlessly clean environment.

10

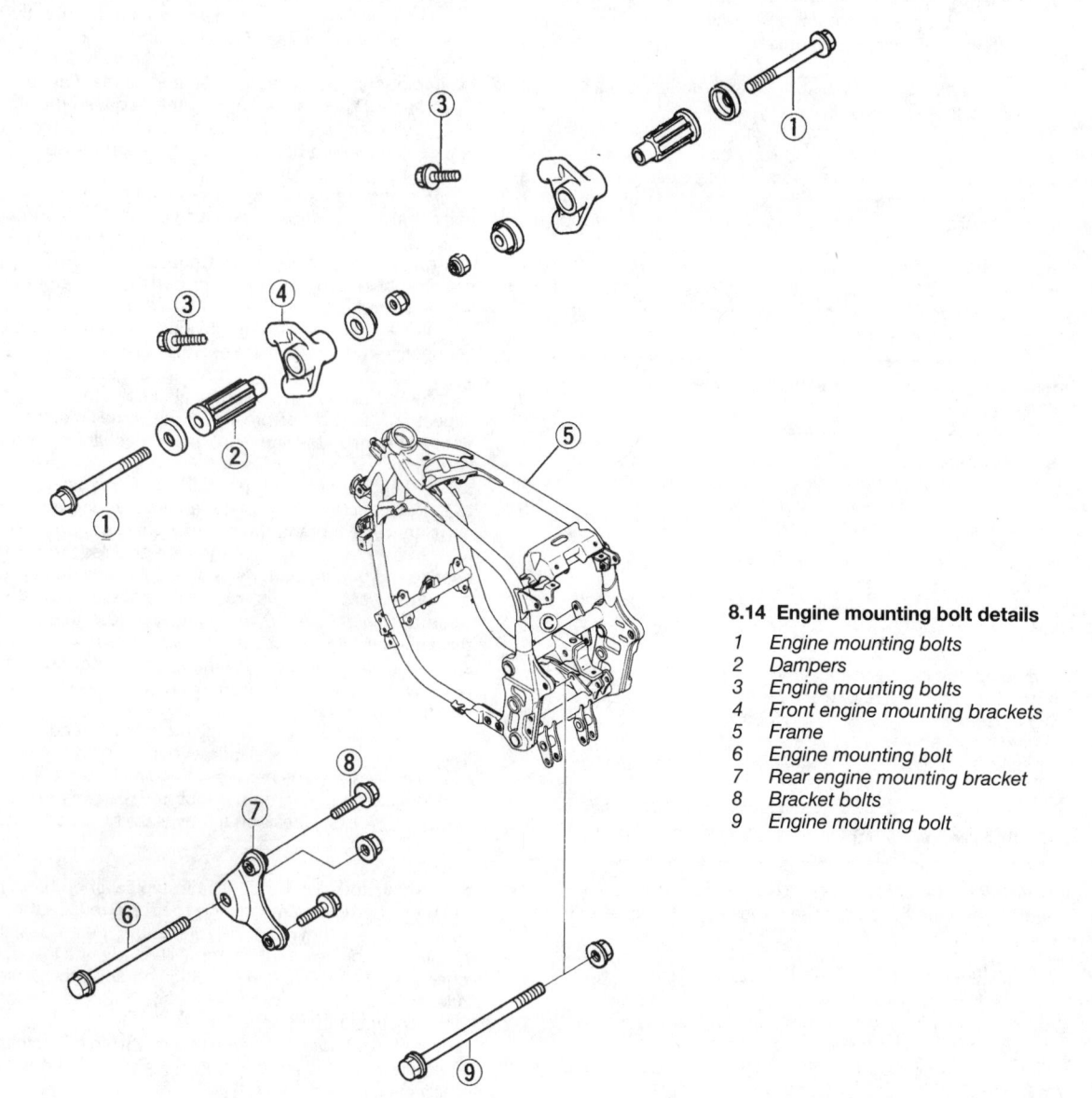

8.12 A ground wire securing bolt goes in this hole at the right rear of the crankcase

---

8   Engine - removal and installation (ZX750 models)

Note: *Engine removal and installation should be done with the aid of an assistant to avoid damage or injury that could occur if the engine is* dropped. A hydraulic floor jack should be used to support and lower the engine if possible (they can be rented at low cost).

Removal

Refer to illustrations 8.12 and 8.14

1   Set the bike on its centerstand.
2   Remove the seat, the fuel tank and the baffle plates (see Chapter 4 and Section 42 of this Chapter).
3   Remove the upper and lower fairings (see Section 42).
4   Drain the coolant and the engine oil (see Chapter 1 and Section 3).
5   Remove the ignition coils (see Section 39).
6   Remove the carburetors (see Chapter 4) and plug the intake openings with rags.
7   Remove the radiator, radiator hoses, oil lines and oil cooler (see Chapter 3 and Section 37).
8   Remove the exhaust system (see Chapter 4).
9   Remove the clutch slave cylinder (see Section 23).
10   Remove the engine sprocket cover, remove the sprocket retaining nut and detach the sprocket and chain from the engine (see Chapter 6 and Section 40). **Note**: *The chain can't be slipped off the output shaft until the engine is removed from the frame.*
11   Mark and disconnect the wires from the oil pressure switch, neutral switch and the starter motor. Unplug the alternator, sidestand and pickup coil electrical connectors (see Chapters 5 and 9).

8.14 Engine mounting bolt details

1   *Engine mounting bolts*
2   *Dampers*
3   *Engine mounting bolts*
4   *Front engine mounting brackets*
5   *Frame*
6   *Engine mounting bolt*
7   *Rear engine mounting bracket*
8   *Bracket bolts*
9   *Engine mounting bolt*

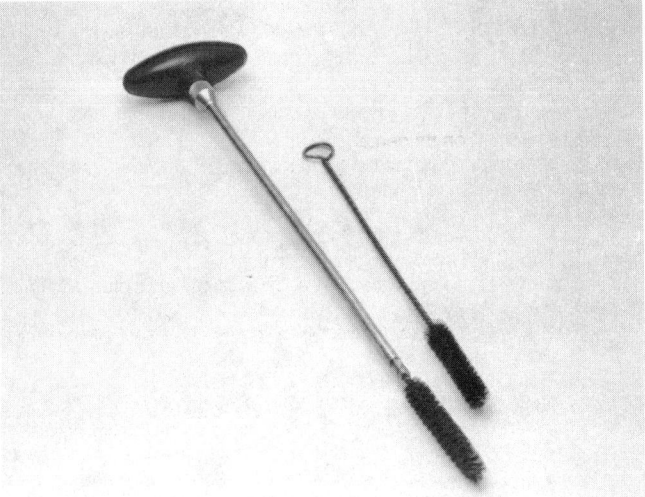

9.2a A selection of brushes is required for cleaning holes and passages in the engine components

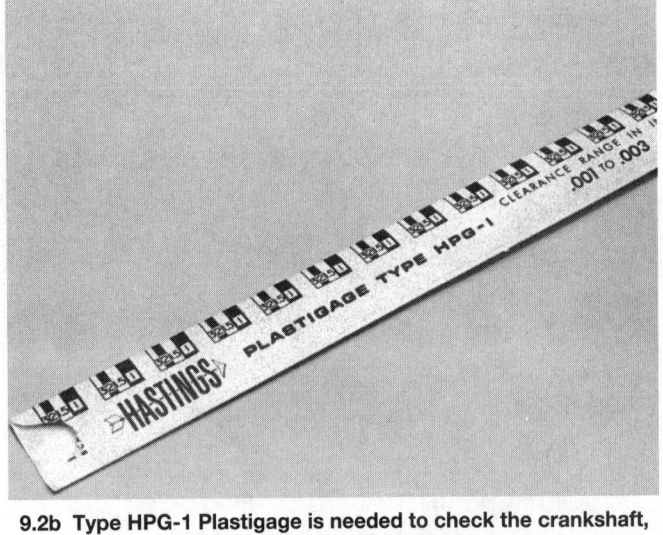

9.2b Type HPG-1 Plastigage is needed to check the crankshaft, connecting rod and camshaft oil clearances

9.3 An engine stand can be made from short lengths of 2 x 4 lumber and lag bolts or nails

12   Remove the bolt securing the ground wire to the right rear of the crankcase **(see illustration)**.
13   Support the engine with a floor jack and a wood block.
14   Remove the engine mounting bolts/nuts and bracket bolts **(see illustration)**.
15   With the engine still supported, make sure no wires or hoses are still attached to the engine assembly.
16   Raise the engine slightly then, with the help of an assistant, slide the engine out to the right so the output shaft clears the drive chain. It would be helpful to have another jack, or a small table or platform that is the same height as the bottom frame tube, which the engine can be slid onto as it is removed.

Installation

17   Installation is basically the reverse of removal. Note the following points:
  a) Don't tighten any of the engine mounting bolts until they all have been installed.
  b) Use new gaskets at all exhaust pipe connections.
  c) Tighten the engine mounting bolts and bracket bolts to the torques listed in this Chapter's Specifications.
  d) Adjust the drive chain, throttle cables and choke cable following the procedures in Chapter 1 and Section 3.

9   Engine disassembly and reassembly - general information

Refer to illustrations 9.2a, 9.2b and 9.3
1   Before disassembling the engine, clean the exterior with a degreaser and rinse it with water. A clean engine will make the job easier and prevent the possibility of getting dirt into the internal areas of the engine.
2   In addition to the precision measuring tools mentioned earlier, you will need a torque wrench, a valve spring compressor, oil gallery brushes, a piston ring removal and installation tool, a piston ring compressor, a pin-type spanner wrench and a clutch holder tool (which is described in Section 22). Some new, clean engine oil of the correct grade and type, some engine assembly lube (or moly-based grease), a tube of Kawasaki Bond liquid gasket (part no. 92104-1003) or equivalent, and a tube of RTV (silicone) sealant will also be required. Although it may not be considered a tool, some Plastigage (type HPG-1) should also be obtained to use for checking bearing oil clearances **(see illustrations)**.
3   An engine support stand made from short lengths of 2 x 4's bolted together will facilitate the disassembly and reassembly procedures **(see illustration)**. The perimeter of the mount should be just big enough to accommodate the engine oil pan. If you have an automotive-type engine stand, an adapter plate can be made from a piece of plate, some angle iron and some nuts and bolts.
4   When disassembling the engine, keep "mated" parts together (including gears, cylinders, pistons, etc. that have been in contact with each other during engine operation). These "mated" parts must be reused or replaced as an assembly.
5   Engine/transmission disassembly should be done in the following general order with reference to the appropriate Sections.
6   Reassembly is accomplished by reversing the general disassembly sequence.

10   Valve cover - removal and installation (ZX750 models)

Note: *The valve cover can be removed with the engine in the frame. If the engine has been removed, ignore the steps which don't apply.*

10

Removal

Refer to illustrations 10.5 and 10.6
1   Set the bike on its centerstand.
2   Remove the fuel tank (see Chapter 4).
3   If necessary for access, remove the upper and lower fairings (see Section 42). Remove the upper and side baffle plates.
4   Remove the air suction valve and the vacuum switching valve (see Chapter 1).

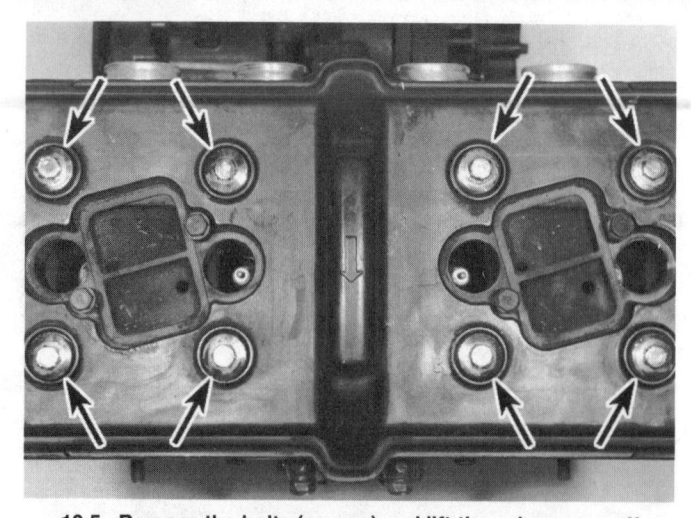

10.5   Remove the bolts (arrows) and lift the valve cover off

10.6   The upper chain guide is mounted inside the valve cover

10.8   Apply a thin film of sealant to the half-circle cutouts (arrows)

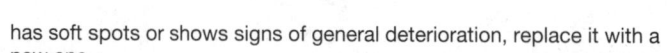

11.1   Loosen the tensioner cap bolt (center arrow), then remove
the tensioner mounting bolts (outer arrows) . . .

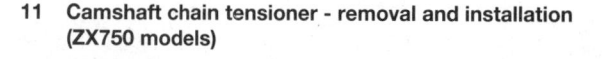

11.2   . . . and take the tensioner off

5   Remove the valve cover bolts **(see illustration)**.
6   Lift the cover off the cylinder head. If it's stuck, don't attempt to pry it off - tap around the sides of it with a plastic hammer to dislodge it. Check the chain guide in the center of the cover - if it's excessively worn, pry it out and install a new one **(see illustration)**.

Installation
Refer to illustration 10.8
7   Peel the rubber gasket from the cover. If it's cracked, hardened,

has soft spots or shows signs of general deterioration, replace it with a new one.
8   Clean the mating surfaces of the cylinder head and the valve cover with lacquer thinner, acetone or brake system cleaner. Apply a thin film of RTV sealant to the half-circle cutouts on each side of the head **(see illustration)**.
9   Install the gasket to the cover. Position the cover on the cylinder head, making sure the gasket doesn't slip out of place.
10   Check the rubber seals on the valve cover bolts, replacing them if necessary. Install the bolts, tightening them evenly, to the torque listed in this Chapter's Specifications.
11   The remainder of installation is the reverse of removal.

**11   Camshaft chain tensioner - removal and installation
       (ZX750 models)**

Refer to illustrations 11.1, 11.2 and 11.3

Removal
Caution: *Once you start to remove the tensioner bolts, you must re-move the tensioner all the way and reset it before tightening the bolts. The tensioner extends and locks in place, so if you loosen the bolts part way and then retighten them, the tensioner or cam chain will be dam-aged.*
1   Loosen the tensioner cap bolt while the tensioner is still installed **(see illustration)**.
2   Remove the tensioner mounting bolts and take it off the engine **(see illustration)**.
3   Remove the tensioner cap bolt and O-ring **(see illustration)**.

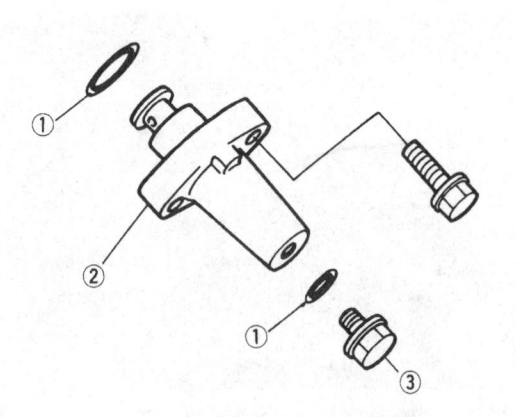

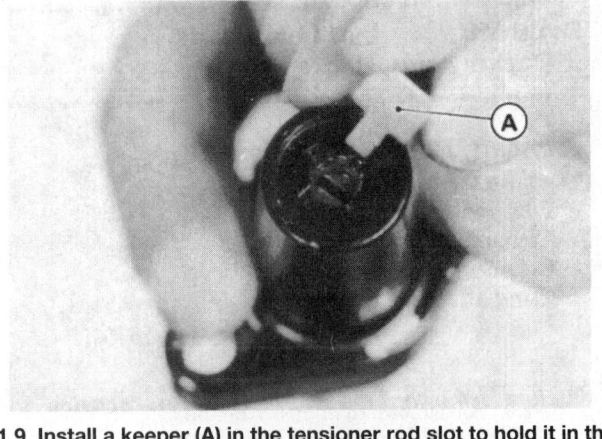

11.3 Cam chain tensioner details

1   O-rings   3   Tensioner cap bolt
2   Tensioner body

11.9 Install a keeper (A) in the tensioner rod slot to hold it in the correct position

12.5a Loosen the cam bearing cap bolts (arrows) evenly . . .

12.5b . . . and lift the caps off, noting the positions of the dowels (arrows)

Installation

4   Check the O-ring on the tensioner body for cracks or hardening. It's a good idea to replace this O-ring whenever the tensioner cap is removed.

Original tensioner

5   Place the tensioner mounting bolts where you can reach them with one hand while the other hand holds the tensioner in position in Step 7.
6   Press the end of the rod that contacts the chain into the tensioner body. At the same time, turn the other end of the rod clockwise with a screwdriver until the rod protrudes about 3/8-inch (10 mm) from the tensioner body. **Caution:** *Don't turn the rod counterclockwise (anticlockwise) or it may separate from the tensioner. If this happens it can't be reassembled.*
7   Place the tensioner in position on the engine. Push it firmly against the engine, remove the screwdriver, and install the mounting bolts finger-tight. **Caution:** *If the tensioner moves away from the engine before you tighten the bolts, the rod will extend too far. If this happens (or you think it might have happened), remove the tensioner and repeat Step 6, then continue with Step 7.*
8   Tighten the mounting bolts to the torque listed in this Chapter's Specifications.

New tensioner

Refer to illustration 11.9
9   New tensioners come with a keeper that fits in the tensioner rod slot and holds the rod in the correct position for installation **(see illustration)**.
10   Place the tensioner on the engine. Install the mounting bolts and

tighten them to the torque listed in this Chapter's Specifications.
11   Pull the keeper out with needle nosed pliers. **Note:** *Save the keeper and place it in your toolbox for future use. You can use it to hold the tensioner rod in position next time you install the tensioner, leaving both hands free.*

Original or new tensioner

12   Install the tensioner cap and O-ring. Tighten the cap to the torque listed in this Chapter's Specifications.

---

12   Camshafts, rocker arm shafts and rocker arms - removal, inspection and installation (ZX750 models)

Note: *This procedure can be performed with the engine in the frame.*

Camshafts

Removal

Refer to illustrations 12.5a, 12.5b, 12.5c, 12.6a, 12.6b and 12.7
1   Remove the valve cover following the procedure given in Section 10.
2   Remove the cam chain tensioner (see Section 11).
3   Remove the pickup coil cover (see Section 39).
4   Position the engine at Top Dead Center (TDC) for cylinders 1 and 4 (see Chapter 1, Valve clearances - check and adjustment, for the TDC locating procedure).
5   Unscrew the bearing cap bolts for one of the camshafts, a little at a time, until they are all loose, then unscrew the bearing cap bolts for the other camshaft **(see illustration)**. **Caution:** *If the bearing cap bolts*

10

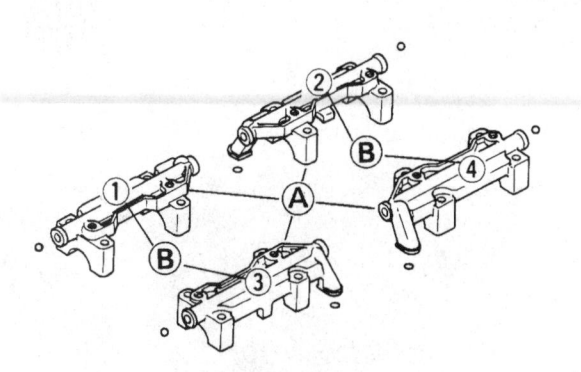

12.5c The camshaft bearing caps (A) and marked with numbers (B) that correspond to numbers on the cylinder head

12.6a Lift the camshaft chain, disengage it from the sprocket and guide the camshaft out

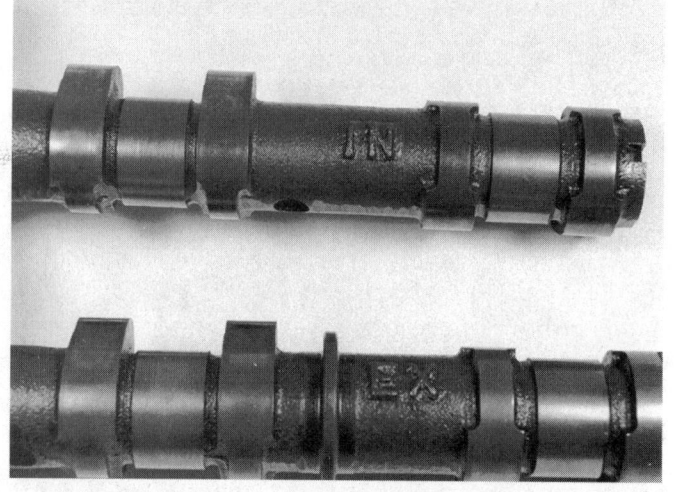

12.6b The intake and exhaust camshafts are identified by cast marks

12.7 Tie the camshaft chain up so it doesn't slip down off the crankshaft sprocket

aren't loosened evenly, the camshaft may bind. *Remove the bolts and lift off the bearing caps* (see illustration). Note the numbers on the bearing caps which correspond to the numbers on the cylinder head (see illustration). When you reinstall the caps, be sure to install them in the correct positions.

6   Pull up on the camshaft chain and carefully guide the camshaft out (see illustration). With the chain still held taut, remove the other camshaft. Look for marks on the camshafts. The intake camshaft should have an IN mark and the exhaust camshaft should have an EX mark (see illustration). If you can't find these marks, label the camshafts to ensure they are installed in their original locations. **Note**: *Don't remove the sprockets from the camshafts unless absolutely necessary.*

7   While the camshafts are out, don't allow the chain to go slack - if you do, it will become detached from the gear on the crankshaft and may bind between the crankshaft and case, which could cause damage to these components. Wire the chain to another component to prevent it from dropping down (see illustration). Also, cover the top of the cylinder head with a rag to prevent foreign objects from falling into the engine.

Inspection

8   Camshaft and sprocket inspection are the same as for ZX600 models (see Chapter 2).

Installation

Refer to illustrations 12.9, 12.10a, 12.10b and 12.11

9   Make sure the bearing surfaces in the cylinder head and the bearing caps are clean, then apply a light coat of engine assembly lube or moly-based grease to each of them (see illustration).

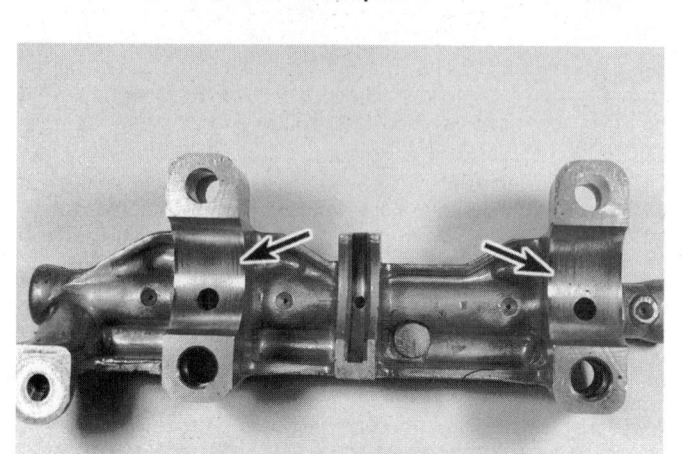

12.9 Check the bearing surfaces (arrows) for wear or damage

10   Apply a coat of moly-based grease to the camshaft lobes. Make sure the camshaft bearing journals are clean, then lay the camshafts in the cylinder head (do not mix them up), ensuring the marks on the cam sprockets are aligned properly (see illustrations).

11   Make sure the timing marks are aligned as described in Step 4, then mesh the chain with the camshaft sprockets. Count the number of chain link pins between the EX mark and the IN mark (see illustration). There should be no slack in the chain between the two sprockets.

12   Carefully set the bearing caps in place in their proper positions (see illustrations 12.5b and 12.5c) and install the bolts. Snug all of the

12.10a Each camshaft has a mark (IN or EX) and a line next to it . . .

12.10b . . . when installing the camshafts, the IN and EX marks on the camshaft sprockets should be positioned like this, with the marks aligned with the valve cover gasket surface on the cylinder head

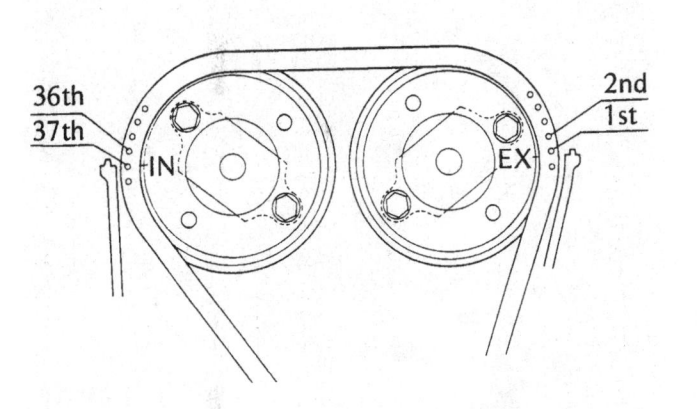

12.11 With no slack in the camshaft chain, there should be 37 pins of the chain between the sprocket marks

12.18a Lift the rocker arms out of the shafts . . .

bolts evenly, then tighten them in a criss-cross pattern to the torque listed in this Chapter's Specifications.

13   Insert your finger or a wood dowel into the cam chain tensioner hole and apply pressure to the cam chain. Check the timing marks to make sure they are aligned (see Step 4) and there are still the correct number of link pins between the EX and IN marks on the cam sprockets. If necessary, change the position of the sprocket(s) on the chain to bring all of the marks into alignment. **Caution:** *If the marks are not aligned exactly as described, the valve timing will be incorrect and the valves may contact the pistons, causing extensive damage to the engine.*

14   Install the cam chain tensioner as described in Section 11.

15   Adjust the valve clearances (see Chapter 1 and Section 3).

16   The remainder of installation is the reverse of removal.

Rocker arm shafts and rocker arms

Removal

Refer to illustrations 12.18a, 12.18b, 12.19, 12.20a, 12.20b and 12.20c

17   Remove the camshafts following the procedure given above. Be sure to keep tension on the camshaft chain.

18   Lift the rocker arms out of the shafts **(see illustration)**. Place the rocker arms in order in a labeled holder so they can be reinstalled in their original positions **(see illustration)**.

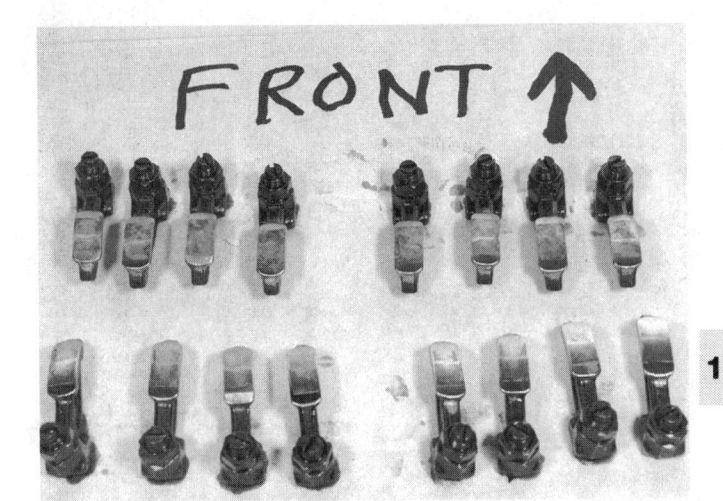

12.18b . . . and place them in order in a holder (a good method is to punch small holes in the side of a cardboard box, then press the ball pivots of the rocker arms into the holes)

10

12.19 Remove the rocker shaft retaining bolts

12.20a Tap the rocker shaft outward with a punch . . .

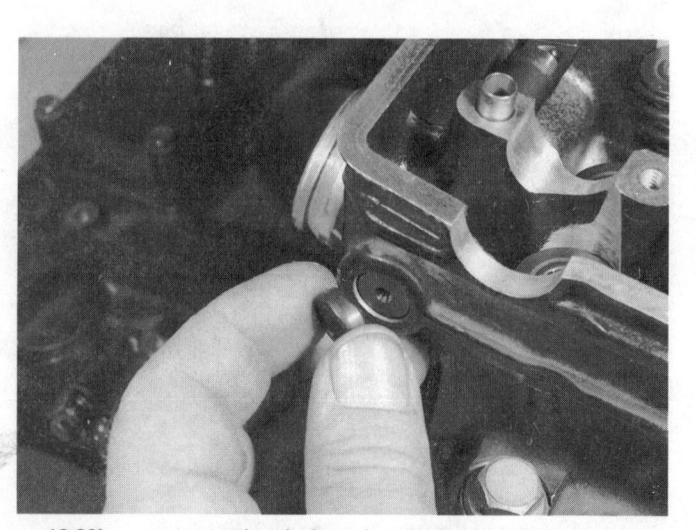

12.20b . . . remove the shaft seal as the rocker shaft pushes
it out . . .

12.20c . . . then grasp the rocker shaft and pull it out the rest of
the way

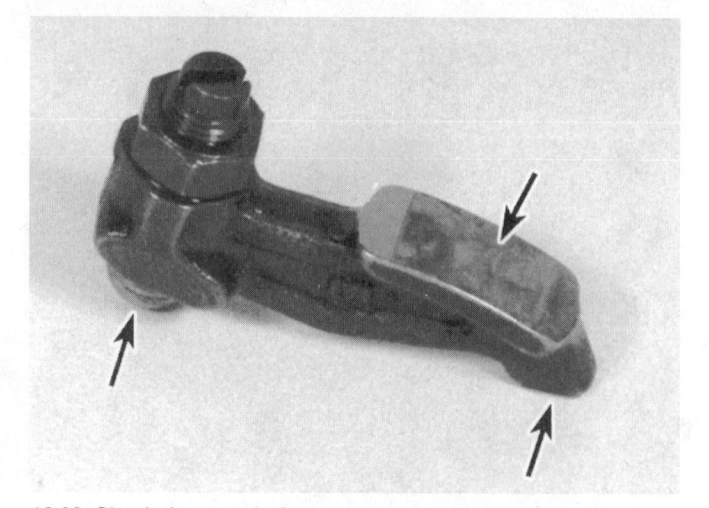

12.22 Check the camshaft contact surface, valve contact surface
and pivot ball (arrows) for wear or damage

19   Remove the rocker shaft retaining bolts **(see illustration)**.
20   Tap the rocker shaft and its end plug out of the engine with a soft
metal drift **(see illustrations)**.
21   Repeat the above Steps to remove the other rocker arm shafts
and rocker arms. Keep all of the parts in order so they can be reinstalled in their original locations.

Inspection

Refer to illustration 12.22

22   Clean all of the components with solvent and dry them off. Blow
through the oil passages in the rocker arms with compressed air, if
available. Inspect the rocker arm faces for pits, spalling, score marks
and rough spots **(see illustration)**. Check the rocker arm-to-shaft contact areas and the adjusting screws, as well. Look for cracks in each
rocker arm. If the faces of the rocker arms are damaged, the rocker
arms and the camshafts should be replaced as a set.

Installation

Refer to illustration 12.23

23   Lubricate the rocker arm shaft with engine oil and slide it into the
cylinder head. Make sure the retaining bolt hole in the shaft is aligned
with the hole in the cylinder head **(see illustration)**. Install the retaining
bolt.
24   Coat the circumference of the rocker shaft plug with a film of silicone sealant, then tap it into its bore in the cylinder head.

12.23 Align the retaining bolt hole in the cylinder head with the corresponding hole in the rocker shaft (arrows)

13.10a Gently pry the oil lines loose from the cylinder head; inspect the O-ring on the fitting and replace it if its condition is in doubt

13.10b Remove the banjo bolts that secure the external oil lines . . .

13.10c . . . there's a sealing washer on each side of the banjo fitting; replace these whenever they're removed

25   Lay the rocker arms in their notches in the shaft.
26   Repeat Steps 23, 24 and 25 to install the remaining rocker arms and shafts.
27   Install the camshafts following the procedure described earlier in this Section.

---

13   Cylinder head - removal and installation (ZX750 models)

Caution: *The engine must be completely cool before beginning this procedure, or the cylinder head may become warped.*
Note: *This procedure can be performed with the engine in the frame. If the engine has been removed, ignore the steps which don't apply.*

Removal

Refer to illustrations 13.10a, 13.10b, 13.10c, 13.11, 13.12a, 13.12b and 13.15

1   Set the bike on its centerstand.
2   Remove the fairing and fuel tank (see Section 42 and Chapter 4).
3   Remove the carburetors (see Chapter 4).
4   Remove the horns (see Chapter 9).
5   Remove the valve cover following the procedure given in Section 10.
6   Remove the cam chain tensioner following the procedure given in Section 11.
7   Remove the radiator (see Chapter 3 and Section 37).
8   Remove the exhaust system (see Chapter 4).
9   Remove the camshafts (see Section 12).

13.11 Cylinder head bolt TIGHTENING sequence

10

10   Detach the oil lines from the top and front of the cylinder head **(see illustrations)**.
11   Loosen the cylinder head bolts, a little at a time, using the **reverse** order of the tightening sequence **(see illustration)**.
12   Lift out the cylinder head bolts and their steel washers once they

13.12a Lift out the cylinder head bolts and washers ...

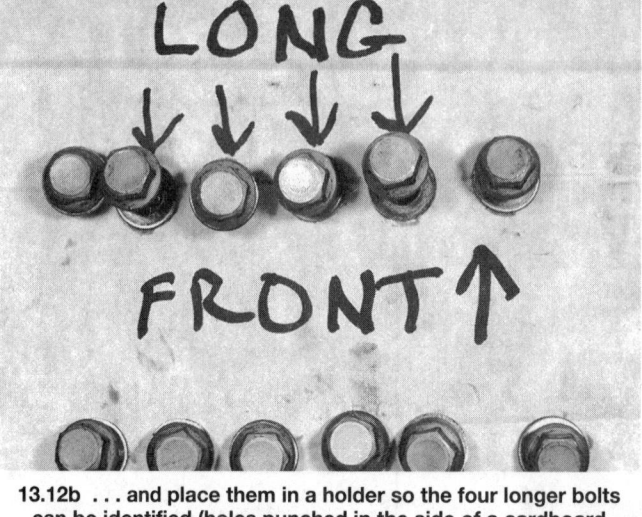

13.12b ... and place them in a holder so the four longer bolts can be identified (holes punched in the side of a cardboard box will work)

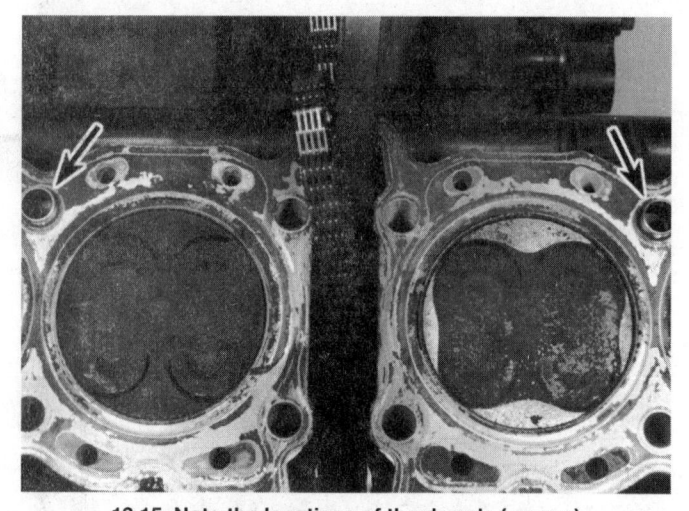

13.15 Note the locations of the dowels (arrows)

have all been loosened **(see illustration)**. **Note:** *Four of the bolts are longer than the others; these are installed in the center holes on the exhaust (front) side of the engine* **(holes 1, 3, 5 and 7 in illustration 13.11)**. *Store the bolts in a holder to keep the four long bolts in their correct locations* **(see illustration)**.

13   Pull the cylinder head off the cylinder block. If the head is stuck, tap around the side of the head with a rubber mallet to jar it loose, or use two wooden dowels inserted into the intake or exhaust ports to lever the head off. Don't attempt to pry the head off by inserting a screwdriver between the head and the cylinder block - you'll damage the sealing surfaces.

14   Stuff a clean rag into the cam chain tunnel to prevent the entry of debris. Remove all of the head bolt washers from their seats, using a pair of needle-nose pliers.

15   Remove the two dowel pins from the cylinder block **(see illustration)**.

16   Check the cylinder head gasket and the mating surfaces on the cylinder head and block for leakage, which could indicate warpage. Refer to Chapter 2 and check the flatness of the cylinder head.

17   Clean all traces of old gasket material from the cylinder head and block. Be careful not to let any of the gasket material fall into the crankcase, the cylinder bores or the water passages.

Installation

18   Install the two dowel pins over their studs, then lay the new gasket in place on the cylinder block. Make sure the UP mark on the gas-

ket is positioned on the right-hand side of the engine. Never reuse the old gasket and don't use any type of gasket sealant.

19   Carefully lower the cylinder head onto the cylinder block. It is helpful to have an assistant support the camshaft chain with a piece of wire so it doesn't fall and become kinked or detached from the crankshaft. When the head is resting against the cylinder block, wire the cam chain to another component to keep tension on it.

20   Lubricate both sides of the head bolt washers with engine oil and place them on the bolts.

21   Install the head bolts, making sure the four longer bolts are installed in the correct holes **(1, 3, 5 and 7 in illustration 13.11)**. Using the proper sequence **(see illustration 13.11)**, tighten the bolts to approximately half the torque listed in this Chapter's Specifications.

22   Using the same sequence, tighten the bolts to the torque listed in this Chapter's Specifications.

23   The remainder of installation is the reverse of the removal steps.

24   Change the engine oil (see Chapter 1).

14   Valves/valve seats/valve guides - servicing (ZX750 models)

1   Because of the complex nature of this job and the special tools and equipment required, servicing of the valves, the valve seats and the valve guides (commonly known as a valve job) is best left to a professional.

2   The home mechanic can, however, remove and disassemble the head, do the initial cleaning and inspection, then reassemble and deliver the head to a dealer service department or properly equipped motorcycle repair shop for the actual valve servicing. Refer to Chapter 2 for those procedures.

3   The dealer service department will remove the valves and springs, recondition or replace the valves and valve seats, replace the valve guides, check and replace the valve springs, spring retainers and keepers (as necessary), replace the valve seals with new ones and reassemble the valve components.

4   After the valve job has been performed, the head will be in like-new condition. When the head is returned, be sure to clean it again very thoroughly before installation on the engine to remove any metal particles or abrasive grit that may still be present from the valve service operations. Use compressed air, if available, to blow out all the holes and passages.

15   Cylinder head and valves - disassembly, inspection and reassembly (ZX750 models)

1   As mentioned in the previous Section, valve servicing and valve guide replacement should be left to a dealer service department or motorcycle repair shop. However, disassembly, cleaning and inspection of the valves and related components can be done (if the neces-

16.2a Remove the Allen bolt from the upper side of the water pipe . . .

16.2b . . . and from the lower side, then pull the pipe fittings out of the block

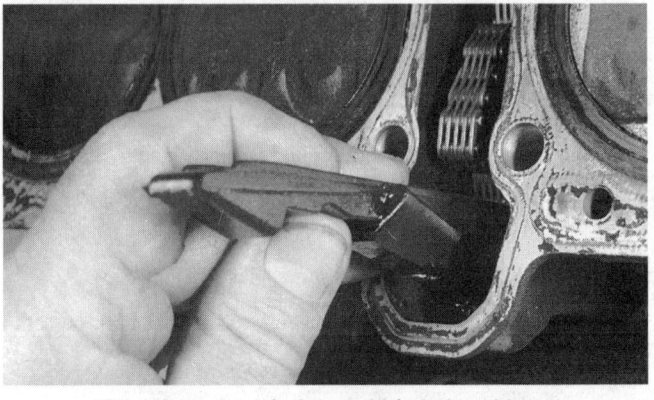

16.3 Lift the front (exhaust side) chain guide out

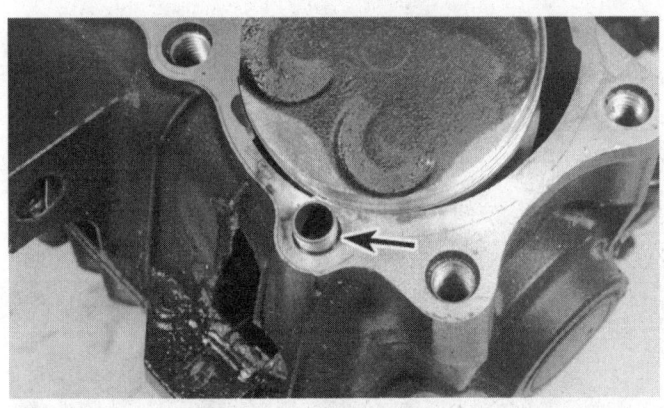

16.5 There's a dowel for the cylinder block at each front corner of the crankcase (arrow)

sary special tools are available) by the home mechanic. This way no expense is incurred if the inspection reveals that service work is not required at this time.

2 Procedures are the same as for the ZX600 cylinder head; refer to Chapter 2 for procedures and this Chapter's Specifications.

16 Cylinder block - removal, inspection and installation (ZX750 models)

Removal

Refer to illustrations 16.2a, 16.2b, 16.3 and 16.5

1 Following the procedure given in Section 13, remove the cylinder head. Make sure the crankshaft is positioned at Top Dead Center (TDC) for cylinders 1 and 4.

2 Remove the water pipe from the rear of the cylinder block **(see illustrations)**.

3 Lift out the camshaft chain front guide **(see illustration)**.

4 Lift the cylinder block straight up off the pistons to remove it. If it's stuck, tap around its perimeter with a soft-faced hammer. Don't attempt to pry between the block and the crankcase, as you will ruin the sealing surfaces.

5 Remove the dowel pins from the mating surface of the crankcase **(see illustration)**. Be careful not to let these drop into the engine. Stuff rags around the pistons and remove the gasket and all traces of old gasket material from the surfaces of the cylinder block and the cylinder head.

Inspection

6 Cylinder block inspection and honing are the same as for ZX600 models. Refer to Chapter 2 for procedures and the Specifications at the beginning of this chapter.

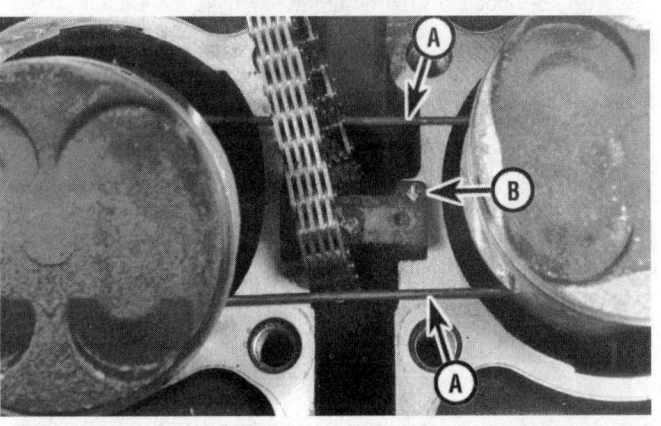

16.9 Slip a rod (A) beneath the front and rear of the pistons; be sure the rear (intake side) cam chain guide is in place (B)

Installation

Refer to illustrations 16.9 and 16.10

7 Lubricate the cylinder bores with plenty of clean engine oil. Apply a thin film of moly-based grease to the piston skirts.

8 Install the dowel pins, then lower a new cylinder base gasket over the studs, with the UP mark on the right-hand side of the engine. Some gaskets also have an arrow, which must point to the front of the engine.

9 Slowly rotate the crankshaft until all of the pistons are at the same level. Slide lengths of welding rod or pieces of a straightened-out coat hanger under the pistons, on both sides of the connecting rods **(see illustration)**. This will help keep the pistons level as the cylinder block is lowered onto them.

10

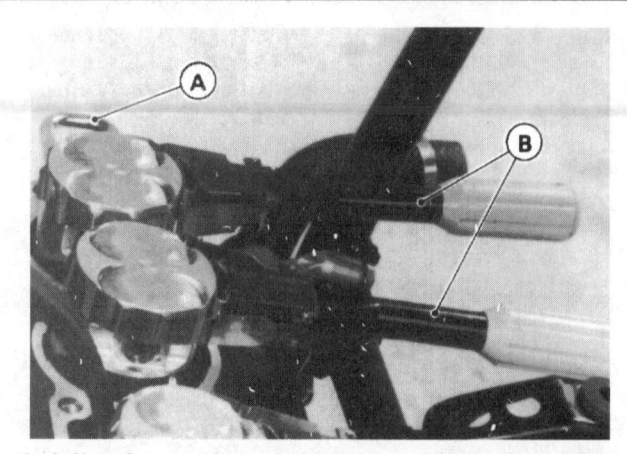

16.10 If you're experienced and very careful, you can guide the cylinder block over the pistons using only a screwdriver, but it's a good idea to use ring compressors

A *Piston support rods*	B *Ring compressors*

19.6 The oil lines are secured to the pan by a banjo bolt (arrow); be sure to use new sealing washers on installation

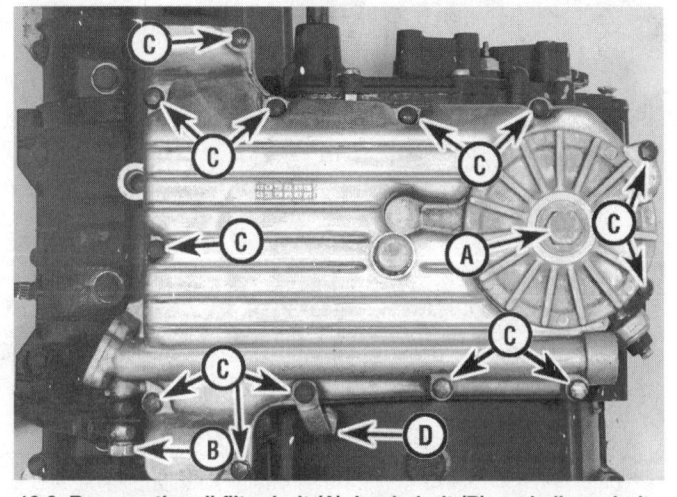

19.8 Remove the oil filter bolt (A), banjo bolt (B), and oil pan bolts (C); one of the bolts secures a wiring harness retainer (D)

10   Attach four piston ring compressors to the pistons and compress the piston rings **(see illustration)**. Large hose clamps can be used instead - just make sure they don't scratch the pistons, and don't tighten them too much.

11   Make sure the intake side cam chain guide is installed **(see illustration 16.9)**.

12   Position the cylinder block over the engine and carefully lower it

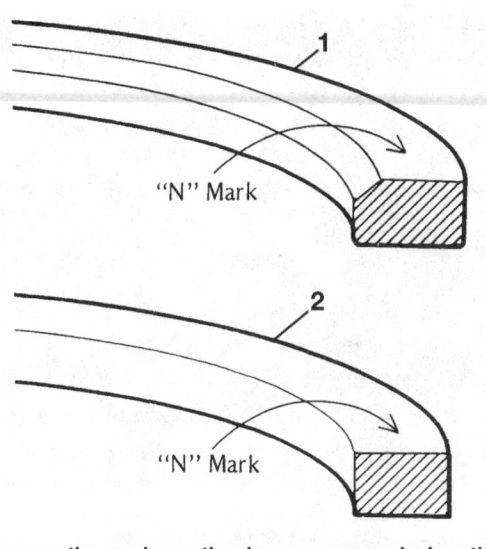

18.1 Make sure the marks on the rings are upward when the rings are installed

1 *Top ring*	2 *Second compression ring*

down until the piston crowns fit into the cylinder liners. While doing this, pull the camshaft chain up, using a hooked tool or a piece of coat hanger. Push down on the cylinder block, making sure the pistons don't get cocked sideways, until the bottom of the cylinder liners slide down past the piston rings. A wood or plastic hammer handle can be used to gently tap the block down, but don't use too much force or the pistons will be damaged.

13   Remove the piston ring compressors or hose clamps, being careful not to scratch the pistons. Remove the rods from under the pistons.

14   Install the cam chain front guide **(see illustration 16.3)**.

15   The remainder of installation is the reverse of removal.

17   Pistons - removal, inspection and installation (ZX750 models)

These procedures are the same as for ZX600 models. Refer to Chapter 2 for procedures and the Specifications at the beginning of this Chapter.

18   Piston rings - installation (ZX750 models)

Refer to illustration 18.1

Piston ring installation is the same as for ZX600 models, except that ring profiles differ **(see illustration)**. Refer to Chapter 2 for details.

19   Oil pan - removal and installation (ZX750 models)

Note: *The oil pan can be removed with the engine in the frame.*

Removal

Refer to illustrations 19.6 and 19.8

1   Set the bike on its centerstand.

2   Drain the engine oil and remove the oil filter (see Chapter 1).

3   Remove the upper and lower fairings (see Section 42).

4   Remove the radiator and oil cooler (see Section 37).

5   Remove the exhaust system (see Chapter 4).

6   Remove the banjo bolt that attaches the oil cooler lines to the oil pan **(see illustration)**.

7   Remove the small screw and disconnect the wire from the oil pressure switch (see Chapter 9).

8   Remove the oil pan bolts and detach the pan from the crankcase **(see illustration)**.

9   Remove all traces of old gasket material from the mating surfaces of the oil pan and crankcase.

19.10 It's a good idea to replace the O-rings (arrows) whenever the oil pan is removed

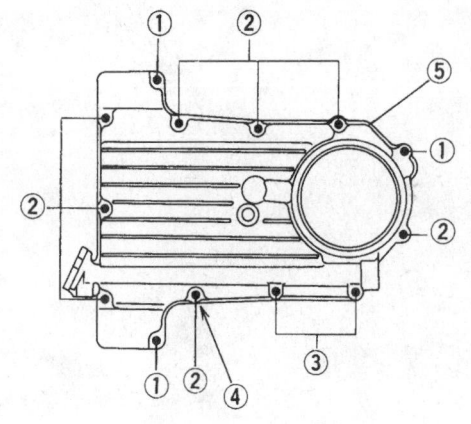

19.11 Oil pan bolt locations

1	40 mm bolts	4	Wiring harness retainer
2	25 mm bolts	5	Oil pan
3	35 mm bolts		

20.2 Remove the oil gallery plug (arrow) and install a pressure gauge

20.9 Work the pickup O-ring free of the crankcase and take the pickup out

Installation

Refer to illustrations 19.10 and 19.11

10   Check the small O-rings in the oil passages in the crankcase and the large O-ring around the oil filter hole (in the pan) for cracking and general deterioration **(see illustration)**. Replace them if necessary. The flat side of the O-rings must face the crankcase.

11   Position a new gasket on the oil pan. A thin film of RTV sealant can be used to hold the gasket in place. Install the oil pan and bolts, making sure the bolts are in the correct holes and the wiring harness retainer is installed on the proper bolt **(see illustration)**. Tighten the bolts to the torque listed in this Chapter's Specifications, using a criss-cross pattern.

12   The remainder of installation is the reverse of removal. Install a new filter and fill the crankcase with oil (see Chapter 1), then run the engine and check for leaks.

20   Oil pump - pressure check, removal, inspection and installation (ZX750 models)

Note: *The oil pump can be removed with the engine in the frame.*

Pressure check

Refer to illustration 20.2

Warning: *If the oil gallery plug is removed when the engine is hot, hot oil will drain out - wait until the engine is cold before beginning this*

check *(it must be cold to perform the relief valve opening pressure check, anyway)*.

1   If necessary for access, remove the lower fairing (see Section 42).

2   Remove the plug at the bottom of the crankcase on the right-hand side and install an oil pressure gauge **(see illustration)**.

3   Start the engine and watch the gauge while varying the engine rpm. The pressure should stay within the relief valve opening pressure listed in this Chapter's Specifications. If the pressure is too high, the relief valve is stuck closed. To check it, see Section 21.

4   If the pressure is lower than the standard, either the relief valve is stuck open, the oil pump is faulty, or there is other engine damage. Begin diagnosis by checking the relief valve (see Section 21), then the oil pump. If those items check out okay, chances are the bearing oil clearances are excessive and the engine needs to be overhauled.

5   If the pressure reading is in the desired range, allow the engine to warm up to normal operating temperature and check the pressure again, at the specified engine rpm. Compare your findings with this Chapter's Specifications.

6   If the pressure is significantly lower than specified, check the relief valve and the oil pump.

Removal

Refer to illustrations 20.9, 20.10, 20.11a, 20.11b, 20.11c, 20.11d and 20.12

7   Remove the oil pan (see Section 19).

8   Remove the clutch assembly (see Section 22).

9   Remove the oil pickup **(see illustration)**.

10

20.10 Place the oil pump drive tab (arrow) and the water pump drive slot in a vertical position, so they'll be aligned on installation of the water pump

20.11a Remove the oil pump sprocket bolt (arrow); it's located behind the clutch housing

20.11b Use a socket (arrow) to remove the chain guide bolt . . .

20.11c . . . lift out the chain guide . . .

20.11d . . . then disengage the oil pump sprocket from the chain and lift it out

Inspection

Refer to illustrations 20.13 and 20.14

13   Remove the oil pump cover screws and lift off the cover **(see illustration)**. Thoroughly clean the mating surfaces.

14   Remove the oil pump shaft, pin, inner rotor and outer rotor from the pump **(see illustration)**. Mark the rotors so they can be installed in the same relative positions.

15   Wash all the components in solvent, then dry them off. Check the pump body, the rotors and the cover for scoring and wear. Make sure the pick-up screen isn't clogged. Kawasaki doesn't publish clearance specifications, so if any damage or uneven or excessive wear is evident, replace the pump. If you are rebuilding the engine, it's a good idea to install new oil pump.

16   Reassemble the pump by reversing the removal steps, but before installing the cover, pack the cavities between the rotors with petroleum jelly - this will ensure the pump develops suction quickly and begins oil circulation as soon as the engine is started. Be sure to use a new gasket.

20.12 Loosen the holder-to-oil pump bolt (A) if you plan to separate the pump and holder, then remove the mounting bolts (B) and lift the oil pump out

Installation

Refer to illustrations 20.18 and 20.20

17   If you removed the oil pump sprocket, engage it with the chain before installing the oil pump.

18   Hold the oil pump and unlatch the stopper from the alternator chain tensioner pushrod **(see illustration)**. Press the alternator chain tensioner pushrod into the oil pump, then slip a piece of thin wire into the pushrod hole to hold the pushrod in the compressed position (the wire will be removed after the oil pump is installed).

19   Position the oil pump on the engine. Coat the threads of the oil pump bolts with non-permanent thread locking agent, then install the bolts and tighten them to the torque listed in this Chapter's Specifications. Remove the wire from the tensioner to allow it to take up chain slack.

10   Turn the crankshaft so the drive slot and tab in the oil pump shaft and water pump shaft are vertical **(see illustration)**.

11   Remove the oil pump sprocket bolt and chain guide bolt, then take out the sprocket **(see illustrations)**.

12   Remove the oil pump mounting bolts, then take the pump and holder out **(see illustration)**.

20.13 Remove the cover screws (arrows); use an impact driver
if necessary

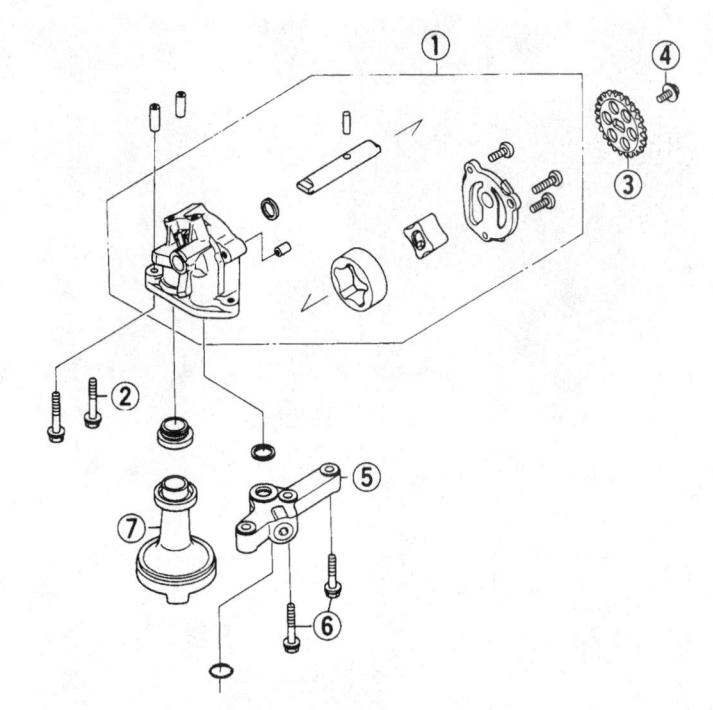

20.14 Oil pump details

1	Rotors and housing	5	Holder
2	Pump mounting bolts	6	Holder and pump
3	Sprocket		mounting bolts
4	Sprocket bolt	7	Oil pickup

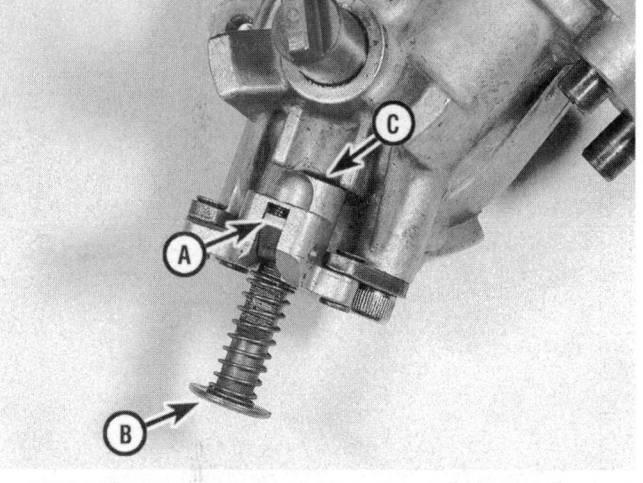

20.18 Lift the latch (A) clear of the grooves in the tensioner
pushrod, then compress the pushrod (B) against the spring -
when the small hole appears at point C, slip a thin piece
of wire into it to hold the pushrod compressed

20.20 Install the pickup with its flat side (arrow) toward the
oil pump

21   Oil pressure relief valve - removal, inspection and installation
(ZX750 models)

Refer to illustration 21.2

Removal
1   Remove the oil pan (see Section 19).
2   Unscrew the relief valve from the oil pan **(see illustration)**.

Inspection
3   Clean the valve with solvent and dry it, using compressed air if
available.
4   Using a wood or plastic tool, depress the steel ball inside the
valve and see if it moves smoothly. Make sure it returns to its seat
completely. If it doesn't, replace it with a new one (don't attempt to
disassemble and repair it).

21.2 The oil pressure relief valve is mounted in the oil pan (arrow)

20   Install the oil pickup so the flat side is toward the oil pump holder
(see illustration).
21   The remainder of installation is the reverse of the removal steps.

10

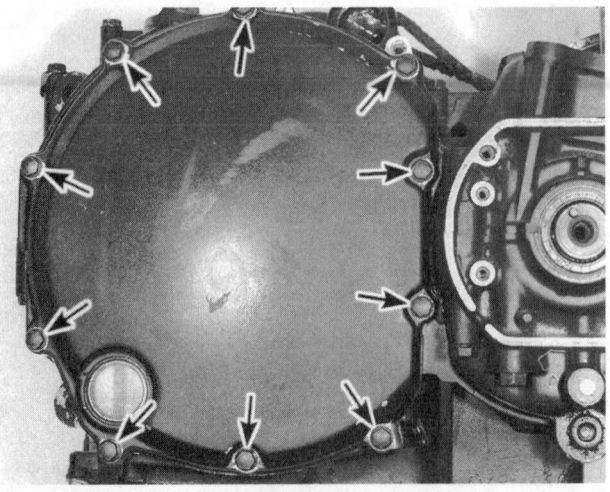

22.3a Loosen the clutch cover bolts (arrows) evenly in a criss-cross pattern . . .

22.3b . . . then remove the cover; one lower bolt secures a wiring harness clip (arrow)

22.4a Remove the clutch spring bolts . . .

22.4b . . . take out the springs . . .

Installation

5   Apply a non-hardening thread locking compound to the threads of the valve and install it into the oil pan, tightening it to the torque listed in this Chapter's Specifications.
6   The remainder of installation is the reverse of removal.

22 Clutch - removal, inspection and installation (ZX750 models)

Note: *The clutch can be removed with the engine in the frame.*

Removal

Refer to illustrations 22.3a, 22.3b, 22.4a, 22.4b, 22.4c, 22.4d, 22.5a, 22.5b, 22.5c, 22.6a through 22.6e, 22.7a through 22.7e, 22.8a, 22.8b, 22.8c and 22.8d

1   Set the bike on its centerstand and remove the lower fairing (see Section 42).
2   Drain the engine oil (see Chapter 1).
3   Remove the clutch cover bolts and take the cover off **(see illustrations)**. If the cover is stuck, tap around its perimeter with a soft-face hammer.
4   Remove the clutch spring bolts **(see illustration)**. Remove the clutch springs, spring plate, bearing and push piece **(see illustrations)**.
5   Remove the outermost clutch friction plate from the clutch housing **(see illustration)**. Note the direction of the oil grooves in the friction plates **(see illustration)**; on some models they are directional and must face the same way during installation. Remove the steel plate **(see illustration)**, then continue removing the friction and steel plates until all are removed.

22.4c . . . and lift off the spring plate

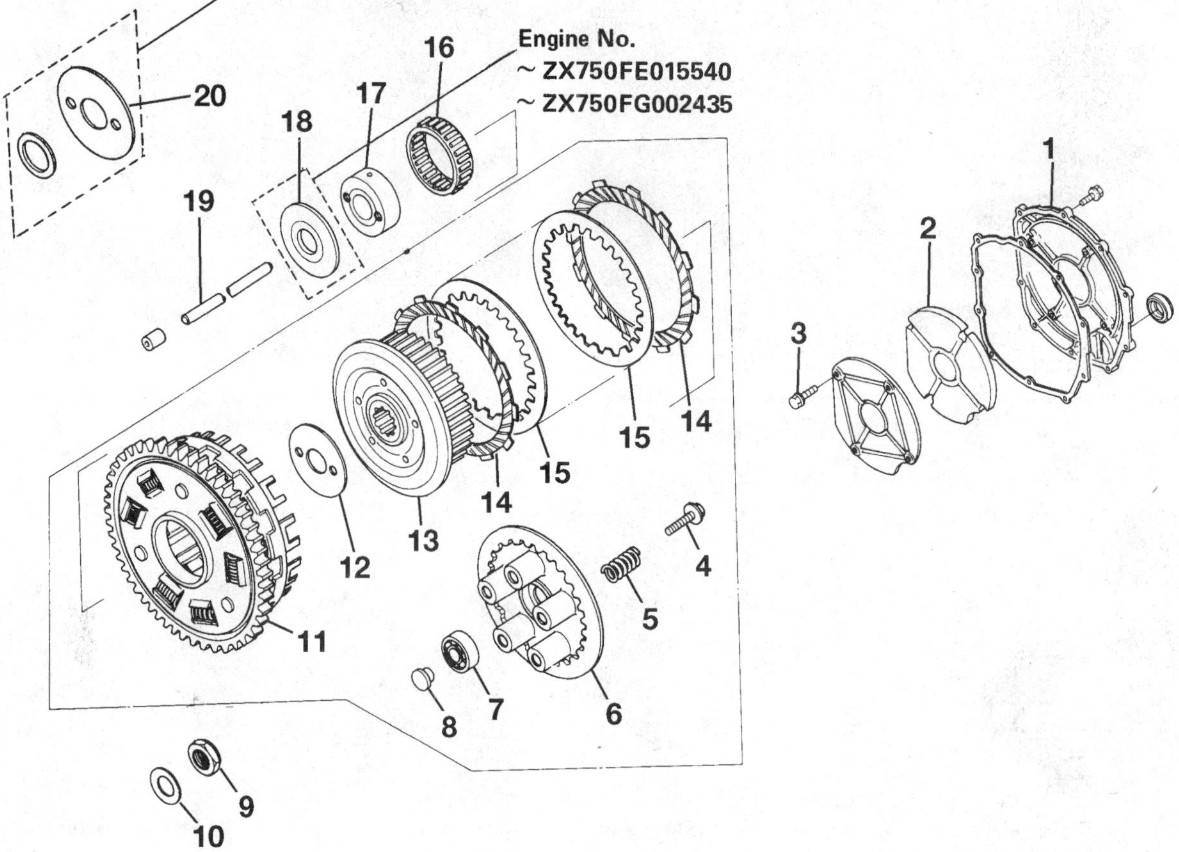

Engine No.
ZX750FE015541 ~
ZX750FG002436 ~
Engine No.
~ ZX750FE015540
~ ZX750FG002435
1
2
3
4
5
6
7
8
9
10
11
12
13
14
15
15
14
16
17
18
19
20

22.4d Clutch details

1 *Clutch cover*
2 *Clutch damper*
3 *Damper bolt*
4 *Clutch spring bolt*
5 *Clutch spring*
6 *Spring plate*
7 *Bearing*
8 *Push piece*
9 *Clutch hub nut*
10 *Dished washer*
11 *Clutch housing*
12 *Thrust washer*
13 *Clutch hub*
14 *Friction plates*
15 *Steel plates*
16 *Bearing*
17 *Collar*
18 *Spacer - earlier models*
19 *Pushrod*
20 *Spacer - later models*

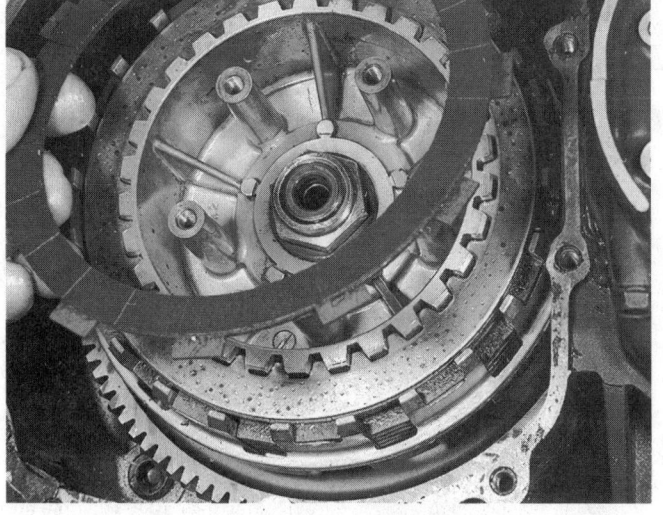

22.5a Take out the first friction plate . . .

①
②

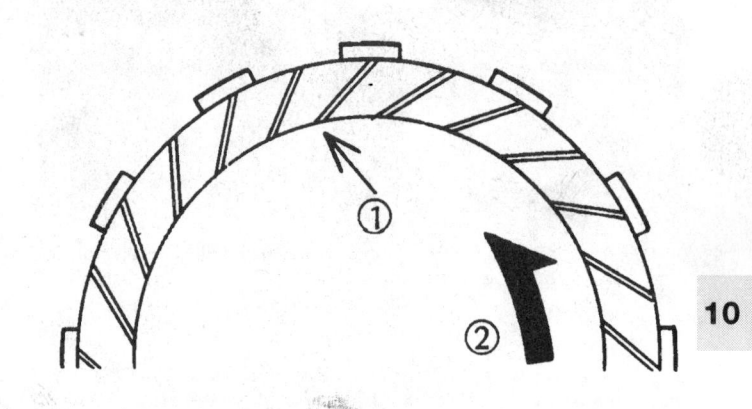

22.5b . . . noting the direction of the oil grooves; some are directional

1 *Oil grooves* 2 *Direction of rotation*

10

22.5c Take out the first steel plate, then continue removing friction and steel plates

22.6a If the clutch hub is secured by a staked nut, bend back the staked portion (arrow) with a hammer and sharp punch

22.6b An old steel plate and friction plate can be drilled and bolted together to make a holding tool . . .

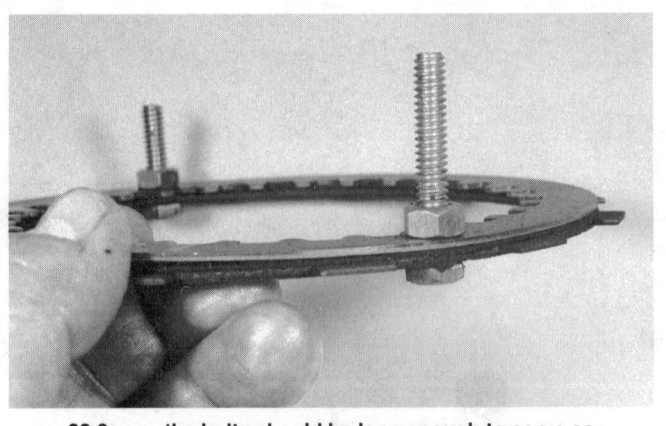

22.6c . . . the bolts should be long enough to serve as removal handles . . .

22.6d . . . slip the bolted plates between the clutch hub and housing in their normal installed position, with the bolt shafts facing outward

22.6e Remove the clutch hub nut

6   Bend back the staked portion of the clutch hub nut with a hammer and sharp punch **(see illustration)**. Remove the clutch hub nut, using a special holding tool (Kawasaki tool no. 57001-305) to prevent the clutch housing from turning **(see illustration 19.7a in Chapter 2)**. An alternative to this tool can be fabricated from some steel strap, bent at the ends and bolted together in the middle **(see illustration 19.7b in Chapter 2)**. If the clutch plates will be replaced, you can drill holes in a friction plate and a steel plate and bolt them together as they would be

when installed **(see illustrations)**. Slip the bolted plates into their installed positions **(see illustration)**; the clutch hub will be locked to the clutch housing. Shift the transmission into a low gear and have an assistant hold the rear brake on. Unscrew the nut and remove it **(see illustration)**.
7   Remove the dished washer, clutch hub and thrust washer **(see illustrations)**. Thread a 6 mm bolt or tap into the collar and pull it out **(see illustration)**.
8   Remove the clutch housing and bearing **(see illustration)**. Re-

22.7a Remove the dished washer . . .

22.7b . . . the clutch hub . . .

22.7c . . . and thrust washer

22.7d Thread a 6 mm bolt or tap into one of the holes in the collar . . .

22.7e . . . and pull the collar out

22.8a Slide the clutch housing sideways to disengage its teeth from the crankshaft . . .

10

22.8b . . . and lift out the bearing . . .

22.8c . . . the clutch housing . . .

22.8d . . . and the thrust washer or spacer

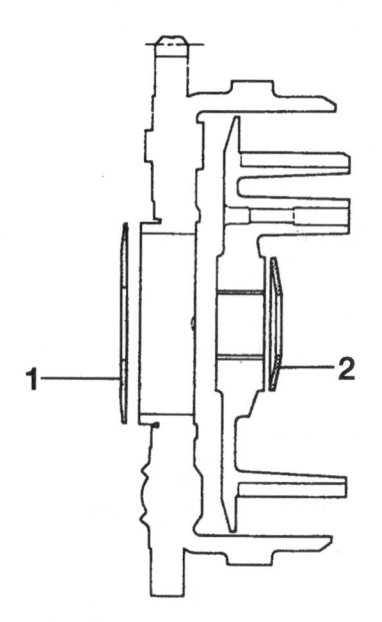

22.10 Install the spacer with its chamfered side toward the
engine; install the washer with its dished side toward the engine

1   Spacer   2   Washer

move the spacer behind the clutch housing **(see illustration 22.4d and
the accompanying illustrations).**

Inspection
9   This is the same as for ZX600 models (see Chapter 2). Wear tol-
erances are listed in this Chapter's Specifications.

Installation
Refer to illustration 22.10
10   Install the spacer over the transmission mainshaft, with the chamfered side facing in **(see illustration)**.
11   Lubricate the collar and the needle bearing with engine oil and
slide them over the mainshaft.
12   Install the clutch housing, thrust washer and the clutch hub. The
dished side of the washer faces in **(see illustration 22.10)**.
13   If the hub nut is a self-locking type, install a new nut. If the hub nut
has a separate lockwasher, install a new lockwasher. Tighten the hub
nut to the torque listed in this Chapter's Specifications. Use the technique described in Step 6 to prevent the hub from turning. After tightening, stake the nut or bend the lockwasher against one of the flats so
the nut can't loosen.
14   Coat the clutch friction plates with engine oil. Install the clutch
plates, starting with a friction plate and alternating them. There are
eight friction plates and seven steel plates. Make sure the oil grooves
in the friction plates are facing the proper direction **(see illustration
22.5b)**.
15   Lubricate the pushrod and install it through the spring plate.
Mount the spring plate to the clutch assembly and install the springs
and bolts, tightening them to the torque listed in this Chapter's Specifications in a criss-cross pattern.

16   Install the clutch cover and bolts, using a new gasket. Tighten the
bolts, in a criss-cross pattern, to the torque listed in this Chapter's
Specifications.
17   Fill the crankcase with the recommended type and amount of engine oil (see Chapter 1).

**23   Clutch hydraulic system - component removal, overhaul and
installation (ZX750 models)**

Master cylinder removal
Refer to illustration 23.2
1   Disconnect the electrical connector for the clutch switch beneath
the master cylinder.
2   Place a towel under the master cylinder to catch any spilled fluid,
then remove the union bolt from the master cylinder fluid line **(see illustration)**. **Caution:** *Brake fluid will damage paint. Wipe up any spills
immediately and wash the area with soap and water.*

23.2 Clutch master cylinder details

1	Rubber cap	11	Cup, spring and piston
2	Banjo bolt	12	Washer
3	Sealing washers	13	Snap-ring
4	Clutch hose	14	Rubber boot
5	Reservoir cover	15	Pushrod
6	Diaphragm	16	Lever pivot bushing
7	Master cylinder body	17	Clutch lever
8	Master cylinder clamp	18	Lever pivot bolt
9	Clamp bolts	19	Clutch line
10	Clutch switch		

3   Remove the master cylinder clamp bolts and take the cylinder body off the handlebar.

Master cylinder overhaul

4   Remove the lever pivot bolt and nut and take off the lever **(see illustration 23.2).**

5   Remove the cover and rubber diaphragm from the reservoir.

6   Remove the rubber boot and pushrod from the master cylinder.

7   Remove the snap-ring, then dump out the piston and secondary cup, primary cup and spring. If they won't come out, blow compressed air into the fluid line hole. **Warning:** *The piston may shoot out forcefully enough to cause injury. Point the piston at a block of wood or a pile of rags inside a box and apply air pressure gradually. Never ooint the end of the cylinder at yourself, including your fingers.*

8   Thoroughly clean all of the components in clean brake fluid (don't use any type of petroleum-based solvent).

9   Check the piston and cylinder bore for wear, scratches and rust. If the piston shows these conditions, replace it and both rubber cups as a set. If the cylinder bore has any defects, replace the entire master cylinder.

23.18 The slave cylinder (A) is secured by two mounting bolts (B)

10   Install the spring in the cylinder bore, wide end first.

11   Coat a new cup with brake fluid and install it in the cylinder, wide end first.

12   Coat the piston with brake fluid and install it in the cylinder.

13   Install the washer. Press the piston into the bore and install the snap ring to hold it in place.

14   Install the rubber boot and pushrod.

15   When you install the clutch lever, align the hole in the lever bushing with the pushrod.

Master cylinder installation

16   Installation is the reverse of the removal steps, with the following additions:

   a Make sure the UP mark on the master cylinder clamp is upright and the arrow points upward.

   b Tighten the clamp bolts to the torque listed in this Chapter's Specifications. Tighten the upper bolt first, then the lower bolt. There will be a small gap between the master cylinder and the clamp at the bottom.

   c Use a new sealing washer on each side of the banjo bolt fitting and tighten the banjo bolt to the torque listed in this Chapter's Specifications.

   d Fill and bleed the master cylinder as described below. Operate the clutch and check for fluid leaks.

Slave cylinder removal

Refer to illustration 23.18

17   If you're removing the slave cylinder for overhaul, loosen the banjo fitting bolt while the slave cylinder is still mounted on the engine. If you're just removing it for access to other components, leave the hydraulic line connected.

18   Remove the mounting bolts and take the slave cylinder off **(see illustration)**.

19   If you're removing the slave cylinder for overhaul, remove the banjo fitting bolt and detach the hydraulic line. Place the end of the line in a container to catch dripping fluid. **Caution:** *Brake fluid will damage paint. Wipe up any spills immediately and wash the area with soap and water.*

20   If the hydraulic line is still connected, push the piston as far into the bore as it will go. Hold the piston in, slowly squeeze the clutch lever to the handlebar and tie the clutch lever in that position. Otherwise, the slave cylinder piston will fall out.

Slave cylinder overhaul

Refer to illustration 23.24

21   Let the pressure of the slave cylinder spring push the piston out of the cylinder, then remove the spring.

22   Separate the spring from the piston.

23   Thoroughly clean all parts in clean brake fluid (don't use any type of petroleum-based solvent).

24   Check the cylinder bore and piston for wear, scratches and rust. If the piston shows these conditions, replace it and the seal as a set. If the cylinder bore has any defects, replace the entire slave cylinder. If

10

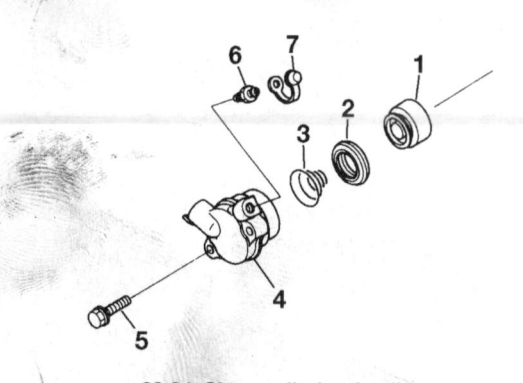

23.24 Slave cylinder details

1	Piston	5	Mounting bolt
2	Seal	6	Bleed valve
3	Spring	7	Bleed valve cap
4	Cylinder body		

the piston and bore are good, carefully remove the seal from the piston and install a new one with its lip facing into the bore **(see illustration)**.

Slave cylinder Installation

25   Installation is the reverse of the removal procedure with the following additions:

 a Use new sealing washers on the clutch fluid line.
 b Tighten the mounting bolts and fluid line banjo bolt to the torques listed in this Chapter's Specifications.
 c Bleed the clutch (see below).
 d Operate the clutch and check for fluid leaks.

Bleeding the clutch

26   Place the bike on its centerstand and point the front wheel straight ahead.
27   Remove the master cylinder cover and diaphragm. Top up the master cylinder with fluid to the upper edge of the fluid level window.
28   Remove the cap from the bleed valve on the slave cylinder. Place a box wrench (ring spanner) over the bleed valve. Attach a rubber tube to the valve fitting and put the other end of the tube in a container. Pour enough clean brake fluid into the container to cover the end of the tube.
29   Slowly squeeze the clutch lever several times. At the same time, tap on the clutch fluid line, starting at the bottom and working your way to the top. Stop when no more air bubbles can be seen rising from the bottom of the reservoir.
30   Squeeze the clutch lever several times until you feel an increase in the effort required to pull the lever, then hold it in.
31   With the lever held in, quickly open the bleed valve to let air and fluid escape, then close it.
32   Repeat Steps 30 and 31 until there aren't any more bubbles in the fluid flowing into the container. **Note**: *Keep an eye on the fluid level in the reservoir. If it drops too low, air will be sucked into the line and the procedure will have to be repeated.*
33   Replenish the master cylinder with fluid, then reinstall the diaphragm and cover and tighten the screws securely.

24   External shift mechanism - removal, inspection and installation (ZX750 models)

Removal

Refer to illustrations 24.7, 24.8a, 24.8b and 24.9a through 24.9e

1   Set the bike on its centerstand.
2   Drain the engine oil and coolant (see Chapter 1 and Section 3).
3   Remove the lower fairing (see Section 42).
4   Remove the clutch slave cylinder (see Section 23).
5   Remove the shift lever, engine sprocket cover and the engine sprocket (see Section 40). Disconnect the wire from the neutral switch.
6   Remove the alternator (see Section 43).
7   Position a drain pan under the shift mechanism cover. Remove

24.7 Remove the cover screws (arrows) with an impact driver

24.8a Compress the shift mechanism arm until the tips are clear . . .

24.8b . . . then take the shift mechanism out

the screws **(see illustration)** and detach the cover from the crankcase. **Note**: *The two flathead screws at the rear of the cover can be very difficult to remove, even with an impact driver. If you need to get the bike back in service quickly, it would be a good idea to start early on a day when your local Kawasaki dealership is open so you can buy new screws if the old ones are ruined during removal.*
8   Pull the shift mechanism arm (against the pressure of the pawl spring) toward the shift shaft until the pointed tips clear the shift drum, then pull the mechanism and shaft off **(see illustrations)**. **Caution:**

24.9a Remove the nuts (arrows) that secure the gear and neutral positioning levers . . .

24.9b . . . remove the collar . . .

24.9c . . . the lever . . .

24.9d . . . the spring . . .

24.9e . . . and the washer

24.14a Check the condition of the pushrod seal (shown with cover installed) . . .

24.14b . . . and the shift shaft seal; remove the cover and replace them if they've been leaking

Don't pull the shift rod out of the crankcase - the shift forks will fall into the oil pan, and the crankcase will have to be separated to reinstall them.

9   Note the positions of the gear and neutral positioning levers and their springs **(see illustration)**. Remove the nuts that secure the levers and lift them off **(see illustrations)**. The levers are interchangeable, but it's a good idea to label them for return to their original locations, since they will take a wear pattern during use.

Inspection

Refer to illustrations 24.14a and 24.14b

10   Check the shift shaft for bends and damage to the splines. If the shaft is bent, you can attempt to straighten it, but if the splines are damaged it will have to be replaced.

11   Check the condition of the return spring and the pawl spring. Replace them if they are cracked or distorted.

12   Check the shift mechanism arm and the overshift limiter for cracks, distortion and wear. If any of these conditions are found, replace the shift mechanism.

13   Make sure the return spring pin isn't loose in the crankcase. If it is, unscrew it, apply a non-hardening locking compound to the threads, then reinstall it and tighten it securely.

14   Check the condition of the seals in the cover **(see illustrations)**. If they have been leaking, drive them out with a hammer and punch. New seals can be installed by driving them in with a socket.

10

24.15 The shift mechanism should look like this when it's installed

24.18 Apply a small amount of sealant to the crankcase parting line where it meets the cover mating surface (arrows)

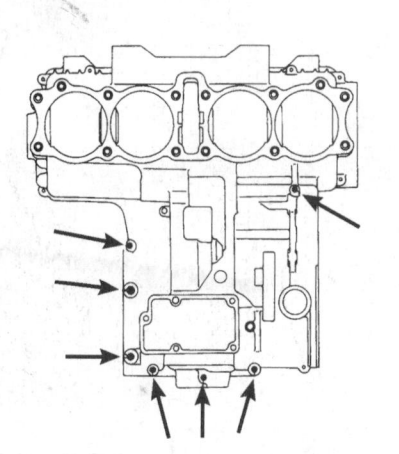

25.7 Upper crankcase bolts

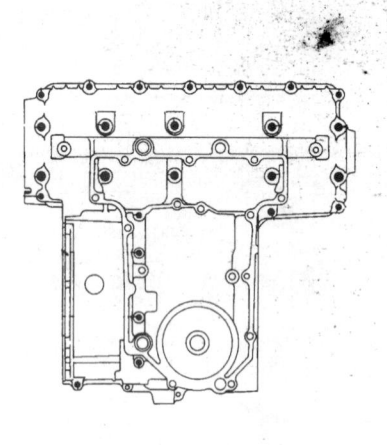

25.9a The lower crankcase 8 mm bolts (A) and 6 mm bolts (B)

Installation

Refer to illustrations 24.15 and 24.18

15   Slide the external shift mechanism into place, lifting the shift arm and the overshift limiter to clear the shift drum **(see illustration)**.
16   Install the gear and neutral positioning levers and make sure the springs are positioned correctly **(see illustration 24.9a)**.
17   Apply high-temperature grease to the lips of the seals. Wrap the splines of the shift shaft with electrical tape, so the splines won't damage the seal as the cover is installed.
18   Apply a thin coat of RTV sealant to the cover mating areas on the crankcase, where the halves of the crankcase join **(see illustration)**.
19   Carefully guide the cover into place. Apply non-permanent thread locking agent to the threads of the two flathead screws along the rear of the cover, then install all of the screws, tightening them securely. Reconnect the neutral switch wire.
20   Install the engine sprocket and chain (see Section 40) and engine sprocket cover.
21   Install the shift lever (see Chapter 6).
22   Check the engine oil level and add some, if necessary (see Chapter 1).

25 Crankcase - disassembly and reassembly (ZX750 models)

Disassembly

Refer to illustrations 25.7, 25.9a, 25.9b, 25.10a, 25.10b and 25.11

1   To examine and repair or replace the crankshaft, connecting rods, bearings, transmission components and idler shaft/starter motor

clutch, the crankcase must be split into two parts.
2   Remove the alternator and starter motor (see Section 43).
3   On the right side of the engine, remove the clutch (see Section 22), pickup coil cover and pickup coils (see Section 39).
4   On the left side of the engine, remove the water pump (see Section 37) and external shift mechanism (see Section 24).
5   On the bottom of the engine, remove the oil filter, oil pan, pump and pickup (see Chapter 1 and Sections 19 and 20).
6   If you're planning to remove the crankshaft, remove the cylinder head, cylinder block and pistons (see Sections 15 and 16 and Chapter 2).
7   Remove the upper crankcase bolts **(see illustration)**.
8   Unbolt the oil pump sprocket, then slide the sprocket and chain off together. Remove the chain guide and separate the sprocket from the chain (see Section 20).
9   Turn the crankcase over and remove the lower crankcase bolts **(see illustration)**. Loosen the 8 mm bolts that secure the crankshaft in the reverse order of the tightening sequence **(see illustration)**.
10   Pry the crankcase halves apart at the pry points only **(see illustrations)**. **Caution:** *Don't pry between the crankcase halves or the mating surfaces will be gouged, resulting in an oil leak.*
11   Lift the lower crankcase half off the upper half **(see illustration)**.
12   Refer to Sections 26 through 34 for information on the internal components of the crankcase.

Reassembly

Refer to illustrations 25.16, 25.17 and 25.18

13   Remove all traces of sealant from the crankcase mating surfaces. Be careful not to let any fall into the case as this is done.

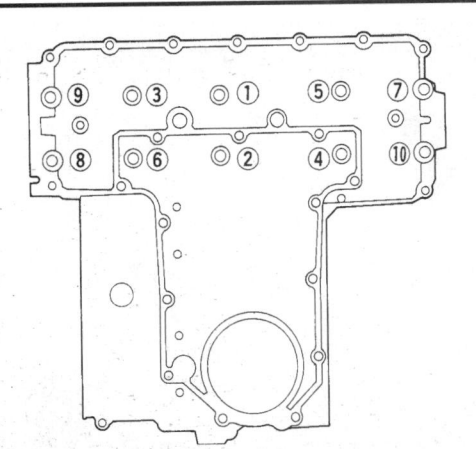

25.9b Crankcase 8 mm bolt TIGHTENING sequence

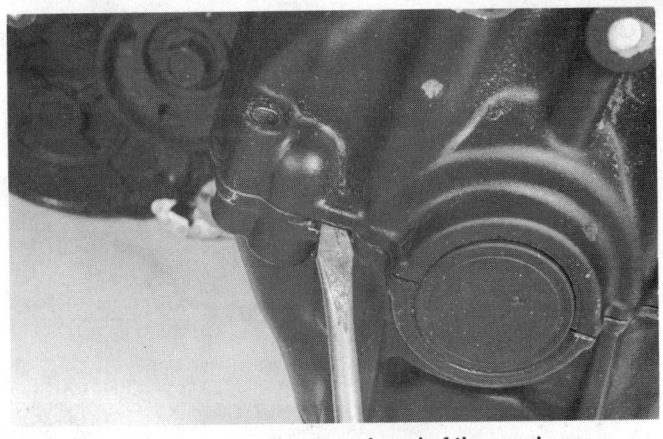

25.10a There's a pry point at each end of the crankcase . . .

25.10b . . . pry only at these points to prevent damaging the gasket surfaces

25.11 Lift the lower case half off the upper half

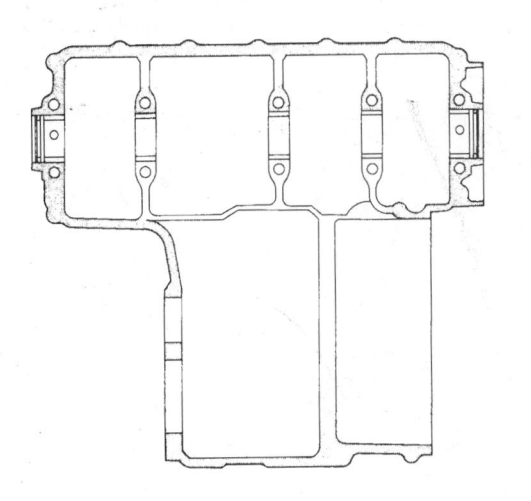

25.16 Apply sealant to the shaded areas

25.17 Position the shift drum and forks in the neutral position

14   Check to make sure the two dowel pins are in place in their holes in the mating surface of the upper crankcase half.

15   Pour some engine oil over the transmission gears, the crankshaft main bearings and the shift drum. Don't get any oil on the crankcase mating surface.

16   Apply a thin, even bead of Kawasaki Bond sealant (part no.

92104-1003) to the indicated areas of the crankcase mating surfaces **(see illustration)**. Also apply RTV sealant to the areas near the ends of the crankshaft seal areas (lay it over the Kawasaki Bond). **Caution:** *Don't apply an excessive amount of either type of sealant, as it will ooze out when the case halves are assembled and may obstruct oil passages.*

17   Check the position of the shift drum - make sure it's in the neutral position **(see illustration)**.

25.18 Make sure the forks engage the gear grooves (arrows)

26.4a Remove the breather cover bolts (arrows) . . .

18   Carefully place the lower crankcase half onto the upper crankcase half. While doing this, make sure the shift forks fit into their gear grooves **(see illustration)**.

19   Install the lower crankcase half bolts and tighten them so they are just snug.

20   In two steps, tighten the larger bolts (8 mm), in the indicated sequence, to the torque listed in this Chapter's Specifications **(see illustration 25.9b)**.

21   Turn the case over and install the upper crankcase half bolts, tightening them to the torque listed in this Chapter's Specifications.

22   Turn the case over again and install the smaller (6 mm) bolts in the lower crankcase half, tightening them to the torque listed in this Chapter's Specifications.

23   Turn the main drive shaft and the output shaft to make sure they turn freely. Install the shift lever on the shift shaft and, while turning the output shaft, shift the transmission through the gears, from first to sixth, then back to first. The positive neutral finder prevents the transmission from being shifted past neutral into second gear unless the output shaft is turning at a fairly high rate of speed, which can be difficult. If the transmission doesn't shift properly, the case will have to be separated again to correct the problem. Also make sure the crankshaft turns freely.

24   The remainder of installation is the reverse of removal.

26   Crankcase components - inspection and servicing (ZX750 models)

Refer to illustration 26.4a, 26.4b and 26.4c

1   After the crankcases have been separated and the crankshaft, shift drum and forks and transmission components removed, the crankcases should be cleaned thoroughly with new solvent and dried with compressed air. All oil passages should be blown out with compressed air and all traces of old gasket sealant should be removed from the mating surfaces. **Caution:** *Be very careful not to nick or gouge the crankcase mating surfaces or leaks will result. Check both crankcase sections very carefully for cracks and other damage.*

2   Check the cam chain and alternator/starter chain guides for wear - one is in the upper case half and the other is in the lower case half. If they appear to be worn excessively, replace them.

3   Check the ball bearings in the case. If they don't turn smoothly, drive them out with a bearing driver or a socket having an outside diameter slightly smaller than that of the bearing. Before installing them, allow them to sit in the freezer overnight, and about fifteen-minutes before installation, place the case half in an oven, set to about 200-degrees F, and allow it to heat up. The bearings are an interference fit, and this will ease installation. **Warning**: *Before heating the case, wash it thoroughly with soap and water so no explosive fumes are present. Also, don't use a flame to heat the case.*

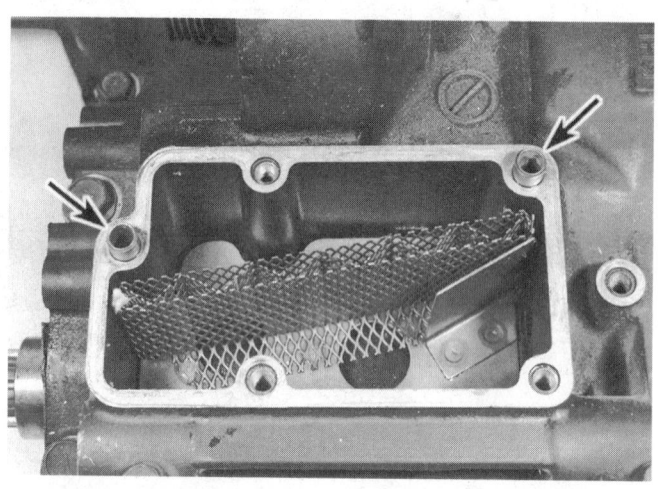

26.4b . . . and lift off the cover, noting the locations of the dowels (arrows) . . .

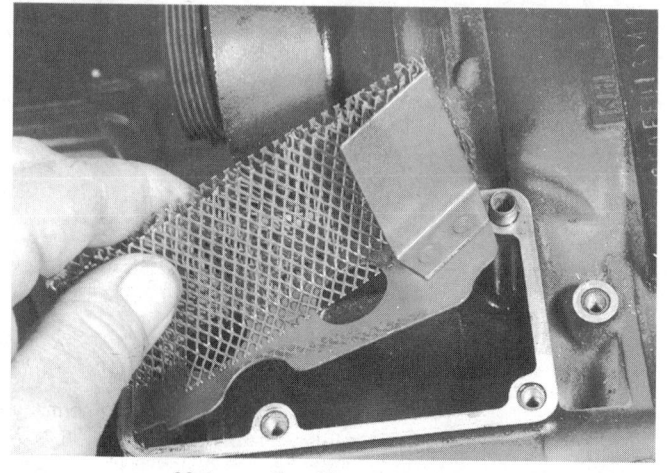

26.4c . . . then lift out the screen

4   Remove the breather cover and lift out the separator screen **(see illustrations)**. Clean the screen with solvent. Replace it if it's clogged or damaged.

5   If any damage is found that can't be repaired, replace the crankcase halves as a set.

30.3 There's an O-ring behind the pulley bolt

30.4 Thread a pair of 6 mm bolts into the holes in the pulley, then with the pulley bolt removed, tighten the 6 mm bolts against the case to push the pulley off

27 Main and connecting rod bearings - general note (ZX750 models)

1   Even though main and connecting rod bearings are generally replaced with new ones during the engine overhaul, the old bearings should be retained for close examination as they may reveal valuable information about the condition of the engine.

2   Bearing failure occurs mainly because of lack of lubrication, the presence of dirt or other foreign particles, overloading the engine and/or corrosion. Regardless of the cause of bearing failure, it must be corrected before the engine is reassembled to prevent it from happening again.

3   When examining the bearings, remove the main bearings from the case halves and the rod bearings from the connecting rods and caps and lay them out on a clean surface in the same general position as their location on the crankshaft journals. This will enable you to match any noted bearing problems with the corresponding side of the crankshaft journal.

4   Dirt and other foreign particles get into the engine in a variety of ways. It may be left in the engine during assembly or it may pass through filters or breathers. It may get into the oil and from there into the bearings. Metal chips from machining operations and normal engine wear are often present. Abrasives are sometimes left in engine components after reconditioning operations such as cylinder honing, especially when parts are not thoroughly cleaned using the proper cleaning methods. Whatever the source, these foreign objects often end up imbedded in the soft bearing material and are easily recognized. Large particles will not imbed in the bearing and will score or gouge the bearing and journal. The best prevention for this cause of bearing failure is to clean all parts thoroughly and keep everything spotlessly clean during engine reassembly. Frequent and regular oil and filter changes are also recommended.

5   Lack of lubrication or lubrication breakdown has a number of inter-related causes. Excessive heat (which thins the oil), overloading (which squeezes the oil from the bearing face) and oil leakage or throw off (from excessive bearing clearances, worn oil pump or high engine speeds) all contribute to lubrication breakdown. Blocked oil passages will also starve a bearing and destroy it. When lack of lubrication is the cause of bearing failure, the bearing material is wiped or extruded from the steel backing of the bearing. Temperatures may increase to the point where the steel backing and the journal turn blue from overheating.

6   Riding habits can have a definite effect on bearing life. Full throttle low speed operation, or lugging (laboring) the engine, puts very high loads on bearings, which tend to squeeze out the oil film. These loads cause the bearings to flex, which produces fine cracks in the bearing face (fatigue failure). Eventually the bearing material will loosen in pieces and tear away from the steel backing. Short trip driving leads to corrosion of bearings, as insufficient engine heat is produced to drive off the condensed water and corrosive gases produced. These products collect in the engine oil, forming acid and sludge. As the oil is carried to the engine bearings, the acid attacks and corrodes the bearing material.

7   Incorrect bearing installation during engine assembly will lead to bearing failure as well. Tight fitting bearings which leave insufficient bearing oil clearances result in oil starvation. Dirt or foreign particles trapped behind a bearing insert result in high spots on the bearing which lead to failure.

8   To avoid bearing problems, clean all parts thoroughly before reassembly, double check all bearing clearance measurements and lubricate the new bearings with engine assembly lube or moly-based grease during installation.

28 Crankshaft and main bearings - removal, inspection, main bearing selection and installation (ZX750 models)

The main journal diameter marks are located on the first, second, fourth, seventh and eighth crank throws (counting from the left end of the crankshaft). Part numbers are available from Kawasaki dealers. Refer to Chapter 2 for service procedures and this Chapter's Specifications.

29 Connecting rods and bearings - removal, inspection, bearing selection and installation (ZX750 models)

The connecting rod journal diameter marks are located on the second, fourth, fifth and seventh crank throws (counting from the left end of the crankshaft). Part numbers are available from Kawasaki dealers. Refer to Chapter 2 for service procedures and this Chapter's Specifications.

30 Idler pulley, shaft and starter motor clutch - removal, inspection and installation (ZX750 models)

Pulley removal
Refer to illustrations 30.3 and 30.4

1   Remove the clutch slave cylinder, engine sprocket cover and alternator (see Sections 23, 40 and 43).

2   Keep the pulley from turning. If the engine is in the bike, shift the transmission into a low gear and have an assistant hold the rear brake on. If the engine has been removed, hold the pulley from turning with a strap wrench.

3   Unscrew the pulley bolt and remove the O-ring **(see illustration)**.

4   Thread a pair of 6 mm bolts into the threaded holes in the pulley and tighten them against the engine to push the pulley off **(see illustration)**.

Idler shaft, gear and starter clutch removal
Refer to illustrations 30.7a, 30.7b, 30.7c, 30.9, 30.10a, 30.10b and 30.11

5   Remove the engine, separate the crankcase halves and remove the transmission shafts (see Sections 8, 25 and 33).

6   Remove the oil pump drive chain guide (see Section 20).

10

30.7a Remove the oil nozzle bolts (arrows) . . .

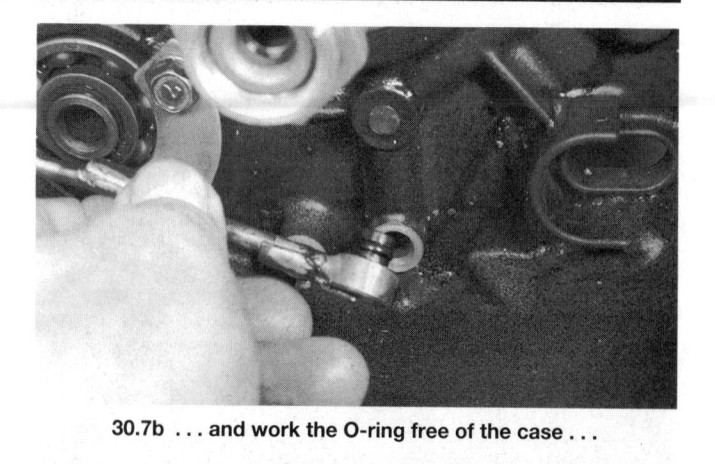

30.7b . . . and work the O-ring free of the case . . .

30.7c . . . then unbolt the bearing retainer (arrow)

30.9 Support the starter clutch and remove the idler shaft

30.10a Lift the starter clutch out

30.10b Disengage the idler shaft sprocket from the chain and remove the sprocket

7   Remove the idler shaft oil nozzle and bearing retainer **(see illustrations)**.

8   Remove the idler shaft pulley (see Steps 2 through 4 above).

9   Support the starter clutch chain with one hand and pull the idler shaft out of the crankcase **(see illustration)**.

10   Lift the starter clutch and idler shaft sprocket out of the crankcase **(see illustrations)**.

11   Remove the snap-ring from the idle gear shaft **(see illustration)**. Pull the shaft out of the crankcase and lift out the starter idle gear.

Inspection

Starter motor clutch

Refer to illustration 30.12

12   Hold the starter motor clutch and attempt to turn the starter motor clutch gear back and forth **(see illustration)**. It should turn in one direction only.

30.11 Starter idle gear details

A   Starter idle gear
B   Long collar
C   Short collar
D   Snap-ring

30.12 Hold the starter clutch and try to rotate the gear; it should turn easily in one direction, but not at all in the other direction

30.16 Inspect the idler shaft splines and sprocket; if the bearing is worn or damaged, have it pressed off

30.18 Replace the idler shaft bearing if it's worn or damaged

13   If the starter motor clutch turns freely in both directions, or if it's locked up, replace it.
14   Remove the snap-ring and washer and slide off the gear. Check the rollers for scoring and pitting and the retainers for damage. Check the gear teeth for cracks and chips. Check the needle roller bearing in the gear for wear or damage. Replace parts as necessary.

Starter motor idler gear

15   Inspect the teeth on the starter motor idler gear for cracks and chips. Turn the idler gear to make sure it spins freely. If the idler gear exhibits any undesirable conditions, replace it. Remove the idler gear as described in Step 11. Coat the shaft with engine assembly lube or moly-based grease before installing it.

Idler shaft and bearings

Refer to illustrations 30.16 and 30.18

16   Check the splines, sprocket, and threads on the shaft for wear or damage **(see illustration)**.
17   Turn the bearing and feel for tight spots and roughness. If necessary, pull the bearing off the shaft, using a bearing puller having removed the snap-ring and washer from the end of the shaft. The new bearing can be tapped onto the shaft, using a piece of pipe with an inside diameter large enough to fit over the shaft and contact the inner

race of the bearing.
18   Check the idler shaft bearing in the crankcase **(see illustration)**. Replace it if it's worn or damaged.

Installation

19   Installation is the reverse of the removal steps, with the following additions:
  a   Coat all parts with clean engine oil.
  b   Be sure to place the long and short idle gear collars on the correct sides of the gear **(see illustration 30.11)**.

---

31   Alternator/starter chain, camshaft chain and guides - removal, inspection and installation (ZX750 models)

Removal

Alternator/starter chain and camshaft chain

Refer to illustration 31.4

1   Remove the engine (see Section 8).
2   Separate the crankcase halves (see Section 25).

10

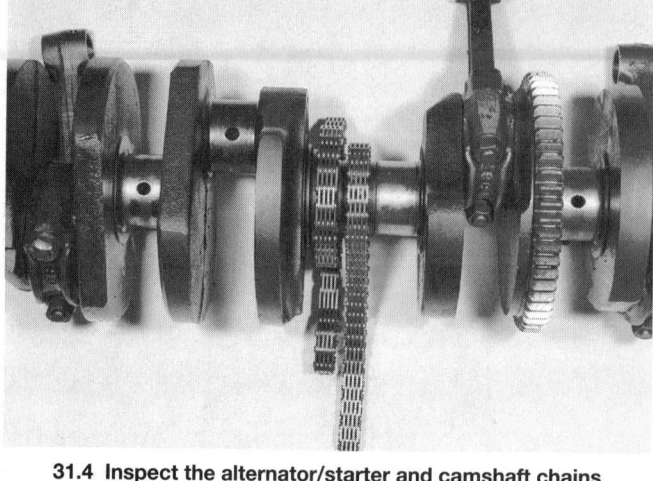

31.4 Inspect the alternator/starter and camshaft chains

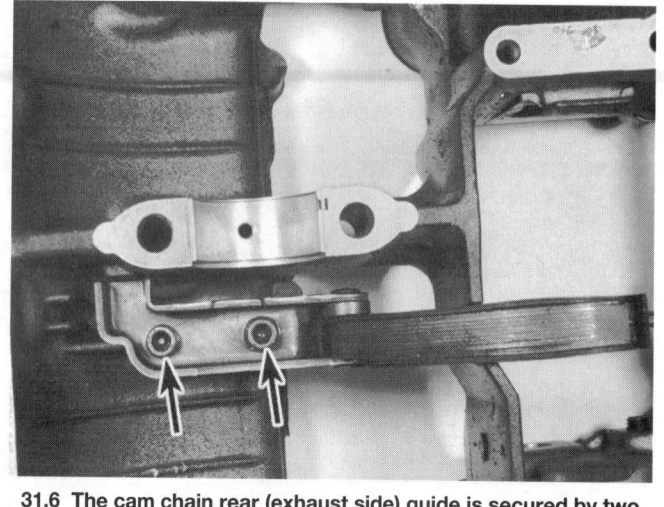

31.6 The cam chain rear (exhaust side) guide is secured by two Allen bolts (arrows)

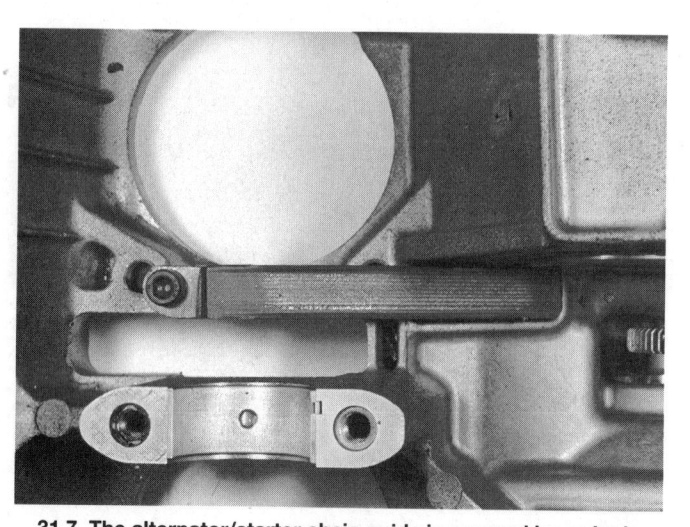

31.7 The alternator/starter chain guide is secured by a single Allen bolt

32.2a Lift out the main drive shaft . . .

3   Remove the crankshaft (see Chapter 2).
4   Remove the chains from the crankshaft **(see illustration)**.

Chain guides

Refer to illustrations 31.6 and 31.7
5   The cam chain front guide can be lifted from the cylinder block after the head has been removed (see Section 16).
6   The cam chain rear guide is fastened to the crankcase with a bracket and two bolts **(see illustration)**. Remove the bolts and detach the guide and bracket from the case.
7   The alternator/starter chain guide in the upper case half is secured by a single Allen bolt **(see illustration)**.

Inspection

Camshaft chain
8   Pull the chain tight to eliminate all slack and measure the length of twenty links, pin-to-pin **(see illustration 28.9 in Chapter 2)**. Compare your findings to this Chapter's Specifications.
9   Also check the chain for binding and obvious damage.
10   If the twenty-link length is not as specified, or there is visible damage, replace the chain.

Chain guides
11   Check the guides for deep grooves, cracking and other obvious damage, replacing them if necessary.

Installation
12   Installation of these components is the reverse of the removal procedure. When installing the bracket for the cam chain rear guide, apply a non-hardening thread locking compound to the threads of the bolts. Tighten the bolts to the torque listed in this Chapter's Specifications. Apply engine oil to the faces of the guides and to the chains.

---

32   Transmission shafts - removal and installation (ZX750 models)

Removal

Refer to illustrations 32.2a and 32.2b
1   Remove the engine and clutch, then separate the case halves (see Sections 8, 22 and 25).
2   The shafts can simply be lifted out of the upper half of the case **(see illustrations)**. If they are stuck, use a soft-face hammer and gently tap on the bearings on the ends of the shafts to free them. The shaft nearest the rear of the case is the output shaft - the other shaft is the main drive shaft.
3   Refer to Section 33 for information pertaining to transmission shaft service and Section 34 for information pertaining to the shift drum and forks.

32.2b . . . and the output shaft

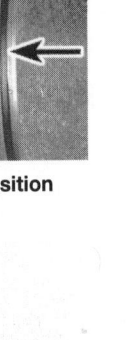

32.4 Be sure the set pins and rings (arrows) are in position

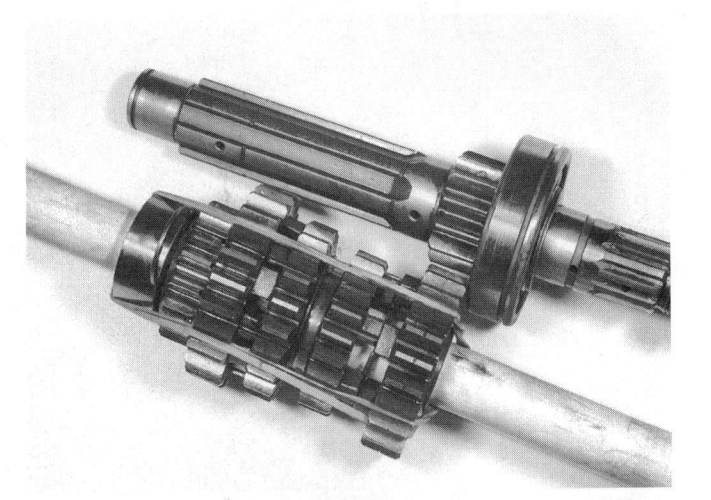

33.1 Place the transmission parts in order on a rod; a large rubber band will keep them from being disturbed

33.2a Slide off the needle bearing outer race . . .

Installation

Refer to illustration 32.4

4   Check to make sure the set pins and rings are present in the upper case half, where the shaft bearings seat **(see illustration).**

5   Carefully lower each shaft into place. The holes in the needle bearing outer races must engage with the set pins, and the grooves in the ball bearing outer races must engage with the set rings.

6   The remainder of installation is the reverse of removal.

---

33   Transmission shafts - disassembly, inspection and reassembly (ZX750 models)

Refer to illustration 33.1

1   Remove the shafts from the case (see Section 32). **Note:** *When disassembling the transmission shafts, place the parts on a long rod or thread a wire through them to keep them in order and facing the proper direction* **(see illustration).**

Main drive shaft

Disassembly

Refer to illustrations 33.2a, 33.2b, 33.3, 33.4a, 33.4b, 33.5a, 33.5b, 33.6, 33.7a, 33.7b and 33.7c

2   Remove the needle bearing outer race, then remove the snap-ring from the end of the shaft and slide the needle bearing off **(see illustrations).**

10

33.2b . . . then remove the snap-ring and bearing

33.3 Remove the thrust washer and second gear

33.4a Slide off sixth gear . . .

33.4b . . . and its bushing

33.5a Remove the snap-ring and toothed washer . . .

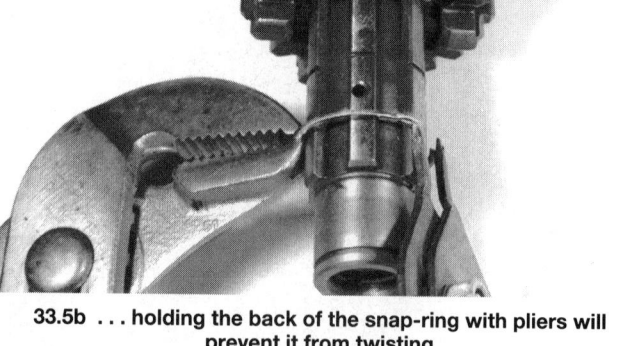

33.5b . . . holding the back of the snap-ring with pliers will
prevent it from twisting

33.6 Slide off third-fourth gear

3   Remove the thrust washer and slide second gear off the shaft **(see illustration)**.
4   Remove sixth gear and bushing **(see illustrations)**.
5   Slide the toothed washer off and remove the snap-ring **(see illustration)**. To keep the snap-ring from bending as it's expanded, hold the back of it with pliers **(see illustration)**.
6   Remove the third/fourth gear cluster from the shaft **(see illustration)**.
7   Remove the next snap-ring, then slide the washer, fifth gear and its bushing off the shaft **(see illustrations)**.

Inspection

Refer to illustrations 33.9 and 33.11

8   Wash all of the components in clean solvent and dry them off. Rotate the ball bearing on the shaft, feeling for tightness, rough spots, excessive looseness and listening for noises. If any of these conditions

are found, replace the bearing. This will require the use of a hydraulic press or a bearing puller setup. If you don't have access to these tools, take the shaft and bearing to a Kawasaki dealer or other motorcycle repair shop and have them press the old bearing off the shaft and install the new one.
9   Measure the shift fork groove between third and fourth gears **(see illustration)**. If the groove width exceeds the figure listed in this Chapter's Specifications, replace the third/fourth gear assembly, and also check the third/fourth gear shift fork (see Section 34).
10   Check the gear teeth for cracking and other obvious damage. Check the bushing and surface in the inner diameter of the fifth and sixth gears for scoring or heat discoloration. If either one is damaged, replace it.
11   Inspect the dogs and the dog holes in the gears for excessive wear **(see illustration 33.9 and the accompanying illustration)**. Replace the paired gears as a set if necessary.

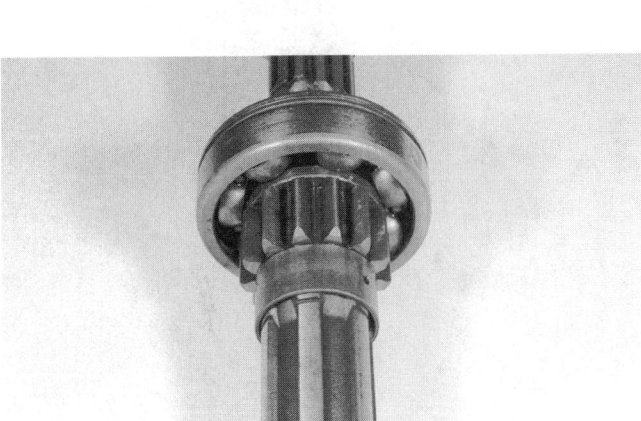

33.7a Remove the snap-ring . . .

33.7b . . . the toothed washer and fifth gear . . .

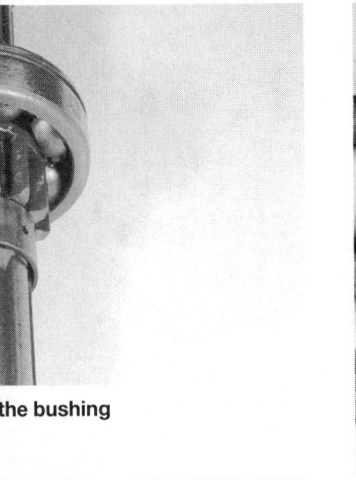

33.7c . . . and the bushing

33.9 Measure the gear grooves; if they're too wide, replace the gear - also replace the gear if the dogs (arrows) are worn

33.11 Inspect the bushing (left arrow) in gears so equipped; replace the gear if it's worn - if the edges of the slots (right arrow) are rounded, replace the gear

33.13 Be sure to align the bushing oil hole with the shaft oil hole (arrows)

10

12 Check the needle bearing and race for wear or heat discoloration and replace them if necessary.

Reassembly

Refer to illustration 33.13

13 Reassembly is the basically the reverse of the disassembly procedure, but take note of the following points:

a Always use new snap-rings and align the opening of the ring with a spline groove (**see illustration 30.21** in Chapter 2). Face the sharp side of the snap-ring toward the gear being secured; the rounded side faces away from the gear.

b When installing the gear bushings on the shaft, align the oil hole in the shaft with the oil hole in the bushing (**see illustration**).

c Lubricate the components with engine oil before assembling them.

33.14a Slide off the bearing outer race . . .

33.14b . . . and the bearing

33.15 Remove the thrust washer (arrow)
and first gear

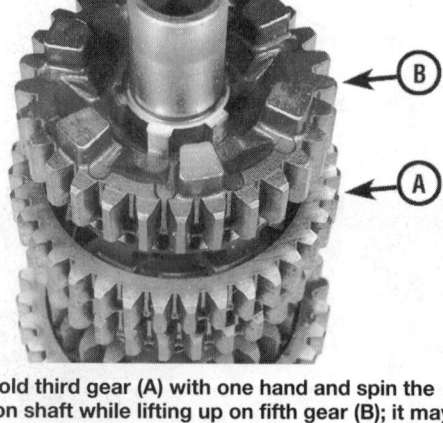

33.16a Hold third gear (A) with one hand and spin the
transmission shaft while lifting up on fifth gear (B); it may
take several tries to disengage fifth gear from the shaft,
but it will slide off easily once it is disengaged

33.16b These three balls ride in slots in the transmission shaft;
they must be flung outward by centrifugal force before
fifth gear can be removed

33.17a Remove the snap-ring . . .

33.17b . . . the toothed washer . . .

33.17c . . . third gear . . .

Output shaft

Disassembly

*Refer to illustrations 33.14a, 33.14b, 33.15, 33.16a, 33.16b, 33.17a,
33.17b, 33.17c, 33.17d, 33.18a, 33.18b, 33.18c, 33.19a, 33.19b,
33.19c and 13.20*

14   Remove the needle bearing outer race and slide the needle bearing off **(see illustrations)**.
15   Remove the thrust washer and first gear from the shaft **(see illustration)**.
16   Remove fifth gear from the shaft. Fifth gear has three steel balls in
it for the positive neutral finder mechanism. These lock fifth gear to the
shaft unless it is spun rapidly enough to fling the balls outward. To remove fifth gear, grasp third gear and hold the shaft in a vertical position with one hand, and with the other hand, spin the shaft back and
forth, holding onto fifth gear and pulling up **(see illustration)**. **Caution:**
*Don't pull the gear up too hard or fast - the balls will fly out of the gear.
After fifth gear is removed, collect the three steel balls* **(see illustration)**.
17   Remove the snap-ring, toothed washer, third gear, bushing and
fourth gear from the shaft **(see illustrations)**.
18   Remove the toothed washer, snap-ring and sixth gear **(see illustrations)**.
19   Remove the next snap-ring, toothed washer, second gear and its
bushing **(see illustrations)**.

33.17d . . . its bushing and fourth gear

33.18a Remove the toothed washer . . .

33.18b . . . the snap-ring . . .

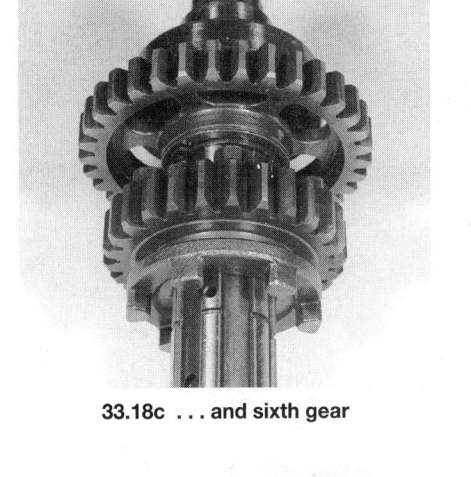

33.18c . . . and sixth gear

33.19a Remove the snap-ring . . .

33.19b . . . the toothed washer and
second gear . . .

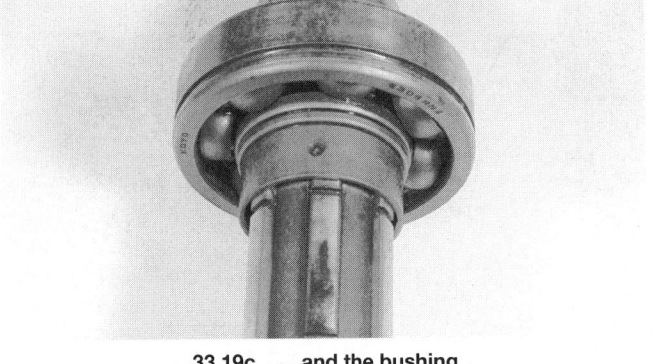

33.19c . . . and the bushing

33.20 The bearing and collar can be left on the shaft unless
they're worn or damaged

20   The ball bearing and collar can remain on the shaft unless they
need to be replaced **(see illustration)**.

Inspection
21   Refer to Steps 8 through 12 for the inspection procedures. They
are the same, except when checking the shift fork groove width you'll
be checking it on fifth gear and sixth gears.

Reassembly
22   Reassembly is the basically the reverse of the disassembly procedure, but take note of the following points:
  a Always use new snap-rings and align the opening of the ring with
    a spline groove **(see illustration 30.21 in Chapter 2)**. Face the

sharp side of each snap-ring toward the gear being secured; face
the rounded side of snap-ring away from the gear.
  b When installing the bushing for third and fourth gear and second
    gear, align the oil hole in the bushing with the hole in the shaft.
  c When installing fifth gear, don't use grease to hold the balls in
    place - to do so would impair the positive neutral finder mecha-
    nism. Just set the balls in their holes (the holes that they can't
    pass through), keep the gear in a vertical position and carefully
    set it on the shaft (engine oil will help keep them in place). The
    spline grooves that contain the holes with the balls must be
    aligned with the slots in the shaft spline grooves.
  d Lubricate the components with engine oil before assembling
    them.

10

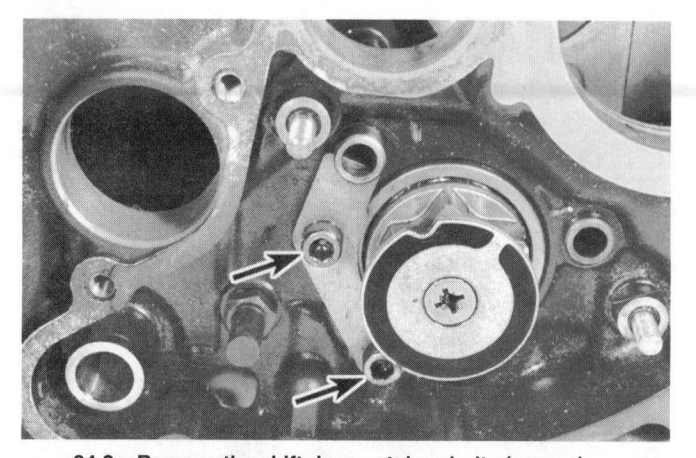

34.2a Remove the shift drum retainer bolts (arrows) . . .

34.2b . . . and the shift rod retainer bolt on the other side of the case

34.3a Slide out the shift rod with the single fork . . .

34.3b . . . and the shift rod with two forks . . .

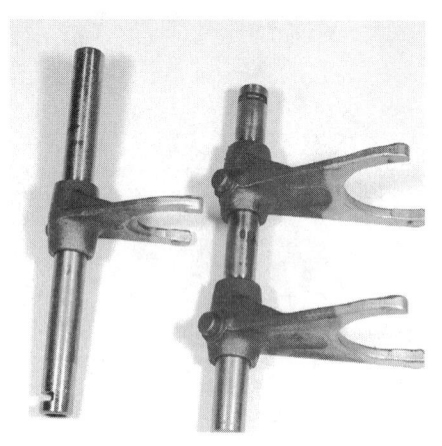

34.3c . . . and reassemble them so they can be returned to their original positions

34.4 Slide the shift drum out of the case

34   Shift drum and forks - removal, inspection and installation (ZX750 models)

Removal

Refer to illustrations 34.2a, 34.2b, 34.3a, 34.3b, 34.3c and 34.4

1   Remove the engine, separate the crankcase halves and remove the external shift mechanism (see Sections 8, 25 and 24).

2   Remove the retaining plates for the shift drum and shift rod **(see illustrations)**.
3   Support the shift forks and pull the shift rods out **(see illustrations)**. The output shaft forks and the shift rods are interchangeable, but it's a good idea to assemble them as they were in the engine so they can be returned to their original positions **(see illustration)**.
4   Slide the shift drum out of the crankcase **(see illustration)**.

Inspection

Refer to illustrations 34.5, 34.6a, 34.6b and 34.7

5   Check the edges of the grooves in the drum for signs of excessive wear **(see illustration)**. Measure the widths of the grooves and compare your findings to this Chapter's Specifications.
6   Remove the Phillips screw from the end of the shift drum and disassemble the drum **(see illustrations)**. Check the pin plate and pins for wear or damage and replace them as necessary. Spin the bearing and check for roughness, noise or looseness. Replace the bearing if defects are found. Reassemble the shift drum, making sure the dowel aligns with the hole in the bearing holder and the one longer pin fits in the recess in the pin plate **(see illustration)**.
7   Check the shift forks for distortion and wear, especially at the fork ears. Measure the thickness of the fork ears and compare your findings with this Chapter's Specifications **(see illustration)**. If they are discolored or severely worn they are probably bent. If damage or wear is evident, check the shift fork groove in the corresponding gear as well. Inspect the guide pins and the shaft bore for excessive wear and distortion and replace any defective parts with new ones.
8   Check the shift fork shafts for evidence of wear, galling and other damage. Make sure the shift forks move smoothly on the shafts. If the shafts are worn or bent, replace them with new ones.

34.5 **Check the fork grooves for wear, especially at their points (arrows)**

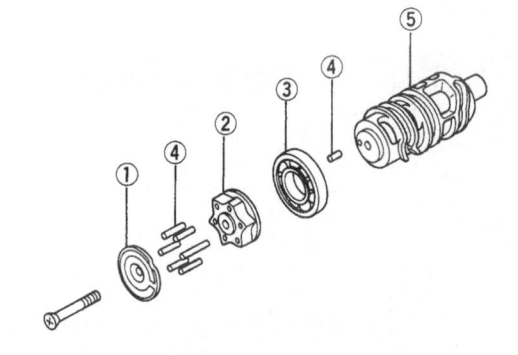

34.6a **Shift drum details**

1	Pin plate	4	Pins
2	Bearing holder	5	Shift drum
3	Bearing		

34.6b **Align the hole in the bearing holder with the shift drum pin**

A	Bearing holder	C	Dowel
B	Hole	D	Shift drum

Installation

9   Installation is the reverse of removal, noting the following points:
    a Lubricate all parts with engine oil before installing them.
    b Use non-permanent thread locking agent on the threads of the shift drum and shift rod retaining plates. Tighten the bolts securely.

35   Initial start-up after overhaul

Note: *Make sure the cooling system is checked carefully (especially the coolant level) before starting and running the engine.*
1   Make sure the engine oil level is correct, then remove the spark plugs from the engine. Place the engine STOP switch in the Off position and unplug the primary (low tension) wires from the coil.
2   Turn on the key switch and crank the engine over with the starter until the oil pressure indicator light goes off (which indicates that oil pressure exists). Reinstall the spark plugs, connect the wires and turn the STOP switch to On.
3   Make sure there is fuel in the tank, then push the button on the fuel tap several times to prime the carburetors and operate the choke.
4   Start the engine and allow it to run at a moderately fast idle until it reaches operating temperature. **Warning**: *If the oil pressure indicator light doesn't go off, or it comes on while the engine is running, stop the engine immediately.*
5   Check carefully for oil leaks and make sure the transmission and controls, especially the brakes, function properly before road testing the machine. Refer to Section 36 for the recommended break-in procedure.

34.7 **Measure the thickness of the shift fork ears and replace the shift forks if they're worn**

6   Upon completion of the road test, and after the engine has cooled down completely, recheck the valve clearances (see Chapter 1).

36   Recommended break-in procedure

1   Any rebuilt engine needs time to break-in, even if parts have been installed in their original locations. For this reason, treat the machine gently for the first few miles to make sure oil has circulated throughout the engine and any new parts installed have started to seat.
2   Even greater care is necessary if the engine has been rebored or a new crankshaft has been installed. In the case of a rebore, the engine will have to be broken in as if the machine were new. This means greater use of the transmission and a restraining hand on the throttle until at least 500 miles (800 km) have been covered. There's no point in keeping to any set speed limit - the main idea is to keep from lugging (labouring) the engine and to gradually increase performance until the 500 mile (800 km) mark is reached. These recommendations can be lessened to an extent when only a new crankshaft is installed. Experience is the best guide, since it's easy to tell when an engine is running freely.
3   If a lubrication failure is suspected, stop the engine immediately and try to find the cause. If an engine is run without oil, even for a short period of time, irreparable damage will occur.

10

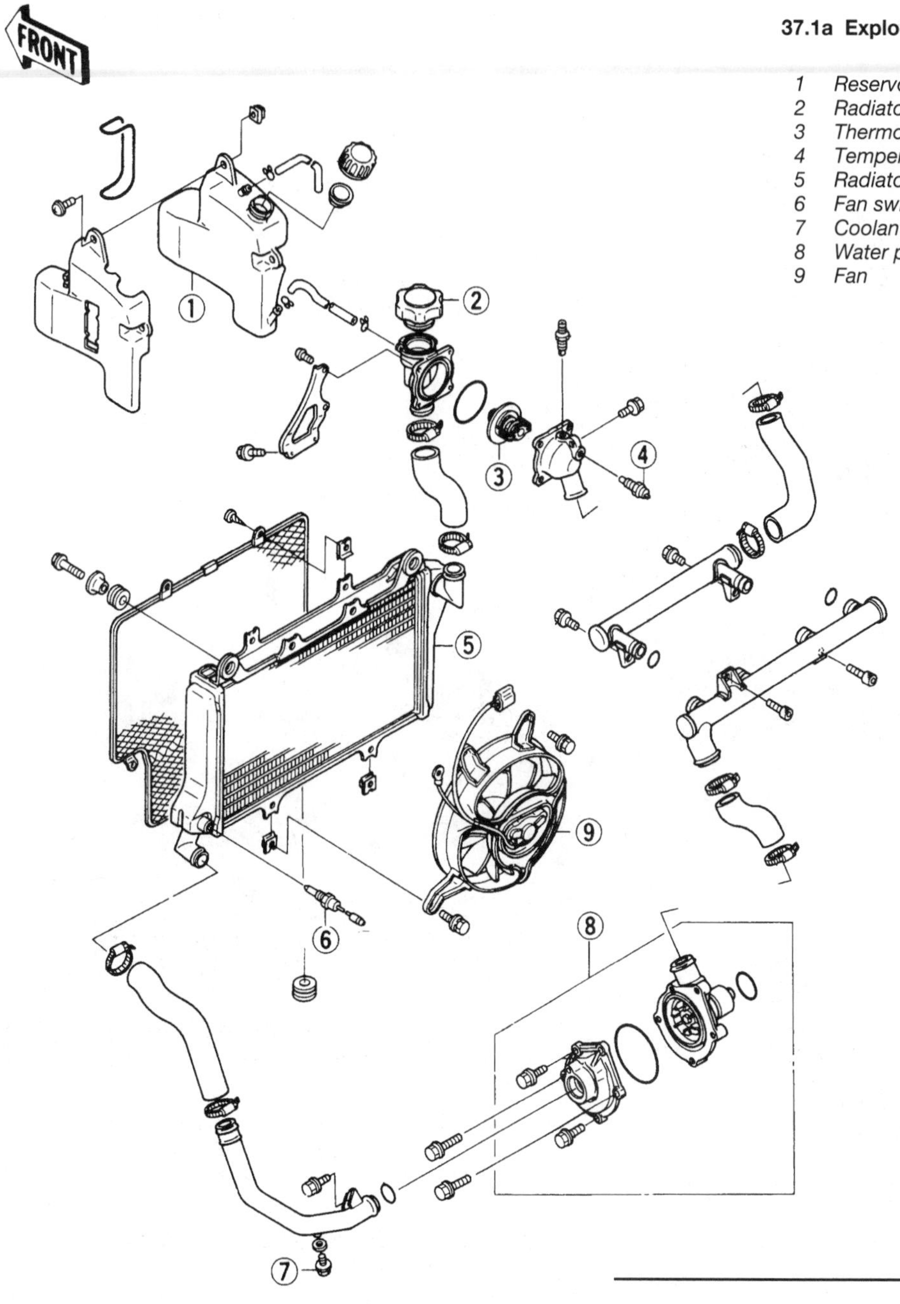

FRONT

**37.1a Exploded view of the cooling system
(ZX750 models)**

1   Reservoir tank
2   Radiator pressure cap
3   Thermostat
4   Temperature sensor
5   Radiator
6   Fan switch
7   Coolant drain plug
8   Water pump
9   Fan

37   Cooling system (Chapter 3) - modified procedures

General information

Refer to illustrations 37.1a and 37.1b
1   The cooling system is similar in design to the ZX600C system, but the locations of some components differ **(see illustrations)**.
2   To gain access to the radiator pressure cap, remove the lower and right fairing panels.

Coolant reservoir - removal and installation

3   To remove the reservoir, remove the lower and right fairing panels.

Fan motor replacement

4   The fan and motor are secured by four bolts and are replaced as an assembly, rather than separately.

Thermostat

Removal
5   If the thermostat is functioning properly, the coolant temperature gauge should rise to the normal operating temperature quickly and then stay there, only occasionally rising above the normal position when the engine gets unusually hot. If the engine doesn't reach normal operating temperature quickly, or if it overheats rapidly, the thermostat should be removed and checked, or replaced with a new one.
6   Refer to Section 3 and drain the cooling system. Remove the upper fairing for access to the thermostat.
7   Unplug the electrical connectors and remove the wiring harness bracket.
8   Unbolt the filler neck from the thermostat housing **(see illustration 37.1a)**. Move the filler neck away from the thermostat housing, lift out the thermostat and remove the O-ring.

Check and installation
9   These procedures are the same as for ZX600 models (see Chapter 3). The thermostat goes into the housing spring end first.

37.1b Coolant flow diagram (ZX750 models)

1 Water pump
2 Hose
3 Water pipe
4 Water jacket
5 Cylinder head
6 Temperature sensor
7 Radiator pressure cap
8 Thermostat
9 Fan
10 Fan switch
11 Radiator

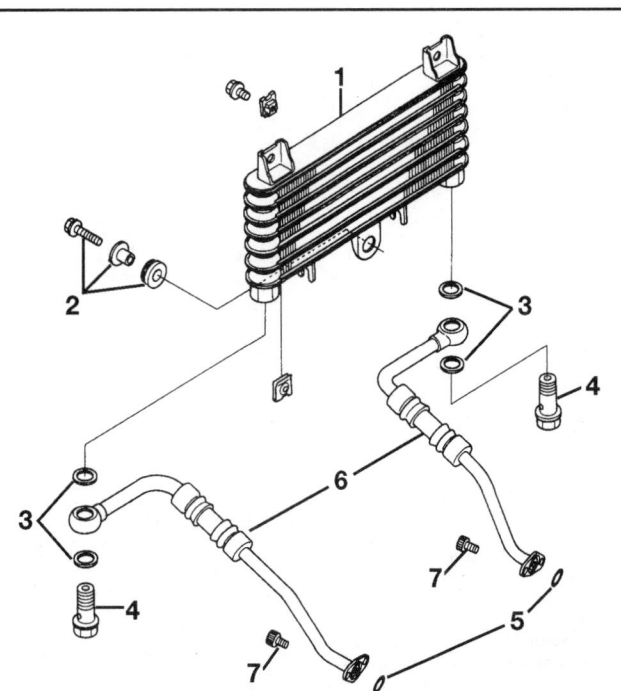

37.16 Oil cooler details (ZX750 models)

1	Oil cooler	4	Banjo bolts
2	Mounting bolt, collar and damper	5	O-rings
		6	Oil lines
3	Sealing washers	7	Mounting bolts

Radiator - removal and installation

10   This is the same as for ZX600C models, but the radiator screen must be removed for access to the lower radiator mounting bolts.

Water pump - check, removal and installation

11   To gain access to check or remove the pump, remove the clutch slave cylinder and engine sprocket cover (see Sections 23 and 40).

Coolant pipes - removal and installation

12   Procedures are the same as for ZX600C models. For details of the ZX750 coolant pipes, refer to **illustrations 16.2a, 16.2b, 37.1a and 37.1b**.

Oil cooler - removal and installation

Refer to illustration 37.16

13   Set the bike on its centerstand and drain the engine oil (see Chapter 1).
14   Remove the lower fairing (see Section 42).
15   Remove the radiator (see Step 10 above and Chapter 3).
16   Place a drain pan under the front of the crankcase and remove the oil line mounting bolts **(see illustration)**. If you're going to detach the oil lines from the cooler, loosen the union bolts at the oil cooler now.
17   Remove the oil cooler mounting bolt and take the cooler out.
18   Installation is the reverse of the removal steps. Use new sealing washers if the oil lines were disconnected from the cooler. Tighten the union bolts to the torque listed in this Chapter's Specifications.

38   Fuel system (Chapter 4) - modified procedures

Carburetor installation

1   This is the same as for ZX600C models, except that the fuel tap doesn't have a PRI position. Instead, press the button on the fuel tap several times to prime the carburetors.

10

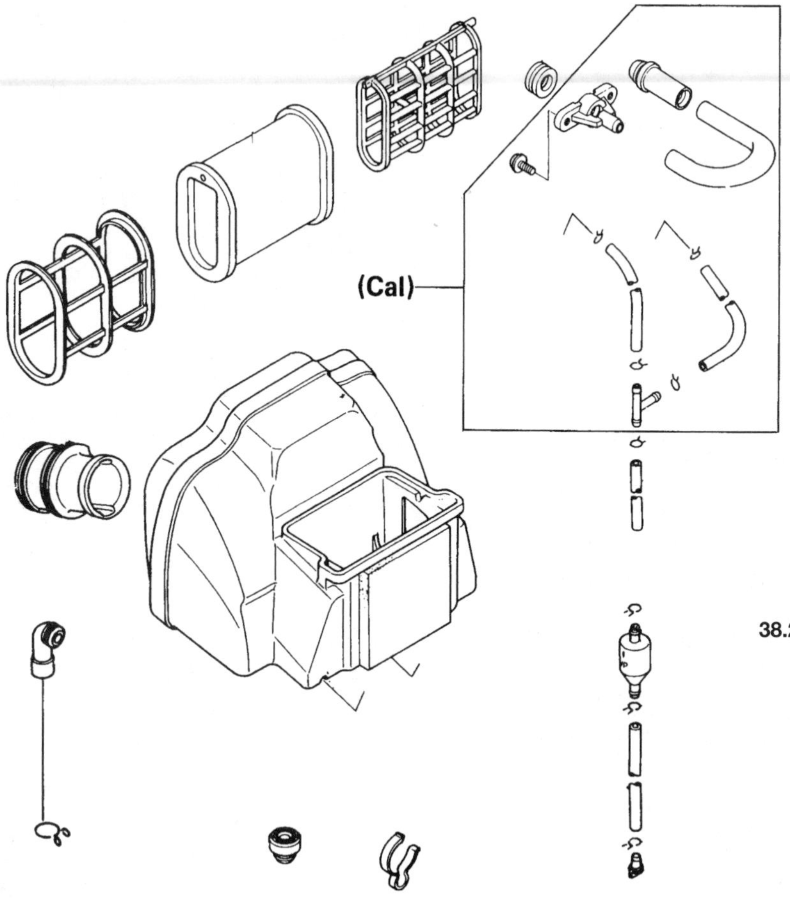

38.2 Air cleaner details (ZX750 models)

(Cal)

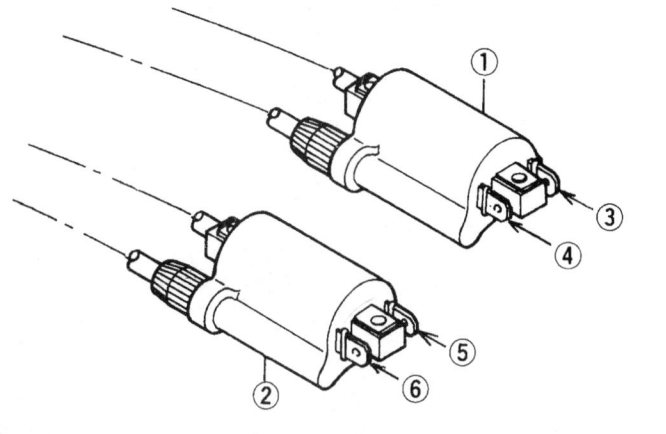

39.1 Ignition coils (ZX750 models)

1	Coil for cylinders 1 and 4	4	Black wire
2	Coil for cylinders 2 and 3	5	Red wire
3	Red wire	6	Green wire

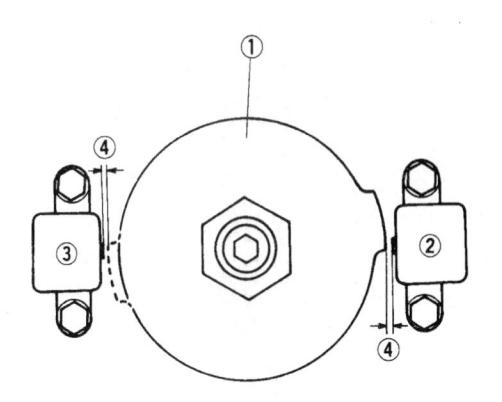

39.3a Set the pickup coil are gaps to specifications

1	Timing rotor	3	Pickup coil for cylinders 2
2	Pickup coil for cylinders 1		and 3
	and 4	4	Air gap

Air filter housing - removal and installation

Refer to illustration 38.2

2   Procedures are generally the same as for ZX600C models; details differ slightly **(see illustration)**.

Exhaust system - removal and installation

3   Procedures are the same as for ZX600 models; the oil cooler must also be removed (see Section 37).

39   Ignition system (Chapter 5) - modified procedures

Ignition coils - check, removal and installation

Refer to illustration 39.1

1   Checking procedures are the same as for ZX600 models (see Chapter 5 and this Chapter's Specifications). Removal and installation procedures are the same as for ZX600 C models, but the mounting differs slightly **(see illustration)**.

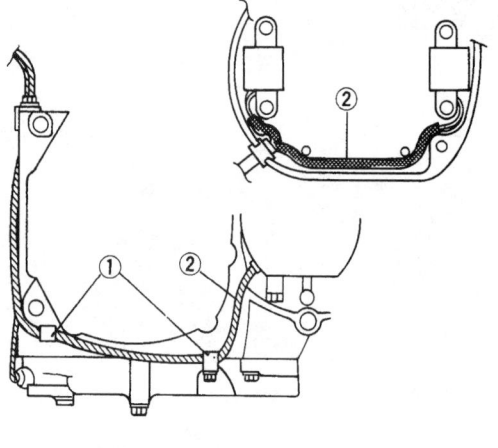

39.3b Pickup coil harness routing

1   Wiring harness retainers   2   Wiring harness

Pickup coils - check, removal and installation

Refer to illustrations 39.3a and 39.3b

2   Procedures are the same as for ZX600 models, except that the lower fairing panel must be removed for access.

3   When you install the pickup coils, make sure the air gaps are as listed in this Chapter's Specifications **(see illustration)**. Route the wiring harness correctly inside the pickup coil housing and under the clutch cover **(see illustration)**.

---

40   Frame, suspension and final drive (Chapter 6) - modified procedures

---

Frame rear section - removal and installation

1   Remove the seat, knee grip covers and side covers.
2   Remove the air cleaner housing cover.
3   Remove the battery (see Chapter 9).
4   Disconnect the wiring connectors for the frame rear section on the right side of the motorcycle, the left side, just forward of the starter relay and at the rear inside the tailpiece.
5   Unbolt the rear master cylinder (but leave the fluid line connected).
6   Support the exhaust system and remove the muffler mounting bolts on both sides of the motorcycle.
7   Unbolt the rear frame section and remove it together with the rear fender.
8   Installation is the reverse of the removal steps.

Forks - removal and installation

9   The procedure is the same as for ZX600 C models, except the fork protrusion from the upper surface of the upper clamp is 0.59 inch (15 mm).

Forks - disassembly, inspection and reassembly

10   Procedures are the same as for ZX600 C models.

Steering head bearings - replacement

11   Procedures are the same as for ZX600 models, except that the brake hose joint must be unbolted and separated from the steering stem (don't disconnect the brake lines).

Rear shock absorber - removal and installation

Refer to illustration 40.12

12   The procedure is the same as for ZX600 models, but details differ slightly **(see illustration)**.

Rear suspension linkage - removal, check and installation

13   Procedures are the same as for ZX600 models, but details differ slightly **(see illustration 40.12)**.

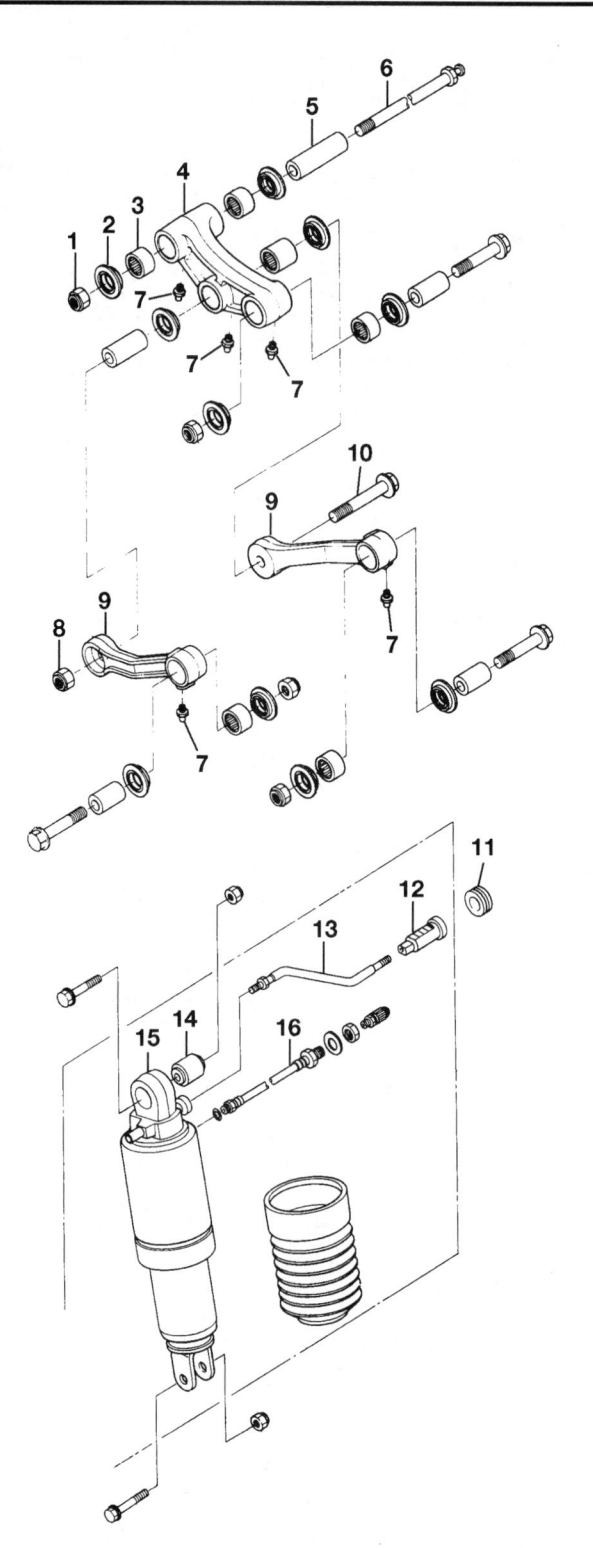

40.12 Rear shock absorber and suspension linkage (ZX750 models) - exploded view

1	Nut	9	Tie-rods
2	Seal	10	Pivot bolt
3	Bearing	11	Cap
4	Rocker arm	12	Damping adjuster
5	Collar	13	Damping adjuster rod
6	Pivot bolt	14	Bearing
7	Grease fitting	15	Shock absorber
8	Nut		

10

40.24a Bend back the lockwasher (arrow) . . .

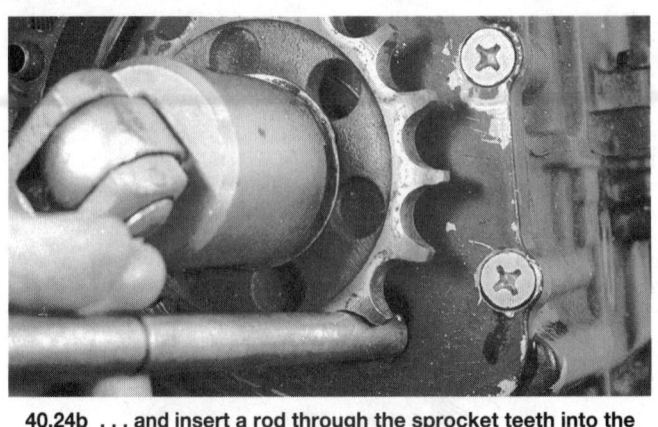

40.24b . . . and insert a rod through the sprocket teeth into the cover slot to prevent the sprocket from turning while the nut is loosened

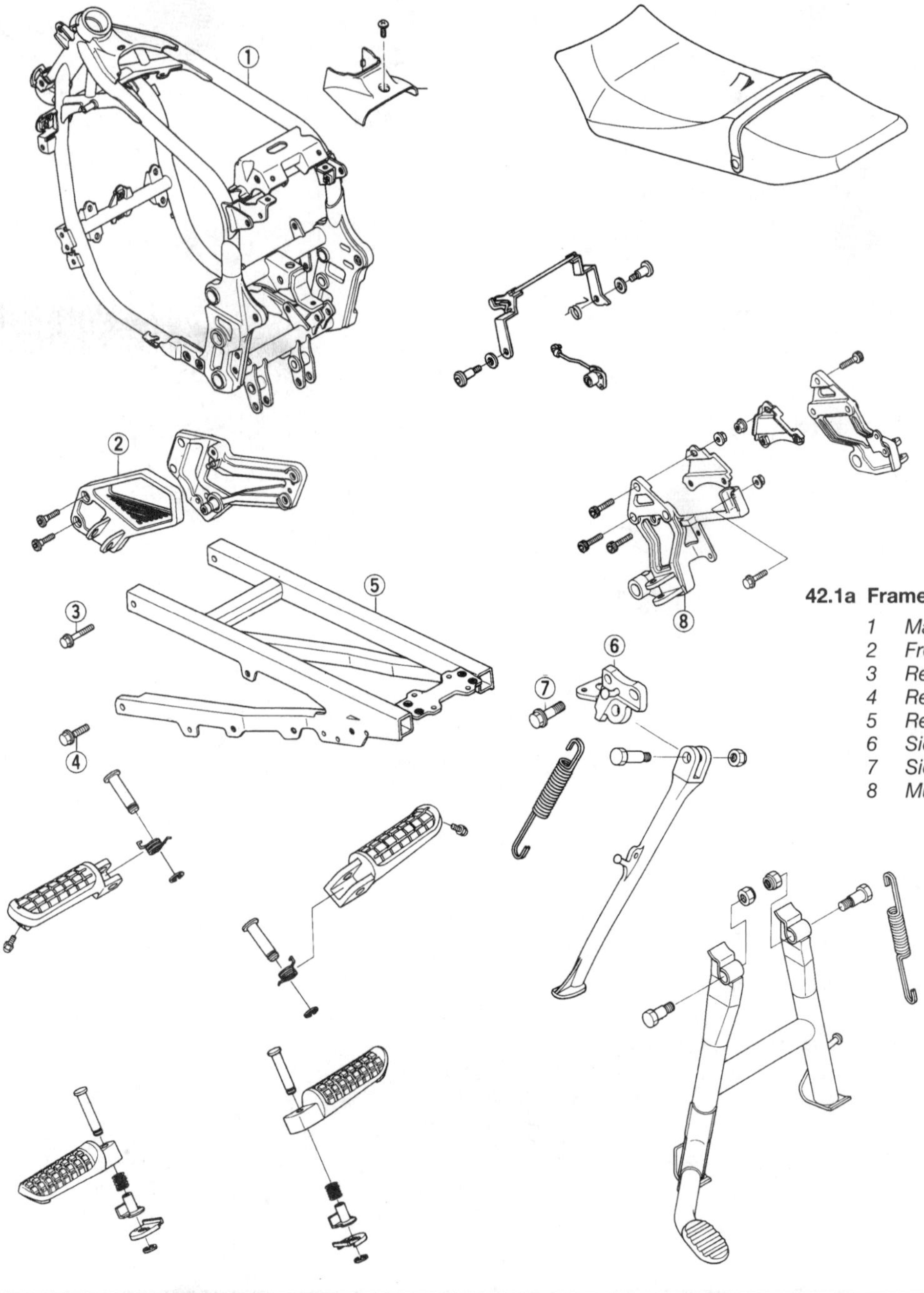

42.1a Frame components (ZX750 models)

1   Main frame section
2   Front footpeg brackets
3   Rear frame upper mounting bolts
4   Rear frame lower mounting bolts
5   Rear frame section
6   Sidestand bracket
7   Sidestand bracket bolts
8   Muffler (silencer) brackets

Swingarm - removal and installation

14   The procedure is the same as for ZX600 models, except that the engine sprocket must be removed first (see Step 24 below).

Drive chain - removal, cleaning and installation

15   Remove the chain guard from the swingarm.
16   Remove the clutch slave cylinder (see Section 23).
17   Remove the screws securing the engine sprocket cover to the crankcase and the alternator lower mounting bracket. Remove the engine sprocket cover, taking note of the dowel positions.
18   Remove the engine sprocket (see Step 24 below).
19   Remove the rear wheel (see Chapter 7).
20   Remove the swingarm (see Chapter 6).
21   Take the chain off the motorcycle.
22   Soak the chain in kerosene or diesel fuel for approximately five or six minutes. **Caution:** *Don't use gasoline or other solvents. Remove the chain, wipe it off, then blow it dry with compressed air immediately. The entire process shouldn't take longer than ten minutes - if it does, the O-rings in the chain rollers could be damaged.*
23   Installation is the reverse of the removal procedure.

Sprockets - check and replacement

Refer to illustrations 40.24a and 40.24b
24   Procedures are the same as for ZX600 models, except that the

engine sprocket is secured by a nut and lockwasher. To remove it, bend back the lockwasher tabs. Insert a rod between two sprocket teeth into the slot in the external shift mechanism cover to hold the sprocket from turning, then loosen the nut **(see illustrations)**. Use a new lockwasher for installation and tighten the nut to the torque listed in this Chapter's Specifications.

---

41   Brakes (Chapter 7) - modified procedures

General information

Brakes are the same as for ZX600 C models, except that the rear caliper is underslung.

---

42   Fairing and bodywork (Chapter 8) - modified procedures

General information

Refer to illustrations 42.1a and 42.1b
1   Fairing and bodywork service procedures are generally the same as for ZX600 models; shapes of parts and locations of fasteners differ **(see illustrations)**.

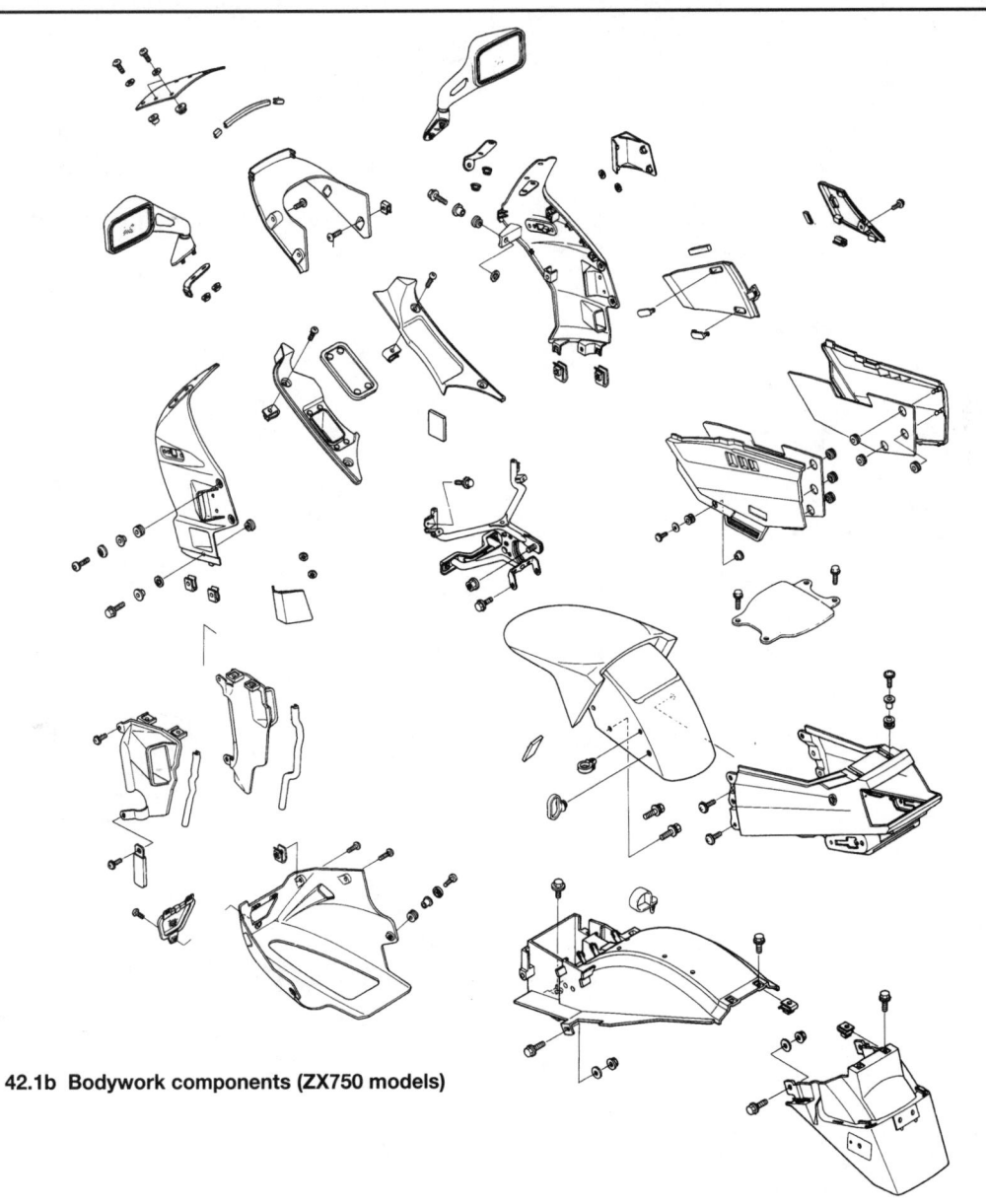

42.1b Bodywork components (ZX750 models)

10

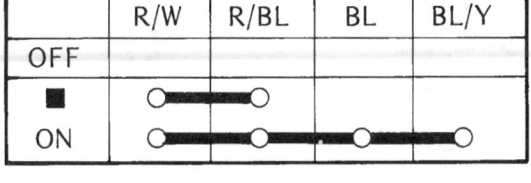

	R/W	R/BL	BL	BL/Y
OFF				
■	o—o			
ON	o—o—o—o			

43.3a Headlight switch connections (other than US, Canada)

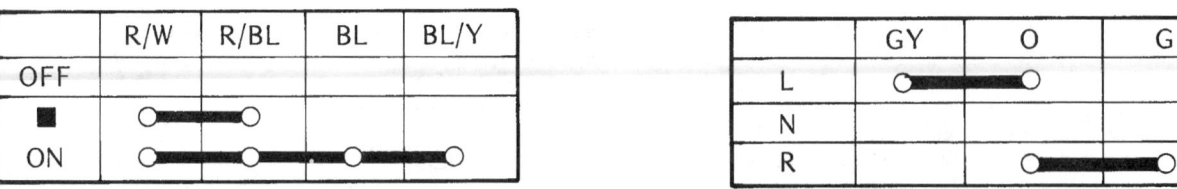

		GY	O	G
L		o—o		
N				
R			o—o	

43.3b Turn signal switch connections

Lower fairing - removal and installation

2   Set the bike on its centerstand.
3   Remove two screws and one Allen bolt on each side of the lower fairing.
4   Carefully maneuver the fairing out from under the bike.
5   Installation is the reverse of removal.

Upper fairing - removal and installation

6   Remove the lower fairing.
7   Remove two Allen bolts at the rear of the upper fairing on each side.
8   Remove the screws and detach the inner fairing panels on both sides.
9   Remove six screws, washers and nuts that secure the windshield. Carefully separate the windshield from the fairing. If it sticks, don't attempt to pry it off - just keep applying steady pressure with your fingers.
10   Remove the headlight lower cover.
11   Remove two bolts at the lower front of the fairing.
12   On the top side of the fairing, remove one bolt on each side.
13   Lift the fairing off, together with the headlight assembly and coolant reservoir. As you ease the fairing forward, disconnect the coolant reservoir hose and the wiring connectors for the headlight and turn signals.
14   Installation is the reverse of the removal steps.

Rear frame section and rear fender - removal and installation

15   Remove the seat.
16   Remove the knee grip covers and side covers on both sides of the bike.
17   Remove the cover from the air cleaner housing.
18   Remove the battery (see Chapter 1).
19   Disconnect the electrical connectors on the left side, on the right side, at the rear inside the tailpiece and just forward of the starter solenoid.
20   Unbolt the rear master cylinder (but leave the brake line connected).
21   Support the exhaust system and remove the muffler mounting bolts on both sides.
22   Unbolt the rear frame section and take it off together with the rear fender **(see illustration 42.1a)**.
23   Unbolt the rear section of the rear fender from the front section and take it off **(see illustration 42.1b)**.
24   Unbolt the front section of the rear fender from the rear frame section.
25   If necessary, detach the rear footpeg brackets from the rear frame section.
26   Installation is the reverse of the removal steps.

---

43   Electrical system (Chapter 9) - modified procedures

Fuses

1   The fuses are located in the junction box inside the left side cover. Replacement and checking procedures are the same as for ZX600 models.

Meters and gauges - check and replacement

2   To check the operation of the fuel gauge, unplug the two-wire connector between the gauge and the sending unit. Turn the ignition switch to the On position. The gauge should read Empty. Connect a jumper wire between the two pins in the gauge side of the connector. The gauge should read Full. **Caution:** Don't leave the wire connected any longer than necessary to take a reading or the gauge may be damaged.

Handlebar switches - check

Refer to illustrations 43.3a and 43.3b
3   Continuity diagrams are the same for all switches except the turn signal switch and the UK headlight switch. Refer to the **accompanying illustrations** to check these two switches **(see illustrations)**.

Starter solenoid - check and replacement

4   This is the same as for ZX600 models, except that the starter solenoid is located behind the battery.

Starter motor - removal and installation

5   This is the same as for ZX600 models, but be careful not to tap or drop the starter body or shaft or the motor may be damaged. Don't tap the motor into position when you install it.

Starter motor - disassembly, inspection and reassembly

6   Remove the starter motor (see Chapter 9).

Disassembly

Refer to illustrations 43.7 and 43.11
7   Mark the position of the housing to each end cover. Remove the two long screws and detach both end covers **(see illustration)**.
8   Pull the armature out of the housing.
9   Remove the brush plate from the housing. Disengage the brushes from the plate and detach the terminal bolt with its brush from the housing.

Inspection

10   This is the same as for ZX600 models, except that only two brushes are used instead of four. Refer to this Chapter's Specifications for brush length.

Reassembly

11   Assembly is the reverse of the disassembly steps, with the following additions:
  a   Be sure to install a large O-ring at each end of the starter housing and a small O-ring on the end that fits into the crankcase.
  b   Align the mark on the starter housing with the notches in the brush cover and plate **(see illustration)**.
  c   Align the cover screw hole with the marks on the starter housing.

Charging system - output test

Caution: Never disconnect the battery cables from the battery while the engine is running. If the battery is disconnected, the alternator and regulator/rectifier will be damaged.
12   To check the charging system output, you will need a voltmeter or a multimeter with a voltmeter function.
13   The battery must be fully charged (charge it from an external source if necessary) and the engine must be at normal operating temperature to obtain an accurate reading.
14   Attach the positive (red) voltmeter lead to the positive (+) battery terminal and the negative (black) lead to the battery negative (-) terminal. The voltmeter selector switch (if equipped) must be in the 0-20 DC volt range.
15   Start the engine.

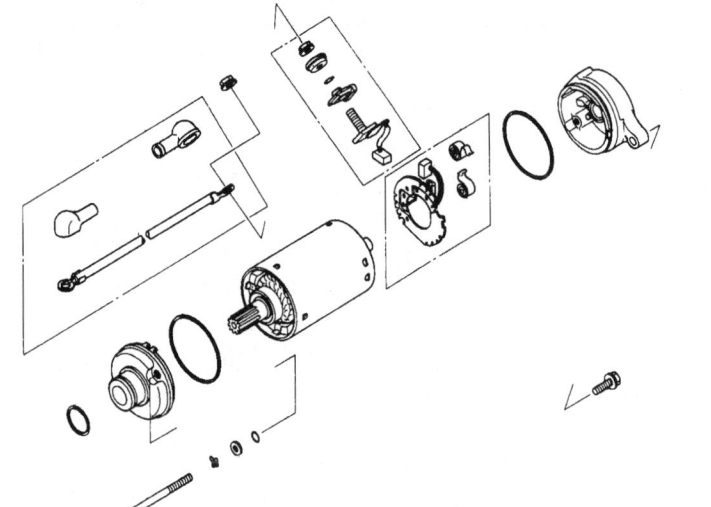

43.7 Starter (ZX750 models) - exploded view

43.28 Alternator (ZX750 models) - exploded view

1   Upper belt cover
2   Mounting bolts
3   Side belt cover
4   Adjusting plate
5   Alternator drive belt
6   Alternator assembly
7   Alternator mounting bolts
8   Pulley mounting nut (if equipped)
9   Pulley
10 Brush assembly
11 Regulator
12 Rectifier

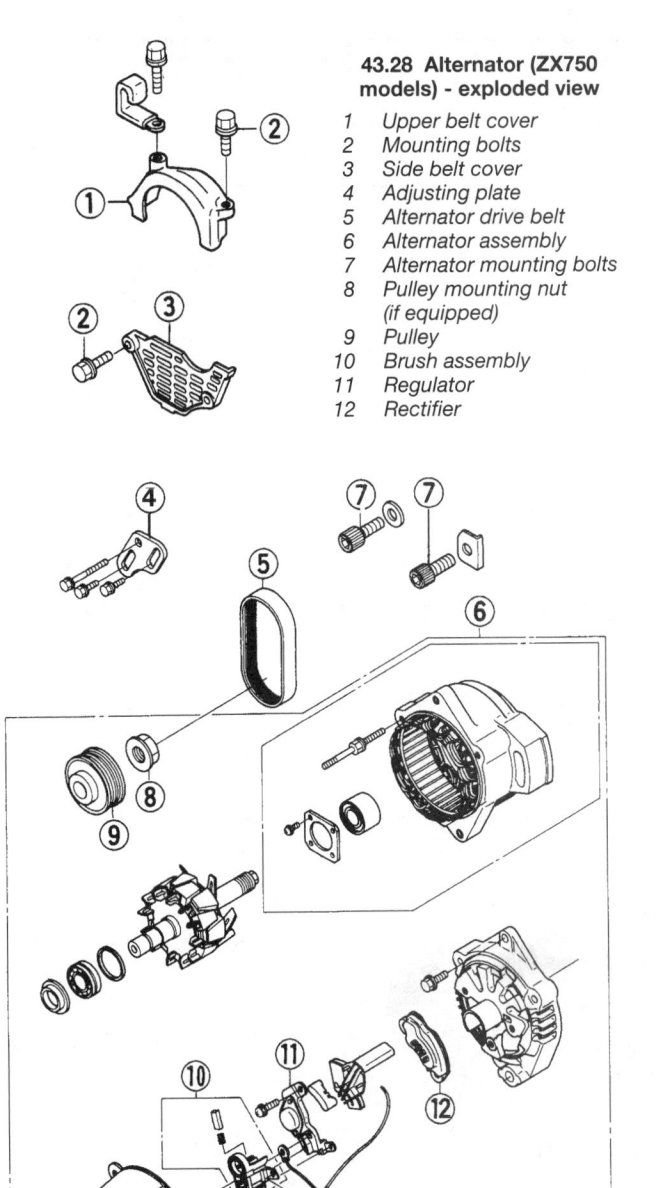

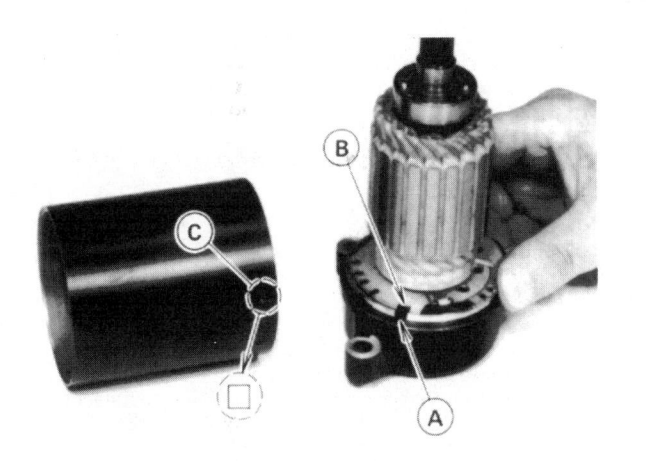

43.11 Align the notches in the cover and brush plate with the housing mark

a   Cover notch
b   Brush plate notch
c   Housing mark

16   The charging system output should be within the range listed in this Chapter's Specifications.
17   If the output is as specified, the alternator is functioning properly. If the charging system as a whole is not performing as it should, refer to Step 26 and check the alternator brushes.
18   Low voltage output may be the result of damaged windings in the alternator stator coils or wiring problems. Make sure all electrical connections are clean and tight, then refer to the following Steps to remove the alternator and inspect the brushes.
19   High voltage output (above the specified range) indicates a defective voltage regulator.

Alternator - removal and installation

20   Disconnect the cable from the negative terminal of the battery.
21   Remove the left side covers and clutch slave cylinder (see Sections 42 and 23).
22   Make a written note of which mark on the alternator scale aligns with the pointer **(see illustration 3.10)**, then remove the alternator bracket and engine sprocket cover **(see illustration 3.11)**.
23   Unplug the alternator electrical connector.
24   Remove the alternator mounting bolts and lift the alternator off the

engine. Disengage the alternator pulley from the drive belt and take the alternator off.
25   Installation is the reverse of the removal steps, noting that the previously noted alignment marks must be matched and the belt tension set (see Section 3). Tighten the alternator mounting bolts to the torque listed in this Chapter's Specifications.

Alternator brushes - inspection and replacement

Refer to illustration 43.28
26   This check, combined with the charging system output test described above, should diagnose most charging system problems. If the brushes are good and alternator output is low, take the alternator to a dealer service department or other repair shop for further checks, or substitute a known good unit and recheck the charging system output.
27   Remove the alternator (see Steps 20 through 25 above).
28   Remove the screws and take the end cover off the alternator **(see illustration)**.

10

29   Remove three screws and lift out the brush assembly.

30   Measure the length of the brushes and compare it to the value listed in this Chapter's Specifications. If the brushes are worn, replace them.

31   Reverse Steps 28 and 29 to reassemble the alternator, then reverse Steps 20 through 24 to reinstall it.

English/American terminology

English	American	English	American
Air filter	Air cleaner	Mudguard	Fender
Alignment (headlamp)	Aim	Number plate	License plate
Allen screw/key	Socket screw/wrench	Output or layshaft	Countershaft
Anticlockwise	Counterclockwise	Panniers	Side cases
Bottom/top gear	Low/high gear	Paraffin	Kerosene
Bottom/top yoke	Bottom/top triple clamp	Petrol	Gasoline
Bush	Bushing	Petrol/fuel tank	Gas tank
Carburettor	Carburetor	Pinking	Pinging
Catch	Latch	Rear suspension unit	Rear shock absorber
Circlip	Snap-ring	Rocker cover	Valve cover
Clutch drum	Clutch housing	Selector	Shifter
Dip switch	Dimmer switch	Self-locking pliers	Vise-grips
Disulphide	Disulfide	Side or parking lamp	Parking or auxiliary light
Dynamo	DC generator	Side or prop stand	Kickstand
Earth	Ground	Silencer	Muffler
End float	End play	Spanner	Wrench
Engineer's blue	Machinist's dye	Split pin	Cotter pin
Exhaust pipe	Header	Stanchion	Tube
Fault diagnosis	Troubleshooting	Sulphuric	Sulfuric
Float chamber	Float bowl	Sump	Oil pan
Footrest	Footpeg	Swing arm	Swingarm
Fuel/petrol tap	Petcock	Tab washer	Lock washer
Gaiter	Boot	Top box	Trunk
Gearbox	Transmission	Two/four stroke	Two/four cycle
Gearchange	Shift	Tyre	Tire
Gudgeon pin	Wrist/piston pin	Valve collar	Valve retainer
Indicator	Turn signal	Valve collets	Valve keepers
Inlet	Intake	Vice	Vise
Input shaft or mainshaft	Mainshaft	Wheel spindle	Axle
Kickstart	Kickstarter	White spirit	Stoddard solvent
Lower leg	Slider	Windscreen	Windshield

Conversion factors

Length (distance)

Inches (in)	X 25.4	= Millimetres (mm)	X 0.0394	= Inches (in)
Feet (ft)	X 0.305	= Metres (m)	X 3.281	= Feet (ft)
Miles	X 1.609	= Kilometres (km)	X 0.621	= Miles

Volume (capacity)

Cubic inches (cu in; in³)	X 16.387	= Cubic centimetres (cc; cm³)	X 0.061	= Cubic inches (cu in; in³)
Imperial pints (Imp pt)	X 0.568	= Litres (l)	X 1.76	= Imperial pints (Imp pt)
Imperial quarts (Imp qt)	X 1.137	= Litres (l)	X 0.88	= Imperial quarts (Imp qt)
Imperial quarts (Imp qt)	X 1.201	= US quarts (US qt)	X 0.833	= Imperial quarts (Imp qt)
US quarts (US qt)	X 0.946	= Litres (l)	X 1.057	= US quarts (US qt)
Imperial gallons (Imp gal)	X 4.546	= Litres (l)	X 0.22	= Imperial gallons (Imp gal)
Imperial gallons (Imp gal)	X 1.201	= US gallons (US gal)	X 0.833	= Imperial gallons (Imp gal)
US gallons (US gal)	X 3.785	= Litres (l)	X 0.264	= US gallons (US gal)

Mass (weight)

Ounces (oz)	X 28.35	= Grams (g)	X 0.035	= Ounces (oz)
Pounds (lb)	X 0.454	= Kilograms (kg)	X 2.205	= Pounds (lb)

Force

Ounces-force (ozf; oz)	X 0.278	= Newtons (N)	X 3.6	= Ounces-force (ozf; oz)
Pounds-force (lbf; lb)	X 4.448	= Newtons (N)	X 0.225	= Pounds-force (lbf; lb)
Newtons (N)	X 0.1	= Kilograms-force (kgf; kg)	X 9.81	= Newtons (N)

Pressure

Pounds-force per square inch (psi; lbf/in²; lb/in²)	X 0.070	= Kilograms-force per square centimetre (kgf/cm²; kg/cm²)	X 14.223	= Pounds-force per square inch (psi; lbf/in²; lb/in²)
Pounds-force per square inch (psi; lbf/in²; lb/in²)	X 0.068	= Atmospheres (atm)	X 14.696	= Pounds-force per square inch (psi; lbf/in²; lb/in²)
Pounds-force per square inch (psi; lbf/in²; lb/in²)	X 0.069	= Bars	X 14.5	= Pounds-force per square inch (psi; lbf/in²; lb/in²)
Pounds-force per square inch (psi; lbf/in²; lb/in²)	X 6.895	= Kilopascals (kPa)	X 0.145	= Pounds-force per square inch (psi; lbf/in²; lb/in²)
Kilopascals (kPa)	X 0.01	= Kilograms-force per square centimetre (kgf/cm²; kg/cm²)	X 98.1	= Kilopascals (kPa)

Torque (moment of force)

Pounds-force inches (lbf in; lb in)	X 1.152	= Kilograms-force centimetre (kgf cm; kg cm)	X 0.868	= Pounds-force inches (lbf in; lb in)
Pounds-force inches (lbf in; lb in)	X 0.113	= Newton metres (Nm)	X 8.85	= Pounds-force inches (lbf in; lb in)
Pounds-force inches (lbf in; lb in)	X 0.083	= Pounds-force feet (lbf ft; lb ft)	X 12	= Pounds-force inches (lbf in; lb in)
Pounds-force feet (lbf ft; lb ft)	X 0.138	= Kilograms-force metres (kgf m; kg m)	X 7.233	= Pounds-force feet (lbf ft; lb ft)
Pounds-force feet (lbf ft; lb ft)	X 1.356	= Newton metres (Nm)	X 0.738	= Pounds-force feet (lbf ft; lb ft)
Newton metres (Nm)	X 0.102	= Kilograms-force metres (kgf m; kg m)	X 9.804	= Newton metres (Nm)

Power

Horsepower (hp)	X 745.7	= Watts (W)	X 0.0013	= Horsepower (hp)

Velocity (speed)

Miles per hour (miles/hr; mph)	X 1.609	= Kilometres per hour (km/hr; kph)	X 0.621	= Miles per hour (miles/hr; mph)

Fuel consumption*

Miles per gallon, Imperial (mpg)	X 0.354	= Kilometres per litre (km/l)	X 2.825	= Miles per gallon, Imperial (mpg)
Miles per gallon, US (mpg)	X 0.425	= Kilometres per litre (km/l)	X 2.352	= Miles per gallon, US (mpg)

Temperature

Degrees Fahrenheit = (°C x 1.8) + 32

Degrees Celsius (Degrees Centigrade; °C) = (°F - 32) x 0.56

*It is common practice to convert from miles per gallon (mpg) to litres/100 kilometres (l/100km), where mpg (Imperial) x l/100 km = 282 and mpg (US) x l/100 km = 235

Index